Lotus® 1-2-3® for Windows™ At Work

David J. Bookbinder
Mark Jacober
Kevin McDonough

Addison-Wesley Publishing Company, Inc.

Reading, Massachusetts Menlo Park, California New York
Don Mills, Ontario Wokingham, England Amsterdam Bonn
Syndey Singapore Tokyo Madrid San Juan
Paris Seoul Milan Mexico City Taipei

Many of the designations used by manufacturers and sellers to distinguish their products are claimed as trademarks. Where those designations appear in this book and Addison-Wesley was aware of a trademark claim, the designations have been printed in initial capital letters.

Library of Congress Cataloging-in-Publication Data

Bookbinder, David J.
     Lotus 1-2-3 for Windows at work / David J. Bookbinder, Mark H.
Jacober.
          p.   cm.
     Includes index.
     ISBN 0-201-56791-1
     1. Lotus 1-2-3 (Computer program) 2. Microsoft Windows (Computer
program) 3. Business--Computer programs.   I. Jacober, Mark H.
II. Title.
HF5548.4.L67B673   1991
650'.0285'5369--dc20   91-34245
                                                                 CIP

Managing Editor: Amorette Pedersen
Set in 10.5-point Garamond by Benchmark Productions

1 2 3 4 5 6 7 8 9-MW-9594939291
First Printing, October 1991

Table of Contents

Chapter 5:   More Worksheet Skills   185

Chapter 6:   Creating a 1-2-3 Database   257

Acknowledgments

Thanks are due to Danielle Albert, Judy Duff, Ed McNierney, Merry Morse, Steve Savage, and Debbie Stolper for their help in providing us with documentation and software. We are also grateful to Amy Pedersen, Chris Williams, Jennifer Noble, and the staff of Benchmark Productions, Inc. for their enthusiasm for the book and care in producing it, and to Sandy Moore for her careful copy editing. Thanks, as well, to Phyllis Staffier, who tested several chapters of this book.

Finally, special thanks are due to the many people who helped with the creation of this book's predecessors, *The Lotus Guide to 1-2-3 Release 3* and *Lotus 1-2-3 for DOS Release 2.3 At Work*. Without their help, the present book would not have been possible.

Preface

What Is Lotus 1-2-3 for Windows?

Lotus 1-2-3 for Windows is an integrated software package used to organize, analyze, and present information. It combines a sophisticated spreadsheet with extensive database and graphics capabilities. It is the most popular electronic spreadsheet product in the world.

The At Work Series

The At Work series is designed to meet the needs of both beginning and intermediate users. Each book provides complete authoritative material on a particular software package. The books in the At Work series have a number of features to make them easy to work with and learn from. At Work sidebars illustrate actual uses of the product in the real world. Adhesive tabs allow you to mark locations that you'll want to refer to frequently. Chapter objectives and summaries help you focus on the important points that you will want to master in each chapter. A special "for the beginner" section covers the basics for the first-time computer user.

Scope of This Book

Lotus 1-2-3 for Windows At Work is a hands-on guide to Lotus 1-2-3 for Windows.

This book helps you learn the most important skills you'll need to make effective use of 1-2-3 for Windows and prepares you for learning more about 1-2-3 on your own. It does not try to teach you everything there is to know about 1-2-3. Instead, it demonstrates, in an easytolearn style, the essential elements of the program and techniques for using them. By the time you are finished with this book, you will be a capable user of 1-2-3, armed with the skills and knowledge you'll need to use 1-2-3 to solve your own problems.

You'll learn by building simple, practical applications and working your way through some basic tasks: creating a worksheet and entering and manipulating data; using multiple worksheets in the same file; generating and manipulating a database; drawing graphs and charts from worksheet data and adding them to the worksheet; and automating your work with macros.

This book is intended to complement the 1-2-3 documentation, not to replace it. As you work through the exercises in this book, you should also take time to explore related information in the 1-2-3 manuals and in the 1-2-3 online Help files on your own.

Although you cannot expect to master 1-2-3 for Windows all at once, it is not a difficult program to learn, and as you'll soon see, you can do much useful work while you are learning.

Getting Familiar with Your Computer System

If you are new to computers, you will want to spend a few minutes exploring this section. You will learn to identify the various components of your computer called *hardware* through the many illustrations in this section. You will also learn the purpose of each hardware component. Once you have identified the various components of your computer you will learn about the instructions called *software* that tell your computer what tasks to perform.

Taking a Look at Computer Hardware

There are many components in your computer. Some components such as the keyboard are visible and can be touched easily. Other components are enclosed in a box and cannot be seen unless the cover is removed from the main computer unit.

Hardware components are made by a number of manufacturers. This helps account for the differences in size, speed, color, price, and capabilities of the same components on different systems.

Exploring the System Unit

The system unit is the most important piece of hardware in your computer system. It contains the brains of your system. A component within the system unit is capable of remembering, at least for the short term. The system unit handles all the processing and computation that you need.

The system unit can take many shapes and sizes; in a desktop unit, it is typically a box on which the monitor or screen sits. Your unit might look something like the IBM PS/2 Model 70 desktop unit in Figure N-1. The *tower* models like the model 60 require less desktop space and are said therefore to have a smaller *footprint.* Portable units frequently have all the components attached directly to the system unit. A laptop or hand-held model would be smaller than any of the system units shown.

The system unit contains a number of components including memory, a central processing unit, slots for adapter cards, adapter cards, ports, and disk drives.

The system unit has an on/off switch to turn the power on to your system. This switch may be in the back of your system, on the side, or on the front. On most systems, the switch is pushed in one direction to turn the system on and in the other to turn it off.

Looking Inside the System Unit The *motherboard* is the main circuit board in your computer. You must open the outer case of the system unit to see it.

Figure N-1: IBM PS/2 Model 70

Figure N-2 provides a look at a motherboard from a popular computer system. Microprocessor chips are attached to this main circuit board. One type of chip applied to the motherboard is the processing unit, frequently called the Central Processing Unit (CPU). It might look something like Figure N-3. The CPU handles mathematical calculations and logical comparisons. Although the entire system unit is commonly thought of as the brains of your computer, it is actually this one component that provides most of this "brain power."

Memory chips are also located on the motherboard. These chips store information as long as the power to your computer is not interrupted. When you purchase a computer, the amount of memory in the unit is stated in either kilobytes (K) or megabytes (MB). A *kilobyte* of memory can store 1,024 characters, but rounding this number and thinking of it as 1 thousand is more common. A *megabyte* of memory can store 1,048,576 characters of information although it is common to think of 1 MB as 1 million. DOS, your application software, and your data will all use some of this memory as you are working with the computer. The memory

Figure N-2: PS/2 Model 70 Motherboard

in your computer system might reside in a bank of chips as shown in Figure N-2. You can also add additional memory that is stored on a card which in turn is placed on a card above the motherboard. This extra memory is either extended or expanded memory.

Slots on the motherboard allow you to add adapter cards. *Adapter cards* allow you to expand the basic capabilities of your system. They are placed in slots on the motherboard which are designed to allow users to define how they want to expand their system. One type of adapter card added to most systems is a video adapter card. This type of card defines whether your monitor displays color or black and white. The card also determines whether the monitor can display only text or text and graphics. Figure N-4 shows an adapter card that can be added to a system.

If your system has a hard disk, it will also be inside the system unit since it is not removable. The size of your hard disk is measured in megabytes with 40 MB and 60 MB the most popular sizes sold today. The information placed on the hard disk will be stored permanently, unlike the information stored in memory which is lost as soon as your system loses its power. Figure N-5 shows a hard disk with the circular plates providing the surface where information is stored. A hard disk is normally referred to as drive C.

Looking at the Outside of the System Unit If you look at the outside of the system unit you will see additional components. These

Figure N-3: Processing Unit

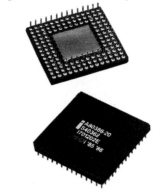

Courtesy Intel

Figure N-4: Adapter Card

Figure N-5: Hard Disk Drive

Courtesy Seagate Technology, Inc.

are important—they include disk drives and ports for connecting other equipment to your system.

On the outside of your system unit you are likely to see one or more drives that allow you to insert a removable diskette. The first one of these drives is called drive A. If you have a second drive as part of the system unit it is called drive B. The B drive can also be attached as an external drive if you do not have a second drive built into the unit. A system configured with a 3 1/2 inch drive and a 5 1/4

Figure N-6: Disk Drive Configuration

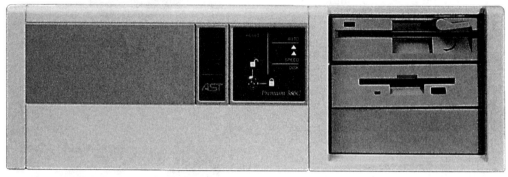

inch drive is shown in Figure N-6.

The most common diskette size in use today are 5 1/4 and 3 1/2 inches. Although the concept behind both types of disks are the same, they differ in the amount of information they hold and the protective covering over the actual disk. The 5 1/4 inch size can hold either 360K or 1.2 MB depending on the disks and the disk drive used to write the data. Figure N-7 shows a 5 1/4 inch disk. The 360K capacity disk is referred to as a double side/double density disk (DS/DD) and the 1.2 MB disk is a high density (HD) disk. The 3 1/2 inch disks hold either 720K or 1.44 MB depending on whether they are double sided, double density or high density disks. Figure N-8 shows a 3 1/2 inch disk.

Figure N-7: 5 1/4 Inch Disk

Figure N-8: 3 1/2 Inch Disk

High density (HD) disk drives can read either double side/double density disks or the high density variety. Double side/double density (DS/DD) disks can only read disks created on a double density drive.

You can write information to a disk as long as it has been prepared with the DOS formatting process. A 5 1/4 inch disk is placed into the drive with the notch on the left side of the disk and the oval cut-out edge placed into the drive first. A 3 1/2 inch disk is placed into the drive label face-up with the metal clip that protects the disk going into the drive first.

Once data has been written on the disk you can physically write-protect the disk to prevent the deletion of the data or the writing of additional information to the disk. On a 5 1/4 inch disk you need to use a write protect tab (these tabs are provided in most disk packages you purchase) over the notch on the left side of the disk. On a 3 1/2 inch disk you need to slide the small shutter toward the protective clip at the front of the disk.

The back of the system unit has ports that you can use to attach other devices to your computer. Figure N-9 provides a closeup look at the connectors for these ports. Cables like the one in Figure N-10 are used to connect the port to the external device. It is important that the cable connector exactly match the port connector. Devices you might attach to these ports include a keyboard, a monitor, printers, a modem, a mouse, or additional disk drives. These ports can be serial ports that accept a stream of characters that you can think of as marching single file from the port to another device or as parallel where parallel lines of characters proceed from the port to the other device.

Figure N-9: Port Connectors on the Back of the System Unit

Figure N-10: Parallel Printer Connector Cable

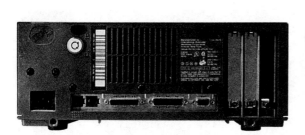

Adding to the Basic System Features You need more than the system unit to have a usable computer system. At a minimum you need a device for communicating your needs to the computer and a way for seeing the output from your computer. A keyboard is the most common method of input and all computers have one. All keyboards have keys that correspond to typewriter keys. These keys always appear in the center area of your keyboard. Other keys appear in different locations on the various keyboards.

Function keys are assigned to request different tasks that vary by the application program you are working with. Function keys are the keys labeled F1 through either F10 or F12. They are located across the top of the IBM Enhanced keyboard shown in Figure N-11 or down the left side of the older model keyboard shown in Figure N-12.

The numeric keypad on the right side of the keyboard has dual functionality. With NUM LOCK on the keys on this pad enter numbers as you press them. Without NUM LOCK on these keys move the cursor from one location to another on your computer screen. Newer keyboards have separate keys to move from one location to another, allowing you to keep the NUM LOCK on at all times for the entry of numbers from the numeric keypad.

A mouse is an optional

Figure N-11: IBM Enhanced Keyboard

Figure N-12: IBM XT Keyboard

Figure N-13: Microsoft Mouse

device that you can use to limit keyboard entries. Figure N-13 shows a Microsoft mouse with two mouse buttons on the top. DOS uses only the left mouse button. Depending upon whether you press the button quickly and release it or hold the button down and move the mouse, you can select an item on the screen or an entire group of items. A mouse provides a shortcut approach to menu selections as well as a way of selecting a group of files in a list.

Monitor screens come in color or monochrome, which only displays one color. They can display only text characters like the ones you type on the keyboard or text and graphics images. Monitors differ greatly in resolution quality depending on the number of pixels in the displays. *Pixels* are dots that can take on an attribute. They are arranged in a grid shape and vary greatly from one type of monitor to another. The capabilities of your monitor are related to the video card installed in the system unit. Figure N-14 shows a monitor screen.

Figure N-14: Monitor Screen

A *modem* is a device that allows you to connect your computer to other computers via the phone lines. You can use either an external modem or a micromodem which is a card inserted into one of your computer's expansion slots. Modems differ in the speed with which they can transmit and receive characters. Figure N-15 shows an external modem.

Exploring Software Options

Figure N-15: External Modem

Software consists of instructions for the computer that are stored as files on disk. There are different types of software. Operating system software such as DOS controls the resources of your computer and provides services to other software programs running on your machine. Operating system software must be the first

software that is placed in your machine during each computer session.

Application software can be used to accomplish a specific business task. It can be general purpose or more specialized to meet the needs of a single industry segment.

General purpose software includes popular packages such as WordPerfect, 1-2-3, and dBASE. WordPerfect is a word processing program that allows you to type memos, letters, tables, and reports. 1-2-3 is a spreadsheet that allows you to create models to forecast sales, plan your monthly budget, or calculate a loan payment. dBASE allows you to create and maintain a database for your clients, a record collection, or inventory. You can use the features of these packages regardless of the business or industry segment that you work in.

Specialized software is tailored to one application. A specialized package might handle a task such as stock portfolio management, medical records, or legal docket control.

When you purchase an application software package you normally receive a manual and one or more disks. If you have a hard disk you will follow the install procedure provided with the software to copy the appropriate information to your hard disk.

Chapter 1

About This Book

This chapter explains how this book is organized and how you can get the most out of it. It also summarizes the new features that Lotus 1-2-3 for Windows adds to previous releases of Lotus 1-2-3.

Organization of This Book

Lotus 1-2-3 for Windows At Work is a tutorial for people new to 1-2-3 for Windows (from here on called either 1-2-3/W or simply 1-2-3). It is a step-by-step guide to learning 1-2-3. *Lotus 1-2-3 for Windows At Work* teaches you how to use 1-2-3 through an integrated set of exercises that demonstrate how to build a set of simple, yet useful, applications.

The book begins with basic worksheet skills and then moves on to more advanced features, such as working with template files, multiple worksheets in the same file, databases, graphs, spreadsheet publishing, multiple-file applications, and macros. In addition to the exercises, many of the chapters also contain short discussions of 1-2-3 tips and techniques.

How to Use This Book

This book was written for three different types of reader:

- Readers new to IBM personal computers (or to computers in general)
- Readers new (or relatively new) to 1-2-3/W, but not to computers
- Readers new to 1-2-3/W but familiar with other releases of 1-2-3

If you have no experience with computers, read "Getting Familiar With Your System" at the beginning of this book before you start working on the exercises. Although you are probably eager to work with 1-2-3 right away, a little delayed gratification now will save you considerable frustration later. If you are new (or relatively new) to 1-2-3, but not to computers, you can skip "Getting Familiar With Your System" or peruse it at your leisure.

In either case, once you have familiarized yourself with the basic hardware and software components of your system, you are ready to start learning 1-2-3. Begin with Chapter 2, then work through Chapters 3, 4, and 5. These chapters are essential to getting a basic understanding of the product. Each of the remaining chapters covers a major area of 1-2-3 knowledge; work through them as you use 1-2-3 to perform your daily tasks.

If you have used earlier releases of 1-2-3, read the summary of 1-2-3/W features further on in this chapter. This summary identifies which chapters in this book deal with what major new 1-2-3/W features. Then skim through the book, paying attention mainly to those sections that deal specifically with 1-2-3/W features or enhancements. You will probably want to read Chapters 5, 7, 8, and 9 in their entirety, since these chapters cover many new 1-2-3/W features.

Read through the "At a Glance" sections at the end of each chapter to make sure you haven't missed anything significant in the other chapters.

A Note on Style and Examples

Like most tools, 1-2-3 can be applied to many different tasks. We have tried to make learning 1-2-3 fun (as it was for us), and at the same time immediately useful, by constructing examples that grow in scope and complexity as your skill in using the product increases. Features are often introduced briefly, then are expanded on and reinforced as the book progresses.

Most of the examples are organized around a kind of modern-day Horatio Alger success story. The story's protagonist is Bob Gordon, an office manager with a young family and a passion for woodworking. As the book progresses, Bob's woodworking hobby grows first into a side business and finally into a full-blown corporation. 1-2-3 accompanies our hero through these various stages, helping him along the way. Initial examples present basic 1-2-3 techniques; they use, as their subject, practical applications for the individual. Later examples use a small business, and still later examples reflect how 1-2-3 is used in larger businesses.

In most cases, this book teaches by leading you through exercises one mouse click or keystroke at a time. Each exercise is preceded by an explanation of what you are about to do and what will happen on the screen. Several chapters also include optional exercises with fewer keystroke instructions; these exercises give you an opportunity to practice newly learned skills on your own.

■ *NOTE:*   To help you move more quickly through the exercises, you can order a diskette that contains all the major examples in this book. See the order form at the back of the book for details.

What's New in 1-2-3 for Windows?

While 1-2-3/W remains compatible with previous releases of 1-2-3, it also offers many new features that substantially extend 1-2-3's basic capabilities, flexibility, and ease of use. Some of the more striking extensions and most useful features include:

■ *Integrated spreadsheet formatting and publishing.*   1-2-3/W, like the most recent DOS versions of 1-2-3, includes enhanced spreadsheet formatting and publishing capabilities. Unlike the DOS versions of 1-2-3, these capabilities—including customizable display colors and fonts, changeable row heights, and the ability to add graphs, graphics, and freehand drawings to the worksheet—are now integrated into a single menu structure.

Graph enhancements include 3-D graph effects, simultaneous on-screen display of graphs and worksheet data in multiple graph windows, a customizable icon palette for graphics editing, and increased control over a graph's appearance.

Printing enhancements include print preview, printing mixed text and graphs, and support of the Microsoft Windows Print Manager and printer drivers. In addition, 1-2-3 comes with the Adobe Type Manager, which adds numerous screen and printer fonts to the Windows font set, and makes screen output even more closely resemble final printed reports.

- *Ease-of-use enhancements* include a customizable icon palette, which lets you execute frequently used commands with a mouse click; greatly expanded on-line help; interactive dialog boxes that simplify entering 1-2-3 commands; Undo; and one-key erasure of both single cells and ranges.
- *Solver and Backsolver.* The Solver and Backsolver commands greatly expand, and at the same time simplify, 1-2-3's what-if problem-solving capabilities. With Solver, you can quickly analyze worksheet data and determine the possible answers to a problem that fit within your specified constraints. With Backsolver, you can automatically change the value of one variable so that a formula evaluates to a specified result.
- *Multiple worksheets, multiple files, and file linking.* The ability to link worksheets to files on disk or in memory (introduced in 1-2-3 Release 3.0) effectively eliminates restrictions on the size of an application and makes consolidation of worksheets from different sources much easier. 1-2-3/W lets you have as many as 256 worksheets in memory, divided among one or more worksheet files. In addition, you can create dynamic links to other Windows applications and to external databases.
- *Macro enhancements* include the Macro Transcript window, which continuously records your 1-2-3 keystrokes, and interactive macro debugging. The Transcript window makes it easy to create your own macros as you perform worksheet tasks. The macro debugger makes it easy to correct macros if they contain errors. In addition, you can add your own macros to the SmartIcon palettes.
- *Compatibility.* Despite the many enhancements of 1-2-3/W, the product is compatible with previous releases of 1-2-3 at the data, cell, macro, and keystroke level. 1-2-3/W reads all worksheet files created with 1-2-3 Releases 1.x, 2.x, 3.x, and Lotus Symphony, and it can run macros created by all previous releases of the product. The 1-2-3 Release 3 menu tree is built into 1-2-3/W, and is available at the touch of the familiar slash key (/). The 1-2-3 Wysiwyg menu, likewise, is available at the press of the colon key (:). 1-2-3/W is also a true Windows product. It conforms to all Windows conventions for menus and mouse movements, and supports Windows Clipboard operations and Dynamic Data Exchange (DDE) links between 1-2-3 and other Windows applications.

Table 1-1 lists the major new or enhanced features of 1-2-3/W that are discussed in this book.

Table 1-1:   New and Enhanced Features of 1-2-3 for Windows

Feature	Chapter
Spreadsheet Formatting	
Control of fonts and color	7
Changing row heights	7
Installing and using Adobe Type Manager	7
Adding graphs and graphics to the worksheet	8

Feature	Chapter
Charts and Graphs	
New graph effects	8
On-screen display of graphs and worksheet data together	8
Control of a graph's appearance	8
Using the Graph SmartIcon palette	8
Printing	
Print preview	9
Printing graphs and text together	9
Using Print Manager and Windows printer drivers	9
Ease-of-use	
Using the SmartIcon palette	2
Using Help	2
Working with dialog boxes	2
Erasing cells and ranges with the Delete key	3
Undoing changes to the worksheet file	3
Solver and Backsolver	12
Multiple worksheets, multiple files, and linking	
Navigating in a multiple-worksheet file	5
Building a multiple-worksheet application	5
Creating links to external databases	6
Navigating multiple files in memory	10
Creating links to other 1-2-3 worksheet files	10
Creating links to other Windows applications	10
Importing and exporting ASCII files	10
Using the Windows Clipboard	10
Macro enhancements	11

Conventions Used In This Book

This section describes the typographical conventions used in *Lotus 1-2-3 for Windows At Work*. If any of the computer terms used here are confusing to you, read "Getting Familiar with Your System" before going any further.

Exercise Steps

Most exercises are divided into steps, with each step given a numbered heading that summarizes what you will be doing. This heading is followed by a detailed explanation of the step, the mouse clicks or keystrokes required to perform the step, and sometimes by an explanation of what should happen after you perform the step. Unless instructed to do otherwise, wait until you reach the actual keystroke instructions before you type anything in or move the mouse. Illustrations that show the results of your actions appear as close as possible to the keystroke instructions to which they apply.

Terms

New terms are defined early on and then repeated throughout the book, so you can grow comfortable with them. The first time a new term is introduced in the body of the book, it is *italicized*.

Keystroke Instructions

In the keystroke and mouse instructions (from here on referred to simply as *keystroke instructions*), keytops showing words or symbols represent the arrow keys, the Enter key, and other special keys such as Tab, Control, Alt, and End. These words and symbols are the same as those that appear on the IBM keyboard. For example, $\boxed{\rightarrow}$ represents the Right arrow key. Function keys are represented by keytops marked with the name of the key followed, in parentheses, by the 1-2-3 name for the key; for instance, $\boxed{\text{F3}}$ (NAME) stands for the Name key. Keystroke instructions appear in **bold** and are followed by a colon. Command names and characters that you are expected to type appear in a `monospaced` typeface, and explanations within keystroke instructions appear in *italics*. Table 1-2 describes the terminology used in keystroke instructions.

Table 1-2: Keystroke Instruction Terminology

Keystroke	Definition
Press:	This means to strike a key. It is used primarily with arrow keys, function keys, the Enter key, and other special keys.
	Press: $\boxed{\rightarrow}$
Type:	**Type** : also means to strike or press a key or series of keys. It is used primarily when you are being instructed to enter words, numbers, or formulas into 1-2-3.
	Type: `Home Budget for 1992`

Keystroke	Definition

Move to:

This directs you to reposition the cell pointer at a certain place on the screen. (The cell pointer is the bar in reverse video or a contrasting color that moves through the worksheet display when you move one of the pointer-movement keys.)

Move to: cell D3

Point to:

This directs you to reposition the mouse pointer at a certain place on the screen. (The mouse pointer moves when you move the mouse. It can take different shapes, depending on what you are doing. Usually, it is an arrow head.)

Point to: *the splitter bar*

Choose:

This directs you to select a specific command from a menu. A menu is a list of commands that appears in a line across the top of the screen. As you will discover in Chapter 2, there are several ways to choose a command from a menu: You can: (1) click on it with the mouse; (2) activate the menu bar, highlight the command you want, and then press the Enter key; or (3) activate the menu bar and press the underlined letter of the command name. Use any of these methods to choose a command when doing the exercises.

Choose: `File`

Many menu commands bring up a submenu from which to choose another command. In this book, all the commands in such a sequence are usually listed on the same line in the keystroke instruction. The commands for saving a file involve such a sequence. The keystroke instructions look like this:

Choose: `File    Save`

Select:

This tells you to pick an item from a list or group of displayed items. You select an item in one of these ways: (1) click on it with the mouse; (2) press Tab until the item is highlighted or surrounded by a dotted box, and then press Enter; or (3) press Alt and the underlined letter in the item's name.

Select: `Format:`

Highlight:

This directs you to define an area of the worksheet. When you define an area, 1-2-3 changes the display of that area to reverse video (with a monochrome display) or a contrasting color (with a color display). You can highlight an area of the worksheet with either the mouse or the keyboard.

Highlight: B109..D119

Keystroke	Definition
Specify:	This tells you to indicate an area of the worksheet, either by typing in the cell addresses or by highlighting the area with the mouse or the keyboard. Keystroke instructions use the term **Specify:** to indicate cell addresses instead of **Type:** or **Highlight:** when it makes no difference which method you use.
	Specify: B109..D119
Click on:	This means to press and then release the left mouse button (or the right mouse button, if you have switched the button meanings with 1-2-3's Install program).
	Click on: OK
Double click:	This means to press and then release the left mouse button two times in rapid succession. (or use the right mouse button, if you have switched the button meanings with 1-2-3's Install program.)
	Double click: `Range:`
Drag to:	This means to move an object on the screen by pointing to it with the mouse, depressing the left mouse button, moving the mouse while still holding down the mouse button, and then releasing the mouse button when the object is where you want it.
	Point to: *the Data Fill dialog box title bar* **Drag to:** *the lower right corner of the window*

Other Conventions

In addition to the conventions used in the keystroke instructions, the following conventions are used in this book.

Table 1-3: Additional Conventions

Convention	Description
Enter Escape Insert	In the text of this book, all keys are referred to by name. For example, the name Enter is used in text to refer to the Enter key, rather than the keytop with the ⏎ symbol that is used in the keystroke instructions.

Convention	Description
READY A:A1 LEDGER @SUM BUDGET.WK3 DIR	Uppercase is used within text for mode indicators, cell and worksheet references, range names, @functions, file names, and operating system commands.
budget.wk3 **dir**	Within keystroke instructions, file names and operating system commands are in lowercase, **monospaced** type.
END **RIGHT**	Unconnected key sequences, such as **END** **RIGHT**, mean you should press and release the first key, then press the second key.
CTRL+RIGHT	Connected key sequences mean that you should hold down the first key while you press the second. For example, **CTRL+RIGHT** means "Hold down the Control key and press the Right arrow key."

Chapter 2

1-2-3 Basics

This chapter is an introduction to 1-2-3. By the time you complete it you will have learned, in a general way, what 1-2-3 can do, and you will have begun to learn how to make 1-2-3 do what *you* want it to.

Concepts and techniques are covered fairly quickly, to give you a broad idea of what 1-2-3 is all about. Don't worry if you don't retain everything you read—most topics mentioned here are expanded on in later chapters. If you try out the exercises and get the gist of the explanations, you'll be a long way toward becoming familiar with the product.

What You'll Learn

This chapter describes the types of work you can do in 1-2-3, each of the main parts of 1-2-3 and how they fit together, and the basic foundation you need in order to work with 1-2-3 effectively. After reading this chapter, besides having a general overview of 1-2-3, you'll know how to perform these tasks:

- **Start 1-2-3**

- **Exit 1-2-3**

- **Choose 1-2-3 commands from menus**

- **Enter data in the worksheet**

- **Fix typing mistakes**

- **Save a worksheet to a file**

- **Erase a worksheet file from memory**

- **Open a previously saved worksheet file**

- **Save a modified worksheet file**

- **Change the default directory setting**

- **Get on-line help with 1-2-3's features and error messages**

- **Change settings in order to tailor 1-2-3 to your individual needs**

A Bird's-Eye View of 1-2-3

This section gives a quick introduction to 1-2-3 and the kinds of tasks for which 1-2-3 is often used.

What You Can Do With 1-2-3

1-2-3 is used by millions of people worldwide, in all walks of life. Managers, accountants, and others in business use 1-2-3 to help them make decisions, generate financial reports, estimate costs, and track inventory and sales. Engineers and scientists use 1-2-3 to gather data, analyze it, and display the results of the analysis. Others use 1-2-3 to calculate their taxes, balance their budgets, manage stock portfolios, and run mail-order businesses. Like other general-purpose tools, the uses of 1-2-3 are limited only by the needs and imaginations of those who work with it.

Typical uses for 1-2-3 include:

- Balance sheets, budgets, and income statements
- Sales forecasts
- Inventory applications
- Statistical analyses
- Loan amortization tables
- What-if tables
- Electronic checkbooks and ledgers
- Employee databases
- Payroll applications
- Forms applications

A few of the less typical uses of 1-2-3 have included:

- Analyzing horse race statistics
- Tracking food intake for patients on special medical diets
- Handling milk-processing information for a dairy farm
- Tracking pollution counts in Boston's Charles River
- Playing games such as "Hangman" and "Adventure"
- Automatically translating numeric grades to letter grades

What Is 1-2-3?

1-2-3 is an integrated software package with spreadsheet, database, and graphics capabilities.

1-2-3 is *integrated* in the sense that all its pieces work together in a coordinated, well-thought-out way. When it was introduced in 1983, integration was 1-2-3's chief innovation over earlier spreadsheet products. It combined into one package capabilities and features that could previously be obtained only by using several separate programs, and it made it easier to use them together. This integration remains one of 1-2-3's chief selling points today.

You can look at 1-2-3 as being made up of three parts, each of which contributes to the whole. They are:

- *Spreadsheet.* 1-2-3 spreadsheets allow you to perform calculations, test assumptions, and analyze results.
- *Database.* 1-2-3 databases allow you to store, organize, and manage information.
- *Graphics.* Graphs drawn from information in spreadsheets and databases allow you to illustrate concepts and visualize results. Graphic images and freehand drawings enhance the appearance and intelligibility of charts and reports.

Because these three parts are integrated into one product, you can move among them freely. For example, you can enter information into a database, manipulate the database information in a spreadsheet, and then graph the results of your spreadsheet analysis, all without leaving 1-2-3. The *user interface*—the way you tell the program what you want it to do through menu commands, mouse clicks, and keystrokes—is the same whether you are creating a spreadsheet, a database, or a graph. All work in 1-2-3 takes place in the 1-2-3 window, rather than in separate spreadsheet, database, and graph environments.

The following sections describe each of these parts of 1-2-3 in more detail.

What Is a Spreadsheet?

A *spreadsheet* is a structure used for numeric or financial calculations. It is an integral tool of most business operations. A traditional paper spreadsheet is a ledger whose columns and rows intersect to form a pattern of boxes, each of which holds a *value*. Many values in a spreadsheet depend on other values entered elsewhere in the spreadsheet.

In a traditional paper spreadsheet, a value is a number. Making a change to one value requires that you manually change all other values related to it. For example, a ledger containing the operating expenses of a company is a spreadsheet. One column contains the salary figures of all employees. The total of that column represents the total compensation paid by the company. That total is then entered in another column that details monthly expenditures. If the salary of an employee changes, you have to go back and recalculate the entire column. You must also recalculate any figure that uses the total compensation, such as the figure for total monthly expenditures.

Figure 2-1: A Traditional Paper Spreadsheet

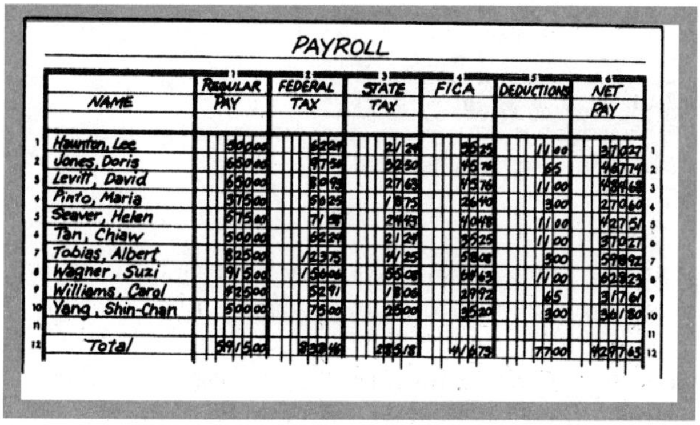

In a traditional spreadsheet, the rows and columns are labeled so that people looking at the spreadsheet can understand their significance. For example, in the payroll spreadsheet in Figure 2-1, the first column contains employee names. Each employee name serves as a label for the salary information to the right of that name (the employee's salary). The columns also have labels that describe the values beneath them.

1-2-3 spreadsheets, such as that shown in Figure 2-2, are created in the *worksheet*, a grid of columns and rows. Although it retains the basic format of the ledger, the 1-2-3 worksheet not only makes the maintenance of the spreadsheet easier, but it also automates operations that would be quite demanding if done manually. Related numbers entered in different sections of the worksheet are dynamically connected to each other—when you change a value, all other values that depend on it change automatically. This interconnection gives the electronic spreadsheet more flexibility than the paper spreadsheet, making it much easier to experiment with figures to see how a change in one area affects other areas.

Figure 2-2:   A 1-2-3 Electronic Spreadsheet

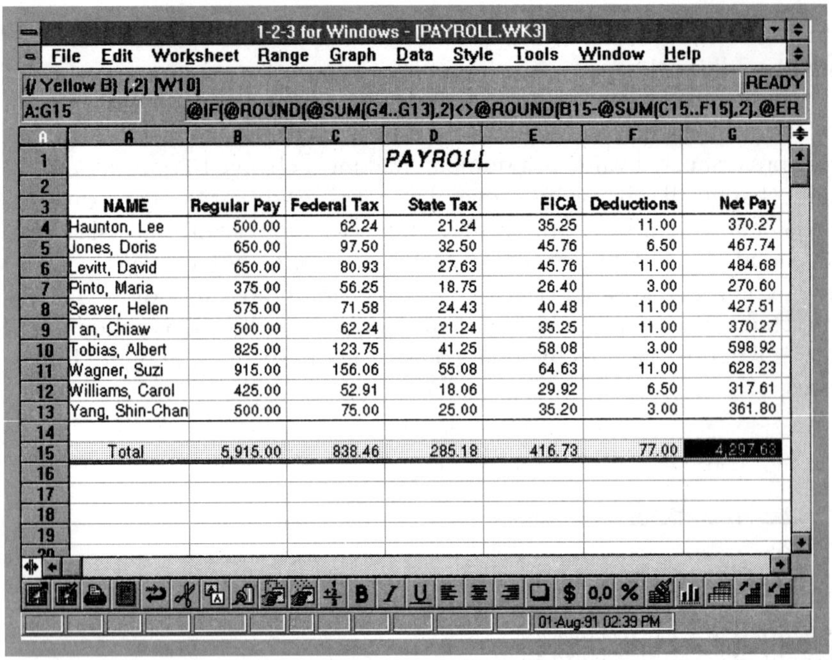

NAME	Regular Pay	Federal Tax	State Tax	FICA	Deductions	Net Pay
Haunton, Lee	500.00	62.24	21.24	35.25	11.00	370.27
Jones, Doris	650.00	97.50	32.50	45.76	6.50	467.74
Levitt, David	650.00	80.93	27.63	45.76	11.00	484.68
Pinto, Maria	375.00	56.25	18.75	26.40	3.00	270.60
Seaver, Helen	575.00	71.58	24.43	40.48	11.00	427.51
Tan, Chiaw	500.00	62.24	21.24	35.25	11.00	370.27
Tobias, Albert	825.00	123.75	41.25	58.08	3.00	598.92
Wagner, Suzi	915.00	156.06	55.08	64.63	11.00	628.23
Williams, Carol	425.00	52.91	18.06	29.92	6.50	317.61
Yang, Shin-Chan	500.00	75.00	25.00	35.20	3.00	361.80
Total	5,915.00	838.46	285.18	416.73	77.00	4,297.63

Worksheet title bar: 1-2-3 for Windows - [PAYROLL.WK3]
Menu: File Edit Worksheet Range Graph Data Style Tools Window Help
{/ Yellow B} [,2] [W10]   READY
A:G15   @IF[@ROUND[@SUM[G4..G13],2]<>@ROUND[B15-@SUM[C15..F15],2],@ER
PAYROLL
01-Aug-91 02:39 PM

What Is a Database?

A *database* is a collection of items of information about a group of people, places, or things. A database typically holds and organizes large amounts of information, or *data*, and makes any item of information immediately accessible.

Most databases are arranged in a pattern. Items of information pertaining to a particular person, place, or thing are grouped together to form *records*, each of which has a similar format. For example, a telephone book is a simple database. It has separate categories for the same kinds of information about each person listed: name, address, and telephone number. This pattern makes it easy to quickly find a particular item, such as a specific person's phone number.

Records in a database are divided into *fields*. Each field contains one item of information about a record. In a phone book database, for example, the name, address, and phone number categories are the fields. In an inventory database, the fields might be the product name, the code number, the number of pieces on hand, the current wholesale cost, and the retail price for each product.

1-2-3 can work with databases created in the 1-2-3 worksheet and also with databases created by other software products. In a 1-2-3 database, the items of information are stored in one or more tables in the worksheet file. Each database record is in a separate row of a table, and each field is in a separate column. The database can expand or contract as new records are added or old ones are removed. The basic form itself can be easily changed if you need to add or remove specific categories of information.

Figure 2-3: A 1-2-3 Database Table

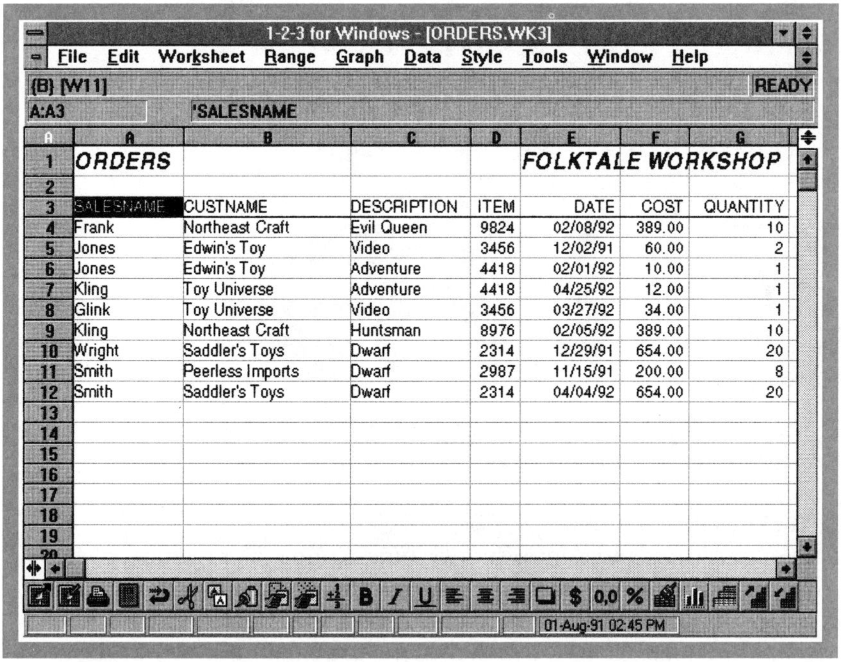

What Is a 1-2-3 Graph?

A 1-2-3 *graph* is a visual representation of spreadsheet or database data.

Often, a graph can reveal patterns in numbers and illustrate overall trends and projections that would be easily missed in pages of numeric data. For this reason, business graphics are frequently used in presentations and reports. Similarly, engineers use graphs to display the relationships between two or more sets of data, or the change in a set of values over time.

A 1-2-3 graph is dynamically connected to the worksheet data it is based on: Change some of that data, and 1-2-3 instantly redraws the graph to reflect the change. You can view a graph on the screen as you create it, and you can modify it or add to it as necessary. Once a graph looks the way you want it, you can display or print it as a chart that can include supporting text, numbers, and additional graphics.

Figure 2-4

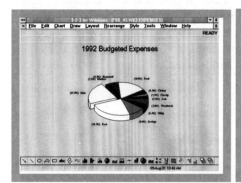

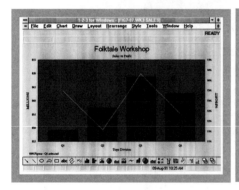

A Note on Reading the Rest of This Chapter

The remainder of this chapter describes and demonstrates some of the major features of 1-2-3. Although at this point you can just keep on reading, you will get the most out of the chapter if you work with 1-2-3 as you go along.

The chapter is divided into sections, each of which presents a unit of information about 1-2-3; a major heading marks the start of each section. The end of a section is a reasonable place for you to stop if you want to take a break or if you need to do something else. Before you stop, save any work you are doing. That way, you can easily continue where you left off when you pick up this book again. (You won't need to save anything before you reach the part of the chapter in which you'll learn how to save your work.)

In general, the exercises include illustrations you can compare to your own work to make sure are "in synch" with the book. If 1-2-3 indicates you have made an error while you are doing these exercises, press F1 (Help) for an explanation of how to fix the problem. (See "The 1-2-3 Help System" later in this chapter for more information on 1-2-3's on-line Help.)

Starting and Exiting 1-2-3

This section describes how to enter and leave 1-2-3.

To start 1-2-3, you must have already installed both Microsoft Windows and 1-2-3/W. If Windows has not yet been installed on your system, follow the instructions in the Windows documentation for installing Windows before you read this section. If 1-2-3/W has not yet been installed on your system, follow the instructions in the 1-2-3 documentation for installing 1-2-3 before you read this section.

Starting 1-2-3 from the Windows Program Manager

If you use other Windows applications, you will probably start 1-2-3 from the Windows Program Manager, rather than from the DOS prompt. The easiest way to do so is to double-click on the 1-2-3/W icon.

1. With Program Manager displayed on your screen, move the mouse pointer to the 1-2-3 for Windows program icon. (The 1-2-3 for Windows program icon and the 1-2-3 for Windows Install icon will both be in the Lotus Applications program group unless you have moved them elsewhere.)

2. Double-click on the 1-2-3 for Windows program icon. The 1-2-3 logo, copyright notice, and licensing information appear on the screen. It takes several seconds for the 1-2-3 program to be loaded into your computer's memory. When this process is finished, the 1-2-3 menu and a blank 1-2-3 worksheet should appear on the computer's screen as shown in Figure 2-5 on the next page.

Exiting 1-2-3

Exiting 1-2-3 means getting out of the 1-2-3 program and returning to the Windows Program Manager or the Windows desktop. Normally, you exit 1-2-3 only after you have permanently recorded any work you have done while using the program. At the moment, since you have not yet done any work, there is no need to make a permanent record of anything; you can exit 1-2-3 with a clear conscience. There will be more about exiting 1-2-3 later on, but for now perform the following steps to see how to exit 1-2-3:

Choose: File   Exit

Windows displays the Program Manager screen (or the Windows desktop, if the Program Manager is minimized).

■ *NOTE:*   When you exit 1-2-3, 1-2-3 removes from memory any files you have been working on. If you have made any changes to a file in memory, 1-2-3 offers to save your work before you exit. If you select Yes from the File Exit dialog box, 1-2-3 saves all modified files and then exits. If you select No, 1-2-3 abandons any work you have done since the last time you saved your work.

Figure 2-5:   A Blank, Untitled Worksheet

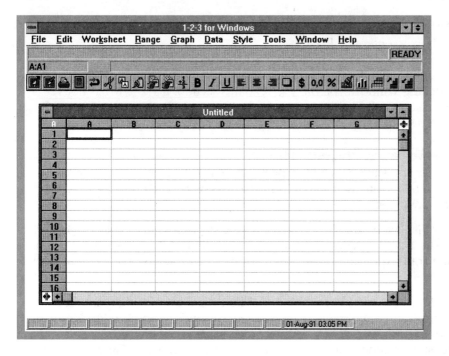

A Note on Starting 1-2-3 from the DOS Prompt

If the only Windows application you run is 1-2-3, you may find it's more convenient to start 1-2-3 directly from the DOS prompt. To do so, you provide the name of the 1-2-3 main program file to Windows when you start Windows.

■ *NOTE:*   The following instructions assume that 1-2-3 is installed in the \123 directory of drive C and that Windows is installed in C:\WINDOWS. If either program is installed in a different drive or directory, substitute the actual location of the 1-2-3 program files for **C:\123** and of the Windows program files for **C:\WINDOWS** in the following instructions.

1. Make sure the current drive is C:.

   Be sure the C> prompt is displayed on the monitor. If you see an A> or B> prompt, this means your computer will look for programs and files on diskette drive A or B. To change to drive C:

   Type: c:

   Press: ⏎

2. Change to the 1-2-3 directory.

Use your operating system's CD (Change Directory) command to change to the 1-2-3 directory. (Be sure you type the name of the actual directory that contains your 1-2-3 program files—the name you specified when you ran Install. For example, if your 1-2-3 program directory is \123W instead of \123, you would type **cd \123W**, and then press the Enter key.)

Type: `cd \123`

Press: ◻

3. Start up 1-2-3.

With the C> prompt on the screen:

Type: `c:\windows\win 123w`

Press: ◻

The computer starts up Windows, and then Windows loads 1-2-3. The 1-2-3 logo, copyright notice, and licensing information appear on the screen.

■ *NOTE:*   When you exit 1-2-3 after you have started 1-2-3 from the DOS prompt, you must also exit Windows before you can return to DOS.

The 1-2-3 Window

When you first start 1-2-3, the screen displays four distinct areas:

- The Worksheet window
- The control panel
- The status line
- The icon palette

Each of these is described in detail in the following pages. Before you go on to the next section, start 1-2-3 again by double-clicking the 1-2-3 for Windows icon in the Program Manager window, and then examine the screen.

The Worksheet Window

The *Worksheet window* is the area in which you display information when you use 1-2-3. It fills most of the screen. Right now, 1-2-3 displays a blank Worksheet window named Untitled, as illustrated in Figure 2-6. Compare this to the illustration of a window containing a nonblank worksheet in Figure 2-7.

The window is bordered by numbers down the left side and letters across the top. The letters identify columns and the numbers identify rows.

When you first start 1-2-3, the letter A appears in the upper left corner, at the intersection of the row and column borders. This is the *worksheet letter*. Initially, 1-2-3 has only one worksheet, but you can add worksheets whenever you like. The worksheet letter lets you know which worksheet is current.

Figure 2-6: A Blank 1-2-3 Window

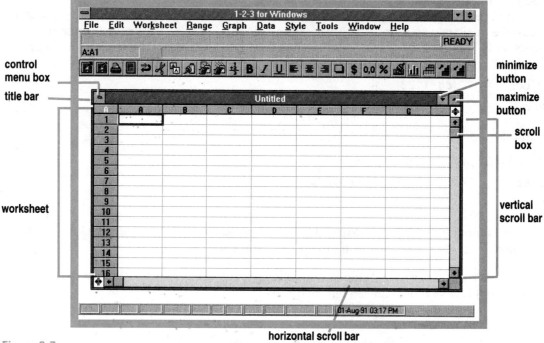

Figure 2-7

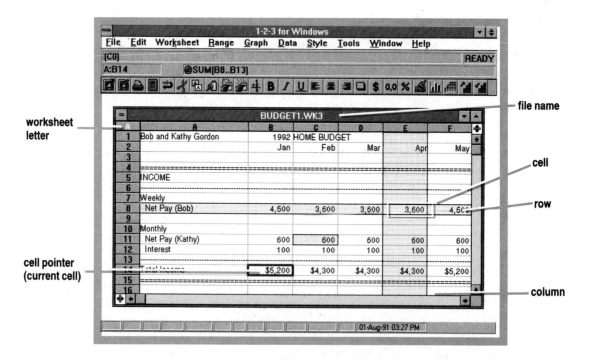

The intersections of columns and rows form a pattern of boxes. These boxes are called *cells*. A cell is the basic building block of a 1-2-3 worksheet. A cell is identified by its *cell address*, which is the cell's location in the grid of worksheet/column/row intersections. The cell address is made up of the worksheet letter, a colon (:), the column letter, and the row number. For example, the cell in the first column and first row of the first worksheet in a file has the cell address A:A1. If you omit the worksheet letter (for example, you refer to the first cell in a worksheet as A1), 1-2-3 assumes you mean the current worksheet.

A 1-2-3 worksheet is much larger than the number of rows and columns that can be displayed even on a very large video screen. The worksheet can contain information in as many as 256 columns (identified by the letters A through IV) and 8192 rows (numbered 1 through 8192). The Worksheet window is a way of looking at this potentially huge area in chunks a computer screen can accommodate.

The Worksheet window is so named because it functions much like a real-life window. When you look out the window of a moving train, you can see different sections of the landscape as you move through the countryside. Similarly, you can use the Worksheet window to look at different sections of a worksheet.

Figure 2-8

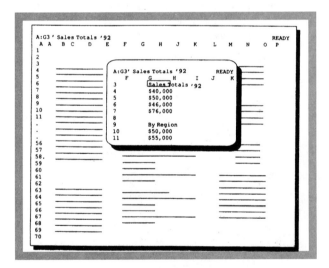

Parts of the Worksheet Window

The parts of the Worksheet window indicated in Figure 2-7 are summarized in Table 2-1 and described in detail in the following pages.

Table 2-1:   Parts of the Worksheet Display

Part	Description
Worksheet	Each worksheet file can contain up to 256 worksheets. Each worksheet is identified by a letter, beginning with A for the first worksheet in a file, B for the second, C for the third, and so on.
Column	Each worksheet contains 256 columns identified by the letters A through IV. The order of the column letters is A through Z, AA through AZ, BA through BZ, and so on. (The 256th column letter is IV.)
Row	Each worksheet contains 8192 rows, numbered 1 through 8192.
Cell	A box formed by the intersection of a column and a row.
Current cell	The currently highlighted cell, whose address and contents are displayed in the control panel.
Cell pointer	The highlight that marks the current cell. By default, this is an outline that surrounds the current cell, but you can change the cell pointer to a solid rectangle in a contrasting color, as in the screen illustrations used in this book. (See "A Note on the Illustrations in this Book" in Chapter 3 for instructions on changing the cell pointer from an outline to a solid.)
Title bar	Displays the Control menu box, the Maximize and Minimize buttons, and the name of the current worksheet file. You can have several files open at once, and each file can contain multiple worksheets (up to a total of 256 worksheets in memory at once).
Control menu box	Lets you move, size, and close the current Worksheet window or switch to another window in 1-2-3.
Maximize button	Enlarges the current window to maximum size.
Minimize button	Shrinks the current window to an icon or, if the window is maximized, to the size it was before you maximized it.
Horizontal scroll bar	Lets you move the Worksheet window from column to column within the worksheet.
Vertical scroll bar	Lets you move the Worksheet window from row to row within the worksheet.
Scroll box	Box in the horizontal or vertical scroll bar that you drag with the mouse pointer to scroll horizontally or vertically through the worksheet.

The highlighted rectangle on the screen is called the *cell pointer*. You can move the cell pointer with the arrow keys and several other keys on the keyboard.

Press: $\boxed{\rightarrow}$ *several times*

$\boxed{\leftarrow}$ *several times*

$\boxed{\downarrow}$ *several times*

$\boxed{\uparrow}$ *several times*

Notice that 1-2-3 beeps each time the cell pointer hits the top or left edge of the worksheet. This is to remind you that you can't move any farther in that particular direction. (If you want to, you can turn off the beep with the Tools User Setup command.)

You can also move the cell pointer with the mouse. To do so, you move the mouse pointer to the cell you want to become the current cell and then click the left mouse button. Try it!

Click on: `cell E11`   *with the left mouse button*

To move to a cell that is not in view, you scroll the display by clicking on the horizontal and vertical scroll bars or by dragging the appropriate scroll box until the cell is in view, and then you click on it. (You'll learn more about scrolling the display in Chapter 3.)

Multiple Worksheets

So far, we've been talking about 1-2-3 in two-dimensional terms; in fact, much of the time you will probably work with 1-2-3 as if it handled only two dimensions. But 1-2-3 is actually a three-dimensional work environment.

When you first start 1-2-3, only one worksheet is in memory; however, you can insert additional worksheets in front of or behind the current worksheet whenever you like, using the "Sheet" option of the Worksheet Insert command. In fact, if your computer has sufficient memory, you can work on as many as 256 worksheets at any time. Each worksheet in a worksheet file is identified by a letter, according to its relative position in the file: the first worksheet in a file is worksheet A, the next is worksheet B, and so on.

You can think of multiple worksheets in a file as if each were a page in a multi-page report. Much as the collection of pages that make up such a report might all be stored in a file folder, so a collection of worksheets whose contents are all related can be stored in a multiple-worksheet file. Conceptually, the worksheets are stacked one behind the other.

Multiple worksheets were introduced with Release 3 of 1-2-3 for DOS. They were introduced for two main reasons:

- To simplify creating consolidations and other three-dimensional applications
- To make it easier to separate logically-distinct parts of an application

Chapter 5 describes multiple worksheets in detail and provides examples of how to use them in each of these ways. Multiple worksheets are also used in examples throughout this book whenever they simplify an application or make it more flexible.

The Control Panel

The *control panel* consists of the top four lines of the 1-2-3 window. It is the area in which you enter data and choose 1-2-3 commands. It can also display the name of the current file, formatting information about the current cell, and indicators that reflect what 1-2-3 is doing at any given moment.

Figure 2-9:   A Multiple-Worksheet File with Three Worksheets Displayed

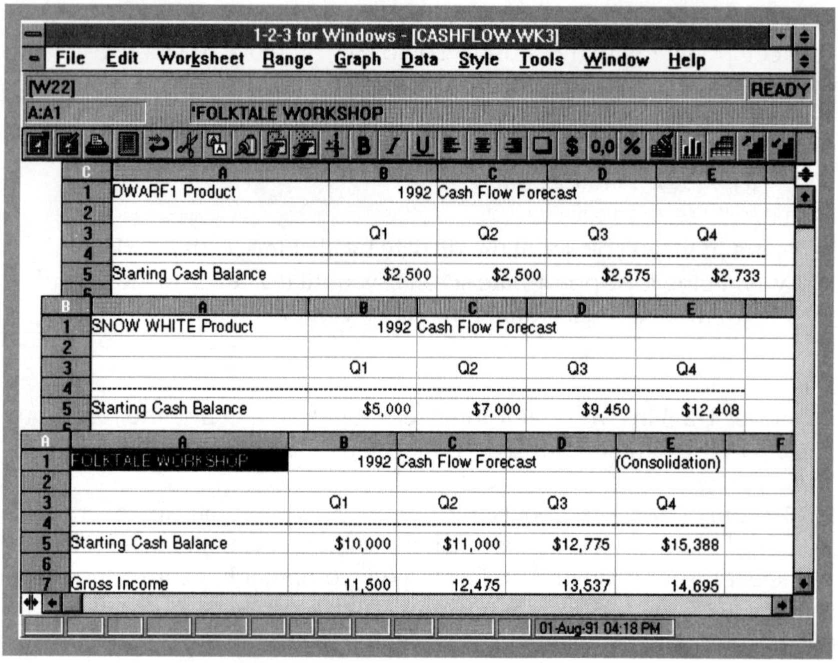

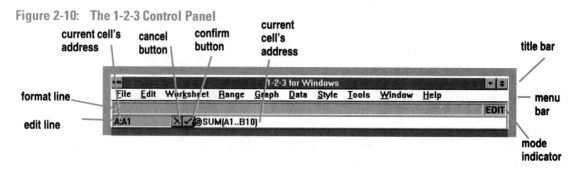

Table 2-2 describes the basic elements of the control panel, which are illustrated in Figure 2-10. You will be working with the control panel extensively throughout this book.

Figure 2-10:   The 1-2-3 Control Panel

Table 2-2:   The 1-2-3 Control Panel

Panel Element	Description
Title bar	Contains the 1-2-3 Control menu box; the area where a command description or icon description appears; the name of the product; the 1-2-3 window's Minimize button; and the 1-2-3 window's Maximize or Restore button.

Panel Element	Description
Menu bar	Displays the 1-2-3 main menu commands (unless you are viewing a graph or a macro transcript window, in which case the menu bar displays commands appropriate to the activities you perform in those windows).
Format line	Shows how the current cell is formatted and displays the current mode indicator. (Mode indicators are described in Table 2-3.)
Edit line	Contains the current cell's address; Confirm and Cancel buttons for accepting or abandoning changes you make to cell entries; and the contents of the current cell. In a new worksheet file, the first line shows the cell address A:A1 and the area for displaying cell contents is blank.

Mode Indicators

The right side of the control panel's format line contains the *mode indicator*. The mode indicator lets you know what 1-2-3 is doing. It displays informational messages, such as WAIT (when 1-2-3 is busy performing some task) or READY (when 1-2-3 is ready for you to enter data or tell it to do something). The standard 1-2-3 mode indicators are listed in Table 2-3, along with short descriptions of their meanings. You will encounter most of them as you work through this book.

Table 2-3:   Mode Indicators

Indicator	What It Means
EDIT	1-2-3 is in EDIT mode. You have pressed F2 (Edit), you have tried to enter data that 1-2-3 couldn't interpret, or 1-2-3 has prompted you to enter a response that may require editing.
ERROR	Something has gone wrong. Either press F1 (Help) to get a detailed explanation of th error, or select OK or press Escape to clear the error and return to where you were before 1-2-3 detected the error.
FILES	1-2-3 is displaying a list of file names while you are in the 1-2-3 Classic menu. (The 1-2-3 Classic menu is described later in this chapter).
FIND	A Data Query Find operation is in progress. (Data Query operations are described in Chapter 6.)
HELP	You are using 1-2-3's on-line Help.
LABEL	You are typing a label entry.
MENU	1-2-3 is presenting you with a menu from which to make a choice, or you are in a dialog box and have pointed to a list box, check box, option button, or command button.
NAMES	1-2-3 is displaying a list of names for graphs, external database tables, @functions, or macro commands.
POINT	You are moving the cell pointer to indicate a cell or a range, or 1-2-3 is prompting you to do so.
READY	1-2-3 is waiting for you to enter data or give it a command.
VALUE	You are typing a number, formula, or @function in the control panel.
WAIT	1-2-3 is busy. You must wait until the WAIT indicator clears before entering data or issuing a command.

The Status Line

The last line of the 1-2-3 window is the *status line*. 1-2-3 uses the status line to convey information about the system and to display the current date and time.

The right side of the status line displays the current date and time (or nothing at all, if you turn off the date/time display with the "None" option of the Tools User Setup dialog box). The left side of the status line is divided into several indicator areas. Initially, each is blank. As you use 1-2-3, however, you will notice that each of these areas displays a different *status indicator*. For instance, the Calc indicator tells you that a cell value has changed since 1-2-3 last recalculated the worksheet, or that 1-2-3 is recalculating formulas in the background. Other status indicators remind you that certain keys have been pressed. For instance, Num means you have pressed the Number Lock key, which causes the arrow keys on the numeric keypad to enter numbers instead of moving the pointer.

Status Indicators

The 1-2-3 status indicators are listed in Table 2-4. You will encounter many of them as you work through this book.

Table 2-4: Status Indicators

Indicator	What It Means
Calc	A cell value has changed since 1-2-3 last recalculated the worksheet, or 1-2-3 is performing background recalculation. If 1-2-3 is set for manual recalculation, you must press F9 (Calc) to obtain the correct values.
Caps	You have pressed the Caps Lock key. Caps Lock reverses the effect of the Shift key on letters. With Caps on, unshifted letters you type are in uppercase, while shifted letters are in lowercase. Press Caps Lock once to turn Caps on and again to turn it off.
Circ	The worksheet file has at least one circular reference; that is, a cell contains a formula that refers to itself directly or indirectly. Choose Help About 1-2-3 to determine the location of the circular reference. NOTE: Since some techniques require circular references, this is not always an error.
Cmd	1-2-3 is running a macro. (If the mode indicator displays anything other than WAIT, 1-2-3 is probably waiting for user input during the macro.)
End	You have pressed the End key. Pressing End before pressing the pointer-movement keys changes where those keys will move the cell pointer. Press End once to turn the End indicator on and again to turn it off.
File	You have pressed the File key, Control+End. Pressing the pointer-movement keys that normally move the cell pointer from one worksheet to another will now move the cell pointer from one file in memory to another.
Group	You have checked the "Group" box in the Worksheet Global Settings dialog box and the current file is now in GROUP mode. (See Chapter 5 for a full discussion of GROUP mode.)
Mem	You are low on available memory.

Indicator	What It Means
Num	You have pressed the Number Lock key. Number Lock allows you to use the numeric keypad to type numbers; it temporarily disables the arrow keys and other pointer-movement keys on the numeric keypad. (Number Lock does not affect pointer-movement keys that are not part of the numeric keypad.) Press Number Lock once to turn Num on and again to turn it off. NOTE: Holding down the Shift key while you press a keypad pointer-movement key allows you to use the key as a pointer-movement key even when the Num indicator is on.
RO	The current worksheet file is read-only. You can look at the file, but you cannot save any changes you make to it. You will see this indicator when you are using 1-2-3 on a network and do not have the file reservation for the current file, or when you have made a file read-only with a DOS command.
Scroll	You have pressed the Scroll Lock key. When Scroll Lock is on, the arrow keys move the Worksheet window one column or row at a time. When Scroll Lock is off, the arrow keys move the cell pointer. Press Scroll Lock once to turn Scroll on and again to turn it off.
Step	You have pressed the Step key (Alt+F2). 1-2-3 will execute macros one step at a time.
Zoom	You have divided the Worksheet window into multiple panes and then pressed the Zoom key (Alt+F6) to get a full-window view of the current window pane.

The Icon Palette

The 1-2-3 *icon palette* is one of the handiest new features of 1-2-3 for Windows. The icon palette is a set of buttons called *SmartIcons* that let you execute commonly used commands just by clicking on the buttons with the mouse. The icon palette is completely customizable: you can move it anywhere in the 1-2-3 window, change its size, hide it, or add icons to it. You can even create icon palettes of your own to use with specific applications.

Figure 2-11a: The Main Menu 1-2-3 Icon Palette

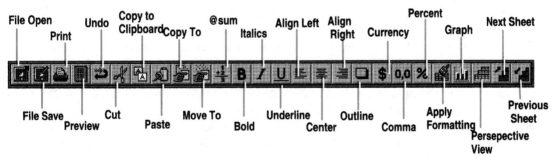

Figure 2-11b: The Graph Window 1-2-3 Icon Palette. (You'll find out how to use these icons in Chapter 8.)

To see what a SmartIcon does, you click on it with the *right* mouse button and a one-line description appears in the 1-2-3 title bar. To choose an icon, you click on it with the *left* mouse button. For example, to see what the "scissors" icon does, click on it with the right mouse button. 1-2-3 displays the phrase "Cut to the Clipboard" in the first line of the 1-2-3 window; to cut highlighted cells to the Windows Clipboard, you would click on the scissors icon with the left mouse button.

Some tasks you perform with icons are executed immediately on the currently highlighted range (for example, "Edit Cut", "File Save", "Undo", "Bold", and "Italics"). Others cause the appropriate dialog box to be displayed (for example, "File Open", "Print", and "Preview"). (Dialog boxes are explained in "Using Dialog Boxes" later in this chapter.) Still others change the mouse pointer to a different kind of pointer and allow you to select a new range (for example, "Copy To", "Move To", and "Apply Formatting").

1-2-3 comes with two different icon palettes. The main menu icon palette lets you perform common 1-2-3 tasks by clicking on an icon. When you are creating or editing a graph in the graph window (described briefly in the next section and in detail in Chapter 8), 1-2-3 displays a palette of graphic tools. You can customize either palette so that it displays only the icons you use, or so that it includes commands you create yourself.

You will use the main menu icon palette throughout this book. You will learn how to customize the palette in Chapter 11.

Other 1-2-3 Windows

Besides the Worksheet window and the icon palette, 1-2-3 provides several other windows you can use to perform various tasks. Each of these is described briefly here and in more detail later in this book.

- *Graph window.* When you create a graph, you do so in another window called the *graph window.* Creating graphs is described in Chapter 8.
- *1-2-3 Classic window.* If you press the slash key (/) or the colon key (:) from READY mode, 1-2-3 displays the *1-2-3 Classic* window, which allows you to enter 1-2-3 Release 3.1 commands. Using the 1-2-3 Classic window is described later in this chapter.
- *Help window.* When you press F1 (Help) or choose Help from the 1-2-3 menu bar, 1-2-3 displays context-sensitive on-line help in the Help window. The Help window contains command summaries, complete descriptions of 1-2-3 procedures, and reference information not found in the printed 1-2-3 documentation. (It's a gold mine of information!) Using Help is described later in this chapter.
- *Print Preview window.* The Print Preview window lets you display an on-screen version of how your worksheet will look when it's printed. Using Print Preview is described in Chapter 9.
- *Transcript window and Macro Trace window.* A *macro* is a collection of 1-2-3 commands, keystrokes, and special instructions that you can execute as if it were a single 1-2-3 command. The Transcript window records your keystrokes and commands and lets you create macros from these recordings. The Macro Trace

window helps you find and correct mistakes in macros. Using both of these windows is described in Chapter 11.

Figure 2-12a: The Graph Window and the Worksheet Being Graphed

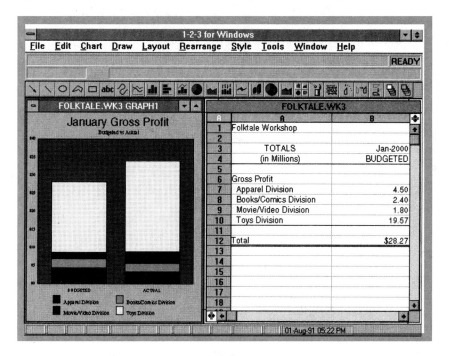

Figure 2-12b: The 1-2-3 Classic Window

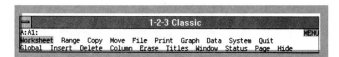

Figure 2-12c: The 1-2-3 Help Window

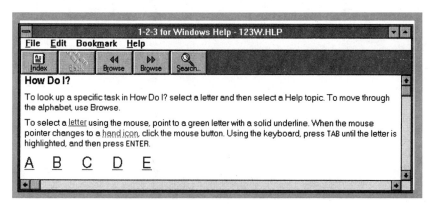

Figure 2-12d: The Print Preview Window

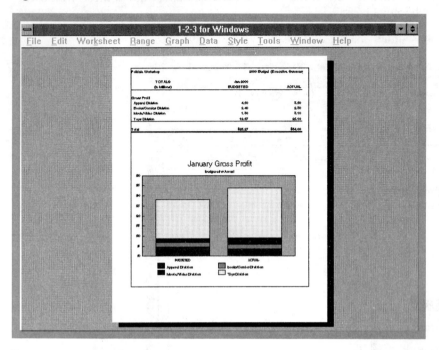

Figure 2-12e: The Transcript and Macro Trace Windows (with an untitled, minimized Worksheet window in the lower left corner of the 1-2-3 window)

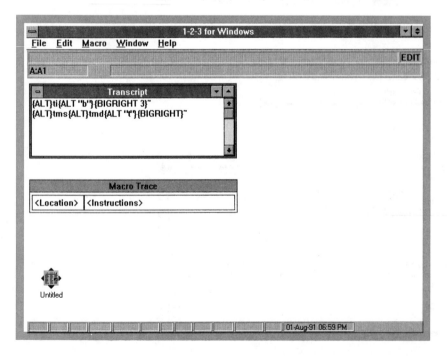

1-2-3 Menus

1-2-3 is a *menu-driven* program. This means that you tell 1-2-3 what you want it to do by making choices from items in *menus*, which are lists of commands you give to 1-2-3.

Figure 2-13:   The Main 1-2-3 Menu

1-2-3 displays the main menu in the second line of the control panel. The main menu lets you choose commands with which you do most of the application-building work in the 1-2-3 program.

- ■ The File commands let you retrieve worksheet files from disk, save them to disk, print them, and exit 1-2-3.
- ■ Edit, Worksheet, and Range commands let you manipulate spreadsheet data.
- ■ Graph commands allow you to create graphs and draw pictures in the worksheet file.
- ■ Data commands allow you to manipulate databases, and to perform data analysis and related operations on worksheet data.
- ■ Style and Window commands control various aspects of the way the worksheet looks.
- ■ Tools commands either let you customize 1-2-3 or solve specialized problems.
- ■ Help provides access to 1-2-3's extensive on-line Help, and it also lets you see 1-2-3 status information, such as the location of circular references.

You can choose 1-2-3 commands with either the keyboard or the mouse. In the next two sections, we'll experiment with both methods; thereafter, you can use whichever method seems most natural to you.

■ *NOTE:*   Later in this chapter, you'll also learn how to use the 1-2-3 Classic menu, which lets you enter 1-2-3 Release 3.1 commands in 1-2-3 for Windows.

Using the Keyboard to Work in 1-2-3 Menus

First, try using the keyboard to navigate 1-2-3 menus. Even if a mouse is attached to your system and you plan to use it most of the time, it is worth familiarizing yourself with the keyboard commands. Once you become fluent in 1-2-3, you may find that using the keyboard for commands you have memorized is quicker. Also, because you can always use the keyboard to enter 1-2-3 commands, you'll have no trouble working in 1-2-3 if you happen to find yourself in front of a mouse-less computer. Finally, when 1-2-3 records commands in the Transcript window, it does so using keyboard commands; some practice with the commands will help you out in Chapter 11, when you learn how to create macros from recorded keystrokes.

Start by activating the main menu.

Press: `ALT` *(or F10)*   *to activate the menu bar*

Figure 2-14:   The Activated 1-2-3 Main Menu

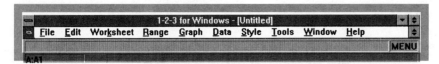

Notice that the first menu choice, the 1-2-3 Control menu box, is now highlighted, and that the mode indicator now reads MENU instead of READY.

Now try using the keyboard to move the menu highlight, which is known as the *menu pointer.*

Press: `→`   *two times, to move the menu pointer to Edit*

The menu pointer moves first to File, and then to Edit, and the title bar displays a general description of the File Edit commands. Pressing the Right arrow key again would highlight Worksheet and display information in the title bar about the Worksheet commands. Pressing the Left arrow key would return the menu pointer to the File menu item.

■ *NOTE:*   You cannot enter data while the 1-2-3 menu is activated. To deactivate the menu, press Escape as many times as you need to for 1-2-3 to display the READY mode indicator, or press Control+Break to immediately return to READY mode.

Each main menu item contains a list of commands. To display the commands listed under a particular main menu item, move the menu pointer to that item and press Enter or the Up or Down arrow keys. See what happens when you press Enter while the menu pointer is on Edit.

Press: `↵`   *with Edit highlighted*

Figure 2-15:   The Edit Commands

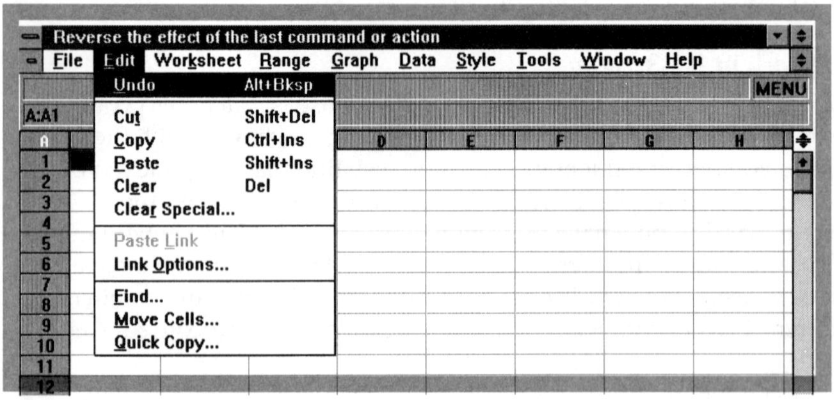

1-2-3 displays a *pull-down menu* of Edit commands. These commands let you copy and move data, create links to others windows applications, and undo (reverse) the effects of a previous action.

Using the keyboard to navigate a pull-down menu works the same way as navigating the main menu, except that you move the menu pointer with the Up and Down arrow keys instead of the Right and Left arrow keys. Use the Down arrow to scroll through the Edit menu. Notice that 1-2-3 displays a description of the currently highlighted command in the title bar, and that when you get to the bottom of the menu, pressing Down once more brings the menu pointer back up to the top.

Take a minute, now, to experiment with using the arrow keys and the Enter key to navigate the 1-2-3 menus. Move the menu pointer through each of the main menu choices and read the explanations for commands. Press Enter to display the pull-down menus associated with a main menu item, and then see what happens when you press Left or Right when a pull-down menu is displayed. Press Escape or Control+Break to return 1-2-3 to READY mode before you go on to the next section.

Choosing a Command with the Arrow Keys   So far, you have used the keyboard only to display menu choices. Now, try choosing a command.

Press: ALT   *(or F10)*   *to activate the menu*

Highlight: Worksheet

Press: ↵

Figure 2-16: The Worksheet Commands

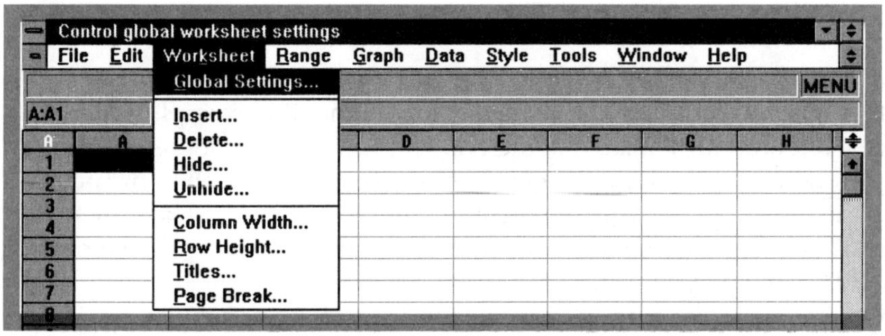

1-2-3 displays the Worksheet commands. The menu pointer is highlighting the Global Settings command. To choose it, press Enter:

Press: ↵

Figure 2-17: **The Worksheet Global Settings Dialog Box**

When you press Enter while the menu pointer is on a command, 1-2-3 executes the command. If the command name in the pull-down menu is followed by an ellipsis (. . .), the command displays a *dialog box*, rather than performing some worksheet operation.

The dialog box is a special window that lets you provide additional information to 1-2-3. In this case, the Worksheet Global Settings dialog box lets you change various settings that affect the current worksheet or worksheet file, such as whether or not 1-2-3 recalculates formulas automatically, how it displays numeric information and aligns text, and so on. You'll learn more about using dialog boxes later in this chapter, in "Using Dialog Boxes." For now, return 1-2-3 to the main menu.

Press: $\boxed{\text{ESC}}$ *to return 1-2-3 to READY mode*

Choosing a Command by Typing its Underlined Letter Notice that each of the main menu and pull-down commands has an underlined letter in the command name. For example, in the main menu, the F in File is underlined; similarly, in the Edit menu, the U in Undo is underlined. You have already seen that you can use the keyboard to choose a command by pressing Alt or F10 to activate the menu bar, moving the menu pointer to a command, and then pressing Enter. You can also choose a command by activating the menu bar and then typing the underlined letter of the command you want to use

Each method of choosing a command has its advantages. If you choose a command by moving the menu pointer to the command and then pressing Enter, you can read the explanations of the menu items before you make a choice. This is handy when you are first learning 1-2-3, or when you are using a part of the product you haven't tried before. Once you are familiar with 1-2-3, however, you may find that pressing Alt or F10 and then typing the underlined letter of the command is faster. Typing the first letter of the command causes 1-2-3 to immediately choose the menu item; you don't have to move the pointer or press the Enter key.

Choose a command by moving the menu pointer to a command and pressing Enter, as you have done before:

Press: |ALT| *to activate the menu bar*

                       |→| *three times, to highlight Worksheet*

                       |↵|

Figure 2-18

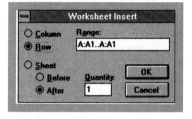

1-2-3 displays the Worksheet pull-down menu again. Now, choose one of the Worksheet menu items by typing its underlined letter:

Type: i   *in either uppercase or lowercase*

Figure 2-19:   The Worksheet Insert Dialog Box

1-2-3 displays the Worksheet Insert dialog box instead of the Worksheet menu. Since you are not going to insert a row, column, or worksheet now, press Escape to remove the dialog box.

Press: |ESC|

■ *NOTE:*   Generally, the first letter of a command is underlined. If there are two commands in the same menu that start with the same letter (as, for example, Wor<u>k</u>sheet and <u>W</u>indow in the main menu), the first letter of one command and a different letter in the other command is underlined.

When the keystroke directions in this book tell you to choose a command with the keyboard, you can use either of the methods you have learned. Remember, though, that if you use one of the arrow keys to choose a command, you must press the Enter key after you high-light the command. (All Enter keystrokes that appear in the keystroke directions are for other purposes and should not be confused with choosing a command.)

Figure 2-20: The Worksheet Global Settings Dialog Box

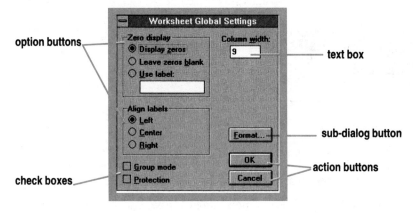

Using a Mouse to Work in 1-2-3 Menus

Besides using the keyboard to navigate through 1-2-3 menus and choose commands, you can use a mouse (assuming one is hooked up to your system and works correctly under Windows). Many people prefer to use the mouse to choose commands, rather than using the keyboard, especially when they are first learning 1-2-3. Table 2-5 explains the mouse procedures for working in menus. Keyboard equivalents are described in Table 2-7.

■ *NOTE:*   The instructions in this table assume that your mouse is configured to use the left button as the "Enter" key. If your mouse buttons work in the reverse fashion, reverse the instructions in the table.

Table 2-5: Mouse Procedures for Working in Menus

Menu Task	How to Do It
Choose a main menu command	Move the mouse pointer to the desired command and click on that command with the left mouse button, then release the mouse button. Or, move the mouse pointer to the menu, hold down the left mouse button, and then, by moving the mouse, drag the menu pointer to the desired command and release the mouse button.
Choose a pull-down menu command	Click on the appropriate main menu command. Then, either drag the menu pointer to the desired pull-down menu command and release the mouse button, or release the mouse button, move the mouse pointer to the command, and click on it.
Return 1-2-3 to READY mode	When 1-2-3 is displaying a menu, click on any part of the 1-2-3 window that is outside the menu. In a dialog box, click on Cancel.

Try experimenting with the mouse. Use the mouse to navigate the main 1-2-3 menu and the pull-down menus and dialog boxes you encountered in the previous section.

1. Choose a command from the main menu.

   Move the mouse pointer to File and click the left mouse button. Notice that instead of merely highlighting File (as 1-2-3 does when you activate the menu by pressing Alt or F10), 1-2-3 also displays the File pull-down menu.

   Clicking a menu item is equivalent to highlighting that menu item and then pressing Enter or the Up or Down arrow key.

2. Navigate the main menu and display pull-down menus.

   With the File pull-down menu still displayed, hold down the left mouse button and slowly drag the mouse across the main menu. (To *drag* means to hold down the button and move the mouse without releasing the button.) Notice that 1-2-3 first highlights each main menu item and then displays the associated pull-down menu.

   Pointing to a menu item, holding down the mouse button, and dragging the mouse is equivalent to moving the pointer along the menu bar with the arrow keys after you have activated a pull-down menu.

3. Choose a pull-down menu command.

   Drag the menu pointer to the Worksheet main menu item. While still holding down the mouse button, move the menu pointer to Global Settings, and then release the button. 1-2-3 displays the Worksheet Global Settings dialog box.

   Dragging the mouse to a main menu item and then to a pull-down menu item combines in one movement numerous presses of the Left or Right and Up or Down arrow keys.

4. Close a dialog box and return 1-2-3 to READY mode.

   Now, instead of pressing Escape to remove the Worksheet Global Settings dialog box, move the mouse pointer to Cancel and click the left mouse button. 1-2-3 returns to READY mode.

5. Choose a command by clicking on menu items.

   Click on Worksheet in the main menu and then release the left mouse button. Notice that 1-2-3 displays the Worksheet pull-down menu even after you have released the mouse button. Now, choose Insert by clicking on the word Insert. 1-2-3 immediately displays the Worksheet Insert dialog box.

   Clicking directly on a menu item without first dragging the mouse is equivalent to activating the menu and then choosing a command by typing its underlined letter.

   Return 1-2-3 to READY mode by selecting Cancel in the Worksheet Insert dialog box.

Using Dialog Boxes

As you saw with the Worksheet Global Settings and the Worksheet Insert commands, some 1-2-3 commands prompt you to specify various options before they actually do anything. For these commands, 1-2-3 displays a *dialog box* that shows you the current settings and gives you an opportunity to change them.

For an example, take a closer look at the dialog box 1-2-3 displays when you choose Worksheet Global Settings.

Choose: Worksheet
                   Global Settings

The Worksheet Global Settings dialog box lets you change many of the characteristics of the current worksheet file. By selecting dialog box options, you can change the way zero values are displayed, determine how text (label) cells are aligned relative to the column borders, adjust the default column width, and modify other *global settings* from their 1-2-3 defaults.

The Worksheet Global Settings dialog box also contains a button that lets you choose the way numeric values are displayed. Click on the button labeled "Format..." and see what happens.

Click on: Format...

Figure 2-21:   The Worksheet Global Settings Format Dialog Box

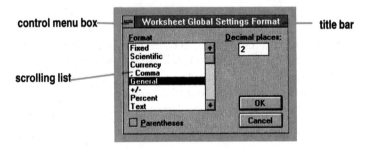

1-2-3 displays the Worksheet Global Settings Format dialog box as well as the Worksheet Global Settings dialog box. These two dialog boxes illustrate most of the dialog box features used in 1-2-3 to display and obtain settings information. The following list describes the basic dialog box elements in some detail. You'll work with them throughout the book.

■ *Action buttons.* Action buttons take effect immediately. For example, almost all 1-2-3 dialog boxes have OK and Cancel, action buttons. When you work with dialog boxes, you make changes to settings and then, if you decide to keep the new settings, you click the OK button and 1-2-3 accepts the changes. If you decide to abandon your changes, you click Cancel, and 1-2-3 leaves the settings and options as they were. Both the OK and the Cancel buttons take effect immediately.

■ *Sub-dialog buttons.* A sub-dialog button is a special kind of action button that brings up another dialog box. Sub-dialog buttons always have ellipses (...) after them. The button labeled "Format..." in the Worksheet Global Settings dialog box is an example. Clicking on the "Format..." button brings up the Worksheet Global Settings Format dialog box.

- *Option buttons.* Option buttons let you choose one of several alternative settings. (Option buttons are also sometimes called *radio buttons* because, like the push buttons on an automobile radio, only one button at a time can be selected). They are organized as groups of round buttons adjacent to descriptive labels. The button with a large black dot in it is the current choice. When you make another choice, that button gets a dot and the former choice becomes blank. For example, the black dot in the middle of the button beside "Display zeros" in the Worksheet Global Settings dialog box means that 1-2-3 will display cells whose value is zero as the numeral 0. To make 1-2-3 display zero values as blank cells, you would click on the button beside "Leave zeros blank" or press Tab until the "Zero display" label is highlighted and then type the letter B.

- *Check boxes.* Check boxes let you make an on/off or yes/no choice. If the check box has an X in it, the choice is selected; an empty box, on the other hand, means that the choice is not selected. Clicking on a check box or pressing Tab until the box is highlighted, and then typing the underlined letter of the label, turns the choice on if it is off and off if it is on. For example, the check box labeled "Parentheses" in the Worksheet Global Settings Format dialog box determines whether or not negative numbers are enclosed in parentheses when they are displayed in the worksheet. Currently, the box is clear, so negative numbers are preceded by a minus sign. If you click on the box to check it and then save the new setting, negative numbers will be enclosed in parentheses.

- *Text boxes.* Text boxes let you type in information. For example, the text box labeled "Decimal places:" lets you specify how many decimal places 1-2-3 will display for numeric data in formats such as Currency format or Comma (,) format. Similarly, the field labeled "Column width:" in the Worksheet Global Settings dialog box is a text box that displays the current default width, in numeric characters, of worksheet columns. To enter a new value in a text box, you double-click on the text box or Tab to it, and then type in a new value. (When the contents of a text box are highlighted, typing in a new value automatically erases the old value.) To edit an existing value, you either click on the text box once or Tab to it and press an arrow key, and then change the value.

- *Scrolling lists.* When you can make many choices, 1-2-3 displays a scrolling list in a dialog box. For example, the list in the box labeled "Format" in the Worksheet Global Settings Format dialog box lets you select the default numeric format from among all the possible numeric formats. To select an item from the list, you click on the item or Tab to the list box, scroll to the item with the arrow keys, and press Enter. If the item you want is not currently displayed, drag the scroll box up or down the scroll bar until the item you want is displayed, and then click on it. (You can also use the arrow keys to scroll through the list.)

Table 2-6 summarizes mouse movements you can use to make selections in dialog boxes. Keyboard equivalents are described in Table 2-7.

Table 2-6: Mouse Movements for Dialog Boxes

Dialog Box Task	Mouse Movement
Select an option button in a dialog box	Click on the option button you want.
Select a check box in a dialog box	Click on a check box to check it (if it is unchecked), or to clear it (if it is checked).
Select a text box in a dialog box	Double-click a text box to highlight it, or click on a text box to edit its contents.
Back out of a dialog box	Click on the Cancel button in the dialog box.
Navigate within a list of names (such as a file-name or range-name list)	Move the mouse pointer to the list's scroll bar, and then click on the scroll bar or drag the scroll box until the name is visible.
Select a name from a displayed list	Move the mouse pointer to the desired name and click the left mouse button.
Accept the displayed response to a prompt in a dialog box	Click on the OK button in the dialog box.

You'll work with dialog boxes in later chapters. For now, return to READY mode by clicking on the Cancel buttons in the two dialog boxes.

Click on: Cancel   *in the Worksheet Global Settings Format dialog box*
                     Cancel   *in the Worksheet Global Settings dialog box*

A Note on Moving Through Menus and Dialog Boxes

Most people find they use both the mouse and the keyboard to move around the worksheet and execute 1-2-3 commands. From now on, the keystroke instructions in this book will assume that both methods are available to you. When the instructions specify either keystrokes or mouse movements, they reflect the way that the authors find is easiest to get a particular job done. However, in most cases, these choices reflect strictly personal preferences. If an instruction calls for a mouse movement and you prefer to use a keyboard command instead, by all means use the keyboard equivalents for mouse movements. Conversely, if the keystroke instructions specify a keyboard command and you prefer to use the mouse for the same action, feel free to do so.

Table 2-7 explains the keyboard equivalents to the mouse movements described in Tables 2-5 and 2-6. For complete information on using the keyboard with 1-2-3, see the 1-2-3 printed documentation, or select Keys from the 1-2-3 Help index.

Table 2-7: Keyboard Equivalents to Mouse Movements

Menu task	How to Do It
Choose a main menu command	Press Alt or F10 and type the underlined letter of the menu name.

Menu task	How to Do It
Choose a pull-down menu command	Choose the appropriate menu command. Then, type the underlined letter of the menu name.
Return 1-2-3 to READY mode	Press Escape as many times as necessary, or press Control+Break.
Select an option button in a dialog box	Tab to the label for the group of buttons from which you want to make a selection and type the underlined letter of the button name, or press Alt and type the underlined letter of the button name.
Select a check box in a dialog box	Tab to the check box and type the underlined letter of the check box name, or press Alt, and type the underlined letter of the button name.
Select a text box in a dialog box	Tab to the text box, or press Alt and type the underlined letter of the text box name.
Back out of a dialog box	Press Escape.
Navigate within a list of names (such as a file-name or range-name list)	Tab to the list and then press Up or Down.
Select a name from a displayed list	Highlight the name with the Up or Down key and then press Enter to select it.
Accept the displayed response to a prompt in a dialog box	Press Enter.

Cascade Menus

Most pull-down menu commands either take effect immediately or present you with dialog boxes so you can further specify what you want 1-2-3 to do. Some commands, however, use *cascade menus* instead.

Somewhat like a cascading waterfall, in which each succeeding step flows to the next, each choice you make in a cascade menu leads to another choice, until an action occurs. To see how this works, choose the Range Name command.

Choose: Range   Name

Figure 2-22: The Range Name Cascade Menu

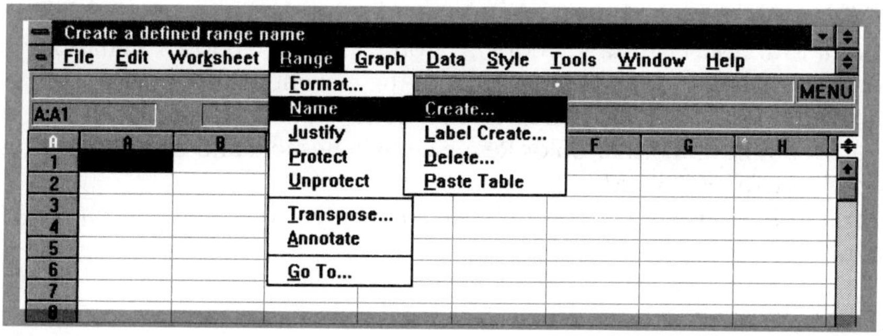

Cascade menus are indicated in pull-down menus by a right-facing black arrowhead. Some of the cascade menu choices lead to additional cascade menu choices, while others lead either to a dialog box or to a command that takes effect immediately.

Press: ESC   *three times, to return 1-2-3 to READY mode*

The 1-2-3 Classic Menu

Besides the normal 1-2-3 for Windows menu, you can also use the *1-2-3 Classic menu* to execute 1-2-3 commands. The 1-2-3 Classic menu appears in its own window near the top of the 1-2-3 Window when you press either the slash key (/) or the less-than symbol (<) when 1-2-3 is in READY mode. (You can move the window elsewhere, if you like, by dragging it with the mouse.)

Figure 2-23:   The 1-2-3 Classic Menu Displaying 1-2-3 Release 3.1 Commands

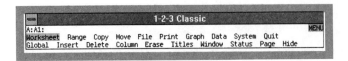

If you are familiar with earlier versions of 1-2-3, you may find the 1-2-3 Classic menu especially useful while you are learning 1-2-3/W. This menu duplicates the 1-2-3 Release 3.1 for DOS command structure. It provides full keystroke compatibility; if your fingers have "memorized" familiar 1-2-3 commands, they will feel quite comfortable with 1-2-3 Classic.

The 1-2-3 Classic menu also lets you execute 1-2-3 Release 3.1 Wysiwyg commands. Just press the colon key (:) with 1-2-3 in READY mode and the Release 3.1 Wysiwyg menu appears.

Figure 2-24:   The 1-2-3 Classic Menu Displaying 1-2-3 Wysiwyg Commands

Besides making it easier to use 1-2-3/W if you are already familiar with previous releases of 1-2-3, the 1-2-3 Classic menus allow you to access some 1-2-3 commands that you can't get to from the regular 1-2-3/W menu. Some of the more useful commands include /Data Table Labeled (lets you create multi-variable cross tabulations), /Worksheet Erase (closes all files in memory), /File Erase (erases a disk file), /File Retrieve (erases the current file from memory and replaces it with a new file), :Display Options Cell-Pointer Solid/Outline (changes cell pointer to either a solid or an outline), :Format Color Reverse (switches text and background colors), and /System (switches to a DOS window).

From time to time, this book will point out 1-2-3 Classic commands you can use as shortcuts for 1-2-3/W commands.

■ *NOTE:*　　When you use the 1-2-3 Classic menus, you must choose commands with the keyboard, rather than the mouse.

Entering Data in the Worksheet

Entering data in a worksheet is different from entering data in some other kinds of software packages. Data that you type is entered into the cell highlighted by the cell pointer (the current cell), but the data doesn't appear in the cell as you type, the way it would if you were using a word processor. Instead, 1-2-3 displays the entry in the edit line of the control panel. When you are through typing an entry, you *complete* it, and it disappears from the edit line and reappears in the current cell. (Although this may seem a little strange if you have never used an electronic spreadsheet, you will soon get used to it. As you work with 1-2-3, you will also find that this method has a number of advantages.)

After you've typed something, there are three ways to complete the entry:

- ■ By pressing Enter
- ■ By clicking on the Confirm button
- ■ By pressing one of the pointer-movement keys

The *Confirm button* is a box that contains a check mark. It appears to the left of the contents of the edit line as soon as you start to enter data. Alongside it is the *Cancel button;* clicking the Cancel button abandons the entry. The *pointer-movement keys* include the arrow keys, the Home key, and the Page Up and Page Down keys. (They are described in detail in Chapter 3, in "Moving Around the Worksheet.")

Figure 2-25: The Confirm and Cancel Buttons

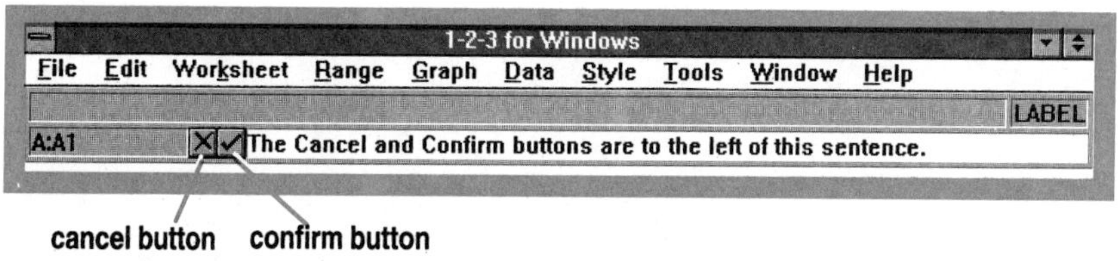

cancel button　　confirm button

If you complete an entry by pressing Enter or by clicking the Confirm button, the cell pointer remains in the current cell. If you complete the entry by pressing a pointer-movement key, the entry is accepted, and then the cell pointer moves in the same direction it would if you had pressed the pointer-movement key from READY mode. For instance, if you complete an entry by pressing the Right arrow key, 1-2-3 inserts the entry in the current cell, then the cell pointer moves right one cell. Similarly, if you complete an entry by pressing the Page Down key, the cell pointer moves down one screen after 1-2-3 accepts the entry.

Try completing some entries now. First, complete an entry by pressing the Enter key:

Press:　　　　　HOME　　*to make sure the cell pointer is in cell A1*

Type:　　　　　3000

Press:　　　　　⏎

Notice that the Confirm and Cancel buttons appear next to the box in which you type data. Pressing Enter puts the number 3000 in cell A1 and leaves the cell pointer in A1. Clicking the Confirm button would have the same effect. Conversely, pressing Escape or clicking the Cancel button would prevent 1-2-3 from accepting the data.

Figure 2-26: Entering Data in the Worksheet

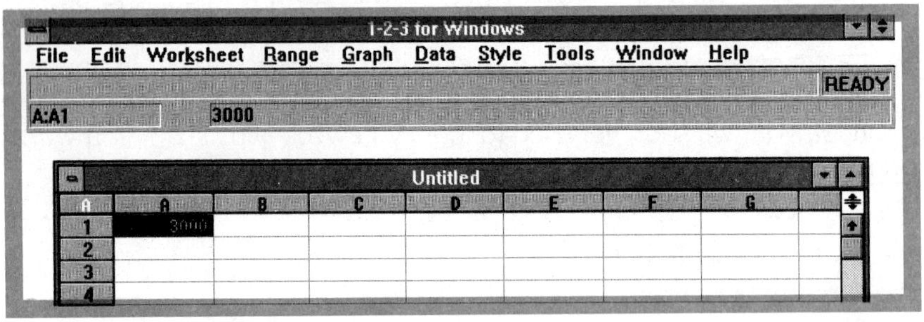

Next, complete some entries by pressing the Right arrow key. Before you begin, maximize the 1-2-3 window so that it displays 20 rows by eight columns.

Click on: the Worksheet window's Maximize button

Now, enter more numbers. Notice what happens as you enter a number in column H: when you press Right, 1-2-3 automatically scrolls the screen so it can display the area the cell pointer is in.

Press: →

Type: 4000

Press: →

Type: 5000

Press: →

Type: 6000

Press: →

Type: 7000

Press: →

Type: 8000

Press: →

Type: 9000

Press: →

Type: 10000

Press: →

Figure 2-27: The Maximized Worksheet Window

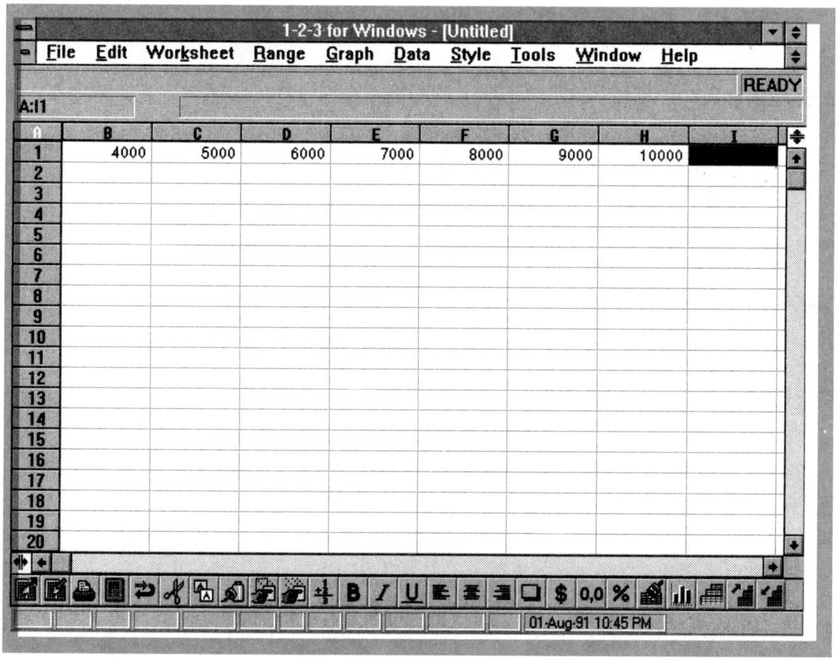

Now, try moving to a cell by clicking on it, and then enter some data in that cell.

Click on: cell C4

Type: I moved here with the mouse

Click on: *the Confirm button (check mark) in the edit line*

Before going on to the next section, take some time to enter data into the worksheet and to experiment with the pointer-movement keys and the mouse. You will not keep this worksheet, so don't type anything you'll want to save.

■ *NOTE:*   In this exercise, the actual information you enter in the worksheet is not really important; however, if you notice a typing mistake before you complete an entry and want to correct it, you can use the Backspace key to erase the error and then retype the text. If you want to correct an error after you have completed an entry, move to the cell and type in a new, correct entry. You'll learn more about entering data and correcting mistakes in Chapter 3.

When you are through experimenting, exit 1-2-3.

Choose: File   Exit

This time, 1-2-3 does not immediately exit when you choose File Exit. Instead, it warns you that you have made changes to a worksheet file but have not saved the file, and it gives you one more chance to change your mind. Since you don't care about the changes you have made, select No.

Select: No

1-2-3 exits and leaves you in the Windows Program Manager (or the Windows Desktop, if you have asked that the Program Manager be minimized on use).

Figure 2-28:   The File Exit Dialog Box

Files

Start up 1-2-3 again. (Restore the Program Manager, if necessary, and then double-click on the 1-2-3 icon). Notice that the information you typed into the worksheet in the previous section is not there when 1-2-3 comes back on your screen. In fact, it's not anywhere, anymore. While you use 1-2-3, your work is stored in the computer's random access memory (RAM). This memory is cleared out when you exit 1-2-3 or whenever the power to the computer is interrupted. Therefore, what you create isn't permanent until you save your work somewhere.

You save your work in *disk files* on a hard disk or a diskette. Storing a worksheet in a disk file makes a copy of the worksheet on the disk's magnetic medium. This copy remains on the disk when the power goes off; it is erased only when you explicitly erase it.

When you start up 1-2-3, the program displays a blank, untitled worksheet; 1-2-3 assumes that you want to start a new worksheet. Often, of course, you will want to use an existing worksheet that you have saved in a file. The following sections explain how to save your worksheets in files, and how to open previously saved worksheet files so you can use them.

■ *NOTE:*   In the following exercises, you are going to create several small worksheet files. You will use these files again in Chapter 10.

Saving a New Worksheet File

You should already have a blank worksheet on your screen. If you don't, exit 1-2-3 and then start up the program again. (You will soon learn how to erase a worksheet without exiting and restarting, but this method will do for now.)

1. Create a small worksheet.

First, maximize the Worksheet window, then enter some text in cell A1 of a blank worksheet:

Click on: the Worksheet window's Maximize button
Type: Folktale Workshop   *in cell A1*

Press: ⏎

This enters the text **Folktale Workshop** into the worksheet. Notice that the part of the text that is wider than column A is displayed in column B.

Figure 2-29:   Creating a New Worksheet File

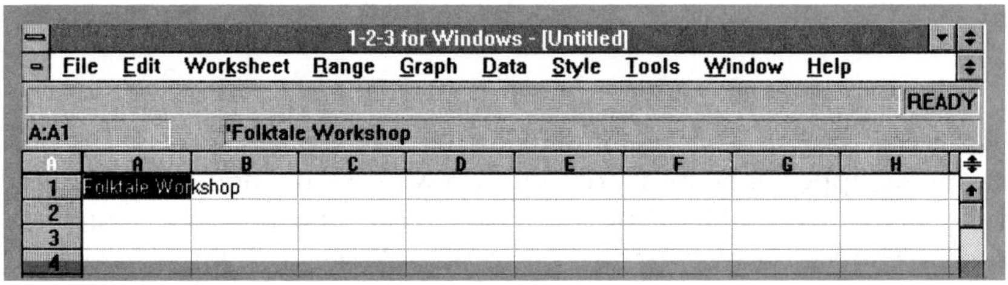

2. Choose a name for the worksheet file.

Before you can save a worksheet in a file, you must give the file a name. Try to give a file a name that readily reminds you of the file's contents. For instance, in this case, the worksheet file's name will be FOLKTALE. The file name can contain up to eight characters. Recommended characters are listed in Table 2-8.

Many disk files are identified not only by their name but also by a *file extension*. File extensions generally tell you something about how a file is used, rather than describing the contents of the file. For example, program files usually have the extension .COM (short for "command") or .EXE (short for "executable"). 1-2-3/W worksheet files have the extension .WK3. 1-2-3 automatically adds this extension when you save the file; you don't have to type it.

Table 2-8:   Recommended File Name Characters

You can use the following characters in file names on any of the systems Lotus supports for running 1-2-3. See your operating system's documentation for other characters that can or cannot be used in file names.

A through Z (uppercase or lowercase)

0 through 9

_(underscore)

3. Save the worksheet in a file.

At the moment, the worksheet is unnamed. To save this worksheet in a new file called FOLKTALE.WK3, you will choose the File Save As command. File Save As saves a file under a new name. (Once the file has been named, you can save any changes to it with the File Save command.)

Choose: File   Save As

(Remember, you can choose commands with either the keyboard or the mouse.)

1-2-3 displays the File Save As dialog box and proposes the system-generated name FILE0001.WK3. The dialog box lets you specify different drives and directories, and it also allows you to protect the file with a password. In this case, however, the only thing you'll change is the file name itself. When you start typing, 1-2-3 will erase the name FILE0001.WK3 and instead display the characters you type. You can type file names in uppercase or lowercase.

Type: `folktale`

Press: ↵

Pressing Enter tells 1-2-3 you have finished naming the file and starts the File Save As operation. The mode indicator in the upper right corner of the 1-2-3 window momentarily changes to WAIT while the worksheet is saved in a file. (You may not even see the indicator change, since the worksheet is small.) The file is saved in the current 1-2-3 directory. Later in this chapter you will learn how to specify a different directory.

The title bar now displays the name FOLKTALE.WK3 instead of Untitled, and the file remains on the screen after you save it.

A Note on 1-2-3 for Windows Files   When you create a worksheet file and save it to disk, 1-2-3 also saves a separate file with the same name but with a .FM3 extension. (For example, when 1-2-3 created FOLKTALE.WK3, it also created a file called FOLKTALE.FM3.) This file contains embedded graphs and drawings as well as formatting information for the .WK3 file with the same name.

Normally, when you work with 1-2-3, you don't have to think about this "shadow" .FM3 file. However, if you copy worksheet files to another disk or directory, make sure you move the .FM3 file along with the .WK3 file with which it is associated. Otherwise, important formatting information and any embedded graphs will not be available to 1-2-3 when you retrieve the copied file.

Opening and Closing Worksheet Files

File Save As and File Save create a copy of your worksheet in a file on disk; conversely, File Open brings a worksheet file from the disk into 1-2-3's memory.

Opening a file does not alter the disk file. Instead, it makes a temporary copy of the file in the computer's memory. Changes you make to this temporary copy are made to the file on disk only if you save the file again. Likewise, unless you choose to save a file before you close it, *closing* an in-memory file removes the file from memory but has no effect on the disk file.

In this example, you are going to remove the current worksheet file from memory, and then create a new in-memory copy of the worksheet file by opening the saved worksheet file from disk.

1. Erase the current worksheet file from memory.

If the FOLKTALE.WK3 worksheet is still on your screen, remove it by closing it.

Choose: `File   Close`

File Close leaves you with a blank, untitled worksheet, as if you had just started 1-2-3.

■ **CAUTION:** File Close erases the current worksheet file from memory. If you have changed a file but have not saved your changes, File Close asks if 1-2-3 should save the file before closing it. If you have made any changes you wish to preserve, make sure you select Yes.

saved worksheet file.

amed FOLKTALE.WK3 to retrieve it from the disk:

Open

File

le Open dialog box, which prompts you for the name of the file to es of worksheet files stored in the current directory, and permits you e, directory, or both.

re 2-30 shows only FOLKTALE.WK3, you may see other file names in s of worksheet files supplied with 1-2-3 and/or worksheet files created by other people who have used the program before you. You may also see one or more irectories:" list box. For the moment, ignore them. Soon, you will you'll create in this book in their own directories, and to instruct 1-2-3 to look for files there.

To select a file to open, you can type in the name of the file or you can highlight the name in the "Files:" list box.

Select: folktale.wk3

1-2-3 displays the size and date of FOLKTALE.WK3 under "File information:" in the dialog box. Open the file by pressing Enter or clicking on OK.

Click on: OK

The disk drive light blinks, and then the file named FOLKTALE.WK3 appears in a new Worksheet window. You can tell it is the same file you saved before because the phrase "Folktale Workshop" is now back on the screen and the title bar reads FOLKTALE.WK3.

■ *NOTE:*   As a shortcut, you can double-click on the name of the file you want to open.

More Practice Saving and Opening Files

The following exercise gives you more practice in the basic skills of saving and opening files. It also creates some small files you will use in the exercises later in this book.

1. Create another small worksheet file and save it to disk.

Now you will create a new worksheet file and save it under the file name TOYS.WK3. The easiest way to do this is to modify the current worksheet file and save it under the new name.

First, enter some new text in cell A1. Notice that when you type an entry into a cell that already has data in it, the new entry replaces the old data.

Move to: cell A1

Type: Toys Division

Press: ⏎

Now, save the file under a new name.

Choose: File   Save As

Figure 2-31:   Saving a File Under a New Name

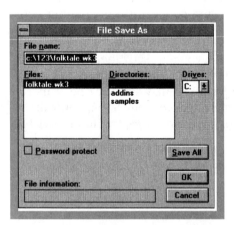

1-2-3 displays the name of the current file in the "File name:" text box. Give the modified worksheet a new file name:

Type: toys

Press: ⏎

This saves the worksheet as a new file named TOYS.WK3. 1-2-3 displays the new file name in the title bar.

2. Create and save four more small worksheet files.

So far, you've created two separate files, FOLKTALE.WK3 and TOYS.WK3. Now, save another small file, following the same technique you just used to create TOYS.WK3.

Type:	`Movie/Video Division` *in cell A1*
Press:	⏎ *to enter text in the new worksheet*
Choose:	`File` `Save As`
Type:	`movie` *to name the new worksheet file*
Press:	⏎ *to save the new worksheet as MOVIE.WK3*

Create three more such files, typing different information into each new worksheet, and naming the worksheet file appropriately. To continue with the set, type Comics Division into the next file and name the file COMICS.WK3, then do the same thing with Apparel Division (APPAREL.WK3), and Books Division (BOOKS.WK3).

3. Open FOLKTALE.WK3.

After you have created a total of six files, open FOLKTALE.WK3 again. This time, use the "File Open" icon on the icon palette. The "File Open" icon depicts a diskette with an arrow pointing upward, as in Figure 2-32.

Figure 2-32

Click on: *the File Open icon in the icon palette*

Your screen should look like Figure 2-33 on the next page (unless there were other worksheet files in the current 1-2-3 directory when you began this chapter). All the files you created are listed in the "Files:" list. Select `folktale.wk3`.

If there were other files in the current 1-2-3 directory, these files are listed too, and you may have to scroll through the list to find `folktale.wk3`. To do so, either drag the list's scroll box until you see the name `folktale.wk3`, or Tab to the "Files:" list and press Down until `folktale.wk3` is highlighted.

Select:	`folktale.wk3`
Click on:	`OK`

The file once again appears on your screen in its own window. BOOKS.WK3 remains in memory, "behind" the new file, as in Figure 2-34 on the next page.

■ *NOTE:*   If you prefer, you can also type the name of the file you want to open in the "File name:" text box and then click OK or press Enter to open the file, or you can double-click the file's name and immediately open the file. If you type the file name, you do not have to type the .WK3 extension.

Figure 2-33:   The Display After Clicking on the "File Open" Icon

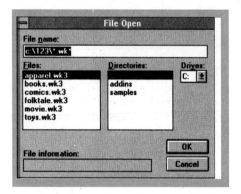

Saving a Modified File

The procedure for saving a modified file is even easier than the procedure for saving a new file. 1-2-3 remembers the original name of the current file and uses it automatically. Take the following steps to modify FOLKTALE.WK3 and save the modified version:

1. Modify FOLKTALE.WK3.

   First, add some text to distinguish the new file:

   Press: →   *three times, to move to cell D1*

   Type: Cash Flow Forecast

   Press: ↵

2. Save the revised file.

   Choose: File   Save

   1-2-3 replaces the existing disk version of the file with the file in memory. That's all there is to it! When you save a file that has already been saved at least once, 1-2-3 does not display a dialog box. It assumes you want to save the modified file under the original file's name.

Figure 2-34: Two Files in Memory at the Same Time

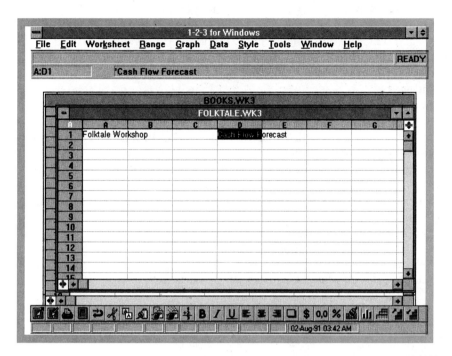

■ *NOTE:*   You can save a modified file with a single mouse click by clicking on the "File Save" icon in the icon palette. The "File Save" icon looks like a diskette with an arrow pointing into it:

When to Save Files

All the work you do in 1-2-3 is stored in your computer's memory. The changes you make are temporary: if you exit 1-2-3, a power failure occurs, or you accidentally unplug the computer before you have saved your file, those changes will be gone.

Therefore, it is a good idea to save your work regularly. Unless you have very few changes to make, don't wait until you have completed all the changes to save your files. Instead, get in the habit of saving your work each time you do something that would take a significant amount of time to re-create, or whenever you leave the computer.

Multiple Files in Memory

As you can see from the preceding exercises, 1-2-3 allows you to have more than one file in memory at a time. Right now, BOOKS.WK3 and FOLKTALE.WK3 are in memory. In fact, if your computer has sufficient memory, you can have numerous files in memory at once, and each file can contain multiple worksheets. The maximum number of worksheets, distributed among all the files in memory, is 256. For example, you could have one file with as many as 256 worksheets; 256 files, each with one worksheet; or any combination in between. (The idea of multiple files in memory is similar to a feature common among many word processors. These programs allow you to have more than one editing window open at a time, and to edit a different file in each window.)

A worksheet file in memory is known as an *active file*. With several files loaded into memory, 1-2-3 becomes the equivalent of an electronic file drawer. Much as you might leaf through the pages of a file folder and then move on to the next file folder in the drawer, you can move quickly from worksheet to worksheet within a file, and from active file to active file.

The electronic file drawer is considerably more flexible than the physical one. You can *tile* the individual file windows so that all files are displayed simultaneously, you can cascade the files (overlap them so that the title bars of each file are exposed) to make it easier to flip from one to another, or you can maximize one file and hide the others behind it. You can also arbitrarily resize any or all worksheet files or shrink them to icons.

Multiple files are explained in detail in Chapter 10.

Figure 2-35:   **Multiple Worksheet Files in Memory**

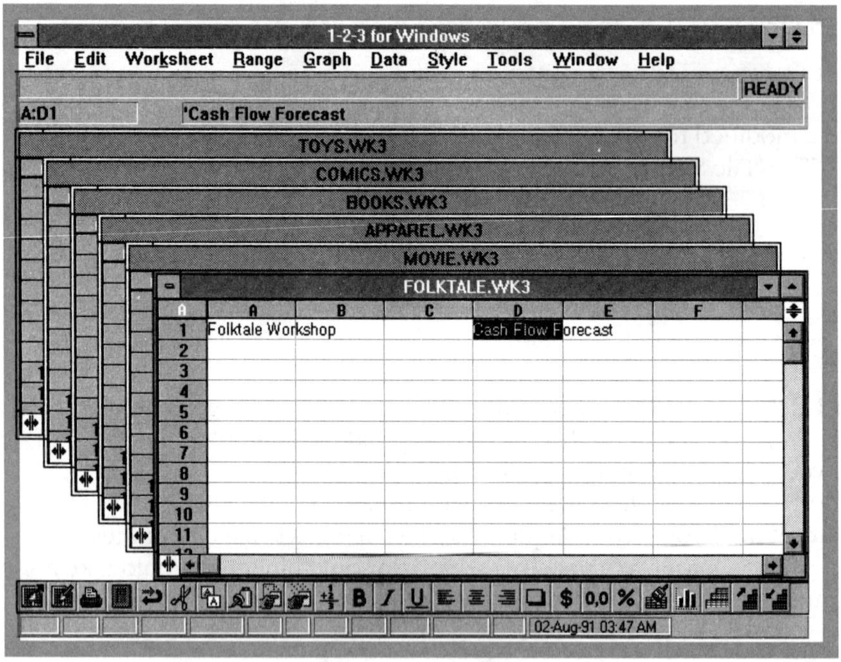

File Linking

The main difference between 1-2-3's electronic file drawer and the more conventional kind is that cells in one file can use information in cells in other files, so that changes you make in one file are automatically reflected in one or more other files. This feature, known as *file linking*, makes it easier for the information in separate files created by different people to be combined into one report, or for one standard table, form, or database to be used by many people.

A worksheet file can have links to other worksheet files either in memory or on disk. A link consists of a formula entered in one worksheet that specifies a cell in another worksheet—for example, +<<TOYS.WK3>>A:C5.

Links are useful for many purposes, one of the most common being *data consolidation*. For example, suppose you have a Q1 total income figure in one worksheet that is the sum of income figures in a number of other files. By creating links in the Q1 total income file to the income figure in each of the other files, you can have 1-2-3 automatically update the total income figure whenever any of the income figures in the subsidiary files change.

Figure 2-36

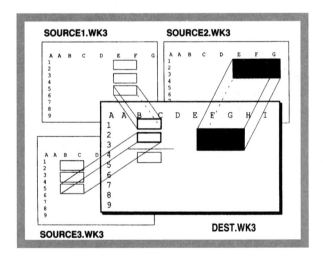

Besides letting you automatically update formulas that are affected by changes in other worksheets, links make it possible to create smaller, more manageable worksheets. You can store a summary worksheet's source data in several small worksheet files instead of storing all the data in a single large file.

You'll learn more about file linking in Chapter 10

Changing the Default File Directory

So far, you have created a number of small worksheet files. When you saved those files, you saved them in the 1-2-3 program directory (unless 1-2-3 was already set up to save files in a different directory, such as WORK). This is okay now, when you have few worksheet files. However, saving all your files in the same directory could prove to be an inconvenience later on when you have dozens or hundreds of worksheet files related to many different projects. Doing so is roughly the same as storing all your printed reports and files in one big pile on your desk. A better idea is to put all data files that are related to one another in the same place, just as you would put related printed reports in the same file folder.

Creating a 123BOOK Directory

The following steps show you how to put some order into your 1-2-3 life. You will first create a directory in which to store the worksheet files you are going to create as you work through this book. The remaining steps lead you through the process of telling 1-2-3 to use this directory each time you File Save or File Open worksheet files.

■ *NOTE:* This exercise uses the Windows File Manager to create the 123BOOK directory. Alternatively, you can temporarily leave 1-2-3 by switching to the Program Manager and starting a DOS session. Then you can create the 123BOOK directory with the MKDIR command. See your DOS manual for more information on using MKDIR.

1. Switch out of 1-2-3.

   One advantage to working with a Windows program like 1-2-3 is that you can switch to other programs without actually exiting 1-2-3. For now, you'll temporarily return to the Program Manager so you can start the File Manager and create a directory. Then you'll resume your work in 1-2-3.

   From 1-2-3's READY mode, press Control+Escape to display the Windows's Task List window. Double-click Program Manager to switch to the Windows Program Manager.

Figure 2-37: The Windows Task List

2. Start File Manager.

   Double-click on the File Manager icon (a two-drawer file cabinet) to start the File Manager. (File Manager should be in your Main program group. If it is not, you can start File Manager by selecting File Run from the Program Manager, typing **winfile**, and pressing Enter or clicking on OK.)

3. Change File Manager to the 1-2-3 program drive.

The File Manager displays a Directory Tree window that contains a list of available disk drives on your system. By default, the drive on which you have installed Windows is highlighted. If necessary, double-click the drive on which you have installed 1-2-3/W to make that the current File Manager drive.

The File Manager displays the files in the root directory of the selected drive.

Figure 2-38: The File Manager Window

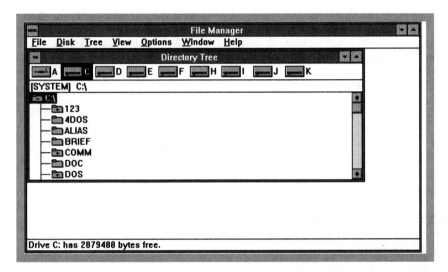

4. Create a 123BOOK directory in the 1-2-3 program directory.

First, change to the 1-2-3 program directory by double-clicking the directory name (for example, 123 or 123W). File Manager displays the 1-2-3 program files.

Then, create the new directory. Choose File Create Directory from the File Manager menu. File Manager displays the Create Directory dialog box. Type in the name of the directory you want to create, 123BOOK.

Figure 2-39: Creating a 123BOOK Directory in the File Manager.

Click on OK in the Create Directory dialog box to accept the new directory name, then choose File Exit and select OK to leave File Manager.

5. Return to 1-2-3.

If necessary, press Control+Escape to redisplay the Task List window, and then double-click 1-2-3 for Windows. Windows returns you to 1-2-3 at the same place you were before you switched out.

6. Change the "Worksheet directory:" setting of the Tools User Setup dialog box.

Now that you've created a directory for the files you'll create in this book, you must tell 1-2-3 to use the new directory as the place to save and open files. To do so, you must change the *default directory* setting. Initially, this setting is the same as the directory in which the 1-2-3 program files are stored (unless you supplied a different directory name when you ran the 1-2-3 Install program). Make sure 1-2-3 is in READY mode, then take the following steps to change the default directory setting to the 123BOOK directory:

Choose: Tools   User Setup

1-2-3 displays the Tools User Setup dialog box. Modify the "Worksheet directory:" text box so that it displays the new directory. The easiest way to do so is to type W or press Tab until the text box is highlighted and then type the complete path, for example, C:\123\123BOOK. When you have finished, your screen should look like Figure 2-40.

Figure 2-40:   The New "Worksheet Directory:" Specification

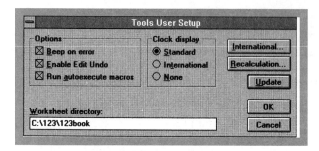

7. Save the new default directory setting.

The *current directory* is now the 123BOOK directory. If you simply pressed Enter or clicked on OK, 1-2-3 would look for and save files in your 123BOOK directory for the remainder of the current session. However, the next time you used 1-2-3, the default directory setting would revert back to its original value. To make the new setting permanent, you must instruct 1-2-3 to revise a file on disk known as a *configuration file*. This file is called 123W.INI and it is stored in your Windows program directory. It is a permanent storage place for default settings you change from the Tools User Setup dialog box.

The process of revising the configuration file is called *updating*. To update the configuration file now, select "Update" from the Tools User Setup dialog box.

Select: `Update`

The disk drive light comes on for a moment as 1-2-3 saves your changes. Click on OK to return 1-2-3 to READY mode.

Select: `OK`

The next time you start 1-2-3, it will automatically look for and save files in your 123BOOK directory.

A Note on File Directories

You can use the techniques presented here to organize your other 1-2-3 worksheet files. For instance, if part of your job entails creating a number of budget worksheets, consider creating a BUDGET directory for these worksheets. When you know you are going to be spending most of your time in 1-2-3 working on budget worksheet files, change the default directory to this BUDGET directory and select "Update" to store this change in the 123W.INI file. 1-2-3 will use the new default directory when it saves or opens files.

If you need to switch from the default directory to another directories during a particular 1-2-3 session, you can temporarily change the current directory with the Tools User Setup command. Follow the same procedure you did in the previous section, but instead of selecting Update after you change the "Worksheet directory:" specification, just click on OK. When you return to READY mode, the new directory will be the current directory, but only for the current 1-2-3 session. When you exit 1-2-3 and start up the program again, 1-2-3 will use the previously saved setting in the 123W.INI file to establish the default directory.

The 1-2-3 Help System

1-2-3's Help system is an electronic reference manual that instantly provides detailed information about how the program works and how to use it.

Unlike a paper reference manual, 1-2-3's on-line Help provides *context-sensitive help*. 1-2-3 senses the activity you are engaged in and tries to provide help appropriate to that activity. You can call Help at any point—even in the middle of a command sequence or while entering information into a cell—and 1-2-3 displays a Help window that explains the choices available to you at that moment. You can also search Help for specific information, including information not found in the printed 1-2-3 documentation. The following sections demonstrate how and when to use Help.

How to Call Up 1-2-3 Help

You call up Help either by selecting Help from the main menu, or by pressing F1, the Help key. Each Help message is tailored to what is currently on the screen. For example, from READY mode, pressing F1 (Help) provides you with a Help index:

Press: F1   **(HELP)**

Figure 2-41: The 1-2-3 Help Window

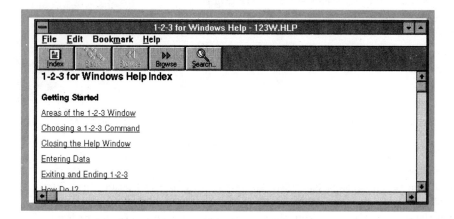

Pressing F1 (Help) from any other point gives you help on the current task. For example, if you are about to create a graph and need help, choose Graph from the main menu, highlight the Graph command on which you need help, and press F1 (Help).

To clear the Help screen, press Alt-F4, choose Close from the Help window's Control menu, or double-click the Control menu. Use one of these methods now to remove Help.

■ *NOTE:*   If you click the 1-2-3 window or the Minimize button on the Help window, Windows restores 1-2-3 to the screen but leaves Help in memory. You can then switch to Help by pressing Alt-Tab or by selecting Help from the Windows Task List. If you reduce the size of the 1-2-3 window, you can even view 1-2-3 and 1-2-3 Help side-by-side.

You can also call up Help by choosing Help from the main menu. Help presents several broad categories to choose from, including the very handy Using Help choice.

How to Navigate Within Help

Often, you press Help when you need specific information, then remove the Help window and go on with what you were doing. Equally often, however, the answer to one question triggers another. The Help system is designed to make it easy for you to follow a line of inquiry.

There are six main ways to move through the Help system. You can:

- *Call up the Help Index and select a topic.*   When you need to refresh your memory about a command, or remind yourself of how to do something, and you know the name of the topic you are looking for, use the Help Index. To get to the Help index, press F1 (Help) from READY mode, select Index from any Help screen, or choose Help Index from the main menu. Once you are in the Help Index, you can go directly to a screen that describes any of the listed topics.

- *Select a highlighted topic from a Help screen.*   Most Help screens, including the Help Index, not only display information, but also provide a way to find out more about a subtopic or a related topic. In the Help screens, clicking on a word that is underlined with a solid line (or tabbing to it and pressing Enter) moves you to a Help screen about that topic. Repeating this process in the new Help screen will move you further into Help screens on the same subject. Selecting a word that is underlined with a dotted line displays a short definition of the term. (You can find the same definition in the on-line glossary, available by selecting Glossary from the main 1-2-3 Help Index.)

Figure 2-42: The Using Help screen explains in detail how to use 1-2-3 Help, as well as how to customize Help and print out help screens.

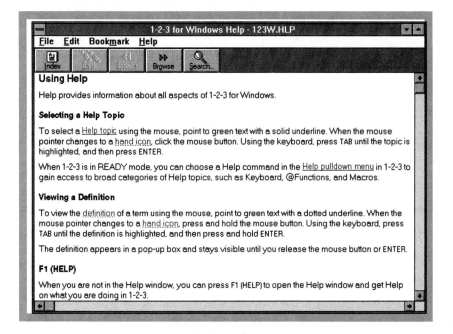

- *Browse through Help topics in sequence.* Selecting the Browse button with the right-pointing arrows lets you move forward through the current set of Help topics one topic at a time. Selecting Browse with the left-pointing arrows lets you move backward through the current set of Help topics.
- *Search for specific information by keyword.* If you select the Search button (magnifying glass), 1-2-3 Help prompts you for a keyword or phrase and then tries to find matching topics. After you type a phrase, you click on the Search button, highlight the topic that seems most likely to contain the information you're looking for, and then select Go To to call up the associated Help screen. (Or, as a shortcut, you can double-click on the keyword and then double-click on the topic.)
- *Return to a previously viewed Help screen.* Sometimes, it's handy to move through a sequence of topics, then go back to where you started and pursue a different path through on-line Help. Clicking on the Back button (leftward-moving footprints)

moves you back to the previously viewed Help screen. Repeatedly clicking on Back eventually returns you to the first screen in the current Help session.

■ *Get help on error messages.* For many people, the most frequent use of 1-2-3's Help system is to get help on errors. When you make certain kinds of errors, 1-2-3 displays an error-message box describing the problem. Pressing F1 (Help) after you get an error message presents you with a screen of information on the error message you received. Many of the information screens also present you with choices of additional Help topics related to commands that could have generated the error message.

Experiment with these techniques on your own to see how they work, and to acquaint yourself with features of 1-2-3 you haven't learned about yet. Get deep into Help, then use Back to return to an earlier screen, or Search to go to a completely different topic. Once you find an area you are interested in, Browse through it. Browsing Help is a good way to acquaint yourself with features of 1-2-3 you have not yet used, or that you'd like to learn more about.

When to Use Help

The 1-2-3 Help system is an often-underused tool. Take advantage of it!

As you work through this book, use Help to find out more about a topic. As you continue to work with 1-2-3, press F1 (Help) to explore the program and to remind yourself of commands and features you have not used recently. Print out Help screens and keep them handy for future reference.

Don't wait until you are stuck or encounter an error to press F1 (Help); use it whenever you are puzzled or just plain curious. Reading a Help screen generally takes much less time than finding the same information in a book, or asking someone. More often than you might suspect, you'll find exactly what you need.

■ *NOTE:* If you have used previous versions of 1-2-3, be sure to read the special section on upgrading in 1-2-3 Help. Choose Help from the main menu, then choose For Upgraders. This section describes how to use the 1-2-3 Classic menu, and details correspondences between 1-2-3/W commands and commands of previous releases of 1-2-3.

Configuring 1-2-3

The installation process adapts 1-2-3 to your equipment, but you can also customize 1-2-3 to the needs of a project and to your working habits. This section describes how to "fine tune" 1-2-3 for your personal preferences and needs.

Changing Global Settings and Global Defaults

There are two basic kinds of settings you can change. These are:

■ *Worksheet Global Settings.* Worksheet global settings apply to the current worksheet or worksheet file. They are saved when you save the file.

■ *Tools User Setup defaults.* Tools User Setup defaults apply to the entire 1-2-3 working environment. They are saved in a file separate from the worksheet, the 1-2-3 configuration file (123W.INI). These defaults apply to every 1-2-3 session.

Worksheet Global Settings 1-2-3 has numerous worksheet global settings that control the basic format of the current worksheet. These settings are the ones 1-2-3 uses as defaults in a worksheet unless you specify something else. For example, a column in a worksheet is set to the global column width unless you specify a different width with the Worksheet Colmn Width command.

You can view and change the 1-2-3 global settings in the Worksheet Global Settings dialog box. Choose Worksheet Global Settings to display the dialog box and the current worksheet global settings now.

Choose: Worksheet   Global Settings

Figure 2-43

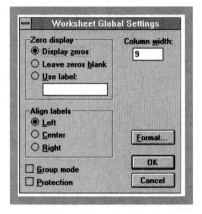

To change any of the worksheet global settings, you select option buttons, select check boxes, enter text in a text box, or select an item from a list box. When you have completed your selections, you apply them to the current worksheet by selecting OK. Each setting you alter remains in effect for this worksheet file until you explicitly change the setting again.

Table 2-9 describes the worksheet global settings. In later chapters you'll learn more about many of them.

Table 2-9: **Worksheet Global Settings**

Setting	Description
Align labels	Specifies whether labels you enter in the worksheet are automatically left-aligned, right-aligned, or centered in cells.

Setting	Description
Column width:	Sets the worksheet's default column width. (You can set the width of individual columns with the mouse or with Worksheet Column Width.)
Format...	Sets the worksheet's global cell format, which determines how 1-2-3 displays numbers and formulas. (Format settings are available through a sub-dialog box you get to by selecting "Format...".)
Group	Turns GROUP mode on or off for the current worksheet file. When GROUP mode is on, changes to the label alignment, row height, column width, cell format, and cell protection affect all worksheets in the file.
Protection	Turns global protection on and off for the worksheet. When global protection is on, you can enter and edit data only in cells you unprotect with Range Unprotect.
Zero display	Controls how 1-2-3 displays and prints worksheet cells that have a value of zero. 1-2-3 can show either 0's or a specified label, or it can make those cells appear blank.

Tools User Setup Defaults   The Tools User Setup dialog box allows you to make changes that affect 1-2-3 itself. Earlier in this chapter, you changed the default directory. You can also change numerous other defaults to suit your personal preferences and requirements. With the exception of Recalculation settings (which are stored in the worksheet file that is current when you make changes, but which affect all worksheets currently in memory), all of these settings can be stored in the 1-2-3 configuration file 123W.INI so that 1-2-3 uses them with each session. The settings are described in Table 2-10.

Table 2-10: 1-2-3 Tools User Setup Settings

Setting	Description
Beep on error	Turns the computer bell on or off for 1-2-3 sessions. Initially, the bell is on, and 1-2-3 will beep when you make an error or try to move the cell pointer beyond the edge of the worksheet. If you prefer a quiet session, turn the beep off. NOTE: This setting also controls whether or not the bell sounds in response to {BEEP} commands in macros.
Enable Edit Undo	Turns the Edit Undo feature on or off. Undo must be on if you want to use the Undo key (Alt-Backspace) to undo mistakes. Initially, undo is on. Undo uses memory, so turn it off if you need the extra memory. Chapter 3 contains more information about the undo feature.
Run auto-execute macros	Tells 1-2-3 to run a macro named \0 when it opens a file that contains such a macro (see Chapter 11 for more information on auto-execute macros).
Worksheet directory...	Sets the directory that 1-2-3 automatically uses for saving and opening files. Initially, this is the directory you told Install to use.
Clock display	Controls what 1-2-3 displays in the date-and-time indicator: the date and time (in either standard or international format), or nothing at all.

Setting	Description
International	Lets you change settings for the currency symbol and the international date and time formats, and controls whether 1-2-3 uses parentheses or a minus sign to indicate negative numbers in Currency and Comma (,) formats. Also lets you choose the decimal and thousands-separator characters for numbers and the argument separator used in @functions and macros.
Recalculation	Specifies the following recalculation settings: the times at which 1-2-3 recalculates the worksheet (whenever a cell value changes or only when you press the Calc key, F9); in what order 1-2-3 recalculates the worksheet (dependent cells first, column by column, or row by row); and how many recalculation passes 1-2-3 performs each time it recalculates the worksheet (from 1 to 50).

You can make changes to default settings permanent by updating the 1-2-3 configuration file. Select "Update" in the Tools User Setup dialog box after you have made your changes, then select OK to return to READY mode.

At a Glance

This chapter has introduced you to 1-2-3 and described many of the program's features and capabilities. You have also learned how, specifically, to perform the 1-2-3 tasks listed in the following table:

Task	How To Do It
Starting 1-2-3	Click on the 1-2-3 for Windows icon in the Lotus Applications group of the Program Manager (or a different group, if you have moved the icon). Or, select File Run from the Program Manager, type the path of the 1-2-3 program (for example, C:\123\123w), and either click on OK or press Enter. Or, from DOS, change to the 1-2-3 directory, and then type the command **win 123w**.
Exiting 1-2-3	Choose File Exit, choose Close from the Control menu of the 1-2-3 window, or press Alt+F4.
Selecting commands from menus	Click on a command, or press Alt or F10 and either (1) highlight the command and press Enter, or (2) type the underlined letter of the command name.
Entering data in the worksheet	Type labels or values in the control panel and then press Enter, click on the Confirm button, or press one of the pointer-movement keys.
Fixing typing mistakes	To fix mistakes while entering data, use Backspace. Otherwise, move to a cell that contains the error and retype the entry. (More ways to fix mistakes are discussed in Chapter 3.)
Saving a worksheet to a file	Choose File Save or click the File Save SmartIcon to save a file with its existing name. Choose File Save As to save a file under a new name.
Erasing a worksheet file from memory	Choose File Close.

Task	How To Do It
Opening a previously-saved worksheet file	Choose File Open and select or type the name of the file you want to open, then press Enter or click on OK. (You can also double-click the file name.)
Getting on-line help with 1-2-3's features and error messages	Press F1 Help or choose Help from the main menu.
Changing the default directory setting	Choose Tools User Setup and then modify the name in the "Worksheet directory:" text box. Click on OK to make the change last only for the current session, or select "Update" and then OK to make the change permanent.

Chapter 3

Worksheet Basics

The heart of 1-2-3 is the worksheet, in which you enter and manipulate all your data, whether you are using 1-2-3's spreadsheet, database, or graphics features.

This chapter teaches you basic worksheet skills you need to know in order to do any kind of work with 1-2-3. You will learn these skills as you build the first part of a practical 1-2-3 application, a Home Budget spreadsheet. In this chapter, you'll construct the framework for the budget application and enter all the required data. You will complete the Home Budget in Chapter 4, "Worksheet Skills." Together, Chapters 3 and 4 present a set of skills that are fundamental to working with 1-2-3. What you learn here and in Chapter 4 will apply to any future work you do with this product.

What You'll Learn

By the time you have finished this chapter, you will know how to:

- **Move around the worksheet**

- **Design a basic spreadsheet application**

- **Enter labels and values in the worksheet**

- **Edit data**

- **Change column widths**

- **Work with ranges**

- **Erase worksheet data**

- **Copy data**

- **Use the Edit Undo feature**

Before You Start

You will get the most out of this chapter if you work with 1-2-3 as you read. Before you go on:

- Start 1-2-3 and make sure it has been set up to save files in your 123BOOK directory (see Chapter 2, page 54).
- If you are already in 1-2-3 when you begin this chapter, save any work that is already on your screen and then close all open files.

To save a single file:

Choose: `File`   `Save`

To save all open files:

Choose: `File`   `Save As`
Select: `SaveAll`   `OK`

To close a file:

Choose: `File`   `Close`

■ *NOTE:*   As a shortcut when you have multiple files in memory, you can close all open files simultaneously by choosing /Worksheet Erase Yes from the 1-2-3 Classic menu. You can also close a file by double-clicking the file's Control menu box, or by pressing Control+F4.

1-2-3 displays a blank, untitled worksheet on the screen. The current cell is cell A:A1 (worksheet A, column A, row 1). Maximize the Worksheet window by clicking on the Maximize button, double-clicking on the title bar, or choosing Maximize from the Worksheet window Control box menu.

A Note on Reading This Chapter   This chapter is divided into sections, each of which presents a group of related worksheet skills. A heading marks the start of each section.

You will be doing a fair amount of typing in this chapter. If you find yourself getting tired, or if you need to interrupt your work for some other reason, continue working until you reach the next heading or numbered step and then File Save your worksheet file. The name for the Home Budget worksheet file you will create is BUDGET1.WK3. When you want to resume working on the exercises, start up 1-2-3, File Open BUDGET1.WK3, and pick up where you left off.

A Note on Keystroke Instructions   By now, you should be pretty used to the idea that you can use either the mouse or the keyboard to execute 1-2-3 commands and make selections from dialog boxes. From now on, keystroke instructions will mostly leave the choice up to you. Where it makes no difference which method you use, this book will say to "choose" a menu item or "select" an item from a dialog box, rather than telling you to use specific keystrokes or mouse movements; the choice of which to use is yours. The exception to this practice will be when the point of the instruction is to illustrate either a mouse or keyboard shortcut, or when there is no "generic" way to express a concept. Even in these cases, however, feel free to do the task in whatever way you feel most comfortable.

In addition, from now on, the symbol for pressing a key to complete data entry will be treated as part of entering the data. Also, instructions to press several keys in a row will all appear as one **Press:** instruction. For example, instead of these instructions for entering a word into a cell and then moving the cell pointer one cell down, one cell to the right, and one window width to the right:

Type: `folktale`
Press: ↓

        →

        TAB

you would see:

Type: `folktale`   ↓
Press: →   TAB

A Note on the Illustrations in This Book   As you've probably noticed by now, the cell pointer and any text you highlight in 1-2-3 is surrounded by an outline in a contrasting color. To make the screen illustrations clearer, this book uses a solid, contrasting color instead of an outline to show the cell pointer or other highlighted cells in the worksheet.

If you like, you can also change the cell pointer from an outline to a solid. Although there is no command in the 1-2-3 main menu to change the cell pointer, the 1-2-3 Classic Wysiwyg menu lets you do so. To change the cell pointer to a solid, execute the following commands:

Press: `:` **(colon)**   *to display the Wysiwyg menu in the 1-2-3 Classic window*
Choose: `Display`   `Options`   `Cell-Pointer`   `Outline`   `Quit`   `Quit`

1-2-3 changes the cell pointer to a solid for the current session. To change the cell pointer back to an outline,

Press: `:` **(colon)**
Choose: `Display`   `Options`   `Cell-Pointer`   `Solid`   `Quit`   `Quit`

To save your cell-pointer changes for future 1-2-3 sessions, execute another Wysiwyg command:

Press: `:` **(colon)**
Choose: `Display`   `Default`   `Update`   `Quit`

Also note that from now on, the illustrations in this book assume that the icon palette is at the bottom of the 1-2-3 window, just above the status line. The examples will, however, work equally well with the icon palette at the top of the window, if that's where you prefer it. (For instructions on moving the icon palette around the 1-2-3 window, see "A Note on the Icon Palette and Maximizing the Worksheet Window" later in this chapter.)

Moving Around the Worksheet

Creating and using a 1-2-3 worksheet involves moving from one cell to another and entering labels, values, and formulas. In Chapter 2, you used the arrow keys to move the cell pointer one cell at a time and the mouse to jump to a specific cell. There are also a number of other ways to move around the worksheet quickly and efficiently. The keys and mouse movements that allow you to do so are described in the following pages and summarized in Table 3-2 on page 72.

Moving to Any Cell

The Goto key, F5, allows you to jump directly to any specific cell in an active file. Press F5 (Goto), then type a cell address and press Enter. Cell addresses can be typed in uppercase or lowercase letters.

Press: |F5| **(GOTO)**

Type: z75 |↵| *to move the cell pointer to cell Z75*

Figure 3-1:   F5 (Goto) Moves the Cell Pointer to Any Specified Cell

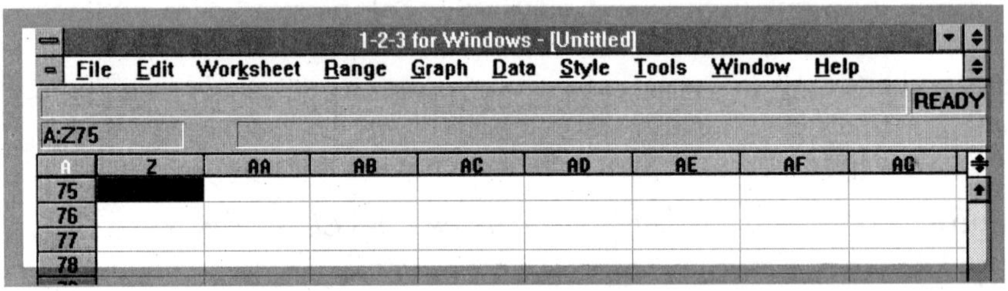

You can also use the mouse to move to any cell by scrolling the screen with the Worksheet window's horizontal and vertical scroll bars until the cell you want is in view, and then clicking on the cell.

Moving to Cell A1 of the Current Worksheet

The Home key returns the cell pointer to cell A1 of the current worksheet:

Press: |HOME| *to move the cell pointer to cell A1*

You can use the mouse to return the cell pointer to the "home" cell by clicking on the worksheet letter at the intersection of the row and column borders.

■ *NOTE:*   If worksheet titles are set, pressing Home or clicking on the worksheet letter moves the cell pointer to the cell just below and to the right of the worksheet titles. You'll learn about setting worksheet titles in Chapter 4.

Moving Up or Down by More Than One Row

The Page Up and Page Down keys move the cell pointer up and down one window height.

Press: |PGDN| |PGUP|

The Worksheet window moves down one window height, then moves back up.

You can use the mouse to move up or down by more than one row in any of these ways:

- *Click above or below the vertical scroll box.* To move the cell pointer up or down one window height using the mouse, click above or below the scroll box of the Worksheet window's vertical scroll bar.
- *Drag the vertical scroll box.* To move the cell pointer up or down an arbitrary number of rows, drag the scroll box in the Worksheet window's vertical scroll bar up or down. When the scroll box is at the top of the scroll bar, the cell pointer is in the first row of the worksheet. When the scroll box is at the bottom of the scroll bar, the cell pointer is at the bottom of the active area of the worksheet (the part that contains data or formatting).
- *Click on the vertical scroll bar's arrow icons.* To move the cell pointer up or down one row at a time, click on the up or down arrow icons in the Worksheet window's vertical scroll bar. To scroll continuously up or down, move the mouse pointer to the up or down arrow in the vertical scroll bar and hold the mouse button down until the cell pointer is where you want it.

Moving Left or Right by More Than One Column

The Control key can be used in combination with the Right or Left arrow keys to move the screen right or left one window width. To use the Control key with an arrow key, hold down Control, press the arrow key, then release both keys. The Tab key moves the window the same way as Control+Right and Shift+Tab moves the window the same way as Control+Left.

Press: CTRL+RIGHT

CTRL+LEFT

TAB

SHIFT+TAB

The Worksheet window moves right one window width, moves left to its original position, then moves right and left once again.

You can use the mouse to move right or left by more than one column in any of these ways:

- *Click to the right or left of the horizontal scroll box.* To move the cell pointer right or left one window width using the mouse, click to the right or left of the scroll box of the Worksheet window's horizontal scroll bar.
- *Drag the horizontal scroll box.* To move the cell pointer right or left an arbitrary number of columns, drag the scroll box in the horizontal scroll bar right or left. When the scroll box is at the right side of the scroll bar, the cell pointer is at the last column of the active area of the worksheet. When the scroll box is at the left side of the scroll bar, the cell pointer is in the first column of the worksheet (column A).
- *Click on the horizontal scroll bar's arrow icons.* To move the cell pointer right or left one column at a time, click on the right or left arrow icons in the horizontal scroll bar. To scroll continuously right or left, move the mouse pointer to the right or left arrow

in the horizontal scroll bar and hold the mouse button down until the cell pointer is where you want it.

Using the End Key with Pointer-Movement Keys

Pressing and releasing the End key before you press Home, Right, or Left temporarily changes how these keys affect cell-pointer movement.

Pressing End followed by Home moves the cell pointer to the bottom right corner of the worksheet's *active area.* The active area is the rectangular block bounded by the top and left edges of the worksheet, and by the bottom-most row and right-most column that have cells containing data or special formatting.

Pressing End followed by one of the arrow keys moves the cell pointer in the direction of the arrow. How far the pointer moves depends on whether the pointer is in a blank cell or a cell that contains data (or formatting), and on whether the next cell in the direction of the arrow is blank or contains data (or formatting). If the pointer is in a blank cell when you press End, it moves in the direction of the arrow either to the first data cell or to the edge of the worksheet. If the pointer is in a data cell when you press End, it moves in the direction of the arrow to either the last data cell before a blank cell, the first data cell after a blank cell, or the edge of the worksheet.

When you press the End key, the End indicator appears in the status line. The End indicator disappears when you press an arrow key or the Home key to complete the keystroke combination. Pressing End a second time also removes the End indicator.

Try using the End key in combination with Home and the arrow keys to move to the four corners of a blank worksheet:

1. Move right along row 1.

   The following sequence of keystrokes brings the cell pointer first to the upper left corner of the worksheet, then to the upper right.

   Press: `HOME`   *to move to cell A1*

                   `END`   `→`   *to move to cell IV1*

   Because row 1 contains only blank cells, pressing End Right moves the cell pointer to the right edge of the worksheet.

2. Move down column IV and left across row 8192.

   Now, move the cell pointer to the lower right corner of the worksheet, then move it leftward until it reaches column A:

   Press: `END`   `↓`   *to move to cell IV8192*

                   `END`   `←`   *to move to cell A8192*

3. Move up to cell A1.

   Finally, use End Up to move back to cell A1:

Press: END ↑

Using the End key in combination with the arrow keys is a very quick way to move to an edge of the worksheet, or to the beginning or end of a data area. If you wish, take some time now to experiment with these keys on your own. Create the worksheet in Figure 3-2. Use End Right and End Left to move across rows 1 and 2, observing where the cell pointer lands each time you press the End key combination. Use End Down and End Up to move up and down column G. Watch what 1-2-3 does, depending on whether the cell pointer is in a blank cell or in a cell that contains data. Press End Home, then Home, to see how these keys affect the cell pointer.

Table 3-1 describes a suggested path through the worksheet.

Figure 3-2

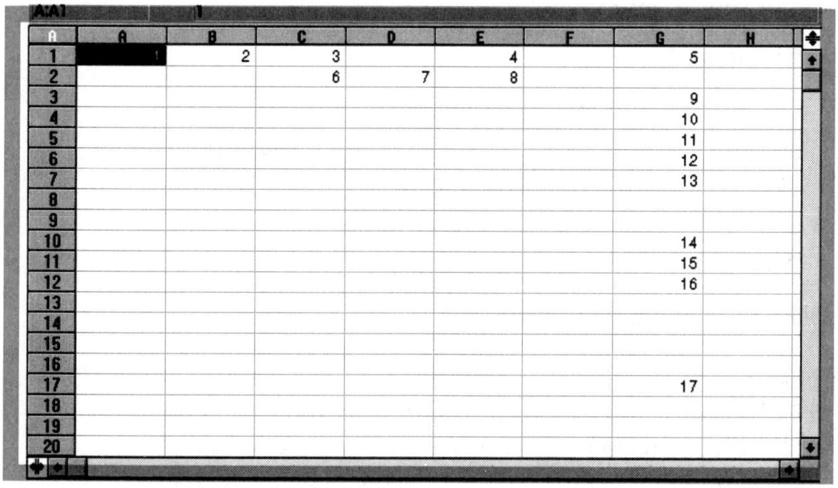

Table 3-1: Experimenting with the End Key

Start Here	Press:	Go to Here
1. From A1	END → *four times*	IV1
	END ←	G1
	HOME	A1
	↓	A2
2. From A2	END → *two times*	E2
	→	E1
	END →	G1

Start Here	Press:	Go to Here
3. From G1	END ↑ *three times*	G10
	END HOME	G17
4. From G17	END ↑ *four times*	G3
5. From G3	↑	G2
	END ← *three times*	A2
6. From A2	END HOME	G17
	HOME	A1

When you are through experimenting, save the file and clear the worksheet:

Choose:	File Save As	
Type:	endkeys ↵	*to name the file ENDKEYS.WK3*
Choose:	File Close	*to close the file*

1-2-3 once again displays a blank, untitled worksheet.

Summary of Pointer-Movement Keys

Table 3-2 describes the keys and key combinations you can use to move around a 1-2-3 worksheet. Keys linked with a plus sign (+) in the table must be pressed simultaneously. Key combinations that begin with END mean to press and release the End key, then press the other indicated key.

Table 3-2: Pointer-Movement Keys

Key	What It Does:
← → ↑ ↓	Moves one cell left/ right or up/down.
PGUP PGDN	Moves up or down one window height.
CTRL+→ or TAB	Moves right one window width.

Key	What It Does:
CTRL+← or SHIFT+TAB	Moves left one window width.
HOME	Moves to the upper left corner of the worksheet.
END HOME	Moves to the lower right corner of the active area of the worksheet.
END → END ← END ↑ END ↓	If the pointer is in a blank cell, moves in the direction of the arrow either to the first data cell or to the edge of the worksheet. If the pointer is in a data cell, moves in the direction of the arrow either to the last data cell before a blank cell, the first data cell after a blank cell, or the edge of the worksheet.
F5 (GOTO)	Moves to the cell address you specify.

Summary of Ways to Use a Mouse to Move Around the Worksheet

Table 3-3 describes the procedures for using a mouse to move around the worksheet.

■ *NOTE:*   The instructions in this table assume that your mouse is configured to use the left button as the "Enter" key. If your mouse buttons work in the reverse fashion, reverse the instructions in the table.

Table 3-3:   Worksheet Navigation with a Mouse

Worksheet Navigation Task	How To Do It:
Move to a different cell	If the cell is currently displayed, move the mouse pointer to the cell and click the left mouse button. If the cell is not currently displayed, move the mouse pointer to the appropriate scroll arrow in the horizontal scroll bar, click (or hold down) the left mouse button until the cell comes into view, and then click on the cell.
Move to cell A1	Move the mouse pointer to the worksheet letter in the upper left corner of the worksheet border (the area where the column-letter border and the row-number border intersect), and click the left mouse button
Move up/down row by row, or right/left column by column	Move the mouse pointer to the appropriate scroll arrow in the vertical or horizontal scroll bar, and then click or hold down the left mouse button until you reach the desired row or column.
Move up/down or right/left quickly	Click the left mouse button on the scroll box in the vertical or horizontal scroll bar, and then drag the scroll box in the appropriate direction.

Moving and Sizing Windows

1-2-3/W windows can be moved, sized, tiled, maximized, and minimized just like the windows in any other Windows application. You'll be given specific instructions for sizing or moving windows as you work through this book. Some of the basic operations, however, are described below. For a complete summary on sizing and moving windows, see the 1-2-3 or Windows documentation, or the 1-2-3 or Windows Help files.

Figure 3-3a: To move a window, choose Move and use the arrow keys to move the window, and then press Enter. Or, click on the title bar and drag the window to its new position.

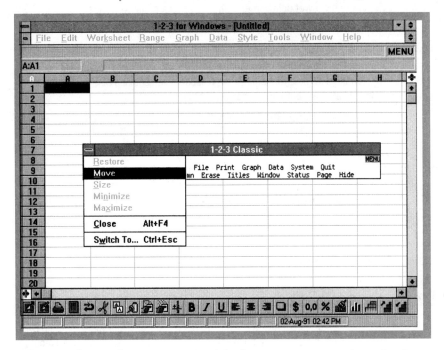

■ **NOTE:** If a window is maximized, before you can move it or size it, you must restore it. To do so, either click on the window's Restore button, or press Alt+spacebar (for the 1-2-3 window) or Alt+hyphen (for other windows) to activate the window's Control menu, and then type R for Restore.

Moving a Window

You can move any of the 1-2-3 windows except the Print Preview window (Worksheet window, Graph window, Help window, dialog box windows, and so on).
To move a window with the mouse:

1. Move the mouse pointer to the window's title bar.

2. Press the left mouse button and drag the window to its new location.

Figure 3-3b: To size a window, choose Size and use the arrow keys to change the window and the press Enter. Or, use the mouse to drag an edge to its new position.

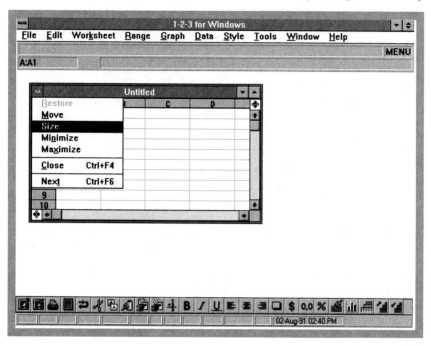

3. Release the mouse button.

To move a window with the keyboard:

1. Press Alt+spacebar to open the Control menu for the 1-2-3 window, a Help window, or a dialog box, or Alt+hyphen to open the Control menu for any other window.

2. Type M to choose Move.

3. Press the Up, Down, Left, or Right arrow key to move the window. (Control+Up, Control+Down, Control+Left, and Control+Right move the window smaller amounts, in some cases.)

4. Press Enter.

Sizing a Window
You can change the size of any 1-2-3 window except dialog box windows, the Print Preview window, and the Macro Trace window.

■ *NOTE:*   If a window is maximized, before you can change its size, you must restore it. To do so, either click on the window's Restore button, or press Alt+spacebar (for the 1-2-3 window or a Help window), or Alt+hyphen (for other windows) to activate the window's Control menu, and then type R for _R_estore.

To size a window with the mouse:

1. Move the mouse pointer to the border you want to move (to change the size in one direction), or to the corner you want to move (to change the size in two directions).

2. Drag the border left, right, up, or down to change the window's size in one direction only. Drag a corner of the border to simultaneously change the window's size both vertically and horizontally.

To use the keyboard to change a window's size:

1. Press Control+F6 until the window you want to resize is the active window.

2. To change the size of a Worksheet, Graph, or Transcript window, press Alt+hyphen and type S to choose _S_ize. To change the size of the 1-2-3 window, press Alt+Spacebar and then type S.

3. Press the Left, Right, Up, or Down arrow key to move the pointer to the left, right, top, or bottom border.

4. Press an arrow key to move the border. (Control+Up, Control+Down, Control+Left, and Control+Right change the window size by smaller amounts, in some cases.)

5. Press Enter when the border is where you want it.

1-2-3 Function Keys

1-2-3 uses the keyboard function keys to make it easier to do frequently performed tasks. You have already learned about two of 1-2-3's function keys, F1 (Help) and F5 (Goto). By the time you complete this chapter, you will have learned to use several more.

Table 3-4 summarizes 1-2-3's function keys. Each 1-2-3 function key is described in this book in some detail. In Table 3-4, each function key is identified by its key name on the keyboard and, if one exists, by its 1-2-3 macro key name (macros are described in Chapter 11). Notice that most function keys can perform two operations: one when you press the function key alone, and another when you hold down the Alt key and press the function key. A few function keys also perform an additional operation when you hold down the Control key and press the function key.

Table 3-4:   Function Keys

Function Key	What It Does
F1 (HELP)	Calls up 1-2-3's on-line Help system.
ALT+F1 (COMPOSE)	Lets you create characters that you can't enter directly from the keyboard.
F2 (EDIT)	Changes the mode indicator to EDIT, and allows you to edit data in a cell.

Function Key	What It Does
ALT+F2 (STEP)	Turns on 1-2-3's Step indicator. Macros will run one step at a time. Pressing Alt+F2 turns the Step indicator off again and restores macro execution to normal.
F3 (NAME)	Displays lists of range names, named graphs, files, macro commands and keys, and @functions.
ALT+F3 (RUN)	Displays a list of range names and then runs the macro whose range name you select.
F4 (ABS)	In READY mode, anchors the cell pointer so that you can highlight a range. In POINT or VALUE mode, changes cell addresses in formulas to absolute, relative, or mixed.
ALT+F4	Ends the current 1-2-3 session. (The same as selecting File Exit.)
F5 (GOTO)	Moves the cell pointer to a specified location in an active file (shortcut for Range Go To).
F6 (PANE)	Moves the cell pointer between window panes created with Window Split.
ALT+F6 (ZOOM)	Toggles between enlarging the current window pane to the full size of the Worksheet window and shrinking it back to its original size.
CTRL+F6	Switches to the next open window
F7 (QUERY)	Repeats the most recent Data Query command. During a Data Query Find operation, toggles between READY and FIND modes.
ALT+F7 (ADD-IN 1)	Activates the add-in application assigned to the Add-in 1 key, if one is assigned.
F8 (TABLE)	Repeats the most recent Data What-if Table command.
ALT+F8 (ADD-IN 2)	Activates the add-in application assigned to the Add-in 2 key, if one is assigned.
F9 (CALC)	In READY mode, recalculates formula cells in the worksheet file. In EDIT or VALUE mode, changes a formula in the edit line to its current value.
ALT+F9 (ADD-IN 3)	Activates the add-in application assigned to the Add-in 3 key, if one is assigned.
F10 (MENU)	Activates the 1-2-3 main menu so you can choose commands. (The same as pressing Alt.)

Creating a Worksheet

If you've completed the exercises in Chapter 2, you have already used some of 1-2-3's worksheet commands. Now, you'll learn more about the basic worksheet commands by building a Home Budget spreadsheet application.

About the Home Budget Example

This example begins the story of Bob Gordon and his rise to fame, fortune, and skill in using 1-2-3.

Picture him: A young man with a small family, an office manager with a secret passion for working with wood. Until now, Bob has been notoriously bad about keeping his finances in order, but with a new baby and with his wife, Kathy, now working only a day or two a week outside their home, Bob knows he must take a more serious stance. He is learning 1-2-3 on the job, and he realizes that the program might help him evaluate his family's spending patterns. Maybe if he and Kathy understood where their money was going, Bob reasons, they would have a better idea of how to manage it.

In this chapter, you are going to look over Bob's shoulder as he uses 1-2-3 to create a simple cash flow budget. The budget is based on a record he and Kathy have been keeping of the family finances. For three months, they have scrupulously used their checkbook as a ledger, funneling all income and expenses through it. From this, they have come up with an approximation of how much they earn, how much they spend, and what they spend it on. As this book progresses, we will see Bob's woodworking hobby grow into a small business, and the business grow into a large corporation. 1-2-3 will accompany Bob and help him on this journey.

We find Bob, now, fiddling with his first spreadsheet, much as you soon will, unaware that this "fiddling" may one day alter the course of his life.

The Home Budget Model

Think of a worksheet as being made up of two parts: One part is the worksheet's basic *structure,* and the other is the *data* you enter into that structure.

The basic structure is designed for a specific purpose, such as a budget, an income statement, an expense report, or a general ledger. It includes labels that describe the kind of information in the worksheet, formatting specifications that control the worksheet's physical appearance (column width, how numbers are displayed, and so on), and formulas that tell 1-2-3 how to calculate the values in certain cells. The data is the information the formulas operate on to generate results.

In this chapter, you will begin to construct the worksheet structure for the Gordons' Home Budget application and to enter the data (the figures for projected income and expenses that Bob and Kathy gathered by using their checkbook as a ledger). Before you type anything, look at the various parts of the completed Home Budget model. Figure 3-4 shows a printed version of the spreadsheet area of the budget worksheet. (This area will not be entirely completed until Chapter 4.)

INCOME Section   This part of the budget displays the Gordons' monthly projected income. Income is divided into **Weekly** and **Monthly** categories. For example, Bob is paid weekly; the amount of money he earns in a particular month is equal to his weekly pay multiplied by the number of paydays in that month. Kathy, on the other hand, is paid monthly; she earns the same amount of money every month.

The row with the label **Total Income** shows the sum, for each month, of Bob's pay, Kathy's pay, and their interest earnings.

EXPENSES Section   This part of the budget displays the Gordons' projected monthly expenses. Expenses are divided into major categories, such as auto, charity, clothes, household (repairs and furniture), and so on.

The row with the label **Total Expenses** shows the monthly sum of all budgeted expense categories.

CASH FLOW Section   This part of the budget displays projected balances for Bob and Kathy's checking and savings accounts. It also shows the total amount of cash they will have available at the end of any given month. Negative values are in parentheses.

Figure 3-4: Bob and Kathy's Home Budget Spreadsheet

Bob and Kathy Gordon   1992 HOME BUDGET

	Jan	Feb	Mar	Apr	May	Jun	Jul	Aug	Sep	Oct	Nov	Dec	Annual
INCOME													
Weekly													
Net Pay (Bob)	4,500	3,600	3,600	3,600	4,500	3,600	4,500	3,600	3,600	4,500	3,600	3,600	46,800
Monthly													
Net Pay (Kathy)	600	600	600	600	600	600	600	600	600	600	600	600	7,200
Interest	100	100	100	100	100	100	100	100	100	100	100	100	1,200
Total Income	$5,200	$4,300	$4,300	$4,300	$5,200	$4,300	$5,200	$4,300	$4,300	$5,200	$4,300	$4,300	$55,200
EXPENSES													
Auto	150	150	150	150	150	150	150	150	150	150	150	150	1,800
Charity	75	75	75	75	75	75	75	75	75	75	75	75	900
Clothes	200	200	200	200	200	200	200	200	200	200	200	200	2,400
Food	875	700	700	700	875	700	875	700	700	875	700	700	9,100
Household	200	200	200	200	200	200	200	200	200	200	200	200	2,400
Medical	150	150	150	150	150	150	150	150	150	150	150	150	1,800
Misc	1,125	900	900	900	1,125	900	1,125	900	900	1,125	900	900	11,700
Rent	1,100	1,100	1,100	1,100	1,100	1,100	1,100	1,100	1,100	1,100	1,100	1,100	13,200
Savings	500	400	400	400	500	400	500	400	400	500	400	400	5,200
Utility	200	200	200	200	200	200	200	200	200	200	200	200	2,400
Woodwork	250	250	250	250	250	250	250	250	250	250	250	250	3,000
Total Expenses	$4,825	$4,325	$4,325	$4,325	$4,825	$4,325	$4,825	$4,325	$4,325	$4,825	$4,325	$4,325	$53,900
CASH FLOW													
Savings Account													
Savings this Month	500	400	400	400	500	400	500	400	400	500	400	400	
Cumulative Savings	2,500	2,900	3,300	3,700	4,200	4,600	5,100	5,500	5,900	6,400	6,800	7,200	
Checking Account													
Opening Balance	1,000	1,375	1,350	1,325	1,300	1,675	1,650	2,025	2,000	1,975	2,350	2,325	
Net Cash Flow	375	(25)	(25)	(25)	375	(25)	375	(25)	(25)	375	(25)	(25)	
Closing Balance	$1,375	$1,350	$1,325	$1,300	$1,675	$1,650	$2,025	$2,000	$1,975	$2,350	$2,325	$2,300	
Total Available Funds	$3,875	$4,250	$4,625	$5,000	$5,875	$6,250	$7,125	$7,500	$7,875	$8,750	$9,125	$9,500	

INCOME section

EXPENSES section

CASHFLOW section

VARIABLES Sections   The INCOME, EXPENSES, and CASH FLOW sections of the budget worksheet are where 1-2-3 displays the Gordon family's budget projections. However, these sections do not contain the actual data you type into the budget worksheet. Instead, they contain formulas that evaluate to the displayed values.

Formulas are mathematical expressions that perform calculations on values in the worksheet. (You will learn more about formulas in Chapter 4.) The Home Budget worksheet, like many other worksheets, is constructed so that the numbers used by the formulas are kept in a separate part of the worksheet. This makes it easier to find and change those numbers. The part of the worksheet where the numbers are kept is called the *variables area*.

Variable is a general term for an item that can have any one of a set of values. A worksheet cell that contains values you assign to it directly is called a variable because you can change (vary) the information in it. For example, a variable intended to contain the current year would contain 1992 if the year were 1992, 1993 if the year were 1993, and so on.

The variables for this particular worksheet are stored in three sections. Each of these is described briefly and illustrated in the next few pages. Although these three worksheet sections are specific to this worksheet, you can apply the concept of separating variables to any application.

Figure 3-5 shows a printed version of the variables area of the Home Budget worksheet.

Figure 3-5: The Variables Area of the Home Budget Application

```
INCOME VARIABLES
-------------------------------------
Weekly
   Net Pay (Bob)            $900

Monthly
   Net Pay (Kathy)         $600
   Interest                $100
=====================================


EXPENSE VARIABLES
-------------------------------------
Weekly
   Food                    $175
   Misc                    $225
   Savings                 $100

Monthly
   Auto                    $150
   Charity                  $75
   Clothes                 $200
   Household               $200
   Medical                 $150
   Rent                  $1,100
   Utility                 $200
   Woodwork                $250
=====================================


MISC. VARIABLES
-------------------------------------
Payday day-of-week:     Friday
Current year:             1992
Last year's checking:   $1,000
Last year's savings:    $2,000
=====================================
```

INCOME VARIABLES section.   The INCOME VARIABLES section contains values for weekly and monthly budgeted income. The values in this section are used in the calculations performed in the INCOME section of the worksheet. For instance, the value for Bob's monthly pay is based on his weekly pay of $900 multiplied by the number of weeks in a given month.

EXPENSE VARIABLES section.   The EXPENSE VARIABLES section contains values for weekly, monthly, and quarterly budgeted expenses. The values in this section are used in the calculations performed in the EXPENSES section of the worksheet. For example, the Gordons' monthly food budget is based on their weekly allocation for food ($175) multiplied by the number of weeks in the month.

MISC. VARIABLES section.   The MISC. VARIABLES section contains values that are not related specifically to income or expenses. These include entries for the day of the week when Bob gets paid, the current year, and last year's checking account and savings account ending balances.

Interrelation of Data in the Home Budget

The electronic worksheet's ability to automatically recalculate interrelated values when any single value is changed is its biggest advantage over a paper spreadsheet.

Notice that many of the values in the Home Budget application are the result of adding or subtracting two or more other values. For example, the row labeled Net Cash Flow in the CASH FLOW section of the worksheet shows the difference between the Gordons' total income (from the INCOME section) and their total expenses (from the EXPENSES section) for each month ($5,200 - $4,825 = $375 for January). If you change any of the income or expense values, the Net Cash Flow adjusts automatically.

Figure 3-6:   Net Cash Flow = Total Income - Total Expenses

(You'll create the 3-D version of the Home Budget in Chapter 5.)

A Note on Constructing the Home Budget Application

The Home Budget application is set up so that while you are building the worksheet, each major worksheet section is on a separate screen. As you create the application, you can move easily from screen to screen using the Page Up and Page Down keys. The keystroke instructions assume that you have maximized the Worksheet window, and that the worksheet displays 20 rows. (You'll maximize the Worksheet window in a moment.)

You will find it easier to follow the keystroke instructions and to match your work to the illustrations if you position the first label of each major worksheet section at the top left corner of the Worksheet window whenever you start on a new section of the budget worksheet. You can do this in any of the following ways:

- Use F5 (Goto) or the Range Go To command to move to the first cell in the section (1-2-3 automatically positions this cell in the top left corner of the Worksheet window).
- Press Page Down or click below the scroll box in the vertical scroll bar to move from worksheet section to worksheet section one window-depth at a time.

If necessary, use the Scroll Lock key in conjunction with the arrow keys to help you position the worksheet. (Scroll Lock causes the arrow keys to move the Worksheet window instead of moving the cell pointer.)

A Note on the Icon Palette and Maximizing the Worksheet Window

When you are working with only one worksheet at a time, as you will be for the remainder of this chapter and the following chapter, it is usually easiest to *maximize* the Worksheet window. When you maximize the window, the 1-2-3 window title bar and the Worksheet window title bar share a common space, and the Worksheet window expands to the margins of the 1-2-3 window. You had a little practice with maximizing the Worksheet window in Chapter 2. Now take a look at this procedure in more detail.

The position of the icon palette affects how many rows are displayed when you maximize the Worksheet window. The icon palette can be displayed at the top, bottom, left, or right border of the 1-2-3 window; it can "float" anywhere in the window; or it can be hidden altogether. The examples and illustrations in this book assume that the icon palette is at the bottom of the screen and that, when both the 1-2-3 window and the Worksheet window are maximized, the Worksheet window displays 20 rows.

The following instructions describe how to make the icon palette appear at the bottom of the 1-2-3 window (as in Figure 3-7 on the next page). While you are doing the exercises in this book, keep the icon palette there unless instructed to do otherwise. (When you are doing other work in 1-2-3, feel free to move the icon palette wherever you want it.) If the palette is already at the bottom of your 1-2-3 window, just above the status line, skip this procedure. Otherwise, move the icon palette there now.

Choose: `Tools`   `SmartIcons`

1-2-3 displays the Tools SmartIcons dialog box. To display the palette at the bottom of the window, select the "Bottom" option button and make sure the "Hide palette" check box is not checked, then select OK to return 1-2-3 to READY mode.

Next, maximize the Worksheet window by clicking on the Maximize button (upward-facing arrow in the upper right corner of the Worksheet window), or by pressing Alt+hyphen to display the Worksheet window's Control menu and pressing X to select Maximize. Notice that the Worksheet window now displays 20 rows and eight columns. Also notice that the Worksheet window's Control menu box and the current file's name have moved from the Worksheet window title bar to the control panel, and that the Worksheet window's Maximize and Minimize buttons have been combined into a single Restore button.

Figure 3-7: The Icon Palette, Displayed at the Bottom of the 1-2-3 Window

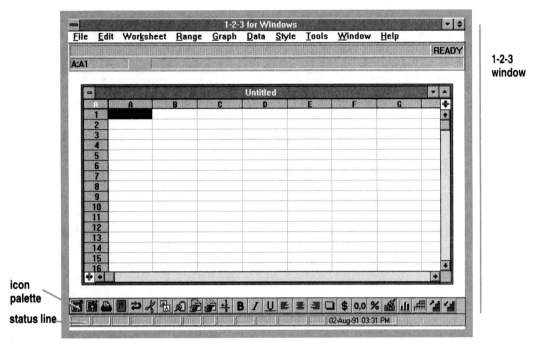

Figure 3-8: The Maximized Worksheet Window

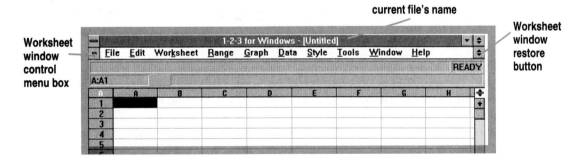

Entering Data in the Worksheet

There are two fundamental kinds of worksheet entries: labels and values. In most cases, *labels* are letters or words; they can be titles, captions that describe what is in a column or row, or special characters. Values can be numbers or formulas.

In general, 1-2-3 distinguishes between a label entry and a value entry by examining the first character. Since labels are usually words and values are either numbers or formulas, 1-2-3 assumes that an entry beginning with a letter is a label and one beginning with a number (or one of several special characters used in formulas) is a value. For example, **Interest** and **Dividends** are labels; **$100** and **1992** are values.

Table 3-5:   1-2-3 Rules for Distinguishing Labels from Values

Data Item	Rule
Value	1-2-3 will interpret an entry as a value if the first character entered is one of the following: 0 1 2 3 4 5 6 7 8 9 – + (. @ # $
Label	1-2-3 will interpret an entry as a label if the first character entered is any character other than those listed for values.

1-2-3 checks to make sure that data entered is valid. If it finds an error—for example, if you tried to enter a number that contains alphabetic characters—1-2-3 beeps and then switches to EDIT mode so that you can correct the error. You can enter a maximum of 512 characters in a cell.

■ *NOTE:*   If you use any characters in an entry other than those you can type directly from the keyboard, the character maximum for that entry is less than 512. See Chapter 5 for details.

What to Do about Typing Mistakes

You will probably make typing mistakes as you create this worksheet. Later in this chapter, in "Editing Data," you will learn a great deal about fixing mistakes. For now, since the entries you will be making are short, use the following techniques:

- *Correcting mistakes while typing an entry.* If you make a mistake while typing an entry, but before completing it, you can fix the error with the Backspace key. Backspace erases characters to the left of the cursor. Use Backspace to erase the characters up to the incorrect part of the entry, then retype the rest of the entry and press Enter to complete it.
- *Correcting mistakes after completing an entry.* If you notice a mistake after you have completed a cell entry, fix it by moving the cell pointer to the cell, typing the correct entry into the control panel, and pressing Enter.
- *Erasing an incorrect cell.* If you complete a cell entry and then realize that you should have left the cell blank, use Edit Clear to erase the contents of the cell: (1) move to the cell you want to erase, (2) make sure 1-2-3 is in READY mode, and (3) choose Edit Clear to erase the cell's contents. As a shortcut, you can also press Delete instead of selecting Edit Clear. (Later in this chapter, you'll learn more about using Edit Clear to erase one or more cells.)

Entering Labels

In this section, you will fill in the labels of the first three screens of the Home Budget worksheet.

Creating the INCOME Section Labels   The first section of the worksheet contains a worksheet title and a projection of Bob and Kathy Gordon's income for 1992. Begin with a blank, untitled, maximized worksheet (with the icon palette at the bottom of the 1-2-3 window).

1. Enter the first label of the Home Budget worksheet

   The cell pointer should already be in cell A1. If it is not, before you start typing, press Home, or click on the worksheet letter (at the intersection of the row and column borders) to move the pointer there. Begin the Home Budget by entering the first label in the worksheet. As you enter the label, notice that the mode indicator reads LABEL.

   Move to: cell A1

   Type: `Bob and Kathy Gordon`   ↵

Figure 3-9

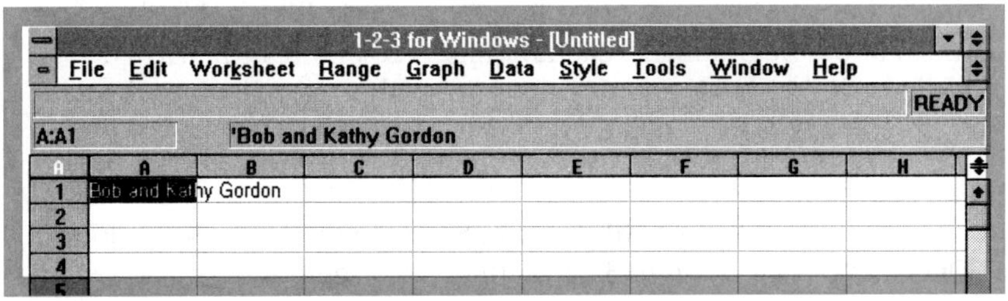

Now look at the text in the edit line of the control panel:

`'Bob and Kathy Gordon`

1-2-3 recognizes that this entry is a label and automatically puts an apostrophe (') before it. The apostrophe is one of three *label prefixes* that control how a label is aligned within a cell. The apostrophe indicates that an entry is a label aligned at the left side of the cell.

The other label-alignment prefixes are the double quotation mark (") and the caret (^). The label-alignment prefixes are described in Table 3-6. Other label prefixes include the backslash (\) and the vertical bar (|). Neither is used for label alignment; both are described later in this book.

Table 3-6: Label-Alignment Prefixes

Prefix	What It Does:
' (apostrophe)	Aligns a label at the left side of a cell.
" (double quote)	Aligns a label at the right side of a cell.
^ (caret)	Centers a label in a cell.

2. Enter the next three labels in the INCOME section (rows 5 through 8, column A).

Use the Down arrow instead of the Enter key to complete the entries.

Move to:	cell A5
Type:	INCOME
Press:	↓ *two times*
Type:	Weekly ↓
Press:	SPACEBAR *two times, to indent the next label*
Type:	Net Pay (Bob)
Press:	↓ *two times*

Notice that pressing the Down arrow completes an entry and moves the cell pointer to the next cell automatically, as if you had pressed Enter or clicked on the Confirm button and then pressed Down. Using pointer-movement keys to enter data and move the cell pointer is usually quicker than pressing Enter or clicking on Confirm and then moving the cell pointer.

3. Enter the remaining labels in the INCOME section (rows 10 through 14, column A).

Type the other four labels in Figure 3-10 into column A. Remember to leave two blank spaces (press the Space bar two times) at the beginning of each indented label. Press the Down arrow to complete the labels in cells A10, A11, and A12, and move the cell pointer to the cell beneath. Press Enter after you type the label in cell A14.

4. Save your work so far.

You have now completed the labels for the INCOME section. Save the work you have done so far in a new file called BUDGET1.WK3 (see Figure 3-11 on the next page):

Choose:	File Save As
Type:	budget1 *in the File name: field*
Press:	↵ *to save the worksheet in BUDGET1.WK3*

Figure 3-10

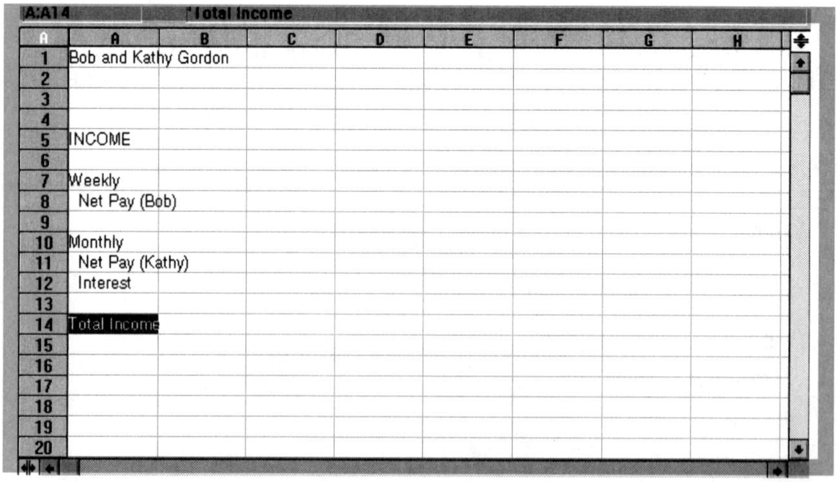

Figure 3-11: Saving BUDGET1.WK3

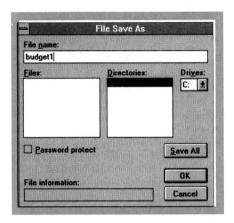

■ *NOTE:*   From now on, save your file before you move on to a new section.

Creating the EXPENSES Section Labels   Now, with the first part of your work safely tucked away in a disk file, complete the labels in the second section of the worksheet. This section contains a projection of the Gordons' expenses for 1992. Figure 3-12, shows how this section will look after you have entered these labels.

Figure 3-12

	A	B	C	D	E	F	G	H	
21	EXPENSES								
22									
23	Auto								
24	Charity								
25	Clothes								
26	Food								
27	Household								
28	Medical								
29	Misc								
30	Rent								
31	Savings								
32	Utility								
33	Woodwork								
34									
35	Total Expenses								
36									
37									
38									
39									
40									

1. Position the cell pointer in cell A21.

   To make sure that what you type agrees with Figure 3-12, move the cell pointer so that the cell in which you will enter the **EXPENSES** label is at the top left corner of the Worksheet window. If you have sized the Worksheet window so that it displays 20 rows, this can be done with two keystrokes. (Notice that when you move up or down using the Page Up or Page Down key, the cell pointer remains in the same relative position it was in before you moved the window.)

Press: `HOME`   *to move the cell pointer to cell A1*

                      `PGDN`   *to move to the next window down*

2. Enter the labels in the EXPENSES section (rows 21 through 35).

Enter the label **EXPENSES** in cell A21, then enter the indented label **Auto** in cell A23:

Type: EXPENSES

Press: `↓`   *two times*

                   `SPACEBAR`   *two times*

Type: Auto   `↓`

Enter the remaining labels in Figure 3-12, pressing the Down arrow to complete each entry except the last. Finish the EXPENSES screen by entering the label **Total Expenses** in cell A35 and pressing Enter.

Remember to leave two blank spaces at the beginning of each indented label. Do this the same way you indented the **Auto** label, by pressing the Space bar two times before typing in the words for the label. These two spaces become part of the label. You will use this technique for indenting labels in the next few screens.

3. Save your work.

You have completed another block of typing, and you should save your file again at this point. As with all computer work, it's a good idea to develop the habit of saving your file whenever you've made any substantial changes and whenever you get up from your computer. Soon, saving your file after you've completed a task will become almost automatic. Should "disaster" strike, you will lose at most only a few minutes of work.

Creating the CASH FLOW Section Labels   The CASH FLOW section of the worksheet displays the amount of cash Kathy and Bob will have in their savings and checking accounts if they follow their budget. The last line of the CASH FLOW section shows how much total cash the Gordons will have available in any given month.

1. Position the cell pointer in cell A41.

The procedure for creating the labels in the CASH FLOW section is quite similar to the one for creating the labels for the INCOME and EXPENSES worksheet sections. Once again, before you start to type, position the cell pointer so that the first cell of the CASH FLOW section is in the top left corner of the Worksheet window. This time, use the Goto key to move the cell pointer:

Press: [F5]   (**GOTO**)

Type: a41   *in the Range: text box*

Press: [↵]

     The cell pointer moves to cell A41, positioned in the top left corner of the Worksheet window.

2. Enter the labels in the CASH FLOW section (rows 41 through 55, column A).

     Enter the label **CASH FLOW** into cell A41, and then fill in the remaining labels on this screen, as indicated in Figure 3-13. Remember to use the Space bar to indent the indented labels two spaces. Finish with the label **Total Available Funds** in cell A55.

Figure 3-13

3. Save your work.

     Creating the Month Column Headings   The second row of the Home Budget worksheet contains column headings for the month of each column's data. Continue your label-entry work by entering these column headings. You will right-align the column headings so they line up with the numbers below them.

1. Move the cell pointer to cell B2.

Press: [F5]   (**GOTO**)

Type: b2   [↵]

2. Enter the worksheet's month column labels (cells B2 through M2).

     Enter the label **"Jan** into cell B2, using the Right arrow key to simultaneously complete the entry and move the cell pointer to cell C2. Be sure to type the quotation mark (") label-prefix so that the label will be right-aligned in the cell. In the same manner, enter the remaining months' names in columns C through M, typing the quotation mark (") label-prefix before each of them: **"Feb, "Mar, "Apr, "May, "Jun, "Jul, "Aug, "Sep, "Oct, "Nov**, and **"Dec**. The final label you will enter, **"Dec**, will be in cell M2.

Figure 3-14

A..M2		Dec						
A	F	G	H	I	J	K	L	M
2	May	Jun	Jul	Aug	Sep	Oct	Nov	Dec
3								
4								
5								
6								

■ *NOTE:* You can change the label alignment of a cell or range by (1) editing the cell and changing the label prefix, or (2) highlighting the cell or range and choosing one of the Style Alignment options, or (3) highlighting the cell or range and clicking on one of the "Style Alignment" SmartIcon buttons. The "Style Alignment" SmartIcons look like this:

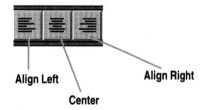

Align Left

Center

Align Right

Entering Labels that Start with Numbers

1-2-3 automatically identifies each entry you type as a label or a value by looking at the first character. Sometimes, however, the first character is misleading.

For example, suppose you want to enter a label that begins with a number, such as the Gordon family's street address, 58 Kettering Drive. To use this kind of label, you must manually type a label prefix before the first character: **'58 Kettering Drive**. This tells 1-2-3 that even though the entry looks like it is a value, you mean it to be a label. The prefix doesn't appear in the cell display, but you will see it in the edit line of the control panel when the cell pointer is in the cell.

To see what 1-2-3 does with a label that begins with a number, try giving the budget worksheet a title that starts with a year:

Move to: cell B1

Type: 1992 HOUSEHOLD BUDGET ⏎

The computer beeps and the mode indicator reads EDIT. The initial **1** in **1992** tells 1-2-3 the entry is a value; however, the program does not accept a value that contains alphabetic characters. A similar problem occurs with items such as telephone numbers or social security numbers; although these items contain only numerals, they are not actually numeric values.

For example, 1-2-3 interprets the telephone number 555-1212 as "five hundred fifty-five minus one thousand two hundred twelve" and produces the result: -657.

Figure 3-15:   Trying to Enter a Label that Begins with a Number

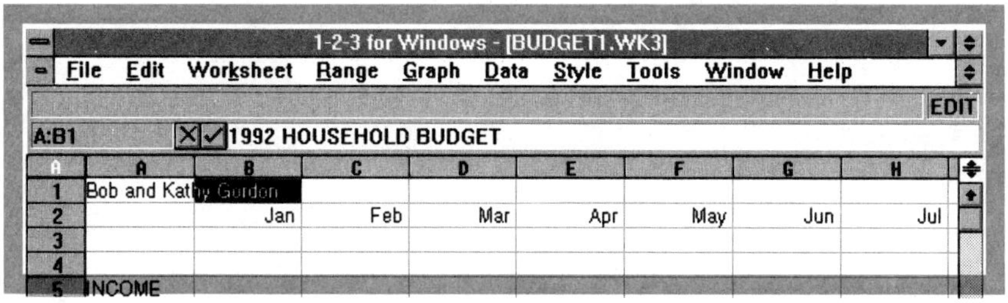

Try the budget title again, but this time begin it with an apostrophe (') label prefix. First, clear the control panel and return to READY mode:

Press: [ESC]   *two times*

Pressing Escape the first time clears the control panel and leaves you in EDIT mode. Pressing Escape the second time returns you to READY mode.

Now, enter the title as a label. Keep your eye on the mode indicator; once you have typed the apostrophe, the indicator will read LABEL.

Type: '1992 HOUSEHOLD BUDGET   [↵]

1-2-3 has no problem accepting the label this time. (It will look as if 1-2-3 has overwritten part of the contents of cell A1 with the entry in cell B1. Don't worry about this—the full text of the label is still there, and you will fix the display later.)

■ *NOTE:*   If you are entering many labels that begin with numbers, you should pre-format the cells into which you will be entering the labels as Label cells, so they will automatically accept numeric and mixed alphanumeric entries as labels without your having to type a label prefix. Formatting cells is described in Chapter 4.

Figure 3-16:   Entering a Label that Begins with a Number

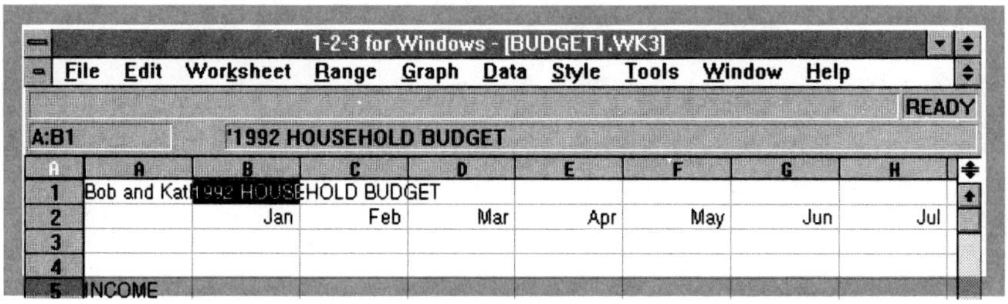

Congratulations! You have finished entering the labels for the spreadsheet portion of the Home Budget worksheet. Before you continue with the next exercise in this chapter, save your worksheet once more.

If you printed the worksheet out at this point, it would look something like Figure 3-17. (Printing worksheets is described in Chapter 9.)

Figure 3-17

```
Bob and K1992 HOUSEHOLD BUDGET
              Jan   Feb   Mar   Apr   May   Jun   Jul   Aug   Sep   Oct   Nov   Dec


INCOME

Weekly
  Net Pay (Bob)

Monthly
  Net Pay (Kathy)
  Interest

Total Income



EXPENSES

  Auto
  Charity
  Clothes
  Food
  Household
  Medical
  Misc
  Rent
  Savings
  Utility
  Woodwork

Total Expenses



CASH FLOW

Savings Account
  Savings this Month
  Cumulative Savings

Checking Account
  Opening Balance
  Net Cash Flow

  Closing Balance


Total Available Funds
```

Entering Values

The basic structure of the Home Budget worksheet is now almost half complete. The next step is to enter the values used in budget calculations. (In Chapter 4, you will enter formulas that reference these variables.)

Two Approaches to Entering Values   In general, there are two ways to go about entering values into a spreadsheet: You can enter data in the spreadsheet area itself, or you can enter data in a separate area of the worksheet and then refer to that data in the spreadsheet. Each method has its merits, and neither is universally preferred.

Entering data directly into the spreadsheet is generally most useful if the spreadsheet is a one-shot deal, something you build for a particular purpose and don't plan to modify. Although constructing a spreadsheet this way is fast, you sometimes have a hard time finding the values later, if you want to change them. Because Bob Gordon will probably want to use this budget in future years (and because we are going to build on this worksheet in future chapters of this book), it makes sense to take the other approach.

Instead of entering income data directly into the INCOME section of the worksheet and expense data directly into the EXPENSES section, you are going to create separate VARIABLES sections for your data. The advantage of this method is that it lets you make changes to worksheet data in only one place and have the changes automatically reflected elsewhere. Though creating variables sections involves more planning and a little more work up front than simply entering data directly into the spreadsheet area of an application, when you use this method it is much easier to try out new values and to modify the worksheet later on.

You are going to create a variables section for income data and refer to that data in the INCOME section. Similarly, you will create a section for expense data and use that information in the EXPENSES section. Finally, you'll create a section for any other variable information you will use in the spreadsheet.

■ *NOTE:*   Chapter 5 contains an example of a worksheet file in which data is directly entered into the spreadsheet area of the worksheet; the example uses a different technique to separate data from calculated values.

Creating the INCOME VARIABLES Section   The INCOME VARIABLES section contains the values that the INCOME section references when it calculates budgeted income for each month of a given year. The INCOME VARIABLES section contains subsections for Weekly and Monthly income.

Figure 3-18:   The INCOME VARIABLES Section, with Data

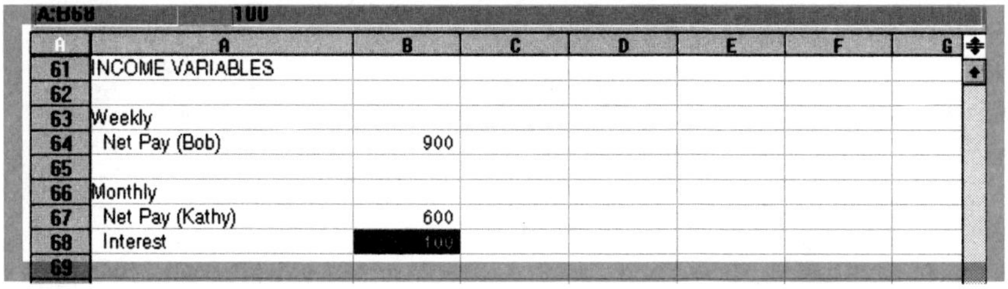

A:B68		100						
A	A	B	C	D	E	F	G
61	INCOME VARIABLES						
62							
63	Weekly						
64	Net Pay (Bob)	900					
65							
66	Monthly						
67	Net Pay (Kathy)	600					
68	Interest	100					
69							

Perform the following steps to create the INCOME VARIABLES section:

1. Position the cell pointer in cell A61.

   First, position cell A61 in the upper left corner of the Worksheet window and move the cell pointer to that cell. You can do this using any of the methods you have learned for moving the cell pointer: Pressing F5 (Goto) or choosing Range Go To; pressing Page Down; or clicking on the vertical scroll bar and the scroll bar arrow.

   Move to: cell A61

2. Enter the labels in column A of the INCOME VARIABLES section (rows 61 through 68).

   Enter the labels in column A so that your screen looks like the one in Figure 3-19. Begin by entering the label INCOME VARIABLES in cell A61. As you have done with previous screens, use the Down arrow to complete each entry and move to the next cell down. Press the Space bar two times to begin indented labels with two blank spaces.

   Figure 3-19

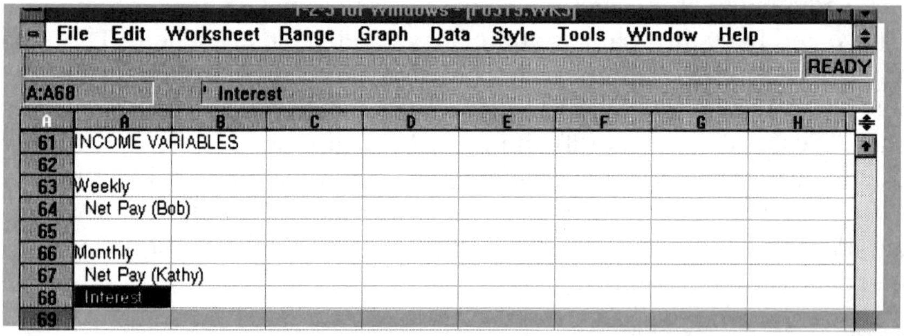

3. Enter the values for the INCOME VARIABLES section (cells B64, B67, and B68).

   Enter the values for Bob and Kathy's income in the cells to the right of the appropriate labels. Use the arrow keys to move to cell B64, rather than using the Goto key, so that cell A61 remains in the top left corner of the Worksheet window. (It will look as if you are overwriting parts of column A when you fill in values for column B. Don't worry about this; the labels in column A will still be intact, and you'll display them again later.) Notice that the mode indicator in the upper right corner of the control panel reads VALUE as soon as you start to type a number.

   Move to: cell B64
   Type: 900
   Press: ↓ *three times*
   Type: 600 ↓

   100 ↵

When you have finished, your screen should look like Figure 3-20. If it does not, correct the labels and values you have entered so far, or the budget figures your worksheet generates will not agree with the text and it will be difficult for you to tell whether you have made an error. Later on, if you want to convert the budget worksheet for your own use, you can change the values in the VARIABLES sections to values appropriate to your situation.

Figure 3-20

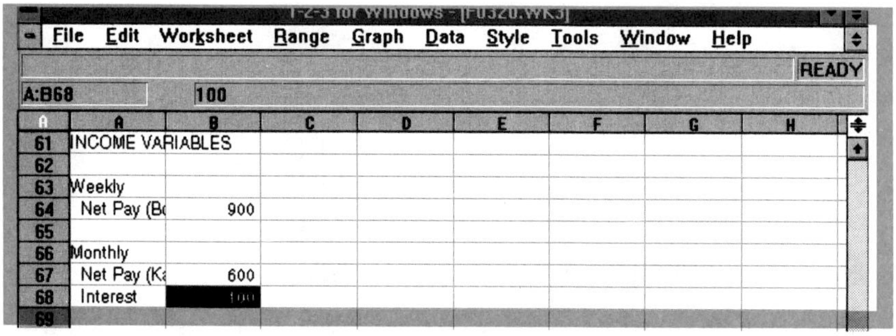

4. Widen column A to 22 characters.

Notice what happened to the labels in column A when you typed values in column B: the text that extended into column B appears to be cut off. The text is still there (you can see it in the control panel if you move the cell pointer to one of the cut-off labels), but 1-2-3 can't display it.

How 1-2-3 handles *long labels* (labels that are longer than the column widths of their cells) depends on the cells to the right of the long label. If the cells to the right of the label are blank, 1-2-3 displays the entire long label. Otherwise, 1-2-3 displays the contents of the cells to the right of the long label, rather than the part of the long label that extends beyond the label's column. In this case, some of the labels in column A are longer than the default column width (measured in the number of numeral characters that can be displayed in the column using the default font). This is no problem when the cells in column B are blank, but when you enter values into those cells, 1-2-3 truncates the long-label display.

To fix the truncated-label problem, make column A wide enough to display the longest label you plan to enter:

Move to:	*any cell in column A*
Choose:	Worksheet Column Width
Select:	Set width to
Type:	22 *in the text box*
Press:	↵ *or select OK*

Column A widens to 22 characters and 1-2-3 displays the complete labels in the INCOME VARIABLES section.

Figure 3-21: **Widening a Column**

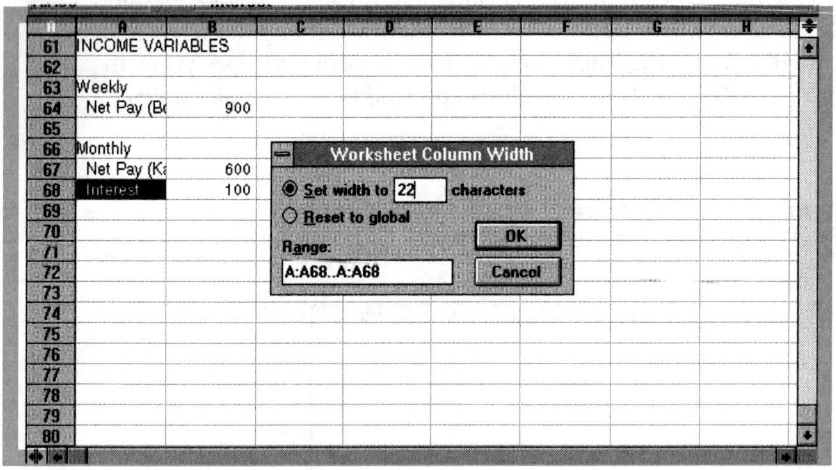

■ *NOTE:*   You can also adjust the column width with the mouse. Move the mouse pointer to the column border to the right of the column letter. When the mouse pointer turns into a dark cross with horizontal arrows, drag the pointer by pressing the left mouse button and moving the mouse to the right or left to change the column width. When the column is the width you want, release the mouse button. Regardless of how you do it, adjusting the column width affects the display of the whole column, from row 1 to row 8192.

5. Save your work.

Creating the EXPENSE VARIABLES Section   Creating the EXPENSE VARIABLES section is similar to creating the INCOME VARIABLES section, though a bit more typing is involved. Like the INCOME VARIABLES section, the EXPENSE VARIABLES section is divided into two parts: Weekly and Monthly expenses. Perform the following steps to complete the EXPENSE VARIABLES section:

1. Position the cell pointer in cell A81.

   Using any of the methods you have learned, position cell A81 in the upper left corner of the Worksheet window and move the cell pointer to that cell.

   Move to: cell A81

2. Enter the labels in column A of the EXPENSE VARIABLES section (rows 81 through 96).

   Enter the labels in column A so your screen looks like Figure 3-22. Don't indent any of the labels yet. Instead, type them into the worksheet exactly as you see them here; you will indent them later. Use the Down arrow to complete each entry and move down to the next cell in the column. Finish by typing the word Woodwork into cell A96 and pressing Enter.

Figure 3-22

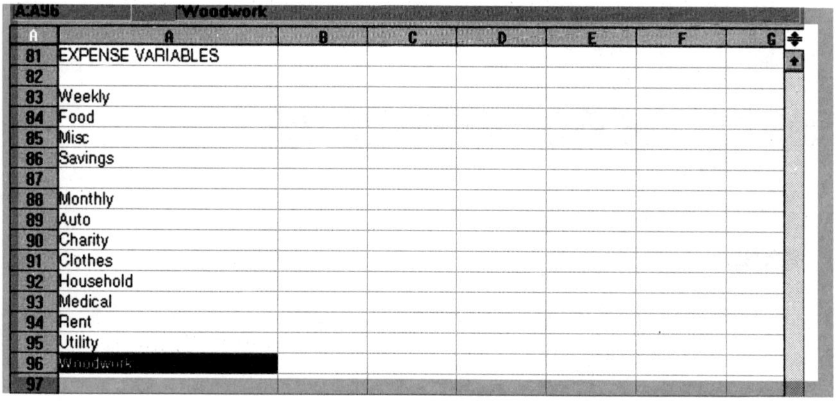

A	B	C	D	E	F	G
81 EXPENSE VARIABLES						
82						
83 Weekly						
84 Food						
85 Misc						
86 Savings						
87						
88 Monthly						
89 Auto						
90 Charity						
91 Clothes						
92 Household						
93 Medical						
94 Rent						
95 Utility						
96 Woodwork						
97						

3. Enter the values for the EXPENSE VARIABLES section (cells B84 through B96).

Enter the values for Bob and Kathy's expenses, using Figure 3-23 as your guide. Begin with the value for Food, in cell B84. Use the Down arrow to complete each entry and move to the next cell down. Finish with **250** in cell B96.

Figure 3-23

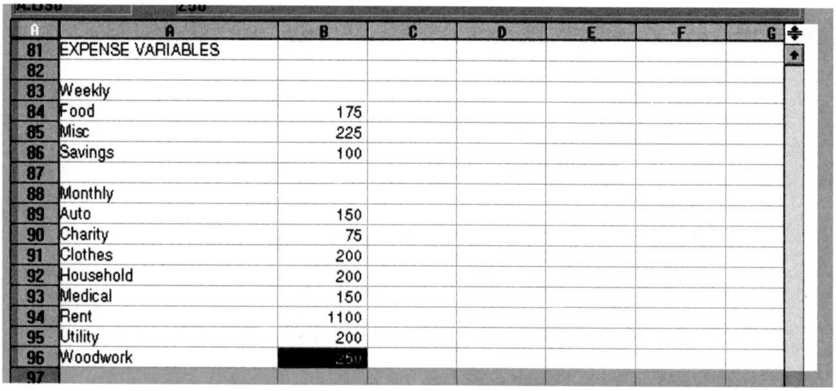

A	B	C	D	E	F	G
81 EXPENSE VARIABLES						
82						
83 Weekly						
84 Food	175					
85 Misc	225					
86 Savings	100					
87						
88 Monthly						
89 Auto	150					
90 Charity	75					
91 Clothes	200					
92 Household	200					
93 Medical	150					
94 Rent	1100					
95 Utility	200					
96 Woodwork	250					
97						

4. Save your work.

Creating the MISC. VARIABLES section   The last section of this worksheet is the MISC. VARI-ABLES section. This worksheet section contains any VARIABLES needed in the worksheet that are neither income nor expenses.

The VARIABLES in this section are straightforward: **1992** is a number and the figures for last year's checking and savings account balances are numbers. The word **Friday** is a label cell. It is not used in calculations, but it is included here because it is used to manually figure out how many paydays fall in a given month. Type in these entries just as you have other labels and values.

Figure 3-24: The Completed MISC. VARIABLES Section

	A	B	C	D	E	F	G
101	MISC. VARIABLES						
102							
103	Payday day-of-week:	Friday					
104	Current year:	1992					
105	Last year's checking:	1000					
106	Last year's savings:	2000					
107							
108							
109							

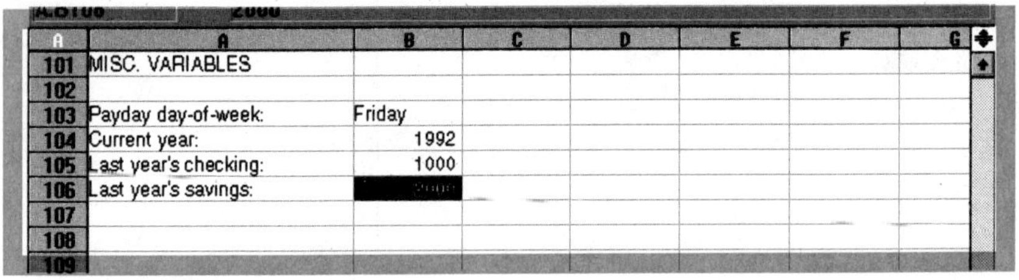

1. Position the cell pointer in cell A101.

   Position cell A101 in the upper left corner of the Worksheet window.

   Move to: cell A101

2. Enter the labels in column A of the MISC. VARIABLES section (rows 101 through 106).

   Use Figure 3-25 as your guide.

Figure 3-25

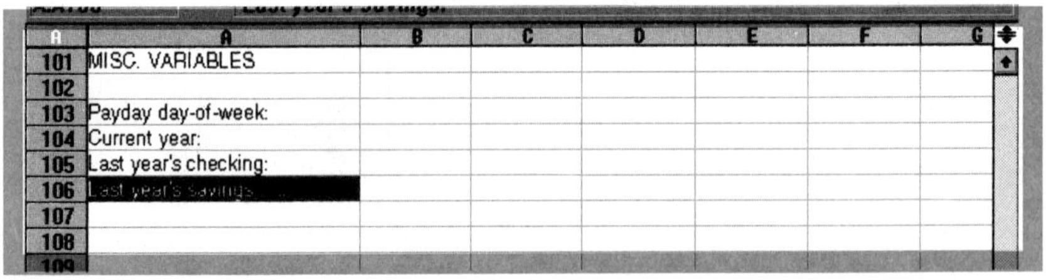

	A	B	C	D	E	F	G
101	MISC. VARIABLES						
102							
103	Payday day-of-week:						
104	Current year:						
105	Last year's checking:						
106	Last year's savings:						
107							
108							
109							

3. Enter the values for the MISC. VARIABLES section (cells B103 through B106).

   Fill in the values for Payday day-of-week, Current year, Last year's checking, and Last year's savings.

   Move to: cell B103

   Type: Friday   [↓]

   1992   [↓]

   1000   [↓]

   2000   [↵]

When you have finished these keystroke instructions, the cell pointer will be in cell B106.

Figure 3-26:   The Completed MISC. VARIABLES Section

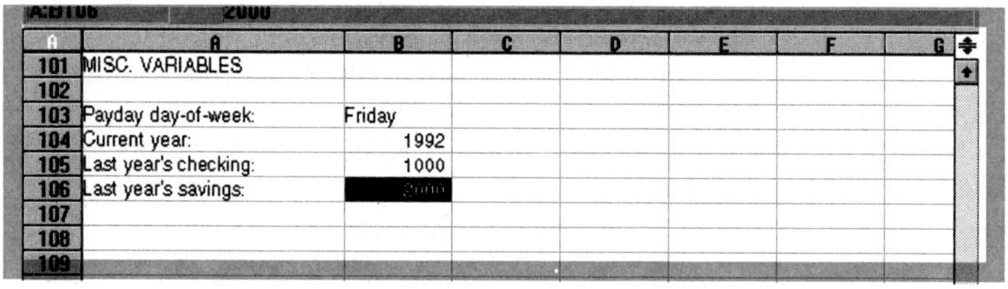

4. Save your work.

Congratulations! You have finished creating the VARIABLES area and entering most of the values for the Home Budget worksheet. If you printed it out, the VARIABLES area would now look something like Figure 3-27.

Figure 3-27:   The VARIABLES Area of the Home Budget Application

```
INCOME VARIABLES

Weekly
     Net Pay (Bob)           900

Monthly
     Net Pay (Kathy)         600
     Interest                100


EXPENSE VARIABLES

Weekly
Food                         175
Misc                         225
Savings                      100

Monthly
Auto                         150
Charity                       75
Clothes                      200
Household                    200
Medical                      150
Rent                        1100
Utility                      200
Woodwork                     250


MISC. VARIABLES

Payday day-of-week:     Friday
Current year:             1992
Last year's checking:     1000
Last year's savings:      2000
```

Completing Data Entry for the Home Budget

The Home Budget uses the number of paydays in each month to calculate the Gordons' anticipated monthly income and expenses. To arrive at a monthly figure for values they have budgeted weekly (such as food expenses), the weekly values are multiplied by the number of paydays in the month. For example, if the weekly budgeted amount for food is $175 and there are five paydays in the month, the month's budget for food is 5 * $175, or $875. If there are four paydays in the month, the food budget for that month is $700.

Enter the number of paydays in the month of January, 1992, in cell B3:

Move to: cell B3

Type: 5   →

Continue to enter paydays/month in row 3, using the list of months and paydays/month in Setup Table 3-1 as your guide. The table assumes payday is Friday.

Congratulations! You have finished entering the labels and values for the Home Budget worksheet. Before going on, save the file again.

Setup Table 3-1: Months and Paydays for 1992

Month	Paydays	Cell Address
January	5	B3
February	4	C3
March	4	D3
April	4	E3
May	5	F3
June	4	G3
July	5	H3
August	4	I3
September	4	J3
October	5	K3
November	4	L3
December	4	M3

■ *NOTE:*   From now on, Setup Tables will be provided instead of keystroke instructions whenever a table will make it easier for you to enter data.

A Note on the Next Several Sections

You have created much of the basic structure of the Gordons' home budget. In the next few sections, you are going to put ordering Bob and Kathy's finances on hold as you learn some additional 1-2-3 skills. You will pick up the construction of the Home Budget application again toward the end of this chapter, and then complete it in Chapter 4.

Editing Data

Earlier in this book, you were told about some simple ways to fix errors in cell entries. In this section, you'll learn more about how to correct typing mistakes and make other changes to the contents of cells.

There are two ways to make changes to a worksheet entry: Replace the entry or edit the entry. Replacing the entry is often the best method for changing a simple entry such as a number or a short label; this is what you have done so far. If, however, you need to change a long or complicated entry, it is usually easier to *edit* the entry—that is, to modify the existing entry, rather than typing in a new one. Editing a cell involves several steps:

1. Move the cell pointer to the cell you want to edit.
2. Press F2 (Edit) or double-click the cell to start editing the entry in the edit line of the control panel.

3. Use the arrow keys and other pointer-movement keys to move the cursor to the incorrect part of the entry.

4. Remove the error with the Backspace or Delete key.

5. Type in the correct information.

6. Complete the entry by pressing Enter or clicking the Confirm button.

To get the feel of editing, try changing a couple of cells in the first row of Bob and Kathy's Home Budget:

1. Edit cell A1.

First, change the label in cell A1 so that it includes Bob and Kathy's son, Tim. Notice that the mode indicator changes to EDIT when you double-click the cell or press F2, the Edit key.

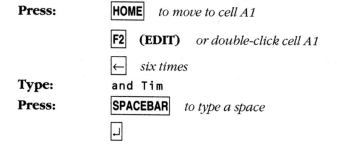

Press: ⬛ HOME *to move to cell A1*

⬛ F2 **(EDIT)** *or double-click cell A1*

⬛ ← *six times*

Type: and Tim

Press: ⬛ SPACEBAR *to type a space*

⬛ ↵

Figure 3-28

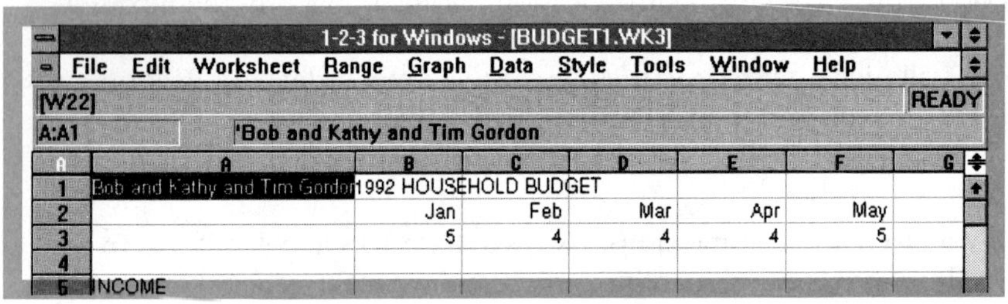

2. Edit cell B1.

Now, change the label in cell B1 from **1992 HOUSEHOLD BUDGET** to **1992 HOME BUDGET**:

Press:	HOME	*to move to cell B1*
	F2 **(EDIT)**	*or double-click cell B1*
	HOME	*to move to the start of the entry*
	→	*eight times, to move to the U in "HOUSEHOLD"*
	DELETE	*seven times, to delete the characters "USEHOLD"*
Type:	ME	*to complete the word "HOME"*
Press:	↵	

Figure 3-29

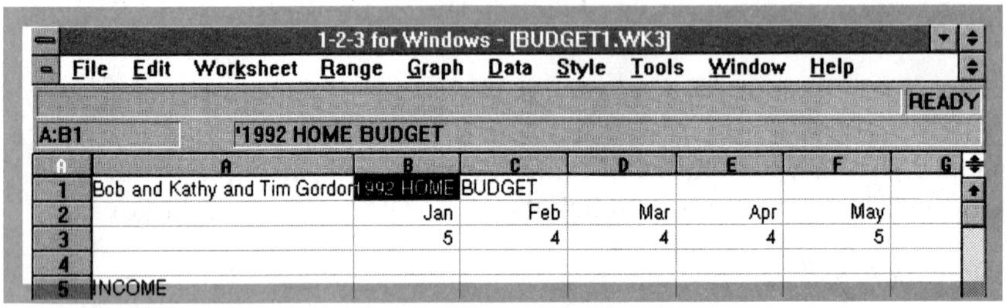

The label **1992 HOME BUDGET** appears in cell B1.

Notice that pressing Home in EDIT mode moves the cursor to the beginning of an entry, rather than completing the entry and moving the cell pointer to cell A1, as it would if 1-2-3 were in VALUE mode or LABEL mode.

3. Restore the previous contents of cell A1.

Looking again at the label in cell A1, you decide to leave Tim off the title, cute as he is.

Press: ⬅ *to move to cell A1*

   F2   **(EDIT)**   *or double-click cell A1*

   ⬅   *six times*

   BACKSPACE   *eight times, to erase "and Tim "*

   ↵

Figure 3-30

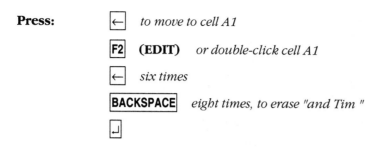

The label once again reads "Bob and Kathy Gordon".

4. Save BUDGET1.WK3.

Keys Used in Editing

The Edit key transforms the control panel into a miniature and somewhat specialized text editor. Besides the Home, Delete, Backspace, and arrow keys, there are many other keys you can use when you are editing an entry. Each is described in Table 3-7.

Table 3-7:   **Keys Used in Editing**

Key	What It Does
F2 (EDIT)	From READY, LABEL, or VALUE mode, changes to EDIT mode so you can edit the current cell's contents. From EDIT mode, switches between EDIT mode and VALUE or LABEL mode, depending on whether the current cell contains a value or a label.
ENTER	Replaces the original cell entry with the edited one.
LEFT / RIGHT	Moves the cursor one space at a time left or right.
BACKSPACE	Erases the character preceding the cursor.
DELETE	Erases the character the cursor is on.
UP / DOWN	Completes an entry and moves the cell pointer up or down one cell.
CTRL+RIGHT or TAB	Moves the cursor right one word at a time.

Key	What It Does
CTRL+LEFT or SHIFT+TAB	Moves the cursor left one word at a time.
ESC	Cancels all characters in the edit line. If you are in LABEL or VALUE mode or the edit line is blank, returns 1-2-3 to READY mode.
PGUP / PGDN	Completes an entry and moves the cell pointer up or down one window height.
HOME	Moves the cursor to the first character of an entry (if the entry is a label, the first character will be an apostrophe or other label-prefix character). If you are in LABEL or VALUE mode, completes an entry and moves the cell pointer to cell A1 of the current worksheet.
END	Moves the cursor to the last character of an entry.

A Note on Using the Editing Keys in VALUE or LABEL Mode

While you are working with 1-2-3, it is helpful to keep in mind how the pointer-movement keys behave in relation to the current mode. Remember that when you are typing in data (1-2-3 is in LABEL or VALUE mode), the pointer-movement keys do not move the cursor in the control panel, as they do when you are editing; instead, they complete a cell entry and move the cell pointer.

If you need to edit an entry when 1-2-3 is in LABEL or VALUE mode, press F2 (Edit) first to change to EDIT mode. Otherwise, you may be surprised by where the cell pointer lands. For example, in EDIT mode, the Home key moves the cursor to the first character in the entry being edited; in VALUE or LABEL mode, the Home key completes the current entry and moves the cell pointer to cell A1 of the current worksheet.

Ranges

A *range* is a cell or a group of cells in the worksheet file. It can be one cell, a single row or column of cells, or a block of cells composed of many rows and columns. A range can also extend through multiple worksheets in the worksheet file. A two-dimensional range must be a rectangle, while a three-dimensional range (a range that extends through more than one worksheet) must be a rectangular solid. Figure 3-31 on the next page shows some examples of 1-2-3 worksheet ranges.

Without ranges, constructing a worksheet would be much more difficult and time-consuming. Later in this section on ranges you will see how a range can be used to speed up entering and erasing data. Ranges can also help you copy or move sections of the worksheet, format an area quickly, and print or graph a group of cells.

Defining a Range

To define a range in a worksheet, you give 1-2-3 the cell addresses of two opposite corners of the range (or, in the case of a single row or column, opposite ends of the range). For example, the month names you entered in the INCOME section occupy the 12 cells in row 2 beginning with cell B2 and moving right. This area is defined as the range B2 to M2. Similarly, the two rows of month names and paydays per month occupy the range B2 to M3.

Figure 3-31a: Two-Dimensional Ranges

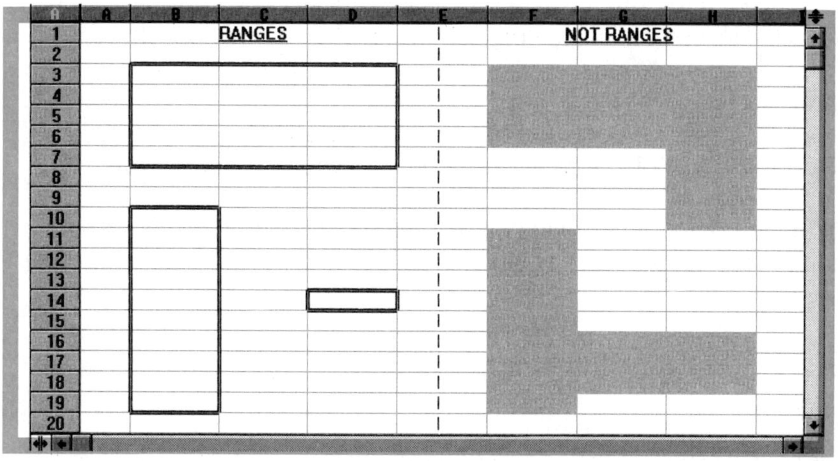

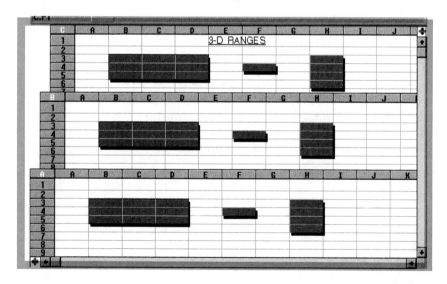

Figure 3-31b: Three-Dimensional Ranges

1-2-3's notation for entering ranges is: **START..END**, where **START** and **END** are the cell addresses of opposite corners of the range. Although 1-2-3 always displays ranges using two periods to separate the start and end cell addresses of the range, you need supply only one period. For instance, the range of month names you entered in row 2 of the Home Budget worksheet can be typed as either **B2.M2** or **B2..M2**; the effect is exactly the same. You can also use either uppercase or lowercase letters for the worksheet or column letters in range addresses.

■ *NOTE:*   When a cell address is in the current worksheet, you don't have to specify the worksheet letter. In this book, worksheet letters will not be mentioned in text and in keystroke instructions unless they are needed to distinguish one worksheet from another. Unless a specific worksheet reference is made, assume that a range applies to the current worksheet.

Filling and Erasing a Range

This section demonstrates how to use ranges to automatically fill part of a worksheet with data, and then to selectively erase part of that new data. You'll experiment with the Data Fill, Edit Clear, and Edit Cut commands.

Besides being useful in their own right, Data Fill, Edit Clear, and Edit Cut are convenient commands for demonstrating the various ways of entering ranges in the worksheet. There are three ways to enter a range:

- ■   By typing in the range address
- ■   By highlighting the range with the pointer-movement keys or the mouse
- ■   By entering a range name

The following exercise demonstrates the first two of these methods. It uses Data Fill to enter some data in a worksheet, and then uses Edit Clear and Edit Cut to erase it, a little at a time, using different methods for defining the ranges to erase. (The third method, entering a range name, is described in "Naming Ranges" in Chapter 4.)

1. Create a scratch worksheet in the current worksheet file.

You will experiment with ranges in a new, empty worksheet. That way, you won't have to worry about erasing something important; you will also start getting used to the idea that there are many worksheets at your disposal. Think of creating this scratch worksheet as reaching for a piece of scrap paper in the middle of some other activity. When you are through using the scratch worksheet, you can delete it.

Use Worksheet Insert to create a new worksheet after worksheet A:

Choose: Worksheet   Insert

Figure 3-32:   The Worksheet Insert Dialog Box

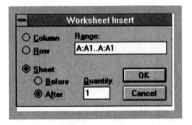

1-2-3 displays the Worksheet Insert dialog box. From here, you can add columns, rows, or worksheets to a worksheet file. In this case, you're going to insert a worksheet, so select the "Sheet" and "After" option buttons and make sure the "Quantity:" text box shows **1**.

Select: OK   *to insert worksheet B*

The WAIT indicator appears briefly, and then you are presented with a new worksheet, worksheet B. (Adding worksheets will be described in more detail in Chapter 5.)

Although the Worksheet window is now blank, you are still in the BUDGET1.WK3 file, and the data you entered in worksheet A is intact. If you like, you can verify this by moving back to worksheet A:

Press: CTRL+PGDN   *to move to worksheet A*

Holding down the Control key while you press Page Down moves the cell pointer to the previous worksheet. Worksheet A appears on your screen, exactly as it was when you left it. Now, return to worksheet B:

Press: CTRL+PGUP   *to move back to worksheet B*

Once again, the blank worksheet B fills the Worksheet window.

2. Fill a range with numbers.

Now that you have a clear place in which to work, fill a couple of screens with numbers, using the Data Fill command. Data Fill is a shortcut method for entering a series of values in a 1-2-3 worksheet. You can use Data Fill to enter sequential numeric data without having to type each entry individually.

When you choose Data Fill, 1-2-3 presents a dialog box that prompts for a fill range, a Start value, a Step value, and a Stop value. The first time you use Data Fill in a worksheet file, 1-2-3 prompts you with the currently highlighted range (if there is one), or the current cell address and it proposes system default values for Start, Step, and Stop. When you subsequently use Data Fill in the same worksheet file, 1-2-3 prompts you with either the currently highlighted range (if there is one) or the most recent fill range, and it proposes the Start, Step, and Stop values you supplied the last time you used Data Fill in the file. In either case, you can supply a different fill range and Start, Step, and Stop values.

Figure 3-33:   The Data Fill Dialog Box

Each of the Data Fill dialog box prompts is described in Table 3-8. The keystroke instructions following Table 3-8 guide you through the Data Fill process.

Table 3-8: Prompts for Entering Data with Data Fill

Prompt	Example	Description
Range:	B:A1.B:M41 or B:A1..B:M41	The area of the worksheet into which you want Data Fill to enter data. In this case, the range begins with cell B:A1 and ends with cell B:M41.
Start:	0	The value you want the first filled cell to contain. In this case, 0.
Step:	1	The amount by which you want each value to increase or decrease as Data Fill moves from one cell to the next. In this case, you want Data Fill to add 1 to the previous entry to get the next one.
Stop:	8191	The last value in the series of values you want Data Fill to create. You can use for the Stop value any value that is greater than the highest value you expect Data Fill to generate. The system default is 8191.

With the cell pointer in cell A1, do the following:

Choose: Data   Fill

1-2-3 prompts you for the fill range, Start value, Step value, and Stop value. In this case, you are going to specify the Range by typing the range address.

Type: a1.m41   *in the Range: text box*

1-2-3 proposes 0 as the Start value, 1 as the Step value, and 8191 as the Stop value. Accept these defaults and your new "Range:" value.

Press: ⏎   *or select OK*

1-2-3 works for a moment, and then the numbers 0 through 532 appear in cells A1 through M41. The first screenful of these values is illustrated in Figure 3-34.

Figure 3-34

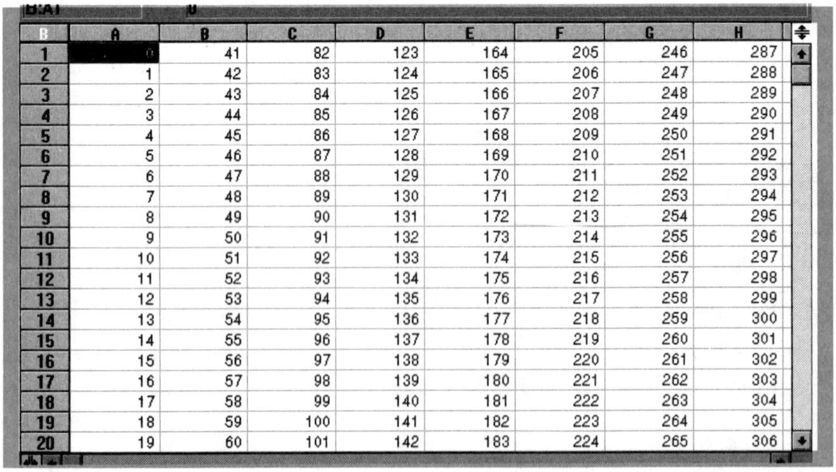

	A	B	C	D	E	F	G	H
1	0	41	82	123	164	205	246	287
2	1	42	83	124	165	206	247	288
3	2	43	84	125	166	207	248	289
4	3	44	85	126	167	208	249	290
5	4	45	86	127	168	209	250	291
6	5	46	87	128	169	210	251	292
7	6	47	88	129	170	211	252	293
8	7	48	89	130	171	212	253	294
9	8	49	90	131	172	213	254	295
10	9	50	91	132	173	214	255	296
11	10	51	92	133	174	215	256	297
12	11	52	93	134	175	216	257	298
13	12	53	94	135	176	217	258	299
14	13	54	95	136	177	218	259	300
15	14	55	96	137	178	219	260	301
16	15	56	97	138	179	220	261	302
17	16	57	98	139	180	221	262	303
18	17	58	99	140	181	222	263	304
19	18	59	100	141	182	223	264	305
20	19	60	101	142	183	224	265	306

3. Erase part of the filled range by pointing and highlighting with the keyboard.

Erasing data with Edit Clear is a two–step process. First, you highlight the range you want to erase (*preselect* the range), and then you choose Edit Clear (or, as a shortcut, press Delete). Erasing data removes worksheet cell contents, as if you had used a pencil eraser to remove the contents of a paper spreadsheet cell.

You can use either the mouse or the keyboard to highlight a range. To use the keyboard, move the cell pointer to the cell at which you want the range to start, press F4, and then move the cell pointer to the cell at which you want the range to end. (1-2-3 changes to POINT mode when you press F4 and highlights the range as you move the cell pointer.) When you have highlighted the range you want, press Enter to anchor the free end of the range and return 1-2-3 to READY mode. Try this on the range B:A1..B:D11.

Move to:	cell B:A1
Press:	F4
Move to:	cell B:D11 *with the Down and Right arrow keys*
Press:	↵

Figure 3-35: Highlighting a Range with F4 and the Arrow Keys

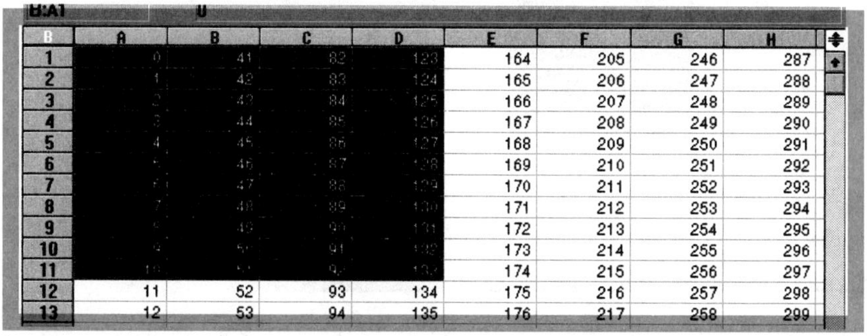

Choose:	Edit	Clear	*or press Delete*	

1-2-3 erases the range A1..D11. Notice that the preselected range remains highlighted. This is so you can perform other commands on it. In this case, however, you won't be performing any other commands on the erased range, so clear the highlighting:

Press:	ESC *to clear the range highlighting*

4. Cut part of the filled range to the Clipboard by pointing and highlighting with the mouse.

To use the mouse to highlight a range, move the mouse pointer to the cell at which you want the range to start, press and hold the left mouse button, and drag the mouse pointer to the cell at which you want the range to end. Try this on the range E1..F15.

Click on:	cell E1 *and hold down the left mouse button*

Move to: cell F14 *and release the left mouse button*

1-2-3 highlights the range. This time, instead of selecting Edit Clear, erase the range by cutting to the Windows Clipboard. (The Clipboard is a temporary storage area used by 1-2-3/W and other Windows applications to hold data.) Choose the Edit Cut command (or, as a shortcut, click on the "scissors" icon in the icon palette).

Choose: Edit Cut *or click on the Cut icon*

Figure 3-36: **Cutting a Range to the Clipboard**

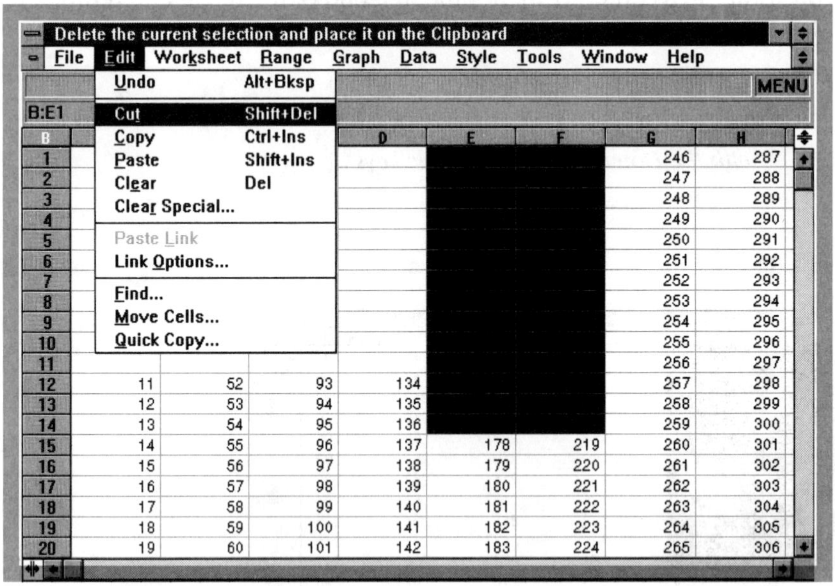

Delete the current selection and place it on the Clipboard							

File	Edit	Worksheet	Range	Graph	Data	Style	Tools	Window	Help

	Undo	Alt+Bksp					MENU

B:E1

	Cut	Shift+Del					
B	Copy	Ctrl+Ins	D	E	F	G	H
1	Paste	Shift+Ins				246	287
2	Clear	Del				247	288
3	Clear Special...					248	289
4						249	290
5	Paste Link					250	291
6	Link Options...					251	292
7						252	293
8	Find...					253	294
9	Move Cells...					254	295
10	Quick Copy...					255	296
11						256	297
12	11	52	93	134		257	298
13	12	53	94	135		258	299
14	13	54	95	136		259	300
15	14	55	96	137	178	219	260	301
16	15	56	97	138	179	220	261	302
17	16	57	98	139	180	221	262	303
18	17	58	99	140	181	222	263	304
19	18	59	100	141	182	223	264	305
20	19	60	101	142	183	224	265	306

1-2-3 copies the range to the Clipboard, erases it from the worksheet, and returns to READY mode.

■ *NOTE:* If you inadvertently erase a range with Edit Clear, you can recover it by immediately pressing Alt+Backspace or selecting Edit Undo. (You'll learn more about Edit Undo later in this chapter.) If you erase a range by cutting it to the Clipboard, you can recover it either by choosing Edit Paste or by choosing Edit Undo.

Experimenting with Secondary Selection of Ranges

As you may have noticed, you can select a range in 1-2-3 either *before* you choose a command (as you did with Edit Clear and Edit Cut), or *after* you choose the command (as you did with Data Fill). With many commands, you can do whichever you prefer.

Selecting a range after you have already chosen a command is called *secondary selection*. When you use secondary selection, you can either type the range in the "Range:" text box, or highlight the range with the mouse or keyboard. Typing the range is usually quickest when the range is relatively large, as it was when you selected the range for the Data Fill command. However, highlighting the range is often more intuitive.

Try using the mouse to perform a secondary selection. Use the Data Fill command again, but this time, fill the range A1..C5 with numbers starting with 100 and increasing by 100.

1. Begin the Data Fill operation.

Without first selecting a fill range, choose the Data Fill command.

Press: `ESC`   *to clear any range highlights*

Choose: `Data`   `Fill`

1-2-3 displays the Data Fill dialog box and proposes the previously selected fill range as the new fill range.

2. Move the Data Fill dialog box out of the way.

Performing a secondary selection is similar to highlighting a range before you choose a command. Before you highlight the new range, however, it is sometimes easier to move the dialog box out of the way. To move the Data Fill dialog box, click on the dialog box's title bar and drag the box to a new position (for instance, the upper right corner of the 1-2-3 window). When you have finished, your screen should look like Figure 3-37.

Figure 3-37: Moving the Data Fill Dialog Box Out of the Way

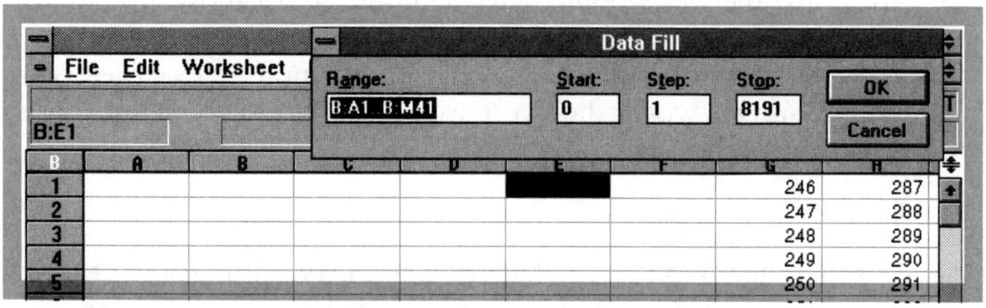

3. Use secondary selection to fill the range.

Now, highlight and fill the new range by dragging the cell pointer with the mouse:

Point to: `cell B:A1`   *and hold down the left mouse button*

Drag to: `cell B:C5`   *and release the left mouse button*

1-2-3 temporarily hides the dialog box as you select the range, then restores it when you have finished. Now, provide Data Fill with new values for Start and Step. (The default Stop value is still greater than the highest value Data Fill will generate, so it's okay to leave it as it is.)

Select: `Start:`

Type: `100`   *in the text box*

Press: `TAB`   *to move to the Step: text box*

Type: 100 *in the text box*

Press: ⏎ *or select OK*

Figure 3-38: **The Results of Using Data Fill with a Secondary Selection**

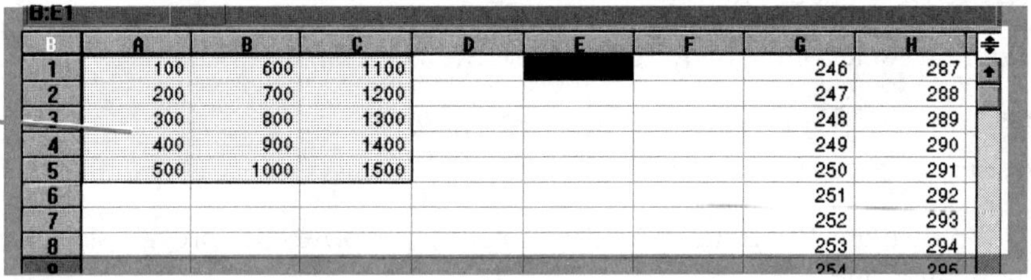

selected range

Experimenting with Anchored and Unanchored Ranges

Many of 1-2-3's commands for manipulating ranges prompt you with either a one-cell range (for example, A:A1..A:A1), or with the same range you used the last time you issued that command (for example, the range initially presented when you performed a secondary selection from the Data Fill dialog box). This range is called an *anchored range*, because the starting point is established and only the end point changes as you move the cell pointer to expand the highlight.

1-2-3 assumes that you want to start the range at the current cell pointer location and extend it from there. Often, however, you want to start the range at a different part of the worksheet file, but still have the convenience of pointing to the range. 1-2-3 allows you to do this by *unanchoring* the range.

Although you can anchor and unanchor ranges you select with the mouse, it's easiest to see how anchored and unanchored ranges work when you use the keyboard commands. Choose Data Fill to fill a different part of the worksheet:

Choose: Data Fill

1-2-3 proposes the previous fill range, B:A1..B:C5. The mode indicator displays POINT, which means you can change the range by highlighting a new one. Suppose you want to extend the range one row down and one row to the right.

Press: ↓

1-2-3 temporarily hides the Data Fill dialog box, then highlights the new range, B:A1..B:C6. It also displays the new range address in the control panel. The range is still anchored—you can't move the starting point, cell B:A1, by moving the cell pointer—but you can move the end point anywhere you like. Move it one row to the right.

Press: → ⏎

1-2-3 redisplays the Data Fill dialog box, but now the new range, B:A1..B:D6, is displayed in the "Range:" text box. If you were to select OK or press Enter, 1-2-3 would fill this range.

Suppose, however, that you changed your mind. Actually, you want to overwrite the range B:A12..B:E20 with new values. To do so, you can unanchor the range, move to the new starting point, and then highlight the new range.

Once again press Down to hide the Data Fill dialog box.

Press: ↓

1-2-3 highlights the previous range, plus one row. Now, unanchor the range:

Press: ESC

Pressing Escape unanchors the cell pointer and leaves it at the range's starting point. Notice that the highlighting disappears and the control panel prompt now displays only the start of the range, to indicate that the range is no longer an anchored range. (Whenever 1-2-3 displays only a single cell address in a prompt, the range is unanchored.) Move the cell pointer to the start of the new range you want to fill and then anchor it there:

Move to: cell B:A12

Press: .   **(Period)**

Pressing the Period key (.) anchors the range in the new location of the cell pointer (in this case, cell B:A12). 1-2-3 displays a one-cell anchored range in the control panel.

■ *NOTE:*   To anchor ranges, use the Period key (.) on the part of the keyboard that contains the alphabetic characters, not the Period key on the numeric keypad. Unless Number Lock is on, the Period key on the numeric keypad serves as the Delete key, rather than as a Period key.

Now, fill the range B:A12..B:E20:

Highlight: B:A12..B:E20   *by moving the Down and Right arrow keys*

Press: ↵ *two times, to complete the range selection and to accept the defaults for Start, Step, and Stop*

1-2-3 fills the range with the values 100 to 4500, as illustrated in Figure 3-39.

Figure 3-39

							253	294	
9							254	295	
10							255	296	
11							256	297	
12	100	1000	1900	2800	3700		257	298	
13	200	1100	2000	2900	3800		258	299	
14	300	1200	2100	3000	3900		259	300	
15	400	1300	2200	3100	4000	219	260	301	
16	500	1400	2300	3200	4100	220	261	302	
17	600	1500	2400	3300	4200	221	262	303	
18	700	1600	2500	3400	4300	222	263	304	
19	800	1700	2600	3500	4400	223	264	305	
20	900	1800	2700	3600	4500	224	265	306	

■ *NOTE:*   Anchoring and unanchoring ranges when you use the mouse works much as it does when you use the keyboard. Press the left mouse button to start highlighting the range. To unanchor the range, press Escape while still holding down the mouse button. Then, while continuing to hold down the mouse button, move the mouse pointer to the new location for the start of the range and press Period (.). Finally, while still holding down the mouse button, drag the mouse pointer to the new end point for the range. When you have finished highlighting the new range, release the mouse button.

Table 3-9 describes the keys you can use when you specify a range in a single worksheet, and the effect each key has if the range is anchored or unanchored.

Table 3-9:   Keys Used to Anchor and Unanchor a Worksheet Range

Key	Anchored Range	Unanchored Range
BACKSPACE	Moves the cell pointer to the anchor cell and removes the anchor.	Returns the cell pointer to the cell it was in before you issued the command (if you moved the cell pointer).
ESC	Moves the cell pointer to the anchor cell and removes the anchor.	Returns you to the previous command or to the dialog box you were last in.
. (Period)	Moves the anchor cell and the free cell clockwise around the corners of the range.	Makes the current cell the anchor cell.

On your own, experiment with anchoring and unanchoring ranges. Use the Data Fill command to fill more of the scratch worksheet. Use all the keys in Table 3-1 when you are highlighting fill ranges, both with the keyboard and with the mouse. When you are comfortable with highlighting, anchoring, and unanchoring, using both the keyboard and the mouse, return 1-2-3 to READY mode and proceed with the next exercise.

Using Undo to Correct Mistakes

Before you do much more work in 1-2-3, you should know about the Edit Undo command.

Edit Undo is 1-2-3's way of letting you change your mind. With Edit Undo, you can reverse the effects of an entry, a command, or another action that changes the worksheet file. For example, if you complete a cell entry and choose Edit Undo or press the Undo key (Alt+Backspace), 1-2-3 restores the cell's previous contents. If you move, copy, or erase a range of cells and then press Undo, 1-2-3 "undoes" those changes, too.

Enabling and Disabling Edit Undo

By default, Edit Undo is enabled; pressing the Undo key or choosing Edit Undo reverses the effects of the most recent command or action that can be undone.

If Edit Undo is disabled, the Edit Undo command is greyed out on the Edit menu. In that case, you'll have to turn it on to complete the exercise in this section. The following keystrokes turn Edit Undo on and save the setting for future 1-2-3 sessions.

Choose:	Tools User Setup
Select:	Enable Edit Undo *and check the check box*
	Update OK

Try out Edit Undo in a blank part of the scratch worksheet. Enter some text into cell B:A101, then write over the entry with a new entry in the same cell:

Move to:	cell B:A101
Type:	This is a test, not an actual alert. ↵
	This is an actual alert ↵

Figure 3-40

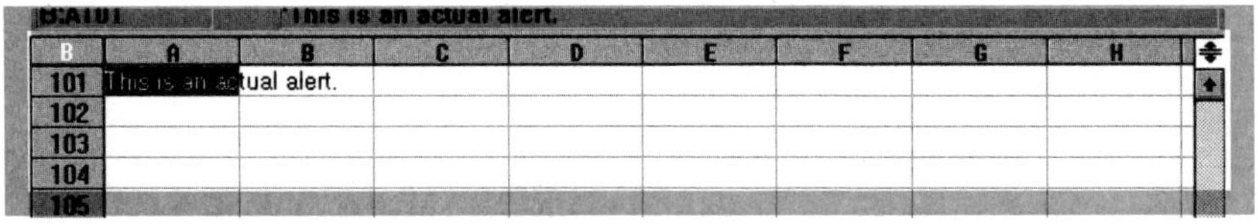

1-2-3 enters the first set of characters you typed into cell B:A101, then replaces this entry with the next set of characters you typed. Now, press Undo:

Press:	**ALT+BACKSPACE** **(UNDO)**

Figure 3-41

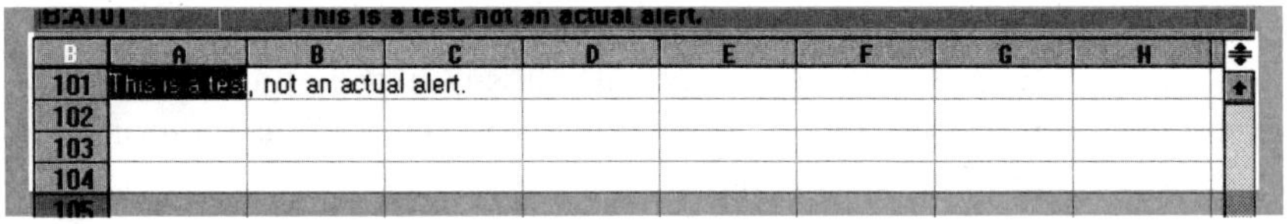

1-2-3 restores the first set of characters to cell A101. The worksheet is exactly the same as it was before you made the second entry.

Now, try something a little more dramatic. First, use the Data Fill command to enter some more data into the scratch worksheet.

Highlight:	B:A101..B:D110 *for the new fill range*
Choose:	Data Fill
Select:	OK

1-2-3 fills the range with the numbers 100 through 4000 (see Figure 3-42 on the next page). Use Edit Undo to cancel the Data Fill and erase the data you just entered:

Press:	**ALT+BACKSPACE** **(UNDO)**

Figure 3-42

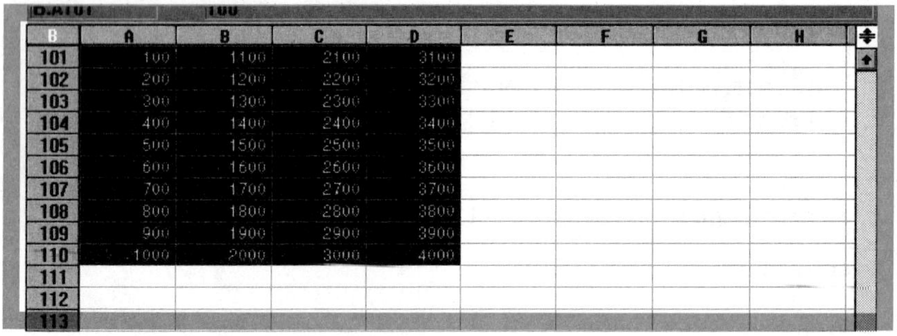

1-2-3 erases all the data you just entered with Data Fill and restores the previous entry in cell B:A101.

How Edit Undo Works

Edit Undo works from READY mode to READY mode. If Edit Undo is turned on, 1-2-3 preserves a trail that it can follow back to the previous READY mode state. This trail is called the *undo history*. Each time you make a change and return to READY mode again, 1-2-3 replaces the undo history with a new undo history. When you press Undo, 1-2-3 uses the current undo history to cancel any changes you have made between the last time it was in READY mode and the moment you press Undo. This restores the working environment to the previous READY mode state.

Because Edit Undo records only the information it needs in order to restore the worksheet to its previous state, Edit Undo uses memory efficiently. Operations that affect only a small number of cells, such as entering a label, use little memory; File Close, on the other hand, requires enough memory to temporarily store the contents of the closed file. (This memory, however, is freed as soon as you do something else that can be undone.)

When to Use and When Not to Use Edit Undo

Saving your work frequently is one way to protect yourself against losing work through mistakes. Edit Undo provides you with another, more immediate, way to recover from errors. You can undo most changes that can be saved in the worksheet file, including cell entry, macros, most menu commands, and most settings. Use Edit Undo before you resort to reissuing a command, retyping work, or going back to an earlier version of a worksheet file. Do not press Undo when you are in the middle of a command and want to cancel it—1-2-3 will let you use Edit Undo only from READY mode. (Press Control+Break or Escape to cancel commands.)

There are a few more things you should know about Edit Undo:

The first is that 1-2-3 does not add to the undo history until you actually make a change to the worksheet environment. If you begin a command and then cancel it, or if you just move the cell pointer, you have not done anything that can be undone. If you press Undo after you move the cell pointer, press a function key that makes no changes to the worksheet file, or cancel a command, 1-2-3 restores the worksheet to the *previous* READY mode state, canceling any changes you made just before you moved the cell pointer, pressed the function key, or started the canceled command. Because returning to the previous READY mode state may not be what you expect or want to happen, be sure to press Undo only when you have made a change to the worksheet file that you want to reverse.

Second, note that Edit Undo can't undo some commands and tasks. Edit Undo can't cancel the effects of commands that affect devices outside 1-2-3, such as printers or disk drives. Consequently, you can't undo File Print commands, File Save commands, or File Extract To commands. (You can, however, undo a File Open or File Close command, since these commands affect only the worksheet files in memory, not disk files.) Similarly, if you undo an operation that copies information to the Windows Clipboard, such as Edit Cut, 1-2-3 restores the worksheet file to its previous state, but it does not restore the previous contents of the Clipboard.

Third, you can't undo formula recalculation caused by pressing F9 (Calc) or by updating file links. For example, if the Calc indicator is on and you press F9 (Calc) to update formula values, then you press Alt+Backspace, the cell values won't revert to their un-recalculated values.

Fourth, although Edit Undo uses memory efficiently, there may be times when you need the memory it does use. If 1-2-3 runs out of memory when you try to do something, turn Edit Undo off (un-check the Enable Edit Undo check box in the Tools User Setup dialog box). After you have performed the operation, turn Edit Undo back on so you can continue to work with the Edit Undo "safety net." Some commands that typically require a lot of memory to maintain an undo history include closing files, Data Fill with a large fill range, Edit Clear of a large range, and any large macro.

Finally, Edit Undo is not a toggle. That is, you can't undo pressing Alt+Backspace or choosing Edit Undo by pressing Alt+Backspace or choosing Edit Undo again.

■ *NOTE:*   Besides choosing the Edit Undo command or pressing Alt+Backspace (Undo), you can activate Edit Undo by clicking on the "Undo" SmartIcon. The "Undo" icon looks like this:

Copying

1-2-3 has two principal ways of transferring information from one part of a worksheet file to another: *copying* and *moving*. Although both can rearrange data and formulas, each has somewhat different uses. You will learn about these commands as you continue to build Bob and Kathy's Home Budget and carry out the other exercises in this book.

Both Edit Quick Copy and Edit Copy (in conjunction with Edit Paste) allow you to duplicate repetitive information without having to retype it. They let you copy existing labels, numbers, and formulas from one location to another, leaving the original version intact. Labels and numbers are copied exactly as they appear in the original location. Formulas are copied exactly unless they contain relative or mixed cell addresses (described in Chapter 4).

Edit Copy and Edit Quick Copy work somewhat differently. When you choose Edit Copy (or press Control+Insert), 1-2-3 copies the highlighted selection to the Windows Clipboard. To copy that data to another location, you move the cell pointer to the new location and select Edit Paste (or press Shift+Insert). Edit Quick Copy, on the other hand, copies information from one part of the worksheet file to another without using the Clipboard.

The main advantage of Edit Quick Copy is that it is essentially a one-step procedure, and it is fast for large amounts of data. On the other hand, using Edit Copy followed by Edit Paste makes it easy to copy the same data to multiple locations, and to perform other operations in between the copies. In addition, you can use Edit Copy and Edit Paste to transfer data between 1-2-3 and other applications running under Windows.

To get the feel for the 1-2-3 copy commands, you are going to use them to draw all the single-ruled and double-ruled lines that appear in the Home Budget worksheet. You will do this by entering repeating labels in cells, and then copying those cells to multi-cell ranges. (Later, in Chapter 7, you will also learn how to underline data cells by formatting the cells themselves, rather than by drawing a line in its own row.)

Before you continue, you need to move back to worksheet A of the Home Budget file. The easiest way to do that is to use the First Cell key combination, Control+Home.

Press: CTRL+HOME

1-2-3 moves the cell pointer to cell A:A1 of the current worksheet file.

A Note on Copying and Range Selection

When you are constructing 1-2-3 applications, you will often copy information from one part of the worksheet to another. Although you can specify the "from" range either before or after you start the copy command, the easiest way to specify the "from" range is usually to highlight the range before you start the copy command.

To specify the range you are copying to (the "to" range), you can type its address, highlight it, or use the "Copy To" SmartIcon described later in this chapter. If you highlight the range, make sure the "To:" text box is selected and that 1-2-3 is in POINT mode before you try to highlight the range. If 1-2-3 beeps instead of highlighting the range, it is probably in EDIT mode (so that you can edit the contents of the text box). If this is the case, clear the "To:" text box, press F2 (Edit) to change to POINT mode, and then highlight the range.

Using Repeating Labels to Draw Lines

Before you can use copy commands to draw lines, you need to learn another 1-2-3 shortcut: using *repeating labels*.

One way to draw a line in a worksheet is to type a row of dashes (for single lines) or equal signs (for double lines) into a cell. For lines containing more than a few characters, however, typing in characters is unnecessarily time-consuming. In addition, entering a fixed number of characters can cause headaches later on, if you decide to change the width of the column that contains the line: Widen the column, and you have to add more characters to the line.

A quicker and more flexible way to draw a line is to enter a *repeating label* in one cell and then copy it to a range of cells.

Specify a repeating label by typing the backslash (\) label prefix character. (Make sure you type the backslash character, not the slash character you use to call up the 1-2-3 Classic menu.) Type the backslash as the first character in a cell, followed by the character or characters you want repeated. After you press Enter, the label repeats across the entire cell.

In the Home Budget worksheet, draw a double line in cell A:A4, above the label INCOME.

Move to: cell A:A4

Type: \=   ⏎

1-2-3 creates a double-ruled line the width of column A. Were you to change the column to a different width, the width of the double-ruled line would change, too.

You can repeat any single character or group of characters using the same technique. A repeated equal sign (=) makes a double line, which is the way totals are often flagged in business spreadsheets. The dash (-), underscore (_), and asterisk (*) are other characters frequently used to create lines and borders.

To create a line that stretches over several columns, you can copy the contents of a cell containing a repeating label to the appropriate range. You will do so in the following pages, as you create the single-ruled and double-ruled lines in the Home Budget worksheet.

Copying One Cell to a Range

In this exercise, you will try out Edit Quick Copy and Edit Copy / Edit Paste. With either method, you can copy:

- A single cell to another cell
- A single cell to a range of cells
- A range of cells to another range

The simplest use of a copy command is to copy labels and values from one cell to another part of the worksheet. You will use Edit Quick Copy to draw a double–ruled line across the top of the INCOME section of the worksheet. You will do this by copying the contents of cell A:A4 (which contains the repeating equal sign) to the range A:B4..A:N4. The same technique can be used to copy any single cell to a range of cells.

1. Start the copy operation.

When you copy data in a worksheet, you first indicate the range to be copied, and then you indicate the place you want it copied to. With the cell pointer still on cell A:A4:

Choose: Edit   Quick Copy

Figure 3-43:   The Edit Quick Copy Dialog Box

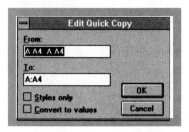

1-2-3 displays the Edit Quick Copy dialog box. Notice that the mode indicator reads POINT, and the dialog box contains two text boxes: "From:" for the range to copy from, and "To:" for the range to copy to.

■ *NOTE:*   The dialog box also contains two check boxes, both of which should remain unchecked for simple copy operations. The "Styles only" check box, if checked, tells 1-2-3 to copy special cell formatting (such as outlining, and different fonts or colors), but not data. The "Convert to values" check box, if checked, tells 1-2-3 to copy the value of a formula, rather than the formula itself.

The notation A:A4..A:A4 appears in the "From:" text box. This shows that the "from" range is an anchored range beginning and ending with the current cell. (Ranges are automatically anchored for many commands, including the Edit Quick Copy command.) In this case, you are copying from the current cell to several cells, so this is okay.

3. Specify the "to" range (A:B4..A:N4).

The "To:" text box displays the unanchored range A:A4, the current cell. Change this by highlighting the range to which you want to copy the double-ruled line in A:A4. Use either the mouse or the keyboard to highlight the range. (Or, if you prefer, type the new range in the text box.)

Select:	**To:**
Specify:	A:B4..A:N4
Press:	↵ *or select OK*

1-2-3 copies the contents of cell A4 to the range B4..N4, creating a double-ruled line the width of the entire Home Budget. This line is one column wider than the range of month labels. Later, you will add another label to row 2 and fill in column N.

Figure 3-44

	A	B	C	D	E	F	G
1	Bob and Kathy Gordon	1992 HOME BUDGET					
2		Jan	Feb	Mar	Apr	May	
3		5	4	4	4	5	
4	================	====	====	====	====	====	
5	INCOME						

■ *CAUTION:*   In general, before copying a range, you should make sure there is no data in the area you want to copy "to". The copy commands will write over any data that is already there, without warning. If you inadvertently copy over data that you wish to retain and Edit Undo is on, you can recover the data by pressing Alt+Backspace or choosing Edit Undo immediately after you issue the erroneous copy command.

Copying a Range to Another Location

Now, you are going to copy the line you just created to another section of the worksheet, beneath the label Total Income. This time, since you will be making more than one copy of the line, it is probably easiest to use Edit Copy and Edit Paste.

1. Highlight the "from" range (A:A4..A:N4).

   Highlight the range A:A4..A:N4, either by clicking on cell A:A4, holding down the mouse button, and then dragging the cell pointer with the mouse, or by pressing F4, pressing End Right, and then pressing Enter.

2. Copy the range to the Windows Clipboard.

   Choose: Edit   Copy   *or press Control+Insert*

3. Highlight the first cell of the "to" range (cell A:A15) and perform the copy.

   Move to: cell A:A15
   Choose: Edit   Paste   *or press Shift+Insert*

   1-2-3 copies the line. Notice that when you are copying a range to another location, you have to indicate only the first cell of the range that will contain the copy.

4. Paste the line to another location.

   Because the line you copied from A:A4..A:N4 is still in the Clipboard, you can paste it to a new location. Try copying the line to row 36:

   Move to: cell A:A36
   Choose: Edit   Paste   *or press Shift+Insert*

5. Create the remaining BUDGET1 ruled lines.

   Finish creating the ruled lines of the BUDGET1 worksheet. These lines will help you visualize the finished worksheet as you fill in formulas.
       Setup Table 3-2 summarizes all the lines in the BUDGET1 worksheet, including the ones you've already created. Notice that the lines in the INCOME and EXPENSES sections extend from column A to column N, while the lines in the CASH FLOW section extend only to column M, and the lines in the VARIABLES sections extend only to column F. (Refer to the screen illustrations in "The Home Budget Model" earlier in this chapter if you need more help positioning the lines.)

Use a repeating hyphen (-) for single-ruled lines, and a repeating equal sign (=) to create double-ruled lines. Sometimes you'll find it is easier to create a line by entering a repeating label in one cell and copying it to a range; other times, you will find it quicker to copy an existing line to a new location. Experiment with both Edit Quick Copy and the Edit Copy and Edit Paste combination as you create these lines, so that you get the feel for which method works better in various situations.

Setup Table 3-2:   Ruled Lines

Worksheet Section	Range	Type of Line
INCOME	A4..N4	Double-ruled
	A6..N6	Single-ruled
	A13..N13	Single-ruled
	A15..N15	Double-ruled
EXPENSES	A22..N22	Single-ruled
	A34..N34	Single-ruled
	A36..N36	Double-ruled
CASH FLOW	A42..M42	Single-ruled
	A46..M46	Double-ruled
	A51..M51	Single-ruled
	A53..M53	Double-ruled
	A56..M56	Double-ruled
INCOME VARIABLES	A62..F62	Single-ruled
	A69..F69	Double-ruled
EXPENSE VARIABLES	A82..F82	Single-ruled
	A97..F97	Double-ruled
MISC. VARIABLES	A102..F102	Single-ruled
	A107..F107	Double-ruled

6. Save BUDGET1.

Congratulations! You have finished entering the labels, values, and ruled lines for the Home Budget worksheet. In the next chapter, you'll complete your work with the Home Budget.

A Note on Using the "Copy To" SmartIcon   If you have a mouse, the quickest way to copy data is often to use the "Copy To" SmartIcon instead of the Edit Quick Copy command or Edit Copy and Edit Paste. The "Copy To" icon looks like this:

The "Copy To" icon lets you specify the "to" range for Edit Quick Copy without having to specify the command itself. To use the "Copy To" icon, highlight the "from" range, click on the "Copy To" icon, and click on the "to" range. (The mouse pointer changes from an arrow to a hand.) When you release the mouse button, 1-2-3 performs the copy operation, exactly as if you had chosen Edit Quick Copy.

If you like, experiment with the "Copy To" icon by copying lines and data in the scratch worksheet before you move on to the next chapter. Whenever the instructions in this book tell you to use Edit Quick Copy to copy cells, you can use the "Copy To" SmartIcon instead.

At a Glance

In this chapter you have learned some of the basic skills and concepts for working with data in the 1-2-3 worksheet. You have also learned how, specifically, to perform the 1-2-3 tasks listed in the following table:

Task	How To Do It:
Moving around the worksheet	The arrow keys let you move one cell at a time. Keys such as Page Down, Control+Right, and End Left let you move a window or a block of data at a time, and F5 (Goto) lets you move to any cell in the worksheet. If you have a mouse, you can also use the mouse to move to a specific cell, or to scroll through the worksheet a row, column, or window at a time.
Changing column widths	Move the mouse pointer to the line to the right of the column letter of the column whose width you want to change, and then drag the line to the width you want. Alternatively, select Worksheet Column Width, type in the width you want, and then press Enter or select OK to change the column width.
Aligning labels	To align a label with the left edge of a cell, use the apostrophe ('). Use the double quotation mark (") to align a label with the right edge of the cell, and the caret (^) to center the label. You can also align ranges with the label-alignment SmartIcons.
Entering labels that start with a number	Type a label prefix before entering a number as a label.
Entering long labels	Labels that exceed the width of the column you enter them in will overlap into the next column only when the adjacent cell is blank. To display an entire long label when the adjacent cell contains data, you must widen the column the label is in. You can do this with Worksheet Column Width, or by stretching the column with the mouse, as described above.
Using repeating labels	Enter a backslash (\) as the label prefix, followed by the character or characters you want to repeat.
Editing data	1-2-3 provides several ways to edit data once you enter it in a cell. You can either erase the entry with the Delete key or the Edit Clear command; write over it with a new entry; or double-click on the cell (or press F2) and correct the existing entry.

Task	How To Do It:
Using ranges	Using ranges, you can perform 1-2-3 commands on many cells at once instead of on one cell at a time. A two-dimensional range can be any rectangular block of cells. Its address consists of the cell addresses of its upper left and lower right cells, separated by two periods (for example, A1..G23). You can specify a range by typing its address, highlighting the range, or (as you will learn in Chapter 4) using its range name. When you are highlighting a range, you can anchor it by pressing the Period key (.), and unanchor it by pressing Backspace or Escape.
Copying data	Highlight the cell or range to copy "from," choose Edit Quick Copy, highlight the cell or range to copy "to", and then press Enter or select OK. Or, highlight the "from" range, click on the "Copy To" SmartIcon, and highlight the "to" range. You can also make copies by copying to the Clipboard with Edit Copy or Control+Insert, moving the cell pointer to the "to" range, and pasting the copied information from the Clipboard to the worksheet by choosing Edit Paste or pressing Shift+Insert.
Erasing a range	Highlight the range you want to erase, then choose Edit Clear or press Delete. Alternatively, cut the range to the Clipboard by highlighting the range and choosing Edit Cut or pressing Shift+Delete. Make sure, before you use Edit Cut, that there is nothing in the Clipboard that you want to preserve.
Entering a sequence of numbers	Choose Data Fill, then provide a range to fill, a Start value, a Step value, and a Stop value that is greater than or equal to the last fill value you want. You can also highlight the range to fill and then choose Data Fill.
Undoing changes to the worksheet	When Edit Undo is enabled (Tools User Setup Enable Edit Undo), you can use the Undo key (Alt+Backspace) or the Edit Undo command to undo the most recent data entry or command that changes the worksheet file.

Chapter 4

Worksheet Skills

This chapter completes the presentation of fundamental worksheet skills begun in Chapter 3. In the process, it also brings to completion the Home Budget application you started in Chapter 3.

What You'll Learn

By the time you have finished this chapter, you will know how to:

- Enter formulas that include cell addresses, range names, and @functions

- Use relative, absolute, and mixed cell references

- Create range names

- Search for and replace cell entries

- Move a range of cells

- Change the appearance of the worksheet and the display of information in worksheet cells

- Use SmartIcons to format ranges and move cells

- Set worksheet titles

- Insert and delete rows and columns

- Perform simple what-if analysis

You'll also learn how to use more of 1-2-3's function keys.

Before You Start

The first several sections of this chapter cover concepts you need to understand in order to work with formulas. In these sections, you are going to be working in a scratch worksheet in the Home Budget worksheet file. In the remainder of the chapter, you will continue to build the Home Budget worksheet, learning additional skills and concepts (and getting more practice with some you've already learned) as you go along. Before you read further:

- Start 1-2-3 and make sure it has been set up to save files in your 123BOOK directory (see Chapter 2).

- If you are already in 1-2-3 when you begin this chapter, but not in BUDGET1.WK3, File Save any work that is already on your screen and then use File Close (or /Worksheet Erase Yes) to close all open files and create a new, Untitled worksheet.
- File Open BUDGET1.WK3 and then maximize BUDGET1.WK3, either by clicking the Worksheet window's Maximize button, or by pressing Alt+hyphen and then pressing X for Maximize.

Figure 4-1: The Home Budget Worksheet File

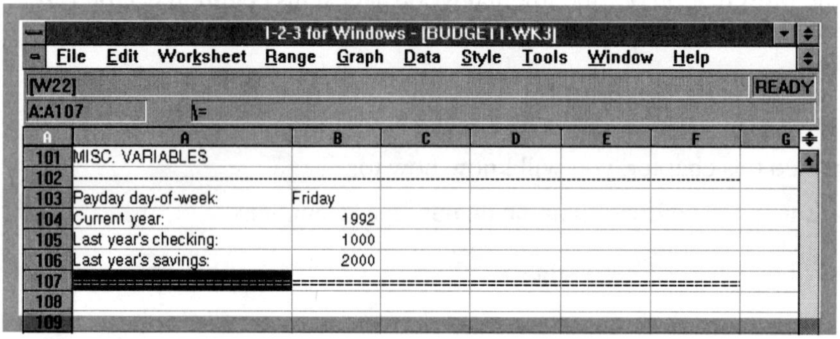

The file name in the title bar reads BUDGET1.WK3. 1-2-3 places the cell pointer where it was just before you last saved the file (for example, in cell A:A107, if the last thing you did was create the double-ruled line in row 107).

A Note on Example Layout   As in previous chapters, the examples in this chapter assume that your screen displays 20 rows and eight columns when the Worksheet window is maximized. If your display does not show 20 rows and eight columns, your screens will look somewhat different from the illustrations, but you can still do all the examples. Just be sure to use the cell addresses and ranges specified in the instructions.

A Note on Keystroke Instructions   The keystroke instructions in this chapter often assume you are using a mouse to perform such operations as highlighting a range or selecting an option in a dialog box. If you prefer, you can also use the keyboard to perform the same operations. Many of the keyboard equivalents to mouse operations were described in previous chapters, and others will be described in this chapter. A few of the most common ones are summarized here. For a complete list of keystroke equivalents to mouse operations, see the 1-2-3 documentation, or the 1-2-3 on-line Help.

Entering Formulas

Formulas are what allow a change in one cell to automatically affect related cells. Without formulas, an electronic spreadsheet would be only a slight improvement over a paper one.

Formulas contain references to other cells and specify the operations to be performed on the values within those cells. With formulas, you can easily perform simple arithmetical opera-

Keyboard Equivalents to Mouse Operations

Operation	Instruction		Keyboard Equivalent	
Complete action and close dialog box	**Select:**	OK	**Press:**	⏎
Cancel action and close dialog box	**Select:**	Cancel	**Press:**	ESC
Highlight a text box	**Select:**	text box	**Press:**	ALT+*underlined_letter*
Edit a range in a text box	**Select:** **Specify:**	Range A:A1..C:D4	**Press:**	ALT+*underlined_letter* F2 (EDIT)
Edit a number or word in a text box	**Select:** **Specify:**	text box new text *(or click on text and edit it)*	**Press:** **Type:**	ALT+*underlined_letter* new text *(or press Left arrow and edit text)*
Highlight a range	**Highlight:** A:A1..C:D4		**Move to:** **Press:** **Move to:** **Press:**	cell A:A1 F4 cell D4 ⏎

tions, such as adding up the figures in a column. However, you can also use formulas to perform sophisticated financial, engineering, and mathematical calculations.

1-2-3 solves formulas when it recalculates the worksheet. During *recalculation,* 1-2-3 examines each cell, determines which cells have been changed since the last recalculation, and evaluates the formulas that are affected by the changed cells. 1-2-3 then redisplays the cells whose values are changed as a result of the recalculation.

Formula Basics

Before you get started entering formulas in the Home Budget worksheet, try out some basic formula concepts in your scratch worksheet.

To enter a formula in the worksheet, type it into a cell, just as you enter labels and numbers. You usually start a formula by typing in a value or a cell address, then a mathematical operator, then another value or address, and so on. This is similar to the way a formula is entered on a calculator; in fact, you can treat a 1-2-3 cell almost as if it were the display area of a calculator.

Try using 1-2-3 as if it were a calculator. First, erase the data in your scratch worksheet. A quick way to do so is to select the entire active area of the worksheet and then press Delete.

Press: CTRL+PGUP   *to move to worksheet B*

| HOME | to move to cell B:A1 |

| F4 | to switch into POINT mode |

| END | | HOME | to select the active area of the worksheet |

| ↵ | to return 1-2-3 to READY mode |

| DELETE | to delete the selected area |

| ESC | to clear the highlighting |

Now, try entering some simple formulas.

Move to: cell B:A2

Type: 2*3   ↵

1-2-3 multiplies 2 by 3 and displays the result (6) in cell B:A2. 1-2-3 displays the formula itself (2*3) in the control panel.

Figure 4-2:   Entering a Simple Formula in the Worksheet

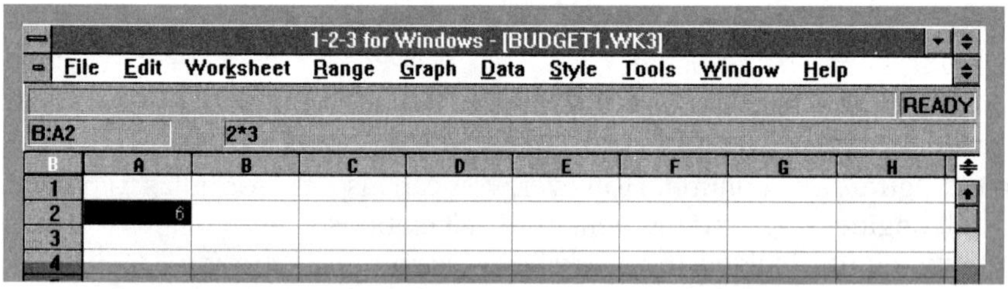

Now continue with the calculation:

Press: F2   **(EDIT)**   *or double-click cell B:A2*

Pressing the Edit key or double-clicking the cell brings the formula into the edit line of the control panel. Add 2 to the existing formula:

Type: +2   ↵

1-2-3 displays the result of the new formula (which multiplies 2 by 3, then adds 2 to the product) in cell B:A2.

1-2-3 checks formulas for correct syntax when you try to enter them. Formulas with incorrect syntax are not accepted. (1-2-3 can only check for syntax errors; it can't tell if the logic of your formula is correct!) Try entering a formula with incorrect syntax by editing the formula in cell B:A2 again:

Press: F2   **(EDIT)**

Type: +(123−4/5(↵

1-2-3 detects that you have typed a left parenthesis character instead of a right parenthesis at the end of the line. It beeps, and then waits for you to correctly complete the arithmetic expression.

Press: | BACKSPACE | *to delete the left parenthesis character*

Type:) | ↵ |

1-2-3 displays the result of the new formula (130.2) in cell B:A2.

You can modify a formula in the same ways you would any other cell entry: Replace it completely by typing over it, or press the Edit key and change the existing formula. Edit this formula to remove the characters **+(123−4/5)**:

Press: | F2 | **(EDIT)**

| BACKSPACE | *ten times*

| ↵ |

1-2-3 once again displays the value 8 in cell B:A2.

Entering Formulas That Begin With Letters

Like a number, a formula is a value. If a formula begins with a number, 1-2-3 automatically enters it as a value when you press Enter or click on the Confirm button. However, if a formula begins with a cell address or a range name, you must tell 1-2-3 that you are entering a formula, not a label. Usually, you do this by beginning the formula with a plus sign (+). (Range names are discussed later in this chapter.)

For example, the formula +A2/2 divides the contents of cell A2 of the current worksheet by two. If you entered this formula without the initial plus sign, 1-2-3 would interpret it as a label. Try this now. Notice that the mode indicator reads LABEL as you start to type the formula.

Move to: cell B:A1

Type: a2/2 | ↵ |

Figure 4-3: A Misguided Attempt to Enter a Formula

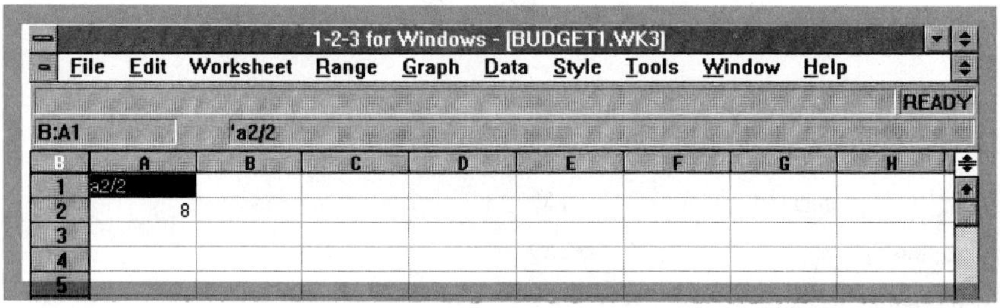

1-2-3 inserts the characters **a2/2** in cell B:A1 instead of displaying the value of cell A2 divided by 2. The edit line of the control panel shows that this cell begins with an apostrophe, indicating that the cell contains a left-aligned label, not a value.

Now, try entering the same formula, but place a plus sign (+) before the first cell address:

Press: |F2| **(EDIT)** *to bring the formula into the edit line*

|HOME| *to move the cursor to the apostrophe*

|DELETE| *to delete the apostrophe*

Type: + |↵|

Figure 4-4: The Corrected Formula

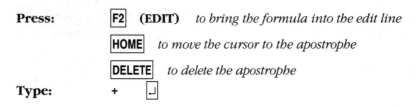

1-2-3 accepts this as a formula. The program divides the contents of cell B:A2 by 2 and displays the result (4) in cell B:A1. The formula itself is displayed in the control panel.

■ *NOTE:* To look at any formula in the worksheet, move the cell pointer to the cell that contains the formula. 1-2-3 displays the formula in the control panel. Another way to view formulas, rather than their values, is to format the cells that contain them as Text. (Cell formatting is discussed later in this chapter.)

Arithmetic Operators and Order of Precedence

Arithmetic is the foundation of all calculations within 1-2-3. Addition, subtraction, multiplication, division, and exponentiation are the basic operations on which the more complicated functions are based.

Table 4-1 shows you 1-2-3's arithmetic operators.

Table 4-1: Arithmetic Operators

Operator	Description	Example	Precedence*
^	Exponentiation (raises to the indicated power)	+A2^2 1	1
+	Unary plus (making something positive)	+A2	2
-	Unary minus (making something negative)	-A2	2
*	Multiplication	+A2*A4	3
/	Division	+A2/A4	3

Operator	Description	Example	Precedence*
+	Addition	+A2+A4	4
-	Subtraction	+A2-A4	4

*Operations with lower precedence numbers are evaluated before operations with higher precedence numbers.

Table 4-1 also lists the *order of precedence* of each of the arithmetic operators. The order of precedence is the order in which 1-2-3 will perform the operation unless you use parentheses to explicitly change that order. 1-2-3 performs operations that have the lowest precedence numbers first. Operations with the same order of precedence are performed sequentially, from left to right. For example, to multiply the value of cell A2 by the value of cell A1 raised to the power of 2, type the formula **+a2*a1^2** into a blank cell in the scratch worksheet:

Move to: cell B:F4

Type: **+a2*a1^2**   ⏎

1-2-3 displays **128** in cell F4. Because exponentiation has a higher order of precedence than multiplication, the exponentiation is automatically performed first. (The initial unary plus sign has the effect of letting 1-2-3 know that **a2** is part of a formula, rather than a label.) Since the value in cell A2 is 8 and the value in cell A1 is 4, the result of this calculation is 8 multiplied by 4 squared (8*16, or 128).

Figure 4-5:   Taking Advantage of Order of Precedence

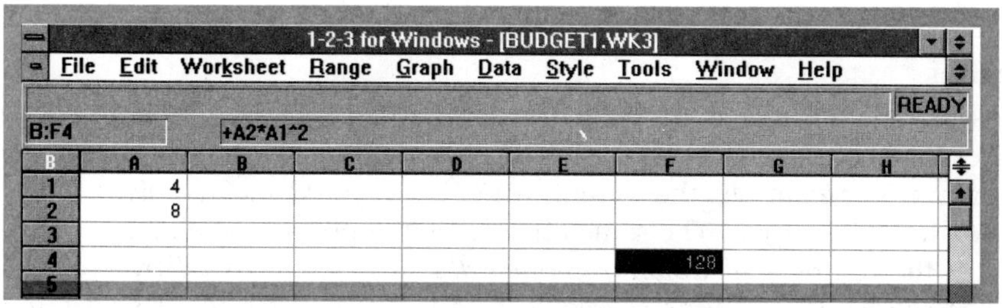

Overriding Order of Precedence   Because 1-2-3 performs operations within parentheses first, you can override the order of precedence by putting parentheses around an operation. For instance, if you want to multiply the value of cell A2 by the value of cell A1 and raise the product of those two values to the power of 2, you have to make your request explicit by enclosing the values you want to multiply together in parentheses, like so: (A2*A1)^2. Enter this formula in another blank cell in the worksheet:

Move to: cell B:G4

Type: **(a2*a1)^2**   ⏎

Using the same values for cell A2 and cell A1, this formula evaluates to (8*4)^2, which is 1024. Notice that in this case, you don't need the plus sign in front of **a2**, since the left parenthesis lets 1-2-3 know you are entering a formula.

Figure 4-6: Overriding Order of Precedence by Using Parentheses

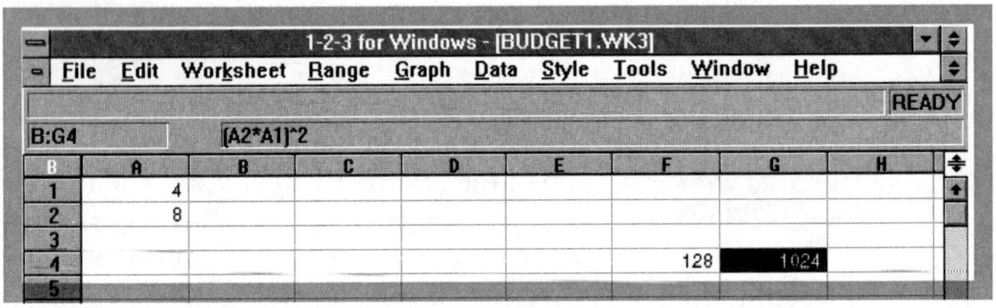

■ *NOTE:*   You can always use parentheses to make 1-2-3 evaluate a formula the way you want it to. If you are unsure of how to use order of precedence when you are constructing a formula, parenthesize the operations you want evaluated first. When the formula works with sample values, you can experiment with removing the excess parentheses to make the formula appear less cluttered and take up less space.

Relative, Absolute, and Mixed Cell References

In a formula, 1-2-3 can refer to another cell by using one or more of the following types of cell references:

- A relative reference
- An absolute reference
- A mixed reference

Relative Cell References

Unless you tell it to do otherwise, 1-2-3 stores cell addresses as *relative cell addresses*. It remembers the distances in terms of how far up, down, right, or left the cell is from the cell in which the reference is made. For example, the formula +A2/2 in cell A1 means "divide the value of the cell *beneath* this cell by two." The same formula, if it appeared in cell B1, would mean "divide the value of the cell *one cell down and one cell to the left of this cell* by two."

A formula reference to a relative cell address is known as a *relative reference*. Using a relative reference in a formula is similar to giving somebody directions to your house by saying something like, "Go up two streets, take a left, and it's the first house on the right," instead of just giving your street address.

The concept of a relative reference to a cell address is important mostly because of the implications it has for the copy commands. The way 1-2-3 stores cell addresses is unimportant with most other 1-2-3 commands.

■ *NOTE:*   The following discussion and exercise uses Edit Quick Copy, but the same principles apply to operations that use Edit Copy and Edit Paste to copy formulas.

You've seen how Edit Quick Copy copies the contents of a cell or a range of cells to another place in the worksheet. Edit Quick Copy works differently when it is copying cells that contain formulas. Rather than copying the value displayed in the cell, it copies the formula itself.

When 1-2-3 copies a formula, the relative cell addresses in the formula change to reflect the location of the new copy of the formula cell. To see how this works, copy the formula in cell A1 of the scratch worksheet to the three cells immediately to the right. First, however, enter some values in cells B2, C2, and D2 of worksheet B:

Move to:	cell B:B2
Type:	11 $\rightarrow$
	16 $\rightarrow$
	23 $\downarrow$
Move to:	cell B:A1
Choose:	Edit Quick Copy
Select:	To:
Specify:	B:B1..B:D1
Press:	$\downarrow$ *or select OK*

Figure 4-7

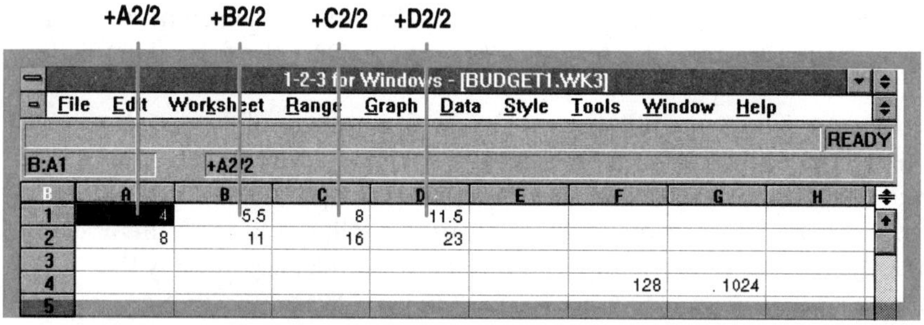

Look at the values in Figure 4-7 that 1-2-3 displays. Notice that each new formula divides the value beneath it by 2, just as the formula in cell B:A1 divides the value in cell B:A2 by 2. If you move the cell pointer to cell B:B1, you will see that the formula in that cell reads **+B2/2**. Similarly, the formula in cell B:C1 reads **+C2/2**, and the formula in B:D1 is **+D2/2**. Copying the formula in cell B:A1 anywhere in the worksheet file would have the same effect: The new formula would divide the value in the cell directly beneath it by 2.

Absolute and Mixed Cell References

By default, 1-2-3 interprets a cell address in a formula, as a relative reference. Relative cell references frequently make it much easier to perform similar calculations on rows and columns of data, because 1-2-3 adjusts them to the new location when you copy the formula cell.

There are also, however, many times when you must refer to a specific location in a formula, and you do not want the cell address to change when you copy the formula. To handle these situations, enter *absolute references* to cell addresses instead of entering relative references. Absolute references, also known as *absolute cell addresses*, do not change when you copy formulas containing them to different parts of the worksheet. Using an absolute reference in a formula is similar to telling somebody, "I live at 58 Kettering Drive, Apartment 21," instead of giving somebody directions for how to get to your house from wherever they happen to be.

The notation in 1-2-3 for absolute cell addresses is a dollar sign ($) in front of the part of the address that is absolute. The worksheet, the column, the row, or any combination of the three can be either absolute or relative. The different ways you can combine absolute and relative column and row addresses follow. (What happens when you make the worksheet letters absolute or relative is discussed in Chapter 5.)

- *Column is absolute, row is absolute.* Placing a dollar sign in front of both the column and the row part of a cell address (for example, $A$2) makes both the column and the row absolute. This means that the cell address does not change at all when you copy the formula cell to another part of the same worksheet. For instance, if you copy the formula 2*$A$2 from cell B1 to cell D10, the formula in cell D10 still reads: 2*$A$2.
- *Column is absolute, row is relative.* Placing a dollar sign in front of the column but not in front of the row part of a cell address (for example, $A2) makes the column absolute and the row relative. This is one form of what is called a *mixed cell address.* The column part of the cell address does not change, no matter where you copy the formula cell, but the row address changes if you copy the cell to a different row. For instance, if you copy the formula 2*$A2 from cell B1 to cell D10, the formula in cell D10 reads: 2*$A11.
- *Column is relative, row is absolute.* Placing a dollar sign in front of the row but not in front of the column part of a cell address makes the row absolute and the column relative. This is another form of mixed cell address. The row part of the cell address does not change, no matter where you copy the formula cell, but the column address changes if you copy the cell to a different column. For instance, if you copy the formula 2*A$2 from cell B1 to cell D10, the formula in cell D10 reads: 2*C$2.

Using Relative and Absolute Cell References

For the remainder of this chapter, you will continue building Bob and Kathy Gordon's Home Budget worksheet. The formulas you are going to enter into the budget worksheet contain relative, absolute, and mixed cell references. In this section, you will enter some formulas with relative and absolute references. Later in the chapter, you will also enter formulas that use mixed cell references.

In general, the budget worksheet uses simple formulas. As you'll soon see, however, one of the advantages of using electronic spreadsheets is that much can be accomplished with simple formulas. Begin by entering formulas in the INCOME section. Figure 4-8 (shown on next page), shows the completed INCOME section.

Figure 4-8: The Completed INCOME Section of the Home Budget Worksheet

A	A	B	C	D	E	F	G
1	Bob and Kathy Gordon	1992 HOME BUDGET					
2		Jan	Feb	Mar	Apr	May	
3							
4	========	========	========	========	========	========	===
5	INCOME						
6							
7	Weekly						
8	Net Pay (Bob)	4,500	3,600	3,600	3,600	4,500	3,
9							
10	Monthly						
11	Net Pay (Kathy)	600	600	600	600	600	
12	Interest	100	100	100	100	100	
13							
14	Total Income	$5,200	$4,300	$4,300	$4,300	$5,200	$4,
15	========	========	========	========	========	========	===
16							
17							
18							
19							
20							

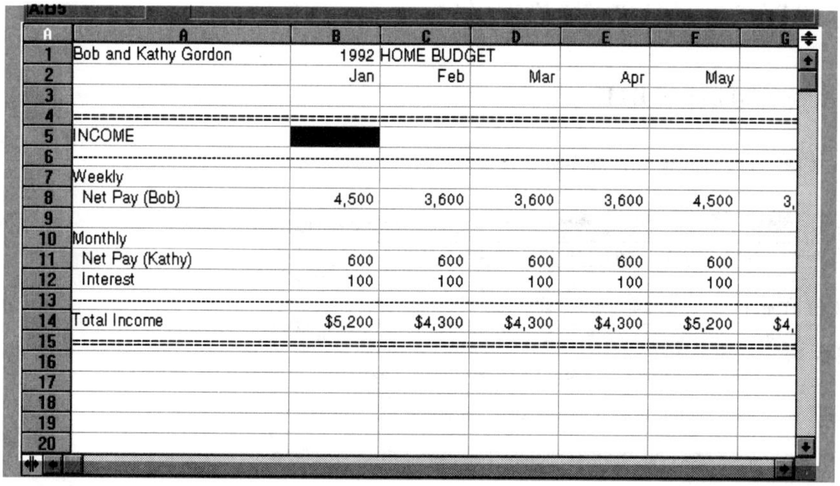

The values displayed in the INCOME section are produced by formulas, rather than by numbers entered into that part of the worksheet. These formulas use absolute references to variables in the INCOME VARIABLES and MISC. VARIABLES sections you created in Chapter 3. They use relative references to the number of paydays in a given month, which you entered in row 3.

The formulas in this part of the worksheet use the following values from the sections for INCOME VARIABLES and MISC. VARIABLES:

Description	Cell Address	Value
Bob's weekly pay	B64	$900
Kathy's monthly pay	B67	$600
Monthly interest	B68	$100

You are going to enter some of these formulas now.

1. Move to the INCOME section of the Home Budget worksheet.

   Press: `CTRL+HOME` *to move to cell A:A1*

   1-2-3 moves the cell pointer from the scratch worksheet to the first cell of the Home Budget worksheet (see Figure 4-9).

2. Reference the variable containing Kathy's net pay (cell B67) in cell B11.

   Kathy's part-time job pays her by the month, rather than by the week, so her pay is the same each month. The formula for her net monthly pay is simply a reference to the variable labeled **Net Pay (Kathy)** in the INCOME VARIABLES section of the worksheet. Enter this formula in cell B11. (You will enter the formula for Bob's net pay later.)

Move to: cell B11

Type: **+b67**   *to reference Kathy's Net Pay value*

Press: ⏎

1-2-3 displays the value 600 in cell B11.

Figure 4-9   The Home Budget Worksheet File's Income Section

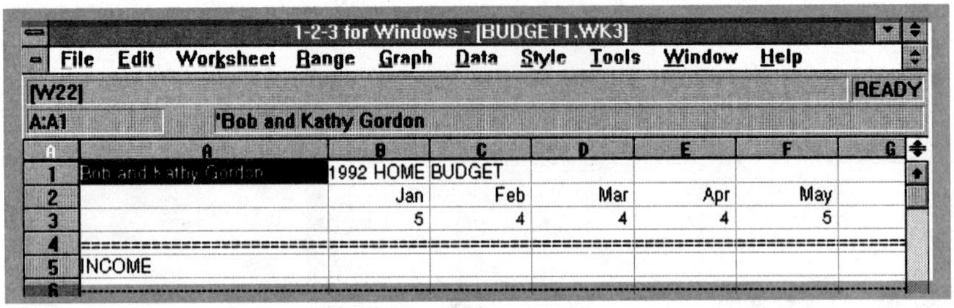

3. Try copying cell B11 across row 11.

Watch what happens when you copy the relative cell address in cell B11 to each month in the budget:

Choose: `Edit`   `Quick Copy`

Select: `To:`

Specify: C11..M11   *in the text box*

Press: ⏎   *or select OK to complete the copy*

1-2-3 copies the cell reference across the range C11..M11. The value 600 is displayed in cell B11, but instead of displaying **600** in the other cells in this row, 1-2-3 displays **0**.

Figure 4-10:   A Misguided Attempt at Copying a Formula

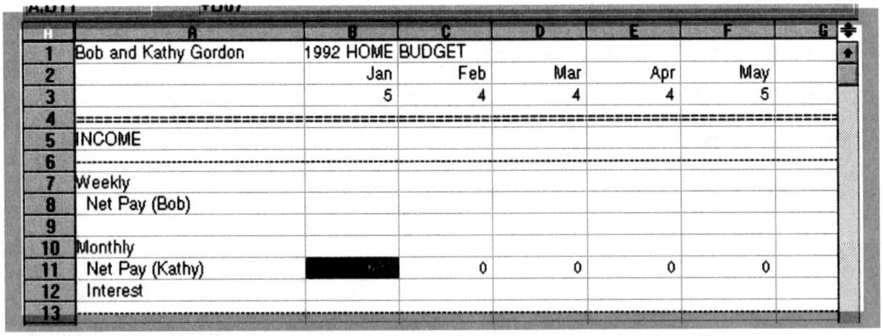

Move the cell pointer to cell C11 to discover why this happened:

Move to: cell C11

1-2-3 displays the formula **+C67** in cell C11. Similarly, cell D11 contains the formula **+D67**. Edit Quick Copy has copied the relative cell address B67 to each month of the budget. However, only cell B67 actually has the value for Kathy's pay; cells C67, D67, and so on through M67 are all blank, and so 1-2-3 displays **0** when it refers to those cells in C11..M11.

4. Use the Absolute key, F4, to create an absolute cell reference.

To use the value for Kathy's pay in each month of the budget, you must make the cell reference in cell B11 an absolute reference.

You can type in an absolute cell reference directly by typing a dollar sign ($) before the row and the column ($B$67). You can also change an address from relative to absolute by using F4 (Abs). F4 serves as the Absolute key when 1-2-3 is in EDIT or POINT mode. It lets you cycle through the parts of a cell address in a formula and change each part from relative to absolute. In a one-address formula like this one, it is just as easy to edit or retype the cell address. However, in a longer formula, where you might want to change several cell addresses, using F4 (Abs) is often quicker than typing dollar signs.

Move to:	cell B11
Press:	F2 **(EDIT)**
	F4 **(ABS)**

Pressing F4 (Abs) changes the relative address B67 to the absolute address $A:$B$67. To familiarize yourself with the operation of the Absolute key, press F4 (Abs) a few more times and notice what happens to the dollar signs in the cell address:

Press:	F4 **(ABS)** *four times*

As you press F4 (Abs), the cell address cycles through the possible combinations of relative, mixed, and absolute cell address. In this case, the formula in the edit line cycles through the following combinations: $A:B$67, $A:$B67, $A:B67, A:$B$67. Continue to press F4 (Abs), observing how each press changes the cell address. Press Enter when the address is $A:$B$67.

Press:	F4 **(ABS)** *until the edit line displays $A:$B$67*
	↵

5. Copy Kathy's net pay (cell B11) across row 11.

Choose:	Edit Quick Copy
Select:	To:
Specify:	C11..M11 *in the text box*
Press:	↵ *or select OK to complete the copy*

1-2-3 copies the absolute cell address $B$67 across the range C11..M11. The value 600 is now correctly displayed across row 11.

■ **NOTE:** 1-2-3 stores the absolute cell address $A:$B$67 as $B$67. The absolute worksheet letter $A: is assumed.

Figure 4-11: Using an Absolute Address with Edit Quick Copy

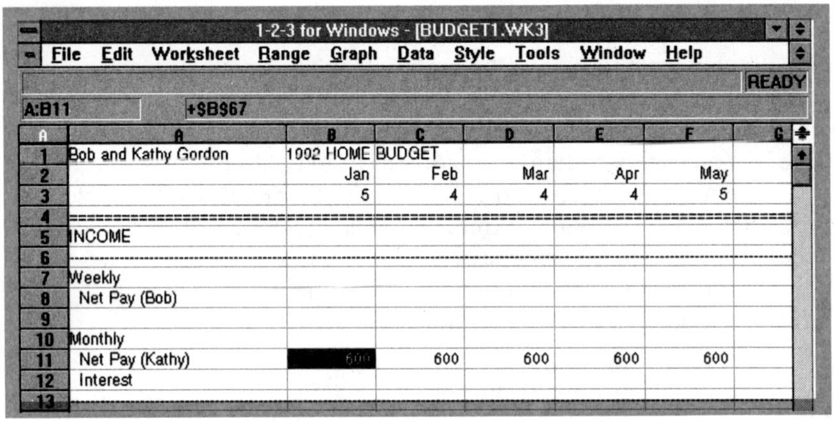

	A	B	C	D	E	F	G
1	Bob and Kathy Gordon	1992 HOME BUDGET					
2		Jan	Feb	Mar	Apr	May	
3		5	4	4	4	5	
4							
5	INCOME						
6							
7	Weekly						
8	Net Pay (Bob)						
9							
10	Monthly						
11	Net Pay (Kathy)	500	600	600	600	600	
12	Interest						
13							

1-2-3 for Windows - [BUDGET1.WK3]
File Edit Worksheet Range Graph Data Style Tools Window Help
READY
A:B11   +$B$67

6. Reference the Interest variable (cell B68) across row 12.

Enter Interest in cell B12 the same way you did Kathy's Net Pay, then copy the cell reference in cell B12 across row 12:

Move to:	cell B12
Type:	b68 *to reference the value for Interest*
Press:	↵
Choose:	Edit Quick Copy
Select:	To:
Specify:	C12..M12 *in the text box*
Press:	↵ *or select OK*

The value 100 is displayed in each cell in the range B12..M12.

7. Enter the formula for Bob's net pay across row 8.

Bob is paid by the week, so his pay for a given month depends on the number of paydays in that month. For example, Bob's net weekly pay is $900. Payday is Friday, and there are five Fridays in January 1992. Therefore, Bob should earn $4,500 in that month. In March, there are four paydays, so Bob's budgeted net pay for March should be $3,600.

In the formula you will create, the number of paydays per month changes with each month, according to the numbers you entered in row 3. Therefore, you should use a relative cell address to refer to the number of paydays per month. On the other hand, the value for Bob's weekly net pay should be an absolute cell reference, since you don't want this value to change when you copy the formula across row 8.

Enter the formula for Bob's net pay in January 1992. This formula multiplies the number of paydays in the current month by Bob's weekly wage.

Move to: cell B8

Type: +b3*b64

Press: ⏎

1-2-3 displays the value 4500 in cell B8. Now, copy this formula across row 8:

Choose: Edit   Quick Copy

Select: To:

Specify: C8..M8   *in the text box*

Press: ⏎   *or select OK*

1-2-3 copies across row 8 the formula that calculates Bob's monthly net pay. Use the mouse or the Right arrow key to move to a few of these cells; verify that the cell addresses that refer to cells in row 3 change, while the ones for Bob's weekly wage do not.

Figure 4-12: Using a Mixed Cell Address with the Edit Quick Copy Command

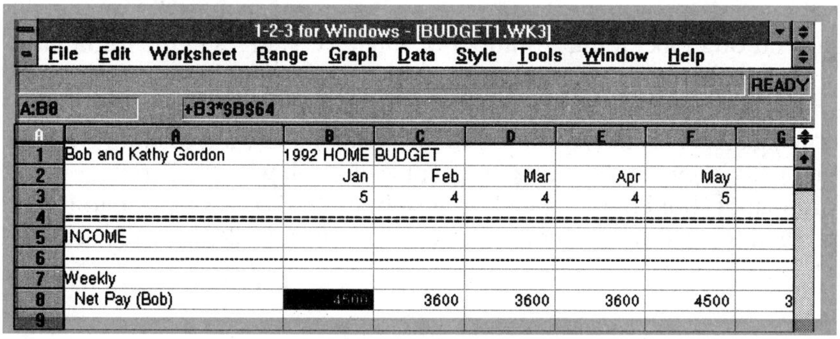

8. Save BUDGET1.

Congratulations! You have finished entering most of the formulas for the INCOME part of the Home Budget worksheet. If you printed the INCOME section at this point, it would look something like Figure 4-13 on the next page. (Printing worksheets is described in Chapter 9.)

Entering Cell Addresses in Formulas by Pointing

So far, you have entered cell addresses into a formula by typing them. You can also enter addresses by pointing to the cells to be included, instead of typing in the addresses.

You are going to enter a formula for Kathy and Bob's Total Income. It will add the values in cells B8, B11, and B12. You'll begin by moving to the cell that will contain the formula, then you will move to the indicated cells. Notice that the mode indicator changes from READY to

VALUE when you start to type, and then to POINT as soon as you start to move the cell pointer.

Figure 4-13:   The INCOME Section of the Home Budget

```
Bob and Kathy Gordon  1992 HOME BUDGET
                 Jan     Feb     Mar     Apr     May     Jun     Jul     Aug     Sep     Oct     Nov
Dec
                   5       4       4       4       5       4       5       4       4       5       4
4
=============================================================================================================
INCOME
-------------------------------------------------------------------------------------------------------------
Weekly
  Net Pay (Bob)   4500    3600    3600    3600    4500    3600    4500    3600    3600    4500    3600
3600

Monthly
  Net Pay (Kathy) 600     600     600     600     600     600     600     600     600     600     600
600
```

■ **NOTE:**   You can use either the arrow keys or the mouse to point to a cell whose address you want to include in a formula. If you use the keyboard, the formula includes the address of the cell you are pointing to. If you use the mouse, the formula (by default) includes the single-cell range you are pointing to. Although including a number of single cell ranges in the formula will make the formula longer, it shouldn't affect the way 1-2-3 evaluates it. If you prefer to use the mouse for pointing *and* you want the formula to include cell addresses rather than single-cell ranges, take the following steps: (1) Move to the cell into which you want to enter the formula; (2) type a plus sign (+) to begin the formula; (3) point to the cell whose address you want to enter into the formula; (4) hold down the left mouse button; (5) press Escape to unanchor the cell pointer; and then (6) release the mouse button. Repeat steps 2-6 for each cell whose address you want to enter into the formula.

Move to:	cell B14
Type:	+
Point to:	cell B8
Type:	+
Point to:	cell B11
Type:	+
Point to:	cell B12
Press:	↵ *or click on the Confirm button*

The value 5200 appears in cell B14 and the formula **+B8+B11+B12** appears in the control panel.

Figure 4-14

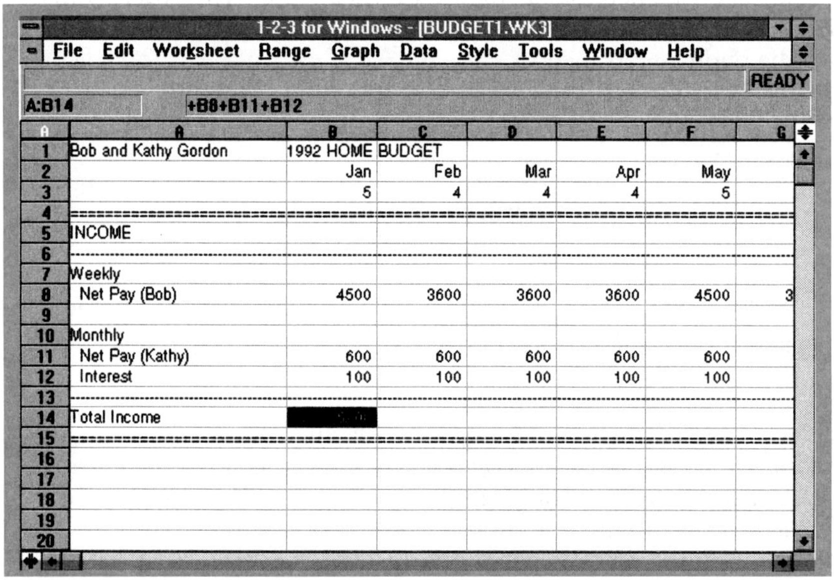

1-2-3 for Windows - [BUDGET1.WK3]						
File Edit Worksheet Range Graph Data Style Tools Window Help						

A:B14   +B8+B11+B12

READY

	A	B	C	D	E	F	G
1	Bob and Kathy Gordon	1992 HOME BUDGET					
2		Jan	Feb	Mar	Apr	May	
3		5	4	4	4	5	
4							
5	INCOME						
6							
7	Weekly						
8	Net Pay (Bob)	4500	3600	3600	3600	4500	3
9							
10	Monthly						
11	Net Pay (Kathy)	600	600	600	600	600	
12	Interest	100	100	100	100	100	
13							
14	Total Income						
15							
16							
17							
18							
19							
20							

Naming Ranges

Instead of typing or highlighting a cell address or a range, you can use a *range name*. A range name is just what it sounds like: A name that represents a cell address or a range of cell addresses.

Naming a range of cells makes a worksheet much easier to create and use. For example, when you entered the formula for Bob's net pay earlier in this chapter, a name such as NETPAY_BOB would have been easier to remember than the cell address B64. Using range names for variables and other ranges also makes formulas much easier to understand, because you don't have to look up the cell addresses to understand what the formula is doing.

You can use a range name with any command that calls for a range, including the Edit Quick Copy and Edit Move Cells commands, the Range commands, and several of the File, Data, and Graph commands. When 1-2-3 prompts you to specify a range, you type the range name in the dialog box or select it from a list of range names, rather than specifying a cell or range address.

Range names are created with the Range Name Create or Range Name Label Create commands. Range names are automatically saved with the worksheet, so they remain available for future work sessions.

Creating Range Names

You are going to create range names to refer to some of the variables you created in the Home Budget worksheet. Then you will use these range names to help you more easily construct the remaining budget worksheet formulas. This section shows you how to create names for single cells. In later chapters, you will also create names for multiple-cell ranges.

Since you have already entered most of the formulas in the INCOME section without the benefit of range names, you will create names only for the values in MISC. VARIABLES and EXPENSE VARIABLES. First, name the variables in MISC. VARIABLES. These names will be used in several sections of the budget worksheet.

1. Move to the MISC. VARIABLES section (cell A101).

2. Name the current year (cell B104).

First, you'll give the name CURRENT_YEAR to the value in cell B104:

Move to:	cell B104
Choose:	`Range   Name   Create`
Type:	`current_year` *in the Range name: text box*
Select:	`Create`

When you select "Create" in the dialog box, 1-2-3 accepts the range name CURRENT_YEAR as the name for cell B104. The dialog box remains on screen so you can define additional range names. If this were the only range name you needed to define, you could select OK or press Enter to return 1-2-3 to READY mode.

You can type the letters in a range name in either uppercase or lowercase; 1-2-3 converts lowercase letters to uppercase when it stores the name.

■ *NOTE:*   Range names, like file names, should be as descriptive as possible. They can be up to 15 characters long. In general, they should begin with a letter, which can be followed by letters, numbers, underscores (_), or other characters. They should not contain spaces or hyphens: Use underscores instead of spaces or hyphens to separate words in a range name. Also, they should not contain any characters 1-2-3 uses in formulas, such as the plus sign (+) or the asterisk (*).

3. Name the checking and savings balances (cells B105 and B106).

Now, name the variables for checking and savings account balances. First, move the Range Name Create dialog box out of the way, so you can get at the cells you wish to name more easily.

Point to:	*the title bar of the Range Name Create dialog box*
Drag to:	*the lower right corner of the 1-2-3 window*

Now, create two more range names. Notice that 1-2-3 lists CURRENT_YEAR in the scrolling list box beneath the "Range name:" text box. When you add a new name, that name is added to the list.

Select:	`Range name:`
Type:	`last_checking`
Select:	`Range:`

Figure 4-15:   Moving the Range Name Create Dialog Box Out of the Way

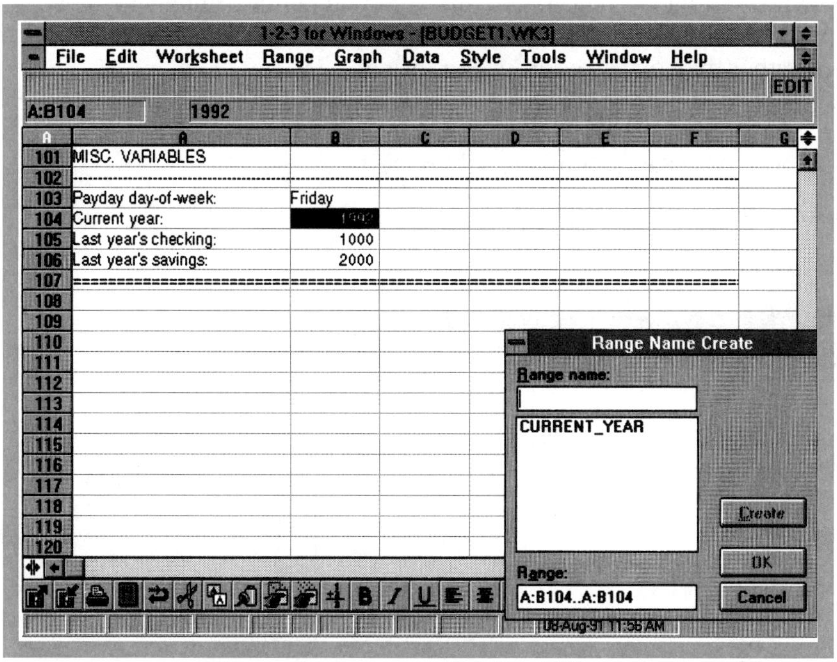

Specify: cell B105   *in the text box*
Select: `Create`

1-2-3 names cell B105 LAST_CHECKING and waits for your next command.

Select: `Range name:`
Type: `last_savings`
Select: `Range:`
Specify: cell B106
Select: `OK`   *to define the name and return to READY mode*

4. Save BUDGET1.

Saving BUDGET1 also saves the range names you created.

Naming Ranges with the Range Name Label Create Command

Although using range names can save you time and trouble, creating range names can be tedious if there are many cells you want to name. Fortunately, 1-2-3 provides a shortcut in the form of the Range Name Label Create command. Range Name Label Create lets you to create range names by using labels in the worksheet to name adjacent cells. You can use label cells above, below, or to the right or left of the cells you want to name.

Naming the EXPENSE Variables The EXPENSE VARIABLES section of the worksheet is a good example of a place where Range Name Label Create comes in handy. When you create formulas in the EXPENSES section of the Home Budget worksheet, you will find it easier to refer to variables by name rather than by cell address. For instance, instead of having to remember that B84 is the address of the variable for budgeted food expenses, you will be able to type **FOOD** in the formula for Bob and Kathy's food allowance. You can name the cells that contain the variables all at once with Range Name Label Create.

1. Move to the EXPENSE VARIABLES section (cell A81).

Figure 4-16

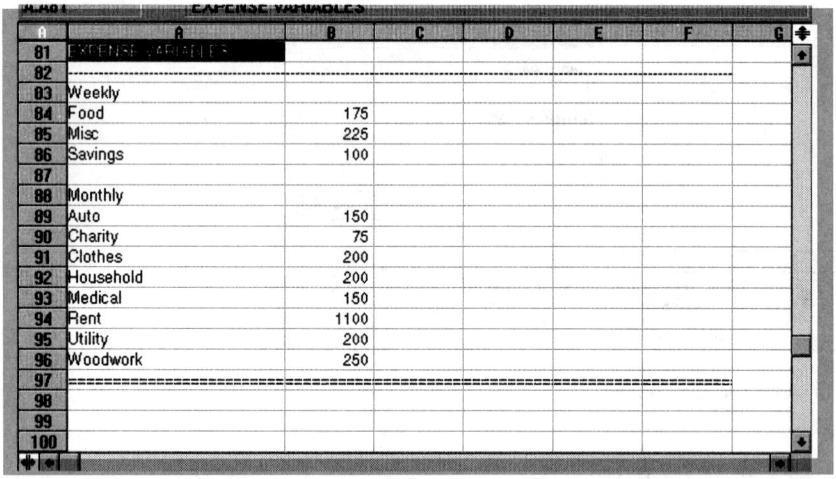

	A	B	C	D	E	F	G
81	EXPENSE VARIABLES						
82							
83	Weekly						
84	Food	175					
85	Misc	225					
86	Savings	100					
87							
88	Monthly						
89	Auto	150					
90	Charity	75					
91	Clothes	200					
92	Household	200					
93	Medical	150					
94	Rent	1100					
95	Utility	200					
96	Woodwork	250					
97							
98							
99							
100							

2. Name the expense section's variables (cells B84 through B96).

There are 11 categories of expenses. Use Range Name Label Create to name all 11 cells at once:

Move to:	cell A84	*(the label for the Food variable)*
Highlight:	A84..A96	
Choose:	`Range` `Name` `Label Create`	

1-2-3 presents a dialog box that prompts you for the range of labels to use as names and for the relationship of the label cells to the cells you want to name. The "Range:" text box displays the highlighted range.

Select:	→ OK	
Press:	ESC	*to clear the highlight*

The expense categories are now appropriately named. For instance, cell B86 is now named SAVINGS and cell B89 is named AUTO. (If you select Range Name Create, you can see these new names displayed in the "Range name:" list box.)

Deleting Range Names

Range names take up space in your computer's memory. When you don't need them, remove them.

When you used Range Name Label Create to name the expense variables, you created a name that corresponds to each label in the range A84..A96. One of these labels—**Monthly**—does not identify a value; consequently, you do not need the range name MONTHLY, and you can delete it with the Range Name Delete command.

1. Delete the MONTHLY range name.

First, call up the Range Name Delete dialog box:

Choose: Range   Name   Delete

Figure 4-17: The Range Name Delete Dialog Box

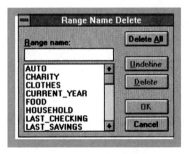

1-2-3 displays the range names you have created, in alphabetical order, in the list box beneath the "Range name:" text box. To delete a range name, point to it with the mouse (or by pressing Alt-R, Tab, and then the Down arrow). When the name you want to delete appears in the "Range name:" text box, select "Delete." If you can't see the name you want to delete, scroll the list box until the name is in view.

Select: MONTHLY   *in the list box*

        Delete

1-2-3 deletes the range name MONTHLY. If you wanted to delete another range name, you could select it and then again select "Delete." In this case, however, you'll need the remaining range names, so return 1-2-3 to READY mode.

Select: Cancel   *or press Escape*

2. Save BUDGET1.

Congratulations! You have finished naming the variables for the Home Budget worksheet. You now have range names for all the variables you are going to use in this chapter. Save BUDGET1 again to make these names a permanent part of the worksheet file.

A Note on Creating Range Names with Absolute Addresses   If you use a range name in a formula and copy the formula cell to other cells, the range will change, just as it would with any other relative cell address. To make a range name refer to an absolute range, put a dollar sign before the range name (for example, $LAST_SAVINGS).

You are going to use both relative and absolute range names as you create the remaining formulas in the Home Budget worksheet.

Using the Name Key to View Range Names

This section doesn't directly add anything to the Home Budget, but it does discuss a technique you will find handy whenever you are using a worksheet that contains range names: Using the Name key, F3.

Pressing the F3 (Name) whenever 1-2-3 prompts you for a range displays a list of range names. For example, try using the Name key in conjunction with Edit Quick Copy.

Choose: Edit   Quick Copy

Press: F3   **(NAME)**   *with the "From:" text box highlighted*

Figure 4-18:   Using F3 (Name) With Edit Quick Copy

1-2-3 initially displays a dialog box that prompts for "from" and "to" ranges. When you press F3 (Name), 1-2-3 displays another dialog box that lets you choose from among a list of existing range names, much as you did when you created and deleted range names. Select one of these names, and then select OK or press Enter to tell 1-2-3 to accept the selection:

Select: CHARITY   OK

1-2-3 removes the Range Names dialog box and redisplays the Edit Quick Copy dialog box. The "from" range is now CHARITY, the range name you selected. Since you are not going to do any copying right now, return 1-2-3 to READY mode.

Select: Cancel

Figure 4-19: Selecting a Range Name

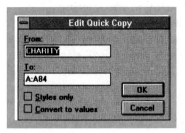

■ **NOTE:** The Name key makes it possible for you to see other kinds of information about the current worksheet file. You can press it whenever you are prompted for a name or cell address of some kind and 1-2-3 is not already displaying a list of range names. You can also press F3 (Name) while you are entering a formula, to display a list of range names, @functions, or macro commands and key names. Experiment with F3 (Name) on your own as you work through this book.

Entering Formulas That Use Range Names

You will continue to build Bob and Kathy Gordon's Home Budget by entering more formulas in the INCOME and EXPENSES sections of the worksheet. The range names you just created will make this task much easier.

1. Reference the current year in the worksheet title.

Right now, cell A:B1 contains the title **1992 HOME BUDGET**. This title is a label. Instead of a label, change it so that the worksheet title refers to the contents of the variable for the current year:

Move to:	cell A:B1	
Type:	+current_year	*(range name for cell A:B104)*
Press:	→	
Type:	HOME BUDGET	←

Figure 4-20

	1-2-3 for Windows - [BUDGET1.WK3]		
□ **File Edit Worksheet Range Graph Data Style Tools Window Help**			
{Page}			READY
A:B1	+CURRENT_YEAR		

A	B	C	D	E	F	G
1 Bob and Kathy Gordon	1992	HOME BUDGET				
2	Jan	Feb	Mar	Apr	May	
3	5	4	4	4	5	
4	======	======	======	======	======	======
5 INCOME						

You can enter the range name CURRENT_YEAR instead of having to remember the address B104. Preceding this name with a plus sign (+) tells 1-2-3 that you are entering a formula—in this case, a range name for a cell in another part of the worksheet. If next year you change the contents of cell B104 to 1993, the worksheet title will read **1993 HOME BUDGET**. Notice that 1-2-3 displays the range name instead of the cell address in the control panel. Displaying range names is one way 1-2-3 helps you clarify the structure of the worksheet.

2. Enter the formulas for monthly expenses in cells B23 through B33.

You can enter the formulas for all the categories of Bob and Kathy's expenses by using the range names you created with Range Name Label Create. The procedure is similar to the one you followed to fill in the Gordons' income, but the job is easier because you can use range names in the formulas instead of having to remember cell addresses, or point to cells.

First, you will type an absolute range name for some of the expenses that were budgeted by the month:

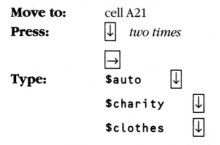

Move to: cell A21

Press: ↓ *two times*

    →

Type: `$auto`   ↓

    `$charity`   ↓

    `$clothes`   ↓

1-2-3 displays the values for auto, charity, and clothing expenses in cells B23, B24, and B25, respectively. Notice that you do not have to type a plus sign in front of the first range name in a formula if you use an absolute range name; 1-2-3 recognizes the dollar sign as a legitimate way to begin a value.

Now enter a formula to calculate one of the expenses that was budgeted weekly, food. This formula multiplies the weekly budgeted amount by the number of paydays in the month. It uses an absolute range name for the expense category ($FOOD), and a relative address for the cell that contains the number of paydays in the month (B3, for January). The method is the same as the one you used to calculate Bob's monthly pay, except that in this case you will use a range name to refer to the budgeted value:

Type: `$food*b3`   ↓

1-2-3 displays the amount of January's food budget, **875**. Now use the information in Setup Table 4-1 to fill in the remaining formulas in column B of the EXPENSES worksheet section. Begin with $HOUSEHOLD in cell B27. When you have finished, 1-2-3 should display the values indicated in the "Value Displayed" column of Setup Table 4-1.

Setup Table 4-1: EXPENSES Section Formulas

Expense	Formula	Enter in Cell:	Value Displayed
Auto	$auto	B23	150
Charity	$charity	B24	75
Clothes	$clothes	B25	200
Food	$food*B3	B26	875 (for January)
Household	$household	B27	200
Medical	$medical	B28	150
Misc	$misc*B3	B29	1125 (for January)
Rent	$rent	B30	1100
Savings	$savings*B3	B31	500 (for January)
Utility	$utility	B32	200
Woodwork	$woodwork	B33	250

3. Copy the EXPENSES formulas across rows 23 through 33.

You can use a single Edit Quick Copy command to copy the formulas you have just entered across the worksheet. Use F4 and the End Down key combination or the mouse to highlight the "from" range before you select the copy command.

Move to: cell B23

Highlight: B23..B33   *("from" range)*

Choose: `Edit   Quick Copy`

Specify: C23..M23   *in the "To:" range text box*

Press: ⏎   *or select OK to complete the copy*

  `ESC`   *to clear the highlight*

1-2-3 copies the column of formulas across the worksheet and displays the budgeted expense values (see Figure 4-21). Notice that you have to specify only the top row of a block of columns when you are copying one column to a range of columns. Also notice that the values for weekly expenses (such as food and savings) reflect the number of paydays in each month.

Using @Functions in Formulas

In addition to formulas you create yourself, 1-2-3 has many built-in formulas that you can use to perform calculations. These built-in formulas are called *at functions,* written *@functions.* They are so named because each function begins with the at-sign character, @.

An @function is made up of three parts:

Figure 4-21:   Using Edit Quick Copy to Copy the Formulas for Budgeted Expense Values

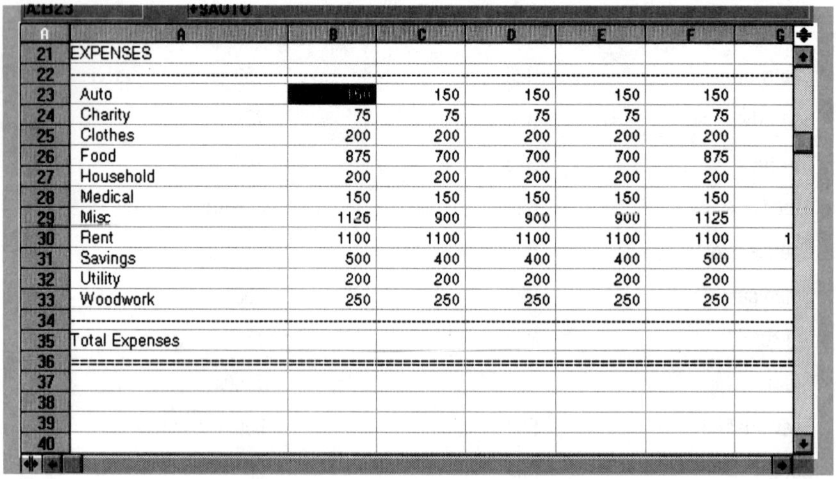

	A	B	C	D	E	F	G
21	EXPENSES						
22							
23	Auto	150	150	150	150	150	
24	Charity	75	75	75	75	75	
25	Clothes	200	200	200	200	200	
26	Food	875	700	700	700	875	
27	Household	200	200	200	200	200	
28	Medical	150	150	150	150	150	
29	Misc	1126	900	900	900	1125	
30	Rent	1100	1100	1100	1100	1100	1
31	Savings	500	400	400	400	500	
32	Utility	200	200	200	200	200	
33	Woodwork	250	250	250	250	250	
34							
35	Total Expenses						
36							
37							
38							
39							
40							

- The at sign (@), which must appear as the first character
- The name of the function, typed in either uppercase or lowercase letters
- One or more *arguments* enclosed in parentheses

The arguments specify the data the @function works on. @Function arguments can be anything from a single value to a range of cells, depending on the requirements of the particular @function. Many @functions can also take a list of arguments, separated by commas. Table 4-2 illustrates some of the ways @functions use arguments.

- *NOTE:*   You can change the argument separator with the Tools User Setup International Style command.

Table 4-2:   Function Arguments

Example	Description
@SQRT(B:A16)	The argument, B:A16, is the address of a cell that contains a value whose square root the @SQRT function will find.
@AVG(A1..A10)	The argument, A1..A10, is the range of cells whose values will be averaged by the @AVG function.
@SUM(A1..A10,B:Z1)	This is an example of a list of arguments. @SUM evaluates to the total of the values in the range A1..A10 in the current worksheet plus the value in cell Z1 in worksheet B.
@DATE(92,1,25)	The @DATE function produces a date value. It takes three arguments: the year, the month, and the day. In this case, @DATE(92,1,25) evaluates to the date value that corresponds to January 25, 1992.

1-2-3 provides many built-in @functions. You are going to use the @SUM function in this chapter, and you will use other @functions throughout the book.

If you select @Function Index from the 1-2-3 Help index, 1-2-3 will display a Help screen that provides an index of all the @functions available to you. When you select one of these @functions, 1-2-3 Help displays a complete discussion of how to use the selected @function. In addition, 1-2-3 Help provides detailed information on @function format, @function arguments, and rules for entering @functions in formulas.

■ *NOTE:*   You can get information on a specific @function by typing its name in the control panel and pressing F1 (Help).

Using @SUM

The @SUM function adds up a series of values in a range or a list. (A list can contain single cells, ranges of cells, and numbers.) @SUM is most often used to add up all the values in a row or a column, or to add up values in a range of cells that extends through several worksheets. You are going to use @SUM to calculate total income, total expenses, and cumulative savings for Kathy and Bob's Home Budget. You will then use this function to create annual figures for the various categories of income and expenses in their budget.

1. Enter formulas for total income in cell B14.

Earlier in this chapter, you calculated the total income for January 1992 by pointing to each cell and building the formula cell by cell. Now you are going to rewrite that formula with the @SUM function. In this case, you will use @SUM to add the values in the range B8..B13.

Move to:	cell B14 *(the location of the formula cell)*
Type:	@sum(

Enter the range by pointing to the start and end cells. Use the arrow keys to move the cell pointer.

Move to:	cell B8
Press:	$\boxed{.}$ **(Period)**
Move to:	cell B13 *(the ruled-line cell)*
Type:	) $\boxed{\hookleftarrow}$

The number 5200 once again appears in cell B14, and the formula @SUM(B8..B13) appears in the control panel. @SUM treats label cells and blank cells as if they contained zeros, so the blank cells between B8 and B11 do not affect the calculation (see Figure 4-22).

Notice that row 13, the ruled line beneath the Interest row, is included in the range. Including this line makes it easier to insert a new row beneath Interest (for example, for dividends) without disturbing the @SUM range. The @SUM function will automatically adjust to the new, expanded range if you do this. (You will learn how to insert a row later in this chapter)

Figure 4-22: Using @SUM to Total a Column of Numbers

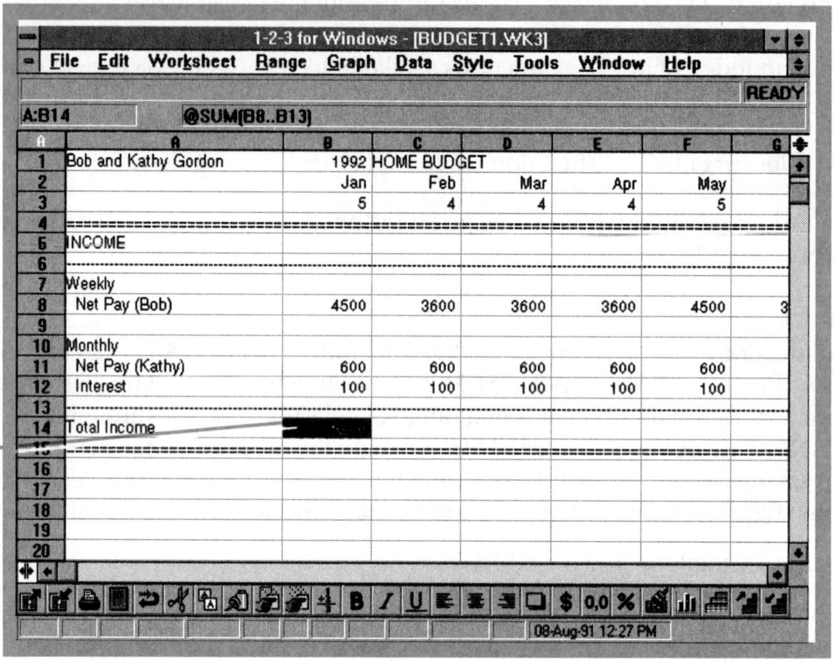

Also notice that this formula uses relative addresses. Copying it across the worksheet allows you to calculate the total income for each month.

Choose:	`Edit   Quick Copy`	*with the cell pointer in B14*
Select:	`To:`	
Specify:	C14..M14	
Press:	↵	*or select OK*

1-2-3 copies the formula across the worksheet and displays the Total Income value for each month (see Figure 4-23).

2. Enter formulas for total expenses in cells B35 through M35.

Total expenses are calculated in the same way as total income. Once again, you will create an @SUM formula that totals a column of data, and then copy that formula across the worksheet. Figure 4-24 on page 154 shows the results of the copy operation.

Move to:	cell B35
Type:	`@sum(`
Highlight:	B23..B34
Type:	`)` ↵

Figure 4-23: Using @SUM to Create Total Income Formulas for Each Month

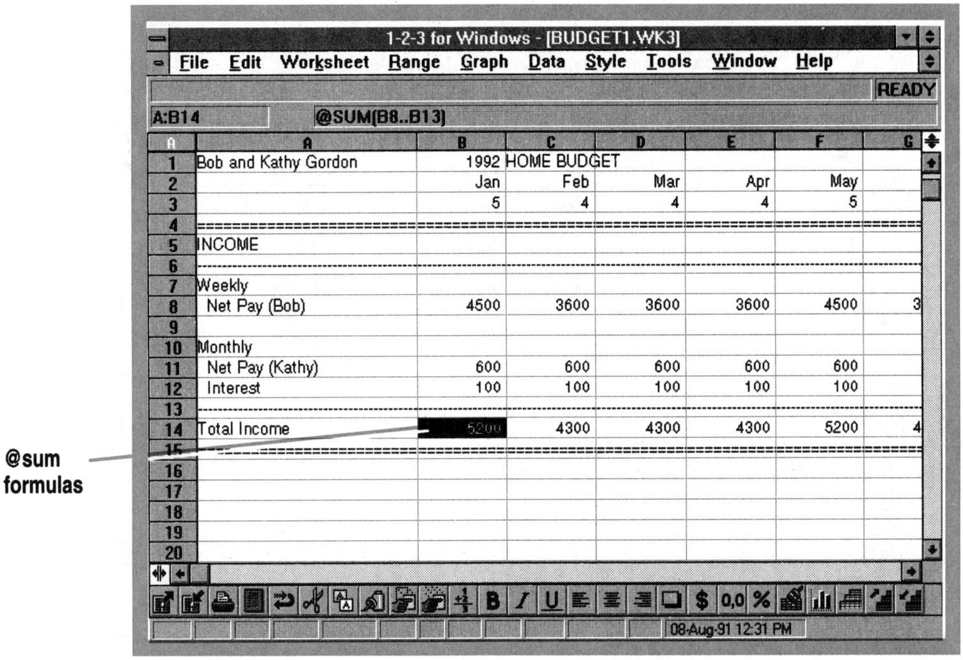

	A	B	C	D	E	F	G
	1-2-3 for Windows - [BUDGET1.WK3]						
	File Edit Worksheet Range Graph Data Style Tools Window Help						
							READY
A:B14	@SUM(B8..B13)						
1	Bob and Kathy Gordon	1992 HOME BUDGET					
2		Jan	Feb	Mar	Apr	May	
3		5	4	4	4	5	
4							
5	INCOME						
6							
7	Weekly						
8	Net Pay (Bob)	4500	3600	3600	3600	4500	3
9							
10	Monthly						
11	Net Pay (Kathy)	600	600	600	600	600	
12	Interest	100	100	100	100	100	
13							
14	Total Income	5200	4300	4300	4300	5200	4
15							
16							
17							
18							
19							
20							

08-Aug-91 12:31 PM

@sum formulas

■ *NOTE:* When the range of values that you want to add together is adjacent to the cell into which you want the @SUM formula to appear, you can use the @SUM icon to quickly create the formula. The @SUM icon looks like this:

To use the icon, move the cell pointer to the cell in which you want the @SUM formula to appear, and then click on the icon. 1-2-3 inserts an @SUM formula in the current cell, and automatically uses the range above, below, to the right, or to the left as the argument.

1-2-3 enters the formula @SUM(B23..B34) in cell B35 and displays the value 4825. Copy this formula across the other monthly expense columns:

Choose:	Edit Quick Copy
Select:	To:
Specify:	C35..M35
Press:	↵

1-2-3 displays total expenses values for the months of January through December 1992.

3. Enter formulas for cumulative savings in cells B45 through M45.

Figure 4-24: Using @SUM to Create Total Expenses Formulas for Each Month.

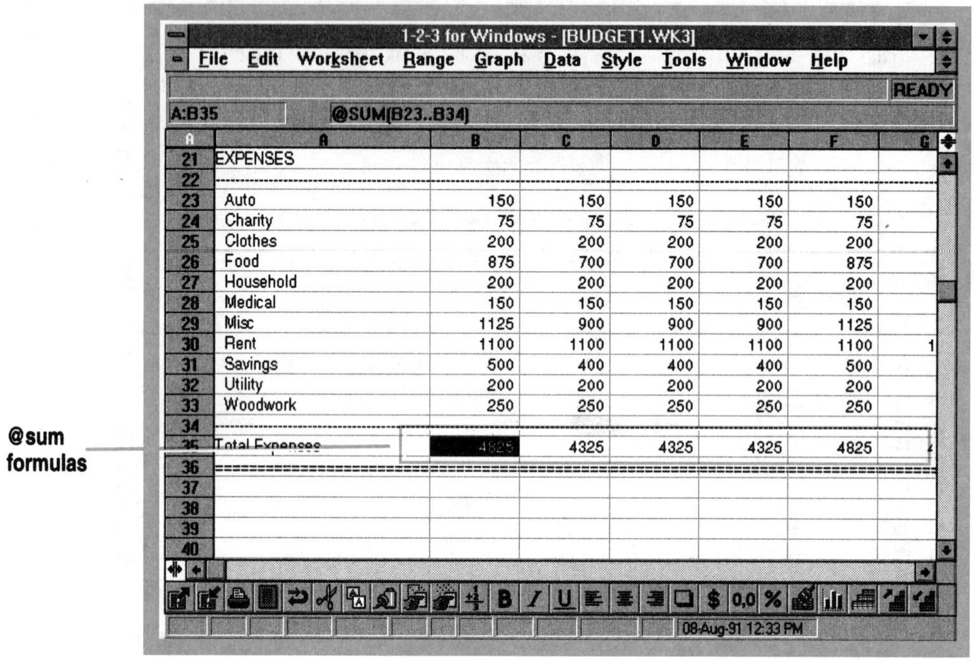

@sum
formulas

To calculate cumulative savings in the CASH FLOW section, you are going to write a formula that uses a combination of relative and mixed cell addresses to create a running total. This formula demonstrates how understanding the way Edit Quick Copy handles cell references can help you use 1-2-3 more efficiently.

The formula is somewhat trickier than the other formulas you have entered so far. If you have trouble following the explanation given here, don't worry about it. Type in the keystrokes, then come back to the explanation some other time, after you have had more of a chance to experiment with formulas, ranges, and different types of cell references.

First, take a look at the cumulative savings row in Figure 4-25 (shown on the next page). It shows how the worksheet will look after you have entered the formulas.

The row labeled **Cumulative Savings** displays the Gordons' savings account balance for each month. This value consists of the amounts deposited up to and including the current month, plus the amount carried over from the previous year. For example, the cumulative savings value for March 1992 consists of the amounts deposited in January, February, and March, plus the amount carried over from 1991. The cumulative savings value for March, therefore, is $500+$400+$400+$2,000, which is $3,300.

The value in the LAST_SAVINGS variable (cell B106) provides the carryover from the previous year. The running total of monthly deposits comes from a slightly tricky use of ranges, cell references, and @SUM.

Figure 4-25:   Combining Relative and Mixed Addresses to Create a Running Total

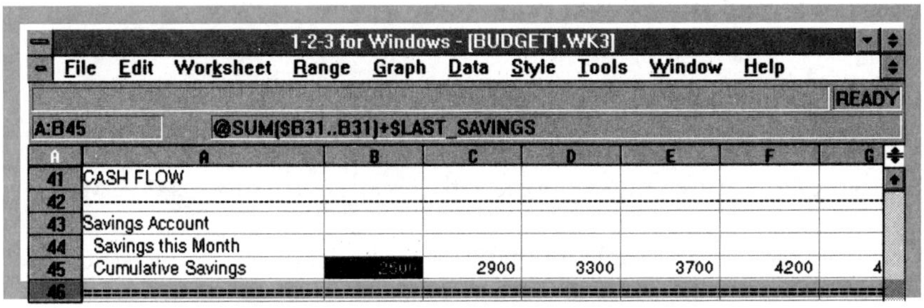

Do the following:

Move to:	cell B45
Type:	@sum($b31.b31)+$last_savings ↵

1-2-3 displays the result: **2500**. Now, watch what happens when you copy this formula across row 45:

Choose:	Edit Quick Copy
Select:	To:
Specify:	C45..M45
Press:	↵ *or select OK*

1-2-3 displays cumulative savings values for each of the remaining months.

Figure 4-26a: Cumulative Savings for the First Part of the Year

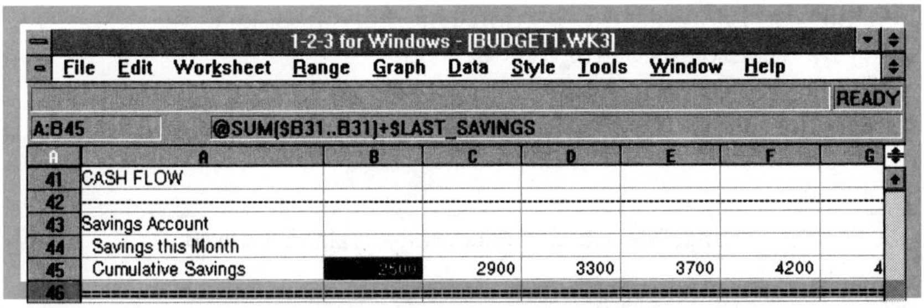

Figure 4-26b: Cumulative Savings for the Latter Part of the Year

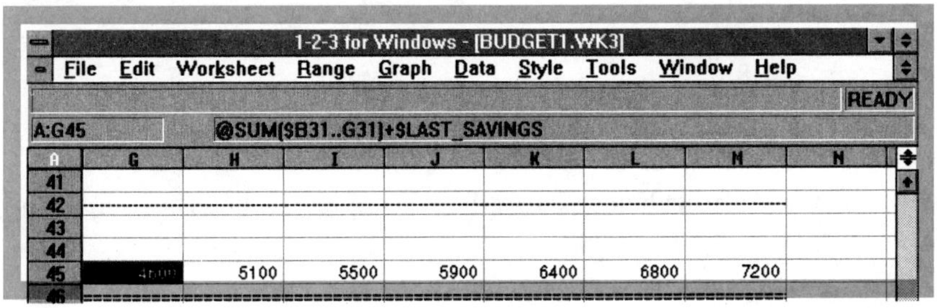

How the Formula Works The key to this formula is the way you have defined the range in the @SUM function. Look at the formula in cell B45 in the control panel:

```
@SUM($B31..B31)+$LAST_SAVINGS
```

This formula adds the savings value for January (500) to last year's savings (2000). The formula refers to last year's savings with an absolute reference to a range name: $LAST_SAVINGS. It refers to the January savings deposit with a somewhat curious @SUM formula: @SUM($B31..B31).

Move the cell pointer across row 45 and look at what Edit Quick Copy did to the @SUM range.

The formula in cell B45 uses both a mixed cell address ($B31) and a relative address (B31) to refer to the contents of cell B31. In the January column, the effect of this formula is the same as if you had entered @SUM(B31). However, when you copy this formula across row 45, 1-2-3 adjusts the cell addresses in the formula. Because the mixed cell address $B31 does not change when you copy the formula cell, each copy of the formula uses cell B31 as the start address of the @SUM range. The end address of the range, however, is a relative address (B31); this address *does* change as you copy the formula across the row.

In column C, the end of the range becomes C31, and the @SUM formula sums the savings for January through February. In column D, the end of the range becomes D31, and the formula in column D sums the savings for January through March. In other words, each formula sums the values in a range that begins with B31 and ends with the current month. This creates a running total of monthly deposits. Adding this total to the carry-over from the previous year ($LAST_SAVINGS) gives you the values for monthly cumulative savings.

Completing the CASH FLOW Section

Entering the remaining cell references in the CASH FLOW section will complete the basic worksheet structure and enable you to predict the Gordons' monthly income, expenses, account balances, cash flow, and total available funds.

You will refer to the following cells in other parts of the worksheet as you complete the CASH FLOW section. (These values are reproduced here as a convenience; you have already created them.)

Description	Range Name or Cell Address	Value Displayed
Last year's savings account balance	LAST_SAVINGS	2000
Last year's checking account balance	LAST_CHECKING	1000
Monthly savings deposit (January)	B31	500
Monthly total income (January)	B14	5200
Monthly total expenses (January)	B35	4825

1. Fill in the values for **Savings this Month** across row 44 to complete savings account information:

Move to:	cell B44
Type:	+b31 ⏎

1-2-3 displays the value of the January savings account deposits. Copy this relative cell reference across row 44:

Choose:	Edit Quick Copy
Select:	To:
Specify:	C44..M44
Press:	⏎ or select OK

1-2-3 displays the savings deposit values for January through December.

2. Fill in the Checking Account information in rows 49, 50, and 52.

The Checking Account information is in the form:

```
  Opening Balance
+ Net Cash Flow
  ─────────────────
= Closing Balance
```

The opening balance for January is the closing balance for the previous year. The opening balance for the remaining months is the closing balance for the previous month.

First, fill in the Checking Account formulas for January:

Move to:	cell B49
Type:	last_checking ⬇
	+b14−b35 *(Total Income - Total Expenses)*
Press:	⬇ *two times*
Type:	+b49+b50 *(Opening Balance + Net Cash Flow)*
Press:	⏎

Figure 4-27:   January's Checking Account Figures

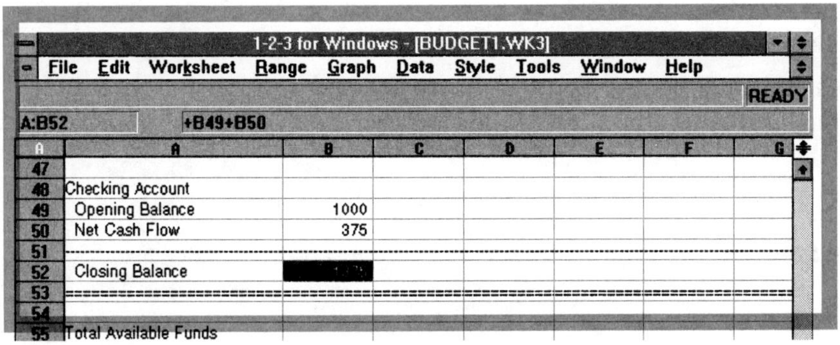

	1-2-3 for Windows - [BUDGET1.WK3]						
File Edit Worksheet Range Graph Data Style Tools Window Help							READY
A:B52	+B49+B50						
A	A	B	C	D	E	F	G
47							
48	Checking Account						
49	Opening Balance	1000					
50	Net Cash Flow	375					
51							
52	Closing Balance	▓▓▓▓					
53							
54							
55	Total Available Funds						

The formulas for the remaining months are slightly different from those for January. Fill in the opening balance for February:

Move to:	cell C49
Type:	+b52 *(refers to the January closing balance)*
Press:	↓

Now copy the formulas for net cash flow and closing balance from column B to column C:

Highlight:	B50..B52
Choose:	Edit Quick Copy
Specify:	C50 *in the To: text box*
Select:	OK *or press Enter to complete the copy*

Figure 4-28: February's Checking Account Values Depend on January's Values

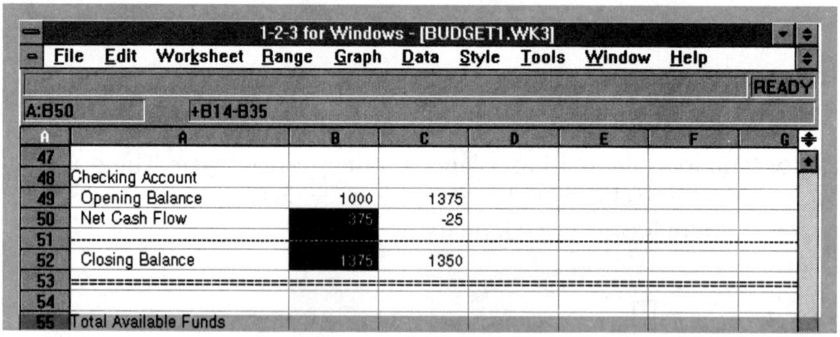

Finally, copy the checking account information from column C to the remaining months:

Highlight:	C49..C52
Choose:	Edit Quick Copy
Select:	To:
Specify:	D49..M49 *in the "To:" text box*
Press:	↵ *or select OK to complete the copy*
	ESC *to clear the highlight*

3. Fill in total available funds formulas in row 55.

Total Available Funds adds up the cumulative savings and the closing balance figures for each month.

Move to:	cell B55
Type:	+b45+b52
Press:	↵

Figure 4-29: **The Remaining Checking Account Values Use the Same Formulas as February's Values**

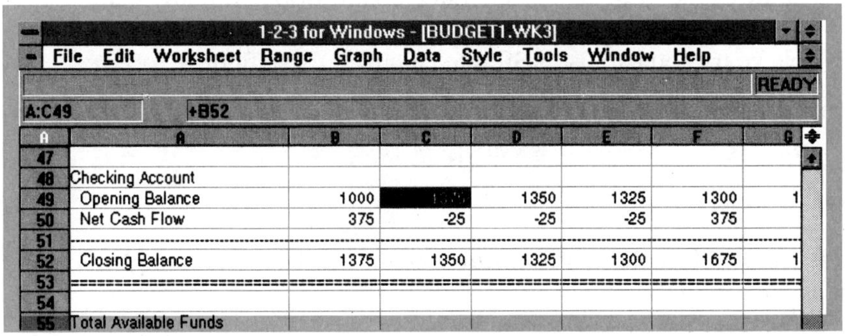

1-2-3 for Windows - [BUDGET1.WK3]						
File **Edit** **Worksheet** **Range** **Graph** **Data** **Style** **Tools** **Window** **Help**						READY
A:C49	+B52					
A	A	B	C	D	E	F	G
47							
48	Checking Account						
49	Opening Balance	1000		1350	1325	1300	1
50	Net Cash Flow	375	-25	-25	-25	375	
51							
52	Closing Balance	1375	1350	1325	1300	1675	1
53							
54							
55	Total Available Funds						

1-2-3 displays the total available funds for January. Copy the formula in cell B55 to the range C55..M55:

Choose:	Edit Quick Copy	
Select:	To:	
Specify:	C55..M55	
Select:	OK *or press Enter*	

Figure 4-30: **Total Available Funds for the Year**

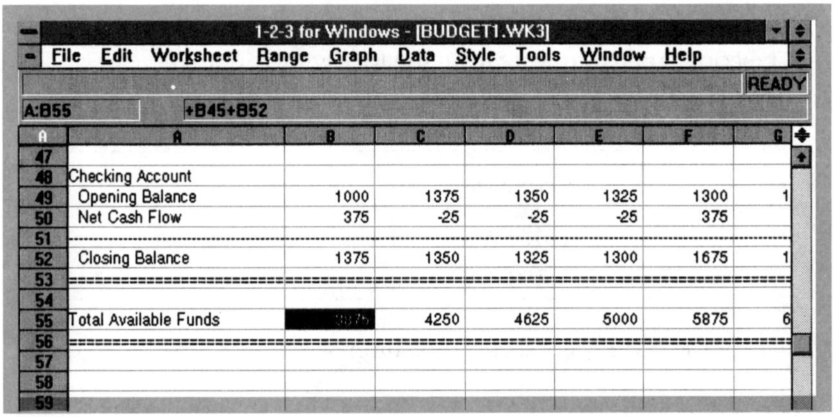

1-2-3 for Windows - [BUDGET1.WK3]						
File **Edit** **Worksheet** **Range** **Graph** **Data** **Style** **Tools** **Window** **Help**						READY
A:B55	+B45+B52					
A	A	B	C	D	E	F	G
47							
48	Checking Account						
49	Opening Balance	1000	1375	1350	1325	1300	1
50	Net Cash Flow	375	-25	-25	-25	375	
51							
52	Closing Balance	1375	1350	1325	1300	1675	1
53							
54							
55	Total Available Funds		4250	4625	5000	5875	6
56							
57							
58							
59							

4. Save BUDGET1.

Congratulations! You have completed the basic structure of the Home Budget worksheet. If you stopped now, you would have a functional budget application. The remainder of this chapter adds a few finishing touches and uses some additional 1-2-3 features to clean up the appearance of the worksheet and make it easier to use.

Using @SUM across Rows to Calculate Annual Amounts

In addition to the monthly figures the budget has generated so far, Bob and Kathy will probably want to know how much they can expect to earn, and how much they will spend, over the course of the whole year. You can use @SUM to calculate these figures, too.

1. Create a column heading called **Annual** in column N:

Move to:	cell N2
Type:	**"Annual** ⏎

The double quotation mark before the word **Annual** aligns this label on the right, so it has the same alignment as the month headings.

2. Fill in annual @SUM formulas for the INCOME section (column N, rows 8 through 14).

Now use @SUM to add up each of the Gordons' sources of income for the year. Start with Bob's net pay for January through December:

Move to:	cell N8
Type:	**@sum(b8.b8)** ⏎ *or click on the @SUM icon*

1-2-3 adds up the monthly values for Bob's net pay and displays the result: **46800**. This @SUM formula contains relative addresses, so you can copy it to the other categories of income and create annual totals for them, too, without having to enter each @SUM formula manually.

Use Edit Quick Copy or Edit Copy and Edit Paste to copy the formula in cell N8 to cells N11..N12 and to cell N14. The copy command will create the following formulas:

Description	Cell Address	Formula Created	Value Displayed
Kathy's annual net pay	N11	@SUM(B11..M11)	7200
Annual interest earned	N12	@SUM(B12..M12)	1200
Gordons' total annual income	N14	@SUM(B14..M14)	55200

3. Fill in annual @SUM formulas for the EXPENSES section (column N, rows 23 through 35).

The EXPENSES section's annual sums can be created even more easily. All you need is one copy command. Copy one of the @SUM formulas from column N of the INCOME section (the formula in cell N14) to the range N23..N35:

Move to:	cell N14
Choose:	**Edit Copy** *or click on the Edit Copy icon*
Highlight:	N23..N35
Choose:	**Edit Paste** *or click on the Edit Paste icon*
Press:	ESC *to clear the highlight*

1-2-3 copies the @SUM formula down column N. Notice that this copy command over-wrote the single-ruled line in cell N34. Fix this, and you are done with the annual expenses!

Move to: cell N34

Type: \‐   ⏎

To check your work, position the window so cell G21 is in the upper left corner:

Press: F5   (GOTO)

Type: g21   ⏎

Your final result should look like Figure 4-31.

Figure 4-31:   The Completed Annual Expenses Formulas

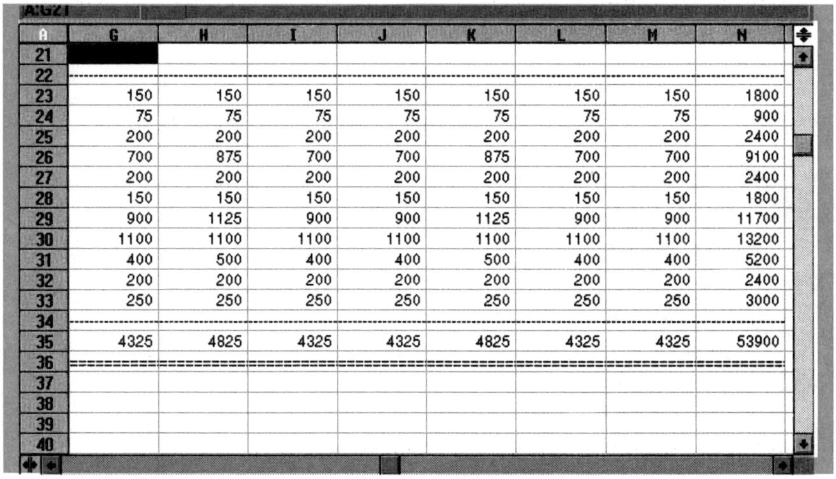

	G	H	I	J	K	L	M	N
21								
22								
23	150	150	150	150	150	150	150	1800
24	75	75	75	75	75	75	75	900
25	200	200	200	200	200	200	200	2400
26	700	875	700	700	875	700	700	9100
27	200	200	200	200	200	200	200	2400
28	150	150	150	150	150	150	150	1800
29	900	1125	900	900	1125	900	900	11700
30	1100	1100	1100	1100	1100	1100	1100	13200
31	400	500	400	400	500	400	400	5200
32	200	200	200	200	200	200	200	2400
33	250	250	250	250	250	250	250	3000
34								
35	4325	4825	4325	4325	4825	4325	4325	53900
36								
37								
38								
39								
40								

Congratulations! You are through entering all the labels, data, and formulas into the Home Budget worksheet. Almost done!

Cleaning up the Worksheet

You have just about finished the Gordon family's Home Budget worksheet. All that remains is a little more cleanup work.

Using Edit Find

1-2-3's Edit Find command allows you either to find, or to find and then modify, the contents of cells.

Edit Find works very much like the search and search and replace commands of word processors and text editors. When you choose Edit Find, 1-2-3 displays a dialog box that prompts you for a *character string* to search for (a character string is any group of contiguous characters), and a range to search. It also asks you if it should search for the string in labels, formulas, or both, and if you want only to find the strings or to find them and replace them with another string. If you choose to find and replace, Edit Find also requires a replacement string. Once you have supplied the command with the search or search-and-replace information, Edit Find searches through the range you supplied for the specified character string and, optionally, replaces it with the replacement string.

Use Edit Find to change the EXPENSE VARIABLES labels so that they are indented two spaces.

1. Highlight the range to search.

   Tell 1-2-3 to search the list of types of expenses:

   Highlight: A84..A96

2. Choose Edit Find.

   Choose: Edit   Find

   1-2-3 displays the Edit Find dialog box.

   Figure 4-32: The Edit Find Dialog Box

   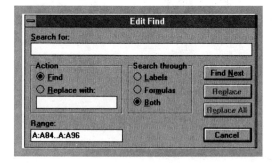

3. Specify the search string and the kind of search to perform.

   Search for label cells beginning with an apostrophe ('). This will cause 1-2-3 to find all the label cells in the highlighted range but to skip the blank cell, cell A87.

   Select: Search for: *(if necessary)*
   Type: '   *(an apostrophe, with no spaces)*

   For each apostrophe the program finds, you want it to substitute an apostrophe followed by two spaces.

   Select: Replace with:
   Type: '   *(an apostrophe)*
   Press: SPACEBAR   *two times, to type two spaces*

3. Select the type of cell contents to search.

1-2-3 asks if you want to search cells that contain labels, formulas, or both.

Select: `Labels`

4. Replace all matching strings except **`Monthly`**.

At this point, you can select "Find Next" to find the first matching string, "Replace" to find the next match and automatically replace it with the replacement string, "Replace All" to change all matching strings in the range to the replacement string, or Cancel to leave Edit Find.

In this case, you want 1-2-3 to replace all the matching strings except the label **`Monthly`**, which should remain flush left. To accomplish this, first select "Find Next" to make sure 1-2-3 has located the correct label—the address and contents of the "found" cell should be displayed in the control panel. Then, select "Replace" for **`Food`**, **`Misc.`**, and **`Savings`**:

Select: `Find Next` *to find cell A84*

`Replace` `Replace` `Replace`

Now select "Find Next" to skip **`Monthly`** (cell A88), and then select "Replace All" to indent the remaining matching labels in the range:

Select: `Find Next` *to skip over cell A88*

`Replace All`

After 1-2-3 replaces the matching strings, the program returns to READY mode. The labels are now indented.

Press: ESC *to cancel the highlighting*

Figure 4-33: The Results of the Edit Find Operation

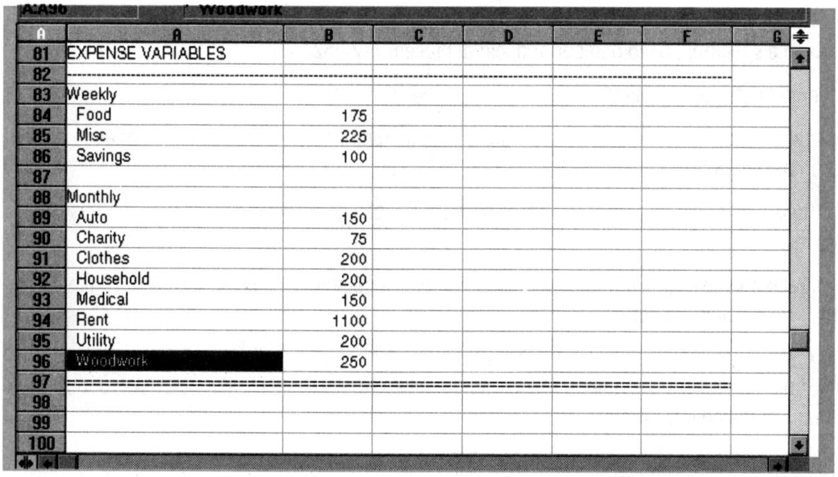

A:A96 'Woodwork

A	A	B	C	D	E	F	G
81	EXPENSE VARIABLES						
82	------------------						
83	Weekly						
84	Food	175					
85	Misc	225					
86	Savings	100					
87							
88	Monthly						
89	Auto	150					
90	Charity	75					
91	Clothes	200					
92	Household	200					
93	Medical	150					
94	Rent	1100					
95	Utility	200					
96	Woodwork	250					
97	==================						
98							
99							
100							

Formatting Values in Cells

Most of the values in the Home Budget worksheet are currency, but they are displayed as unformatted numbers. To make it easier to distinguish different kinds of values, values can be *formatted.* For example, you can add dollar signs, insert thousands separators, or round off decimal places. You can format one cell or a range of cells, and you can alter the default format for the worksheet.

The Worksheet Global Settings Format dialog box allows you to choose a default format for the whole worksheet. This global format is the format a cell will have unless you change the format of the cell with the Range Format command. Range Format allows you to apply formats to a single cell, or to a range of cells.

Formatting a specific cell or range of cells gives that cell or group of cells a *local format.* If a cell has a local format, 1-2-3 uses that format when it displays the cell's values. If a cell does not have a local format, 1-2-3 displays the cell according to the global format in effect at the time.

You can change the local or global format settings whenever you want to. Formats established with Range Format always take precedence over the current global format, and changing the global format does not affect the format of cells that have been locally formatted. Formatting a value changes only the way it is displayed; the value itself is not changed

Table 4-2 describes the formatting choices available to you. With the exception of Reset, these choices are available in both the Range Format and the Worksheet Global Settings Format dialog boxes.

■ *NOTE:*   You can change the color or font, and add outlining, shading, and underlining to cells with the Style menu commands. You'll learn how to use these commands in Chapter 7.

Table 4-2:   Cell Formats

Format	What It Does:
Fixed	Rounds to a specified, fixed number of decimal places: 1125.62
Scientific	Exponential notation: 1.13E+03
Currency	Dollars and cents. Adds thousands separators to long numbers: $1,125.62; places negative values in parentheses: ($25)
, Comma	Adds thousands separators to long numbers: 1,125.62; places negative values in parentheses: (25)
General	The initial worksheet global format. No fixed number of decimal places; rounds to fit column width or uses scientific notation.
+/-	Horizontal bar graph (+++ or ---). The number of plus or minus signs displayed equals the integer value of the entry. Displays a period (.) for numbers between +1 and -1, and asterisks for numbers greater than the column width.
Percent	Multiplies by 100 and adds a % sign: .42 = 42%

Format	What It Does:
Text	Displays formulas instead of the values to which the formulas evaluate
Date (1: through 5:)	Formats in one of several Date formats, for example, DD-MMM-YY (01-Sep-92)
Time (6: through 9:)	Formats in one of several Time formats, for example, HH:MM:SS (14:30:25)
Hidden	Does not display specified cells.
Automatic	Formats cells into which you enter numbers, dates, and times according to how the values are entered. For example, if you enter the number $100.00 into a cell that has been formatted Automatic, the cell acquires the Currency, 2 decimal places format. Labels that begin with numbers are automatically prefixed with the default label prefix. NOTE: Once an Automatic cell acquires a new format, it is no longer Automatic; any future entries into the cell are displayed in the acquired format.
Label	Automatically adds the default label prefix to new entries.
Reset	Returns a range to the global default format (General, if not changed).

■ *NOTE:*   You can change the currency symbol, the thousands separator, and the decimal separator through the Tools User Setup International dialog box.

In this section, you are going to use three local formats—Currency, Fixed, and Hidden—and one global format, Comma (,). You will use others as you work through this book.

1. Change the format of the totals rows (14, 35, 45, 52, and 55) to currency, no decimal places.

With many formats, you are asked to choose the number of decimal places you'd like displayed. 1-2-3 can display up to 15 decimal places. No matter how many decimal places are displayed, however, 1-2-3 always remembers the number at maximum precision, and will use the stored value in calculations.

You are going to format the rows containing totals in the INCOME, EXPENSES, and CASH FLOW worksheet sections to display their contents as currency with no decimal places. Begin with the total income row, row 14:

Highlight:	B14..N14
Choose:	`Range` `Format`
Select:	`Currency` *from the Format: list box*
	`Decimal places:`
Type:	0 *in the text box*
Select:	`OK` *or press Enter*
Press:	`ESC` *to clear the highlighting*

Figure 4-34: Formatting a Range of Cells as Currency with Zero Decimal Places

	A	B	C	D	E	F	G
5	INCOME						
6							
7	Weekly						
8	Net Pay (Bob)	4500	3600	3600	3600	4500	3
9							
10	Monthly						
11	Net Pay (Kathy)	600	600	600	600	600	
12	Interest	100	100	100	100	100	
13							
14	Total Income	$5,200	$4,300	$4,300	$4,300	$5,200	$4,
15							
16							
17							

(Control panel: 1-2-3 for Windows - [BUDGET1.WK3]; File Edit Worksheet Range Graph Data Style Tools Window Help; (C0); A:B14 @SUM(B8..B13); READY)

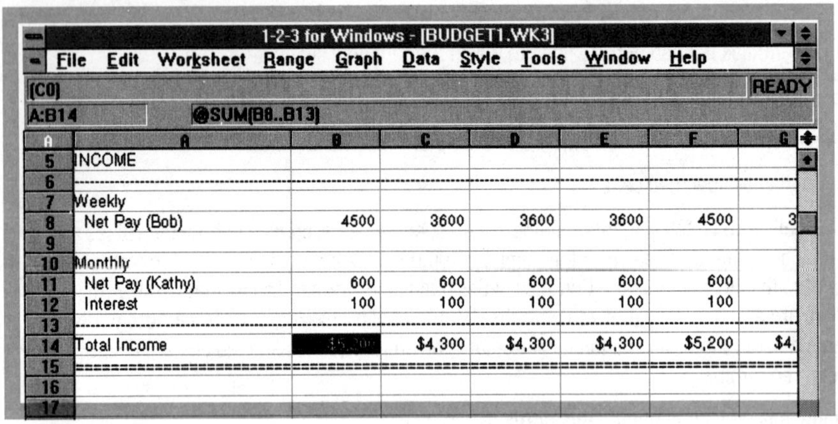

Move through the cells in the row you just formatted and look at the control panel. Notice that (C0) now appears in the format line of the control panel. This means the format is "Currency, zero decimal places."

Repeat this procedure on the following ranges: B35..N35, B45..N45, B52..M52, and B55..M55.

2. Change the global format to Comma (,) format.

In most financial worksheets, a column of currency values with a total beneath it is formatted so that the numbers in the column look like currency values (they have thousands separators), but the values are not prefixed with a dollar sign. In these worksheets, only the totals are formatted to have dollar signs, to make these values stand out better.

The cell format that displays numbers with commas but without dollar signs is called *Comma format* and is indicated in the "Format:" list of the Range Format dialog box with a comma (,) followed by the word `Comma`.

You could format each of the rows of numbers that are not totals so that they are in Comma (,) format, but each time you added a new row to a column you would have to format that row, too. There is an easier way. Change the global format setting to Comma (,) format with zero decimal places:

Choose:	`Worksheet    Global Settings`
Select:	`Format...`
	`Comma` *from the Worksheet Global Settings Format Format: list box*
	`Decimal places:`
Type:	`0` *in the text box*
Select:	`OK` *two times, to return to READY mode*

Figure 4-35: Changing the Global Cell Format to Comma (,)

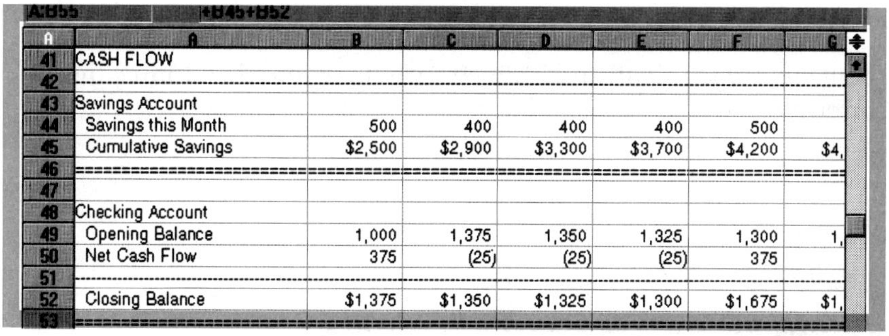

A	B	C	D	E	F	G
41 CASH FLOW						
42						
43 Savings Account						
44 Savings this Month	500	400	400	400	500	
45 Cumulative Savings	$2,500	$2,900	$3,300	$3,700	$4,200	$4,
46						
47						
48 Checking Account						
49 Opening Balance	1,000	1,375	1,350	1,325	1,300	1,
50 Net Cash Flow	375	(25)	(25)	(25)	375	
51						
52 Closing Balance	$1,375	$1,350	$1,325	$1,300	$1,675	$1,
53						

1-2-3 changes the display of all numbers that have not been formatted locally to Comma (,) format. Notice that negative numbers are now surrounded by parentheses instead of being preceded by a minus sign. In addition, values greater than 999 have commas.

Changing the global format instead of the individual ranges has two advantages: First, it allows you to add new rows or columns of formulas without having to format each new range as Comma (,) format. Second, if you later decide to change the format of these cells (for instance, to include decimal values), you can just change the global format setting instead of having to reformat the specific cells; 1-2-3 automatically changes the display of all the cells that have not been locally formatted.

3. Clean up remaining formats.

Cells B1 and B104 both display the value 1992. Now that the global format is Comma (,), this number is displayed with a comma: **1,992**. Since you intend 1992 to represent a year, not a sum of money, format cells B1 and B104 as Fixed format, zero decimal places:

Move to:	cell A:B1
Choose:	`Range` `Format`
Select:	`Fixed`
	`Decimal places:`
Type:	`0` ⏎

From now on, changes to the global format will not affect the display of the current year in cell B1. You could also change cell B104 in the same way. Another way to duplicate an existing cell format is to use the "Apply Formatting" SmartIcon. The icon looks like this:

You can specify the cell to which the formatting is to be appied either by typing its address in the control panel or by clicking on it.

Click on:	*the Apply Formatting icon*
Specify:	cell B104

1-2-3 applies the formatting information in cell B1 to cell B104.

4. Format the currency values in the variables sections as Currency, zero decimal places.

Highlight the range that contains the INCOME and EXPENSE variables and then format the values in that range as Currency:

Move to: cell B64

Highlight: B64..B96

Figure 4-36: **Highlighting the INCOME and EXPENSE Variables**

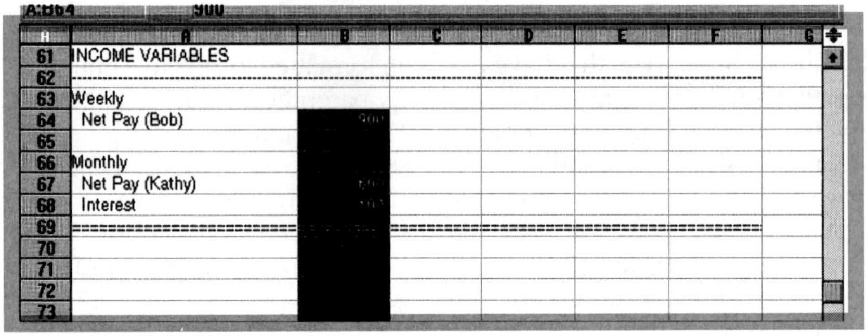

Choose: Range   Format

Select: Currency

          Decimal places:

Type: 0   ⏎

Figure 4-37: **The INCOME and EXPENSE Variables Formatted as Currency, Zero Decimal Places (Window Split Into Two Panes)**

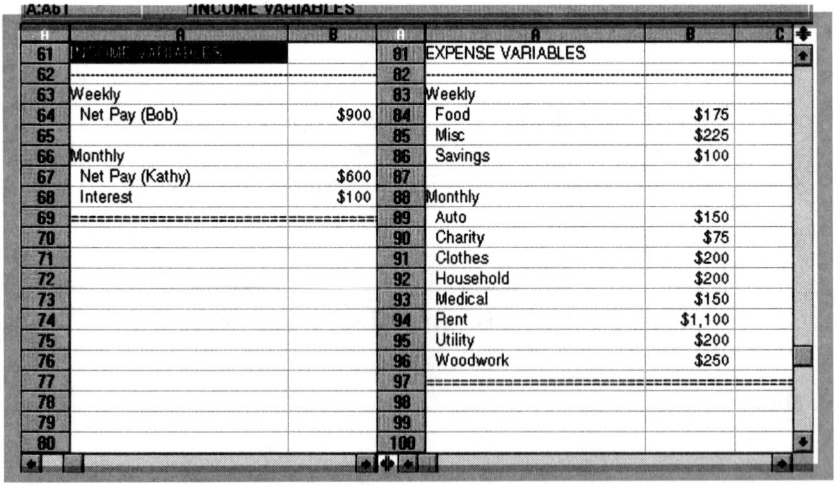

1-2-3 formats the preselected range. Now, format the two currency values in the MISC. VARIABLES section.

Move to:	cell B105
Highlight:	B105..B106
Choose:	`Range     Format`
Select:	`Currency`
	`Decimal places:`
Type:	`0` ⏎

Finally, if you like, you can prevent 1-2-3 from displaying the numbers of paydays/month in row 3 by giving them the Hidden format:

Highlight:	B3..M3
Choose:	`Range     Format`
Select:	`Hidden` *(scroll the Format: list box until Hidden is visible)*
	`OK`

Figure 4-38: Hiding the Values in Row 3

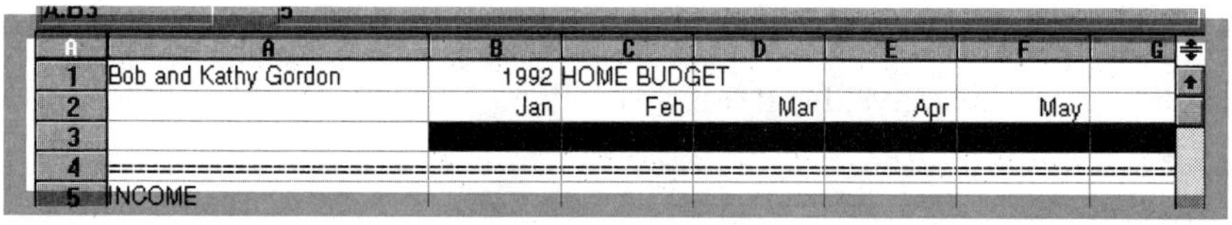

	A	B	C	D	E	F	G
1	Bob and Kathy Gordon	1992 HOME BUDGET					
2		Jan	Feb	Mar	Apr	May	
3							
4	==
5	INCOME

Notice that no values for the Hidden cells are displayed in the worksheet. The symbol (H), for Hidden format, is displayed in the format line of the control panel when the cell pointer is in a Hidden cell. Hidden cells still retain their values, can be referenced in formulas, and so on. They have not been erased; they are simply not displayed.

■ *NOTE:*   To make the contents of Hidden cells visible again, you must either reset the range format (with the "Reset" option in the Range Format dialog box), or format the cells with a different format. In this case, Fixed with zero decimal places would be the most appropriate, since the numbers are whole numbers.

A Note on Using SmartIcons to Format Ranges   In addition to the "Apply Formatting" icon, which you used to apply the format of one cell to another, you can use other icons as shortcuts for cell formatting operations. On your own, experiment with using the "Currency", "Comma," and "Percent" SmartIcons to change the display of cells and ranges in the scratch worksheet. These icons look like this:

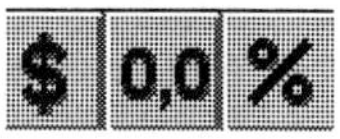

To use a SmartIcon to change the format of a cell or range, point to the cell or highlight the range, and then click on the appropriate icon. 1-2-3 immediately formats the cell or range.

Setting Worksheet Titles

It often happens that labels identifying columns and rows are placed at the top or left edges of a worksheet, and that these labels scroll off the screen as you move around the worksheet. The Worksheet Titles command lets you freeze the rows or columns (or both) of labels at these edges. The labels stay in place when you move around the worksheet, making it easier for you to identify the contents of cells by their row or column headings. For example, in a worksheet with the months of the year entered in the top row, setting the top row as a title keeps the labels visible no matter how far down in the worksheet you move.

Before setting worksheet titles, you must move the cell pointer to a cell just to the right of the column you want to set as a vertical title, or just below the row you want to set as a horizontal title. If you want to set both horizontal and vertical titles, place the pointer in the cell to the right of the column to be set and beneath the row.

You are going to use the "Both" option of the Worksheet Titles command to make it easier to use the Home Budget worksheet. You will freeze the labels in column A, and in rows 1 through 4.

Press: |HOME|

Move to: cell B5

Choose: **Worksheet   Titles**

The Worksheet Titles dialog box displays these options:

Horizontal   Vertical   Both   Clear

Select: **Both   OK**

The dialog box disappears and the titles are frozen. Figure 4-39 shows how you can scroll the worksheet down and to the right, and still have 1-2-3 display the worksheet titles.

Figure 4-39: **Worksheet Titles Freeze One or More Border Rows, Columns, or Both**

	A	G	H	I	J	K	L
1	Bob and Kathy Gordon						
2		Jun	Jul	Aug	Sep	Oct	
3							
4							
21	EXPENSES						
22							
23	Auto	150	150	150	150	150	
24	Charity	75	75	75	75	75	
25	Clothes	200	200	200	200	200	
26	Food	700	875	700	700	875	
27	Household	200	200	200	200	200	
28	Medical	150	150	150	150	150	
29	Misc	900	1,125	900	900	1,125	
30	Rent	1,100	1,100	1,100	1,100	1,100	1,
31	Savings	400	500	400	400	500	
32	Utility	200	200	200	200	200	
33	Woodwork	250	250	250	250	250	
34							
35	Total Expenses	$4,325	$4,825	$4,325	$4,325	$4,825	$4,
36							

1-2-3 will not allow you to move the cell pointer to the rows and columns you have frozen except with the Goto key or the Range Go To command. For example, the cell pointer does not move to cell A1 when you press Home, but moves instead to the new home position, below and to the right of the worksheet titles you froze (cell B5). Experiment with moving the cell pointer around, then press Home to return the cell pointer to B5:

Press: |HOME|

■ *NOTE:* You can clear worksheet titles with the "Clear" option of the Worksheet Titles command, described later in this chapter.

Inserting and Deleting Rows and Columns

This section demonstrates how to insert and delete rows and columns. It uses the Worksheet Insert and Worksheet Delete commands to complete the budget worksheet.

Inserting One Row You are going to insert a blank row in a worksheet. Begin by placing the cell pointer in the row above which you want the new row to appear.

Move to: *any cell in row 13* *(notice that you can't move to A13)*

Choose: Worksheet Insert

Select: Row OK

Figure 4-40: Inserting a Row

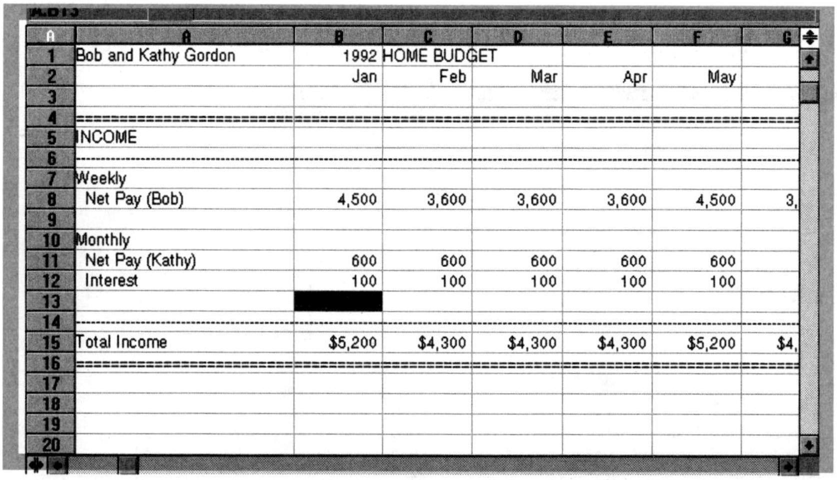

As you can see in Figure 4-40, this command adds a new, blank row above the original row 13. Notice that each cell in the worksheet below the new row has a new cell address. The label Total Income, for example, was in cell A14 and is now in cell A15.

Also notice that if the worksheet contains formulas that refer to a range and you insert or delete a row or column within that range, the cell addresses in the formulas change to reflect the new range. For example, the @SUM formula that calculates total income for January now refers to the range B8..B14 instead of the range B8..B13. This convenient feature makes it easy to insert entries in columns of figures without having to rewrite the formulas that operate on those figures. For instance, the blank row you just inserted does not affect the values for total income; however, if you were to put values in row 13 (to indicate a new source of monthly income for Bob and Kathy), the new values would automatically be added to the total income values in row 15.

Finally, notice that any cells with local formats (such as the cells formatted as Currency in the **Total Income** row) retain their local formats when the cells shift position. Newly-inserted rows, on the other hand, are completely blank and unformatted, even if the rows they displace contain locally formatted cells.

Inserting More than One Row   To insert more than one row, highlight the area in which you want the rows inserted, and then choose the "Row" option of the Worksheet Insert command. For example, try inserting two rows below the row labeled **Net Pay (Bob)**:

Move to: *any cell in row 9*

Highlight: *at least one cell in each of rows 9 and 10*

Choose: **Worksheet   Insert**

Select: **Row   OK**

This procedure inserts new, blank rows in rows 9 and 10, and moves everything else down two rows.

Figure 4-41:   Inserting More Than One Row

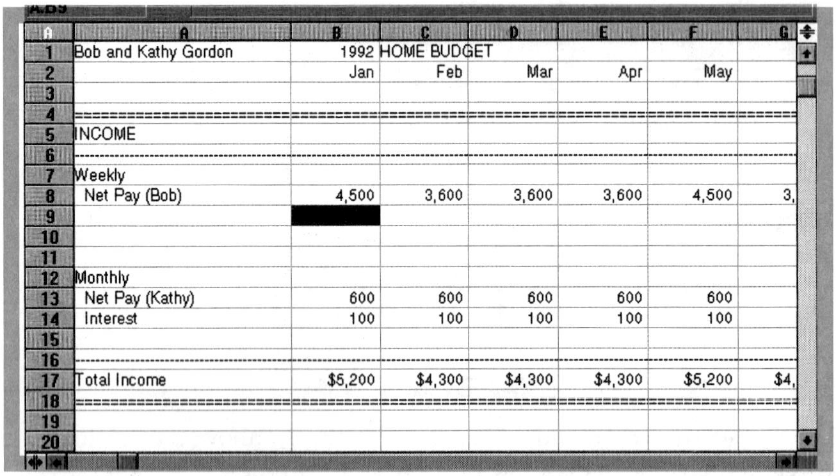

	A	B	C	D	E	F	G
1	Bob and Kathy Gordon	1992 HOME BUDGET					
2		Jan	Feb	Mar	Apr	May	
3							
4							
5	INCOME						
6							
7	Weekly						
8	Net Pay (Bob)	4,500	3,600	3,600	3,600	4,500	3,
9							
10							
11							
12	Monthly						
13	Net Pay (Kathy)	600	600	600	600	600	
14	Interest	100	100	100	100	100	
15							
16							
17	Total Income	$5,200	$4,300	$4,300	$4,300	$5,200	$4,
18							
19							
20							

Notice how 1-2-3 has again adjusted the formulas in the row labeled **Total Income** to reflect the new range.

Move to: cell B17

The control panel shows that this cell now contains the formula @SUM(B8..B16), which includes the rows you just inserted.

■ *CAUTION:*   Be careful when you insert or delete rows. Rows are inserted or deleted all the way across the worksheet, out to column IV. Make sure that inserting or deleting one or more rows in one part of the worksheet will not disturb a part of the worksheet to the right or the left of the part you are viewing.

Deleting Rows

Deleting rows works just like inserting rows, but in reverse. Use the "Row" option of the Worksheet Delete command to eliminate the extra rows you just added:

Move to: *any cell in row 15*
Choose: Worksheet   Delete
Select: Row   OK

1-2-3 deletes the blank row 15 and moves everything below it up one row. Now delete the two blank rows you inserted beneath row 8:

Move to: *any cell in row 9*
Highlight: *at least one cell in each of rows 9 and 10*
Choose: Worksheet   Delete
Select: Row   OK

1-2-3 deletes these rows and restores the cell references in the formulas in row 14 to their original addresses.

Move to: cell B14

The control panel displays the original formula: @SUM(B8..B13)

Inserting and Deleting Columns

The procedures for inserting and deleting columns are similar to the ones for inserting and deleting rows.

To insert one or more columns, (1) highlight at least one cell in the range in which you want the new column or columns to appear; (2) select the "Column" option of the Worksheet Insert command; and then (3) select OK or press Enter to complete the command. 1-2-3 shifts all the columns to the right of the highlighted area to make room for the new column or columns and adjusts cell references as needed.

To delete one or more columns, (1) highlight at least one cell in each of the columns you want to delete; (2) select the "Column" option of the Worksheet Insert command; and then (3) select OK or press Enter to complete the command. 1-2-3 deletes the highlighted column or columns and shifts all the columns to the right of the highlighted area to fill in the gap left by the deleted column(s). 1-2-3 also adjusts cell references as needed.

■ *CAUTION:*   Be careful when you insert or delete columns. Columns are inserted or deleted all the way down the worksheet, to row 8192. Make sure that inserting or deleting one or more columns in one part of the worksheet will not disturb a part of the worksheet above or below the part you are viewing.

Before you go on to the next section, move the cell pointer to the scratch worksheet (by pressing Control+Page Up), and practice inserting and deleting columns and rows on your own. When you have finished practicing, return to the Home Budget worksheet by pressing Control+Page Down.

Using Edit Move Cells

The last clean-up task is to adjust the CASH FLOW section of the worksheet so that it lines up better when you page down through the worksheet. You are going to do this by using Edit Move Cells.

Edit Move Cells allows you to rearrange worksheets and worksheet files. In effect, you can lift a piece of the worksheet from one area and replace it in a different area. Using Edit Move Cells with labels and numbers is similar to using Edit Quick Copy followed by Edit Clear (or Edit Cut followed by Edit Paste). However, if the cells you are moving contain formulas, the effect is quite different.

As you recall, Edit Quick Copy adjusts relative references so that copied formulas are in the same relationship to the cells they refer to as the original formula is to the cells it refers to. For example, if a formula refers to the cell two rows down and one row to the right, each copy of the formula cell refers to the cell one row down and two rows to *its* right. This address adjustment is convenient when you want to apply the same basic formula to different data.

Edit Move Cells, on the other hand, adjusts relative references so that moved formulas operate on the same data they operated on before. 1-2-3 assumes that you want the formula to perform exactly as it did—you just want it to appear somewhere else in the worksheet file.

Consequently, if you want to rearrange a worksheet file, it is usually easier to use Edit Move Cells than it is to use either Edit Quick Copy and Edit Clear, or Edit Cut and Edit Paste, since 1-2-3 makes sure that moved formula cells still refer to the original cells; you don't have to worry about formula references changing. Also, you can accomplish this rearrangement in one simple operation.

■ *CAUTION:*   Like Edit Quick Copy, Edit Move Cells overwrites the cells in the "to" range with the data in the "from" range. Before you complete an Edit Move Cells operation, make sure there is nothing in the "to" range that you care about. If you do inadvertently overwrite important data, press Alt+Backspace before you do anything that changes the worksheet environment, so that you can undo the move.

To see how Edit Move Cells works, press Home and then page down to the CASH FLOW section:

Press: HOME

                    PGDN   *two times*

Figure 4-42:   The "Unimproved" View of the CASH FLOW Section

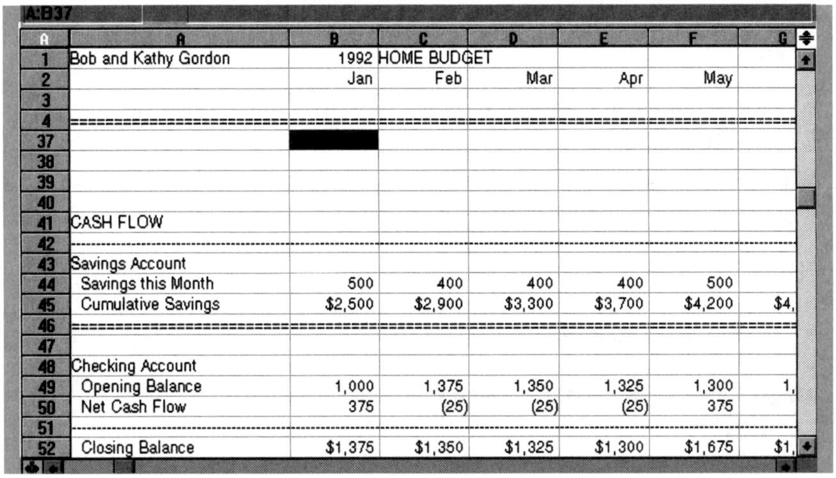

A	B	C	D	E	F	G
A:B37						
	A	**B**	**C**	**D**	**E**	**F**	**G**
1	Bob and Kathy Gordon	1992 HOME BUDGET					
2		Jan	Feb	Mar	Apr	May	
3							
4	=================	=====	=====	=====	=====	=====	====
37							
38							
39							
40							
41	CASH FLOW						
42	--------						
43	Savings Account						
44	Savings this Month	500	400	400	400	500	
45	Cumulative Savings	$2,500	$2,900	$3,300	$3,700	$4,200	$4,
46	=================	=====	=====	=====	=====	=====	====
47							
48	Checking Account						
49	Opening Balance	1,000	1,375	1,350	1,325	1,300	1,
50	Net Cash Flow	375	(25)	(25)	(25)	375	
51	--------						
52	Closing Balance	$1,375	$1,350	$1,325	$1,300	$1,675	$1,

Notice that, because of the worksheet titles you established earlier, paging down to the CASH FLOW section now produces a display with a few extra blank rows below the titles. To clean up the CASH FLOW display, use Edit Move Cells to move the formulas and labels in the CASH FLOW section up four rows.

1. Clear worksheet titles.

First, clear the worksheet titles, so that you will be able to move the cell pointer into column A:

Choose: Worksheet   Titles
Select: Clear   OK

1-2-3 unfreezes the titles. After you have made your changes, you can reestablish worksheet titles.

2. Move the CASH FLOW section up four rows.

Highlight: A41..M56   *(the CASH FLOW section)*
Choose: Edit   Move Cells
Specify: A37   *in the To: text box*
Select: OK

1-2-3 moves the section up four rows.

3. Reestablish worksheet titles.

Finally, restore the worksheet titles to their former setting.

Remember that 1-2-3 always sets worksheet titles from the current cell position; therefore, to freeze the same rows and columns you froze before, you must return to the cell from which you initially set worksheet titles.

Press: |HOME|

Move to: cell B5

Now reestablish the worksheet titles, and then page down to the CASH FLOW section again to see the results of your handiwork.

Choose: Worksheet Titles

Select: Both OK

Press: |PGDN| *two times*

Figure 4-43:   The "Improved" View of the CASH FLOW Section

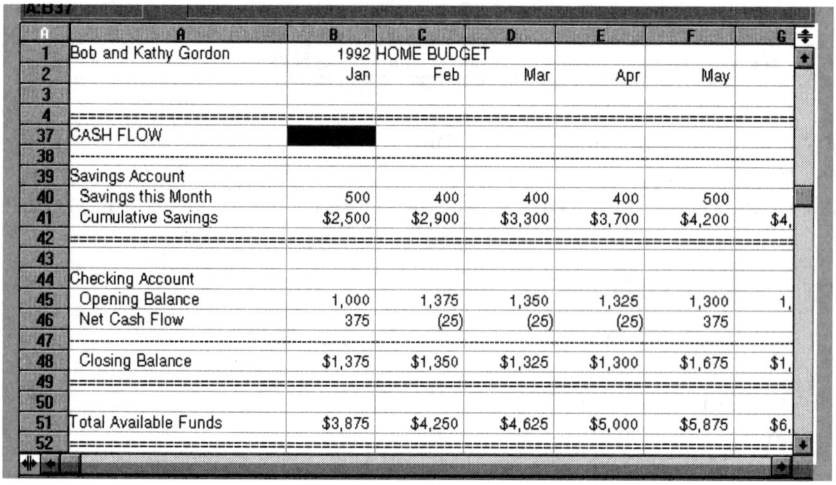

	A	B	C	D	E	F	G
1	Bob and Kathy Gordon	1992 HOME BUDGET					
2		Jan	Feb	Mar	Apr	May	
3							
4	======	======	======	======	======	======	
37	CASH FLOW						
38							
39	Savings Account						
40	Savings this Month	500	400	400	400	500	
41	Cumulative Savings	$2,500	$2,900	$3,300	$3,700	$4,200	$4,
42	======	======	======	======	======	======	
43							
44	Checking Account						
45	Opening Balance	1,000	1,375	1,350	1,325	1,300	1,
46	Net Cash Flow	375	(25)	(25)	(25)	375	
47							
48	Closing Balance	$1,375	$1,350	$1,325	$1,300	$1,675	$1,
49	======	======	======	======	======	======	
50							
51	Total Available Funds	$3,875	$4,250	$4,625	$5,000	$5,875	$6,
52	======	======	======	======	======	======	

4. Save BUDGET1.WK3.

Congratulations! At last, you are finished building this version of the Home Budget worksheet. Save the file, and bill Bob Gordon for your time.

Press: |HOME|

Choose: File Save

Press: ⏎

If you printed out the spreadsheet area of the worksheet at this point, it would look something like Figure 4-44. (Printing worksheets is described in Chapter 8.)

Figure 4-44 The Completed Home Budget Spreadsheet

Bob and Kathy Gordon — 1992 HOME BUDGET

	Jan	Feb	Mar	Apr	May	Jun	Jul	Aug	Sep	Oct	Nov	Dec	Annual
INCOME													
Weekly													
Net Pay (Bob)	4,500	3,600	3,600	3,600	4,500	3,600	4,500	3,600	3,600	4,500	3,600	3,600	46,800
Monthly													
Net Pay (Kathy)	600	600	600	600	600	600	600	600	600	600	600	600	7,200
Interest	100	100	100	100	100	100	100	100	100	100	100	100	1,200
Total Income	$5,200	$4,300	$4,300	$4,300	$5,200	$4,300	$5,200	$4,300	$4,300	$5,200	$4,300	$4,300	$55,200
EXPENSES													
Auto	150	150	150	150	150	150	150	150	150	150	150	150	1,800
Charity	75	75	75	75	75	75	75	75	75	75	75	75	900
Clothes	200	200	200	200	200	200	200	200	200	200	200	200	2,400
Food	875	700	700	700	875	700	875	700	700	875	700	700	9,100
Household	200	200	200	200	200	200	200	200	200	200	200	200	2,400
Medical	150	150	150	150	150	150	150	150	150	150	150	150	1,800
Misc	1,125	900	900	900	1,125	900	1,125	900	900	1,125	900	900	11,700
Rent	1,100	1,100	1,100	1,100	1,100	1,100	1,100	1,100	1,100	1,100	1,100	1,100	13,200
Savings	500	400	400	400	500	400	500	400	400	500	400	400	5,200
Utility	200	200	200	200	200	200	200	200	200	200	200	200	2,400
Woodwork	250	250	250	250	250	250	250	250	250	250	250	250	3,000
Total Expenses	$4,825	$4,325	$4,325	$4,325	$4,825	$4,325	$4,825	$4,325	$4,325	$4,825	$4,325	$4,325	$53,900
CASH FLOW													
Savings Account													
Savings this Month	500	400	400	400	500	400	500	400	400	500	400	400	
Cumulative Savings	$2,500	$2,900	$3,300	$3,700	$4,200	$4,600	$5,100	$5,500	$5,900	$6,400	$6,800	$7,200	
Checking Account													
Opening Balance	1,000	1,375	1,350	1,325	1,300	1,675	1,650	2,025	2,000	1,975	2,350	2,325	
Net Cash Flow	375	(25)	(25)	(25)	375	(25)	375	(25)	(25)	375	(25)	(25)	
Closing Balance	$1,375	$1,350	$1,325	$1,300	$1,675	$1,650	$2,025	$2,000	$1,975	$2,350	$2,325	$2,300	
Total Available Funds	$3,875	$4,250	$4,625	$5,000	$5,875	$6,250	$7,125	$7,500	$7,875	$8,750	$9,125	$9,500	

A Note on Using the "Move To" SmartIcon   As a shortcut to using Edit Move Cells, you can use the "Move To" SmartIcon to move data and formulas. The "Move To" icon looks like this:

The "Move To" icon lets you specify the "to" range for Edit Move Cells without having to specify the command itself. To use the "Move To" icon, highlight the "from" range, click on the "Move To" icon, and click on the upper left corner of the "to" range. When you release the mouse button, 1-2-3 performs the move operation, exactly as if you had chosen Edit Move Cells.

If you like, experiment with the "Move To" icon by moving data in the scratch worksheet, before you move on to the next section. Whenever the instructions in this book tell you to use Edit Move Cells to move cells, you can use the "Move To" SmartIcon instead.

What-If Analysis

Now that you have created Bob and Kathy's Home Budget, you can use it to illustrate the what if potential of 1-2-3.

What-if analysis asks the question "What would happen if I change some of my assumptions?" It uses the worksheet to predict a new situation, based on the effects of changing one or more variables. For instance, the owner of a business can see how net profit would be affected if he or she switched to a different supplier of materials. A prospective home owner can try out different combinations of term, interest rate, and down payment to see how monthly mortgage payments will vary. The different versions of projected situations are known as *what-if scenarios.*

In this section, you will use what-if analysis to see how changing some of the Home Budget variables affects the opening balance of Bob and Kathy's checking account.

Bob and Kathy decide that they want to take a vacation toward the end of the year, and that the vacation will probably cost them about $2,000. They don't want to take this money out of savings, and as things now stand, they won't have enough cash available by December to take their vacation and still have a little money in reserve. They would like to have at least $3,000 in their checking account before they start their vacation. Currently, their budget shows that they will have $2,325 at the beginning of December (cell M45).

Figure 4-45:   Bob and Kathy's December Checking Account Opening Balance

	A	J	K	L	M	N	
1	Bob and Kathy Gordon						
2		Sep	Oct	Nov	Dec	Annual	
3							
4	================	=====	=====	=====	=====	=====	
37	CASH FLOW						
38							
39	Savings Account						
40	Savings this Month	400	500	400	400		
41	Cumulative Savings	$5,900	$6,400	$6,800	$7,200		
42	================	=====	=====	=====	=====		
43							
44	Checking Account						
45	Opening Balance	2,000	1,975	2,350	2,325		
46	Net Cash Flow	(25)	375	(25)	(25)		

A:M45   +L46

Two methods of acquiring this extra money occur to them: (1) They could cut back on their other expenses (for example, Bob's woodworking hobby), and (2) they could find new sources of income (for instance, Kathy could work an extra morning a week). In the following two examples, they try out each of these what-if scenarios.

■ *NOTE:*　　This section shows the simplest application of 1-2-3's what-if capability. For information on creating what-if tables, see Chapter 6. For an example of how to use graphs for what-if analysis, see Chapter 8. For information on using 1-2-3's Backsolver and Solver, see Chapter 12.

What If Scenario 1: Cutting Back on Expenses

What if Bob cuts his woodworking expenses in half, from $250 a month to $125 a month? What effect would this have on the Gordons' checking account's December Opening Balance?

Move to:　　cell B96　　*(range name WOODWORK)*

Type:　　125　　↵

Figure 4-46:　Changing Bob's Woodworking Expenses

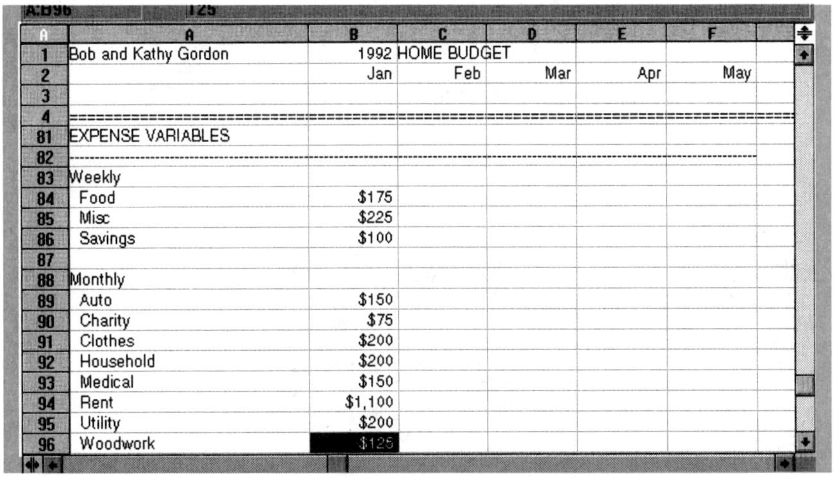

Now move to the CASH FLOW screen and look at the figure for the checking account's December Opening Balance (cell M45):

Figure 4-47:　The New December Balance

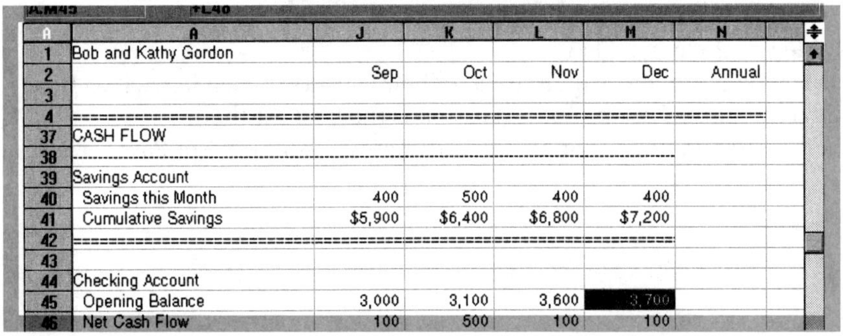

1-2-3 displays the value $3,700 in cell M45. Cutting back on Bob's hobby will allow them to take their vacation.

Notice how other values related to the contents of cell B96, such as the figures for net cash flow in the other months and for opening balance and closing balance, are also updated to reflect the change you made. Compare the current values to those in Figure 4-44.

What-If Scenario 2: Increasing Income

What if Kathy works an extra morning a week? Kathy figures that she could earn another $200 a month if she worked an extra morning. (She thinks she can probably leave Tim with her parents.) Will this allow the Gordon family to take their vacation?

First, restore the original value for Bob's woodworking hobby:

Move to:	cell B96
Type:	250 ↵

Now add $200 to the figure for Kathy's monthly net pay:

Move to:	cell B67
Press:	F2 (EDIT)
Type:	+200 *to increase the value in cell B67 by $200*
Press:	↵

Figure 4-48: Changing Kathy's Earnings

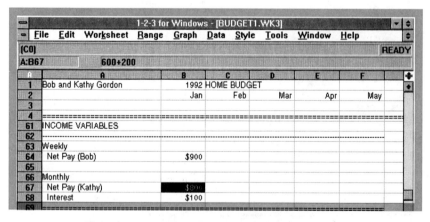

1-2-3 displays the value $4,525 in cell M45.

Increasing Kathy's hours will also allow them to take their vacation. We'll leave it to Bob and Kathy to decide which method of saving for a vacation is the best for them.

To complete this chapter, restore the original figure for Kathy's monthly Net Pay:

Move to: cell B67

Press: ⌕F2⌕ **(EDIT)**

⌕BACKSPACE⌕ *four times, to remove +200*

⌕⏎⌕ ⌕HOME⌕

Finally, save the file either by choosing File Save or clicking the "File Save" SmartIcon.

Figure 4-49: The New December Balance

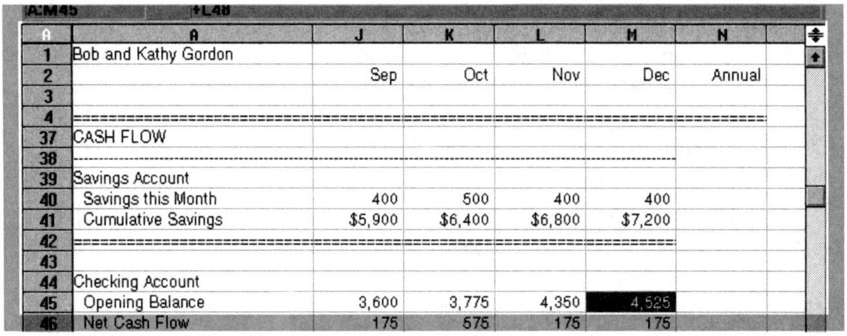

A	J	K	L	M	N
Bob and Kathy Gordon					
	Sep	Oct	Nov	Dec	Annual
====	====	====	====	====	====
CASH FLOW					
Savings Account					
Savings this Month	400	500	400	400	
Cumulative Savings	$5,900	$6,400	$6,800	$7,200	
Checking Account					
Opening Balance	3,600	3,775	4,350	4,525	
Net Cash Flow	175	575	175	175	

At a Glance

In this chapter you have continued your exploration of the 1-2-3 worksheet, completing the Home Budget application you started in Chapter 3 and learning a number of new skills and concepts along the way. Some of these skills and concepts are listed in the following table.

Task	How to Do It:
Entering formulas that include cell addresses, range names, and @functions	Besides entering labels and numbers in a worksheet, you can enter formulas that calculate values based on the values in other worksheet entries. To enter a formula that starts with a cell address or a range name, type a plus sign (+) and then the formula. To use an @function in a formula, type an at-sign (@), followed by the function name, followed by any arguments to the function enclosed in parentheses. (See 1-2-3's on-line Help for detailed information on @functions.)
Overriding order of precedence	If you want a formula to be evaluated in an order different from the one 1-2-3 ordinarily uses, put parentheses around the operations you want 1-2-3 to evaluate first.
Using relative, absolute, and mixed cell references	1-2-3 uses relative references by default. To create absolute or mixed cell references, precede the part of the cell reference that you want to be absolute (worksheet letter, column letter, row number, or any combination of the three) with a dollar sign ($). To change between types of cell references, use the Absolute function key (F4 in POINT or EDIT mode). To make a range name absolute, precede it with a dollar sign ($).

Task	How to Do It:
Creating range names	You can use range names instead of cell addresses in commands and formulas. Range names are easier to remember than their corresponding cell addresses and they clarify the meaning of formulas. You create range names with the Range Name Create or the Range Name Label Create commands. You delete range names with Range Name Delete.
Searching for and replacing cell entries	To quickly locate (and, if desired, change) specific entries in a worksheet, you can use the Edit Find commands. Edit Find lets you find, or find and replace, entire entries or parts of entries in label and formula cells.
Changing cell formats	To improve the appearance of a worksheet and clarify the meaning of its numbers, you can use 1-2-3's formatting commands. The Worksheet Global Settings "Format" options change the default cell format for the worksheet file. The Range Format options change the format of specified cells. Changes made with Range Format are not affected by later changes to the global format.
Preselecting ranges	For many 1-2-3 commands, it's easiest to preselect the range you want to change. To preselect a range with the mouse, move to the first cell in the range, press the left mouse button, and hold down the button while you drag the mouse to highlight the range. When you have finished, release the mouse button. To use the keyboard, make sure you are in READY mode or POINT mode, then press F4. Use the pointer-movement keys to specify the range you want to preselect, then press Enter to complete the selection. 1-2-3 automatically uses that range in commands that require a range specification. To clear a highlighted range, either move the cell pointer or press Escape. To use the same range with another command, execute the command without first pressing Escape or moving the cell pointer.
Setting worksheet titles	Use the Worksheet Titles options to "freeze" rows and columns at the beginning of the worksheet so they remain in view as you scroll through the rest of the worksheet. To set horizontal titles, position the cell pointer below the title row or rows, choose Worksheet Titles, select "Horizontal", and then select OK. To set vertical titles, position the cell pointer to the right of the title column or columns, choose Worksheet Titles, select "Vertical", and then select OK. Select "Both" in the Worksheet Titles dialog box to simultaneously set horizontal and vertical titles, and select "Clear" to clear worksheet titles.
Inserting and deleting rows and columns	The Worksheet Insert and Delete commands let you add and remove rows and columns in the worksheet. For example, to insert one or more rows, highlight at least one cell in each row of the area in which you want a blank row inserted, choose Worksheet Insert, select "Row", and then select OK. To delete one or more rows, highlight at least one cell in each row you want to delete, choose Worksheet Delete, select "Row", and then select OK. When you insert and delete rows and columns, 1-2-3 automatically adjusts cell references in formulas as necessary.

Task	How to Do It:
Moving a range of cells	Edit Move Cells provides a quick and easy way to reorganize data in the worksheet. Highlight the range to move "from," choose Edit Move Cells, specify the "to" range in the "To:" text box, and then select OK. You can also move cells by highlighting the "from" range, clicking the "Move To" SmartIcon, and then clicking the "to" range. In either case, unlike Edit Quick Copy, Edit Move Cells does not adjust relative cell references in formulas.
Performing simple what-if analysis	Change the value of one or more worksheet variables to see how the results of formulas that refer to those variables change. What-if analysis can help in budgeting, home buying, and sales planning decisions, or in any other matter in which you must make decisions about costs, expenditures, allocations, or other factors involving numbers. NOTE: There are many ways to perform what-if analysis in 1-2-3. In addition to the simple method presented in this chapter, Chapter 6 shows you how to create what-if tables, Chapter 8 shows you how to graph a what-if scenario, and Chapter 12 shows you how to use 1-2-3's Backsolver and Solver.

Chapter 5

More Worksheet Skills

There are many ways to make 1-2-3 spreadsheet applications efficient and easy to use. You learned a number of application-building techniques for single-worksheet files in Chapters 3 and 4, as you created a Home Budget model. In this chapter, you'll practice some of those techniques and familiarize yourself with several important new ones as you create a multiple-worksheet application: A Cash Flow Forecast for a small business Bob Gordon is thinking of starting.

What You'll Learn

Much of this chapter is dedicated to teaching you about one of the most powerful features of 1-2-3—the ability to create and use more than one worksheet in a file. You will learn to navigate in a multiple-worksheet environment and to construct applications that take advantage of this feature. Along the way, you'll also learn some new principles for setting up 1-2-3 applications, and several additional 1-2-3 skills. By the time you have finished this chapter, you will know how to:

- **Construct and use worksheet templates**

- **Insert and delete worksheets**

- **Move information from one worksheet to another**

- **Change the width of specified columns over several worksheets**

- **Group similar worksheets together**

- **Consolidate information from several worksheets**

- **Copy a range to multiple worksheets**

- **Find data within a range of worksheets**

- **Use window panes and perspective view**

- **Center labels in a range**

- **Correct the display of numbers displayed as asterisks**

- **Change the global column width**

- ■ Protect a worksheet

- ■ Unprotect specific cells within a protected worksheet

In addition, at the end of the chapter, you'll learn some techniques for avoiding, finding, and correcting errors in a worksheet's logic and structure, and you will acquire a new store of tips that apply to any work you do in a 1-2-3 worksheet.

Before You Start

Before you begin the exercises in this chapter, start 1-2-3. Make sure that the cell pointer is in cell A:A1 of a new, blank worksheet file, and that 1-2-3 is set up to save files in your 123BOOK directory.

A Note on Example Layout   As in previous chapters, the examples in this chapter assume that your screen displays 20 rows and eight columns when the Worksheet window is maximized. If your display does not show 20 rows and eight columns, your screens will look somewhat different from the illustrations, but you can still do all the examples. Just be sure to use the cell addresses and ranges specified in the instructions.

A Note on Keystroke Instructions   The keystroke instructions in this chapter often assume you are using a mouse to perform such operations as highlighting a range or selecting an option in a dialog box. You can also use the keyboard to perform the same operations. Many of the keyboard equivalents to mouse operations have been described in previous chapters. A few of the most common ones are summarized here. For a complete list of keystroke equivalents to mouse operations, see the 1-2-3 documentation or the 1-2-3 on-line Help.

Keyboard Equivalents to Mouse Operations

Operation	Instruction		Keyboard Equivalent
Complete action and close dialog box	**Select:**	OK	**Press:** ⏎
Cancel action and close dialog box	**Select:**	Cancel	**Press:** ESC
Highlight a text box	**Select:**	text box	**Press:** ALT+*underlined_letter*
Edit a range in a text box	**Select:** **Specify:**	Range A:A1..C:D4	**Press:** ALT+*underlined_letter* F2 (EDIT)
Edit a number or word in a text box	**Select:** **Specify:** *(or click on text and edit it)*	text box new text	**Press:** ALT+*underlined_letter* **Type:** new text *(or press Left arrow and edit text)*
Highlight a range	**Highlight:** A:A1..C:D4		**Move to:** cell A:A1 **Press:** F4 **Move to:** cell D4 **Press:** ⏎

Multiple Worksheets in Memory

So far, your use of 1-2-3 has been confined mostly to a single, two-dimensional worksheet. However, 1-2-3 is actually a three-dimensional spreadsheet product. If your computer has enough memory, you can have as many as 256 separate worksheets available to you in any session. Any cell in any of these worksheets can refer to any other cell, and any command that uses a two-dimensional range can also use a three-dimensional range.

Figure 5-1: Highlighting a Three-Dimensional Range

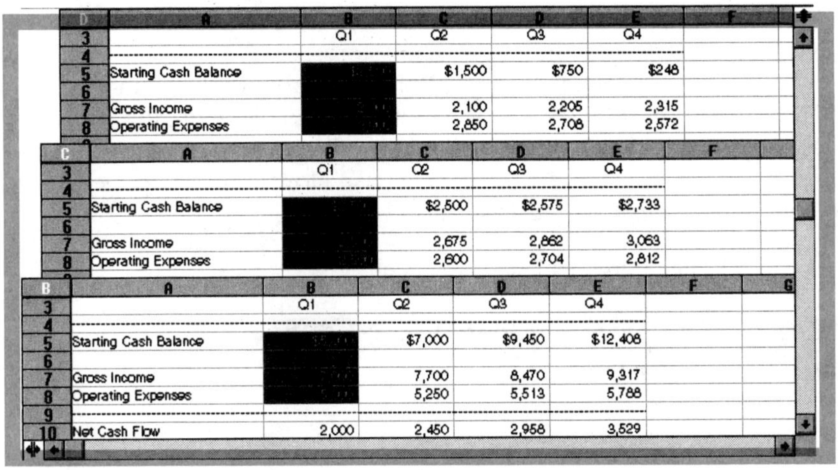

Multiple worksheets were introduced with 1-2-3 Release 3 for DOS. They make it easier for you to do two things: (1) Create consolidations and other applications best constructed in three dimensions; and (2) physically separate logically distinct sections of an application. This chapter shows you how to do each of these operations, first by leading you through the process of creating a new multiple-worksheet application (a Cash Flow Forecast), and then by showing you how to rearrange a two-dimensional worksheet (the Home Budget application) so that it takes advantage of multiple worksheets to simplify its design.

The Cash Flow Forecast Model

The multiple-worksheet application you will build in this chapter continues the saga of Bob Gordon and his rise to wealth, power, and fluency with 1-2-3.

In Chapters 3 and 4, Bob took some steps toward organizing his finances by building a Home Budget. Now, he wonders if he can turn his hobby, woodworking, into a profit-making enterprise. One day, while watching his son pit robots from outer space against plastic dinosaurs, an idea hits him. Although Bob has never much cared for the strange toys children play with, he knows kids like them better than the more wholesome-looking toys their parents prefer. It occurs to him that he has the skills and equipment to create toys that appeal to both generations: toys with a dual identity.

Bob's toys would be made of wood and painted in simple, primary colors. In their "normal" state, they would resemble characters in tales from Mother Goose, the Brothers Grimm, and other classic children's stories. However, in their "magic" state, Bob's figures change into superhuman robots with nearly invincible powers.

As he looks over the Annual column of the Home Budget, Bob figures he has about $10,000 to play with: The $3,000 he was already planning to spend on woodworking, the $5,200 he and Kathy planned to save this year, and another $1,800 from a bonus he expects to receive in May. $10,000 isn't a lot to start with, but it might be enough. Besides, there is always the possibility of attracting investors or taking out loans. Bob decides to give it a go, at least on paper.

He will design his first characters around the Snow White story.

Sitting in his workshop, roughing out the first dwarf, Bob thinks about the fortune he'll make—his toys in every department store, the book, the movie, the comic book, the T-shirts. Then he shakes off fantasy and decides to see what he might be able to do with the resources at hand. Stand in his shoes, now, as he uses 1-2-3 to create a Cash Flow Forecast application for the little company he tentatively calls Folktale Workshop.

Figure 5-2: Summary Worksheet of Bob Gordon's Completed Cash Flow Forecast

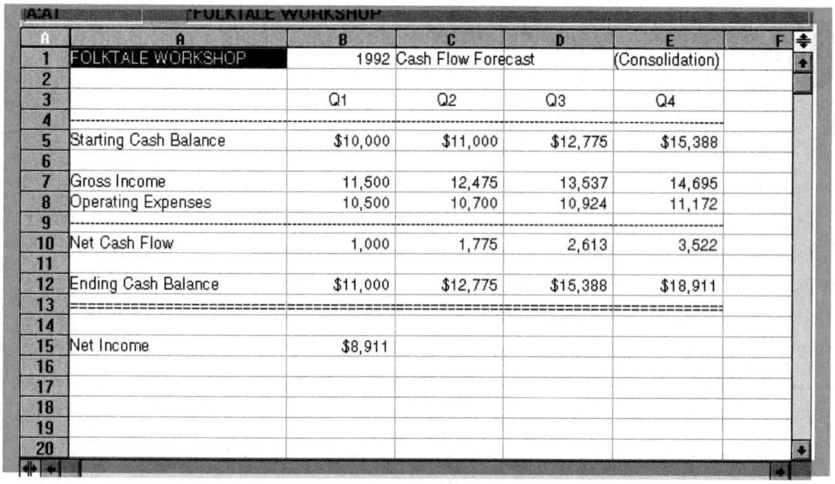

A	B	C	D	E	F
1 FOLKTALE WORKSHOP	1992 Cash Flow Forecast			(Consolidation)	
2					
3	Q1	Q2	Q3	Q4	
4					
5 Starting Cash Balance	$10,000	$11,000	$12,775	$15,388	
6					
7 Gross Income	11,500	12,475	13,537	14,695	
8 Operating Expenses	10,500	10,700	10,924	11,172	
9					
10 Net Cash Flow	1,000	1,775	2,613	3,522	
11					
12 Ending Cash Balance	$11,000	$12,775	$15,388	$18,911	
13					
14					
15 Net Income	$8,911				
16					
17					
18					
19					
20					

Creating the Cash Flow Forecast Application

The Cash Flow Forecast application consists of five worksheets in a single worksheet file:

- One worksheet for each of the three products Bob intends to build in 1992
- A summary forecast worksheet
- A template forecast for one more product Bob's not sure he'll get to this year

To build this application, you are going to do the following:

1. *Create a single forecast for one product, the Snow White toy.* You'll use this forecast as a model for the other forecasts.

2. *Create a template for the remaining product forecasts.* You'll build the template from a copy of the SNOW WHITE forecast.

3. *Duplicate the template for the remaining products.* You will use the "Sheet" option of the Worksheet Insert command to add additional worksheets to the worksheet file, then you'll copy the template to each of the new worksheets.

4. *Create a summary forecast.* The summary forecast rolls up the income, expenses, and cash balances for all the products Bob will make, creating totals for the whole company. You will make this worksheet the first in the file.

5. *Fill in some of the templates.* You will fill in forecast values for two more products, DWARF1 and DWARF2. These values will be reflected in the summary forecast.

Building the First Forecast

Bob decides that a Snow White doll will be his first creation. He makes some rough calculations and comes up with what is known as an order-of-magnitude estimate. (An order-of-magnitude estimate is the first—and the coarsest—of several types of estimates someone might normally make in the process of planning a new product.)

Bob calculates a unit cost for each toy, a trial price, and the number of toys he thinks he can sell in the first quarter. From these figures, he arrives at estimates for his gross income and operating expenses for the quarter. Finally, he estimates how much his operating expenses and gross income will increase or decrease each subsequent quarter.

With these rough figures in hand, Bob builds a worksheet to help him forecast his net income (profit or loss) for each quarter of 1992. Figure 5-3 shows how this worksheet will look when the Cash Flow Forecast is finished.

Figure 5-3: The Snow White Product Cash Flow Forecast

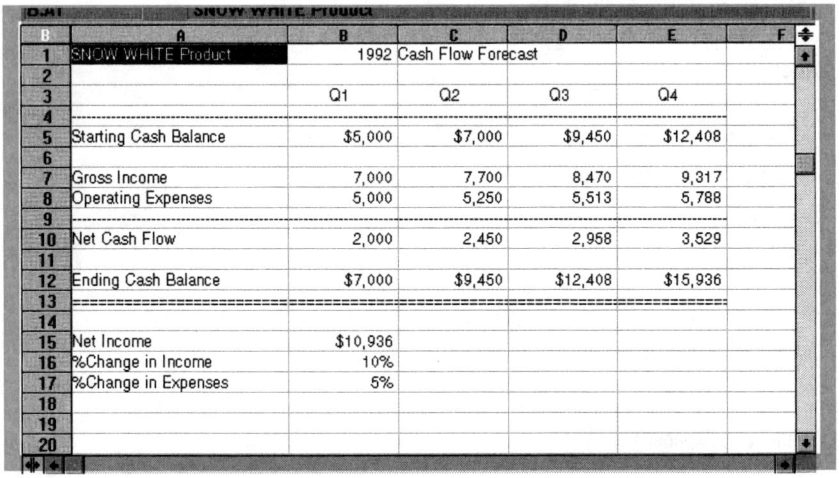

	A	B	C	D	E	F
1	SNOW WHITE Product	1992 Cash Flow Forecast				
2						
3		Q1	Q2	Q3	Q4	
4						
5	Starting Cash Balance	$5,000	$7,000	$9,450	$12,408	
6						
7	Gross Income	7,000	7,700	8,470	9,317	
8	Operating Expenses	5,000	5,250	5,513	5,788	
9						
10	Net Cash Flow	2,000	2,450	2,958	3,529	
11						
12	Ending Cash Balance	$7,000	$9,450	$12,408	$15,936	
13						
14						
15	Net Income	$10,936				
16	%Change in Income	10%				
17	%Change in Expenses	5%				
18						
19						
20						

Since this forecast is a quick-and-dirty projection (and to keep the example simple), you will not create a separate section for variables as you did with the Home Budget. Instead, you are going to enter many of the values directly into the forecast itself. However, to make it easier to experiment with the values for %Change in Income and %Change in Expenses, you will create variables for these numbers.

Building this forecast is the most time-consuming step in the process of creating the Cash Flow Forecast. Once you have completed this forecast, you will be nearly finished with the structure of the application.

1. Change the width of column A to 22.

You will be entering long labels into column A; widen it so they'll be displayed correctly. With the cell pointer in cell A:A1 of a blank, untitled worksheet file:

Choose:	Worksheet Column Width
Select:	Set width to
Type:	22 *in the text box*
Select:	OK

The new width of the column appears in the format line of the control panel, above the current cell's address.

■ *NOTE:*   You can also use the mouse to change the width of a column. Point to the line to the right of the column letter in the top worksheet border and then drag the line until the column is the width you want.

2. Enter the labels in the SNOW WHITE forecast.

Use Setup Table 5-1 to help you enter the labels in the SNOW WHITE forecast. When you are finished, your worksheet should look like Figure 5-4 (shown on next page).

Setup Table 5-1:   SNOW WHITE Forecast Labels

Cell Address	Label
A1	SNOW WHITE Product
A5	Starting Cash Balance
A7	Gross Income
A8	Operating Expenses
A10	Net Cash Flow
A12	Ending Cash Balance
A16	%Change in Income
A17	%Change in Expenses

Cell Address	Label
C1	Cash Flow Forecast
B3	Q1
C3	Q2
D3	Q3
E3	Q4

Figure 5-4

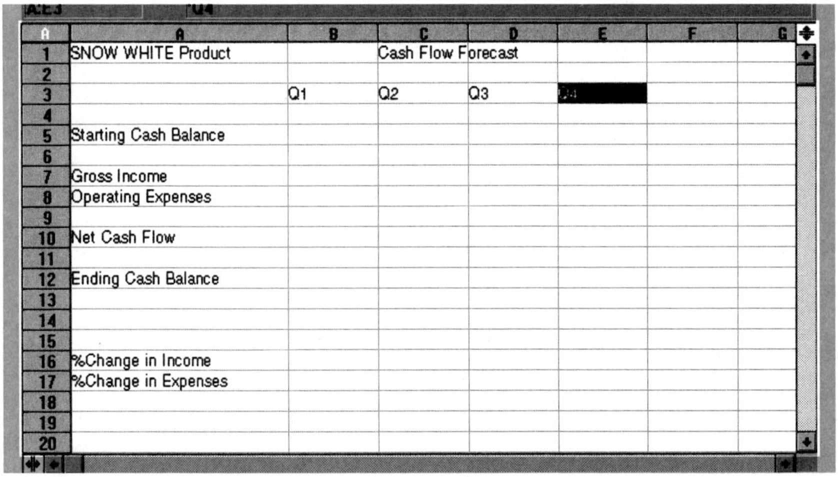

3. Center the Q1 - Q4 labels.

Normally, 1-2-3 uses the default label prefix to determine how to place labels over columns. Unless you have changed the default system setting, 1-2-3 has left-aligned the labels you entered. Use the "Align label" option of the Style Alignment command to center the labels for Q1 through Q4.

Highlight: B3..E3
Choose: `Style`   `Alignment`
Select: `Center`   `OK`

1-2-3 changes the existing label prefix characters in the specified range from the apostrophe (') to the caret (^), centering the labels.

You can also use a SmartIcon to align labels. For example, to center the Q1 - Q4 labels, highlight the range B3..E3 and then click on the "Align Center" icon. If you wish, experiment with these SmartIcons now, while B3..E3 is still highlighted. The icons for aligning labels look like this:

4. Enter the SNOW WHITE values and variables.

Bob puts half of his available $10,000 toward SNOW WHITE. He estimates that he will take in $7,000 in the first quarter, with operating expenses for the quarter totalling $5,000. He also estimates that earnings will increase by 10% each quarter, while expenses will go up only 5%.

Enter the year in cell B1, then enter the values for the SNOW WHITE forecast in column B of the worksheet. When you are finished, your worksheet should look like Figure 5-5.

Move to:	cell B1
Type:	1992
Press:	↓ *four times*
Type:	5000
Press:	↓ *two times*
Type:	7000 ↓
	5000 ↵
Move to:	cell B16
Type:	10% ↓
	5% ↵

Figure 5-5

	A	B	C	D	E	F	G
1	SNOW WHITE Product		1992 Cash Flow Forecast				
2							
3		Q1	Q2	Q3	Q4		
4							
5	Starting Cash Balance	5000					
6							
7	Gross Income	7000					
8	Operating Expenses	5000					
9							
10	Net Cash Flow						
11							
12	Ending Cash Balance						
13							
14							
15							
16	%Change in Income	0.1					
17	%Change in Expenses	0.05					
18							
19							
20							

A:B17   0.05

Notice that 1-2-3 automatically enters 10% as 0.1 and 5% as 0.05. You'll format all of the numbers later.

5. Enter the formulas for Q1 in column B.

The forecast uses formulas to figure out net cash flow and ending cash balance. Net cash flow is calculated as follows:

```
Net Cash Flow = (Gross Income)-(Operating Expenses)
```

Net cash flow is a positive number if Bob makes a profit in the quarter, and negative if he takes a loss. For example, the net cash flow for Q1, the first quarter of 1992, is $7,000-$5,000 = $2,000.

Move to:	cell B10
Type:	+b7−b8
Press:	↓ *two times*

Ending cash balance uses the following formula:

```
Ending Cash Balance = (Starting Cash Balance) + (Net Cash Flow)
```

Type:	+b5+b10 ↵

1-2-3 displays the calculated values for net cash flow and ending cash balance.

Figure 5-6:   Net Cash Flow and Ending Cash Balance Values

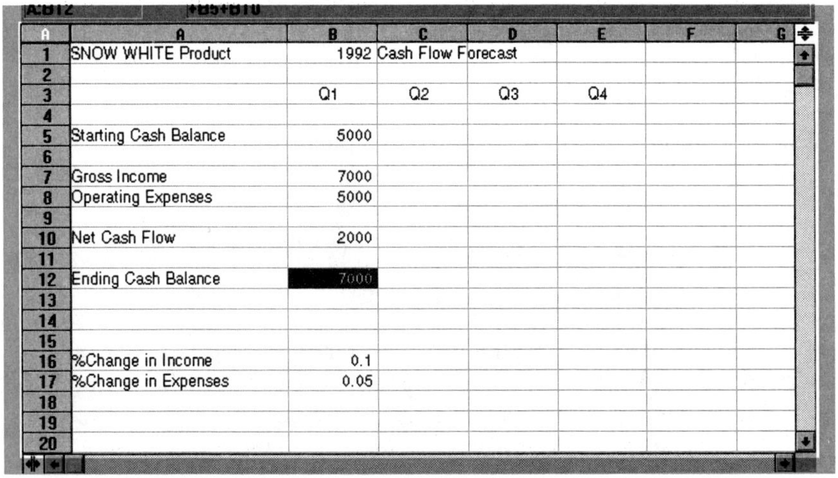

	A	B	C	D	E	F	G
1	SNOW WHITE Product	1992 Cash Flow Forecast					
2							
3		Q1	Q2	Q3	Q4		
4							
5	Starting Cash Balance	5000					
6							
7	Gross Income	7000					
8	Operating Expenses	5000					
9							
10	Net Cash Flow	2000					
11							
12	Ending Cash Balance	7000					
13							
14							
15							
16	%Change in Income	0.1					
17	%Change in Expenses	0.05					
18							
19							
20							

6. Enter the formulas for Q2 in column C.

The Cash Flow Forecast also uses formulas to arrive at projected values for the second, third, and fourth quarters. You will create these formulas in column C, and then copy them to columns D and E.

    The Q2 starting cash balance is equal to the ending cash balance for Q1. Enter the cell reference as a relative cell address. When you copy this cell reference to columns D and E, each copy will point to the ending cash balance of the previous quarter.

Move to:	cell C5
Type:	+b12
Press:	↓ *two times*

    The formula to calculate gross income for Q2, Q3, and Q4 is:

```
Gross Income =
(Gross Income for previous quarter) +
(Gross Income for previous quarter * %Change in Income)
```

    For example, gross income for Q2 is equal to the gross income for Q1 plus 10% of that figure. That is, $7,000 + ($7,000*0.1) = $7,700.

    Enter the cell address for Q1's gross income as a relative address. Enter the cell address of the `%Change in Income` variable as a mixed cell address, with the row and column absolute and the worksheet letter a relative address. When 1-2-3 copies this formula to columns D and E, the relative address will point to the gross income figure for the previous quarter, while the mixed cell address will always point to the same cell in the current worksheet, cell B16.

Type:	+b7+b7*a:b16 ↓

    1-2-3 displays the result: **7700**. Since 1-2-3 performs addition before multiplication, you don't have to enclose **b7*a:b16** in parentheses.

    Operating expenses for the first quarter are calculated in a similar way:

Type:	+b8+b8*a:b17 ↵

    In this case, operating expenses for Q2 are equal to $5,000 + ($5,000*.05) = $5,250.

7. Copy the formulas for net cash flow and ending cash balance.

The formulas for net cash flow and ending cash balance are the same for all quarters. Copy the formulas you created for these values in column B across rows 10 and 12. When you have finished, your worksheet will look like Figure 5-7 (shown on next page).

Highlight:	B10..B12
Choose:	Edit Quick Copy
Specify:	C10..E10 *in the To: text box*
Select:	OK

■ **NOTE:** If you wish, you can use the "Copy To" SmartIcon instead of the Edit Copy command. To do so, highlight the "from" range, click on the icon, and then highlight the "to" range with the "hand" mouse pointer. As you work through this chapter, experiment with using the various means to copy data and formulas that you have learned (Edit Quick Copy, Edit Cut and Edit Paste, and the "Copy To" icon), so that you become comfortable with each one.

Notice that the formulas in columns B and C produce meaningful values, while the formulas in columns D and E display zeros. These formulas will also produce meaningful values as soon as you put values in the cells above them.

Figure 5-7

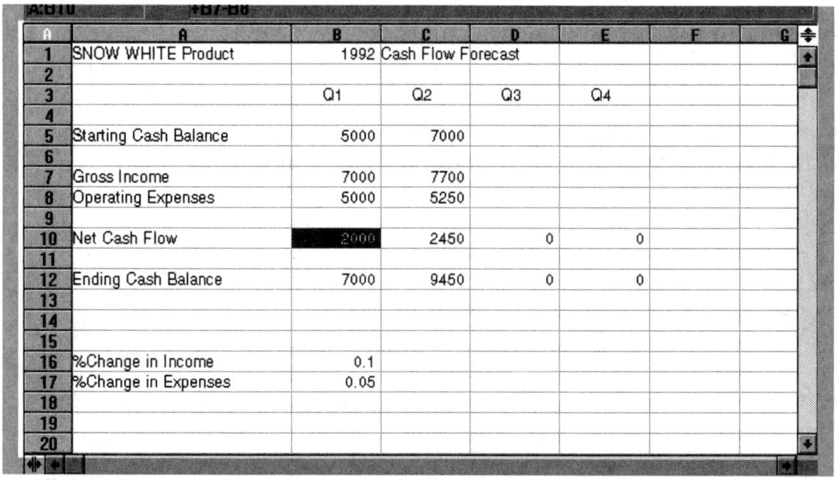

	A	B	C	D	E	F	G
1	SNOW WHITE Product	1992 Cash Flow Forecast					
2							
3		Q1	Q2	Q3	Q4		
4							
5	Starting Cash Balance	5000	7000				
6							
7	Gross Income	7000	7700				
8	Operating Expenses	5000	5250				
9							
10	Net Cash Flow	2000	2450	0	0		
11							
12	Ending Cash Balance	7000	9450	0	0		
13							
14							
15							
16	%Change in Income	0.1					
17	%Change in Expenses	0.05					
18							
19							
20							

8. Copy the remaining formulas for Q2 to columns D and E.

Copying the remaining formulas in column C across the worksheet completes the formulas for SNOW WHITE:

Highlight:	C5..C8
Choose:	Edit Quick Copy
Specify:	D5..E5 *in the To: text box*
Select:	OK

9. Format the worksheet values.

Right now, the values don't look like dollar amounts, but you can fix that in a moment or two. First, change the global format to Comma (,), with zero decimal places:

Choose:	Worksheet Global Settings
Select:	Format...
	, Comma

	Decimal places:
Type:	0 *in the text box*
Select:	OK *two times*

Then format the values in rows 5 and 12 as Currency with zero decimal places.

Highlight:	B5..E5
Choose:	Range Format
Select:	Currency
	Decimal places:
Type:	0 ⏎

If you have a mouse, you can use the "Apply Formatting" icon to format row 12. To do so, click on the icon (it looks like a paintbrush on top of a grid) and then move the mouse pointer into the worksheet. The pointer becomes a paintbrush. Use it to highlight the range B12..E12. When you release the mouse button, the range is formatted.

If you do not have a mouse, use the following keystrokes to format the range:

Highlight:	B12..E12
Choose:	Range Format
Select:	Currency
	Decimal places:
Type:	0 ⏎

Notice that the current year no longer looks like a date. Format it as Fixed with zero decimal places:

Move to:	cell B1
Choose:	Range Format
Select:	Fixed
	Decimal places:
Type:	0 ⏎

And finally, format the values in cells B16 and B17 as Percent with zero decimal places. Do this the same way you formatted other values: highlight the range B16..B17, choose Range Format, select Percent, type 0 in the "Decimal places:" text box, and then select OK to complete the operation. Figure 5-8 shows the results.

10. Create ruled lines to separate sections of the forecast.

Single-ruled lines in the Cash Flow Forecast separate tables from titles and indicate subtotals, while double-ruled lines emphasize final totals.

Setup Table 5-2 describes the ruled lines for the forecast. For now, use the technique you learned in "Using Repeating Labels to Draw Lines" in Chapter 3 to draw ruled lines. (You'll learn some new techniques in Chapter 7.) For each row that is to contain a line, enter either a repeating hyphen (for single-ruled lines) or a repeating equal sign (for double-ruled lines) in the first cell of the row, and copy the cell to the indicated range. If you have a mouse, experiment with using the "Copy To" SmartIcon to create the lines. When you are finished, the worksheet should look like Figure 5-9.

Figure 5-8:   The Cash Flow Forecast Worksheet With Globally and Locally Formatted Values

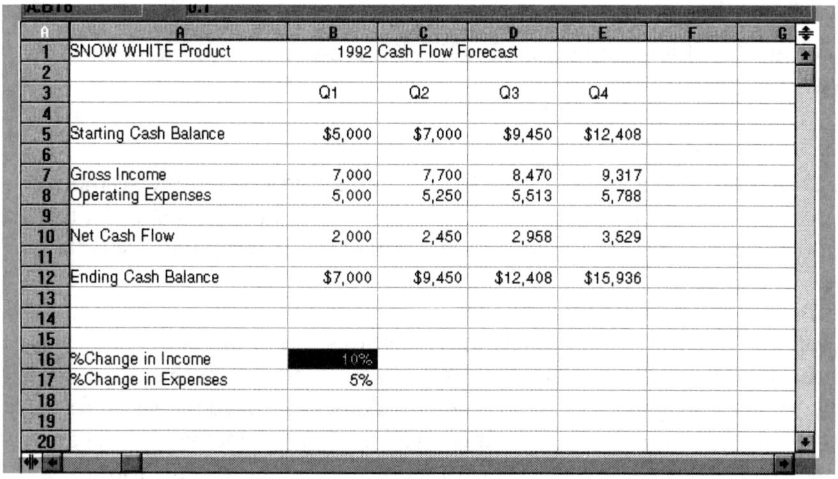

	A	B	C	D	E	F	G
1	SNOW WHITE Product	1992 Cash Flow Forecast					
2							
3		Q1	Q2	Q3	Q4		
4							
5	Starting Cash Balance	$5,000	$7,000	$9,450	$12,408		
6							
7	Gross Income	7,000	7,700	8,470	9,317		
8	Operating Expenses	5,000	5,250	5,513	5,788		
9							
10	Net Cash Flow	2,000	2,450	2,958	3,529		
11							
12	Ending Cash Balance	$7,000	$9,450	$12,408	$15,936		
13							
14							
15							
16	%Change in Income	10%					
17	%Change in Expenses	5%					
18							
19							
20							

Setup Table 5-2:   Ruled Lines for the SNOW WHITE Forecast

Range	Type of Line
A4..E4	Single-ruled
A9..E9	Single-ruled
A13..E13	Double-ruled

Figure 5-9:   The SNOW WHITE Forecast With Ruled Lines Drawn

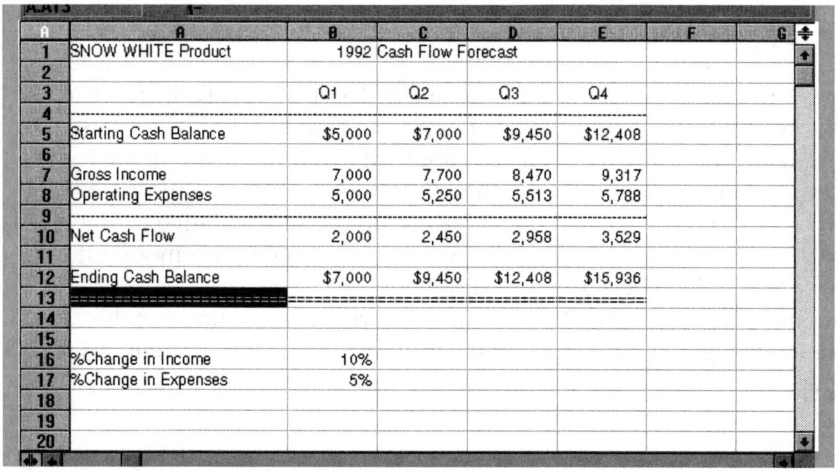

	A	B	C	D	E	F	G
1	SNOW WHITE Product	1992 Cash Flow Forecast					
2							
3		Q1	Q2	Q3	Q4		
4		--------	--------	--------	--------		
5	Starting Cash Balance	$5,000	$7,000	$9,450	$12,408		
6							
7	Gross Income	7,000	7,700	8,470	9,317		
8	Operating Expenses	5,000	5,250	5,513	5,788		
9		--------	--------	--------	--------		
10	Net Cash Flow	2,000	2,450	2,958	3,529		
11							
12	Ending Cash Balance	$7,000	$9,450	$12,408	$15,936		
13		========	========	========	========		
14							
15							
16	%Change in Income	10%					
17	%Change in Expenses	5%					
18							
19							
20							

11. Save the Cash Flow worksheet file.

Choose:	`File  Save As`
Select:	`Filename:` *(if necessary)*
Type:	`cashflow` ⏎

1-2-3 saves the worksheet in a file named CASHFLOW.WK3 in your 1-2-3BOOK directory. [CASHFLOW.WK3] appears in the title bar.

Using GROUP Mode

In Chapter 3, you inserted a scratch worksheet in the Home Budget worksheet file so that you could freely experiment with Data Fill, Edit Clear, and Edit Undo. At that time, it did not matter if the scratch worksheet had the same cell formats, global formats, or column widths as the budget itself.

For many applications, it is desirable for worksheets in a multiple-worksheet file to have different formats; therefore, by default, 1-2-3 uses its initial settings (column width of 9, General format, and so on) for new worksheets. However, when you construct a consolidation or other three-dimensional application, you often want each worksheet to have the same format.

Manually ensuring that any changes to the format or organization of one worksheet are propagated to the rest would be a tedious process. Fortunately, 1-2-3 provides a shortcut method for creating, modifying, and using worksheet files where you want all the worksheets to look the same. This shortcut method, called *GROUP mode*, allows you to make changes in one worksheet and have the changes reflected throughout the other worksheets in the file. The worksheets are grouped together and treated as parts of a logical whole as long as GROUP mode is on.

Turning On GROUP Mode

By default, GROUP mode is off. Turn on GROUP mode now by checking the "Group mode" option of the Worksheet Global Settings command:

Choose:	`Worksheet  Global Settings`
Select:	`Group mode` *and check the check box*
	`OK`

1-2-3 displays the Group indicator in the status line.

When GROUP mode is on, all worksheets in the file immediately take on the characteristics of the current worksheet, and new worksheets you insert also inherit the characteristics of the current worksheet. In addition, while the file is grouped, changes you make to the format of the current worksheet are automatically made to the other worksheets in the file.

Also, while GROUP mode is on, the cell pointer is always in the same relative position when you page from worksheet to worksheet in a file. When you turn GROUP mode off, you can manipulate and format the worksheets independently.

Table 5-1 lists the menu commands that affect grouped worksheets. Notice that this table includes commands that control global format and local format, and commands that insert or delete rows and columns.

■ *NOTE:* Putting a file in GROUP mode does not affect the data in the file. Only the commands and settings described in Table 5-1 are affected by GROUP mode.

Table 5-1: Commands that Affect GROUP Mode Worksheets

Command	Options	What Happens
Worksheet Global Settings	Zero display, Align Labels, Protection, Column Width, Format	Worksheets take on the global settings of the current worksheet.
Worksheet Column Width	All	Worksheets take on the corresponding column widths of the current worksheet. If you change the column width with the mouse, all worksheets are also affected.
Worksheet Delete	Column, Row	Deleting a column or row in the current worksheet causes the corresponding columns or rows to be deleted from the other worksheets in the file.
Worksheet Insert	Column, Row	Inserting a column or row in the current worksheet causes the corresponding columns or rows to be inserted in the other worksheets in the file.
Worksheet Page Break	All	Causes a page break to be inserted (or removed) at the corresponding location in all worksheets in the file.
Worksheet Row Height	All	Worksheets take on the corresponding row heights of the current worksheet. If you change the row height with the mouse, all worksheets are also affected.
Worksheet Titles	All	Worksheets take on the title settings of the current worksheet.
Range Format	All	Cells in all worksheets take on the cell formats of the corresponding cells in the current worksheet.
Range Protect Range Unprotect	All	Cells in all worksheets take on the cell protection of the corresponding cells in the current worksheet.
Style	Font, Alignment, Border, Color, Shading	Cells in all worksheets take on the style attributes of the corresponding cells in the current worksheet.

At the moment, there is only one worksheet in the Cash Flow worksheet file, but you will soon be adding several more. Because you will add these worksheets while the file is in GROUP mode, the new worksheets will inherit the global format, the cell format, and the column width settings of the SNOW WHITE worksheet.

Turning Off GROUP Mode

Clearing the "Group mode" check box in the Worksheet Global Settings dialog box breaks the formatting connection between the grouped worksheets. Once the file is no longer in GROUP mode, changing global settings or format settings in any worksheet in the file has no effect on any other worksheets in the file.

Turning off GROUP mode also unsynchronizes the worksheets. When GROUP mode is off, 1-2-3 keeps track of the cell pointer position in each worksheet; if you move to a worksheet by using Next Sheet or Prev Sheet (or the equivalent SmartIcons, described soon), the cell pointer moves to the position it was in when you last visited the worksheet.

While you are constructing this application, you will leave GROUP mode *on*, since each worksheet is intended to have the same format. When you are nearly finished building the application, you will turn GROUP mode *off* to allow for some local cell formatting.

■ *CAUTION:*   Format changes made to worksheets as a result of putting a worksheet file in GROUP mode cannot be reversed by turning off GROUP mode. If you put a worksheet file in GROUP mode by mistake, and Edit Undo is enabled, press Alt+Backspace (Undo) to restore the worksheet file to its previous READY mode state before you do anything else to the worksheet file.

Inserting Worksheets After the Current Worksheet

When 1-2-3 first comes up on your screen, you have one 256-column by 8192-row worksheet. However, as you learned earlier in this book, you can insert additional worksheets whenever you like.

Now, you will add worksheets to the Cash Flow worksheet file. With the file still in GROUP mode, insert three worksheets after the SNOW WHITE worksheet. These new worksheets will inherit the format of the SNOW WHITE worksheet.

Choose: Worksheet   Insert

Select: Sheet   After

The "Quantity:" text box prompts you for the number of worksheets to insert. You want three:

Type: 3   *in the Quantity: text box*

Press: ⏎   *or select OK*

Figure 5-10:   The First of the New Worksheets, Worksheet B

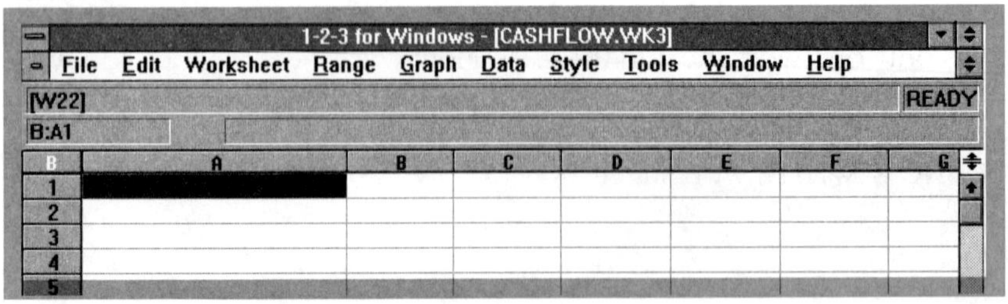

1-2-3 inserts three worksheets after worksheet A and leaves the cell pointer in the first inserted worksheet, worksheet B. The worksheet letter at the intersection of the row and column borders reads B, and the current cell address in the control panel now reads B:A1 instead of A:A1. Notice that this new, blank worksheet has the same column-width settings as the SNOW WHITE worksheet.

■ *NOTE:* 1-2-3 will not permit more than 256 worksheets in memory at one time.

Moving Among Multiple Worksheets

The action of moving the cell pointer among multiple worksheets is somewhat like leafing through the pages of a report. You can move through the file a worksheet at a time, and you can jump directly to the first or last worksheet. You can also use the Goto key or Range Go To command to move directly to any cell in any worksheet in memory.

Table 5-2 describes the pointer-movement keys for moving among multiple worksheets. You will use these keys throughout this chapter. They will be referred to as *worksheet navigation keys.*

■ *NOTE:* You can also move through a stack of worksheets by clicking on the "Next Sheet" and "Previous Sheet" SmartIcons. These icons look like this:

Table 5-2: Worksheet Navigation Keys

Key Name	What It Does:
CTRL+PGUP (NEXTSHEET)	Moves to the next higher worksheet in the current file (away from worksheet A). If the cell pointer is in the last worksheet in the file and there is more than one file in memory, moves to the first worksheet in the next file (if any). 1-2-3 beeps if you try to move beyond the last worksheet in the last or only file.
CTRL+PGDN (PREVSHEET)	Moves to the next lower worksheet in the current file (toward worksheet A). If the cell pointer is in the first worksheet in the file, moves to the last worksheet in the previous file (if any). 1-2-3 beeps if you try to move before the first worksheet in the first or only file.
CTRL+HOME (FIRSTCELL)	Moves to cell A1 in worksheet A in the current file.
END CTRL+HOME (LASTCELL)	Moves to the lower right corner of the last worksheet in the active area of the current file.
END CTRL+PGUP (END NEXTSHEET)	Similar to End Right, except it moves the cell pointer through worksheets toward the last worksheet in the file, instead of across columns.
END CTRL+PGDN (END PREVSHEET)	Similar to End Left, except it moves the cell pointer through worksheets toward the first worksheet in the file, instead of across columns.

Key Name	What It Does:
F5 (GOTO)	Moves to any cell or worksheet you specify. If the worksheets are not grouped and you specify only the worksheet letter and a colon, moves to the previous location of the cell pointer in the specified worksheet.

The following steps give you some practice with the worksheet navigation keys as you add titles to the worksheets you just inserted:

1. Move to the previous worksheet.

   To convince yourself that the SNOW WHITE worksheet is still there, move back to it with the Prev Sheet key:

   Press: CTRL+PGDN

   1-2-3 displays the SNOW WHITE worksheet.

2. Add a title to worksheet B.

   Now, move to worksheet B again and type some text in the worksheet to further identify it:

   Press: CTRL+PGUP   *to move to worksheet B*
   Type: DWARF1 Product   *in cell B:A1*
   Press: ↵

3. Move to worksheet C and enter a title in that worksheet.

   Type a title in worksheet C. Instead of pressing Enter to complete the entry, use Next Sheet to enter the title and move to worksheet D:

   Press: CTRL+PGUP
   Type: DWARF2 Product
   Press: CTRL+PGUP

   1-2-3 enters the words **DWARF2 Product** in cell C:A1, and then moves the cell pointer to the next worksheet, worksheet D. Enter a title in the last worksheet you created.

   Type: EVIL QUEEN Product
   Press: ↵

4. Experiment with the worksheet navigation keys and icons.

   Your worksheet file now contains four worksheets: One has data and formulas, while the others contain only titles. Experiment with the worksheet navigation keys (and, if you have a mouse, the worksheet navigation SmartIcons) until you get the feel of moving around in a file with multiple worksheets. When you are done, move back to the SNOW WHITE worksheet:

Figure 5-11: Entering a Label in Worksheet D (File is in Perspective View)

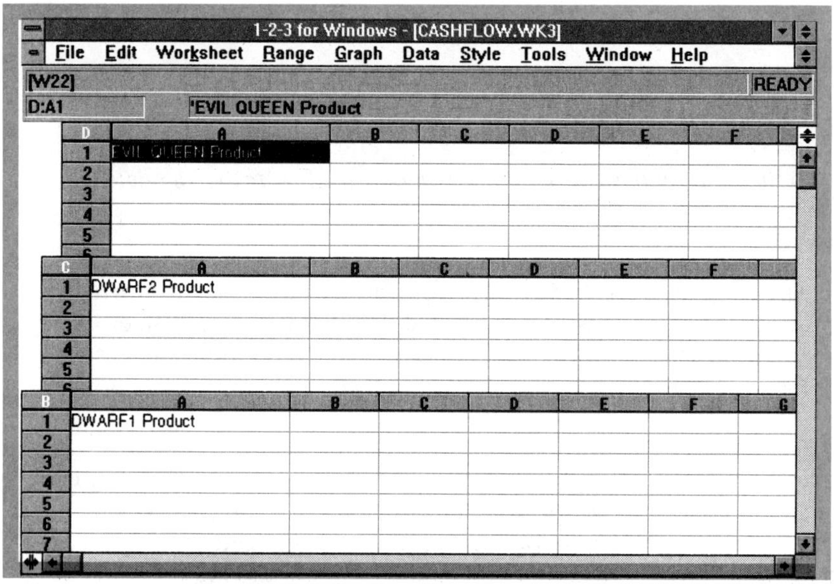

Press: CTRL+HOME

5. Save the CASHFLOW worksheet file.

You have completed the basic framework of this multiple-worksheet file. Save the file again.

A Note on Finding Data in Other Worksheets   Besides using the worksheet navigation and Goto keys to move from worksheet to worksheet, you can use Edit Find to move from one worksheet to another. Use Edit Find when you know something is in the worksheet file, but you don't know where it is.

For example, suppose you want to find the EVIL QUEEN worksheet, but you can't remember the worksheet letter. Instead of paging through the worksheet file, let Edit Find do the work.

First, highlight the entire active area of the file, and then choose Edit Find:

Press: CTRL+HOME   *to move to cell A:A1 (if necessary)*

                 F4   *to switch to POINT mode and anchor the range*

                 END   CTRL+HOME   *to move to the last active cell*

                 ⏎ *to return to READY mode*

Choose: Edit   Find

Edit Find prompts you for a string to search for. Have it search for EVIL QUEEN in label cells.

Type:	`evil queen` *in the Search for: text box*
Select:	`Find   Labels   Find Next`

1-2-3 finds EVIL QUEEN in cell D:A1.

Press:	ESC *two times, to return 1-2-3 to READY mode and clear the highlight*

Creating a Template

You are going to use the structure of the SNOW WHITE forecast as a *template* from which to create the remaining product-specific forecasts. Like a physical template, a worksheet template is used as a model from which to form one or more completed worksheets. It contains the structure of the final worksheets—the labels and formulas—but it does not contain the actual data.

■ *NOTE:*   When you are constructing this application, you will often copy information from one part of the worksheet file to another. To specify the "to" range, you can type its address, highlight it, or use the "Copy To" SmartIcon. If you highlight the range, make sure the "To:" text box is selected and that 1-2-3 is in POINT mode before you attempt to highlight the range. If you have put 1-2-3 in EDIT mode (so that you could modify the contents of the text box), erease the contents of the text box, press F2 (Edit) to change to POINT mode, and then highlight the "to" range.

1. Copy the contents of worksheet A to worksheet B.

   First, copy everything but the titles of the SNOW WHITE worksheet from worksheet A to worksheet B. The copy commands work the same between worksheets as they do within one worksheet. Try using Edit Copy and Edit Paste here:

Move to:	cell A:A3
Highlight:	A:A3..A:E17
Choose:	`Edit   Copy` *or press Contrl+Insert*
Press:	CTRL+PGUP *to move to cell B:A3*
Choose:	`Edit   Paste` *or press Shift+Insert*

   1-2-3 copies the range. Except for the title row and the worksheet letter, worksheet B now looks exactly the same as worksheet A.

2. Zero the values in column B.

   You will use this worksheet as a template from which to create the other product-specific worksheets. Replace the values copied from worksheet A with 0s, so it will be obvious that these worksheets do not yet have useful data in them. Do *not* replace the formulas in the worksheet with 0s.

Figure 5-12: The Template Worksheet With SNOW WHITE's Values

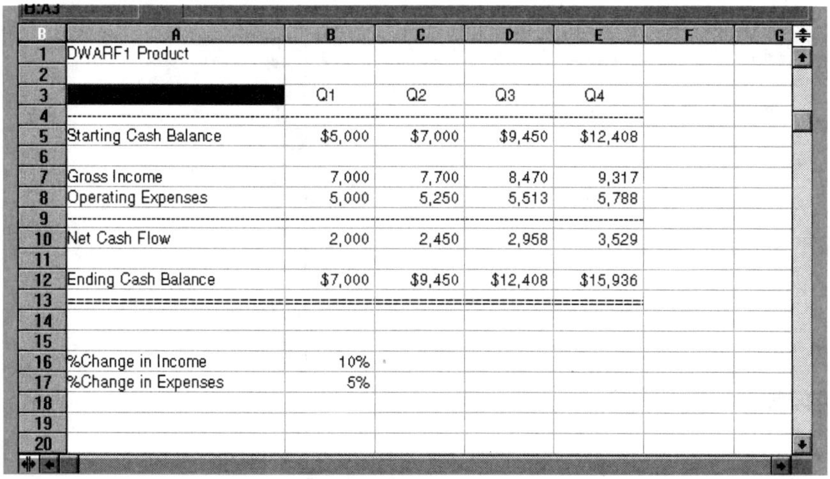

	A	B	C	D	E	F	G
1	DWARF1 Product						
2							
3		Q1	Q2	Q3	Q4		
4							
5	Starting Cash Balance	$5,000	$7,000	$9,450	$12,408		
6							
7	Gross Income	7,000	7,700	8,470	9,317		
8	Operating Expenses	5,000	5,250	5,513	5,788		
9							
10	Net Cash Flow	2,000	2,450	2,958	3,529		
11							
12	Ending Cash Balance	$7,000	$9,450	$12,408	$15,936		
13							
14							
15							
16	%Change in Income	10%					
17	%Change in Expenses	5%					
18							
19							
20							

Move to:	cell B:B5
Type:	0
Press:	↓ *two times*
Type:	0
Press:	↓
Type:	0
Press:	↵
Move to:	cell B:B16
Type:	0
Press:	↓
Type:	0
Press:	↵

1-2-3 recalculates the formula cells, using the new 0 values. The result is 0 values for starting cash balance, gross income, and operating expenses. The worksheet should look like Figure 5-13 (shown on next page).

3. Save the Cash Flow worksheet file.

The template is now complete. Save your work.

Copying the Template

The next step in creating this application is to make two additional copies of the template.

1. Copy the template to worksheets C and D.

Figure 5-13: The Template Worksheet, Completed

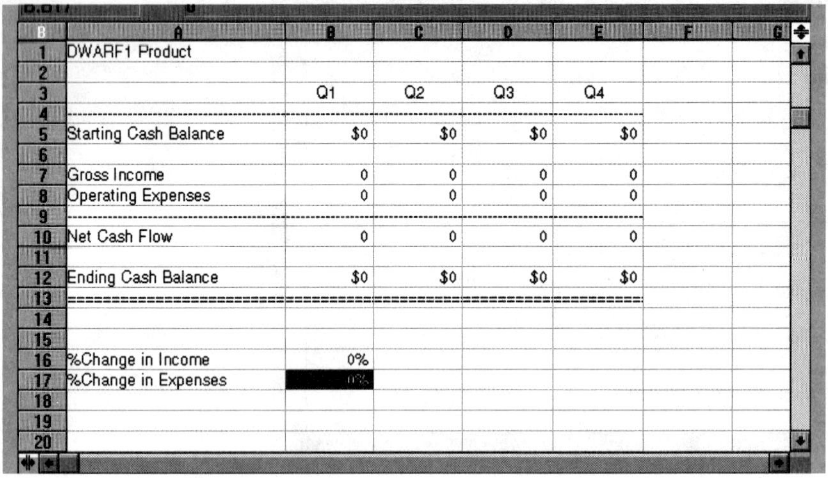

	A	B	C	D	E	F	G
1	DWARF1 Product						
2							
3		Q1	Q2	Q3	Q4		
4							
5	Starting Cash Balance	$0	$0	$0	$0		
6							
7	Gross Income	0	0	0	0		
8	Operating Expenses	0	0	0	0		
9							
10	Net Cash Flow	0	0	0	0		
11							
12	Ending Cash Balance	$0	$0	$0	$0		
13							
14							
15							
16	%Change in Income	0%					
17	%Change in Expenses	0%					
18							
19							
20							

This time, make a duplicate of all but the first row of the DWARF1 worksheet in worksheets C and D:

Move to:	cell B:A3
Highlight:	B:A3..B:E17
Choose:	Edit Quick Copy
Specify:	C:A3..D:A3 *in the To: text box*
Press:	↵ *or select OK*

1-2-3 copies the template to the other worksheets. Page back and forth through the file to verify this, using the Control+Page Up (Next Sheet) and Control+Page Down (Prev Sheet) keys, or the equivalent SmartIcons.

2. Copy the current year and the application title.

To complete the templates, copy the current year and the application title from worksheet A to worksheets B through D:

Move to:	cell A:B1
Highlight:	A:B1..A:C1
Choose:	Edit Quick Copy
Select:	To: *(if it is not already highlighted)*

So you can more easily see what the copy command does when you copy across worksheets, use the keyboard to highlight the "to" range this time.

Press:	CTRL+PGUP *to move to worksheet B*

.　**(Period)**　*to anchor the range at B:B1*

CTRL+PGUP　*two times*

◻ *two times, to accept the range B:B1..D:B1 and then complete the copy*

1-2-3 copies the current year and the worksheet title from worksheet A to the corresponding positions in worksheets B through D.

Figure 5-14:　Perspective View of Worksheets B Through D After Copying the Worksheet Title

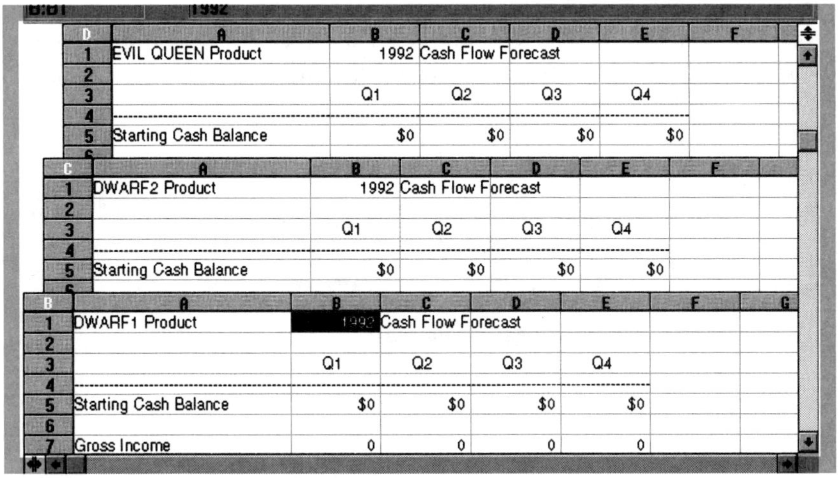

3. Save the Cash Flow worksheet file again.
   Congratulations! You have completed a major piece of work on this application.

Using Worksheet Window Panes

Paging back and forth between worksheet areas is an easy way to look at the different parts of an application, but sometimes you need to see two or more separate areas simultaneously. 1-2-3 allows you to do this by dividing the Worksheet window into *panes*. Using the Window Split commands, you can split the window horizontally or vertically to view two parts of a worksheet file at the same time, or you can create a *perspective view* that allows you to view any three consecutive worksheets simultaneously.

In the next several sections, you will use the "Horizontal" option of the Window Split command to create two horizontal window panes in the CASHFLOW Worksheet window, and then you will use the "Perspective" option of Window Split to create a perspective view of the window. Your experimentation with window panes will have no direct effect on the Cash Flow worksheet application, but it will come in handy any time you want to modify one part of a worksheet and see the effects on another part, or when you need to view a three-dimensional range. After you have experimented with these commands, you will continue building CASHFLOW.WK3.

Splitting the Screen

Using the "Horizontal" and "Vertical" options of the Window Split command, you can divide a window into two panes. Having two panes allows you to keep track of more than one area at a time. For instance, in the Home Budget worksheet you created in Chapters 3 and 4, you could display the CASH FLOW section of the worksheet in one pane and the INCOME VARIABLES section in another. As you change values in the variables section, you can see the effects of the changes reflected in the formulas in the CASH FLOW section.

The "Horizontal" option of Window Split splits the screen horizontally at the current row. The "Vertical" option splits the screen vertically at the current column. With either type of window pane, you can synchronize scrolling in the two panes or scroll the panes independently by checking or clearing the "Synchronize" check box. You can display any part of a worksheet file in memory in either window pane.

Experiment with window panes now:

1. Split the screen.

   To see how window panes operate, split the SNOW WHITE forecast horizontally, then scroll the lower pane to the next forecast:

Press:	`CTRL+HOME`	*to move to cell A:A1*
Move to:	cell A:A11	*with the Down arrow or the mouse*
Choose:	`Window  Split`	
Select:	`Horizontal  OK`	

   1-2-3 splits the window at row 11. (See Figure 5-15.)

■ *NOTE:*   When you choose Window Split Horizontal or Vertical, 1-2-3 splits the active Worksheet window at whatever row or column the cell pointer is in, unless the cell pointer is in the first or last row or column of the window, in which case 1-2-3 just beeps.

2. Scroll the top window pane.

   At first, it looks as if the only real difference is a row of column letters inserted in the middle of the screen display. However, if you try to move the cursor down past this row of letters, you'll see immediately that this is not all that has changed:

Press:	↓	*two times*

   The top half of the screen scrolls up, while the lower half remains stationary. (See Figure 5-16.)

3. Move to the lower window pane.

   To scroll the lower pane, you have to move the cell pointer to it. The Pane key (F6) moves the cell pointer from one pane to another.

Figure 5-15: Splitting a Window Into Two Horizontal Panes

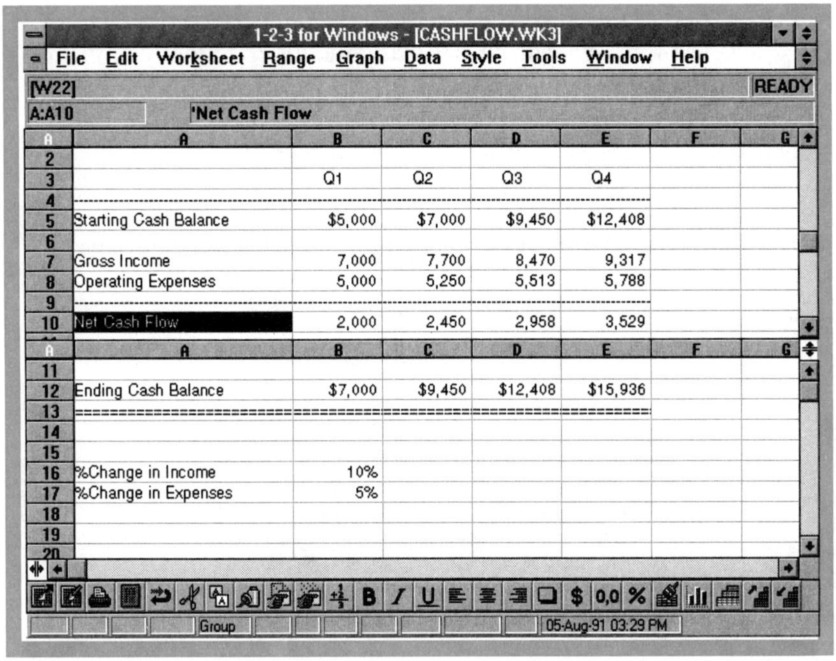

Figure 5-16: Scrolling One Pane of a Split Window

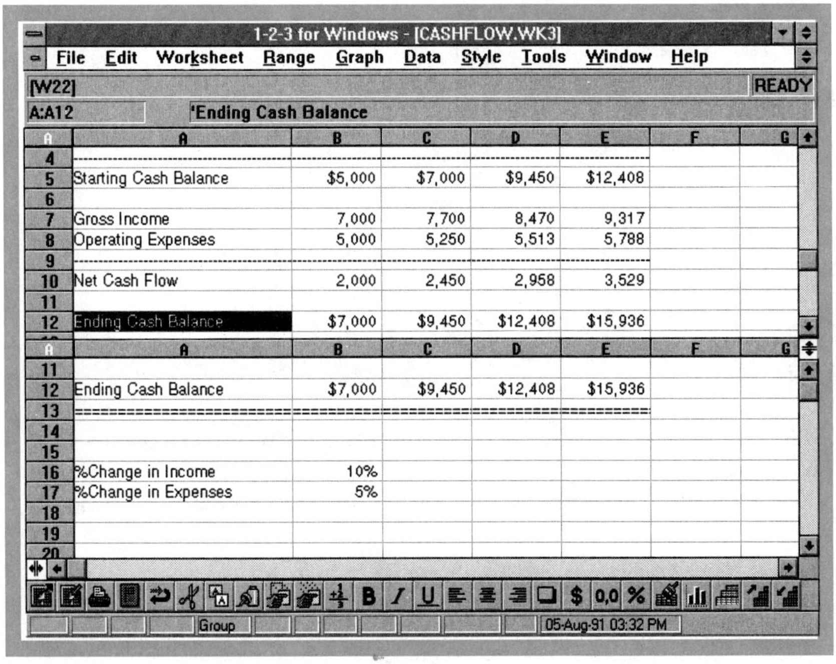

Press: F6   **(PANE)**

The cell pointer jumps to the part of the screen below the second line of column letters. The pointer-movement keys allow you to move around in this pane independently of the top pane.

Use Home to display the top part of the worksheet in the lower pane:

Press: HOME

1-2-3 now displays the top part of the worksheet in each pane. Scroll the lower pane to the next forecast:

Press: F5   **(GOTO)**

Type: b:b1   ↵

Figure 5-17:   Displaying Two Worksheets in the Same Window

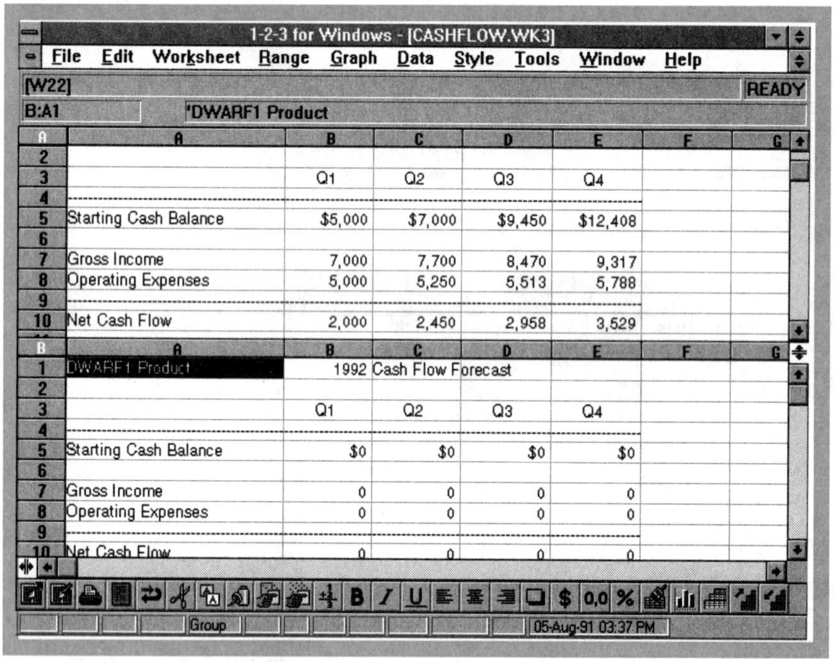

1-2-3 displays the DWARF1 forecast in the lower pane and the SNOW WHITE forecast in the upper pane. Experiment with the Pane key and the pointer-movement keys to see how you can move within and between the two window panes, and then read the next section.

Using the Mouse to Work with Window Panes

As a shortcut, you can split the window horizontally or vertically with the mouse. Both the horizontal and the vertical scroll bars contain *splitters.* To split the window, you drag the appropriate splitter to the place where you want the split to occur. You can also use the mouse to adjust windows that are already split. To split a window into horizontal panes, do the following:

1. Move the mouse pointer to the horizontal splitter at the top of the right scroll bar. The mouse pointer will change to a two-headed vertical arrow.

2. Press the left mouse button, drag the mouse pointer to the row at which you want to split the window horizontally, and then release the mouse button.

To "un-split" a window divided into horizontal panes, drag the splitter to the top or bottom edge of the window.

Figure 5-18:   Using the Mouse to Split a Window Into Horizontal Panes

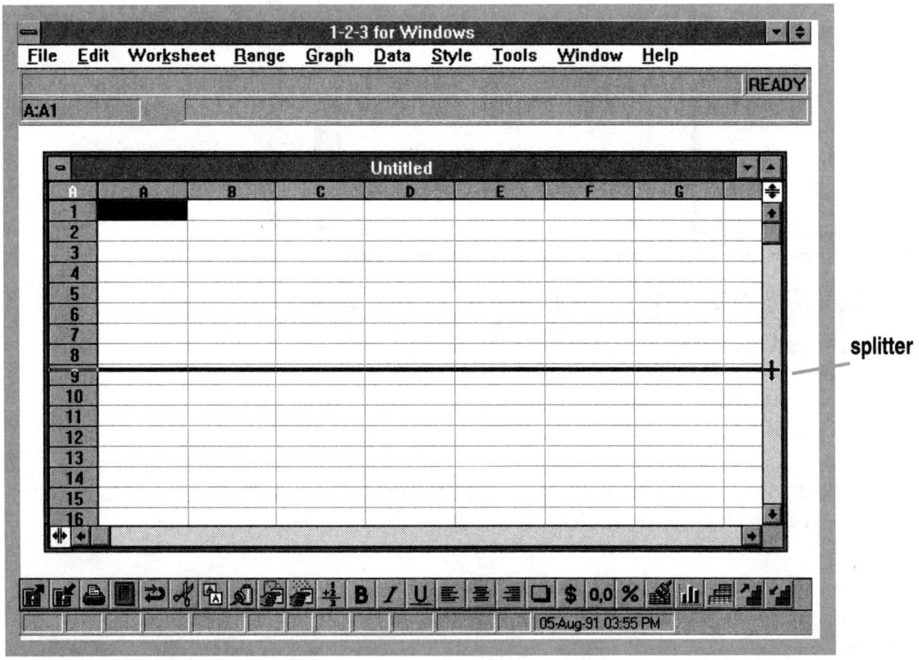

To split a window into vertical panes, do the following:

1. Move the mouse pointer to the vertical splitter at the left side of the bottom scroll bar. The mouse pointer will change to a two-headed horizontal arrow.

2. Press the left mouse button drag the mouse pointer to the column at which you want to split the window vertically, and then release the mouse button.

To "un-split" a window divided into vertical panes, drag the splitter to the left or right edge of the window.

Figure 5-19: Using the Mouse to Split a Window Into Vertical Panes

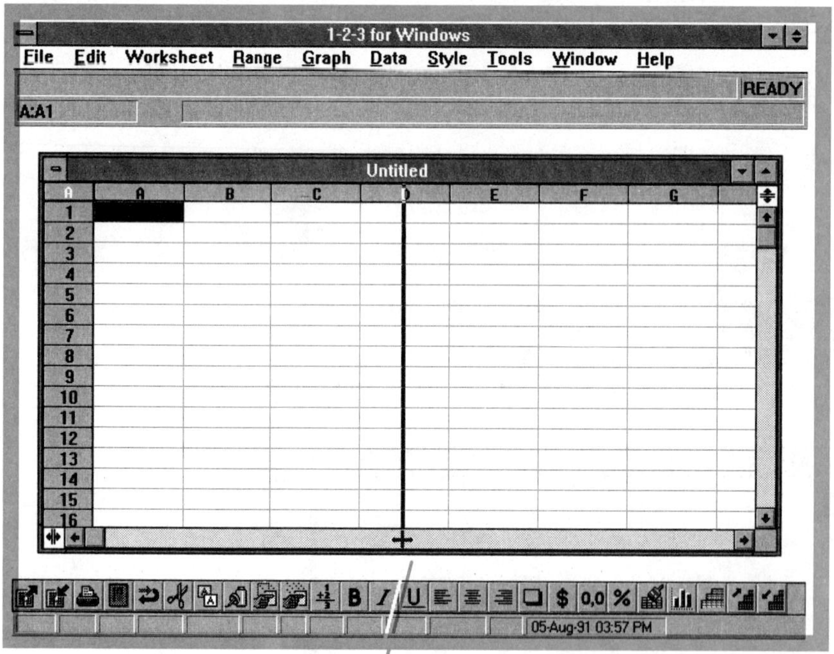

splitter

■ *NOTE:* If you like, experiment with the splitter by changing the size of the CASHFLOW window panes before you go on to the next section.

Synchronizing or Unsynchronizing Window Panes

You can make the two panes scroll together or separately by checking or clearing the "Synchronize" check box of the Window Split command.

When you first divide a worksheet into panes, 1-2-3 assumes that you want both panes to scroll together. The panes are synchronized: horizontal panes are synchronized horizontally, and vertical panes are synchronized vertically. Try scrolling horizontally:

Press: |CTRL+RIGHT| *or Tab, to move one screen right*

Both panes move right one screen.

Figure 5-20: Synchronized window panes scroll together

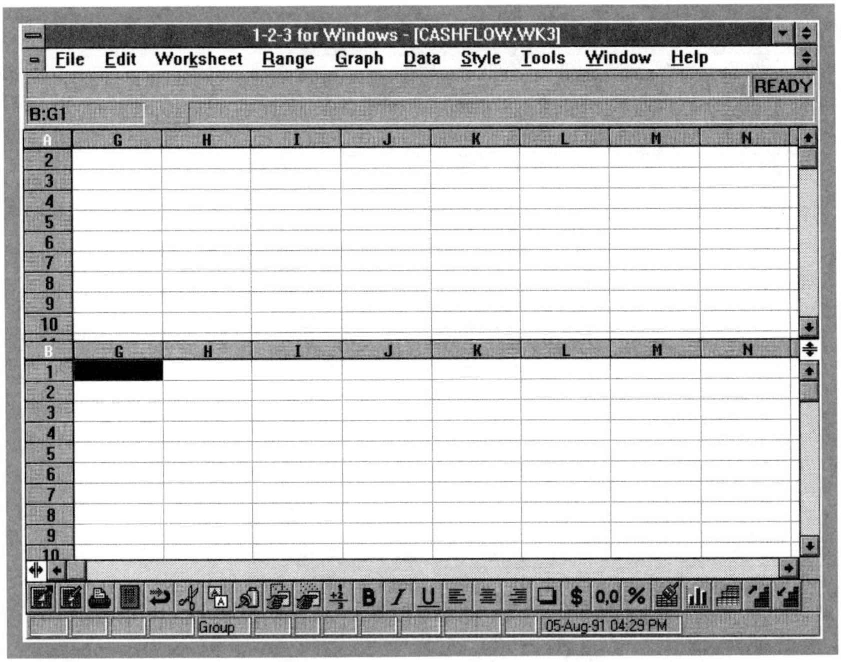

Press: `CTRL+LEFT`   *or Shift+Tab*

Both panes move back to the original display. Now, unsynchronize the panes and see what happens:

Choose: Window   Split

Select: Synchronize: *and clear the check box*
                  OK

Press: `CTRL+RIGHT`

                  `CTRL+LEFT`

The bottom pane scrolls independently of the top pane (see Figure 5-21).

Clearing Window Panes

When you are through moving around the two panes, restore the window to a single pane.

Choose: Window   Split

Select: Clear   OK

Figure 5-21:   Unsynchronized Window Panes Scroll Separately

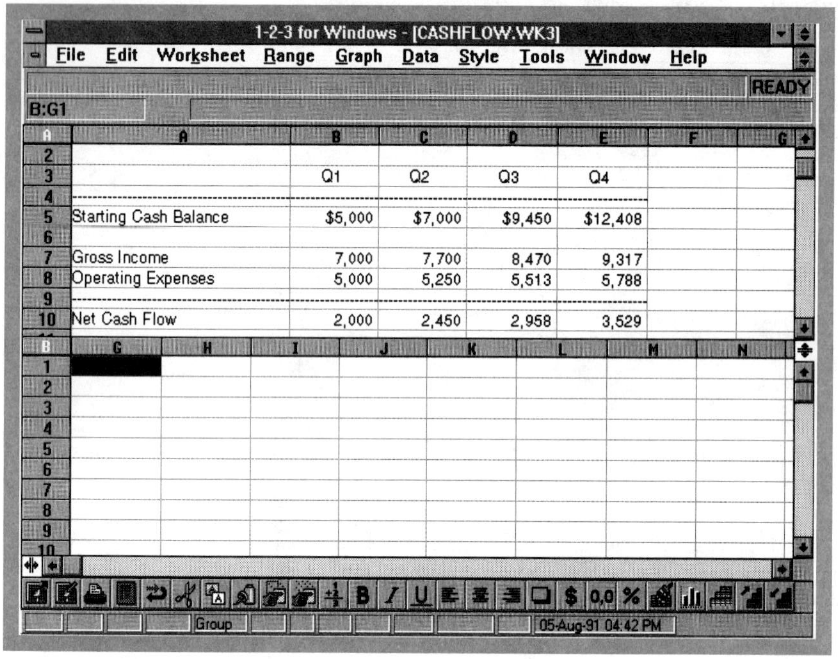

With the cell pointer in either pane, the "Clear" option of the Window Split command restores the single-pane display and leaves the cell pointer in the cell it most recently occupied in the top or left pane.

■ *NOTE:*   1-2-3 saves window pane settings with the worksheet file. For instance, if you save a worksheet file with the screen split horizontally, the screen will still be split horizontally when you retrieve that file later.

Using Perspective View

Perspective view allows you to look at several rows from three consecutive worksheets simultaneously. Each pane in perspective view is approximately the same size.

Changing to Perspective View

To change to perspective view, use the "Perspective" option of the Window Split command:

Press:　　　　 `CTRL+HOME`   *to move to cell A:A1 (if necessary)*

Choose:　　　　 Window   Split

Select:　　　　 Perspective   OK

1-2-3 displays the first three worksheets in the Cash Flow worksheet file.

Figure 5-22:   The Cash Flow Forecast in Perspective View

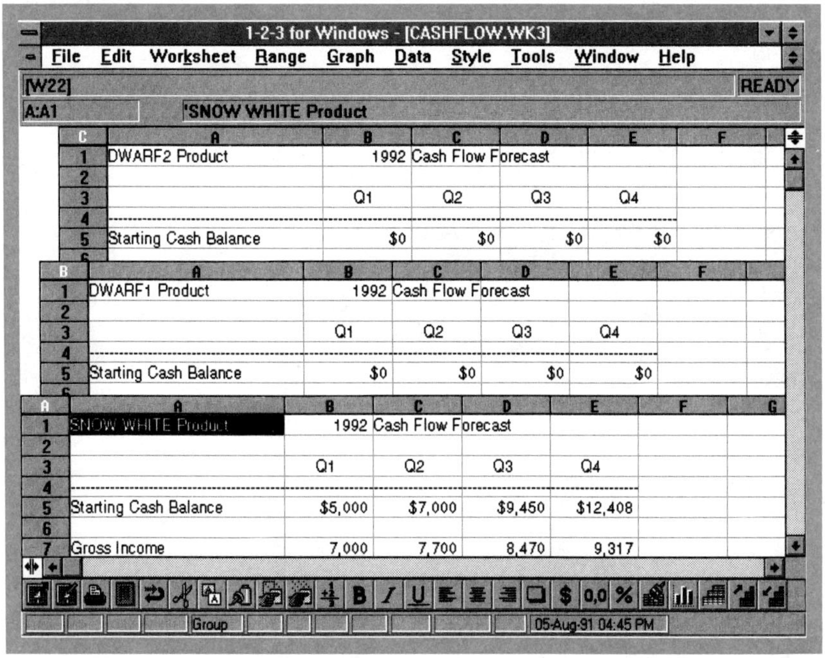

	1-2-3 for Windows - [CASHFLOW.WK3]					
File Edit Worksheet Range Graph Data Style Tools Window Help						
[W22]						READY
A:A1	'SNOW WHITE Product					

C
	A	B	C	D	E	F
1	DWARF2 Product		1992 Cash Flow Forecast			
2						
3		Q1	Q2	Q3	Q4	
4						
5	Starting Cash Balance	$0	$0	$0	$0	

B
	A	B	C	D	E	F
1	DWARF1 Product		1992 Cash Flow Forecast			
2						
3		Q1	Q2	Q3	Q4	
4						
5	Starting Cash Balance	$0	$0	$0	$0	

A
	A	B	C	D	E	F	G
1	SNOW WHITE Product		1992 Cash Flow Forecast				
2							
3		Q1	Q2	Q3	Q4		
4							
5	Starting Cash Balance	$5,000	$7,000	$9,450	$12,408		
6							
7	Gross Income	7,000	7,700	8,470	9,317		

Group		05-Aug-91 04:45 PM

■ *NOTE:*   You can toggle between a single-pane view and perspective view by clicking on the "Perspective View" SmartIcon. The icon looks like this:

Moving Among Worksheets in Perspective View

In perspective view, you can still move from worksheet to worksheet by using Control+Page Up (Next Sheet), Control+Page Down (Prev Sheet), and other worksheet navigation keys, as well as the "Next Sheet" and "Previous Sheet" icons. Try moving from worksheet A to worksheet D:

Press: CTRL+PGUP   *three times, or click on the Next Sheet icon three times*

Notice that the cell pointer first moved from worksheet A to worksheets B and C. When you pressed Next Sheet a third time, the cell pointer stayed at the top of the worksheet display; however, instead of displaying parts of worksheets A, B, and C, 1-2-3 now displays parts of worksheets B, C, and D.

You can cycle the cell pointer through the currently displayed panes by using the Pane key, F6:

Press: F6   **(PANE)**   *three times*

As with windows that have been split horizontally or vertically, you can move from worksheet to worksheet when a file is in perspective view by clicking on any cell in the worksheet you want to move the cell pointer to:

Click on: *any cell in worksheets B, C, and D*

Figure 5-23:   Each Press of Control+Page Up Moves the Cell Pointer One Worksheet up, Even in Perspective View

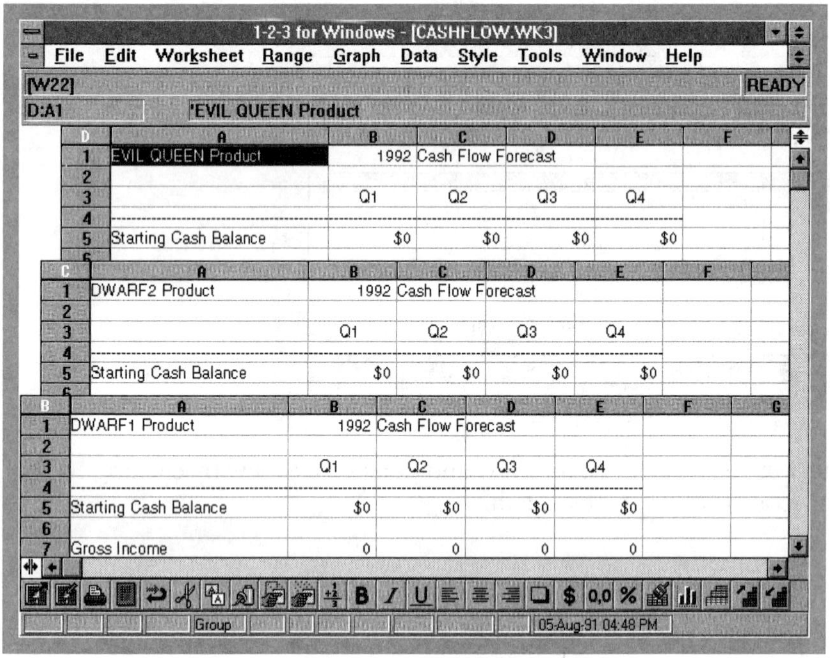

Moving Within Worksheets in Perspective View

In perspective view, you can still use the pointer-movement keys and the mouse to move around in a worksheet. Move from worksheet to worksheet and practice scrolling while in perspective view. Try out the Goto key, the scroll bars, and the pointer-movement keys, and observe how the worksheets scroll. See what happens when you toggle the "Synchronize" check box on and off.

Notice, as you scroll, that the worksheets all move together. When a file is in GROUP mode and 1-2-3 is in perspective view, the worksheets are *always* synchronized, regardless of the "Synchronize" setting; all the panes scroll simultaneously when you move one pane left, right, up, or down. When a worksheet file is not in GROUP mode and 1-2-3 is in perspective view, clearing the "Synchronize" check box in the Worksheet Global Settings dialog box tells 1-2-3 to move only the pane that contains the cell pointer, while checking the check box synchronizes the panes.

Using the Zoom Key with Window Panes

When you are using or building a complex application with more than one active file or with several worksheets in a file, it is easy to get lost and inadvertently modify data in one worksheet when you mean to be in another. Perspective view and window panes make it easy to "place" yourself within the application. When you want to work exclusively in one worksheet, but still be able to switch back and forth between a single-pane and multiple-pane view, use the Zoom key, Alt+F6.

Somewhat like a zoom lens on a camera, the Zoom key (Alt+F6) lets you quickly switch between different ways of looking at the worksheet file. The first time you press Zoom while more than one pane is on the screen, 1-2-3 expands the current pane to the full screen. The next time you press Zoom, 1-2-3 restores the previous view. Zoom restores the current pane to a full-window view without "forgetting" the current Window Split settings. When you want to resume the multiple-pane view, you press Zoom again. (Pressing Alt+F6 when the window is not split into panes has no effect.)

With the Worksheet window still in perspective view, experiment with the Zoom key:

Press: | ALT+F6 | **(ZOOM)**

Figure 5-24:   Zooming a Pane

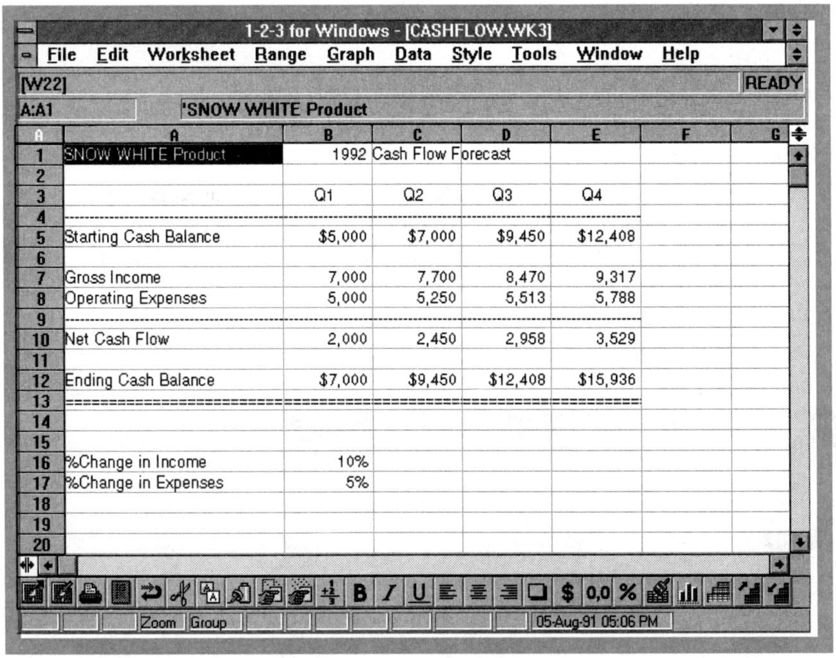

1-2-3 expands the current pane to the whole Worksheet window. Notice the Zoom indicator in the status line. If you page through the worksheet file, the pane remains zoomed and the Zoom indicator remains in the status line.

Although the view of the current pane now looks the same as it would if the worksheet were not in perspective view, there are some differences. The Pane key still works to move between worksheets:

Press: F6   **(PANE)**   *three times*

1-2-3 switches from one worksheet another. Now, unzoom the current window pane:

Press: ALT+F6   **(ZOOM)**

1-2-3 restores the horizontal window display.

Clearing Perspective View
Now, clear perspective view the same way you cleared horizontal panes:

Choose: Window   Split
Select: Clear   OK

Figure 5-25:   **Clearing Perspective View**

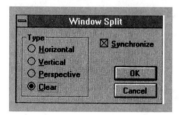

1-2-3 restores the single worksheet screen display and displays the current worksheet.

Creating a Summary Forecast
Now that you have created templates for each of the products Bob Gordon is thinking about building, and you are used to moving among multiple Worksheet windows and panes, create a summary forecast so Bob can see how the business as a whole is shaping up. The summary forecast adds up each of the figures for each quarter, for all the products, and displays the results.

When you have finished this exercise, your summary forecast will look like Figure 5-26.

Figure 5-26:   **The Completed Summary Forecast Worksheet**

A	B	C	D	E	F	G
1 FOLKTALE WORKSHOP		1992 Cash Flow Forecast		(Consolidation)		
2						
3	Q1	Q2	Q3	Q4		
4						
5 Starting Cash Balance	5,000	7,000	9,450	12,408		
6						
7 Gross Income	7,000	7,700	8,470	9,317		
8 Operating Expenses	5,000	5,250	5,513	5,788		
9						
10 Net Cash Flow	2,000	2,450	2,958	3,529		
11						
12 Ending Cash Balance	7,000	9,450	12,408	15,936		
13						
14						
15						
16						
17						
18						
19						
20						

1. Insert a blank worksheet before the SNOW WHITE forecast.

   You will create the summary forecast worksheet by inserting a new worksheet in front of the SNOW WHITE worksheet. Conceptually, this is similar to stapling a summary to the first page of a report.

   First, move the cell pointer to cell A:A1:

   Press: CTRL+HOME

   Now, insert a blank worksheet in front of worksheet A. This time, accept the default of **1** when you are prompted for the number of worksheets to insert:

   Choose: Worksheet   Insert

   Select: Sheet   Before   OK

   1-2-3 inserts a blank worksheet and gives it the letter A. The cell pointer moves to the new worksheet. Because the worksheet file is still in GROUP mode, this worksheet has the same format as the other worksheets.

2. Examine the file's new structure.

   Take a look at the worksheet file with perspective view to see the new structure. If you have a mouse, use the "Perspective View" SmartIcon (three worksheets, stacked like stairs) to change to perspective view. Otherwise, do the following:

   Choose: Window   Split

   Select: Perspective   OK

Figure 5-27:   The Cash Flow Forecast with a Blank Worksheet for the Summary

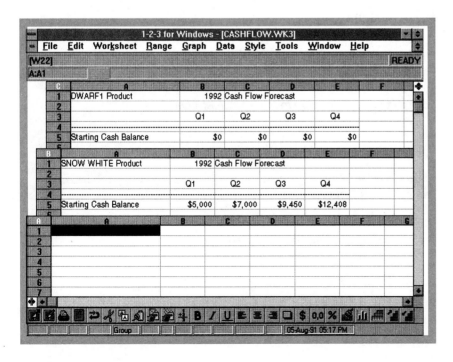

When 1-2-3 inserts a new worksheet in front of other worksheets, it effectively moves the current worksheet (and any worksheets behind it) back, to make room for the new worksheet. In this case, 1-2-3 has inserted the new, blank worksheet in front of the SNOW WHITE worksheet. SNOW WHITE, formerly worksheet A, is now worksheet B; DWARF1, formerly worksheet B, is now worksheet C; and so on. Had you inserted two worksheets instead of one, 1-2-3 would have moved the existing worksheets back two worksheet letters.

■ *NOTE:*   When you have finished with this exercise, experiment on your own to see what happens when you insert worksheets "Before" or "After" a worksheet that is in the middle of a group of worksheets.

Clear perspective view before going on to the next step. Again, if you have a mouse, click on the "Perspective View" icon; the icon toggles between perspective view and a full-window view of the current worksheet. Otherwise, do the following:

Choose:	`Window`	`Split`
Select:	`Clear`	`OK`

3. Fill in the first row of the summary forecast.

Like the other forecasts in this worksheet, the first row will contain a title in the upper left corner, followed by the current year in cell B1, and the application title in cell C1. You will also add a label identifying this worksheet as a consolidation of the other worksheets.

With the cell pointer in cell A:A1, type in the following. Be sure to type a label prefix before the parenthetical phrase "(Consolidation)," or 1-2-3 will try to interpret this entry as a value.

Type: `FOLKTALE WORKSHOP` →

`1992` →

`Cash Flow Forecast`

Press: → *two times*

Type: `'(Consolidation)`   *(be sure to type the apostrophe)*

Press: ↵

4. Copy the forecast structure from a template to the summary forecast worksheet.

The easiest way to create the basic structure of the summary forecast is to copy the forecast template you created earlier to worksheet A:

Move to:	cell C:A3
Highlight:	C:A3..C:E13 *(the body of the DWARF1 forecast)*
Choose:	`Edit` `Quick Copy`
Specify:	cell A:A3 *in the To: text box*
Select:	`OK`

1-2-3 copies information from the DWARF1 template to the summary forecast worksheet.

Press: CTRL+HOME

Figure 5-28: **The Summary Worksheet With Template Data**

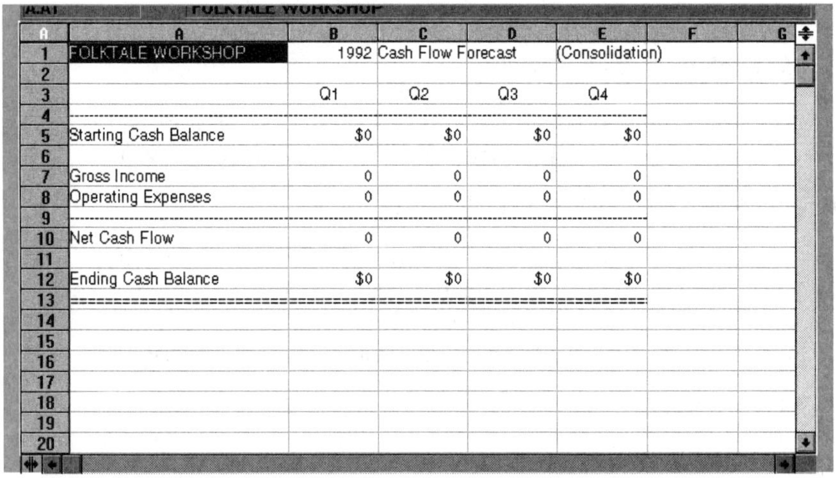

5. Erase the formula cells in the summary forecast worksheet.

The formulas for the summary forecast are different from those of the other forecasts. To avoid confusion when you enter the new formulas, erase the existing values and formulas:

Highlight: A:B5..A:E12

Choose: Edit Clear *or press Delete*

Figure 5-29: **Making the Worksheet Ready for New Formulas**

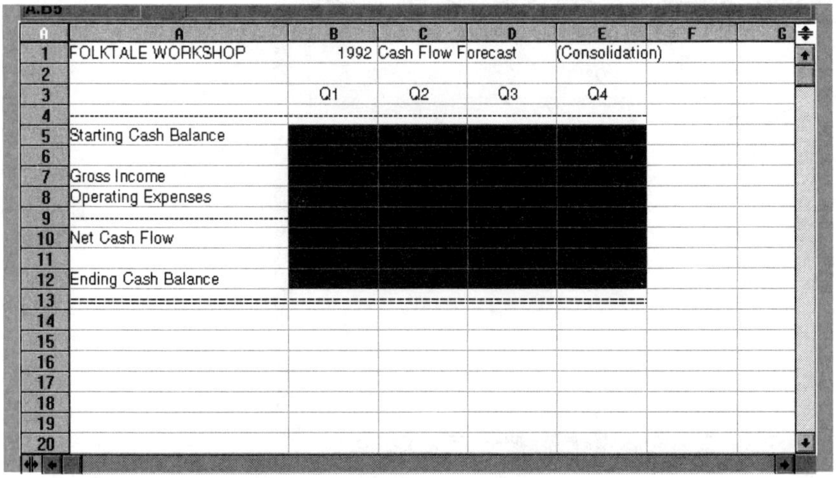

6. Enter the formula for Starting Cash Balance in the summary forecast.

Each value displayed in the summary forecast is a formula, and each formula is a variation on the same theme. For example, the formula in cell A:B5 is @SUM(B:B5..E:B5). This formula adds up the starting cash balance in each of the product-specific forecasts. Enter this formula now:

Move to: cell A:B5   *(if necessary)*
Type: `@sum(b:b5.e:b5)` ⏎

    1-2-3 adds up the values in the range and displays **5,000** in cell A:B5. (For now, because the other referenced cells contain 0s, the formula reflects only the value in cell B:B5.)

7. Copy the formula in A:B5 to the remaining formula cells in column B.

To complete the summary forecast, you can copy the formula in cell A:B5 to the remaining formula cells in the forecast. Because this formula uses relative cell addresses, the cell references will automatically adjust; each @SUM formula in the summary forecast will total the values in corresponding cells in the individual forecasts. First, copy the formula down column B:

Choose: `Edit`   `Quick Copy`
Select: `To:`
Specify: A:B7..A:B12   *in the To: text box*
Select: `OK`

    1-2-3 copies the formula in cell A:B5 to the range you highlighted. Cells B7, B8, B10, and B12 in worksheet A add up the values in the corresponding cells in the individual forecasts in the worksheets behind worksheet A. Cells A:B9 and A:B11 display 0s, because those formulas refer to cells that contain no data.

Figure 5-30: The Summary Forecast, With Formulas in Column B

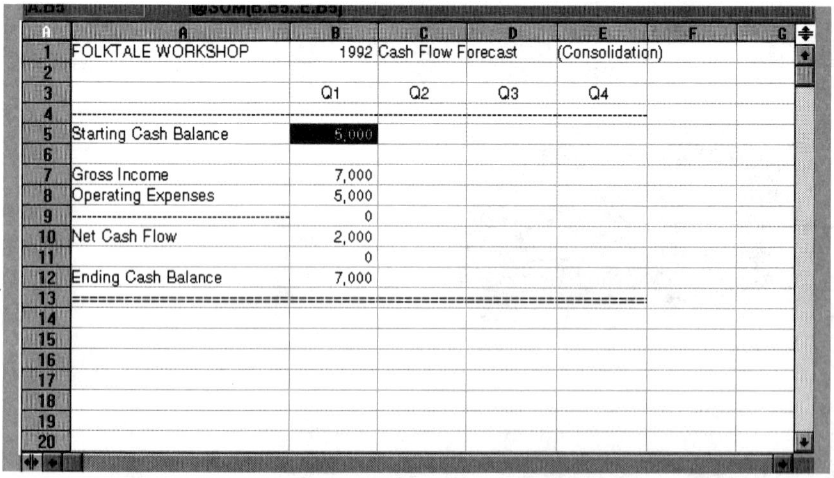

8. Fix up column B formulas and cell formats.

Copying the formula in cell A:B5 copies formulas to two cells that should not contain formulas: cells A:B9 and A:B11. Before you copy column B to columns C and D, correct these small problems. First, put a repeating hyphen in cell A:B9, and then erase cell A:B11:

Move to:	cell A:B9
Type:	\-
Press:	↓ *two times*
	DELETE

9. Copy the formulas in column B to columns C, D, and E.

Now that the first-quarter column is the way you want it, copy it to the Q2, Q3, and Q4 columns:

Move to:	cell A:B5
Highlight:	A:B5..A:B12
Choose:	Edit Quick Copy
Specify:	A:C5..A:E5 *in the To: text box*
Select:	OK

1-2-3 copies the formula cells (and the repeating hyphen) and completes the summary forecast. At the moment, the results displayed in the summary are the same as the figures for SNOW WHITE, since the other product-specific forecasts still contain 0s instead of actual values. However, as you fill in values for these other forecasts, the summary forecast will automatically reflect the new totals.

Figure 5-31:   The Completed Summary Forecast

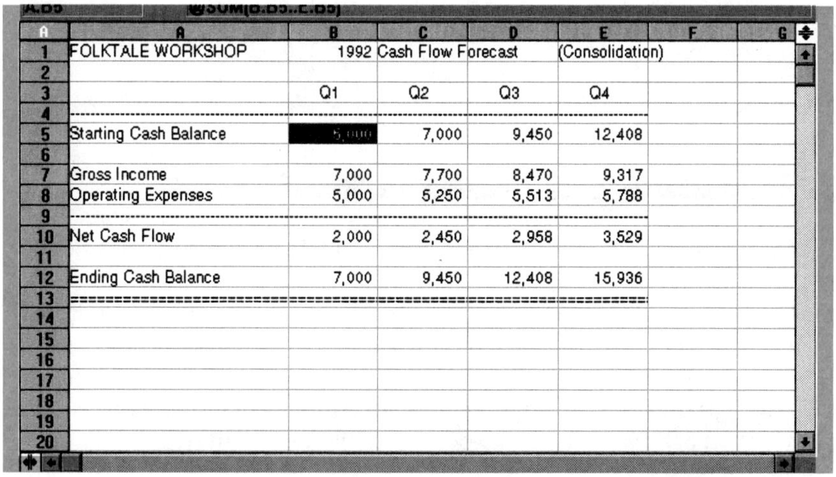

10. Save the Cash Flow worksheet file.

Congratulations! You have finished creating the structure of the Cash Flow Forecast application.

Filling in the Templates

All that remains to complete this worksheet is to fill in sample values for some of the other forecasts, and to do a little cleaning up. You will fill in values for two of the templates: DWARF1 and DWARF2. You'll leave the EVIL QUEEN template blank for now, though you can keep it in the worksheet file in case Bob wants to try out a different scenario later on.

1. Fill in sample values for the DWARF1 product.

Bob has allocated half of his startup fund of $10,000 to the SNOW WHITE toy. He decides to split the remaining $5,000 between DWARF1 and DWARF2.

Move to: cell C:B5

Type: 2500

Press: ↓ *two times*

Figure 5-32: **Entering Values in the DWARF1 Spreadsheet**

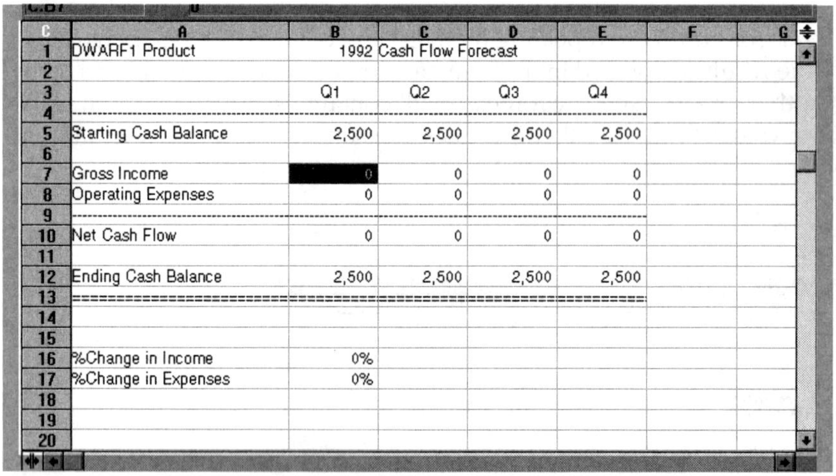

C	A	B	C	D	E	F	G
1	DWARF1 Product		1992 Cash Flow Forecast				
2							
3		Q1	Q2	Q3	Q4		
4							
5	Starting Cash Balance	2,500	2,500	2,500	2,500		
6							
7	Gross Income	0	0	0	0		
8	Operating Expenses	0	0	0	0		
9							
10	Net Cash Flow	0	0	0	0		
11							
12	Ending Cash Balance	2,500	2,500	2,500	2,500		
13							
14							
15							
16	%Change in Income	0%					
17	%Change in Expenses	0%					
18							
19							
20							

Notice that this value is immediately reflected across rows 5 and 12, as the formulas begin to do their work.

Bob figures he'll spend the whole $2,500 in the first quarter, but that he'll also make it back. He's less optimistic about sales for DWARF1 than he was for SNOW WHITE, since he doesn't intend to advertise the product as heavily. He estimates that sales for DWARF1 will increase at a rate of only 7% per quarter. He also figures that DWARF1's operating expenses will go up a little more slowly than SNOW WHITE's expenses, at 4% per quarter.

Enter first-quarter values for gross income, operating expenses, and anticipated change in income and expenses. With the cell pointer in cell C:B7:

Type:	2500	*(the value for gross income)*
Press:	↓	
Type:	2500	*(the value for operating expenses)*
Press:	↵	*or click on the Confirm button*
Move to:	cell C:B16	
Type:	7%	*(the value for %Change in Income)*
Press:	↓	
Type:	4%	*(the value for %Change in Expenses)*
Press:	↵	

1-2-3 displays values in all the formula cells. Because this product's initial income and expenses are the same and they diverge only slightly, each quarter shows only a small positive cash flow.

Figure 5-33: The Completed DWARF1 Forecast

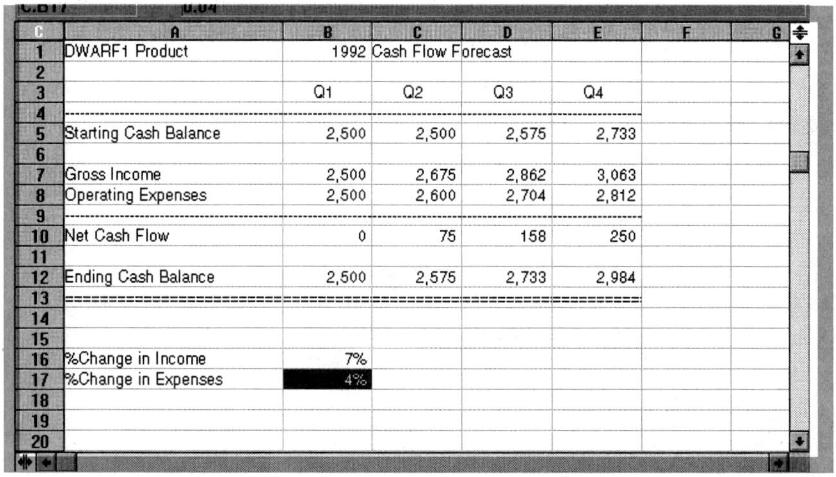

	A	B	C	D	E	F	G
1	DWARF1 Product	1992 Cash Flow Forecast					
2							
3		Q1	Q2	Q3	Q4		
4							
5	Starting Cash Balance	2,500	2,500	2,575	2,733		
6							
7	Gross Income	2,500	2,675	2,862	3,063		
8	Operating Expenses	2,500	2,600	2,704	2,812		
9							
10	Net Cash Flow	0	75	158	250		
11							
12	Ending Cash Balance	2,500	2,575	2,733	2,984		
13							
14							
15							
16	%Change in Income	7%					
17	%Change in Expenses	4%					
18							
19							
20							

2. Fill in sample values for the DWARF2 product.

Bob puts the remaining $2,500 into DWARF2. He plans to incorporate some metal parts into the toy, so he estimates that initial expenses will be greater than income. However, he plans to absorb most of the additional costs of these parts in the first quarter, so he assumes his expenses will go down as the year progresses. Move to the DWARF2 forecast and enter the values:

Move to:　　cell D:B5

Type:	2500	
Press:	↓ *two times*	
Type:	2000 ↓	
	3000 ↵	
Move to:	cell D:B16	
Type:	5% ↓	
	−5% ↵	

Figure 5-34: The Completed DWARF2 Forecast

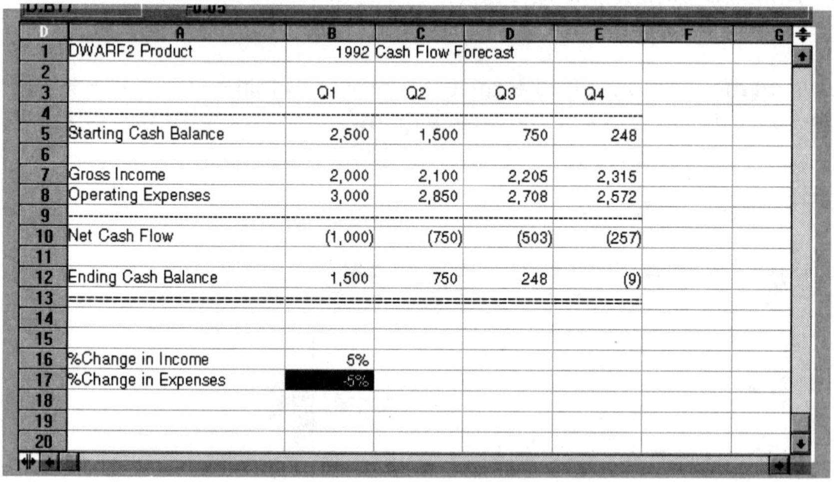

D	A	B	C	D	E	F	G
1	DWARF2 Product	1992 Cash Flow Forecast					
2							
3		Q1	Q2	Q3	Q4		
4							
5	Starting Cash Balance	2,500	1,500	750	248		
6							
7	Gross Income	2,000	2,100	2,205	2,315		
8	Operating Expenses	3,000	2,850	2,708	2,572		
9							
10	Net Cash Flow	(1,000)	(750)	(503)	(257)		
11							
12	Ending Cash Balance	1,500	750	248	(9)		
13							
14							
15							
16	%Change in Income	5%					
17	%Change in Expenses	-5%					
18							
19							
20							

1-2-3 calculates new values for the DWARF2 product. Notice that although Bob loses money on DWARF2 each quarter, his loss steadily decreases. (If you were to extend the forecast into the following year, you could find out when Bob should expect to start making money on DWARF2.)

3. Examine the summary forecast.

Look at the summary forecast to see how the values you have entered are reflected there:

Press: CTRL+HOME

Notice that the summary forecast now displays the sum of the corresponding values in the SNOW WHITE, DWARF1, and DWARF2 forecasts (see Figure 3-35).

4. Save the Cash Flow worksheet file.

With the templates filled in, you've completed another significant piece of this application.

Figure 5-35: The Summary Forecast Now Reflects the Filled-in Values of the Other Forecasts

	A	B	C	D	E	F	G
1	FOLKTALE WORKSHOP		1992 Cash Flow Forecast		(Consolidation)		
2							
3		Q1	Q2	Q3	Q4		
4							
5	Starting Cash Balance	10,000	11,000	12,775	15,388		
6							
7	Gross Income	11,500	12,475	13,537	14,695		
8	Operating Expenses	10,500	10,700	10,924	11,172		
9							
10	Net Cash Flow	1,000	1,775	2,613	3,522		
11							
12	Ending Cash Balance	11,000	12,775	15,388	18,911		
13							
14							
15							
16							
17							
18							
19							
20							

Cleaning Up the Cash Flow Forecast

All that remains to complete the Cash Flow Forecast for Folktale Workshop are a few refinements and a little cleanup work.

1. Enter a label and a formula for net income.

The summary forecast shows Bob ending up the year with a cash balance of $18,911. So that Bob doesn't have to do any arithmetic in his head, create a place on the forecast to hold the year's net income (profit or loss). Format this cell as Currency, zero decimal places:

Move to:	cell A:A15
Type:	Net Income →
Choose:	Range Format
Select:	Currency
	Decimal places:
Type:	0
Select:	OK
Type:	+e12-b5 ↵

1-2-3 displays the value $8,911, Folktale Workshop's total projected profit for 1992 (as illustrated in Figure 5-36, on the next page).

2. Create net income figures for the product-specific forecasts.

Copy the net income formula to the individual forecasts. The copied labels and formulas will identify and display the annual net income for each of the products.

Highlight:	A:A15..A:B15
Choose:	Edit Quick Copy

Specify: B:A15..E:A15   *in the To: text box*

Select: OK

Figure 5-36: **Adding a Net Income Formula to the Forecast**

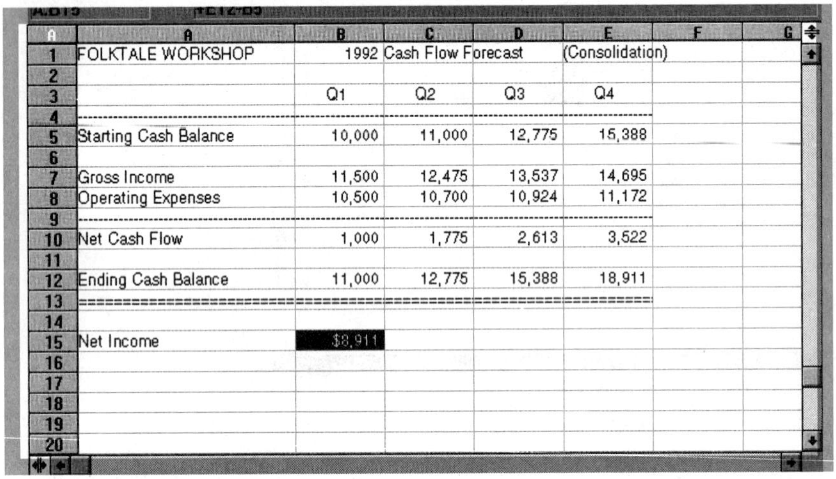

Page through CASHFLOW.WK3 with the Next Sheet key or the "Next Sheet" icon to verify that the forecasts in worksheets B, C, D, and E all contain the **Net Income** label and formula. Or, use perspective view to examine your handiwork, as in Figure 5-37.

Figure 5-37: **The Net Income Figures for Three Forecasts**

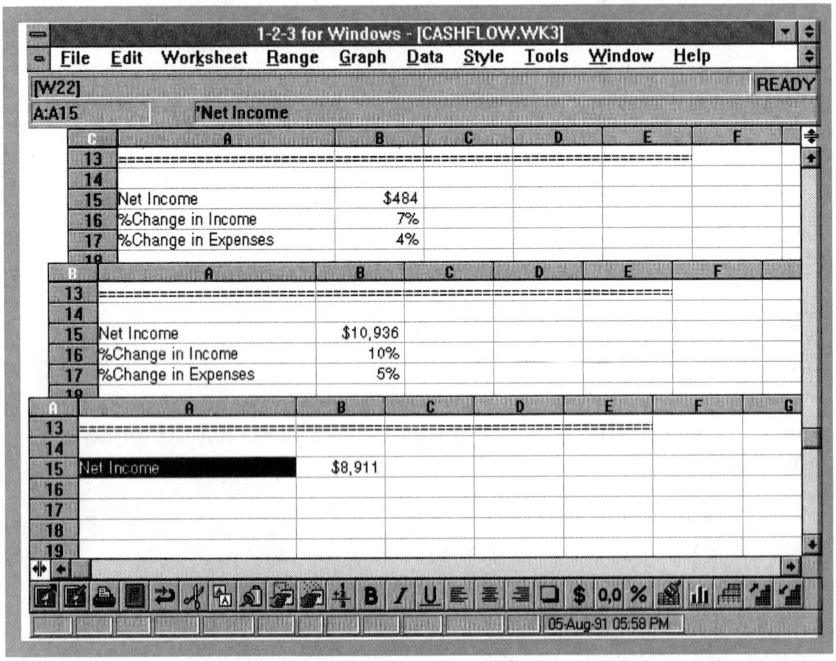

3. Format the starting and ending cash balance figures as currency.

In applications of this type, it is common practice for the beginning and ending figures to be formatted as Currency, and the intervening figures to be displayed in Comma (,) format. You've already changed the global format to Comma (,) with no decimal places. Now, format the starting and ending cash balance figures. Because the worksheet file is in GROUP mode, formatting the summary forecast worksheet also automatically formats the corresponding figures in the other forecasts.

Highlight:	A:B5..A:E5
Choose:	`Range    Format`
Select:	`Currency`
	`Decimal places:`
Specify:	0
Select:	`OK`

If you have a mouse, use the "Apply Formatting" icon to format the row that contains ending cash balance values. Otherwise, use the following keystrokes:

Highlight:	A:B12..A:E12
Choose:	`Range    Format`
Select:	`Currency`
	`Decimal places:`
Specify:	0
Select:	`OK`

4. Change the global column-width setting.

As a final clean-up task, change the global column-width setting from the default (9) to 11. This will create a more balanced display.

Choose:	`Worksheet    Global Settings`
Select:	`Column width:`

1-2-3 offers the default column width. You will change the **9** to **11**. Before you do so, however, look at what happens when you narrow the column width too much to adequately display some of the wider numbers:

Specify:	5 *in the Column width: text box*
Select:	`OK`

The column width for all columns except column A changes from 9 to 5, and 1-2-3 displays asterisks in many of the worksheet cells in which it had previously displayed values. This is 1-2-3's way of letting you know that a column is too narrow to display the current values in the cell format and font you have selected. If you increase the column width, choose a numeric format that requires fewer characters, or use a smaller font, 1-2-3 can again display the values instead of asterisks. Increase the column width to 11:

Choose: `Worksheet   Global Settings`

Select: `Column width:`

Specify: 11

Select: `OK`

Figure 5-38: **1-2-3 Displays Asterisks Instead of Values if the Column is Too Narrow for the Current Value, in the Current Format and Font**

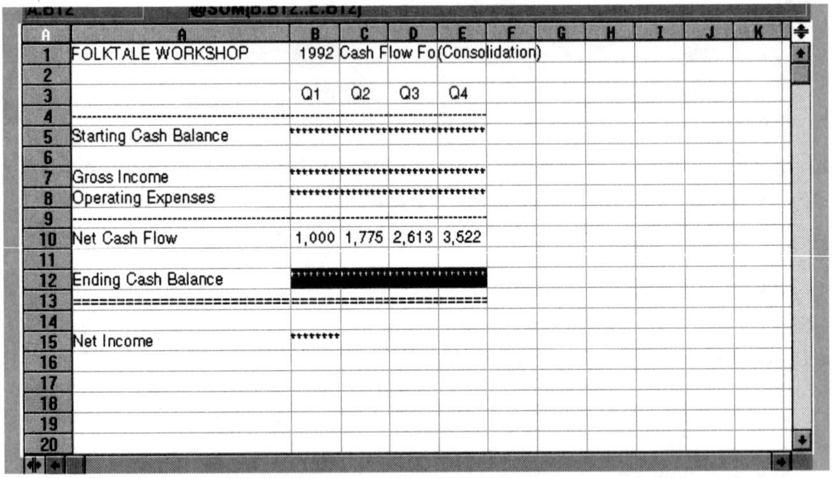

1-2-3 widens columns A through E and redisplays the numbers, as in Figure 5-39.

Figure 5-39: **Increasing the Global Column Width Redisplays the Numbers**

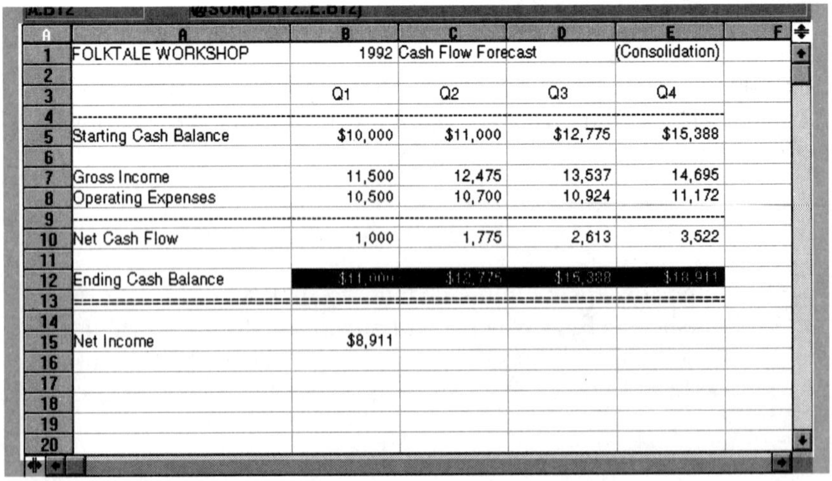

5. Save the Cash Flow worksheet file.

Protecting and Unprotecting Cells and Worksheets

Now that you have finished building the Cash Flow application, you can *protect* the final version and *unprotect* cells that might need to be altered.

When you create a new worksheet, all of the cells are unprotected; you can enter data into any of them. Protecting a worksheet tells 1-2-3 not to permit changes to worksheet cells. This helps prevent you from inadvertently modifying or erasing formulas or other important cell contents. 1-2-3's protection feature is global: The program protects all the cells in the worksheet.

Of course, after you have protected a worksheet, you may still need to change some of the cells. Once global protection is turned on, you can unprotect specific cells or ranges of cells that you want to be able to change. Unprotecting a cell allows you to modify an entry even if a worksheet is protected.

In this section, you will learn first how to protect a worksheet, and then how to unprotect specific cells.

Protecting Worksheets

Turn on global protection:

Choose:	`Worksheet`	`Global Settings`
Select:	`Protection`	*and check the check box*
	`OK`	

1-2-3 protects the worksheet. The only immediate evidence that this has happened is that 1-2-3 displays the letters PR in the format line, above the current cell address. However, if you try to edit any cell in the worksheet or change its format, 1-2-3 beeps and displays an error message.

As you scroll through the worksheet file, you will see that protecting the current worksheet also protects the other worksheets in the file. Because the Cash Flow Forecast worksheet is still in GROUP mode, changes to the global protection of one worksheet affect all worksheets in the file. If you had turned off GROUP mode before you enabled global protection, only the current worksheet would have been affected.

■ *NOTE:* To turn off global protection, clear the "Protection" check box. If you turn off global protection while a file is in GROUP mode, protection will be disabled in all the worksheets in the file. If you turn off global protection in a file that is not in GROUP mode, only the current worksheet's global protection status will be affected.

Unprotecting Cells

With global protection turned on, you will not be able to change any of the cells in the worksheet (or, in this case, in any of the worksheets). To alter specific cells, you must *unprotect* the cells you want to change. For instance, Bob Gordon may want to change the cells containing percentages and first-quarter estimates in the product-specific forecasts.

One way to change these numbers is to turn off global protection, make the changes, and then turn protection back on. This is a sensible way to proceed when you are making major modifications to a protected worksheet. However, selectively unprotecting cells is much easier and safer when you are likely to change only specific cells.

Cell-protection settings affect all the worksheets in a grouped worksheet file. In this particular application, the summary forecast contains only formulas, whereas the product-specific forecasts contain data that is likely to change. It is best to unprotect some of the cells in the product-specific worksheets without unprotecting the corresponding cells in the summary worksheet.

To do so, you must turn off GROUP mode before you unprotect the cells:

Choose:	`Worksheet` `Global Settings`	
Select:	`Group mode`	*and clear the check box*
	`OK`	

1-2-3 turns off GROUP mode for the CASHFLOW.WK3 file and removes the Group indicator from the status line. You will leave the file ungrouped so that the protection status of the product-specific worksheets is not applied to the summary worksheet, or *vice versa.*

All the calls Bob may need to change in order to experiment with different cash flow scenarios contain numbers, not formulas. Unprotect data cells in the product-specific forecasts.

First, unprotect the figures for %Change in Income and %Change in Expenses in worksheets B through E:

Move to:	cell B:B16
Choose:	`Range` `Unprotect`
Specify:	B:B16..E:B17
Select:	`OK`

1-2-3 unprotects these cells. Notice that unprotecting cells causes them to be highlighted (on a monochrome monitor) for to appear in a different color (on a color monitor). These cells are highlighted to make it easier to identify the cells (usually called *input cells*) into which to enter data. Also notice that the letter U appears in the format line of the control panel when the cell pointer is in an unprotected cell. (The letters PR still appear in the format line when the cell pointer is in a protected cell.)

Now, unprotect the other data cells that Bob may want to change frequently:

Move to:	cell B:B5
Choose:	`Range` `Unprotect`
Specify:	B:B5..E:B8
Select:	`OK`

Figure 5-40: Unprotected Cells Are Highlighted or Displayed in a Different Color

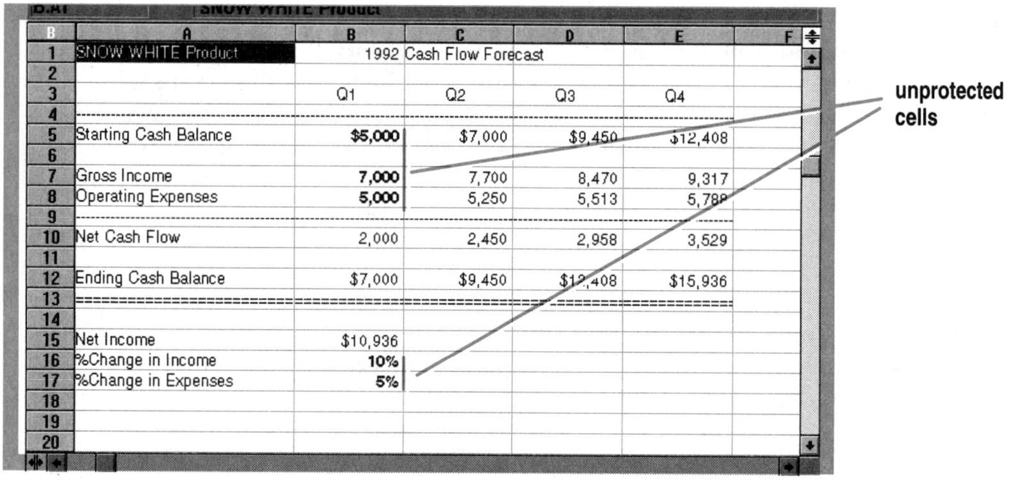

	A	B	C	D	E	F
1	SNOW WHITE Product		1992 Cash Flow Forecast			
2						
3		Q1	Q2	Q3	Q4	
4						
5	Starting Cash Balance	$5,000	$7,000	$9,450	$12,408	
6						
7	Gross Income	7,000	7,700	8,470	9,317	
8	Operating Expenses	5,000	5,250	5,513	5,788	
9						
10	Net Cash Flow	2,000	2,450	2,958	3,529	
11						
12	Ending Cash Balance	$7,000	$9,450	$12,408	$15,936	
13						
14						
15	Net Income	$10,936				
16	%Change in Income	10%				
17	%Change in Expenses	5%				
18						
19						
20						

unprotected cells

Using global protection and selectively unprotecting input cells is a way to separate data from formulas logically and visually. The effect is similar to the one you achieved in Chapter 3, when you created separate sections for variables and formulas in the Home Budget application. In both cases, you have made it easy to distinguish cells that shouldn't be modified from cells that you intend to change.

■ *NOTE:*   To reprotect cells you have unprotected, use the Range Protect command.

Save CASHFLOW.WK3.   Congratulations! You have completed the Cash Flow Forecast. Press Control+Home to move the cell pointer to the first cell in the summary forecast and save the completed file. You will use this file again in Chapters 7 and 8, where you will enhance the formatting, add another report, graph values, perform what-if analysis, and graph the results of the what-if analysis.

Converting a File to Multiple Worksheets

Keeping parts of an application that are logically distinct from each other in separate worksheets often makes it easier to keep track of them, to move among them, and to modify them. To get the feel for how multiple worksheets can simplify an application and to give yourself a chance to try out some of the skills you have learned in this chapter and in Chapters 2, 3 and 4, you'll convert Bob and Kathy Gordon's Home Budget from a single-worksheet application to one that takes advantage of multiple worksheets.

Multiple worksheets will make the Home Budget more flexible to use and easier to modify. For example, right now it is easy to move around in the budget worksheet by using the Page Up and Page Down keys, since each major section occupies one maximized worksheet window. However, if you insert or delete rows in any of these sections, worksheet navigation becomes more awkward. Placing each section in its own worksheet lets you page from section to section with the Next Sheet and Prev Sheet keys or icons, regardless of how many rows each section occupies.

In the following section, you will convert the budget worksheet to a multiple-worksheet application by putting the main spreadsheet sections in their own worksheets. Since the point of this exercise is, in part, to help you become familiar with using the worksheet commands you have learned so far, individual keystrokes are not provided. You have already done all of the operations required in this exercise. If you need a reminder of how to perform a particular operation, either refer to the "At a Glance" sections at the end of each chapter, or press F1 (Help) and select "Search" to scan 1-2-3's excellent on-line Help for the procedures you need help with.

■ *NOTE*   These instructions also use a shorthand way to refer to command options. For example, step 2 says to clear worksheet titles with Worksheet Titles Clear rather than telling you to select the "Clear" option of the Worksheet Titles command.

1. Retrieve BUDGET1.WK3 and save it as BUDGET3D.WK3.

   You'll work in a copy of the file you created in Chapters 3 and 4, rather than in the original file. File Open BUDGET1.WK3, maximize the worksheet, and choose File Save As to save the file as BUDGET3D.WK3

2. Clear worksheet titles with Worksheet Titles Clear.

3. Delete the scratch worksheet.

   You don't need the scratch worksheet anymore, so get rid of it. Choose Worksheet Delete and select the "Sheet" option. Specify, as the range to delete, any cell in worksheet B, then select OK.

4. Insert three new worksheets after worksheet A.

   Use Worksheet Insert Sheet to insert new worksheets for the EXPENSES, CASH FLOW, and VARIABLES sections. You will leave the INCOME section in the original worksheet.

5. Widen column A of worksheets B, C, and D.

   Highlight the range B:A1..D:A1 and then choose Worksheet Column Width. Set the width to 22 characters.

6. Move the EXPENSES section to worksheet B.

   Use Edit Move Cells (or the "Move To" icon) to move the EXPENSES section "from" A:A21..A:N36 "to" B:A5.
   Edit Move Cells is the key to reorganizing a worksheet file. Moving part of a worksheet to another worksheet is similar to cutting a paragraph from one page of a report and pasting it down on another page. When you are finished, the information appears on the new page and is no longer on the original page. Unlike the copy commands, Edit Move Cells adjusts relative cell addresses so that formulas still operate on the same data they did before the move took

place. When you "pick up" part of one worksheet and move it to another, you do not invalidate any of the formulas in the moved part, or any of the formulas that depend on values in the moved part; 1-2-3 automatically adjusts the row, column, and worksheet addresses so that the formulas still work the same as they used to.

Figure 5-41: The EXPENSES Section in Its New Location

B	A	B	C	D	E	F	G
1							
2							
3							
4							
5	EXPENSES						
6							
7	Auto	150	150	150	150	150	
8	Charity	75	75	75	75	75	
9	Clothes	200	200	200	200	200	
10	Food	875	700	700	700	875	
11	Household	200	200	200	200	200	
12	Medical	150	150	150	150	150	
13	Misc	1125	900	900	900	1125	
14	Rent	1100	1100	1100	1100	1100	1
15	Savings	500	400	400	400	500	
16	Utility	200	200	200	200	200	
17	Woodwork	250	250	250	250	250	
18							
19	Total Expenses	$4,825	$4,325	$4,325	$4,325	$4,825	$4,
20							

7. Move the CASH FLOW section to worksheet C.

   Again, use Edit Move Cells or the "Move To" icon. Use a "from" range of A:A37..A:M52 and a "to" range of C:A5.

Figure 5-42: The CASH FLOW Section in Its New Location

C	A	B	C	D	E	F	G
1							
2							
3							
4							
5	CASH FLOW						
6							
7	Savings Account						
8	Savings this Month	500	400	400	400	500	
9	Cumulative Savings	$2,500	$2,900	$3,300	$3,700	$4,200	$4,
10							
11							
12	Checking Account						
13	Opening Balance	1000	1375	1350	1325	1300	1
14	Net Cash Flow	375	-25	-25	-25	375	
15							
16	Closing Balance	$1,375	$1,350	$1,325	$1,300	$1,675	$1,
17							
18							
19	Total Available Funds	$3,875	$4,250	$4,625	$5,000	$5,875	$6,
20							

8. Move the VARIABLES sections to worksheet D.

Move the INCOME VARIABLES, EXPENSE VARIABLES, and MISC. VARIABLES sections as one block and place them at the top of worksheet D. Use A:A61..A:F107 as the "from" range and D:A1 as the "to" range.

Figure 5-43:   The INCOME VARIABLES Section in Its New Location

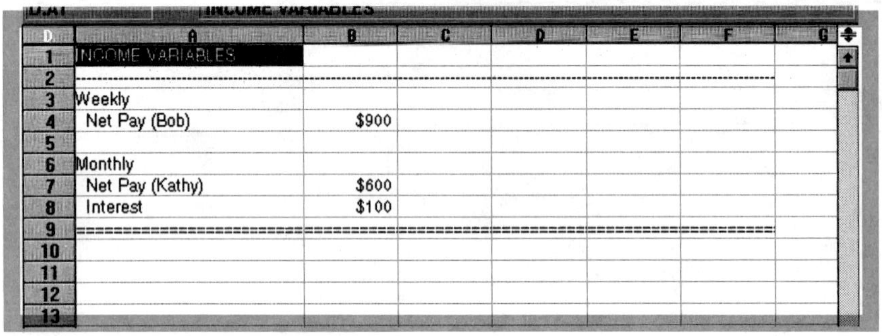

9. Copy the title rows of worksheet A to worksheets B and C.

Almost finished! Now that they are in different worksheets, the EXPENSES and CASH FLOW sections of the new Home Budget need their own worksheet titles and column headings. Copy the first two rows of worksheet A to each of the new worksheets. Before you make the copy, however, make the range-name reference in cell A:B1 into an absolute range name ($CURRENT_YEAR), so that the copies of cell A:B1 in worksheets B and C all refer to the same cell.

As the "from" range, use A:A1..A:N2. As the "to" range, use B:A1..C:A1.

10. Copy the double-ruled line in row 4 of worksheet A to worksheets B and C.

As the "from" range use A:A4..A:N4. As the "to" range, use B:A4..C:A4. Figure 5-44 (shown on the next page), shows how the worksheet file should look in perspective view after titles have been copied.

■ *NOTE:*   You do not need to copy row 3, which contains the hidden values for the number of paydays in each month, because all the formulas in the worksheet that reference these values reference worksheet A. To prove this to yourself, look at cells B:B10, B:B13, and B:B15. Each of these cells now references cell A:B3, which contains the value for the number of paydays in January.

11. Clean up any remaining formatting problems.

Use Worksheet Global Settings Format to set the global format for worksheets B and C to Comma (,), with 0 decimal places. Then look over the worksheet file carefully and clean up any stray formatting problems. (For example, worksheet C now has a useless **Annual** label in cell C:N2.)

12. Test out the new worksheet arrangement.

Figure 5-44: Perspective View of BUDGET3D.WK3 After Titles Have Been Copied

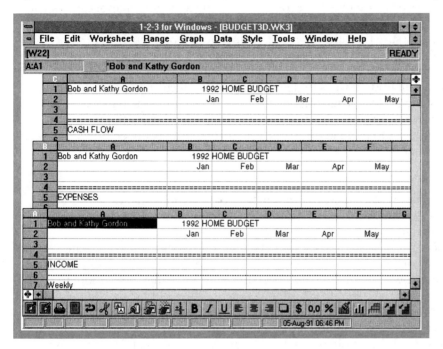

Use the Next Sheet and Prev Sheet keys (or the equivalent icons) to page back and forth among the worksheets of the new Home Budget. Examine some of the formulas to see how moving them to new worksheets changed the cell references in them. Make sure none of the formulas evaluate to ERR, and that there are no spurious 0 values. If you find any errors, fix them now.

Then try changing some budget variables to see how modifying them changes the values displayed elsewhere in the file. If the new budget doesn't behave the same as the old one, check the formula cells and make sure they still point to the right places.

13. Set worksheet titles in worksheets A, B, and C.

When you have assured yourself that the conversion from single-worksheet to multiple-worksheet application is complete and accurate, use Worksheet Title Both to set worksheet titles for worksheets A, B, and C at cell B5. This freezes column A and rows 1 through 4. Worksheet D is fine just the way it is.

14. Save the modified BUDGET3D.WK3 file.

Congratulations! You are finished with the new version of Bob and Kathy Gordons' Home Budget, and you are now reasonably proficient in the major uses of multiple-worksheet files.

The rest of this chapter contains a collection of tips, techniques, and "gotchas" that apply to any work you'll be doing in 1-2-3.

Avoiding and Detecting Worksheet Errors

In the last few chapters you have created two spreadsheet applications. In the process, along with learning many 1-2-3 skills, you may have formulated some ideas about applications you want to build for your own use. As you begin to develop your own applications, it will be your responsibility to make sure they are error-free. As mentioned previously in this book, 1-2-3 knows whether the formulas you enter are valid, but it can't tell whether they are working as you intended them to.

Much is often said about finding ways to detect errors in an electronic spreadsheet, but the truth is that the best method for detecting errors is to avoid creating them in the first place. This section contains a few pointers on keeping out of trouble—how to set things up so it is easy to avoid errors, and what to do to keep errors from getting too deeply embedded in your application if they do occur.

Planning Your Applications

Before you actually start to build a 1-2-3 application, take the time to plan it out:

First, write down what you want the application to accomplish, who besides you will be using it, and what those other users need to know in order to run it.

Next, figure out how the application breaks down logically. Do you need separate sections for different groups of data? How will these sections relate to each other? For example, will formulas link them? How large do the areas need to be, and will they need room to expand? Do all of them need to be in memory at the same time, or could some of them be relegated to separate files? Given the answers to the questions above, map out the application on paper. You do not have to be exact in your allocation of worksheet files, worksheets, rows, and columns, but you should sketch out the general locations of groups of data and how big an area each group will occupy.

Next, make a record of the assumptions involved in building the application. You can do this either on the screen or on paper. Note any additional sources of information on which your application depends, and any applications that depend on it.

Build and test the application. After you have completed it, consider printing out a document that lists only the cell contents line by line, and another that prints the forecasts with the worksheet frame. These printouts will give you information on all the material in each cell— formula, label, format, and so on—and will provide a reference for tracking down problems and making changes.

To print cell contents, use the 1-2-3 Classic /Print menu. First, choose /Print Printer Range and specify the print range. Then, while still in the /Print Printer menu, choose Options Other Cell-Formats to tell 1-2-3 to print formulas rather than values. Finally, choose Align Go Page Quit to print the range and return to READY mode. (See the 1-2-3 documentation for more information on using the 1-2-3 Classic menu.)

To print the worksheet frame as well as the displayed contents, choose File Page Setup and select the "Show worksheet frame" and "Show grid lines" options. Then highlight the range you want to print and choose File Print. (See Chapter 9 for more information on printing.)

Avoiding and Detecting Errors

The more careful and consistent your work habits become, the more likely you are to notice when your worksheet file deviates from them. Following are some techniques that can help you trap errors before they become deeply embedded in your work.

No matter how careful you are, however, eventually some errors will probably creep into your work. This section describes some of the techniques you can use to detect errors when they do creep in.

Document Your Work   Be generous in your use of labels for value and formula cells, and of ruled lines or other separators between different areas of the application. Create tables of contents for large applications so that you can easily find major sections of the application, and give range names to the upper left corner of these sections so you can use the Goto key to move to them quickly.

Name cells that you refer to frequently. Range names provide insurance against referencing the wrong cell in a formula. It is always a good idea to name variables, and it is also a good idea to name formulas that you refer to elsewhere.

Use Range Name Paste Table to create a table of range names and their addresses in the worksheet file. This procedure is especially useful when you have a large number of range names; the table provides a quick way to refresh your memory on the ranges those names refer to.

■ *CAUTION:*   Make sure the location you choose for a range name table is blank; 1-2-3 writes over any existing information in the cells it needs to create the table. Once you have established a safe location, name the upper left corner of the table range. When you want to re-create the table, provide the Range Name Paste Table command with the range name. 1-2-3 will overwrite the old table with the new one.

Establish Naming Conventions and Stick to Them   Name files, ranges, variables, and macros consistently. If all of your macros begin with the same character, you are unlikely to accidentally try to run a random worksheet range as a macro. If all your print ranges begin with "P_" and your graph ranges begin with "G_", they will be easy to locate and easy to associate with print settings and graphs. The same principle holds for linked worksheet files associated with a multiple-file application: name them in a consistent manner, and make it clear that subordinate files are related. (Multiple-file applications are discussed in Chapter 10.) The actual scheme you develop for naming is not nearly as important as your consistency in using it.

Protect Worksheets and Unprotect Input Cells   When you have finished creating an application, protect the worksheets and unprotect only the cells that contain data you plan to change. Do this even if you are the only one who will be using the application. Unprotecting cells highlights them and makes it easy to see which cells contain data that may change. Protecting the cells containing constants, formulas, and labels prevents you from inadvertently changing them. It is very easy to accidentally type a value on top of a formula, thus creating a "dead spot" in the worksheet that no longer responds to changes in variables. Protecting formula cells prevents this type of error.

Use Formats and Column Widths to Spot Errors   1-2-3 displays asterisks if a value in a cell is too large for the current column width and cell display format. You can use this to your advantage to identify values that are larger than they should be.

Design your spreadsheets so that columns containing values are just wide enough to display the largest value you anticipate. If, after you have worked with your application a while, a cell suddenly displays asterisks, it is likely there's some sort of problem. The asterisks provide an early warning of trouble.

Use "1"s to Find Errors in Formulas   One of the simplest techniques you can use to prevent errors in formulas is to plug values into them that will generate easy-to-interpret results. For example, suppose you created a table of values with @SUM formulas in the right-most column and @AVG formulas in the bottom row. To test these formulas, use 1s as the values being summed and averaged. The @SUM formulas should contain values equal to the number of columns being summed and the @AVG formulas should each contain the value 1. Since you can do the math in your head if you use 1s, this technique provides a quick visual check on your formulas. When you are confident that the formulas are okay, use the actual data.

Use Crossfoot Totals to Flag Formula Errors   Many spreadsheet applications are organized as rows of data with a row of totals beneath the data, and another row of totals to the right of the data. An easy way to be sure that the totals are correct is to create a "grand total" cell that compares the sum of the values in the row of totals with the sum of the values in the column of totals. This effectively adds up all the values in two different orders. The formula should round the two sums to the number of significant digits in the calculations. If the two rounded sums agree, the cell displays one of them as the grand total. If they do not agree, the cell either displays an error message (if you are not going to use this total in subsequent calculations), or evaluates to ERR (so that if the value is an error, ERR will be propagated to any formulas that use this value).

Figure 5-45 (shown on thew next page) illustrates this technique. The formula in cell E28 adds up the values in the range B28..D28 (the range named ROWS), and compares that sum to the total of the values in the range E24..E26 (the range named COLS). If the two sums agree, the formula displays one of them—in this case, @SUM(ROWS). If the two sums don't agree, the formula displays ERR.

The formula uses the @ROUND function to round both values to zero decimal places, the @ERR function to produce the value ERR if the two sums disagree, and the @IF function to make the comparison. (See 1-2-3's on-line Help for complete information on using these @functions.)

Use a Spreadsheet Auditor   A number of spreadsheet auditor programs exist that contain additional tools for managing worksheet applications, and that dramatically extend your ability to document and also to debug a 1-2-3 application. Spreadsheet auditors typically contain commands to let you examine the formulas behind worksheet cells; list cell dependencies, range names, and other settings; trace circular references; locate the original formulas from which copies were made; report on overlapping or other suspicious ranges; and perform other useful analyses of worksheet structure. If much of your daily work is in developing 1-2-3 applications, consider investing in, and learning how to use, a spreadsheet auditor.

Figure 5-45: Using Crossfoot Totals. The formula in cell E28 compares the values in the row of totals and the column of totals to see if they agree. (They should!)

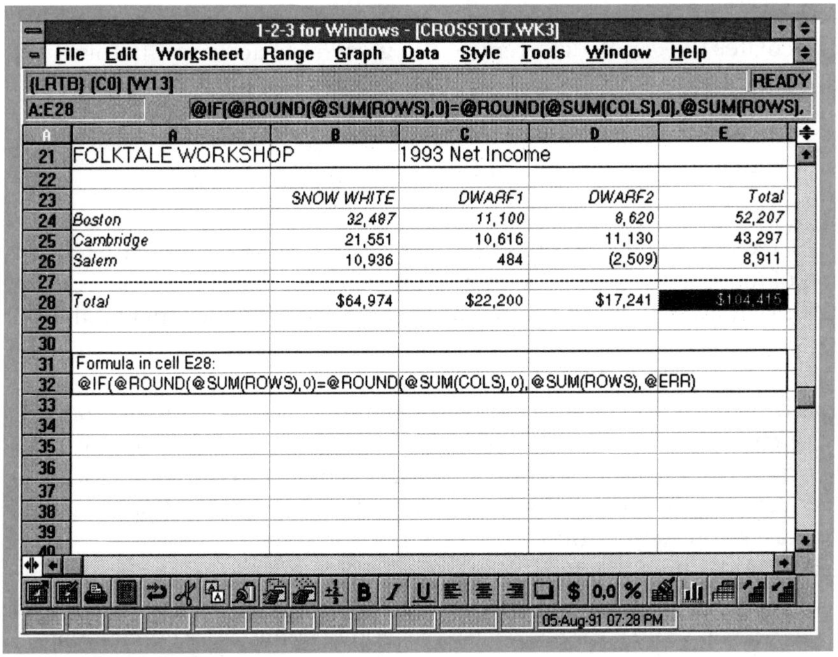

Identify Circular References   A worksheet file contains circular references when one or more formulas refer to themselves either directly or indirectly. The simplest case is a formula that directly references its own cell: For example, cell B2 contains the formula +B2/B3 or @SUM(B2..B5). A more common case is where a formula references another formula, which in turn references another formula, which in turn eventually refers back to the initial formula cell.

Except in circumstances where you are intentionally using 1-2-3 to repeatedly recalculate the same cell (see note on the next page), a circular reference is an error. When 1-2-3 detects one or more circular references, it displays the Circ indicator in the status line. If you see the Circ indicator, you should examine the worksheet to find and eliminate the circular reference or references.

In the Help About 1-2-3 dialog box, 1-2-3 displays the cell address of the first circular reference it encounters. To remove a circular reference, choose Help About 1-2-3, note the address of the reference, and go to that cell to correct the error. If 1-2-3 still displays the Circ indicator after you have corrected the error, you have another circular reference in the worksheet. Repeat this process until the Circ indicator disappears.

■ *NOTE:*   Sometimes, *intentional* circular references are the only way to solve a problem. For example, to figure out bonuses based on after-tax profits, you may need to create intentional circular references. Imagine that bonuses are a tax-deductible expense set at 8% of a company's after-tax profits. To compute a bonus, you need to know the after-tax profits, but you can't compute the after-tax profits until you know how much you are paying out in bonuses. To solve this sort of problem, you must create circular references and recalculate the formulas iteratively. With each successive recalculation pass, you home in on the final result; the more times 1-2-3 recalculates the circular references, the greater the accuracy. In this case, you would use the "Iterations" option of Tools User Setup Recalculation to set the number of recalculation cycles in a recalculation pass to the number necessary to achieve the degree of accuracy you need.

Worksheet Tips

This section describes tips, techniques and gotchas that apply to 1-2-3 worksheets and to the product in general. Some of these have already been introduced or mentioned in Chapters 3 and 4, or in earlier sections of this chapter. This information will serve as review material.

Read the Manual

No kidding, this is probably the best tip in this book. Although you may have bought *Lotus 1-2-3 for Windows at Work* because you wanted more step-by-step instructions than the 1-2-3 documentation provides, now you know what you are doing. It's time to have another look at that manual. This book covers only a portion of what 1-2-3 has to offer; the 1-2-3 printed documentation describes tasks you can perform with the whole product.

Tackle the manual a piece at a time, going where your interests and the needs of your current projects lead you. Commands and procedures that may have looked intimidating when you first started learning 1-2-3 will seem easier and easier as you become more familiar with the product.

Many users never familiarize themselves with more than about 20% of 1-2-3's features. If you take the trouble to learn what's in this book, you'll already be beyond that category. But why stop then? Each new command, @function, or technique you learn increases the opportunity you have to solve a problem quickly and easily; each new skill you master increases both the value of 1-2-3 to you, and your value in your work. A few minutes spent learning something new whenever you work with 1-2-3 will pay off in hours saved when you apply an easy, elegant solution to a problem instead of a more obvious, but more cumbersome, method.

Mouse Tips

Perhaps the easiest way to speed up your work with 1-2-3 is to take advantage of the things you can do with the mouse. This section recommends a few places to start.

Use SmartIcons   In general, using SmartIcons is quicker and easier than using either the menus or the keyboard to perform 1-2-3 operations. While some icons may not save you much time relative to the time it takes to complete the task—for example, it takes only a moment more to choose the File Open or File Print commands than it does to click their respective icons—some icons are much quicker and easier. For instance, using the "Copy To" and "Move To" icons greatly simplifies copying and moving information, and the "Apply Formatting" icon lets you handle repetitive formatting operations with a few clicks and drags.

Once you get used to thinking of the icons as another interface, you'll find yourself using them all the time, particularly when you start to customize the icon palette, and to add your own icons. (See Chapter 11 for information on customizing the icon palette.)

Double-Click to Edit   The quickest way to edit a cell entry is to double-click on the cell you want to edit. Double-clicking brings the cell contents into the control panel's edit line and switches 1-2-3 to EDIT mode.

You can also cut and paste text between the Clipboard and the edit line by clicking and dragging with the mouse.

Keyboard Tips

Another easy way to speed up your work with 1-2-3 is to take advantage of the function keys, the pointer-movement keys, and other 1-2-3 special keys.

Use F1 (Help)   The Help system is the most painless way to familiarize yourself with features you have not yet used, and to refresh your memory on features you have. It describes every command in the product, often in more detail than the manual. Use it!

In addition to the ways to use Help described in Chapter 2, you can also use 1-2-3's context-sensitive Help when you are entering formulas or creating macros.

You can get Help on a particular @function in two ways: (1) type an at-sign (@) in the control panel and press F1 (Help), or (2) press Help, select @Functions, and then select @Function Index. With either method, 1-2-3 displays a list of built-in @functions. Highlight the name of the @function you need and press Enter; 1-2-3 displays a Help screen on that @function.

Getting help on macro commands and keywords is similar. Either (1) type an open brace ({) in the control panel and press F1 (Help), or (2) press Help, select Macros, and then select Macro Command Index. In either case, 1-2-3 displays a list of macro commands and keywords.

Convert a Formula to a Value with F2 (Edit) and F9 (Calc)   You can convert the formula in a single cell to a value by moving to the cell, pressing F2 (Edit), pressing Calc (F9), and then pressing Enter. This is usually faster than using Edit Quick Copy with the "Convert to values" option checked when all you want to do is convert a single formula to a value. If you use this technique, before you press Enter, make sure you no longer need the formula.

■ *NOTE:*   See "What to Do When You Run Out of Memory" later in this chapter for more on using the "Convert to values" option of Edit Quick Copy.

Use F3 (Name)   Like F1 (Help), F3 (Name) is context-sensitive. Whenever a 1-2-3 prompt in a dialog box expects a cell address or a file name, you can press F3 (Name) to display the appropriate list of names. Selecting a name from the list inserts it in the text box.

Use F5 (Goto) to Edit Worksheet Titles   Ordinarily, you can't move the cell pointer to rows or columns frozen by the Worksheet Titles command. To edit the titles, you usually turn Worksheet Titles off, and then turn them back on when you have finished. This is fine if your changes are extensive, but to make a quick change, there's a faster way:

You can use the Goto key to move to any cell, even if that cell is part of a worksheet title row or column. 1-2-3 will display two rows or columns of worksheet titles: One containing the cell pointer, and one without the cell pointer. Edit the cells you want to change, press Enter, then press End Home Home to move the cell pointer to the last active cell in the worksheet and then back to the cell just below and to the right of the worksheet titles. Only the new, edited version of the worksheet titles will be displayed.

■ *NOTE:*   You can also edit titles by making your changes to cells outside the title area and then using Edit Move Cells to move the changed cells into the titles area.

Use F7 (Query) and F8 (Table)   F7 (Query) repeats the last Data Query command and F8 (Table) repeats the last Data Table command. Both of these keys allow you to change values in the worksheet file and obtain new results without having to go through the Data commands. (You'll learn more about Data Query and Data Table commands in Chapter 6.)

Use End to Navigate Worksheets Quickly   Worksheet navigation is considerably faster once you get the hang of using the End key in combination with the pointer-movement and worksheet navigation keys. Remember the basic rules:

1. If the cell pointer is in a nonblank cell, it moves in the direction of the pointer-movement key either to the last nonblank cell before a blank cell, to the first nonblank cell after a blank cell, or to the edge of the worksheet.

2. If the cell pointer is in a blank cell, it moves in the direction of the key either to the first non-blank cell, or to the edge of the worksheet.

Experiment with End and the pointer-movement and worksheet navigation keys. Soon you will be building into your applications opportunities to simplify worksheet navigation by using End key combinations. For example, you can use End in conjunction with the arrow keys or the Next Sheet and Prev Sheet keys to quickly define ranges in a worksheet file. Or, you can move to a column you know to be blank, and press End Down to move to the last row of the worksheet. Pressing End Home move you immediately to the end of the active area of a worksheet, and End in a macro can help you expand or contract ranges when you don't know actual cell addresses. (Macros are described in Chapter 11.)

Adjust Ranges with the Period, Escape, and Backspace Keys   The Period key (.) moves the free corner of an anchored range to each of the four corners of the range, changing the part of the range that you can expand or contract with the pointer-movement keys. Backspace and Escape unanchor a range, so that you can re-anchor it somewhere else. These keys work the same whether you are highlighting a range with the keyboard or the mouse.

Enter Characters that Aren't on the Keyboard   Alt+F1 (Compose) can be used to create characters that cannot be typed from the keyboard. For English-language versions of 1-2-3, these include accented characters, special symbols, and graphics characters. To create these characters, you enter *compose sequences* consisting of two or more ordinary characters, preceded by pressing the Compose key. For example, to create the symbol for the Japanese Yen sign, you press Compose and then type Y=. The compose sequences you can use in 1-2-3 are listed in the LMBCS (Lotus Multibyte Character Set) appendix in the 1-2-3 *User's Guide*.

■ *NOTE:*   Depending on your printer, you may not always be able to print characters you have created using compose sequences. Also, if Windows can't display a LMBCS character, it will display an approximation known as a *fallback character*. See the Windows documentation for a list of the characters Windows can display.

Use @Functions

Before you create a formula from scratch, see if there is an @function available to do the job. Using @functions is almost always faster and simpler than writing your own formulas. For example, the following formula calculates the amount of a periodic payment necessary to pay off a loan, given the interest rate and number of payments:

```
+PRINCIPAL*INTEREST/(1-(INTEREST+1)^-TERM)
```

where:

PRINCIPAL is a range name for the value of the loan
INTEREST is a range name for the periodic interest rate
TERM is a range name for the number of payments

The following formula uses the @PMT function to obtain the same result:

```
@PMT(PRINCIPAL,INTEREST,TERM)
```

Therefore, to determine the interest on a three-year, $6000 car loan at an annual interest rate of 10%, you could use either of the following formulas. (In both cases, annual interest is divided by 12 to arrive at a figure for monthly payment.)

Without @PMT: `(6000*.1/12)/(1-(.1/12+1)^-36)`
With @PMT: `@PMT(6000,.1/12,36)`

Besides being shorter and simpler, the @PMT formula also executes many times faster than the version that does not use an @function.

1-2-3 has more than 100 built-in @functions. These @functions can be grouped into eight categories: database, date and time, financial, logical, mathematical, special, statistical, and string. All of the @functions are fully described in the 1-2-3 on-line Help, so information on using them is literally only a few keystrokes away.

Use Range Names to Simplify 1-2-3 Operations

The ability to name a range of cells is one of 1-2-3's most helpful features. With a little practice, you can easily learn to use range names in most places that call for ranges.

Use range names to identify variables, values, print and graph ranges, ranges used in macros, and cells in other files. Range names make formulas much easier to understand, and specifying range names is more convenient than pointing to cells or remembering their addresses.

Because 1-2-3 always uses the current definition of a range name, range names can also help prevent errors. If a named range changes between the time you create the range and the time you use it to print, draw a graph, or in a formula or macro, 1-2-3 still uses the correct worksheet range. This is not always the case when you use cell addresses. (More on this in "Worksheet Gotchas" later in this chapter.)

Use Worksheet Window Panes

Worksheet window panes can speed up worksheet development and, by juxtaposing two distant parts of an application, simplify user interaction with the application.

For example, when you work with a large spreadsheet, it can be time-consuming to move or copy data from one distant part to another. If you break the worksheet display area into two windows, you can display the source area in one window, and the target area in the other. During the copy or move operation, you can switch between panes instead of having to page back and forth through the worksheet file.

In an application, you sometimes need to display totals in one part of the screen and data input cells in another. You can create a narrow pane at the top or bottom of the screen to display the totals, and use the other pane for entering data. If necessary, you can change the column widths of one pane without affecting the column widths of the other.

When you are developing a macro (described in Chapter 11), it is often helpful to look at the variables or at the macro code itself while the macro executes. You can do this by creating one pane to hold the macro, and another to display the part of the worksheet file that the macro acts on.

Copy Shortcuts

This section describes a few copying tricks. You may not need them often, but if you do, they'll save you time.

Making an Exact Copy of a Formula   Sometimes, after you enter a formula, you find that the formula is not working as it should. You may want to experiment with the formula. At the same time, you may also want to look at the original version. In this particular case, you can have your cake and eat it, too, by making an exact copy of the formula in another location.

If the formula contains relative references, simply using Edit Quick Copy will not work: The relative references in the copy will differ from the references in the original. One way around this is to convert the formula to a label by prefixing it with an apostrophe or other label prefix. Then use Edit Quick Copy to copy the formula to another cell, and remove the label prefix from the original formula. By converting the formula to a label, you preserve relative cell addresses in the copy.

Converting a formula to a label is fine if all you are copying is a few cells, but if you want to make an exact duplicate of many formulas that contain relative cell references, the process of putting label prefixes in front of cells, copying the cells, and then removing the label prefixes could get tiresome. Fortunately, there is an easier way. The following four-step process will accomplish the same task without editing any cells:

1. Copy the formulas to a scratch area of the worksheet with Edit Quick Copy, or Edit Copy and Edit Paste.

2. Use Edit Move Cells to move the original formulas to the location where you want an exact copy.

3. Copy the formulas in the scratch area back to the original location.

4. Erase the copied formulas from the scratch area with Edit Clear.

The first copy operation creates a temporary copy of the formulas; relative addresses in this temporary copy adjust to the scratch area location. The move operation moves the original formulas to the location where you want an exact copy; relative references still point to the original cell addresses. The second copy operation copies the scratch area's copies back to the original location, restoring the formulas that were moved by Edit Move Cells; relative addresses that were adjusted by the initial copy once again adjust, this time back to what they originally were.

Doubling   If you are building a spreadsheet that is to have a number of areas with identical rows or columns, you can construct it rapidly with a technique known as "doubling". When you use doubling, you first copy a range to an adjoining range, then you copy both the original and the copy to a third range. Next, you copy the doubled range to another range, and so on. Each copy command copies twice as much information as the previous one.

For example, suppose you have a worksheet that has quarterly values interspersed with monthly values. You could create such a worksheet by setting up the labels and formulas for the first quarter, and then copying that quarter to the second, third, and fourth quarters with separate copy operations. It is faster, however, to copy the first quarter to the second in one operation, and then to copy the first and second quarters to the third and fourth with another copy command.

Copying to Every Other Cell   Occasionally it is useful to copy a cell, row, or column to every other row, or to every other column. To do so, you can make the "to" range a single cell and locate the "to" range within the "from" range.

For example, suppose cell A1 contains a formula that you want to copy to cells A3, A5, A7, and so on down to cell A23. To do this in one copy operation, highlight the range A1..A22, choose Edit Quick Copy, specify a "to" range of A3, and select OK. 1-2-3 will copy the contents of cell A1 to every other cell in the range, beginning with cell A3. If you need to copy to every third cell, use the same "from" range but change the "to" range to A4.

Date and Time Arithmetic

Because 1-2-3 stores dates and times as numbers, you can perform arithmetic on them in much the same way as you can any other numbers. In addition, you can extract part of a date or time from a date or time number by using @functions. This section introduces you to date and time arithmetic.

Dates for the Years 2000 to 2099   1-2-3 assigns a value to a date (a *date number*) that represents the number of days from the beginning of this century to the date. You can enter the date number directly, or with the @DATE or @DATEVALUE function. For example, the entries `4-feb-01`, `@DATEVALUE("04-Feb-01")`, `@DATE(1,2,4)`, or `401` all stand for February 4, 1901. The value 401 stands for 401 days from January 1, 1900. The value 401 appears in the cell unless you format the cell to display its contents as a date or give the cell Automatic format and enter the date in one of 1-2-3's date formats.

1-2-3 can display dates for any year from 1900 to 2099. For years after 1999, you must identify the year with all four digits when you enter it in one of 1-2-3's date formats, or you must add 100 to the last two digits when you use the @DATE function. For example, to enter the date October 31, 2042, you type `31-oct-2042`, `@DATE(142,10,31)`, or `@DATEVALUE("31-Oct-2042")`.

Years from 2000 to 2099 display as four digits when the cell is formatted to display dates, so be sure the cell is wide enough to accommodate the longer entry.

Finding the Month, Day, Year, and Day of the Week   To determine the number of days between any two dates, subtract the later date from the earlier date. For example, if cell A1 contains the date number for 25-Dec-92, and cell A2 contains the date number for 04-Jul-92, the formula +A1-A2 tells you how many days there are between July 4, 1992 and December 25, 1992.

You can also use @functions to find out information about a date. @DAY tells you the day of the month for any given date: 1 for the first day of the month, 2 for the second, and so on. @YEAR calculates the number of the year, from 0 (for 1900) to 199 (for 2099). The @MONTH function tells you what month a given date falls in. It takes as an argument a date number and evaluates to a number corresponding to the month: 1 for January, 2 for February, 3 for March, and so on. @NOW evaluates to the date and time number for the current date and time, and @TODAY evaluates to the current date.

There is no @function that directly gives you the day of the week from a date, but the @MOD function will do the trick. The formula: @MOD(*datenumber*,7) evaluates to 0 if the date is a Saturday, 1 if the date is a Sunday, 2 if the date is a Monday, and so on (*datenumber* is any date number). If you combine the @MOD function with an @IF or an @CHOOSE function, you can directly display the day of the week for any date between January 1, 1900 and December 31, 2099.

In all of the examples just mentioned, the date number can come from a date number you type in, a formula that evaluates to a date number (including @DATE, @DATEVALUE, @NOW, and @TODAY), or a reference to a cell containing a date number. You can combine these @functions to find out anything you like about any date from January 1, 1900 to December 31,

2099. For example, you could use the @MOD function in conjunction with the @DATE and @INT functions to calculate the number of paydays in each month for any given year.

Time Format   Like dates, 1-2-3 stores time values as numbers. Time numbers range from 0.00000000 to 0.99998843, where 0 stands for midnight and .999988 stands for 11:59:59. The time formats, available through the Range Format and the Worksheet Global Settings commands, control the display of time numbers as times. The following table lists the four time formats and shows how each of them displays the time value .774479167:

Time Format		Example
6	HH:MM:SS AM/PM	06:35:15 PM
7	HH:MM AM/PM	06:35 PM
8	HH:MM:SS (Long Intn'l)	18:35:15
9	HH:MM (Short Intn'l)	18:35

You can manipulate time numbers in much the same way as date numbers. You can enter time numbers directly into the worksheet, or you can use the @TIME and @TIMEVALUE functions to create time numbers. Once you have created the numbers, you can manipulate them with arithmetic operators: For example, you can determine the number of hours worked in a day by subtracting the value in a cell containing the start time from the value of a cell containing the end time. You can find out the hour, minute, and second parts of a time number with the @HOUR, @MINUTE, and @SECOND functions.

Using Date and Time Values with Data Fill

The easiest way to enter a sequence of dates or times in a worksheet file is to use date or time values with the Data Fill command.

Because dates are stored as numbers, they can be used as the start, step, or stop values for Data Fill operations. For example, to create the time values for 9:00 AM to 5:00 PM, you would highlight a fill range of nine cells, use Range Format to format the range for **11:59AM**, and then perform the following operations:

Choose:	`Data   Fill`	
Type:	`9:00`	*(the Start value)*
Press:	TAB	
Type:	`1h`	*(the Step value)*
Press:	TAB	
Type:	`17:01`	*(a value just larger than the Stop value)*
Press:	↵	

The same technique applies to entering minutes, days, weeks, months, quarters, years, or other divisions of time. Abbreviate time as: s for seconds, min for minutes, and h for hours. Abbreviate dates as: d for day, w for week, m for month, q for quarter, and y for year. For example, to create a sequence of 12 months, you could use a fill range of 12 cells, begin with the date value 1-jan-92, use a step value of 1m (for 1 month), and use a stop value of 1-jan-93. (The stop value must be greater than the last value you want to use.)

Leave the Formatting to 1-2-3

Most 1-2-3 cell formats take any valid numeric data and display it in the applied format. For example, when you enter a number into a cell formatted in Currency format, the number looks like dollars and cents, whether or not you included a dollar sign when you typed it in.

Automatic format, on the other hand, works in reverse: Cells formatted in Automatic format are somewhat chameleon-like, in that they change to the format that looks like the number you entered. In other words, if you enter a number preceded by a dollar sign into an Automatic format cell, the number is displayed as Currency. Enter a number that looks like a date or time into the Automatic format cell beside it, and that cell becomes a date number or time number, formatted as a date or time.

Besides speeding up numeric data entry, Automatic format can make it easier to enter labels that begin with numbers, such as street addresses. If the local or global format of a cell is Automatic, 1-2-3 interprets entries that start with numbers but contain non-numeric characters as labels and changes the cell format to Label.

You can change the global format to Automatic format by choosing Worksheet Global Settings and selecting "Format..." and then "Automatic." You can change the format of a range to Automatic by highlighting the range, choosing Range Format, and selecting "Automatic."

You can't really appreciate the beauty of Automatic format until you try it. Format a range of blank cells as Automatic, then move the cell pointer to one of them. 1-2-3 displays the characters (A) in the format line of the control panel, confirming that the cell is in Automatic format. Next, enter a currency value such as $1000.00 into the cell. (Be sure to include the dollar sign and the decimal point.) 1-2-3 displays the value exactly as if the cell has been formatted as Currency. And in fact it has, by Automatic format: Look again at the format line in the control panel and you'll see it now displays (C2), for Currency format, 2 decimal places.

■ *NOTE:*   The chameleon act is a one-time-only event. Once 1-2-3 gives a new format to a cell that was in Automatic format, the cell is no longer in Automatic format. Instead, it keeps its new format until you either reset the format to the global format or change it to something else.

How to Let Yourself Know that 1-2-3 is Finished Processing

If you are doing work that will take 1-2-3 considerable time to complete, you can get the program to alert you when it is finished by taking advantage of the *typeahead buffer*, an area of computer memory that stores incoming keystrokes.

To get 1-2-3 to beep when it has finished processing, issue your command and then type several inappropriate keystrokes. For example, suppose you have set recalculation to "Manual" and are sorting a large, complex worksheet. After you start the sort, press Backspace several times. Pressing Backspace won't affect the sort; 1-2-3 stores the Backspace keystrokes in the typeahead buffer until the operation is finished. When the sort is done, 1-2-3 beeps once for each Backspace you typed, since Backspace is an illegal character in READY mode.

Worksheet Gotchas

Although most operations in 1-2-3 are straightforward, the product is complex, and it is not without its quirks. Following are a few things to watch out for as you use the 1-2-3 worksheet environment:

What to Do When You Run Out of Memory   If you create a large enough application, you will eventually find yourself running up against memory limits. There are a number of things you can do to free up more memory:

- *Turn off Edit Undo.* Turning off Edit Undo can save considerable worksheet memory when you are running long macros, closing files, or performing large Data Fill operations.
- *Close other Windows applications.* 1-2-3 gets its memory from Windows, which manages memory for all Windows applications. If you run out of memory while you are working in 1-2-3, you may be able to free up memory by closing other Windows applications.
- *Increase the Windows swap file size.* Windows can use part of the hard disk as if it were memory. If you are low on memory, save your work, exit 1-2-3, and exit Windows. Then, either create a permanent swap file for Windows (if you are running Windows in 386 Enhanced mode), or increase the amount of space allocated to swap files (if you are running Windows in Standard mode). See the Windows documentation for information on creating a permanent swap file or increasing swap file space.
- *Make as much physical memory available to Windows programs as you can.* Examine your CONFIG.SYS and AUTOEXEC.BAT files. Eliminate RAM disks such as RAMDRIVE.SYS, and minimize the amount of memory used by SMARTDRV.SYS, other drivers, or TSR programs that you start before you load Windows.

If these suggestions don't help sufficiently for you to do your work, try making some changes to your worksheet files. To free more memory:

- Close any worksheet files you are not actually using at the moment.
- Erase unneeded data and formula cells, range names, and named print settings.
- Delete rows, columns, and worksheets that contain no data but do contain formatted cells (formatted cells take up memory, even when the cells are otherwise blank), or reset the format of all blank but formatted cells with Range Format Reset. After you have deleted rows and columns or reset the formats of cells, save your worksheet and then retrieve it again.
- Use the "Convert to values" option of the Edit Quick Copy command to convert formulas to numbers wherever you can. Numbers take up much less memory than formulas, and using numbers for constants also speeds up recalculation time.

Converting formulas to values works just the same as the Edit Quick Copy command, except that it copies only the values in a range, not the formulas that created them. To convert formulas to their current values, select the same range as both the "from" range and the "to" range.

■ *CAUTION:* Make sure you no longer need the formulas before you replace them with their current values.

If, after taking all the preceding steps, you still do not have enough memory for your application, you will have to either install more memory, or redesign the application by breaking it into separate files and using file linking to connect the part in memory to parts on disk. File linking is described in Chapter 10.

Ranges and Range Names Ranges and range names are a boon to building and using 1-2-3 applications. They can also get you into trouble unless you watch out for the "gotchas" described here. The following are some tips to keep in mind when you use ranges:

■ *Don't move data into the first or last cell of a range.* As you work with 1-2-3, you may find that a range that was once perfectly valid now causes formulas that use it to evaluate to ERR. Using Edit Move Cells to move data into the first or last cell of a range is the most common cause of this problem. The range address changes to ERR, and formulas that use the invalid range evaluate to ERR. Editing a cell used as the first or last coordinate of a range does *not* cause this problem. If you must move data into the first or last cell of a range instead of editing the cell, use the copy commands instead of the Edit Move Cells command or the "Move To" icon.

■ *When named ranges are preferable.* Most of the time, you can use cell coordinates and named ranges interchangeably. However, it is preferable to use range names instead of cell addresses for ranges you refer to in file links, macros, and print settings. Although cell coordinates will work fine initially, you may run into trouble with them later on, if you move the data to a different range.

■ *Range names to avoid.* 1-2-3 is very flexible in how it allows you to name ranges. This flexibility, however, can sometimes get you into trouble. You will avoid most potential problems with range names if you follow the guidelines listed here when you name ranges. (These guidelines are also good ones to follow when you name files.)

Don't begin range names with numbers. If you give a cell a range name that begins with a number (for example, 3A), you can use that range name in a formula only if you refer to it in as an absolute range name (+$3A, not +3A). Don't use range names that look like cell addresses (for example, T1 or FY90). If you do, 1-2-3 will use the cell address instead of the range name, and your formula won't be doing what you think it is doing.

Don't use range names that look like macro commands. If you do, 1-2-3 will try to execute the contents of the range whenever it encounters the macro command name in a macro.

Don't use range names that contain space characters, dollar signs, or any of the symbols used in formulas (+, -, *, /, #, @). Although these range names may work fine in many situations, they can cause problems in macros and formulas. For example, the range name CITY-TAX would work fine as a print range, but in a macro or formula, 1-2-3 would try to subtract the value in a range named TAX from the value in a range named CITY.

@AVG and Non-Numeric Cells   Be sure that your @AVG ranges do not include cells with labels. Including label cells in an @AVG formula effectively averages in a 0 for each label cell, resulting in a wrong answer if one or more labels is in the @AVG range.

Unequal Numbers That Should Be Equal   Because 1-2-3 stores numbers in a *binary* (base 2) format, creating the same number in different ways does not always produce precisely the same result. For example, try entering the value 10.1 in the following ways:

- Type the number 10.1 into cell A1
- Type the formula @SQRT(5.05)^2+@SQRT(5.05)^2 into cell A2

Cells A1 and A2 display the same number, 10.1. Now, enter the following formula in cell A3: @IF(A1=A2,"Equal","Not Equal"). The formula displays the string "Not Equal" even though the numbers appear to be the same.

Although the two numbers should be the same, (@SQRT (5.05)^2=5.05+5.05=10.1) 1-2-3 stores them slightly differently in the last decimal place. Most of the time, slight differences such as this one have no noticeable effect on calculations. However, if you compare numbers in an @IF function or {IF} macro command, 1-2-3 may complain that two numbers that should be identical are not.

To avoid problems with unequal numbers, use @ROUND to round the numbers to the actual number of decimal places in your calculations. For example, if you are performing arithmetic on numbers where the maximum number of decimal places is two, use @ROUND(*number*,2) to round all the numbers to two decimal places, and use @ROUND(*number*,2) on the result. This will eliminate the "ghost" part of the fraction, and ensure that equal results really are equal.

Note that @ROUND rounds numbers up or down, depending on whether the fraction is smaller than one-half, or greater than or equal to one-half. To always round down, use @INT(*number*) instead of @ROUND. To always round up (as you might when estimating staffing), use the following formula:

```
@IF(number>@INT(number),@INT(number)+1,number)
```

If the referenced number is greater than its integer value, the formula adds one to the integer part of the value, effectively rounding it up. Otherwise, the number must already be an integer, so the formula uses the number as is.

When 512 Characters are Not 512 Bytes   Throughout this book, the limit on the number of characters you can put in a cell entry has been given as 512 characters. The physical limit, however, is actually 512 bytes. Most of the time, each character takes up only one byte. However, in some circumstances, a character requires more than one byte.

Any character you type directly from the keyboard without using Alt+F1 (Compose) takes up one byte. Characters you create with the Compose key use from one to three bytes. Therefore, if you have characters created with compose sequences in a cell, the cell will still contain up to 512 bytes, but it will contain fewer characters.

Column Widths, Row Heights, and Fonts   1-2-3 defines the column width as the number of numeric characters in the default font that will fit across a column. The default column width is nine characters in the default font, a 10-point san-serif font. Although most of the fonts you use in 1-2-3 are proportional (each letter takes up only as much space in the column as it needs), the numeric characters 0 through 9 each take up the same amount of space.

As you'll see in Chapter 7, you can change the font with the Style Font command. When you change the font, 1-2-3 does not adjust the column width. Therefore, if you change the font to a larger font (for instance, 14 point), you will be able to fit fewer than nine numeric characters in a nine-character column. Conversely, if you use a smaller font, you will be able to fit more numeric characters in the column.

1-2-3 also handles row heights differently. If you have not explicitly set a row height, 1-2-3 adjusts the row height to automatically accommodate a larger or smaller font. For example, if you enter text in the default font into a row and then change to a larger font, 1-2-3 increases the row height to a size appropriate to that font. Conversely, if you change to a smaller font, 1-2-3 shrinks the row.

Re-enabling GROUP Mode   GROUP mode is great for situations in which all worksheets have exactly the same format. However, if you want to make formatting changes to selected worksheets in a file, be sure that GROUP mode is turned off. After you have made your changes, do *not* turn GROUP mode back on. If you do, all the worksheets in the file will take on the formatting characteristics of the worksheet the cell pointer is in when you re-enable GROUP mode, eradicating any formatting differences you have established.

If you have created a series of worksheets, all of which have the same format, and you want to add one or more worksheets that look different, consider putting these different worksheets in a separate worksheet file and using file links to connect them to the grouped worksheets in the GROUP mode file. That way, you can make any changes you like to the nongrouped worksheets and still retain the advantages of GROUP mode for the grouped worksheets. (File linking is described in Chapter 10.)

At a Glance

This chapter has completed your introduction to worksheet skills and concepts. The chapter's main focus has been on learning to use multiple worksheets in the same file. In this chapter, you built a multiple-worksheet spreadsheet application—a Cash Flow Forecast that includes both individual product forecasts and a summary forecast for the entire product line—and you converted a single-spreadsheet application to multiple worksheets. In creating and modifying these applications, you learned a number of new skills and 1-2-3 features, including the following:

Task	How To Do It:
Constructing worksheet templates	Many applications contain several individual spreadsheets, each of which has the same structure, but different data. An easy way to construct such an application is to build and test one sample spreadsheet, and then copy the spreadsheet to other worksheets in the file, or to other worksheet files.
Inserting and deleting worksheets in a file	To add one or more worksheets, move the cell pointer to the worksheet that is to be in front of or behind the new worksheets, and choose Worksheet Insert. Select "Sheet", "Before" to insert new worksheets in front of the current worksheet, or "Sheet", "After" to insert new worksheets behind the current worksheet. To insert worksheets with the same format as the current worksheet, turn on GROUP mode, then insert the desired number of worksheets. All worksheets will have the format of the current worksheet.
	To delete one or more worksheets, choose Worksheet Delete, select "Sheet", and specify the range of worksheets you want to delete (you must specify a valid cell address as both the start and end addresses of the range).
Moving information from one worksheet to another	Copying and moving works the same from worksheet to worksheet as it does within a single worksheet. Use Edit Quick Copy, Edit Copy and Edit Paste, or the "Copy To" icon to duplicate labels, numbers, and formulas where you want relative references to adjust. Use Edit Move Cells or the "Move To" icon to rearrange a worksheet file.
Changing column width over several worksheets	Highlight a three-dimensional range of worksheets, choose Worksheet Column Width, and specify the new column width. Or, if the file is in GROUP mode, change the width of the column or columns in one worksheet, and the corresponding column or columns in the other worksheets will automatically change to the same width.
Grouping similar worksheets together	Use GROUP mode primarily when you are working with a file whose worksheets all have the same structure and format. Check the "Group mode" check-box of Worksheet Global Settings to turn on GROUP mode when you want changes to one worksheet to affect all the worksheets in the file. Clear the "Group mode" check-box when you no longer want changes you make in the current worksheet to affect other worksheets in the file.
Consolidating information from several worksheets	Move the cell pointer to worksheet A, choose Worksheet Insert Sheet Before to add a blank summary worksheet, and copy relevant column and row labels from one of the other worksheets to the summary worksheet. Then, use three-dimensional formulas in the summary worksheet to total the information in the worksheets to be consolidated.
Copying a range to multiple worksheets	Highlight the range to copy "from," choose Edit Quick Copy, specify the three-dimensional range to copy to, and select OK. (It's usually easiest to specify the three-dimensional range either by typing it or by using the keyboard, rather than using the mouse and the "Next Sheet" or "Prev Sheet" icons.)
Finding data within a range of worksheets	Highlight the entire worksheet file by pressing Control+Home, F4, End Control+Home. Choose Edit Find and search for the data you want in labels, formulas, or both.

Task	How To Do It:
Using window panes and perspective view	Move the cell pointer to the row or column at which you want to divide a window, and choose Window Split Horizontal or Vertical to divide the active Worksheet window into horizontal or vertical panes. Or, drag the horizontal or the vertical splitter to divide a window into panes or adjust the size of existing panes.
	Choose Window Split Perspective view, or click on the "Perspective View" icon to look at three consecutive worksheets simultaneously.
	Move from pane to pane using F6 (Pane), or by clicking in the pane you want with the mouse. Move from worksheet to worksheet using F5 (Goto), the Next Sheet and Prev Sheet keys or icons, and the other worksheet navigation keys.
	Choose Window Split Clear to return the worksheet display to a single window. Press Alt+F6 (Zoom) to toggle between a full-window display of the current pane and a split view.
Centering labels in a range	To center labels, highlight the labels you want to change, choose Style Alignment, and select "Center". Select "Left" or "Right" to left-align or right-align labels.
Correcting the display of numbers displayed as asterisks	1-2-3 displays numbers as asterisks when it doesn't have enough room in the column to display the numbers in their current cell format and font. To correct the display, either widen the columns, change to a numeric format that takes less space, or use a smaller font.
Changing global column width	Choose Worksheet Global Settings and select the "Column width" option. Type in the width you want and select OK. 1-2-3 uses this width setting for all columns that have not been explicitly set with either the mouse or with the Worksheet Column Width command. Columns you have already set retain their pre-set widths.
Protecting a worksheet	Check the "Protection" check box in the Worksheet Global Settings dialog box to prevent worksheet cells from being changed. Clear the check box to unprotect the entire worksheet.
Unprotecting specific cells within a protected worksheet	Highlight the range of cells you want to modify and then choose Range Unprotect to remove cell protection.

In the closing sections of this chapter, you learned ways both to prevent and to remedy errors in your spreadsheet applications, and you acquired a collection of tips and techniques for using 1-2-3 as efficiently (and painlessly) as possible.

Chapter 6

Creating a 1-2-3 Database

A database allows you to store, organize, and manage information about a group of people, places, or things.

This chapter introduces you to using 1-2-3's database capabilities. You will learn database concepts and skills as you create and manipulate a database of Bob Gordon's business contacts. In this chapter, you will work with a database you create in a 1-2-3 worksheet file. You'll enter names, addresses, and other information about Bob's contacts; sort data records; and find, extract, modify, and delete records using a variety of selection criteria. You'll see examples of other database operations you may want to learn later.

The "What is a Database?" section in Chapter 2 contains a basic introduction to databases. A "Tips and Techniques" section at the end of this chapter briefly describes additional database concepts and skills not covered in the chapter exercises and examples.

What You'll Learn

By the time you finish this chapter, you'll know how to perform the following database tasks:

- **Create a database table**

- **Sort database records**

- **Use input ranges, criteria ranges, and output ranges to perform queries**

- **Search a database table to find records that match specified criteria**

- **Edit records during a database search**

- **Extract specified records to another part of the worksheet file**

- **Modify a block of records that match specified criteria**

- **Delete records from a database table**

- **Use different types of criteria for database queries**

- **Use the F7 (Query) function key**

- **Perform queries with multiple tables**

- **Use external database tables**

- Modify a block of records at a time

- Split a database table into multiple tables

- Use database @functions to analyze a database table

- Set up tables to perform "what-if" analyses

- Include computed and aggregate fields in output ranges

- Connect to database tables outside 1-2-3 and perform queries

- Convert database files between 1-2-3 and other products

You'll also know some additional tips and techniques for using 1-2-3's database capabilities, as well as some ways to aviod problems.

Before You Start

Before you begin the exercises in this chapter, start 1-2-3. Make sure that the cell pointer is in cell A:A1 of a new, maximized, blank worksheet file, and that 1-2-3 has been set up to save files in your 123BOOK directory.

As you work through the exercises in this chapter, you will create files named CONTACTS.WK3, CONTACT3.WK3, CUST_DB.WK3, SUP_DB.WK3, and ADV_DB.WK3. (A disk containing the worksheets created in this book is also available from the authors.) As in previous chapters, stop at the end of a numbered step or just before the next section heading when you are tired or have something else to do. Be sure to save any modified worksheet files before you stop. If you have more than one active file, write down the names of the files in memory and the order in which they are stored. When you want to continue with the exercises, start up 1-2-3, read in the worksheet files you last used, making sure they are in the same order they were in before you stopped, then pick up where you left off.

A Note on Example Layout   As in previous chapters, the examples in this chapter assume that your screen displays 20 rows and eight columns when the Worksheet window is maximized. If your display does not show 20 rows and eight columns, your screens will look somewhat different from the illustrations, but you can still do all the examples. Just be sure to use the cell addresses and ranges specified in the instructions.

A Note on Keystroke Instructions   The keystroke instructions in this chapter often assume you are using a mouse to perform such operations as highlighting a range or selecting an option in a dialog box. You can also use the keyboard to perform the same operations. Many of the keyboard equivalents to mouse operations were described in previous chapters. A few of the most common ones are summarized here. For a complete list of keystroke equivalents to mouse operations, see the 1-2-3 documentation or the 1-2-3 on-line Help.

Keyboard Equivalents to Mouse Operations

Operation	Instruction		Keyboard Equivalent	
Complete action and close dialog box	**Select:**	O K	**Press:**	↵
Cancel action and close dialog box	**Select:**	Cancel	**Press:**	ESC
Highlight a text box	**Select:**	text box	**Press:**	ALT+*underlined_letter*
Edit a range in a text box	**Select:**	Range	**Press:**	ALT+*underlined_letter*
	Specify:	A:A1..C:D4		F2 (EDIT)
Edit a number or word in a text box	**Select:**	text box	**Press:**	ALT+*underlined_letter*
	Specify:	new text	**Type:**	new text
	(or click on text and edit it)		*(or press Left arrow and edit text)*	
Highlight a range	**Highlight:** A:A1..C:D4		**Move to:**	cell A:A1
			Press:	F4
			Move to:	cell D4
			Press:	↵

   Throughout this chapter, the Edit Copy and Edit Paste commands are used in the exercises whenever you copy data from one range to another. In all these places, using the Edit Quick Copy command or the "Copy To" icon are perfectly viable alternatives to Edit Copy and Edit Paste. This chapter also instructs you to highlight a range and use the Delete key whenever you have to clear cells. The Edit Clear command or the "Cut" icon would work equally well. In all tasks, feel free to use the approach you find most comfortable.

1-2-3 Databases

1-2-3 works with two types of database: *1-2-3 databases* are databases entered in the worksheet file itself that can be manipulated just like any other worksheet data. *External databases* are databases created by one of the supported database products, such as Ashton Tate's dBASE IV or Borland's Paradox. 1-2-3 can manipulate external database tables in much the same way it manipulates 1-2-3 database tables, without requiring that you change the external databases in any way.

Database Operations

You can manipulate 1-2-3 databases with the following Data operations:

Operation	What It Does:
Sort	The Data Sort command rearranges the order of records by ordering any of the fields alphabetically, numerically, or chronologically. Sorting makes it easier to find a record when you are looking through the database.
Query	The Data Query command locates, changes, makes copies of, and removes specific records in the database by matching criteria that you set up. The "Find" option locates records and allows you to edit them. The "Extract" option finds records that match the criteria you set up and copies them to another worksheet file location. The "Delete" option removes records you no longer need from the database. The "Modify" option extracts records to another worksheet file location so you can edit them, then lets you place the edited records back in the database table.

For example, if an ordinary phone book were a computerized database, you could sort the list according to name, address, or phone number and print out the results. Using Data Query "Extract", you could query the telephone book database and extract the records for all people who live on Kettering Drive or whose phone number begins with 835.

Figure 6-1 shows how a phone book looks in the 1-2-3 worksheet.

Figure 6-1: A Telephone Book as a 1-2-3 Database

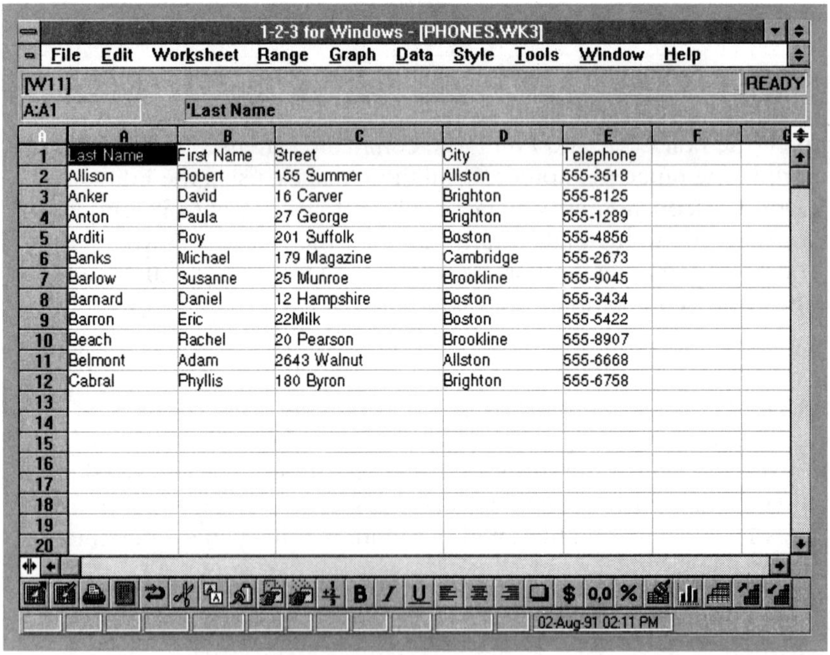

	A	B	C	D	E
1	Last Name	First Name	Street	City	Telephone
2	Allison	Robert	155 Summer	Allston	555-3518
3	Anker	David	16 Carver	Brighton	555-8125
4	Anton	Paula	27 George	Brighton	555-1289
5	Arditi	Roy	201 Suffolk	Boston	555-4856
6	Banks	Michael	179 Magazine	Cambridge	555-2673
7	Barlow	Susanne	25 Munroe	Brookline	555-9045
8	Barnard	Daniel	12 Hampshire	Boston	555-3434
9	Barron	Eric	22Milk	Boston	555-5422
10	Beach	Rachel	20 Pearson	Brookline	555-8907
11	Belmont	Adam	2643 Walnut	Allston	555-6668
12	Cabral	Phyllis	180 Byron	Brighton	555-6758

The Business Contacts Database Model

The database application you will build here continues the Bob Gordon story. It is an electronic address book of Bob's business contacts: advertisers, customers, and suppliers. Bob plans to use this electronic address book as a business phone book and as a master list from which to generate promotional and other types of mailings.

Bob starts out by collecting the names from his card file, address books, order forms, and the scraps of paper he has been using to keep track of his contacts. He decides to consolidate all names into one master list, confident that he will be able to use 1-2-3 to organize the list later in any form he wants. As a 1-2-3 database table, before any of the data has been sorted or otherwise processed, the completed list would look something like Figure 6-2, on the next page.

Creating a 1-2-3 Database Table

1-2-3 databases consist of one or more *database tables*. A 1-2-3 database table is a collection of related data in a worksheet file. The database you will build for Bob Gordon's business contacts initially contains only one database table. However, a worksheet file can contain many different database tables, and each of them can be treated as part of the same database.

A 1-2-3 database table uses the column-row structure of the worksheet to store information. The first row of the database table contains *field names*. These names identify the kind of information stored in each column. For example, the database table illustrated in Figure 6-2 starts in row 4, which contains the field names Last Name, First Name, Telephone, Type, Company, Street, City, State, and Zip. No two fields in the same database table can have the same name.

The subsequent rows contain records. Each record has a similar format and holds all the items of information that pertain to one entry in the database table. For instance, the first record of the database table in Figure 6-2 is in row 5. This record contains the name Edwin P. Fletcher, Edwin's telephone number (**617-555-3210**), a code for the type of business contact Edwin is (**CUS**), the name of Edwin's company (**Edwin's Toy Emporium**), and the company's address.

Visually, each row in a 1-2-3 worksheet is divided into cells by the columns. Logically, the worksheet columns divide each record in a database table into fields, one per column. Each field contains one piece of a record's data. A field can contain any kind of information that can be entered in a worksheet (labels, values, or formulas); however, the kind of data in a particular field must be the same for all records. For example, part numbers in an inventory database could be entered as numbers or as numeric labels, but they should not be entered as a mixture of numeric labels and numbers.

The size of a database table is limited only by the amount of memory available to store data and by the size of the worksheet. Each database table can be up to 256 columns wide (one field per column) and 8192 rows deep (one row for the field names and the rest for data).

In the following pages, you will create, modify, and manipulate records in a simple database. In this section, you will start to create that database.

1. Create a title for the database table.

Begin by entering title information for the database table in the blank worksheet on your screen:

Figure 6-2a: Left Screen of Bob's Initial Business Contacts Database

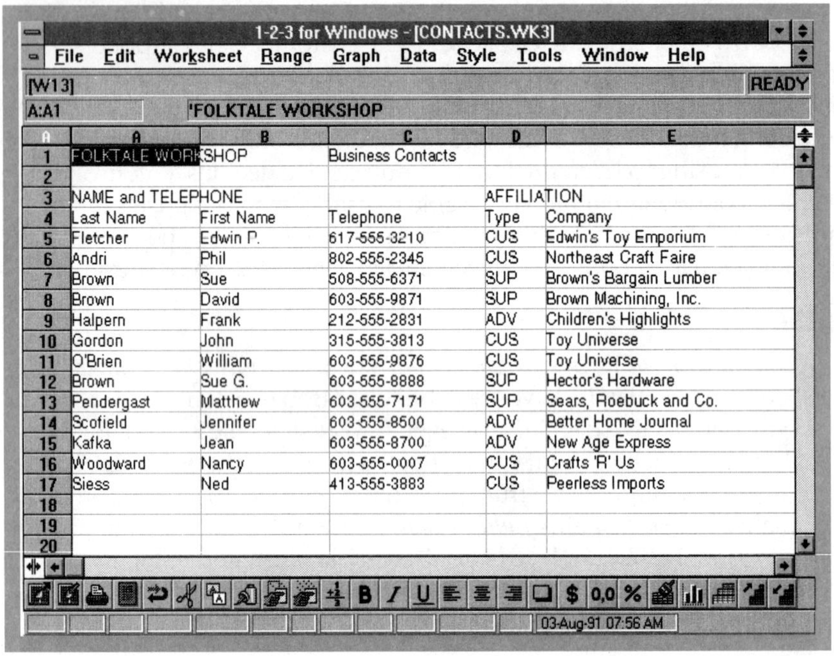

	A	B	C	D	E
1	FOLKTALE WORKSHOP		Business Contacts		
2					
3	NAME and TELEPHONE			AFFILIATION	
4	Last Name	First Name	Telephone	Type	Company
5	Fletcher	Edwin P.	617-555-3210	CUS	Edwin's Toy Emporium
6	Andri	Phil	802-555-2345	CUS	Northeast Craft Faire
7	Brown	Sue	508-555-6371	SUP	Brown's Bargain Lumber
8	Brown	David	603-555-9871	SUP	Brown Machining, Inc.
9	Halpern	Frank	212-555-2831	ADV	Children's Highlights
10	Gordon	John	315-555-3813	CUS	Toy Universe
11	O'Brien	William	603-555-9876	CUS	Toy Universe
12	Brown	Sue G.	603-555-8888	SUP	Hector's Hardware
13	Pendergast	Matthew	603-555-7171	SUP	Sears, Roebuck and Co.
14	Scofield	Jennifer	603-555-8500	ADV	Better Home Journal
15	Kafka	Jean	603-555-8700	ADV	New Age Express
16	Woodward	Nancy	603-555-0007	CUS	Crafts 'R' Us
17	Siess	Ned	413-555-3883	CUS	Peerless Imports
18					
19					
20					

Figure 6-2b: Right Screen of Bob's Initial Business Contacts Database

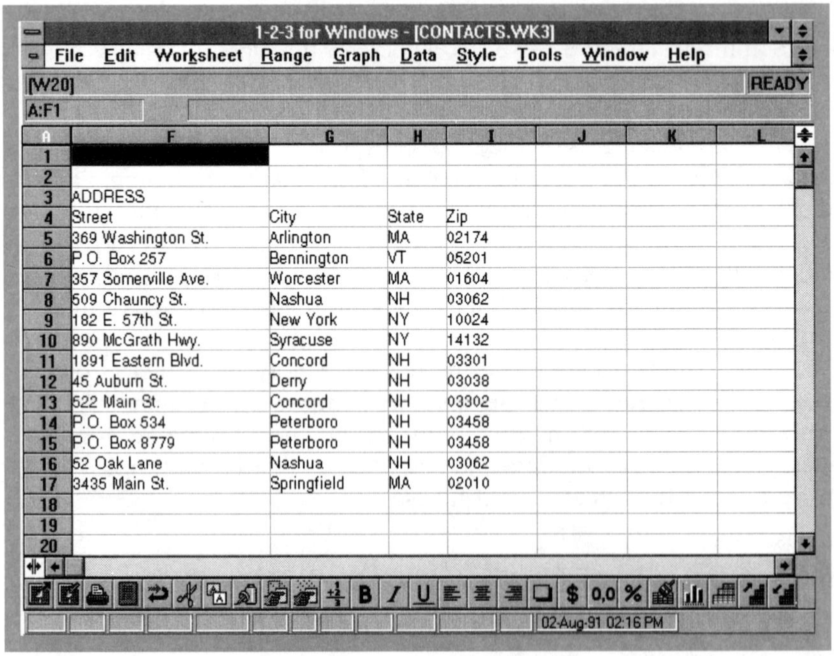

	F	G	H	I	J	K	L
1							
2							
3	ADDRESS						
4	Street	City	State	Zip			
5	369 Washington St.	Arlington	MA	02174			
6	P.O. Box 257	Bennington	VT	05201			
7	357 Somerville Ave.	Worcester	MA	01604			
8	509 Chauncy St.	Nashua	NH	03062			
9	182 E. 57th St.	New York	NY	10024			
10	890 McGrath Hwy.	Syracuse	NY	14132			
11	1891 Eastern Blvd.	Concord	NH	03301			
12	45 Auburn St.	Derry	NH	03038			
13	522 Main St.	Concord	NH	03302			
14	P.O. Box 534	Peterboro	NH	03458			
15	P.O. Box 8779	Peterboro	NH	03458			
16	52 Oak Lane	Nashua	NH	03062			
17	3435 Main St.	Springfield	MA	02010			
18							
19							
20							

Move to:	cell A1
Type:	FOLKTALE WORKSHOP
Press:	→ *two times*
Type:	Business Contacts ↵

Figure 6-3: Titles for the Database Table

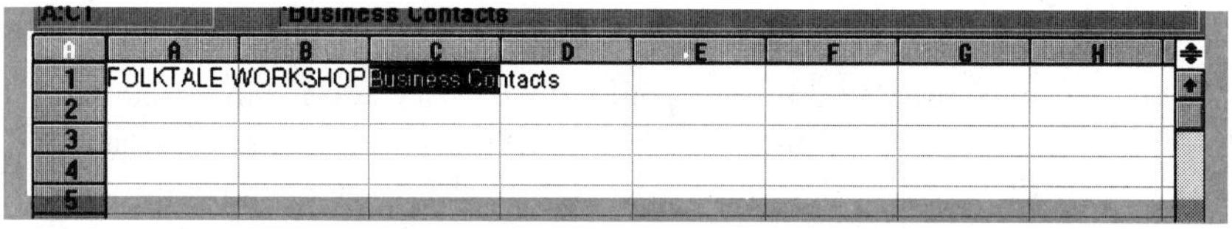

2. Enter field names in row 4 of the worksheet.

The first row of a 1-2-3 database table always contains labels that serve as field names. These field names organize the database by identifying the contents of each column. They are also necessary for many of the database commands.

There are two important guidelines concerning field names: (1) No two fields in the same database table can have the same name; and (2) no field name should have leading or trailing spaces (1-2-3 treats spaces as part of the name).

The database table you will build has records with nine fields. Each field of each record contains a different piece of information about one of Bob's business contacts. Each field is appropriately named: a contact's telephone number is in the Telephone field, company name in the Company field, and so on. The database uses two fields for the contact's name—one for the first name and one for the last name. Having separate fields for each part of the name makes it easier to sort and search the database by name.

The following keystroke instructions lead you through the process of creating a row of field names for Bob Gordon's database.

Move to:	cell A4
Type:	Last Name →
	First Name →
	Telephone →
	Type →
	Company →
	Street →
	City →
	State →
	Zip ↵

Figure 6-4:   Field Names Entered for the Contacts Table

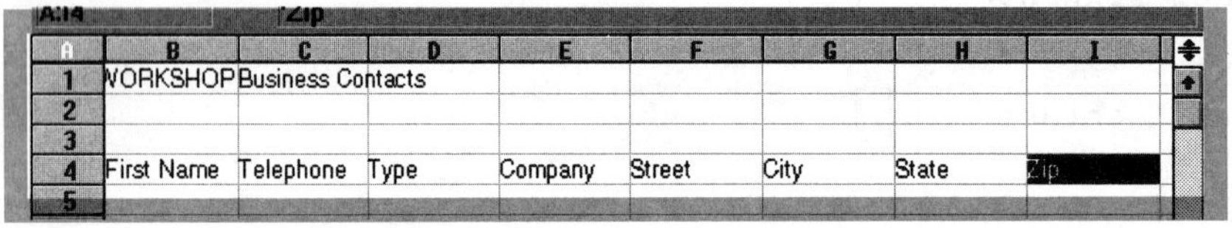

A	B	C	D	E	F	G	H	I
1	WORKSHOP	Business Contacts						
2								
3								
4	First Name	Telephone	Type	Company	Street	City	State	Zip
5								

3. Enter the first record in row 5 of the worksheet.

The row directly below the row containing field names is always the first record in a database table. Do not leave a blank row or insert a separator line between the row containing field names and the first database record; doing so can throw off certain database operations.

Enter the first record. Be sure to precede the entries in the Telephone, Street, and Zip fields with an apostrophe (') so that 1-2-3 knows these entries are labels, not values.

Move to: cell A5

Type: Fletcher   →

Edwin P.   →

'617-555-3210   →

CUS   →

Edwin's Toy Emporium   →

'369 Washington St.   →

Arlington   →

MA   →

'02174   ↵

Figure 6-5:   First Record Entered in the Table

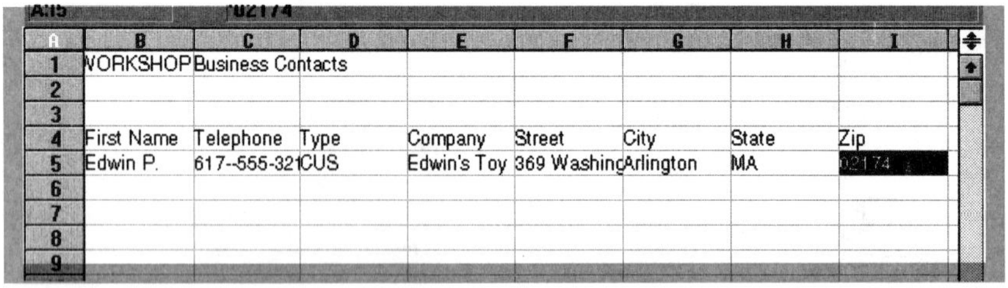

A	B	C	D	E	F	G	H	I
1	WORKSHOP	Business Contacts						
2								
3								
4	First Name	Telephone	Type	Company	Street	City	State	Zip
5	Edwin P.	617--555-321	CUS	Edwin's Toy	369 Washing	Arlington	MA	02174
6								
7								
8								
9								

Refining the Appearance of a Database Table

The physical appearance of the database table is important. It must be easy to read for you and for anyone else who works with it. Look at the record you just entered. Right now, 1-2-3's display of the information in the database is a mess: several of the fields run together, making them illegible. Also, because there are so many fields, it is hard to group related fields together at a glance. Before you enter any more records, refine the appearance of the database table by changing column widths and adding additional titles. Then preformat the cells in the Telephone, Street, and Zip fields so you can type those fields without using a label prefix each time.

Changing Column Widths

The first improvement you will make is to change the column widths of several fields. The current global column-width setting (nine characters) does not allow enough space for all of the names and addresses in Bob's database, but it allows too much space for the Type and State fields. Adjusting the column widths will make the database easier to read.

1. Widen columns A and B to 13 characters.

The first step is to make columns A and B wider. A column width of 13 should be enough to display the last name or first name and middle initial of most people. You can use Worksheet Column Width to set the width of more than one column at a time. Use this command to change the widths of columns A and B to 13:

Highlight:	*any combination of cells in columns A and B*
Choose:	Worksheet Column Width
Type:	13 *in the Set width text box*
Select:	Range
	OK *or press Enter*

Figure 6-6:   Column Widths Adjusted for Names

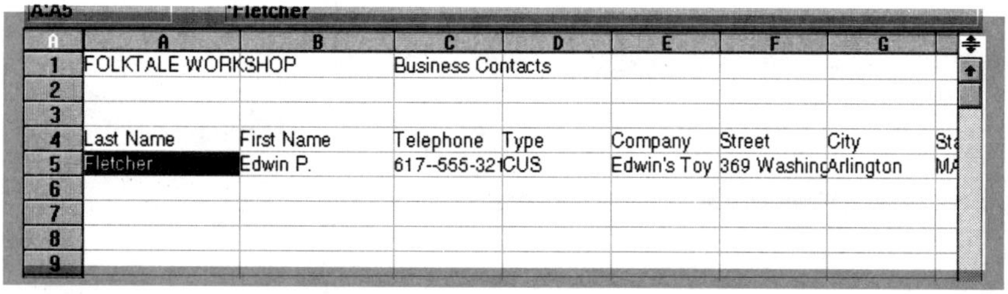

1-2-3 widens columns A and B to 13 characters.

2. Widen column C to 16 characters.

Use Worksheet Column Width to widen column C, the Telephone field:

Move to:	*any cell in column C*
Choose:	Worksheet Column Width
Type:	16 *in the Set width text box*

Press: ⮐ *or select OK*

3. Adjust other columns to make the database more readable.

Setup Table 6-1 summarizes how you should set other column widths in the database table to make the data you enter more readable and the database easier to use. When you are done, your worksheet should look like the illustrations in Figure 6-7.

Setup Table 6-1:   Database Table Column Widths

Field Name	Column Letter	New Width
Type	D	6
Company	E	25
Street	F	20
City	G	12
State	H	6

Figure 6-7a: Left Screen of Bob's Business Contacts Database with Adjusted Column Widths

Figure 6-7b: Right Screen of Bob's Business Contacts Database with Adjusted Column Widths

■ *NOTE:*   You can also use the mouse to adjust a column's width by dragging the right border of the column in the worksheet frame until the column looks good to you. You use the appearance of the worksheet, rather than numbers, to control the width. In these exercises we use the Worksheet Column Width command to ensure that your columns are exactly the same width as those shown in the book.

Adding Titles that Group Related Fields Together

Another way to make a database easier to use is to add titles that help you visually group together related fields. Give Bob's eyes a break by entering titles in columns A, D, and F of row 3 like those in Figure 6-8. (In Chapter 7, you'll learn many techniques you could apply to improve the appearance and legibility of these titles, including font changes, shading, and others.)

■ **NOTE:**   These titles must go above the database table field names. They are not part of the database itself; they are there only to make the database table easier to read.

Figure 6-8a: Using Titles to Indicate Related Fields (Left Screen)

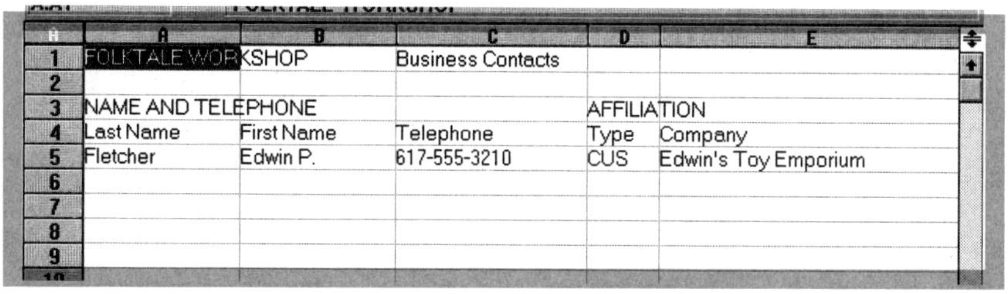

Figure 6-8b: Using Titles to Indicate Related Fields (Right Screen)

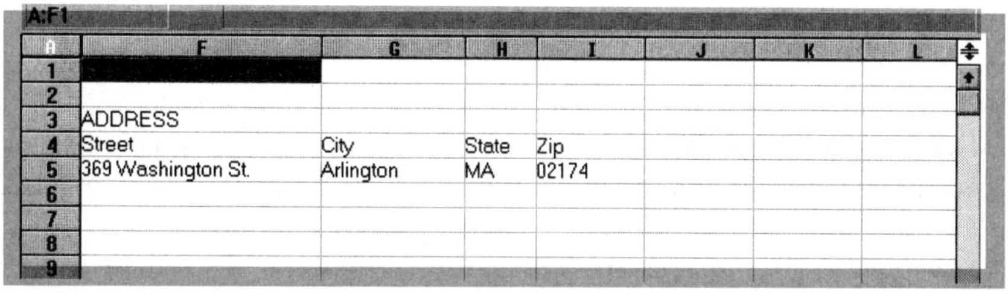

Preformatting Cells as Labels

In Chapter 4, you used Range Format to change the format of cells that contain values. You can also use Range Format to give blank cells a format, so that data is properly displayed as soon as you enter it. This makes it easier for you to check your work as you're typing from a printed report or list, because your data immediately looks the way you want it to appear. For instance, if you were entering a column of dates, you would want 1-2-3 to display the values you entered in a date format, rather than as a date number, so you could be sure you had typed in the proper date.

With this particular database, all the cells contain labels; however, because the data in three fields will almost always begin with a number, preformatting can save you some typing. When you entered data in columns C, F, and I, you had to prefix the entries with an apostrophe to prevent 1-2-3 from trying to interpret the entries as values. Although typing an apostrophe is a small thing, having to remember to do so whenever you enter a new record is tedious. Fortunately, the Range Format command provides a way to automatically insert a label prefix in front of an entry.

You will use Range Format to format cells in the columns for telephone numbers, street addresses, and zip codes. 1-2-3 will automatically format data you enter into each of these columns as labels. As you add more records to the database, you won't need to use a label prefix in these cells.

Highlight:	C5..C20	
Choose:	Range	Format
Select:	Label	*in the Format list box*
	OK	
Highlight:	F5..F20	
Choose:	Range	Format
Select:	Label	*in the Format list box*
	OK	
Highlight:	I5..I20	
Choose:	Range	Format
Select:	Label	*in the Format list box*
	OK	

1-2-3 formats all these cells as labels (see figure 6-9). Notice that 1-2-3 now displays (L) in the control panel's format line. This signifies that the current cell is formatted using the Label format.

Now that the formatting is complete, save the worksheet file. Since this is the first time you have saved the file, you will have to give it a name. Name it CONTACTS:

Choose:	File	Save As
Type:	contacts	↵

1-2-3 saves the file.

Figure 6-9:   Column Preformatted to Treat Numbers As Labels

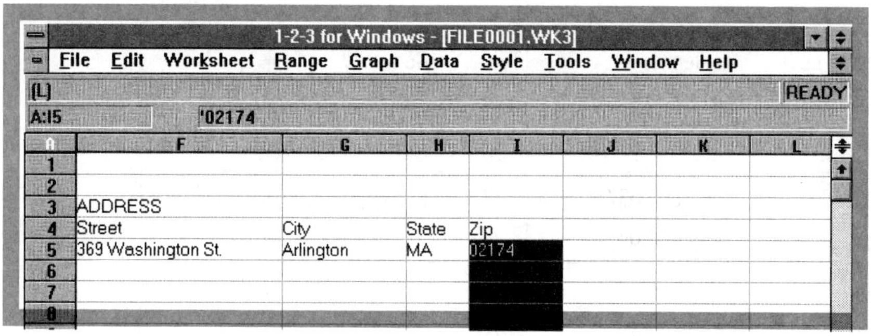

A Note on Database Appearance

Try to keep in mind how a database is going to be used when you design your own field names and titles. Make the database easy to use for its intended purposes.

For example, Bob will use this database as both a telephone book and a master list for mailing labels. Because he will most often use the database as a telephone book, the database has been set up so that a business contact's name, phone number, type, and company name fit on one screen. Bob will need his contacts' addresses only when he is generating some kind of mailing list, so this information is entered one screen-width to the right; pressing Tab or Control+Right moves the worksheet window to that screen. Setting worksheet titles to freeze column A and the first few rows (as described in Chapter 4) would make the database even easier to use once it was complete.

Entering Records

Now that you have set up the database, adjusted the column widths, and preformatted three fields, you can enter the remaining records. Enter the data in rows 6 through 17 of columns A through I, using Setup Table 6-2 your guide. To help line up the rows and columns, you can place a ruler or other straight edge under each record in Figure 6-10 as you type it in. (If you are pressed for time, you can enter only the data in the Last Name, First Name, Type, and State fields. These are the fields you must fill in to do the exercises.)

Setup Table 6-2: Data to Enter in Bob's Contacts Database

A	A	B	C	D	E
4	Last Name	First Name	Telephone	Type	Company
5	Fletcher	Edwin P.	617-555-3210	CUS	Edwin's Toy Emporium
6	Andri	Phil	802-555-2345	CUS	Northeast Craft Faire
7	Brown	Sue	508-555-6371	SUP	Brown's Bargain Lumber
8	Brown	David	603-555-9871	SUP	Brown Machining, Inc.
9	Halpern	Frank	212-555-2831	Adv	Children's Highlights
10	Gordon	John	315-5553813	CUS	Toy Universe
11	O'Brien	William	603-5559876	CUS	Toy Universe
12	Brown	Sue G.	603-555-8888	SUP	Hector's Hardware
13	Pendergast	Matthew	603-555-7171	SUP	Sears, Roebuck and Co.
14	Scofield	Jennifer	603-555-8500	ADV	Better Home Journal
15	Kafka	Jean	603-555-8700	ADV	New Age Express
16	Woodward	Nancy	603-555-0007	CUS	Crafts 'R' Us
17	Siess	Ned	413-555-3883	CUS	Peerless Imports

The Figures 6-10a and 6-10b show how the data should look after you've entered the data in Setup Table 6-2.

Figure 6-10a: Left Screen of Completed Database Table

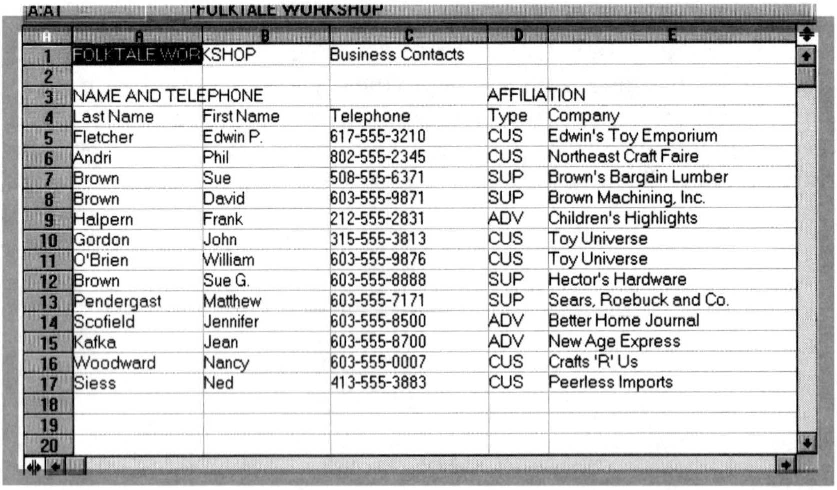

Setup Table 6-2 : (Continued)

F	G	H	I
Street	City	State	Zip
369 Washington St.	Arlington	MA	02174
P.O. Box 257	Bennington	VT	05201
357 Somerville Ave.	Worcester	MA	01604
509 Chauncy St.	Nashua	NH	03062
182 E. 57th St.	New York	NY	10024
890 McGrath Hwy.	Syracuse	NY	14132
1891 Eastern Blvd.	Concord	NH	03301
45 Auburn St.	Derry	NH	03038
522 Main St.	Concord	NH	03302
P.O. Box 534	Peterboro	NH	03458
P.O. Box 8779	Peterboro	NH	03458
52 Oak Lane	Nashua	NH	03062
3435 Main St.	Springfield	MA	02010

Figure 6-10b Right Screen of Completed Database Table

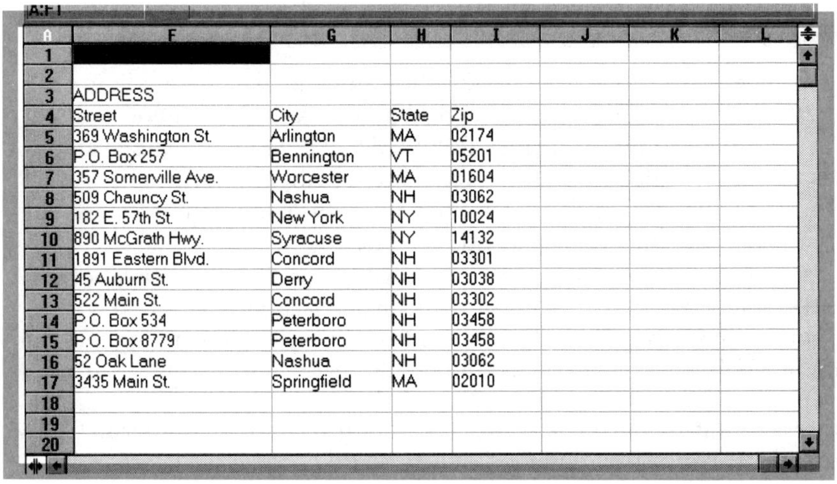
A:F1

A	F	G	H	I	J	K	L
1							
2							
3	ADDRESS						
4	Street	City	State	Zip			
5	369 Washington St.	Arlington	MA	02174			
6	P.O. Box 257	Bennington	VT	05201			
7	357 Somerville Ave.	Worcester	MA	01604			
8	509 Chauncy St.	Nashua	NH	03062			
9	182 E. 57th St.	New York	NY	10024			
10	890 McGrath Hwy.	Syracuse	NY	14132			
11	1891 Eastern Blvd.	Concord	NH	03301			
12	45 Auburn St.	Derry	NH	03038			
13	522 Main St.	Concord	NH	03302			
14	P.O. Box 534	Peterboro	NH	03458			
15	P.O. Box 8779	Peterboro	NH	03458			
16	52 Oak Lane	Nashua	NH	03062			
17	3435 Main St.	Springfield	MA	02010			
18							
19							
20							

Congratulations! You have completed the database. Save the file again.

Sorting Records

When you first set up a database, records are arranged in the order in which you enter them. The Data Sort command lets you rearrange those records by sorting them into an order determined by one or more of the fields. Each *sort* can be done in either *ascending* order (smallest to largest) or *descending* order (largest to smallest).

For example, you could sort Bob's database in ascending order by last and first name. The sorted database would be in alphabetical order: the first record would be the one containing the name closest to the beginning of the alphabet (Andri) and the last record the one containing the name closest to the end of the alphabet (Woodward).

Figure 6-11: Bob's Database Sorted by Last Name and First Name

	A	B	C	D	E
1	FOLKTALE WORKSHOP		Business Contacts		
2					
3	NAME AND TELEPHONE			AFFILIATION	
4	Last Name	First Name	Telephone	Type	Company
5	Andri	Phil	802-555-2345	CUS	Northeast Craft Faire
6	Brown	David	603-555-9871	SUP	Brown Machining, Inc.
7	Brown	Sue	508-555-6371	SUP	Brown's Bargain Lumber
8	Brown	Sue G.	603-555-8888	SUP	Hector's Hardware
9	Fletcher	Edwin P.	617-555-3210	CUS	Edwin's Toy Emporium
10	Gordon	John	315-555-3813	CUS	Toy Universe
11	Halpern	Frank	212-555-2831	ADV	Children's Highlights
12	Kafka	Jean	603-555-8700	ADV	New Age Express
13	O'Brien	William	603-555-9876	CUS	Toy Universe
14	Pendergast	Matthew	603-555-7171	SUP	Sears, Roebuck and Co.
15	Scofield	Jennifer	603-555-8500	ADV	Better Home Journal
16	Siess	Ned	413-555-3883	CUS	Peerless Imports
17	Woodward	Nancy	603-555-0007	CUS	Crafts 'R' Us
18					
19					
20					

You can sort any worksheet data, not just database tables. In general, an ascending sort arranges records so that labels are in alphabetical order and numbers are in numerical order, smallest to largest; blank cells in a column come first, followed by labels and then by values. A descending sort reverses this order: values come first, followed by labels, followed by blank cells, with labels in reverse alphabetical order and numbers in order of largest to smallest. 1-2-3 ignores capitalization in both ascending and descending sorts.

In a 1-2-3 database table, each record contains the same kind of data (values or labels) in a particular field; no field should contain values in some records and labels in other records. Therefore, fields containing values can be sorted into either ascending or descending numerical order. Fields containing labels can be sorted into alphabetical or reverse alphabetical order.

■ *NOTE:*   You can choose the exact *collating sequence* for sorting when you run Install (or by running it again, if you want to change the sequence). The collating sequence determines how labels are sorted (numbers before letters, letters before numbers, or by character values).

When you sort, you specify: (1) The range that contains the records you want sorted; and (2) the field or fields on which you want the sort to be based. In the following pages, you will use the Data Sort command to sort records in Bob Gordon's database in several ways.

Specifying the Data Range

The range of cells containing the records to be sorted is called the *data range*. Usually, the data range includes all the records in the database table, although you can also sort only some of the records. Be sure to include *only* cells that contain records; otherwise, the other cells you include will be sorted into the database. Be especially careful *not* to include the row of field names in the data range, or 1-2-3 will sort this row, too.

When you specify a data range, you must specify all the fields of each record you want to sort. If you do not (for instance, if you specify only the first three fields), 1-2-3 will sort only the fields you specified. The result will be a scrambled database: The fields you specified will be sorted, but they won't be matched up with the remaining fields of the records.

Using Sort Keys

When 1-2-3 sorts a database, it needs to know which field or fields to base the sort on. The *sort keys* specify these fields. The *primary key* is the main sort key. It affects the order of all the records in the database. Use a *secondary key* to sort records that have the same primary key.

In Bob's Business Contacts database, the Type field groups people according to Bob's relationship to them: **CUS** in the Type field means that the person is a customer; **SUP** means that he or she is a supplier; and **ADV** identifies advertising contacts. Sorting the records by Type groups each kind of contact together: Customer records with other customer records, supplier records with those of other suppliers, and advertisers with advertisers.

The following steps show you how to sort Bob's database by Type, and then by Last Name within each Type category.

1. Sort the database using the Type field as the primary key.

Highlight:	A5..I17
Choose:	Data Sort
Select:	Primary key:
Specify:	*any cell in column D* *(the Type field)*

Figure 6-12:   Data Sort Dialog Box with Data Range and Primary Key

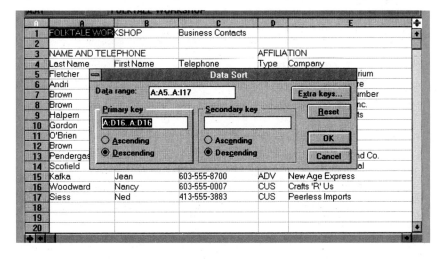

Press: ⏎ *or select OK, to sort in descending order*

    1-2-3 groups all the business contacts together according to the Type field. The Data Sort dialog box disappears from the screen, and 1-2-3 returns to READY mode.

Figure 6-13: Bob's Database Sorted by the Type Field

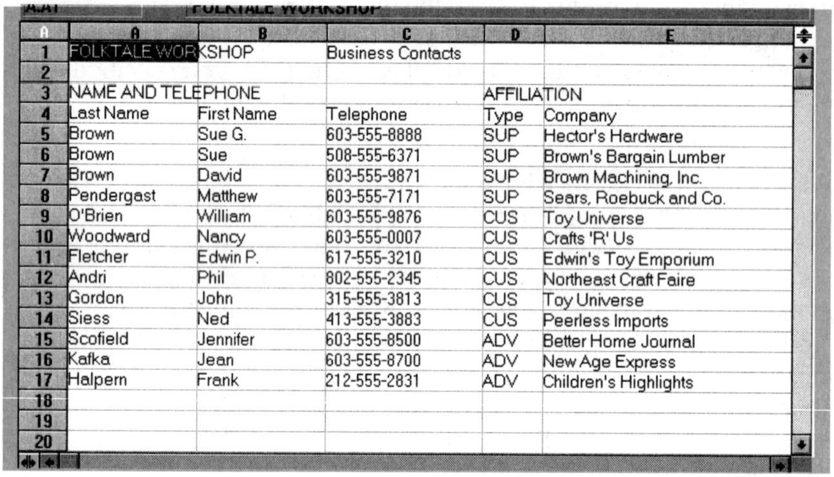

	A	B	C	D	E
1	FOLKTALE WORKSHOP		Business Contacts		
2					
3	NAME AND TELEPHONE			AFFILIATION	
4	Last Name	First Name	Telephone	Type	Company
5	Brown	Sue G.	603-555-8888	SUP	Hector's Hardware
6	Brown	Sue	508-555-6371	SUP	Brown's Bargain Lumber
7	Brown	David	603-555-9871	SUP	Brown Machining, Inc.
8	Pendergast	Matthew	603-555-7171	SUP	Sears, Roebuck and Co.
9	O'Brien	William	603-555-9876	CUS	Toy Universe
10	Woodward	Nancy	603-555-0007	CUS	Crafts 'R' Us
11	Fletcher	Edwin P.	617-555-3210	CUS	Edwin's Toy Emporium
12	Andri	Phil	802-555-2345	CUS	Northeast Craft Faire
13	Gordon	John	315-555-3813	CUS	Toy Universe
14	Siess	Ned	413-555-3883	CUS	Peerless Imports
15	Scofield	Jennifer	603-555-8500	ADV	Better Home Journal
16	Kafka	Jean	603-555-8700	ADV	New Age Express
17	Halpern	Frank	212-555-2831	ADV	Children's Highlights
18					
19					
20					

2. Sort the database using a primary and a secondary key.

    Look at the list of names in Figure 6-13. Notice that, although all the suppliers are grouped with other suppliers, all the customers with customers, and so on, there is no consistent order within each category.

    The database in this example is small enough so that Bob can scan it easily even when it is only partially sorted. However, it would be still easier to find a particular contact if the records were in alphabetical order within each business contact Type. To sort by Last Name within Type, you assign a secondary key and then repeat the Sort command (the data range and the primary key remain the same):

Choose: `Data   Sort`

Select: `Secondary key:`

Specify: *any cell in column A (the Last Name field)*

                `Ascending`   *as the secondary key sort order*

Press: ⏎ *or select OK to perform the sort*

    Now the records are sorted first by Type and then alphabetically by Last Name within each Type.

Figure 6-14:   Bob's Database Sorted by Type and Last Name Fields

	A	B	C	D	E
1	FOLKTALE WORKSHOP		Business Contacts		
2					
3	NAME AND TELEPHONE			AFFILIATION	
4	Last Name	First Name	Telephone	Type	Company
5	Brown	Sue	508-555-6371	SUP	Brown's Bargain Lumber
6	Brown	David	603-555-9871	SUP	Brown Machining, Inc.
7	Brown	Sue G.	603-555-8888	SUP	Hector's Hardware
8	Pendergast	Matthew	603-555-7171	SUP	Sears, Roebuck and Co.
9	Andri	Phil	802-555-2345	CUS	Northeast Craft Faire
10	Fletcher	Edwin P.	617-555-3210	CUS	Edwin's Toy Emporium
11	Gordon	John	315-555-3813	CUS	Toy Universe
12	O'Brien	William	603-555-9876	CUS	Toy Universe
13	Siess	Ned	413-555-3883	CUS	Peerless Imports
14	Woodward	Nancy	603-555-0007	CUS	Crafts 'R' Us
15	Halpern	Frank	212-555-2831	ADV	Children's Highlights
16	Kafka	Jean	603-555-8700	ADV	New Age Express
17	Scofield	Jennifer	603-555-8500	ADV	Better Home Journal
18					
19					
20					

Sorting with a Third Key

The list is now much easier to use than it was before. Notice, however, that there are three suppliers with Brown for a last name, and that these suppliers are not in strict alphabetical order. To completely alphabetize the list, use Data Sort once more with a third key. When you sort with three or more keys, you use the Data Sort Extra Keys command. This time, use the First Name field as a third key:

Choose:	Data Sort
Select:	Extra keys
	Key range *in the Extra Keys dialog box*
Specify:	any cell in column B *(the First Name field)*
Select:	Ascending *as the Sort direction option*
	OK *in the Extra Keys dialog box*
	OK *in the Data Sort dialog box*

1-2-3 once again sorts the database, this time using all three keys. Now all the names are categorized by Type (in descending order) and alphabetized by last and first names within each Type (in ascending order). Since Bob has no contacts who have exactly the same name and the same Type, the database is completely ordered. Had you specified all three keys the first time you sorted the database, 1-2-3 would have sorted the records by all three keys.

Save the file again.

Adding a Record and Re-sorting the Database

The entire database is now sorted according to the Type, Last Name, and First Name fields. From now on, however, any new record you add has to be incorporated into the database in the proper place. You can do this easily by (1) entering the record at the end of the database; (2) redefining the data range so it includes the new row; and (3) sorting the list with the previously defined sort keys.

Figure 6-15: Bob's Database Sorted by Type, Last Name, and First Name

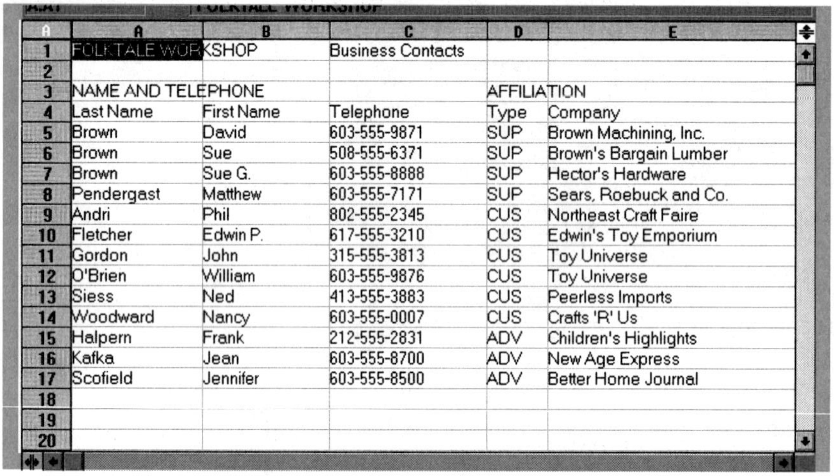

	A	B	C	D	E
1	FOLKTALE WORKSHOP		Business Contacts		
2					
3	NAME AND TELEPHONE			AFFILIATION	
4	Last Name	First Name	Telephone	Type	Company
5	Brown	David	603-555-9871	SUP	Brown Machining, Inc.
6	Brown	Sue	508-555-6371	SUP	Brown's Bargain Lumber
7	Brown	Sue G.	603-555-8888	SUP	Hector's Hardware
8	Pendergast	Matthew	603-555-7171	SUP	Sears, Roebuck and Co.
9	Andri	Phil	802-555-2345	CUS	Northeast Craft Faire
10	Fletcher	Edwin P.	617-555-3210	CUS	Edwin's Toy Emporium
11	Gordon	John	315-555-3813	CUS	Toy Universe
12	O'Brien	William	603-555-9876	CUS	Toy Universe
13	Siess	Ned	413-555-3883	CUS	Peerless Imports
14	Woodward	Nancy	603-555-0007	CUS	Crafts 'R' Us
15	Halpern	Frank	212-555-2831	ADV	Children's Highlights
16	Kafka	Jean	603-555-8700	ADV	New Age Express
17	Scofield	Jennifer	603-555-8500	ADV	Better Home Journal
18					
19					
20					

1. Enter a new customer record in row 18.

   Move to: cell A18

   Type: Saddler →

   Albert →

   313-555-7000 →

   CUS →

   Saddler's Toys by Mail →

   3498 Ford Blvd. →

   Detroit →

   MI →

   48219 ↵

2. Re-sort the records, adding the new record to the data range.

   When you choose Data Sort, 1-2-3 first offers the data range that you specified in the last sort, if any. (1-2-3 remembers the previously defined range even if you have saved the file and opened it again later.)

Choose: Data   Sort

Press: $\boxed{.}$ **(period)**   *to anchor the current data range*

$\boxed{\downarrow}$ *to include new record in range*

$\boxed{\lrcorner}$ *two times, to accept new range and sort*

$\boxed{\text{HOME}}$ *to have a look at the sorted records*

The new record is repositioned (in row 13, between O'Brien and Siess). You can add as many new records as you need, up to 1-2-3's row limit of 8192. You will always be able to re-sort the list to put new records in their proper places.

Congratulations! You have once again successfully ordered Bob's Business Contacts database. Save the file again.

Querying a Database

One of the biggest advantages of an electronic database over card files and other paper databases is the ease and speed with which it allows you to locate specific records. To locate records in a 1-2-3 database, you use the Data Query commands. When you *query* a 1-2-3 database, you ask 1-2-3 to find the records that match criteria you have specified. You can examine matching records, change them, extract them to another part of the worksheet file, or delete them from the database. The Data Query dialog box offers several different query operations. These operations are summarized in Table 6-1.

Table 6-1:   Data Query Operations

Command	What It Does:
Find	1-2-3 locates records that match the selection criteria. Then, as you move the pointer down the rows in the database, 1-2-3 moves to and highlights the next matching record. You can look at or edit the highlighted records.
Extract	1-2-3 finds the records that match the selection criteria and copies them to a designated worksheet location. The original records remain in the database.
Extract Unique	1-2-3 extracts records that match the selection criteria to a designated worksheet location, but does not include any duplicate records.
Modify	1-2-3 extracts the selected records into a worksheet. After editing the extracted records, you place them back into the table from which they were extracted.
Delete	1-2-3 finds and deletes the selected records. The other records shift to fill in the blank rows.

Basic Steps in Data Query Operations

Before you sorted Bob Gordon's database, you had to let 1-2-3 know which fields you wanted to use as sort keys and how you wanted to sort them (ascending or descending). Similarly, you must do some setup work before you can perform a Data Query operation. For all Data

Query operations, you specify as the input range the database table or tables you want the command to act on. For all Data Query operations, you must set up a criteria range (to tell 1-2-3 which records to select). For Data Query operations that produce output separate from the database table, such as Data Query Extract, you must also set up an output range (to tell 1-2-3 where to copy records that match the selection criteria).

Although the analogy is not perfect and the techniques are quite different, the logic behind querying a database is not unlike the logic you use when you go grocery shopping. When you go grocery shopping, you go into the supermarket with a shopping list and put items in a shopping cart. Imagine that the supermarket is a database, the shopping list is a set of selection criteria, and the shopping cart is an output range. As you walk through the aisles, you search the shelves, matching items from your "selection criteria" to items in the "database"; you select the ones that match and deposit them in the "output range." Eventually, you have a shopping cart full of the items in the grocery store that matched the items on your list. (The analogy breaks down only in the sense that when you copy records from a database to an output range, the original records remain in the database.)

Earlier releases of 1-2-3 restricted database operations to single database tables. All the information pertaining to a particular database entry, such as an employee record, had to be contained in one database table if it was to be accessed by a single Data Query command. In this chapter, you'll continue to work with Bob Gordon's Business Contacts database table as you learn the Data Query commands. "Working with Multiple Database Tables" later in this chapter will demonstrate how you use the Data Query commands with more than one table.

This following sections briefly describe the steps needed to perform a find, extract, modify, or delete operation.

Finding Records   To perform a Find, you must let 1-2-3 know what selection criteria you want to use, and which database records you want to search. The basic steps are:

1. Set up a criteria range and enter selection criteria.

   The *criteria range* includes a row with the names of one or more fields in the database table to be searched, as well as one or more rows of selection criteria. Essentially, you set up a criteria range by creating a row of field names and then entering selection criteria beneath it.

2. Choose Data Query Find, specifying the input range to be searched and the criteria range to be used.

   The *input range* is the database table 1-2-3 is to search. (The Find operation only works with one table at a time.) Selecting "Find" in the Data Query dialog box causes 1-2-3 to locate the first record in the input range that matches the criteria in the criteria range. (Pressing Down highlights the next matching record.) The mode indicator changes to FIND.

Extracting Records   To perform an Extract, you must perform the same steps you do for a Find. In addition, you must tell 1-2-3 where the selected records should be copied to. The basic steps are:

1. Set up a criteria range and enter selection criteria (just as you would for Find).

2. Set up an output range.

The *output range* is the part of the worksheet file to which 1-2-3 copies the records that match the selection criteria in the criteria range. You set up an output range by creating a row of field names in an empty area of the worksheet file. The field names you include in the output range determine which fields will be extracted from the records that match the selection criteria.

3. Select "Extract" in the Data Query dialog box and specify which input range, criteria range, and output range to use.

Selecting "Extract" in the Data Query dialog box tells 1-2-3 to search the input range for records that match the criteria in the criteria range. The input range can include one or more database tables. 1-2-3 erases any data in the output range and then copies the selected records to the output range. If you check "Extract Unique Only", 1-2-3 extracts only one copy of any duplicate records to the output range.

Modifying a Block of Records   To modify a block of records, you must perform the same preliminary steps as when you extract records. The basic steps are:

1. Set up a criteria range and enter selection criteria.

2. Set up the output range.

As you perform the Modify operation, 1-2-3 will copy the selected records to the output range, where you will edit them.

3. Choose Data Query and specify the input, criteria, and output ranges.

4. Select "Modify" in the Data Query dialog box.

1-2-3 displays the Data Query Modify dialog box.

5. Select "Extract" in the Data Query Modify dialog box.

6. Edit the extracted records in the output range.

7. Select "Replace" in the Data Query Modify dialog box to put the changed records back in the database.

Deleting Records   Deleting records from a database requires the same preliminary steps as finding records. You do not need to define an output range in order to delete records. However, before you actually delete them, you may want to either Find or Extract the records you plan to delete, to make sure you have set up the criteria range correctly.

The basic steps for deleting records from a 1-2-3 database are:

1. Set up a criteria range and enter selection criteria (just as you would for Find or Extract).

2. Select "Delete" in the Data Query dialog box, specifying the input range and criteria range to use.

When you select "Delete", 1-2-3 gives you one last chance to verify that you really want to delete the records. Selecting Cancel returns you to the Data Query dialog box; selecting "Delete" causes 1-2-3 to delete the records.

■ *CAUTION*   Once records have been deleted, they are no longer part of the worksheet file. Unless you immediately return to READY mode and press Undo to restore the records (assuming Undo is on), they are permanently deleted from the database.

The following sections describe how to set up and perform Data Query Find, Extract, Modify, and Delete operations using Bob Gordon's Business Contacts database.

Working with Input and Criteria Ranges

All of the Data Query commands require that you specify an input range and criteria range. This section describes how you specify an input range to 1-2-3 and how to set up criteria ranges. Setting up an output range is described in "Extracting Records" later in this chapter.

Specifying the Input Range   Whenever you use a Data Query command, you must let 1-2-3 know where the database table is. You do this by specifying the input range. Specifying the input range is similar to specifying the data range for the Sort command, except that unlike the Sort data range, the Data Query input range must include the row of database table field names. The input range does not have to include all the records in the database; there may be times when you want to search only a particular group of records.

Figure 6-16 shows Bob Gordon's contacts table defined as the input range in the Data Query dialog box. After you perform a Data Query operation, 1-2-3 remembers the input range you defined. If you close the worksheet file, 1-2-3 will remember the input range the next time you open the worksheet file.

Figure 6-16:   Specifying an Input Range for a Data Query Command

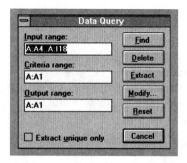

Setting up the Criteria Range Before you can query a database, you have to establish the criteria 1-2-3 will use when it performs the query. You do this by creating and defining a *criteria range*. The criteria range consists of two or more rows. The first row contains an exact copy of some or all of the field names (to a maximum of 256 field names) from the input range. The second row and any additional rows contain the actual criteria 1-2-3 is to use in queries.

When 1-2-3 searches a database, it looks for records that match the information you entered in the criteria range fields. A blank cell in a criteria range field matches every record. A label or value in a criteria range field matches only records that contain the same label or value in that field. A formula in a criteria range field matches records that cause the formula to evaluate to TRUE. (Using formulas in criteria ranges is described later in this chapter.)

For example, to find Bob's Massachusetts business contacts, you would set up a criteria range with two rows. The first row would contain some or all of the field names from the database, including the State field name. The second would contain the letters MA in the cell below the State field name (MA is how Massachusetts is listed in the database) and blank cells in any other cells in that row. 1-2-3 would match all records that contain the letters MA in the State field.

Setting up the criteria range for the first time is a two-step process: (1) Copy field names to another location in the worksheet file; (2) enter the criteria for a particular operation in the row or rows beneath the copy of the field names. Once you have specified a criteria range in one Data Query command, all you have to do for 1-2-3 to search for different records in the same database is change the criteria. 1-2-3 remembers the last criteria range specified from query to query, even after you close and reopen the worksheet file.

In the following steps, you are going to set up a criteria range. Later on in this chapter, you will fill in selection criteria and perform database searches.

Figure 6-17a: Field Names Set Up for Criteria Range (Left Screen)

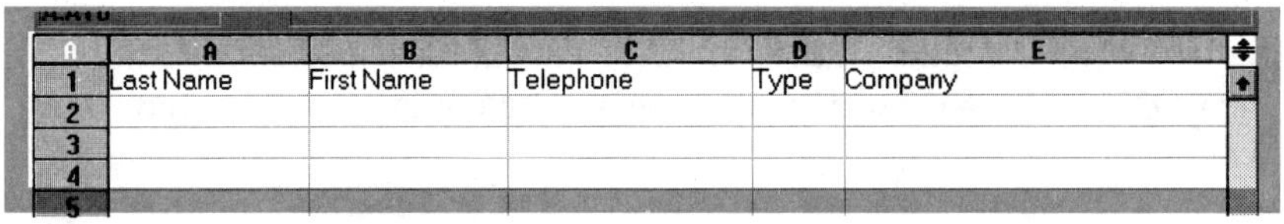

Figure 6-17b: Field Names Set Up for Criteria Range (Right Screen)

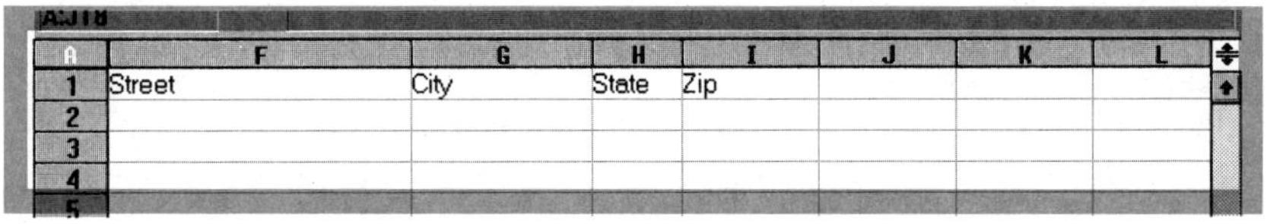

1. Insert a new worksheet for the criteria range.

You can place the criteria range anywhere in the worksheet file. Although you could use part of the database table worksheet for this purpose, using a second worksheet gives you more flexibility and helps keep the worksheet file organized.

Before you insert the second worksheet, you will put the CONTACTS file in GROUP mode. Putting the file in GROUP mode is a shortcut way of applying the column width and cell format settings of the database table worksheet to the new worksheet. After you have inserted the new worksheet, you will turn GROUP mode off. (The concepts of inserting worksheets and putting a worksheet file in GROUP mode are described in Chapter 5.)

First, from READY mode, turn on GROUP mode:

Choose: `Worksheet`   `Global Settings`

Select: `Group mode` *and check the check box*

               `OK`

1-2-3 puts the worksheet file in GROUP mode. The Group indicator appears in the status line. Now insert a new worksheet in front of the current worksheet:

Choose: `Worksheet`   `Insert`

Select: `Sheet` `Before`

Press: ⏎ *or select OK*

Choose: `Window`   `Split`

Select: `Perspective` `OK` *or click the Perspective icon*

1-2-3 inserts a new worksheet in front of the database table and moves the cell pointer there. This worksheet is now worksheet A, and the database table is now worksheet B. The new worksheet inherits the column and cell format settings of the database table worksheet. Figure 6-18 shows how the CONTACTS.WK3 file looks in perspective view after you have inserted the new worksheet.

Finally, turn off GROUP mode, since you do not want any subsequent changes you make to either the new worksheet or the database table to affect the other worksheet in the file.

Choose: `Worksheet`   `Global Settings`

Select: `Group mode` *and clear the check box*

               `OK`

The Group indicator disappears from the status line. Although worksheet A retains the column widths and cell formats of the database table worksheet, the two worksheets are now independent of each other.

2. Copy the database field names to the criteria range.

Figure 6-18: Inserting a New Worksheet Before the Database Table (Perspective View)

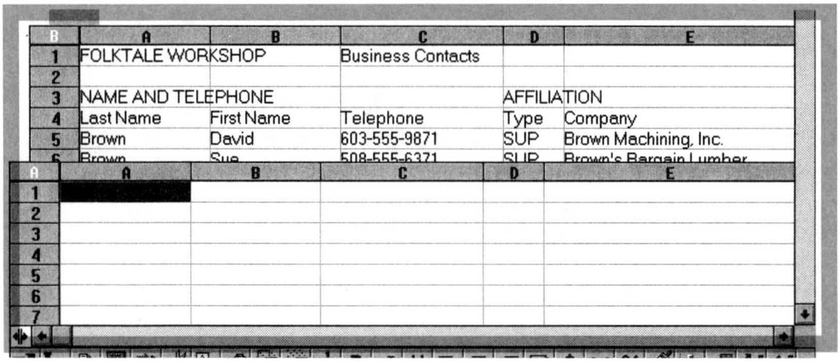

Copy the field names from the database table to the first row of the criteria range. To make sure that these new labels are exact duplicates of the originals, use the Edit Copy command instead of typing in the field names. (If the field names for the input range and the criteria range do not match exactly, 1-2-3 will not be able to query the database successfully.)

Highlight:	B:A4..B:I4 *field names*
Choose:	Edit Copy
Move to:	cell A:A1 *start of criteria range*
Choose:	Edit Paste

The new row of field names appears in row 1 of worksheet A.

Figure 6-19: Field Names Copied to Set Up Criteria Range

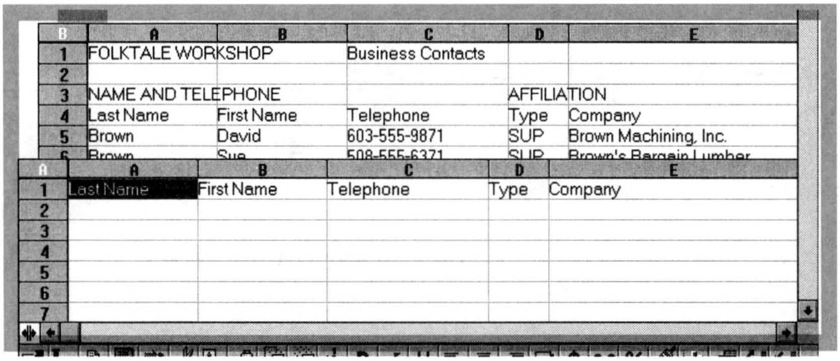

■ *NOTE:* You need to copy only the names of the fields in which you will be entering criteria. However, copying the entire row of field names makes it easier to change criteria whenever you want.

You will use this criteria range in the remaining exercises in this chapter.

4. Save CONTACTS.WK3.

Finding Records

The Data Query Find command allows you to view and edit selected records. When you select "Find", 1-2-3 highlights the first record that satisfies the selection criteria. You can then use the Up and Down keys to move the cell pointer among the entire group of matching records. 1-2-3 skips all non-matching records when you move the cell pointer.

The following steps give you some practice finding records.

1. Enter selection criteria in the criteria range.

To use Data Query Find, you must specify an input range and a criteria range in which you have entered selection criteria. You set up the criteria range earlier, so the only remaining step before using Data Query Find is to enter the actual selection criteria.

Your first task is to locate the records of Bob's Massachusetts business contacts. Specify "located in Massachusetts" as the only criterion by (1) entering the letters MA in the State field of the criteria range, and (2) leaving the other fields in the criteria range blank. You'll want to use the Find command in a full-sized window, so turn off Perspective view before you enter the criterion.

Choose: Window   Split

Select: Clear   *to clear Perspective view*
          OK

Move to: cell A:H2

Type: MA   ⏎

Figure 6-20:   Criterion to Match Contacts in Massachusetts

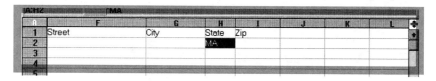

■ *NOTE:*   You can enter search criteria in either uppercase or lowercase.

2. Find the first matching record.

Having set up the criteria range, you are now ready to choose Data Query, specify the input and criteria range, and select "Find". Notice, as 1-2-3 starts the operation, that the mode indicator now reads FIND:

Choose: Data   Query

Specify: B:A4..B:I18   *in the Input range text box*

                A:A1..A:I2   *in the Criteria range text box*

Select: Find

■ *NOTE:*   You could also pre-select the input range.

Figure 6-21: 1-2-3 Finds and Highlights the First Matching Record

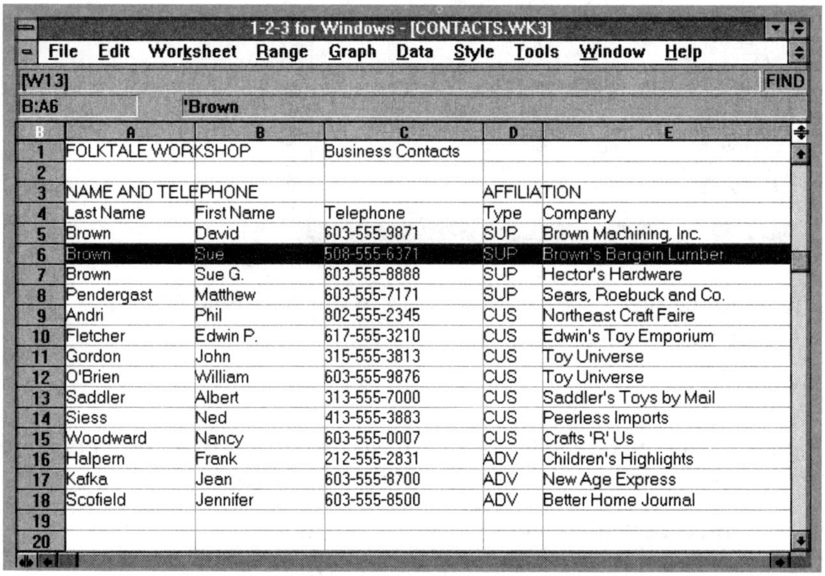

1-2-3 moves to worksheet B and goes to the first record that matches the criterion (Sue Brown of Worcester, MA), highlighting the entire record from columns A to I. 1-2-3 disables the mouse in FIND mode, so you can only navigate with the keys described in this section. Move along the record to verify that Sue Brown is indeed from Massachusetts:

Press: [→]   *six times, to shift the State field into view*

■ *NOTE:*   Because all the fields are highlighted in the "found record," you must look at the edit line to determine the location of the cell pointer within the highlighted field.

3. Find the remaining matching records.

Press: [↓]   *to move to the next matching record*

Figure 6-22: Navigating While in FIND Mode

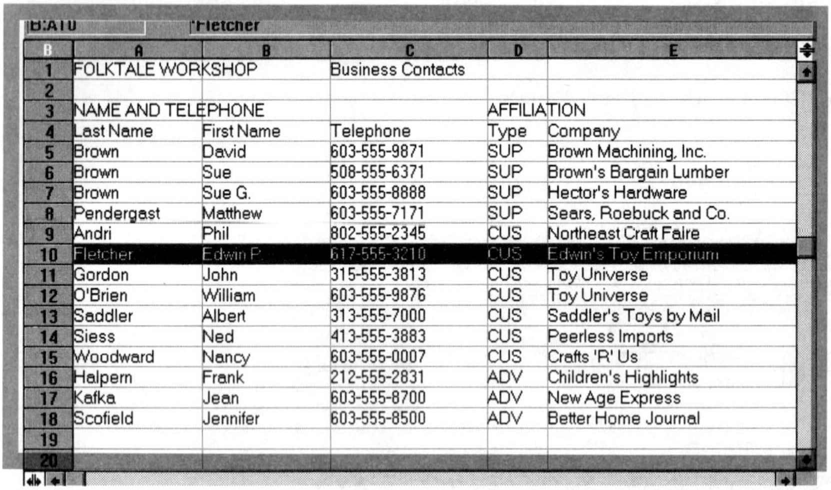

	A	B	C	D	E
1	FOLKTALE WORKSHOP		Business Contacts		
2					
3	NAME AND TELEPHONE			AFFILIATION	
4	Last Name	First Name	Telephone	Type	Company
5	Brown	David	603-555-9871	SUP	Brown Machining, Inc.
6	Brown	Sue	508-555-6371	SUP	Brown's Bargain Lumber
7	Brown	Sue G.	603-555-8888	SUP	Hector's Hardware
8	Pendergast	Matthew	603-555-7171	SUP	Sears, Roebuck and Co.
9	Andri	Phil	802-555-2345	CUS	Northeast Craft Faire
10	Fletcher	Edwin P	617-555-3210	CUS	Edwin's Toy Emporium
11	Gordon	John	315-555-3813	CUS	Toy Universe
12	O'Brien	William	603-555-9876	CUS	Toy Universe
13	Saddler	Albert	313-555-7000	CUS	Saddler's Toys by Mail
14	Siess	Ned	413-555-3883	CUS	Peerless Imports
15	Woodward	Nancy	603-555-0007	CUS	Crafts 'R' Us
16	Halpern	Frank	212-555-2831	ADV	Children's Highlights
17	Kafka	Jean	603-555-8700	ADV	New Age Express
18	Scofield	Jennifer	603-555-8500	ADV	Better Home Journal

The highlight moves down to the next record that lists MA in the State field (Edwin P. Fletcher, of Edwin's Toy Emporium in Arlington).

Press: ↓   *two times*

1-2-3 moves the cell pointer to the next matching record (Ned Siess), then beeps when you press Down a second time, because there are no more matching records.

4. Experiment with other ways pointer-movement keys work in FIND mode.

Pressing Up moves the cell pointer up the list of matched records; Home moves the cell pointer to the first matching record in the input range; and End moves it to the last matching record in the input range. Experiment with these keys on your own, then leave Find mode and the Data Query dialog box by pressing Escape or Enter:

Press: ESC   *or Enter, to leave FIND mode*

Select: Cancel   *to exit the Data Query dialog box*

Notice, when you leave FIND mode by pressing Escape or Enter, that the cell pointer returns to the location in worksheet A that it was in before you entered FIND mode.

Using the Query Key with Data Query Find   Now perform another search, this time for Bob's contacts who are customers located in New Hampshire.

You will leave the input and criteria ranges for the Find operation the same as for the last search, but change the actual selection criteria. You will use two criteria this time: change the State criterion from MA to NH, and then enter CUS into the Type field. A record must match both criteria in order for 1-2-3 to find it: 1-2-3 will match all records whose Type field reads CUS *and* whose State field reads NH.

Move to:	cell A:H2	*if the cell pointer is not already there*
Type:	NH ⏎	
Move to:	cell A:D2	
Type:	CUS ⏎	

Figure 6-23: Entering Two Search Criteria

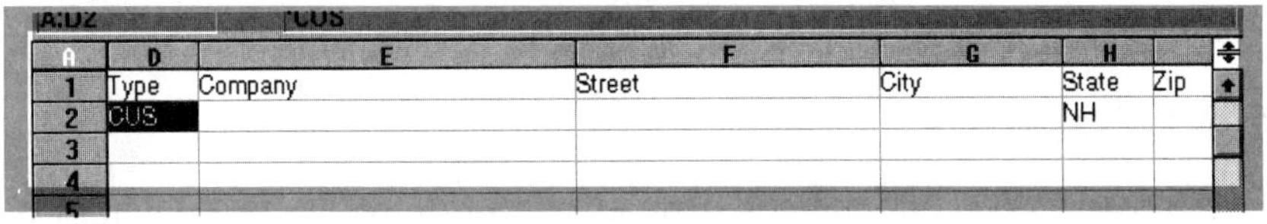

Now start the Find operation. This time, instead of selecting Data Query Find, press F7 (Query). Pressing the Query key from READY mode repeats the last Data Query command. Since the last command you selected was a Find, the Query key will also initiate a Find, using the same input and criteria ranges. Using the F7 (Query) key is particularly useful when you want to examine the same input range using different sets of selection criteria. After entering new criteria in the same criteria range, you can press F7 (Query) to find the records that match your new criteria. The input and criteria ranges are the same.

Press: F7   **(QUERY)**

1-2-3 selects the first matching record, that of William O'Brien from Concord, New Hampshire.

Figure 6-24: Find Operation Performed Using the F7 (Query) Key

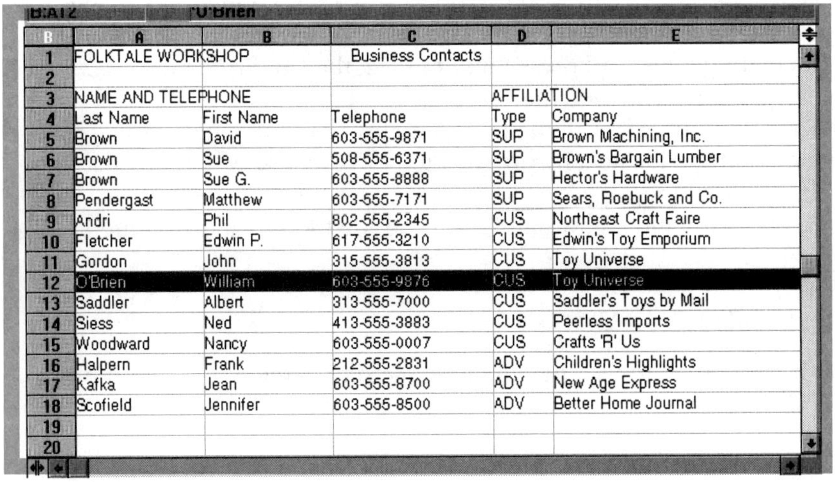

Use the Down and Up keys to move among the records that contain NH in the State field and CUS in the Type field. (Use the Right arrow to display the Type and State fields in the worksheet window, to verify 1-2-3's selections.) Notice that 1-2-3 selects only records that match both criteria; it skips partial matches, such as customers in states other than New Hampshire.

When you are through experimenting, return to READY mode. Earlier in this chapter, you returned to READY mode by pressing Enter or Escape to leave FIND mode and then selecting Cancel to exit the Data Query dialog box. You can return directly to READY mode from FIND mode by pressing the Query key instead of Escape or Enter:

Press: F7   **(QUERY)**

1-2-3 returns to READY mode. Notice that this time, instead of returning the cell pointer to where it was before you started the Find operation, 1-2-3 leaves the cell pointer in the position it was in when you were in FIND mode (the O'Brien record). Leaving FIND mode by pressing the Query key is handy when you want to move the cell pointer to a particular record and then do other worksheet operations in that part of the database table.

■ *NOTE:*   Pressing F7 (Query) from FIND mode will always return you to READY mode. However, the result of pressing Enter or Escape in FIND mode depends on how you entered FIND mode. If you entered it by using the Data Query Find command, pressing Enter or Escape will return you to the Data Query dialog box. If you entered FIND mode by using the Query key, pressing Enter or Escape will return you to READY mode.

Editing in FIND Mode   1-2-3 allows you to edit records that match specified criteria while you are still in FIND mode. As you've learned, you can move the cell pointer from field to field in a highlighted record using the Right and Left arrow keys. The program displays the current cell's contents in the control panel.

By moving the cell pointer along a record, you can go to any fields you wish to change. To edit a cell, you can type in new data and press Enter, or you can press F2 (Edit), modify the cell contents with the usual editing keys, and press Enter or click the Confirm button. 1-2-3 remains in FIND mode after you have changed the cell.

If you like, experiment on your own by editing the Company fields of some of the records. First, use Data Query Find to locate a record, using the current selection criteria, then use the F2 (Edit) key to change the located record.

When you are through experimenting, return to READY mode by pressing F7 (Query):

Press: F7   **(QUERY)**   *to exit FIND mode*
Select: Cancel   *to exit the Data Query dialog box*

Congratulations! You have learned to use the Find command to maneuver through Bob's database. Save CONTACTS.WK3.

Extracting Records

The Data Query Extract command finds records that match the criteria in the criteria range and then copies them to the designated output range. The copied records in the output range are not part of the original database. Therefore, you can edit them, sort them, print them, include them in calculations, or do anything else you would do with worksheet cells, without affecting the cells in the original database.

Working with Output Ranges   Before you can use Data Query Extract you must create an output range to which matching records will be copied. Like the first row of the criteria range, the first row of the output range contains field names from the input range. These names must exactly match the field names in the input range, though they do not have to be in the same order. You can include all of the field names or only those for fields you want to extract. The remaining rows in the output range will hold extracted records after you perform the Data Query Extract. 1-2-3 copies only the parts of matched records whose fields you include in the output range.

In this exercise, you are going to set up the output range directly below the criteria range, so you can view the criteria and output ranges at the same time. In a real-life situation, you might extract records to a different location where, for example, you would incorporate them into a graph or a printed report.

The first step is to copy the row of field names to the output range. You can copy them from either the input range or the criteria range. Copy them from the criteria range:

Highlight:	A:A1..A:I1	*the field names*
Choose:	Edit Copy	
Move to:	cell A:A10	*start of the output range*
Choose:	Edit Paste	

The row of field names appears below the criteria range.

Figure 6-25:   Field Names Copied for Output Range

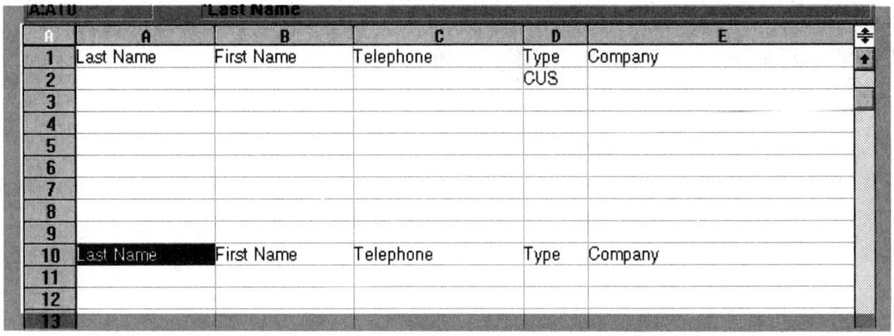

	A	B	C	D	E	
1	Last Name	First Name	Telephone	Type	Company	
2				CUS		
3						
4						
5						
6						
7						
8						
9						
10	Last Name	First Name	Telephone	Type	Company	
11						
12						
13						

When you use a Data Query command that requires an output range, such as Extract or Modify, you can designate either a multiple-row range as the output range or a range that is just one row deep (the row of field names). If you designate a multiple-row output range, 1-2-3 extracts only as many records as will fit in the range, then ends the Extract operation with an error message. To avoid this, you should make sure there is sufficient room for the records you expect to extract. If you designate a single-row output range, 1-2-3 uses the entire area directly below that row for the output range. In either case, to prevent you from confusing previously extracted data with the new extraction, 1-2-3 erases the output range before it extracts the records.

■ *CAUTION:*   Before you extract records, make sure there is no data that you care about in the output range. This is particularly important with single-row output ranges: before it performs an Extract, 1-2-3 erases data in *all* the cells below the output range field names, down to row 8192. Try to construct your worksheets so there is no important information below the output range field names. If you must place important information below the output range field names, do *not* use a single-row output range. Instead, define the output range as a group of rows that you know contain no important data.

Extracting the Records   Once you have set up the criteria and output ranges and have entered the selection criteria, you can use the Data Query Extract command. When you did a Find operation earlier in this chapter, the last criteria you specified were customer contacts who are located in New Hampshire. You'll use those criteria again for this Extract operation. In the Find operation, 1-2-3 highlighted the records of customer contacts who are located in New Hampshire. In the Extract operation, 1-2-3 finds those same records and copies them to the output range. You'll specify a one-row output range.

Choose:	`Data   Query`	
Select:	`Output range`	
Specify:	`A:A10..A:I10`	*as a one-row output range*
Select:	`Extract`	*to perform the query*
	`Cancel`	*to exit the Data Query dialog box*

Figure 6-26: Records of New Hampshire Customers Extracted to Output Range

	A	B	C	D	E	
1	Last Name	First Name	Telephone	Type	Company	
2				CUS		
3						
4						
5						
6						
7						
8						
9						
10	Last Name	First Name	Telephone	Type	Company	
11	O'Brien	William	603-555-9876	CUS	Toy Universe	
12	Woodward	Nancy	603-555-0007	CUS	Crafts 'R' Us	
13						

After you select "Extract", 1-2-3 copies the extracted records to the output range. These records contain C U S in the Type field and N H in the State field. Extracted records have the same cell format in the output range as they had in the database table.

Rearranging the Output Range Fields   You can create as many output ranges as you need, and each one can hold a different group of extracted records. You can also rearrange the fields of an output range so that the extracted records conform to a particular need.

When you use Data Query Extract, specify the output range that will generate the results you want. For example, it is common practice to extract information from a database to generate a report or to create some kind of list, such as a mailing list. 1-2-3 helps you do this by letting you select only certain fields to extract and by allowing you to specify the order in which the fields appear in the output range.

Say, for instance, that Bob really wants to extract just the name, company name, city, and telephone number of each of his New Hampshire customers, instead of the entire record. He can do this by creating an output range that contains only the fields he wants, and then performing an Extract. Create such an output range now in another part of the worksheet file.

1. Move to an empty area of the worksheet file.

You will create a new output range a few columns to the right of the current output range. Begin by moving the cell pointer to the first cell of the new output range:

Move to: cell A:O1

2. Create the output range field names.

Since the field names in this output range are in a different order than the field names in the input range, it is easier to type the names than it is to copy them one at a time from the input or criteria range. Make sure, however, that you type them *exactly* as indicated here. Unless the field names are exact duplicates of those in the input range (including label prefixes and blank spaces), the Extract won't work.

Type: First Name   →

                   Last Name   →

                   Company   →

                   City   →

                   Telephone   ↵

Figure 6-27:   Output Range with Fields Names Organized for Mailing List

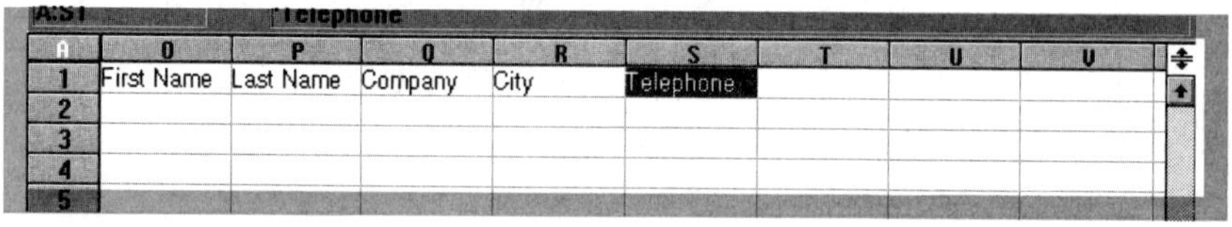

A	O	P	Q	R	S	T	U	U	
1	First Name	Last Name	Company	City	Telephone				
2									
3									
4									
5									

3. Adjust the column widths for the output range.

Adjust the column widths of the output range so that the mailing list records Bob creates will be no wider than one screen. Use the column-width settings in Setup Table 6-3. Notice that the widths for `Telephone` and `City` are slightly narrower than the widths of the same fields in the database itself. (HINT: To save time, use Worksheet Column Width to set the five field widths to 12, then use Worksheet Column Width a second time to set the Company field's width to 24.)

Setup Table 6-3:   Output Range Column Widths

Field Name	Column Letter	New Width
First Name	O	12
Last Name	P	12
Company	Q	24
City	R	12
Telephone	S	12

4. Perform the Extract using the new output range.

You will use the current input range, criteria range, and selection criteria for this Extract. All you need to change is the output range.

Choose: `Data    Query`
Select: `Output range`
Specify: `A:O1..A:S1`
Select: `Extract`
                `Cancel`   *to exit the Data Query dialog box*

Figure 6-28:   Output Range with Selected Field Names Extracts Those Fields from Contacts Table

1-2-3 selects the same records as in the previous exercise. This time, however, only the First Name, Last Name, Company, City, and Telephone fields are extracted from those matching records into the output range.

5. Save CONTACTS.WK3.

Congratulations! You have learned to set up output ranges and to extract records. Save the file.

Adding a New Field to a Database

As Bob's business starts to grow, he decides he'd like to keep track of how frequently he uses a particular supplier or advertiser, and how often a particular customer places orders with him. For example, he would like to know who his best customers are so he can send them catalogs or announcements of special sales; he would like to know how often he buys from a particular supplier so he can bargain for better prices on materials. Bob realizes he can use his Business Contacts database for this purpose if he adds a new field. This field will record the number of times Bob does business with each contact.

In this section, you are going to add a new field to the database and fill in this frequency-of-contact information. You will use the new information later on, in "Using a Formula as a Criterion," to demonstrate how 1-2-3 can use formulas to select records.

1. Add a field named Freq to the database table.

Bob decides to name this new field Freq, for "frequency of contact." First, enter a field name for the Freq field in the database table, to the right of the Zip field name. This field will contain values; prefix it with the right-alignment label prefix, so that the values and the field name will line up properly.

Move to: cell B:J4

Type: `"Freq` ⏎ *to right-align the field name*

2. Fill in sample data for the Freq field.

Enter the numbers shown in column J of Figure 6-29. These represent the number of times Bob has done business with each customer, supplier, or advertiser.

Figure 6-29:   Values to Place in the Freq Field

	Street	City	State	Zip	Freq		
4	Street	City	State	Zip	Freq		
5	509 Chauncy St.	Nashua	NH	03062	12		
6	357 Somerville Ave.	Worcester	MA	01604	3		
7	45 Auburn St.	Derry	NH	03038	3		
8	522 Main St.	Concord	NH	03302	8		
9	P.O. Box 257	Bennington	VT	05201	2		
10	369 Washington St.	Arlington	MA	02174	0		
11	890 McGrath Hwy.	Syracuse	NY	14132	6		
12	1891 Eastern Blvd.	Concord	NH	03301	0		
13	3498 Detroit Blvd.	Detroit	MI	48219	10		
14	3435 Main St.	Springfield	MA	02010	8		
15	52 Oak Lane	Nashua	NH	03062	12		
16	182 E. 57th St.	New York	NY	10024	5		
17	P.O. Box 8779	Peterboro	NH	03458	11		
18	P.O. Box 534	Peterboro	NH	03458	10		
19							
20							
21							
22							
23							

4. Copy the new field name to the criteria and output ranges.

To use the information in this new field in future Data Query operations, you must include the field name in the criteria range and in an output range (you will extend the first output range you set up, rather than create a new output range). This time, since there is only one label to create, copy the label to the appropriate rows instead of typing it:

Move to:	cell B:J4
Choose:	`Edit   Copy`
Move to:	cell A:J1 *for the criteria range*
Choose:	`Edit   Paste`
Move to:	cell A:J10 *for the output range*
Choose:	`Edit   Paste`

Figure 6-30: Adding a New Field to the Criteria and Output Ranges

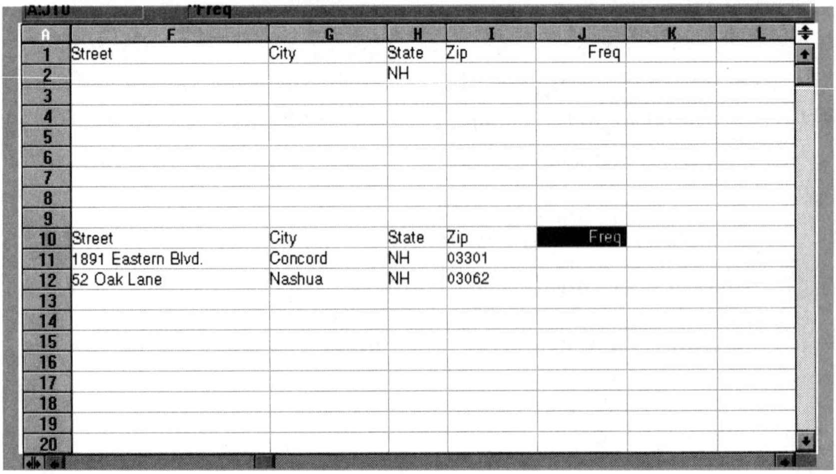

■ *NOTE:*   Adding a new field name to the criteria and output ranges does not automatically change the definition of these ranges. The next time you perform a Data Query operation, you need to redefine the criteria and output ranges to include the new field (you will do so later in this chapter).

More on Using Database Criteria

This section shows you some additional ways you can use criteria to select records in a database.

Using a Formula as a Criterion

Besides matching records by using exact criteria, you can also find or extract records from a 1-2-3 database using formulas for criteria. For example, say Bob is planning a sale for his best customers and wants to send out an announcement to that effect. He decides that anyone who has placed orders with him more than six times in the last few months should get an announcement. He uses 1-2-3 to extract a list of these customers.

You are going to enter a formula in the Freq field of the criteria range (cell A:J2). 1-2-3 will use this formula to test each cell in column J of the database table to see if it contains a value greater than or equal to 6.

This formula has three parts:

- The field to be tested (the Freq field, column J of the database)
- The logical operator "greater than or equal to" (>=)
- The value to which the field values are compared (6)

The following sections describe how to specify cells to be tested by a formula and logical operators you can use in formula criteria.

Specifying the Field to be Tested

There are three ways to indicate which field to test against a formula. You can:

- *Use the field name.* Type a field name in the formula criterion as if it were a range name. If you use this method, 1-2-3 will search the field in the input range whose name is specified in the formula. For example, +freq in the formula +freq>=6 tells 1-2-3 to search the Freq field of the input range for cells that contain a value greater than or equal to 6.
- *Use the relative address of the first data cell in the field.* If you use this method, 1-2-3 will search the field in the input range that is in the same column as the cell address you provide. For example, +J5 in the formula +J5>=6 tells 1-2-3 to search column J of the database table for cells that contain a value greater than or equal to 6. Be sure to specify the address of the field in the *first* record of the input range (immediately below the field name).

> **NOTE:**   When you specify a cell address in a formula criterion that refers to a value outside the database, you must use an absolute cell address. When you specify a cell address that refers to a database field, you must use a relative cell address.

- *Use a shorthand method.* With this method, you do not provide a cell address to identify the field to be tested. 1-2-3 assumes that the field to be tested in the input range is the same as the criteria range field in which you are entering the criterion. For instance, the formula '>=6 in the Freq field of the criteria range means "test the input range cells in the input range Freq field and match cells that contain a value greater than or equal to 6." Note that the shorthand formula starts with a label prefix. 1-2-3 stores these shorthand formulas as labels, but treats them as a special kind of formula during database operations.

Table 6-2 summarizes the three ways you can enter a formula. Each way will select exactly the same records when you perform a Data Query Find or Extract.

Table 6-2: Ways to Enter Formula Criteria

Example	Method	Description
+freq>=6	Field name	1-2-3 uses the field name to identify the column of cells to be tested.
+B:J5>=6	Relative address of first cell in column	1-2-3 uses the relative address to identify the column of cells to be tested.
'>=6	Shorthand	You have not supplied a field name or a relative address, so 1-2-3 assumes that the column of cells to be tested is the one with the same field name as the column containing the formula. (If you enter 6 without any logical operator at all, 1-2-3 tests for values of 6 in the cells.)

In this particular example, there is no strong reason to prefer one method over the other. However, that is not always the case.

The shorthand method involves the least typing and is the most convenient if you are using criteria that are already in fields in the criteria range.

The field name method of entering formula criteria is the most descriptive. When you query with more than one database table at a time, this method also allows you to perform certain operations that could not otherwise be performed. (Performing data query operations on multiple database tables is described later in this chapter.)

The relative cell address method is not as self-documenting as the field name method, but it is the only method compatible with all earlier releases of 1-2-3.

Keep in mind the following additional points as you work with 1-2-3 database criteria:

- If you change a field name in a database table, remember to change the field name in any formula criteria that use the changed field name.
- If you rearrange the order of the database table fields, you may have to change formula criteria that use the relative cell address method so that the formulas refer to the new field locations.
- The shorthand method cannot be used with formulas that contain arithmetic or compound logical operators. For example, `'>6+MIN` is not allowed, nor is `'>6#AND#<9`. (Logical operators are described in the following section).

Using Logical Operators in Formula Criteria   The formula you will enter uses the "greater than or equal to" operator (>=). Table 6-3 provides a complete list of the *logical operators* you can use in formula criteria.

Table 6-3:   Logical Operators

Operator	Description	Example	Precedence*
=	Equal to	+J5=6	5
<>	Not equal to	+J5<>6	5
<	Less than	+J5<6	5
>	Greater than	+J5>6	5
<=	Less than or equal to	+J5<=6	5
>=	Greater than or equal to	+J5>=6	5
#NOT#	Logical NOT	#NOT#J5=6	6
#OR#	Logical OR	+J5>6#OR#J5<3	7
#AND#	Logical AND	+J5>6#AND#J5<9	7

Operations with lower precedence numbers are evaluated before operations with higher precedence numbers. 1-2-3 evaluates an operator whose precedence is 5 before an operator with a precedence of 6 or 7.

■ *NOTE:*   To accommodate certain keyboards, 1-2-3 allows you to type the left angle bracket key (<) instead of the slash key (/) as an alternate way to call up the 1-2-3 Classic menu. If you use the shorthand method for entering formulas and you use the "less than" operator (<), be sure to precede the operator with a label prefix. If you do not, 1-2-3 will display the 1-2-3 Classic menu instead of entering the character.

The operators <, <=, >, >=, =, and <> compare values. They are sometimes called *simple logical operators*. #NOT#, #OR#, and #AND# are sometimes called *compound logical operators*. The #NOT# operator negates a logical expression. For example, the expression #NOT#J5=6 matches cells in the Freq column of a database whose values are not equal to 6. The #OR# and #AND# operators join two logical expressions. The expression +J5>6#OR#J5<3 matches values whose frequency is either greater than 6 or less than 3 (it does not match 3 through 6). The expression +J5>=6#AND#J5<30 matches Freq values that are both greater than or equal to 6 and less than 30.

Table 6-3 also lists the order of precedence of the logical operators. Notice that the simple logical operators all have a lower precedence number than the compound logical operators. Therefore, the simple logical operators are evaluated before the compound logical operators. Consequently, expressions such as +J5>=6#AND#J5<30 do not require parentheses, since the expressions on each side of the #AND# operator are each evaluated before the #AND# operator, as if the formula were written: +(J5>6)#AND#(J5<30).

All the logical operators have higher precedence numbers than the arithmetic operators. Therefore, logical operators are evaluated *after* all arithmetic operations have been performed. (Arithmetic operators are described in Chapter 4 and summarized in Table 4-1.)

Entering the Formula   In this example, use the address of the first data cell in the field you want 1-2-3 to search (Freq) as the left side of the equation. When you perform a Data Query Extract or Find, 1-2-3 searches through each cell in the Freq field of the database table and matches any cells that contain the value 6.

Move to: cell A:J2

Type: +freq>=6 ⏎

Figure 6-31: 1-2-3 Displays ERR Instead of the Formula.

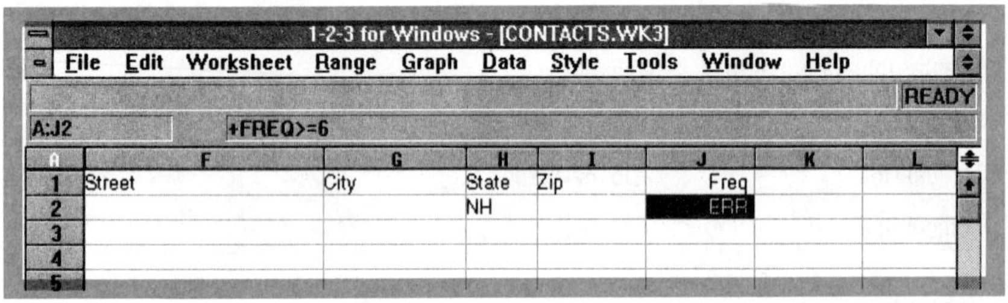

			1-2-3 for Windows - [CONTACTS.WK3]					▾ ▲
	File Edit Worksheet Range Graph Data Style Tools Window Help							▲
								READY
A:J2		+FREQ>=6						

A	F	G	H	I	J	K	L	
1	Street	City	State	Zip	Freq			▲
2			NH		ERR			
3								
4								
5								

Notice that 1-2-3 displays ERR in cell A:J2 while displaying the formula in the edit line. There is actually no error in the worksheet. 1-2-3 displays ERR whenever it encounters a formula that it can't evaluate. The field name Freq has meaning to 1-2-3 only during database operations, so 1-2-3 displays ERR to indicate that it can't evaluate the formula now. At this point, it's more important to see the formula than the formula's result, so format cell A:J2 as Text to display the formula:

Choose: Range   Format

Select: Text   *in the Format list box*
OK

Figure 6-32: Formula Formatted as Text

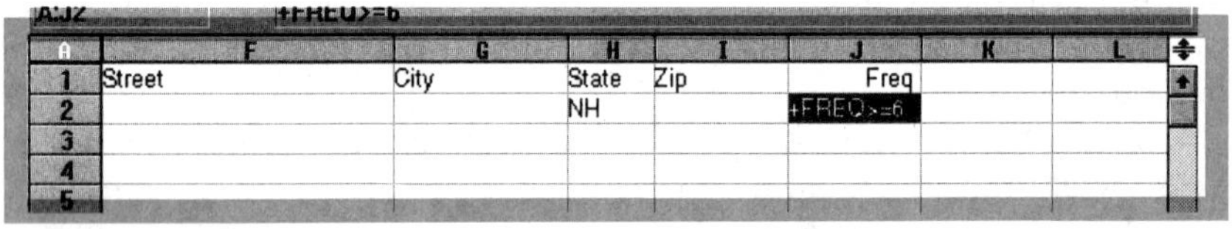

A:J2		+FREQ>=6						
A	F	G	H	I	J	K	L	
1	Street	City	State	Zip	Freq			▲
2			NH		+FREQ>=6			
3								
4								
5								

Performing the Extract   Now extract the records of Bob's preferred customers, using the formula you just entered.

1. Make sure the other criteria are correct.

This extraction will include customers who have had six or more business transactions with Bob. You set up the first criterion (the word **CUS** in the Type field) earlier in this chapter. You also set up the second (**+freq>=6**) criteria. All the other fields should be blank, or 1-2-3 will use their contents as selection criteria. The State field still has NH in it, from the previous Extract. Erase this:

Move to: cell A:H2

Press: DELETE

The selection criteria are now correct.

3. Perform the Extract, including column J in the input, criteria and output ranges.

To get some experience with multiple-row output ranges, you'll specify a ten-row output range. If there are more records to be extracted than will fit in the output range, 1-2-3 will extract as many records as will fit; it will then beep and display an error message indicating that there are too many records for the output range.

Choose: `Data Query`

Specify: B:A4..B:J18 *in the Input range text box*

Select: `Criteria range`

Specify: A:A1..A:J2

Select: `Output range`

Specify: A:A10..A:J20

Select: `Extract` CANCEL *to exit the Data Query dialog box*

Figure 6-33: Output range shows customers with whom Bob has six or more contacts.

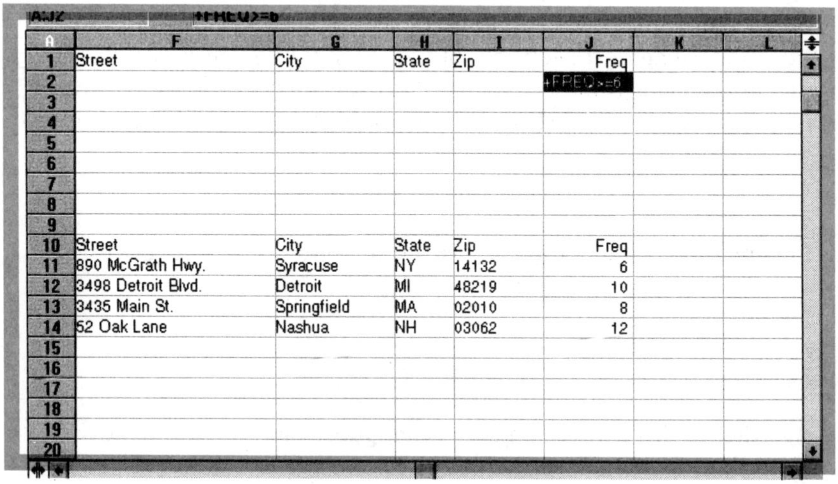

A	F	G	H	I	J	K	L
1	Street	City	State	Zip	Freq		
2					+FREQ>=6		
3							
4							
5							
6							
7							
8							
9							
10	Street	City	State	Zip	Freq		
11	890 McGrath Hwy.	Syracuse	NY	14132	6		
12	3498 Detroit Blvd.	Detroit	MI	48219	10		
13	3435 Main St.	Springfield	MA	02010	8		
14	52 Oak Lane	Nashua	NH	03062	12		
15							
16							
17							
18							
19							
20							

The records in the output range from a previous extraction are replaced by new ones. These new records match two criteria: They contain `CUS` in the Type field, and a value greater than or equal to 6 in the Freq field.

Using More than One Row in the Criteria Range

So far, the database searches you have done have used only a two-line criteria range; one line for the field names and one line for the selection criteria. In some cases, one line is not enough to uniquely identify the desired records.

When you want 1-2-3 to search only for records that match *all* criteria, enter the criteria in the same row. For example, in the previous section, you extracted all the records for people who are customers *and* who did business with Bob at least six times. 1-2-3 was able to find these records by performing what is known, in database parlance, as an *AND search*:

```
(Type equal to CUS)   AND   (Freq greater than or equal to 6)
```

Similarly, earlier in this chapter you extracted all the records for customers who are located in New Hampshire:

```
(Type equal to CUS)   AND   (State equal to NH)
```

Sometimes, however, what you want to do is match all the records that meet *any* of the criteria you supply. A simple example might be to extract all the business contacts in either Massachusetts or New Hampshire. This type of search requires what is known, in database parlance, as an *OR search*. A record must match either one criterion OR another; in this case, the State field must contain either MA *or* NH:

```
(State equal to MA)   OR   (State equal to NH)
```

One way to perform an OR search is to use the #OR# operator in the relevant field. For example, +H5="MA"#OR#H5="NH" in the State field of the criteria range would match records that contained either MA or NH in that field of the input range.

Another way to perform an OR search is to use more than one row in the criteria range: 1-2-3 matches records in the database against each row of the criteria range and extracts the records that match *any* of the criteria rows. To see how this works, modify the criteria range so that 1-2-3 searches for records of contacts in Massachusetts or New Hampshire, then extract those records.

1. Erase any existing criteria.

   Start with a clean slate by erasing the existing criteria in the current criteria range. (Do not erase the field names!)

   Highlight: A:A2..A:J2
   Press: `DELETE`

   1-2-3 erases any existing criteria. (If you performed a Data Query Find or Extract now, 1-2-3 would match all the records in the database, since a completely blank criteria range matches any record.)

2. Enter new criteria in the criteria range.

Now enter new criteria in the State field. Enter the criterion for Massachusetts contacts in row 2, and for New Hampshire contacts in row 3:

Move to:	cell A:H2
Type:	MA ↓
	NH ↵

4. Perform the Extract, using the extended criteria range and an extended output range.

Now that you have set up the criteria range, you can perform the Extract. Since you don't know how many records the operation will put into the output range, you'll enlarge the output range to 20 rows to cover the possibility of all 18 records matching.

Choose:	Data Query
Select:	Criteria range
Specify:	A:A1..A:J3 *enlarge by one row*
Select:	Output range
Specify:	A:A10..A:J31 *for twenty-row output range*
Select:	Extract
	Cancel *to exit the Data Query dialog box*

Figure 6-34:   Multiple-row criteria range extracts Massachusetts and New Hampshire contacts.

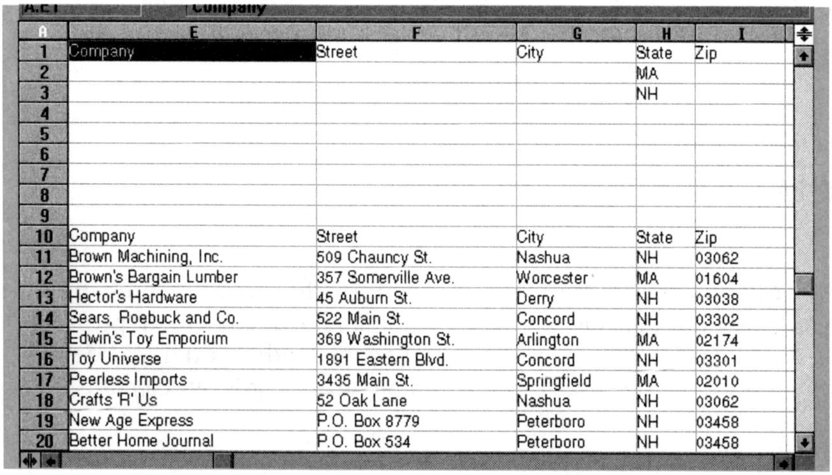

A	E	F	G	H	I
1	Company	Street	City	State	Zip
2				MA	
3				NH	
4					
5					
6					
7					
8					
9					
10	Company	Street	City	State	Zip
11	Brown Machining, Inc.	509 Chauncy St.	Nashua	NH	03062
12	Brown's Bargain Lumber	357 Somerville Ave.	Worcester	MA	01604
13	Hector's Hardware	45 Auburn St.	Derry	NH	03038
14	Sears, Roebuck and Co.	522 Main St.	Concord	NH	03302
15	Edwin's Toy Emporium	369 Washington St.	Arlington	MA	02174
16	Toy Universe	1891 Eastern Blvd.	Concord	NH	03301
17	Peerless Imports	3435 Main St.	Springfield	MA	02010
18	Crafts 'R' Us	52 Oak Lane	Nashua	NH	03062
19	New Age Express	P.O. Box 8779	Peterboro	NH	03458
20	Better Home Journal	P.O. Box 534	Peterboro	NH	03458

■ *NOTE:*   1-2-3/W ignores blank rows in the criteria range, as long as at least one cell in the criteria range contains an entry. However, it is good practice to avoid including blank criteria rows. Blank criteria rows in some earlier releases of 1-2-3 caused all records in the input range to be matched.

Using Criteria Ranges with Multiple Fields and Multiple Rows

It is sometimes necessary to enter criteria in more than one field of a criteria row and, at the same time, to use more than one row of criteria. For example, suppose Bob wants to limit his preferred-customer sale to Massachusetts and New Hampshire customers. In order to send announcements to only those customers, he must extract a list of all the customers in New Hampshire and Massachusetts who have bought toys from him six or more times. He does this by filling in the appropriate criteria for two rows; one for the Massachusetts preferred customers, and one for the New Hampshire preferred customers.

You can generate this list by modifying the selection criteria you entered in the previous section. The two rows of selection criteria you must create will be identical except for the State field (which has already been filled in).

1. Enter the remaining criteria for row 2 of the criteria range.

   First, fill in the criteria for the Massachusetts row. This time, use the shorthand method for filling in the Freq field's criterion:

Move to:	cell A:D2
Type:	CUS
Press:	→ six times, to cell A:J2
Type:	>=6 ↵

2. Enter the remaining criteria in row 3 of the criteria range.

   Now complete the New Hampshire criteria:

Press:	↓
Type:	>=6
Press:	← six times, to cell A:D3
Type:	CUS ↵

3. Perform the Extract.

   If you have just completed the previous exercise, you can perform the Extract by pressing F7 (Query), rather than by reissuing the Data Query Extract command. Remember that pressing Query causes 1-2-3 to re-execute the most recent Data Query command. If you have been experimenting on your own since the previous exercise, extract the records by selecting Data Query Extract:

Choose:	Data Query
Select:	Extract Cancel

   1-2-3 extracts a short list of customers who are located in Massachusetts or New Hampshire, and who have bought toys from Bob at least six times.

Figure 6-35: Customers in MA and NH Who've Bought Toys Six Times or More

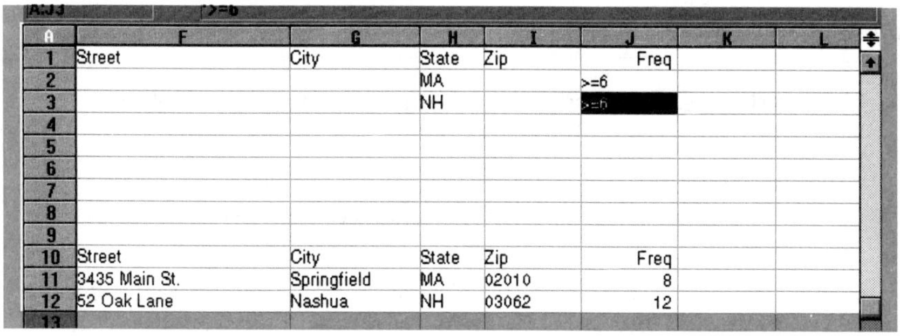

	Street	City	State	Zip		Freq		
1	Street	City	State	Zip		Freq		
2			MA			>=6		
3			NH			>=6		
4								
5								
6								
7								
8								
9								
10	Street	City	State	Zip		Freq		
11	3435 Main St.	Springfield	MA	02010		8		
12	52 Oak Lane	Nashua	NH	03062		12		

Table 6-4 summarizes the kinds of searches 1-2-3 will perform when you set up different kinds of criteria ranges.

Table 6-4: Ways to Use Criteria Ranges

Search	What Happens
AND	Entering two or more criteria in one row finds records that match *all* criteria in the row. 1-2-3 performs an AND search: criterion 1 AND criterion 2 AND criterion 3...
OR	Entering several criteria, each in a different row, finds records that match *any one* of the criteria. 1-2-3 performs an OR search: criterion 1 OR criterion 2 OR criterion 3...
AND/OR	Entering two or more criteria in each of several rows finds records that match *all* criteria in *any* of the rows. 1-2-3 performs an AND search on the criteria in each row, but an OR search on all the rows.

Using Wildcard Characters in Label Criteria

When setting up the criteria range in a database, you usually have to make sure that the characters in the range exactly match the characters you are trying to find in the database. Any incorrect characters will throw off the search.

Three *wildcard characters* enable you to match labels that do not match exactly. Wildcard characters in 1-2-3 work somewhat the same way the wildcard does in a game of poker. When the dealer declares "deuces wild," a deuce card can match any number or any suit: Three jacks and a deuce are equivalent to four jacks. Similarly in 1-2-3, the asterisk (*), question mark (?), and tilde (~) match different combinations of characters in a label.

Table 6-5 describes how to use wildcards in label fields in a criteria range. You can use wildcard characters in any number of label fields.

Table 6-5: Using Wildcards in the Criteria Range

Character	Description
*	An asterisk matches all characters to the end of the label; **dum*** will match "dumpling" and "DUM9124", but not "drum".
?	A question mark matches any single character within a label; **t?p** will match "tap" and "T/P," but not "tips". You can use more than one ? in a label; **s??r** will match "Sear" and "SOUR," but not "soul".
~	The tilde at the beginning of a label is the equivalent of "not equal": it instructs 123 to accept any label except the one following the tilde. For example, **~Brown** will select all records that do not have **Brown** in the indicated field. **~B*** will select all records that do not have a label starting with **B** in the indicated field.

In the following exercises, you will use wildcard characters to search the Last Name, First Name, and Type fields of Bob's database.

Using the Asterisk Wildcard in Criteria   Begin by finding all the records of business contacts whose last names begin with S.

1. Erase any existing criteria in rows 2 and 3, columns A through J.

   This search will use only one row of criteria and one field in that row. However, to avoid possible confusion later on, erase all the fields in both rows of criteria:

   Highlight: A:A2..A:J3
   Press: ⌷DELETE⌷

2. Fill in new criteria.

   Use the asterisk (*) wildcard in the Last Name field so that 1-2-3 will scan the database for names that begin with S. Enter the criterion in cell A2:

   Move to: cell A:A2
   Type: s*   ⌷↵⌷

3. Perform the Find operation, using the smaller criteria range.

   Choose: Data   Query
   Select: Criteria range
   Specify: A:A1..A:J2
   Select: Find

   1-2-3 highlights the record that contains the first occurrence of a Last Name that starts with S (Saddler). Pressing Down will move the highlight to any subsequent records that start with S.

Using the Question Mark Wildcard in Criteria   Now modify the criteria so that 1-2-3 will find all the contacts whose first name begins with J, contains only four letters, and ends with the letter N:

1. Erase the existing criteria.

   Leave FIND mode and erase the criterion in the Last Name field:

Press:	F7 **(QUERY)**	*to leave FIND mode*
Select:	Cancel *to exit the Data Query dialog box*	
Move to:	A:A2 *if necessary*	
Press:	DELETE	

2. Enter new criteria.

   Enter new criteria in the First Name field:

Press:	→	*to move to cell A:B2*
Type:	j??n ↵	

3. Perform the Find.

Press:	F7 **(QUERY)**	*to repeat the previous Find*

   1-2-3 highlights the first record that matches the criteria, *John* Gordon from Toy Universe.

4. Move the cell pointer to the next match.

Press:	↓

   1-2-3 highlights the next matching record, which contains the name *Jean* Kafka. Now press Down again:

Press:	↓

   1-2-3 beeps to signal that there are no more matching records. Notice that the program does not match the name Jennifer, which begins with J and has N as the fourth letter, but which is longer than four characters.

5. Return to READY mode.

Press:	F7 **(QUERY)**	*to return to READY mode*

Using the Tilde Wildcard in Criteria   Finally, this time do a Data Query Extract, using the tilde (~) to extract every record *except* the customer records.

1. Erase the existing criteria.

Move to:	A:B2

Press: [DELETE]

2. Enter new criteria in the Type field.

Move to: A:D2

Type: ~cus   ↵

■ *NOTE:*   If you don't have a tilde on your keyboard, you can create it with the Compose key: Press Compose (Alt-F1), then type two hyphens.

4. Perform the Extract using a single-row output range, and return to READY mode.

Choose: Data   Query

Select: Output range

Specify: A:A10..A:J10

Select: Extract   Cancel

1-2-3 copies all records except the customer records to the output range. Move to the output range and take a look.

Figure 6-36:   Extracting All Records Except Customers

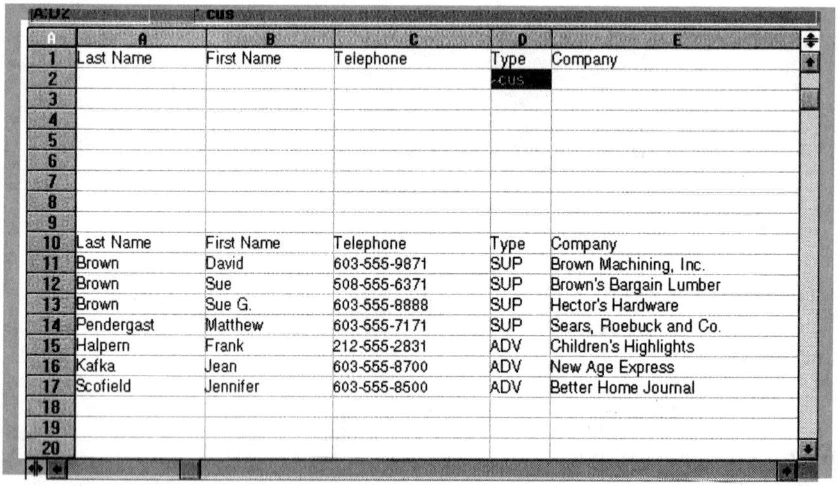

	A	B	C	D	E
1	Last Name	First Name	Telephone	Type	Company
2				CUS	
3					
4					
5					
6					
7					
8					
9					
10	Last Name	First Name	Telephone	Type	Company
11	Brown	David	603-555-9871	SUP	Brown Machining, Inc.
12	Brown	Sue	508-555-6371	SUP	Brown's Bargain Lumber
13	Brown	Sue G.	603-555-8888	SUP	Hector's Hardware
14	Pendergast	Matthew	603-555-7171	SUP	Sears, Roebuck and Co.
15	Halpern	Frank	212-555-2831	ADV	Children's Highlights
16	Kafka	Jean	603-555-8700	ADV	New Age Express
17	Scofield	Jennifer	603-555-8500	ADV	Better Home Journal
18					
19					
20					

Combining WildCard Characters   You can use the asterisk (*), question mark (?), and tilde (~) in various combinations. You can use wildcard characters to specify a particular criterion (for example, ~B* in the Last Name field matches all contacts whose last names do not start with B), or you can use several of them in separate criteria range fields (for example, ~CUS in the Type field and 02* in the Zip field would match all non-customer records with Zip codes that start with 02). Experiment on your own with combining wildcard characters in Data Query operations.

Modify a Block of Records

On a rainy day during a visit to New Hampshire, Bob decides to pay courtesy calls on his New Hampshire suppliers and see what new things they have. As it happens, all the suppliers have items Bob likes, and he places orders with all of them. When Bob returns to work, he needs to update the Freq field for his New Hampshire suppliers.

You can use Data Query Find to modify records in a 1-2-3 database table in an active file, but if you want to edit a group of records quickly, it is usually easier, especially in a large database, to extract the records from the database, make your changes, and then update the database with the changed records. To perform this kind of operation, Bob will use the Data Query Modify command. (You can also use Data Query Modify commands to modify records in external database tables, which cannot be modified with Data Query Find.)

In this section, you are going to use Data Query Modify to: (1) extract the records of the New Hampshire suppliers to the output range, (2) edit the frequency-of-contact information there, then (3) place the edited records back into the Business Contacts table.

1. Set up the criteria range to include all the suppliers in New Hampshire.

   Since Bob needs to update the records of all his New Hampshire suppliers, there will be two criteria: the Type field must be SUP and the State field must be NH. Before you enter these criteria, delete the existing criteria and records in the output range, then enter the new criteria.

Highlight:	A:A2..A:J2
Press:	DELETE
Highlight:	A:A11..A:J17
Press:	DELETE
Move to:	cell A:D2 *the Type field*
Type:	SUP ↵
Move to:	cell A:H2 *the State field*
Type:	NH ↵

2. Extract all the records of New Hampshire suppliers for modification.

Choose:	Data Query

   You must specify the ranges you want to use in the Data Query dialog box before selecting Modify. In this operation, you can use the input, criteria, and output ranges from the last Data Query command.

Select:	Modify

   1-2-3 displays the Data Query Modify dialog box. Notice that it shows the same input, criteria, and output ranges that were established in the Data Query dialog box.

Figure 6-37:   Data Query Modify Dialog Box

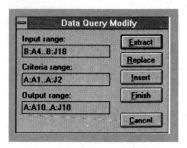

Now, you're going to extract the set of records to be modified.

Select: Extract

Cancel   *to exit the Data Query dialog box*

1-2-3 places the matching records into the output range.

■ *NOTE:*   Do not change any of the ranges in the Data Query dialog box between the time you Extract the records you want to modify and the time you select "Replace" in the Data Query Modify dialog box to place the records you've edited back into the database table (which you'll do in a later step). If you do, 1-2-3 will not be able to replace the records in the database table with the copies you have edited.

3. Edit the Freq fields in the output range to increase the value of each by one.

Move to: A:J11

Type: 13   ⬇

4   ⬇

9   ⏎

4. Replace the originals in the database table with copies you've edited. Notice, as you do this, that 1-2-3 has changed the output range to include the three records you extracted and then modified:

Choose: Data   Query

Select: Modify

Select: Replace   *in the Modify dialog box*

Cancel   *to exit the Data Query dialog box*

Move to worksheet B. You can see in the Business Contacts table that the Freq fields of the New Hampshire suppliers have been increased by one.

Congratulations! You've learned to use Data Query Modify to perform batch updates of database tables. Save the file.

Figure 6-38:   Modified records include higher Freq values.

	F	G	H	I	J	K	L
4	Street	City	State	Zip	Freq		
5	509 Chauncy St.	Nashua	NH	03062	13		
6	357 Somerville Ave.	Worcester	MA	01604	3		
7	45 Auburn St.	Derry	NH	03038	4		
8	522 Main St.	Concord	NH	03302	9		
9	P.O. Box 257	Bennington	VT	05201	2		
10	369 Washington St.	Arlington	MA	02174	0		
11	890 McGrath Hwy.	Syracuse	NY	14132	6		
12	1891 Eastern Blvd.	Concord	NH	03301	0		
13	3498 Detroit Blvd.	Detroit	MI	48219	10		
14	3435 Main St.	Springfield	MA	02010	8		
15	52 Oak Lane	Nashua	NH	03062	12		
16	182 E. 57th St.	New York	NY	10024	5		
17	P.O. Box 8779	Peterboro	NH	03458	11		
18	P.O. Box 534	Peterboro	NH	03458	10		
19							
20							
21							
22							
23							

Deleting Records from a Database

Data Query Delete lets you delete records you no longer need. The deleted records are permanently erased from the database, so use this command with care!

To delete one or more records, set up input and criteria ranges just as you would with the Data Query Find and Data Query Extract commands. In the criteria range, specify criteria that enable you to select only the records you want to delete. For example, suppose Bob decides to eliminate from his database those contacts he has listed as customers, but who have never actually ordered anything from him. The records for those customers would have a 0 in the Freq field.

As it happens, two of the customer records in this small database do have a 0 in the Freq field: Fletcher and O'Brien. In the following steps, use Data Query Delete to delete these records.

1. Save CONTACTS.WK3.

   In the following steps, you are going to permanently delete records from the Business Contacts database. Just to be on the safe side, it is a good idea to save a database before you perform any delete operation.

2. Set up the criteria for deleting records.

   In this case, you will only need one row of criteria to select the record to be deleted. Prepare this row so that 1-2-3 can use it to find customers to whom Bob has never sold anything. First, clear any existing criteria:

   Highlight: A:A2..A:J2
   Press: DELETE

Next, type in the new criteria and then move back to the database table:

Move to:	cell A:D2
Type:	CUS ⏎
Move to:	cell A:J2
Type:	0 HOME

3. Delete the records.

Since you are using the same input range and criteria range (though with different criteria), you could perform the delete without changing any ranges. However, you should check to make sure the criteria range is properly defined (as A:A1..A:J2) before you delete anything.

| **Choose:** | Data   Query |
| **Select:** | Delete   *after checking the criteria range* |

Deleting records makes a permanent change to the database, so 1-2-3 gives you one last chance to cancel or continue the Delete operation. Selecting Cancel returns you to the Data Query dialog box; selecting "Delete" starts the operation. Select "Delete" and then return to READY mode:

| **Select:** | Delete   *to confirm that you want to delete* |
| | Cancel   *to exit the Data Query dialog box* |

1-2-3 deletes the records for Edwin P. Fletcher and William O'Brien and closes up the space in the database.

Figure 6-39:   Bob's Database Minus the Fletcher and O'Brien Records

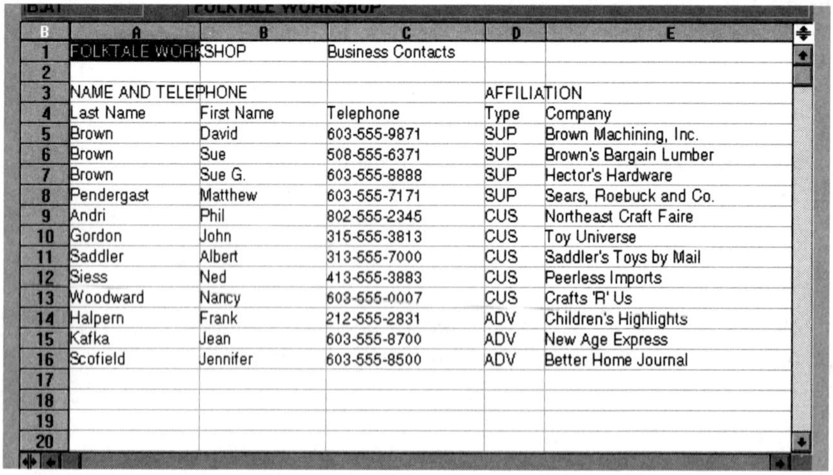

	A	B	C	D	E
1	FOLKTALE WORKSHOP		Business Contacts		
2					
3	NAME AND TELEPHONE			AFFILIATION	
4	Last Name	First Name	Telephone	Type	Company
5	Brown	David	603-555-9871	SUP	Brown Machining, Inc.
6	Brown	Sue	508-555-6371	SUP	Brown's Bargain Lumber
7	Brown	Sue G.	603-555-8888	SUP	Hector's Hardware
8	Pendergast	Matthew	603-555-7171	SUP	Sears, Roebuck and Co.
9	Andri	Phil	802-555-2345	CUS	Northeast Craft Faire
10	Gordon	John	315-555-3813	CUS	Toy Universe
11	Saddler	Albert	313-555-7000	CUS	Saddler's Toys by Mail
12	Siess	Ned	413-555-3883	CUS	Peerless Imports
13	Woodward	Nancy	603-555-0007	CUS	Crafts 'R' Us
14	Halpern	Frank	212-555-2831	ADV	Children's Highlights
15	Kafka	Jean	603-555-8700	ADV	New Age Express
16	Scofield	Jennifer	603-555-8500	ADV	Better Home Journal
17					
18					
19					
20					

■ *NOTE:*   Before you delete records, you may want to use either the Data Query Find or Extract command to make sure that the criteria you set up will delete only the records you want to remove. Once you are satisfied with the criteria, perform the Delete with confidence. If you do accidentally delete records in the active worksheet file that you intended to keep, you can undo the deletion (if Undo is on) by immediately returning to READY mode and pressing the Undo key.

4. Save the database file.

Congratulations! You have learned how to use wildcards and how to delete records. Save the contacts database file again.

Other Ways to Select Records to Delete

Using 1-2-3's wildcards and formulas as selection criteria is an easy way to delete records that have something in common. Sometimes, however, you need to remove a number of records with randomly different characteristics. In that case, it is often easier to physically mark the records for deletion, rather than developing an elaborate criteria range.

For example, to remove records from the Business Contacts database, you could move the cell pointer to one of the fields (for instance, Type) and put an X or other marker in the records you want to delete. When you set up the criteria, simply have 1-2-3 search for any record with an X in the Type field. Since you are deleting the records anyway, it doesn't matter if you modify them first.

If you want to save a copy of the records to be deleted before you delete them, extract the records to another part of the worksheet file and then delete them from the database. Use a new field to indicate the records to save and then delete. The following steps outline this procedure.

1. Add a field to the database to mark records to be deleted. Name that field something like "Remove". Include the new field in the input range.

2. Mark each record that you want to delete by entering an X in the new Remove field.

3. Copy the new Remove field name to the first line of the criteria and output ranges and extend the criteria and output ranges to include the field. Make sure there is only *one* row of criteria.

4. Erase the criteria row of the criteria range and enter an X in the Remove field of that row.

5. Select the "Extract" option of the Data Query command to extract all the records you marked with an X. Look at the output range to verify that these extracted records are the ones you want to delete.

6. Select the "Delete" option of the Data Query command and confirm that you want to delete the records you marked with an X.

7. Exit the Data Query dialog box.

If you follow these steps, 1-2-3 will extract all the "to be deleted" records to the output range and then delete the records from the database.

Splitting a Database Table

As Bob's business expands, he realizes that he needs to keep track of different kinds of information for advertisers, customers, and suppliers. For advertisers, he finds that the Freq field is not especially useful, but he would like to add a field to those records to store information on the kind of advertising they do (magazines, newspapers, television, flyers, and so on). For suppliers, he's interested in keeping his credit limit handy; for customers, on the other hand, he wants to know how much volume they're handling and when they last ordered.

Bob realizes that trying to keep all this information in a single database table could get cumbersome and confusing. As a first step toward restructuring the Business Contacts database, he decides to split the current database table into three database tables in separate worksheet files. (This is as far as you and Bob will go with the database in this chapter.)

To split the CONTACTS database table into three parts, complete the following steps:

1. Make a new copy of the database worksheet file.

   For this exercise, you'll use a copy of the CONTACTS database instead of the original version. That way, you can easily go back to the old version if you decide to use it again (for example, to adapt it to your personal phonebook). Create the copy by saving the database worksheet file under a new name, CONTACT3.WK3:

   Select: F i l e   S a v e A s
   Type: c o n t a c t 3   ⏎

   1-2-3 saves the file under the new name and makes the new file the current file; all changes in this exercise will be made to CONTACT3.WK3.

2. Create the customer database table.

   To create a customer-only database table, delete all records containing SUP or CUS in the Type field. You can continue to use the input, criteria, and output ranges you have already established. First, clear the criteria range of any existing criteria:

   Highlight: A:A2..A:J2
   Press: DELETE

   Before going on, save CONTACT3.WK3 in its current state (with the criteria range blank). This will save you a step in creating the second and third database tables.

   Choose: F i l e   S a v e

   Now enter the criterion for the Data Query Delete operation. This time, try using the #NOT# operator instead of the tilde (~) to specify "everything except records with CUS in the Type field."

   Move to: A:D2   *the Type field*

Type: #NOT#type="cus"   ⏎

■ *NOTE:*   Notice that 1-2-3 displays ERR in cell A:D2 while displaying the formula in the edit line. There is actually no error in the worksheet. 1-2-3 displays ERR whenever it encounters a formula that it can't evaluate. Use Range Format Text to see the formula displayed.

Before performing the Delete, do an Extract to confirm that the criterion you entered is correct. You'll change the output range back to a single-row to accommodate *all* records that 1-2-3 extracts. (The last Modify changed the output range to hold only the records extracted during that operation.)

Choose:	Data Query	
Select:	Output range:	
Specify:	A:A10..A:J10	*to undo change made by Modify*
Select:	Extract	
	Cancel	*to exit the Data Query dialog box*

1-2-3 extracts the supplier and advertiser records to the output range. Look at the output range to verify that this is so. Now delete the supplier and advertiser records from the database table:

Choose:	Data Query	
Select:	Delete	
	Cancel	*to exit the Data Query dialog box*

Move to worksheet B to confirm that only the customer records remain.

Figure 6-40:   Table After All But Customer Records Are Deleted

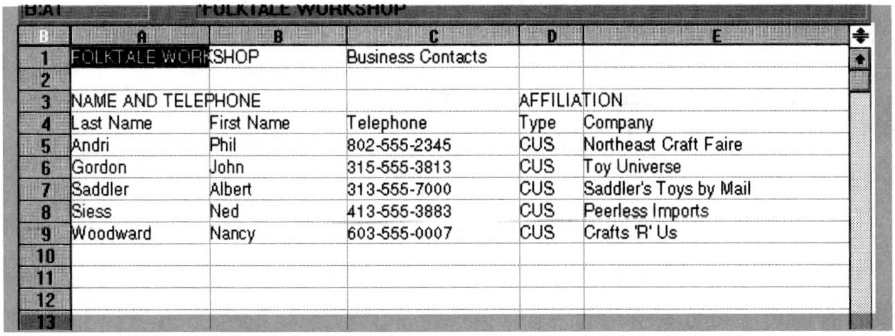

	A	B	C	D	E
1	FOLKTALE WORKSHOP		Business Contacts		
2					
3	NAME AND TELEPHONE			AFFILIATION	
4	Last Name	First Name	Telephone	Type	Company
5	Andri	Phil	802-555-2345	CUS	Northeast Craft Faire
6	Gordon	John	315-555-3813	CUS	Toy Universe
7	Saddler	Albert	313-555-7000	CUS	Saddler's Toys by Mail
8	Siess	Ned	413-555-3883	CUS	Peerless Imports
9	Woodward	Nancy	603-555-0007	CUS	Crafts 'R' Us
10					
11					
12					
13					

3. Change the title line for the database table.

Change the title line so it reflects the new database table's contents:

Move to:	cell B:C1
Type:	Customers ⏎

4. Save the new database table in a separate file.

   Save the customer-only database in a file named CUST_DB.WK3, leaving the CONTACT3 file intact:

Choose:	`File   Save As`
Type:	`cust_db` ⏎

5. Create the supplier database table.

   Open CONTACT3.WK3 and follow the same procedure to create a supplier-only database:

Choose:	`File   Open`
Type:	`contact3` ⏎ *(or select it in the list box)*
Move to:	cell A:D2 *the Type field*

   This time, use the tilde (~) wildcard to create the criterion:

Type:	`~sup` *as the new criterion*
Press:	⏎
Choose:	`Data   Query`
Select:	`Delete`
	`Delete` *to confirm that you want to delete*
	`Cancel` *to exit the Data Query dialog box*
Move to:	cell B:C1
Type:	`Suppliers` ⏎
Choose:	`File   Save As`
Type:	`sup_db` ⏎

6. Create the advertiser database table.

   And finally, to create the advertisers-only database table, use Data Query Delete to delete all the records from CONTACT3.WK3 that are not advertisers.

Choose:	`File   Open`
Type:	`contact3` ⏎ *(or select it in the list box)*
Move to:	cell A:D2 *the Type field*
Type:	`~adv` ⏎
Choose:	`Data   Query`
Select:	`Delete   Delete   Cancel`
Move to:	cell B:C1

Type:	Advertisers ⏎
Choose:	File Save As
Type:	adv_db ⏎

7. Save all modified files and exit 1-2-3. (You can use the "Save All" option of the File Save As command for this.)

Congratulations! You've split the original database into three separate files. In the "More Database Features" section that follows, you'll see how Bob could apply additional database techniques to running his business.

More Database Features

This section introduces some of the additional database features available to you in 1-2-3, and describes tips, techniques, and gotchas that apply to 1-2-3 databases. It doesn't step you through the operations, but you will probably want to try these operations when you have more database experience.

Using Database @Functions

Database @functions (often referred to as *@D functions,* because they all start with the letter D) are specialized @functions that work with database tables. You can use them to find the average, maximum, or minimum value in a database field (@DAVG, @DMAX, @DMIN); the sum, standard deviation, or variance of values in a database field (@DSUM, @DSTD, @DVAR); or the total number of entries in a database field (@DCOUNT). To perform a database @function calculation, 1-2-3 examines the specified input range, selects the records that match the criteria in the specified criteria range, and then, for the selected records, performs the @function calculation on the specified field. The selection of records is an internal operation—1-2-3 does not actually copy extracted records to an output range, as it would with Data Query Extract.

Bob is thinking about hiring a company representative to work in the field, and wants to find out in which state he is doing the most business. By hiring a local representative to handle customer and supplier contacts in the busiest state, Bob hopes to be able to spend more time in the office, managing the growth of the business.

Bob will use the information in his Business Contacts database table to see how much business he's doing in each state. He has a feeling he's doing more business in New Hampshire than anywhere else, so he'll first check how many business contacts he's had in that state. In cell B:F18 of the CONTACTS.WK3 worksheet file, Bob uses the @DSUM function. He specifies an input range, the name of a field in that range, and a criteria range as arguments to the function. The contacts table (A4..J16) is the input range 1-2-3 will examine. 1-2-3 will find the records that match the criteria in the range Bob specifies (H18..H19), and then calculate the contents of the Freq fields in the matching records. You can see the @function Bob entered in the edit line in Figure 6-41. 1-2-3 displays the function's result in cell F18.

Figure 6-41: @DSUM Calculates Total Number of New Hampshire Contacts

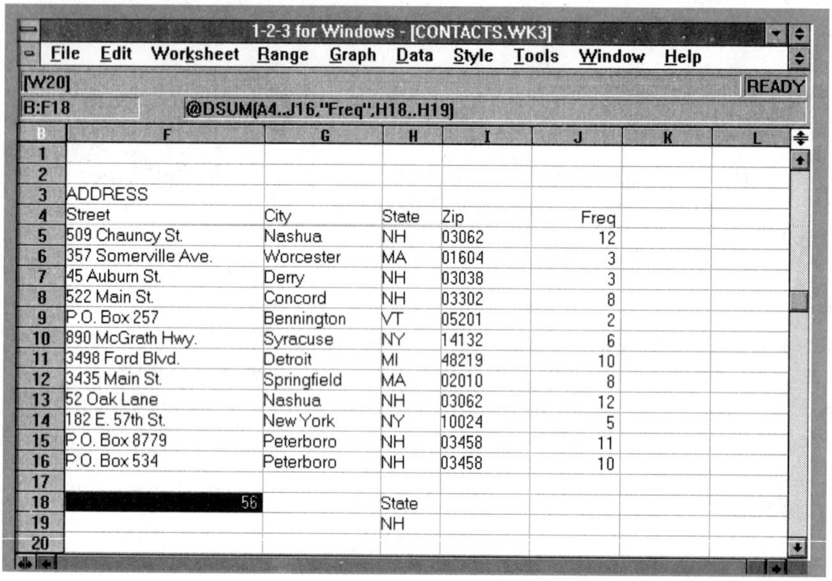
1-2-3 for Windows - [CONTACTS.WK3]

File Edit Worksheet Range Graph Data Style Tools Window Help

[W20] READY

B:F18 @DSUM(A4..J16,"Freq",H18..H19)

B	F	G	H	I	J	K	L
1							
2							
3	ADDRESS						
4	Street	City	State	Zip	Freq		
5	509 Chauncy St.	Nashua	NH	03062	12		
6	357 Somerville Ave.	Worcester	MA	01604	3		
7	45 Auburn St.	Derry	NH	03038	3		
8	522 Main St.	Concord	NH	03302	8		
9	P.O. Box 257	Bennington	VT	05201	2		
10	890 McGrath Hwy.	Syracuse	NY	14132	6		
11	3498 Ford Blvd.	Detroit	MI	48219	10		
12	3435 Main St.	Springfield	MA	02010	8		
13	52 Oak Lane	Nashua	NH	03062	12		
14	182 E. 57th St.	New York	NY	10024	5		
15	P.O. Box 8779	Peterboro	NH	03458	11		
16	P.O. Box 534	Peterboro	NH	03458	10		
17							
18	56		State				
19			NH				
20							

Bob can compute the number of contacts in other states by changing the label in H19 to another state where he does business. As he changes the state name in H19, 1-2-3 will recalculate the value in F18 for the new state.

Describing all the individual database @functions is beyond the scope of this book, but you can read about them and their uses in the 1-2-3 documentation and on-line Help. (The @functions are particularly useful in combination with what-if tables, described next.)

What-if Tables

What-if tables provide a way to quickly substitute a list of values in a formula. You supply the formula and the values, and 1-2-3 plugs the values into the formula and displays the result as a table. In effect, 1-2-3 simultaneously performs a series of what-if analyses.

There are three variants of the Data What-if Table command: Selecting 1-Way allows you to substitute a list of values for one variable into one or more formulas. 2-Way lets you specify two lists for two variables; 1-2-3 plugs the values into a formula that depends on both variables. 3-Way lets you work with three variables in a three-dimensional worksheet. 1-2-3 plugs the values into a formula that depends on all three variables.

You use 1-Way when you want to play "what-if" with one variable but with one or more formulas. You use 2-Way when you want to play "what-if" with a formula that depends on two variables and you want to see the effects of changing both of them. You use 3-Way when you want to play "what-if" with a formula that depends on three variables and you want to see the effects of changing all of them.

The following example shows how to use Data What-if Table 2-Way to calculate the monthly payment for a $6,000 auto loan, using interest rates of from 8% to 14%, and a payment period of from three to five years (36 months to 60 months). The command creates a what-if table from a formula that calculates a single value for a monthly payment.

Figure 6-42 shows the table before you issue the 2-Way command. At the upper left corner of the table (cell B7) is an @PMT formula (in this case, a reference to the formula in cell B4) that references variables for the principal, interest rate, and term of the loan. In column B, below the formula reference, are sample values for the interest rate variable. To the right of the formula reference, across row 7, are the values for the term of the loan. The what-if table uses two cells as input cells for the formula (cells into which 1-2-3 temporarily substitutes the values in column B and in row 7 as it creates the what-if table).

Figure 6-42:   Two-way What-if Table

	1-2-3 for Windows - [WHAT_IF1.WK3]						
File Edit Worksheet Range Graph Data Style Tools Window Help							
[C2] [W10]							READY
A:B4	@PMT[PRINCIPAL,RATE/12,TERM]						
A	A	B	C	D	E	F	G
1	Principal	$6,000					
2	Interest rate	8.0%	(input cell 1)				
3	Term (months)	36	(input cell 2)				
4	Monthly payment	$188.02					
5							
6			TERM (MONTHS)				
7		+B4	36	42	48	54	60
8	INTEREST	8.0%					
9	RATE	8.5%					
10		9.0%					
11		9.5%					
12		10.0%					
13		10.5%					
14		11.0%					
15		11.5%					
16		12.0%					
17		12.5%					
18		13.0%					
19		13.5%					
20		14.0%					

Once you've completed the worksheet, you create the what-if table by performing the following steps:

1. Choose Data What-if Table 2-Way.

2. Supply the range B7..G20 as the Table range.

3. Supply cell B2 as the address of input cell 1.

4. Supply cell B3 as the address of input cell 2.

After you supply the address for the second input cell and press Enter, 1-2-3 creates the table. The results look like Figure 6-43.

Figure 6-43: Two-Way Table After Using Data What-if Table 2-Way

	A	B	C	D	E	F	G
1	Principal	$6,000					
2	Interest rate	8.0% (input cell 1)					
3	Term (months)	36 (input cell 2)					
4	Monthly payment	$188.02					
5							
6			TERM (MONTHS)				
7		+B4	36	42	48	54	60
8	INTEREST	8.0%	188.02	164.26	146.48	132.67	121.66
9	RATE	8.5%	189.41	165.66	147.89	134.10	123.10
10		9.0%	190.80	167.07	149.31	135.54	124.55
11		9.5%	192.20	168.48	150.74	136.98	126.01
12		10.0%	193.60	169.90	152.18	138.43	127.48
13		10.5%	195.01	171.33	153.62	139.90	128.96
14		11.0%	196.43	172.76	155.07	141.37	130.45
15		11.5%	197.86	174.20	156.53	142.85	131.96
16		12.0%	199.29	175.65	158.00	144.34	133.47
17		12.5%	200.72	177.11	159.48	145.84	134.99
18		13.0%	202.16	178.57	160.96	147.35	136.52
19		13.5%	203.61	180.04	162.46	148.86	138.06
20		14.0%	205.07	181.52	163.96	150.39	139.61

The information in a what-if table is not automatically recalculated when the worksheet is recalculated or when input values change. To recalculate the most recently calculated what-if table, use the Table (F8) key or select the appropriate Data Table command. For example, to find out what the monthly payments would be if the loan was for $8,000 instead of $6,000, you would type the value 8000 into cell B1 and press Table.

For more information on using what-if tables, see the 1-2-3 documentation.

Working with Multiple Database Tables

Some earlier releases of 1-2-3 restricted database operations to single database tables. All the information pertaining to a particular database entry, such as an employee record, had to be contained in the same database table if it was to be accessed by a single Data Query operation.

1-2-3/W databases are true relational databases. Data queries can simultaneously be done against multiple database tables and information from separate database tables can be combined into a single output range, provided there are fields in the tables that have data in common. In database terms, the combining of data from multiple tables is known as *joining* the tables. The commands you use to work with multiple database tables are the same Data Query commands you used to work with Bob Gordon's Business Contacts database table. There are differences, though, in the input, criteria, and output ranges you use.

The input range you specify will consist of more than one database table. The criteria range must contain a *join formula* that tells 1-2-3 which fields in the tables being joined have values in common. The output range will contain field names from the multiple tables in the input range. Another difference is that database tables that will be used in multiple-input perations should be given range names, so that 1-2-3 can distinguish a field in one database table from an identically named field in another.

Figures 6-44 through 6-46 show how you could use Data Query Extract to create a shipping report by combining data from two database tables. In this case, the input range consists of one database table that holds customer names and addresses and another database table that holds records of customer orders. The tables have customer names in common, which makes the join possible. In the address database table, the customer names are listed in the field named Customer. In the orders database table, the customer names appear in the field named CUSTNAME. The criteria range contains a single formula, +CUSTOMER=CUSTNAME, which tells 1-2-3 to join the records whenever the contents of the Customer field in the address table is the same as the value of the CUSTNAME field in the orders table. The field names in the output range determine which fields from these joined records appear in the output range.

NOTE: If the fields were identically named in both database tables (for example, both were named CUSTNAME), you would prefix the field name with the name of the database table. A join formula for two identical field names would look like this if the database tables were named ADDRESS and ORDERS: +ADDRESS.CUSTNAME=ORDERS.CUSTNAME.

Figure 6-44 shows the Address Database Table. Figure 6-45 (shown on the next page), shows the Orders Database Table

Figure 6-44: The Address Database Table

B:A1 'ADDRESS

B	A	B	C	D	E
1	ADDRESS			FOLKTALE WORKSHOP	
2	----------------	----------------	----------------	--------	--------
3	Customer	Street	City	State	Zip
4	Northeast Craft	P.O. Box 257	Bennington	VT	05201
5	Edwin's Toy	369 Washington St.	Arlington	MA	02174
6	Toy Universe	890 McGrath Highway	Syracuse	NY	14132
7	Saddler's Toys	3498 Ford Blvd.	Detroit	MI	48219
8	Pearless Imports	3435 Main St.	Springfield	MA	02010
9	Crafts 'R' Us	52 Oak Lane	Nashua	NH	03062
10					
11					
12					
13					

Figure 6-46 (shown on the next page), shows both the criteria range (cells B2..B3), which contains the join formula, and the output range. After the query, the output range contains the shipping database table. Notice that the information in the Customer field is the only information that appears in both of the database tables used as the input range. Notice also that the output range contains fields from both tables. The Customer, City, and State fields come from the Address database table. The Data, Item, and Quantity fields come from the Orders table.

Figure 6-45:   The Orders Database Table

	A	B	C	D	E	F	G
1	ORDERS					FOLKTALE	WORKSHOP
2							
3	SALESNAME	CUSTNAME	DESCRIPTION	ITEM	DATE	COST	QUANTITY
4	Frank	Northeast Craft	Evil Queen	9824	02/08/90	389.00	10
5	Jones	Edwin's Toy	Video	3456	12/02/89	60.00	2
6	Jones	Edwin's Toy	Adventure	4418	02/01/90	10.00	1
7	Kling	Toy Universe	Adventure	4418	04/25/90	12.00	1
8	Glink	Toy Universe	Video	3456	03/27/90	34.00	1
9	Kling	Northeast Craft	Huntsman	8976	02/05/90	389.00	10
10	Wright	Saddler's Toys	Dwarf	2314	12/26/89	654.00	20
11	Smith	Peerless Imports	Dwarf	2987	11/15/89	200.00	8
12	Smith	Saddler's Toys	Dwarf	2314	04/04/90	654.00	20
13	Walker	Toy Universe	Prince	8763	03/14/90	289.00	10
14	Walker	Saddler's Toys	Prince	8763	11/18/89	289.00	10
15							
16							
17							
18							
19							
20							

Figure 6-46:   1-2-3 joins Address and Orders tables to produce the shipping database table.

	A	B	C	D	E	F	G
1	CRITERIA FOR JOIN						
2		Customer					
3		+CUSTNAME=CUSTOMER					
4							
5							
6	SHIPPING SCHEDULE						
7							
8	Date	Customer	City	State	Item	Quantity	
9	02/01/90	Edwin's Toy	Arlington	MA	4418	1	
10	12/02/89	Edwin's Toy	Arlington	MA	3456	2	
11	02/05/90	Northeast Craft	Bennington	VT	8976	10	
12	02/08/90	Northeast Craft	Bennington	VT	9824	10	
13	12/26/89	Saddler's Toys	Detroit	MI	2314	20	
14	04/04/90	Saddler's Toys	Detroit	MI	2314	20	
15	11/18/89	Saddler's Toys	Detroit	MI	8763	10	
16	03/27/90	Toy Universe	Syracuse	NY	3456	1	
17	03/14/90	Toy Universe	Syracuse	NY	8763	10	
18	04/25/90	Toy Universe	Syracuse	NY	4418	1	
19							
20							

■ **NOTE:**   When you set up database tables, you should do so with an eye to how you will join tables. For 1-2-3 to perform joins, one field in the join formula should be free of duplicate values. When you join tables, you join a table in which a value occurs once with a second table in which that value may occur many times. In this example, the Address database table should contain only one address for a customer. (If it contained more, how could you know which is correct?) Thus, each value in the Customer field should occur only once. The Orders table, on the other hand, can contain many orders for the same customer, so the same value will appear in the CUSTNAME field multiple times.

Advantages to Working with Multiple Tables Performing queries that combine information from multiple tables offers many advantages over single-table queries, where all relevant data resides in one table.

- *Avoids redundancy in database tables.* If you place information in only one table, rather than in multiple tables, it is easier to set up your database, since you only have to enter the information once.
- *Easier to keep database up to date.* By isolating information in single tables, you only need to change one table when the information changes. If you include the same information in many tables, you need to keep them all up-to-date. This leads to errors where different tables show different values, with no easy way to determine which value is correct.
- *Combines database information from different sources.* The multiple tables you specify in the input range need not all be 1-2-3 database tables. 1-2-3 database tables can be joined with tables created using other database management products. "Working with External Databases," later in this section, describes how to work with database tables created with other programs.

Analyzing Data As It Is Extracted

In the exercises in this chapter, you placed field names in the output range to control which fields were extracted from the selected records to the output range. In 1-2-3/W, you can also include formulas in the output range that analyze the matching records in the database table (or tables) in the input range as you perform a query. This means that, in addition to retrieving records from one or more database tables, you can cause 1-2-3 to analyze the information in the matching records.

A *computed field* is a formula you include in an output range to extract data and do something to the extracted data in one step. An *aggregate field* is a formula you include in an output range to combine into one step extracting data and generating statistics about the data.

Using Computed Fields in Your Output Range Computed fields provide additional information as you extract matching records. For example, as you extract sales records, you can use a computed field to calculate the commission owed on each sale. You create a computed field by including a formula alongside the field names in the output range. The formula you specify should refer to other fields in the output range.

Consider the table in Figure 6-47 (shown on the next page). It contains a number of orders placed with Folktale Workshop. Each order includes the price of the item and the quantity ordered. The name of the salesperson who made the sale appears in column 1. In the range A16..F17, there is a blank criteria range that will match all records in the table. A19..G19 is the output range. It contains the field names from the table, and a computed field with the formula (PRICE * QUANTITY) * 0.15. (The formula has been formatted as Text.) For each matching record, this formula will calculate the total cost of the items sold by multiplying the price by the number sold, then multiplying that total by the commission rate of 15 percent to calculate the commission owed on the sale.

Figure 6-47: Output range includes a computed field.

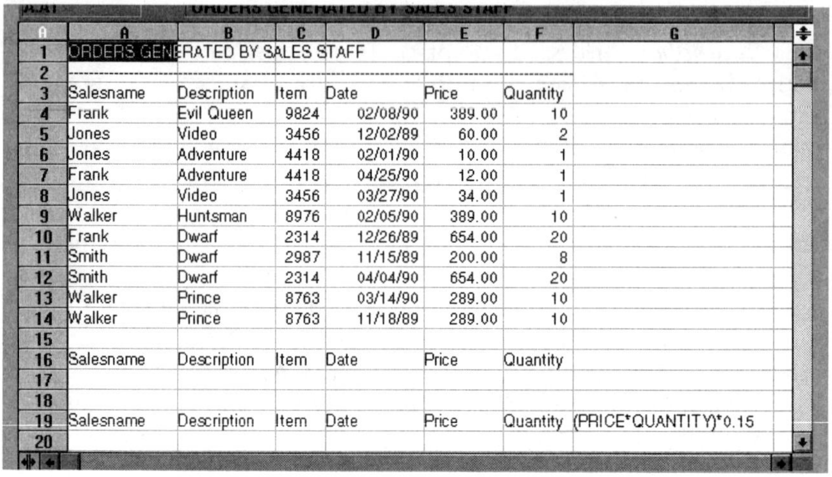

	A	B	C	D	E	F	G
1	ORDERS GENERATED BY SALES STAFF						
2							
3	Salesname	Description	Item	Date	Price	Quantity	
4	Frank	Evil Queen	9824	02/08/90	389.00	10	
5	Jones	Video	3456	12/02/89	60.00	2	
6	Jones	Adventure	4418	02/01/90	10.00	1	
7	Frank	Adventure	4418	04/25/90	12.00	1	
8	Jones	Video	3456	03/27/90	34.00	1	
9	Walker	Huntsman	8976	02/05/90	389.00	10	
10	Frank	Dwarf	2314	12/26/89	654.00	20	
11	Smith	Dwarf	2987	11/15/89	200.00	8	
12	Smith	Dwarf	2314	04/04/90	654.00	20	
13	Walker	Prince	8763	03/14/90	289.00	10	
14	Walker	Prince	8763	11/18/89	289.00	10	
15							
16	Salesname	Description	Item	Date	Price	Quantity	
17							
18							
19	Salesname	Description	Item	Date	Price	Quantity	(PRICE*QUANTITY)*0.15
20							

Figure 6-48 shows the results of a Data Query Extract operation. The computed field has generated a value for each record in the input range that matched the selection criteria (all of them, in this example),

Figure 6-48: Computed field calculates commission owed for each sale.

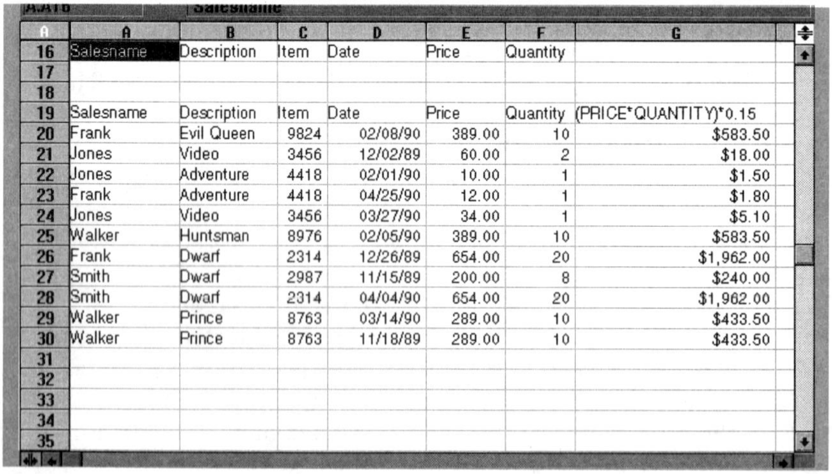

	A	B	C	D	E	F	G
16	Salesname	Description	Item	Date	Price	Quantity	
17							
18							
19	Salesname	Description	Item	Date	Price	Quantity	(PRICE*QUANTITY)*0.15
20	Frank	Evil Queen	9824	02/08/90	389.00	10	$583.50
21	Jones	Video	3456	12/02/89	60.00	2	$18.00
22	Jones	Adventure	4418	02/01/90	10.00	1	$1.50
23	Frank	Adventure	4418	04/25/90	12.00	1	$1.80
24	Jones	Video	3456	03/27/90	34.00	1	$5.10
25	Walker	Huntsman	8976	02/05/90	389.00	10	$583.50
26	Frank	Dwarf	2314	12/26/89	654.00	20	$1,962.00
27	Smith	Dwarf	2987	11/15/89	200.00	8	$240.00
28	Smith	Dwarf	2314	04/04/90	654.00	20	$1,962.00
29	Walker	Prince	8763	03/14/90	289.00	10	$433.50
30	Walker	Prince	8763	11/18/89	289.00	10	$433.50
31							
32							
33							
34							
35							

■ *NOTE:*   You can use arithmetic operators and most @functions in computed fields. See the 1-2-3 documentation for more information.

Using Aggregate Fields in Your Output Range   Aggregate fields differ from computed fields in that they generate one piece of information that summarizes the matching records, rather than producing a value for each matching record. Aggregate fields can use the @AVG, @COUNT, @MAX, @MIN, and @SUM @functions.

In Figure 6-49, the output produced earlier with the computed field has been made into a table by replacing the formula with the Commission field name. B:A16..B:G17 is a blank criteria range that will match all records in the database table. B:A18..B:B18 is the output range that contains the Salesname field name and an aggregate field with the formula @SUM(COMMISSION).

Figure 6-49:   Output range includes an aggregate field.

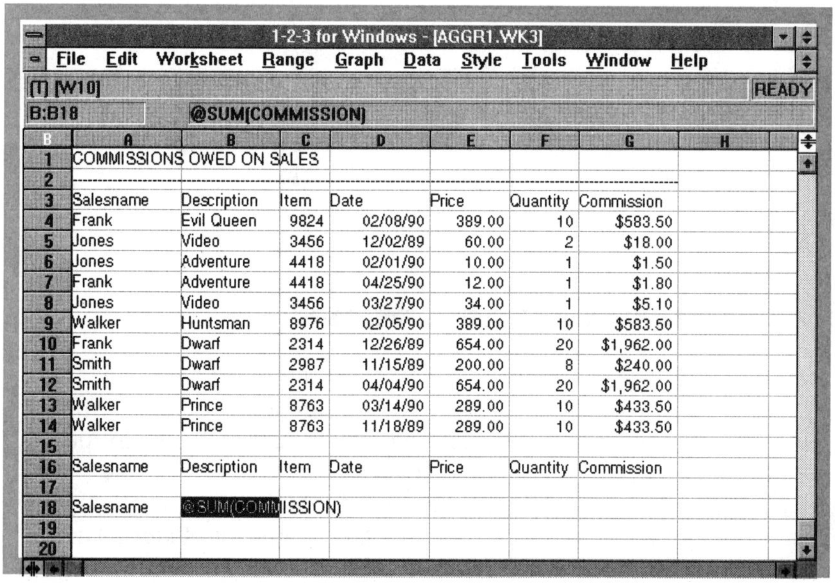

When you perform the Extract, 1-2-3 analyzes the Salesname field of the matching records to determine how many different sales reps appear in the table, then totals the commissions owed to each sales rep by summing the individual commissions. Figure 6-50 shows the results.

Working with External Databases

In the exercises in this chapter, you used the Data Query commands to extract and delete records from a 1-2-3 database table. Except for Data Query Find and Data Sort, you can also use the Data Query commands to work with external database tables. *External database tables* are database tables created with other products, that you work with in 1-2-3 using Data commands. 1-2-3 comes with Datalens drivers that make it possible for you to work inside

1-2-3 with database tables created with Ashton Tate's dBASE IV, Borland's Paradox, and OS/2 Microsoft SQL Server. Additional Datalens drivers are available from manufacturers of database management systems; these let you work in 1-2-3 with database tables created using those systems.

Figure 6-50: Results Produced by Aggregate Field

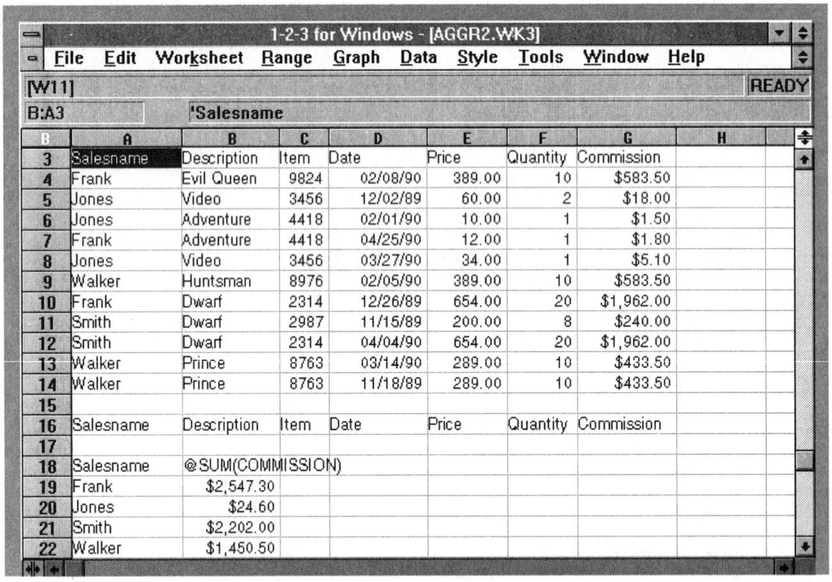

1-2-3 for Windows - [AGGR2.WK3]

File Edit Worksheet Range Graph Data Style Tools Window Help

[W11] READY

B:A3 'Salesname

B	A	B	C	D	E	F	G	H
3	Salesname	Description	Item	Date	Price	Quantity	Commission	
4	Frank	Evil Queen	9824	02/08/90	389.00	10	$583.50	
5	Jones	Video	3456	12/02/89	60.00	2	$18.00	
6	Jones	Adventure	4418	02/01/90	10.00	1	$1.50	
7	Frank	Adventure	4418	04/25/90	12.00	1	$1.80	
8	Jones	Video	3456	03/27/90	34.00	1	$5.10	
9	Walker	Huntsman	8976	02/05/90	389.00	10	$583.50	
10	Frank	Dwarf	2314	12/26/89	654.00	20	$1,962.00	
11	Smith	Dwarf	2987	11/15/89	200.00	8	$240.00	
12	Smith	Dwarf	2314	04/04/90	654.00	20	$1,962.00	
13	Walker	Prince	8763	03/14/90	289.00	10	$433.50	
14	Walker	Prince	8763	11/18/89	289.00	10	$433.50	
15								
16	Salesname	Description	Item	Date	Price	Quantity	Commission	
17								
18	Salesname	@SUM(COMMISSION)						
19	Frank	$2,547.30						
20	Jones	$24.60						
21	Smith	$2,202.00						
22	Walker	$1,450.50						

To use the Data Query commands with an external database, you first connect from 1-2-3 to the external database table. In the process of connecting, you assign a range name to the external table. You use this range name to include the external database table in the input range of your Data Query operations.

In some early releases of 1-2-3, you had to translate external database tables into 1-2-3 format, work with them, and then translate them back. Using the Data Connect to External and the Data External Options commands in 1-2-3/W, you can connect to an external table without any translation. Then, you can:

- *Perform Data Query Extract, Modify, and Delete operations.* Once you've connected to an external database table, you can extract records from the table into your worksheet; use Data Query Modify to extract a block of records from the external table, edit the records, and place the edited records back into the external table; or delete records from the external table.
- *Include the external table in multi-table queries.* If an external table meets the requirement of having values in common with values in another table or tables, you can join information in the external table with information from other table(s).

- *Use computed and aggregate fields.* You can use computed and aggregate fields (described earlier in "Analyzing Data as it is Extracted") to analyze data in the external table as you perform queries.
- *Send database commands from 1-2-3 to the external database.* Using the Data External Options commands, you can send commands from 1-2-3 to the external database by using the command language of the product that created the table. You also can create new external database tables.

A full discussion of using external databases with 1-2-3 is beyond the scope of this chapter. However, the following steps show how to use Data Query Extract to extract records from an external database table that was created using dBASE IV. The procedure for using the other Data Query commands with external databases is similar. If you want to follow along with this procedure, make sure that:

- You've installed the Datalens driver for dBASE.
- The sample dBASE file EMPLOYEE.DBF is present in C:\123\SAMPLES (or the Samples directory in your 1-2-3 program directory, if you installed 1-2-3 in a directory other than C:\123).

If you meet these conditions, you can follow these steps to extract data from an external database table into a worksheet.

1. Move to cell A1 in an empty worksheet.
2. Choose Data Connect to External.

   1-2-3 displays the Connect to External dialog box. At first, it presents the names of the available (installed) DataLens drivers.

Figure 6-51:   **Connect to External Dialog Box Showing Available Drivers**

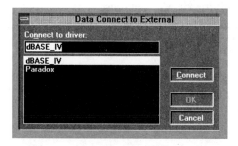

3. Connect to the dBASE_IV driver.

   Highlight the dBASE_IV driver (if it isn't already) and select "Connect". 1-2-3 inserts the selected driver in the text box and prompts for the database you want to connect to.
4. Connect to the database that contains the table you want to connect to.

   When working with dBASE database tables, 1-2-3 views the .DBF file as the database table, and the directory that contains the file as the database. Therefore, when 1-2-3 prompts you to

"Connect to database:", you need to specify the directory that contains the dBASE file. In this case, that directory is C:\123\SAMPLES. Change 123BOOK in the text box to SAMPLES and select "Connect".

Figure 6-52:   After connecting to driver, 1-2-3 prompts for dBASE database.

Figure 6-53:   After connecting to database, 1-2-3 prompts for database table.

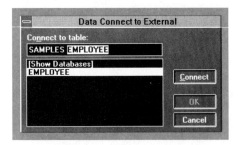

After you specify the database (directory), 1-2-3 lists all the dBASE database tables in that directory. Since only one table comes with 1-2-3, only the EMPLOYEE table appears in the list box.

5. Highlight EMPLOYEE and select "Connect".

Figure 6-54:   After connecting to table, 1-2-3 prompts for range name.

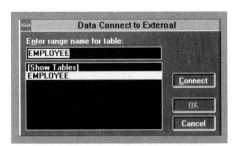

After you've selected the table to which you want to connect, 1-2-3 prompts for a range name for the table. You can accept EMPLOYEE as the range name by selecting "Connect" or pressing Enter.

6. Specify EMPLOYEE as the range name for the external table by selecting "Connect" again.

At this point, you've connected to EMPLOYEE.DBF and assigned it the range name EMPLOYEE. 1-2-3 keeps the dialog box open to offer you the option of connecting to additional database tables.

Figure 6-55:   1-2-3 Offers the option of connecting to additional tables.

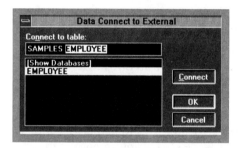

7. Select OK to exit the Connect to External dialog box.

Since you won't be connecting to more tables at the moment, leave the dialog box.

8. Paste the field names from EMPLOYEE.DBF into cell A1 of your worksheet.

You need to set up criteria and output ranges to perform a query. (The EMPLOYEE range name that represents the external table will be the input range.) Since the field names don't exist anywhere in your worksheet, you need to retrieve them from the external table. To do so, you use the Paste Fields command in the Data External Options menu. Highlight EMPLOYEE and select OK.

Figure 6-56:   Using Paste Field Command to Bring Field Information into the Worksheet

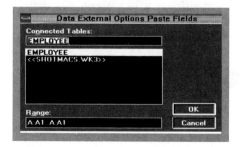

1-2-3 pastes both the field names and additional information about the fields into the worksheet.

Figure 6-57: Field Information Retrieved From External Database Table

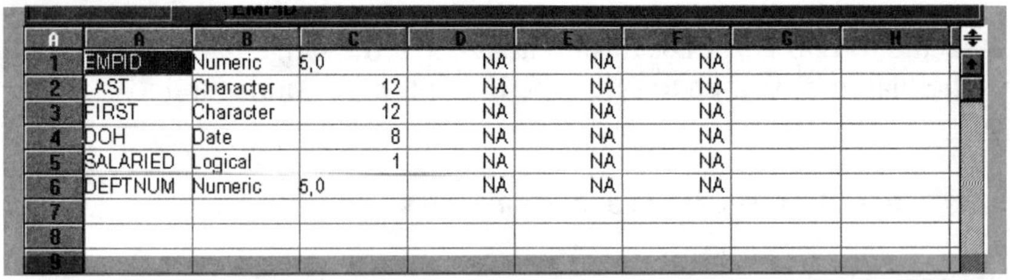

	A	B	C	D	E	F	G	H
1	EMPID	Numeric	5,0	NA	NA	NA		
2	LAST	Character	12	NA	NA	NA		
3	FIRST	Character	12	NA	NA	NA		
4	DOH	Date	8	NA	NA	NA		
5	SALARIED	Logical	1	NA	NA	NA		
6	DEPTNUM	Numeric	5,0	NA	NA	NA		
7								
8								
9								

9. Create a row of field names from the column of database fields.

Use Range Transpose to create a row of field names from the column of external database field names that you created in step 8. Range Transpose copies data from one range to another, converting formulas to their current values; in addition, it transposes the rows and columns of the copied data. Columns of data become rows, and rows of data become columns.

Choose Range Transpose. Specify the column of external database field names (A1..A6) as the "from" range. Specify cell A1 as the "to" range. Afterwards, delete the information beneath the transposed row of field names. These field names (A1..F1) will serve as the criteria range.

Figure 6-58: Transposed Field Names with Unneeded Information Highlighted for Deletion

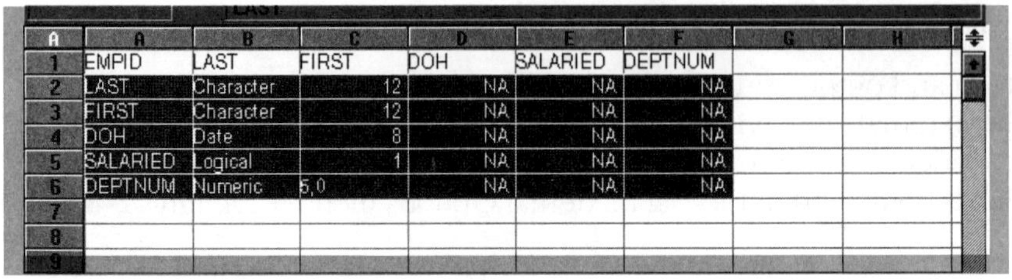

	A	B	C	D	E	F	G	H
1	EMPID	LAST	FIRST	DOH	SALARIED	DEPTNUM		
2	LAST	Character	12	NA	NA	NA		
3	FIRST	Character	12	NA	NA	NA		
4	DOH	Date	8	NA	NA	NA		
5	SALARIED	Logical	1	NA	NA	NA		
6	DEPTNUM	Numeric	5,0	NA	NA	NA		
7								
8								
9								

10. Copy the row of field names to cell A4 for the output range.

You will use the row of field names you created in step 9 as the first row of the criteria range. Copy the field names to A4..F4 to create a one-row output range.

Figure 6-59: Criteria and Output Ranges Ready to Perform the Query

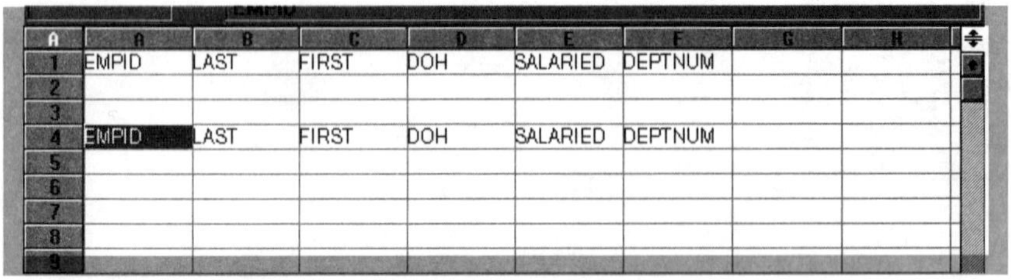

	A	B	C	D	E	F	G	H
1	EMPID	LAST	FIRST	DOH	SALARIED	DEPTNUM		
2								
3								
4	EMPID	LAST	FIRST	DOH	SALARIED	DEPTNUM		
5								
6								
7								
8								
9								

11. Perform the Data Query Extract, using the database table's range name (EMPLOYEE) as the input range, and the criteria and output ranges you set up in steps 9 and 10. By using a blank criteria range (A1..F2) and including all the field names in the output range (A4..F4), all the records and fields in the table are extracted.

Figure 6-60: Extracting Records from the EMPLOYEE Table

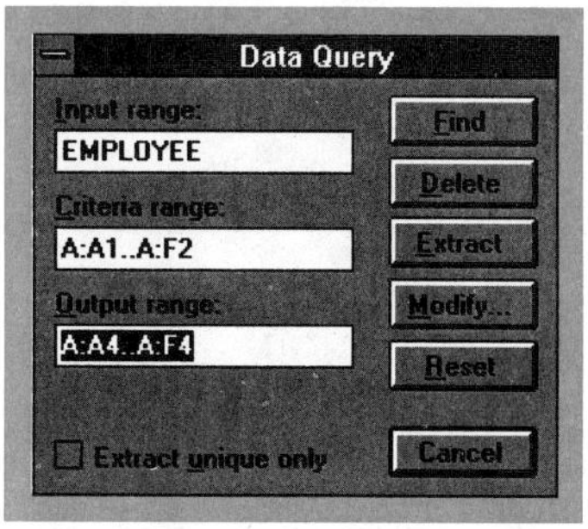

Figure 6-61: Records Extracted from External Table into the Worksheet

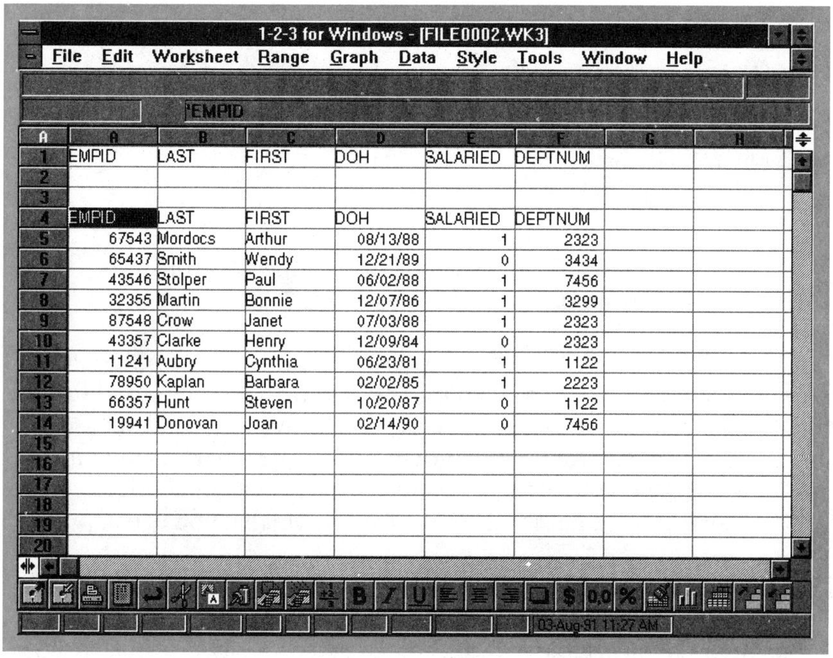

Translating Databases and Worksheets Between 1-2-3 and Other Products

While 1-2-3's ability to work with external database tables allows you to use external database tables without importing them into 1-2-3, there may be times you want to permanently convert external database tables into 1-2-3 database tables, or to convert your 1-2-3 database tables to external database tables for use with a different product. 1-2-3 provides a Translate utility that lets you convert database tables. You can also use this utility to translate 1-2-3/W worksheet files (with a .WK3 file extension) into worksheet files that you can use with other spreadsheet products. This includes converting multiple-sheet worksheet files into separate single-sheet files for use with earlier versions of 1-2-3 or Symphony.

Table 6-6 shows the products whose files you can translate into 1-2-3/W files, and vice versa.

Table 6-6: Products Supported by Translate

Product	Translations
1-2-3 Release 1A	.WK3 files to .WKS files
1-2-3 Release 2	.WK3 files to .WK1 files
dBASE II	.WK3 file database tables to .DBF files and vice versa
dBASE III and III+	.WK3 file database tables to later-version .DBF files and vice versa
DIF	.WK3 to .DIF files and vice versa (DIF files used by several products)
Enable Version 2.0	.WK3 to .SSF files and vice versa
Multiplan 4.2	.WK3 to .SLK files and vice versa
SuperCalc4	.WK3 files to .CAL files and vice versa
Symphony 1 and 1.01	.WK3 files to .WRK files
Symphony 1.1, 1.2, and 2	.WK3 files to .WR1 files

■ *NOTE:*   You don't need to use open to translate worksheets from earlier versions of 1-2-3, Symphony, or Microsoft Excel. You simply open the files in 1-2-3/W.

Translating the Contacts Database Table to a dBASE File   As you've learned in this chapter, a 1-2-3 database table is an area in one worksheet containing one row of field names and some number of rows of records. When you want to convert a 1-2-3 database table to a database table you can use with another product, such as dBASE, you must restrict the translation to only the table. This means that if your worksheet file contains anything at all beyond the database table, you will have to give a range name to the database table that you can supply to Translate.

Since the CONTACTS.WK3 file contains criteria and output ranges, as well as titles for the database table, you have to create a range name for the table itself. For the purpose of translating Bob Gordon's Business Contacts table to a dBASE database file, assume that you've already used Range Name Create to give the range name CONTACTS_DB to the range B:A4..B:J16 in CONTACTS.WK3. (You learned about range names in Chapter 4.) Here are the steps you would take to translate the Business Contacts table to a .DBF file you can use with dBASE:

■ *NOTE:* This description assumes that you have installed 1-2-3/W in the C:\123 directory, and have created the CONTACTS.WK3 worksheet file in the C:\123\123BOOK directory. If you haven't, you will have to adjust these steps accordingly.

1. Start Translate.

   Translate is a separate program from 1-2-3. If you installed Translate as an option when you installed 1-2-3, its "apples-to-oranges" icon should appear in the same Program Group as 1-2-3 for Windows. Double-click the icon to start the program. If the icon does not appear in the program group, use the File Run command of the Windows Program Manager to run C:\123\TRANS.EXE. If that file is not in your 1-2-3 directory, install Translate by running Install again, specifying "Install with options" so that Install will offer Translate as an installation option.

2. Highlight "1-2-3 Release 3" (as the product you want to translate from), and press Enter.

3. Highlight "dBASE III and III+" (as the product you want to translate to), and press Enter.

4. Read the message screens 1-2-3 displays about translating 1-2-3 files to dBASE files by pressing Enter. Press Escape when you've finished.

   In steps 4 and 5, 1-2-3 displays the rules that govern the translation you've selected. In many translations, you are translating from a product that supports more options than the product to which you are translating, or *vice versa*. These screens describe the way Translate adapts to these differences.

5. Edit the "Source file:" field to read "C:\123\123BOOK" and press Enter.

6. Select CONTACTS.WK3 from the list of files and press Enter two times (the second time to accept CONTACTS.DBF as the output file).

7. Select "Named range" in the next menu and press Enter.

8. Type "contacts_db" as the range name, and press Enter two times to start the translation.

   Assuming all your specifications were correct, Translate performs the file conversion and displays a "Translation Successful" message when it's done. Press Escape twice to display the "Do you want to leave Translate?" prompt, then select Yes to return to the Windows Program Manager (or the place from which you started Translate, if not from the Program Manager). Check in the 123BOOK directory for the newly created CONTACTS.DBF.

   For more information on Translate, see the 1-2-3 documentation. If you have many translations to perform, look at the 1-2-3 documentation of the translate commands that you can include in DOS batch files to automate the translation process.

Database Tips, Techniques, and Gotchas

This section contains some useful tips and techniques you may want apply when you are working with database tables. It also some describes some potential pitfalls you will want to avoid.

Tips and Techniques
You may find these tips helpful as you work with database tables in 1-2-3.

Inverting a Column of Data   Occasionally, you may need to invert the order of a series of records. If the records are sorted, reversing the sort order might do the trick. However, if you have used multiple sort keys, or if the records are not sorted, the problem is slightly more difficult.

The solution is to add a new field to each record and number the records sequentially, in ascending order. Use Data Fill to enter the numbers in the new field, beginning with 1 and using a step value of 1. Choose a number greater than the number of records in the database table as the Stop value. To reverse the sort order, use Data Sort to sort the records, using the new field as the primary sort key and choosing Descending as the sort order. After you have completed the sort, the order of the records is exactly reversed. To restore the original order, sort the records again, this time sorting by the new field in Ascending order.

This technique is also useful when you need to sort a database table for the first time, since it always gives you the opportunity to return the records to the order in which they were entered. (For example, when you want to compare a sequence of records to a paper copy from which the records were entered.)

■ *NOTE:*   This tip is in this chapter because the Sort commands appears in the Data menu, but it can be applied to any column of data, whether it is numeric, alphabetic, or mixed.

Finding Embedded Text   You can find database entries that begin with a series of letters by using the asterisk (*) wildcard character. For example, using B* as a selection criterion in a field called Last Name finds all entries that begin with the letter B. However, you cannot use the asterisk to match text *within* an entry. For instance, the selection criterion *St.* would *not* find all the entries that contain the substring "St.". Instead, it would match all entries in the field.

To match embedded text, use the @FIND function in the selection criteria. @FIND finds the starting position of a substring in a string. It returns 0 or a positive number if the string is found, and ERR if the string is not found. To find the substring "St." in Street field entries in the CONTACTS database, you would enter the following formula in the Street field of the criteria range:

`@FIND("St.",F5,0)>=1` (where F5 is the first data cell in the Street field)

Unlike an ordinary string match in a database criterion, @FIND is case-sensitive. To perform a case-insensitive search, combine @FIND with @UPPER:

`@FIND("ST.",@UPPER(F5),0)>=1`

Database Gotchas
Most of the 1-2-3 database operations are straightforward, but there are a few things to watch out for to ensure a peaceful relationship with your database tables. This section outlines some of these potential gotchas.

Don't Use Blank or Divider Rows Beneath Field Names   There should be no intervening blank rows or divider rows between the row containing field names and the first data record of a database table. Using a blank row can cause some database operations and database @functions to work unpredictably.

Use Absolute Cell Addresses for Ranges Outside a Database Table   In selection criteria formulas, you must use absolute cell addresses and range names to refer to any values outside the input range. The selection criteria will not work correctly if you use relative or mixed cell addresses to refer to these values.

Use Absolute Cell Addresses in Records That Will be Sorted   If a database table includes records that contain cell addresses, and you intend to sort these records, use absolute cell addresses. If you use relative cell addresses, 1-2-3 will adjust the addresses to the new location, much as if you had copied the records there, and your formulas will be incorrect.

International Characters Don't Match English Characters   In database queries, similar international characters will not match English characters (for instance, an international "é" will not match "e"). Likewise, similar English characters will not match international characters (for instance, an English "e" will not match "é").

Don't Overlap the Output Range with the Input or Criteria Ranges   The output range must not overlap the input or the criteria range. If you overlap the output range with the input range, 1-2-3 will destroy data in the input range. If you overlap the output range with the criteria range, 1-2-3 will destroy data in the criteria range.

You Can't Undo a Delete in an Off-sheet or External Database Table   You can only undo a Data Query Delete that involves a 1-2-3 database table in an active worksheet file. If you delete records from a 1-2-3 database table in an on-disk file, or from an external database table, the deletion is permanent. You should always perform an Extract to test your selection criteria before you perform the Delete.

At a Glance

In this chapter, you've learned basic skills and concepts for working with 1-2-3 databases, including the following:

Task	How To Do It:
Creating a database table	Enter field names, one per column, across the worksheet. Set column widths and add additional titles, if necessary, so that the database table is easy to use and the data is easy to enter. Then enter the database records, staring in the row below the field names.

Task	How To Do It:
Sorting database records	Sorting database records requires three steps: (1) Define the range you want to sort (Data Sort Data-Range), *excluding* the row of field names; (2) specify the sort keys (Primary-Key, Secondary-Key, and extra keys if desired), and the sort order for each key (Ascending or Descending).
Using input, criteria, and output ranges	When you perform queries, you must specify an input range, a criteria range, and (for most operations) an output range. The input range is the range to be queried, *including* the row of field names; the criteria range contains the criteria you want to match in the query; and the output range specifies where you want 1-2-3 to place a copy of matching records (for extra operations).
Specifying single-row or multiple-row output ranges	If you designate a single-row output range, 1-2-3 will erase all the data in all the cells below the output range field names, down to the bottom of the worksheet (row 8192), and the write the extracted records. If you designate a mutiple-row output range, 1-2-3 will not perform the extract if you have not designated enough rows.
Specifying search criteria	You can use a single criterion or multiple criteria for a database query. To find records that match *all* the criteria you set for a query, enter the criteria in the same row of the criteria range. To find records that match any of the criteria you set, enter the criteria in different rows of the criteria range. Criteria can consist of labels, numbers, or arithmetic or logical fomulas. These are formulas that contain the logical operators >, <, =, >=, <=, <>, #AND#, #OR#, and/or #NOT#, and which can include @functions. Label criteria can include wildcard characters: * to match all characters to the end of the label, ? to match any character in that position within the label, and ~ (tilde) to match anything *except* the label that follows the tilde.
Editing records during a database search	After you have defined the input, criteria, and output ranges, and have entered criteria, choose Data Query Find to enter FIND mode and locate the first record that matches the criteria in the criteria range. Press Edit (F2) to change a found record. Press Up or Down to find the next or previous matching record. Press Query (F7), Enter, or Escape to return to READY mode from FIND mode.
Extracting records from a database	After you have defined the input, criteria, and output ranges, and have entered criteria in the Data Query dialog box, select "Extract" to copy matching records to the output range.
Deleting records from a database table	After you have defined the input and criteria ranges in the Data Query dialog box, select "Delete". You should test the Delete before you do it by extracting the records that match your criteria. You can also delete specific records that do not easily conform to search criteria from a database by marking the individual records for deletion by placing an X or other unique marker in one of the fields and then using Data Query Delete to search for and delete all records with the marker in that field.
Using different types of criteria	You can use values, labels, formulas, and wildcards in a criteria range to describe the records to be matched by the query.

Task	How To Do It:
Using the F7 (Query) key	Pressing F7 (Query) from READY mode repeats the last Data Query command. Pressing Query from FIND mode returns you to READY mode
Performing queries with multiple tables	Using a join formula in the criteria range allows you to query multiple tables with one command. The ability to work with multiple tables in a query requires good database design, where information is stored in only one place and combined by queries.
Using external database tables	You can connect to external database tables and work with them as if they were in a 1-2-3 spreadsheet. This allows you to work with tables in their native format, without the need to convert the tables to worksheets and then back to database tables when you have finished using them
Modifying blocks of records	After you have defined the input, criteria, and output ranges in the Data Query dialog box, select "Modify". In the new dialog box, select "Extract" to copy matching records to the output range. Edit the records in the output range and place them back into the table by selecting Data Query Modify Replace.
Splitting a database table into multiple tables	Using the ~ (tilde) or #NOT# operator in a criteria range makes it possible to remove all records from the table *except* for a set you want to keep in a separate table.
Using database @functions to analyze a database table	The database @functions examine the records in a database table that match specified criteria, and calculate a value based on the records' contents.
Creating What-if tables	The Data What-if Table commands show the effects of changing variables in one or more formulas. Before you execute the command you must set up the appropriate table range and input cell(s).
Including computed and aggregate fields in output ranges	Computed and aggregate fields are formulas included with the field names in the output range. When records are extracted to the output range, the formula analyzes the records being extracted, and calculates a value (aggregate) or values (computed).
Translating 1-2-3 database files to other product files and *vice versa*	The Translate utility can translate files created with other products to 1-2-3 worksheets, or 1-2-3 worksheets to files that can be used with other products.

Besides learning the database building, sorting, and querying skills listed above, you learned a number of additional database (and worksheet) concepts in the Tips section at the end of this chapter. Try putting these concepts into practice as you continue exploring 1-2-3.

Chapter 7

Worksheet Formatting

1-2-3 provides many ways to change the way a worksheet looks and the way data in that worksheet is displayed. Although you've largely been concerned with mastering the procedures you need to build spreadsheets and database tables, you've already looked at some ways that you can format the data in those files to make it easier to interpret. You'll recall, for example, that in Chapter 5 you used Range Format and Worksheet Global Settings Format to format the numeric data in a range of cells as Currency, Percent, and Comma(,). You have also changed the overall appearance of the worksheet. In Bob Gordon's Home Budget and Cash Flow Forecast applications, you used rows of hyphens and equal signs to divide the worksheets into sections.

Formatting such as this is important to the presentation of your data. As anyone who has had to work with poorly organized and formatted worksheets can tell you, the way data is presented is sometimes just as important as the data itself. In this chapter, you will begin further experiments with changing the way the data in spreadsheets and databases is displayed. You'll use 1-2-3's Style commands to apply style formats to data, and you'll use the Window Display Options commands to change the overall look of the worksheet.

■ *NOTE:*   You can use the Style and Window Display Options commands discussed in this chapter in both spreadsheets and database applications.

What You'll Learn

By the time you finish this chapter, you'll know how to perform the following formatting tasks:

■ **Change the font of text in a range**

■ **Change the attributes of text in a range (for example, using bold or italicized text)**

■ **Change the color of text in a range**

■ **Put a border and a drop shadow around a range**

■ **Add shading to a range**

■ **Copy and move formats among cells and ranges**

■ **Use a named-style setting**

■ **Separate sections of the worksheet with graphical elements**

- **View a larger/smaller portion of the worksheet**

- **Change overall worksheet window display characteristics (such as the look of the frame or presence or absence of a grid)**

- **Align a label over single and multiple columns**

- **Use the Lotus Classic Wysiwyg menu**

Before You Start

Before you begin the exercises in this chapter, start 1-2-3. Make sure that the cell pointer is in cell A:A1 of a new, maximized, blank worksheet file, and that 1-2-3 has been set up to save files in your 123BOOK directory.

As you work through the exercises in this chapter, you will modify files named CASHFLOW.WK3 and CONTACT3.WK3 that you created in previous chapters. (A disk containing the worksheets created in this book is also available from the authors.) As in previous chapters, stop at the end of a numbered step or just before the next section heading when you are tired or have something else to do. Be sure to save any modified worksheet files before you stop. If you have more than one active file, write down the names of the files in memory and the order in which they are stored. When you want to continue with the exercises, start up 1-2-3, read in the worksheet files you last used, making sure they are in the same order they were in before you stopped, then pick up where you left off.

- *NOTE:*   The exercises assume that you have installed the Adobe Type Manager (ATM) and the ATM fonts that are included with 1-2-3/W, and that you turned on the Adobe Type Manager using the ATM Control Panel. Since you will be using the Adobe Type Manager for exercises in this chapter, if you have not installed or turned on the Adobe Type Manager, do so now by using the procedures in "1-2-3 and the Adobe Type Manager" at the end of this chapter.

A Note on Example Layout   As in previous chapters, the examples in this chapter assume that your screen displays 20 rows and eight columns when the Worksheet window is maximized. If your display does not show 20 rows and eight columns, your screens will look somewhat different from the illustrations, but you can still do all the examples. Just be sure to use the cell addresses and ranges specified in the instructions.

A Note on Keystroke Instructions   The keystroke instructions in this chapter often assume you are using a mouse to perform such operations as highlighting a range or selecting an option in a dialog box. You can also use the keyboard to perform the same operations. Many of the keyboard equivalents to mouse operations were described in previous chapters. A few of the most common ones are summarized here. For a complete list of keystroke equivalents to mouse operations, see the 1-2-3 documentation or the 1-2-3 on-line Help.

Keyboard Equivalents to Mouse Operations

Operation	Instruction		Keyboard Equivalent	
Complete action and close dialog box	**Select:**	OK	**Press:**	⏎
Cancel action and close dialog box	**Select:**	Cancel	**Press:**	ESC
Highlight a text box	**Select:**	text box	**Press:**	ALT+*underlined_letter*
Edit a range in a text box	**Select:** **Specify:**	Range A:A1..C:D4	**Press:**	ALT+*underlined_letter* F2 (EDIT)
Edit a number or word in a text box	**Select:** **Specify:** *(or click on text and edit it)*	text box new text	**Press:** **Type:** *(or press Left arrow and edit text)*	ALT+*underlined_letter* new text
Highlight a range	**Highlight:** A:A1..C:D4		**Move to:** cell A:A1 **Press:** F4 **Move to:** cell D4 **Press:** ⏎	

Throughout this chapter, the Edit Copy and Edit Paste commands are used in the exercises whenever you copy data from one range to another. In all these places, using the Edit Quick Copy command or the "Copy To" icon are perfectly viable alternatives to Edit Copy and Edit Paste. This chapter also instructs you to highlight a range and use the Delete key whenever you have to clear cells. The Edit Clear command or the "Cut" icon would work equally well. In all tasks, feel free to use the approach you find most comfortable.

Working with the Formatting Commands

In this chapter you will be formatting Bob Gordon's Cash Flow Forecast worksheet. Along the way, you'll learn how to change the appearance of selected data on the worksheet, ways to add highlights (such as color and shading) to selected ranges, and commands that change the look of the overall worksheet display. You'll be using both the Style commands and the Window Display Options commands.

1-2-3's Style commands let you add many kinds of style formats to ranges in your worksheet. *Style formats* refer to the way a range looks when it is displayed. For example, you can add style formats that surround a range with a border, add color to it, shade it, or drop a shadow from the range to make it stand out. You can change the typeface used in a range, or select from several other types of special formatting, including bold, underlined, and italic.

1-2-3's Window Display Options commands let you control the way the worksheet is displayed in the Worksheet window. For example, you can zoom the window in or out to view a smaller or larger portion of the worksheet; change the colors of individual components of the worksheet (such as its frame, cell background, cell contents, and range borders); hide or change the look of the worksheet frame; and establish the palette of colors that are used for displaying and printing worksheets and graphs.

In this chapter, you'll learn the basic Style and Window Display Options commands as you work with Bob Gordon's Cash Flow Forecast worksheet to improve the clarity of Bob's data. When you are finished, you will be able to format a worksheet so that it looks like the one in Figure 7-1. As you can see, the extra formatting really improves the appearance and the legibility of the data.

In later chapters, you'll learn how to use other formatting commands to enhance graphs (Chapter 8) and printed data (Chapter 9).

Figure 7-1:   The Worksheet Formatted by Using Styles and Window Display Option Commands

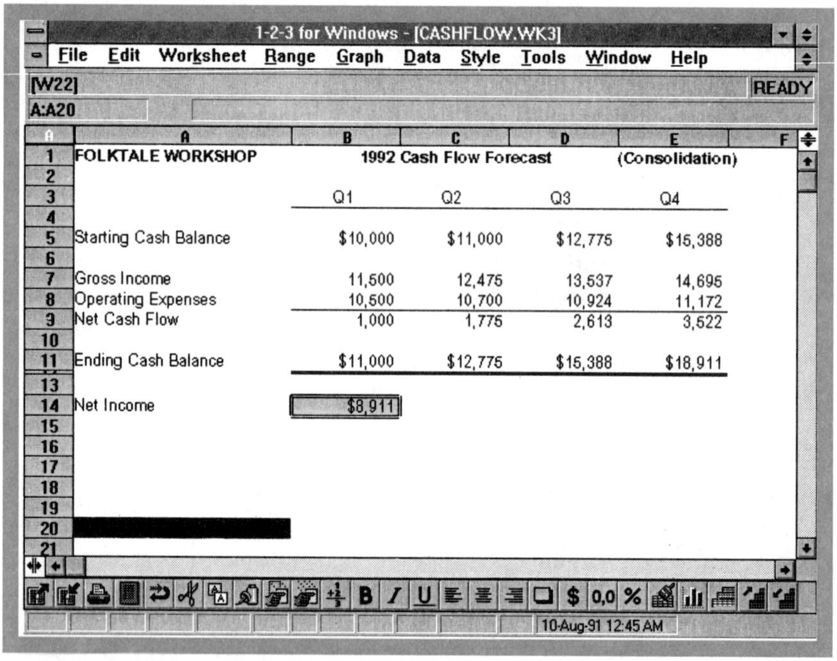

■ *NOTE:*   If you are familiar with 1-2-3 Release 3.1 or Release 2.3, you may have already used many of 1-2-3's formatting commands. In those versions of the product, "style" formats are provided by the Wysiwyg add-in.

In addition to commands that you've already learned, you will use the commands described in Table 7-1 to format the worksheet. (You will print the worksheet in Chapter 9.)

Table 7-1: Commands Used to Format the Worksheet

Command	What It Does:
Style commands:	
Font	Specifies the font for a range; selects and replaces font sets.
Alignment	Aligns a label above a range.
Border	Adds a border around a range.
Color	Specifies the color of entries in a range.
Shading	Adds shading to a range.
Style 1-8	Formats a range with the format settings in the specified named-style setting.
Name	Defines a named-style.
Window commands:	
Display Options	Changes how the current window is displayed, including its color, whether it is zoomed (enlarged or reduced), the look of the frame, and other options.
Edit commands:	
Move Cells	Moves a format (and optionally the data) to another range.
Quick Copy	Copies a format to another range.
1-2-3 Classic Wysiwyg commands:	
Text Edit	Lets you edit a block of text directly in the worksheet.

Formatting Cells and Ranges

You format cells and ranges using the commands in the Style menu. These commands change the look of the entries in the range. For example, you can use Style commands to change the font or color used in a range of cells, make entries in a range bold or underlined, add shading to a range, or add borders around a range. (See Figures 7-2 and 7-3 on the following page.)

Using Fonts

The first style formatting you'll do will change the font of the title in Bob Gordon's Cash Flow Forecast worksheet file.

1. Open the Cash Flow Forecast worksheet file.

First, open Bob Gordon's Cash Flow Forecast and move to the first cell of the worksheet file.

Choose: `File   Open`
Select: `CASHFLOW.WK3`
            `OK`   *to read in the file*

Figure 7-2:   The Cash Flow Forecast Before Formatting

	A	B	C	D	E	F
1	FOLKTALE WORKSHOP		1992 Cash Flow Forecast		(Consolidation)	
2						
3		Q1	Q2	Q3	Q4	
4						
5	Starting Cash Balance	$10,000	$11,000	$12,775	$15,388	
6						
7	Gross Income	11,500	12,475	13,537	14,695	
8	Operating Expenses	10,500	10,700	10,924	11,172	
9						
10	Net Cash Flow	1,000	1,775	2,613	3,522	
11						
12	Ending Cash Balance	$11,000	$12,775	$15,388	$18,911	
13						
14						
15	Net Income	$8,911				
16						
17						
18						
19						
20						

Figure 7-3:   The Cash Flow Forecast After Formatting

	A	B	C	D	E	F
1	FOLKTALE WORKSHOP		1992 Cash Flow Forecast		(Consolidation)	
2						
3		Q1	Q2	Q3	Q4	
4						
5	Starting Cash Balance	$10,000	$11,000	$12,775	$15,388	
6						
7	Gross Income	11,500	12,475	13,537	14,695	
8	Operating Expenses	10,500	10,700	10,924	11,172	
9	Net Cash Flow	1,000	1,775	2,613	3,522	
10						
11	Ending Cash Balance	$11,000	$12,775	$15,388	$18,911	
13						
14	Net Income	$8,911				
15						
16						
17						

Press: CTRL+HOME   *to move to cell A:A1*

1-2-3 opens a Worksheet window entitled CASHFLOW.WK3, makes it current, and moves the cell pointer to A:A1.

Before you continue, maximize the Worksheet window.

Click on: *the Maximize button in the Worksheet window*

2. Turn off global protection for all worksheets.

When you completed the Cash Flow Forecast application in Chapter 5, you turned on global protection. Turn it off now for each of the worksheets so you can add style formatting and edit some of the information. You must turn off global protection for each sheet individually. First, turn off global protection for worksheet A:

Move to:	*any cell in worksheet A*
Choose:	`Worksheet` `Global Settings`
Select:	`Protection` *and clear the check-box*
	`OK`

1-2-3 turns off global protection for worksheet A. Now, turn off global protection for each of the other worksheets by moving to each worksheet in turn and executing these keystrokes:

Choose:	`Worksheet` `Global Settings`
Select:	`Protection` *and clear the check-box*
	`OK`

■ *NOTE:*   From now on, we'll leave global protection off, to simplify changing the worksheet.

3. Change the font of the worksheet title.

To make the worksheet title stand out from the rest of the worksheet, change the font of the title to a larger one. The default font is Arial MT 10 (Arial MT typeface with a size of 10 points). Try Arial MT 14 (14-point Arial MT).

Highlight:	A:A1..A:E1	*to select the title range*
Choose:	`Style` `Font`	

1-2-3 displays a dialog box that lists the currently available fonts. The default font (Arial MT 10) is listed first. Choose "Arial MT 14" for the title.

Select:	`Arial MT 14`
	`OK`

The text in the range you specified is changed to the larger size font. However, you'll also notice that this has caused a problem with the first label, **FOLKTALE WORKSHOP**. Although the title fit perfectly in cell A:A1 before, changing to the larger font has made the label longer than the cell is wide. To remedy this problem, you'll adjust the column width.

4. Adjust the column width for column A.

Figure 7-4: The title is now set in Arial MT 14.

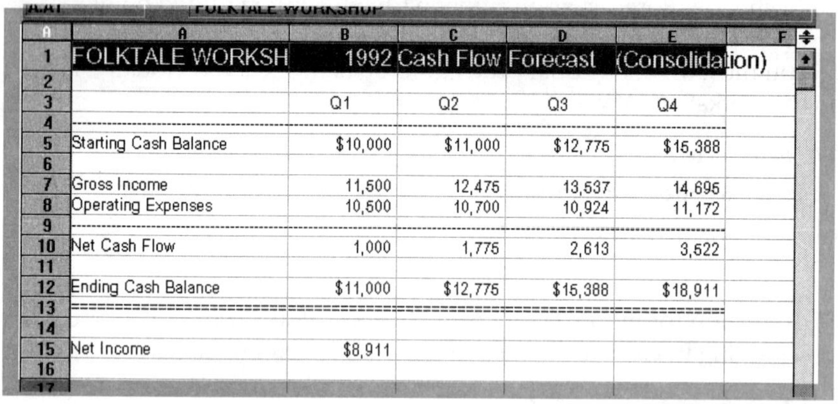

	A	B	C	D	E	F
1	FOLKTALE WORKSH	1992 Cash Flow Forecast		(Consolidation)		
2						
3		Q1	Q2	Q3	Q4	
4						
5	Starting Cash Balance	$10,000	$11,000	$12,775	$15,388	
6						
7	Gross Income	11,500	12,475	13,537	14,695	
8	Operating Expenses	10,500	10,700	10,924	11,172	
9						
10	Net Cash Flow	1,000	1,775	2,613	3,522	
11						
12	Ending Cash Balance	$11,000	$12,775	$15,388	$18,911	
13						
14						
15	Net Income	$8,911				
16						
17						

Although you could use the Worksheet Column Width command (and you *will* do that in a later step), you will use the mouse this time to adjust column A to a width that accommodates the complete **FOLKTALE WORKSHOP** label. First, move the mouse pointer to the right border of column A in the worksheet frame. The mouse pointer changes to a two-headed arrow. Now, drag the mouse pointer to the right to widen the column. When you release the mouse button, 1-2-3 adjusts the column to the new width. See if the label fits well now. If the label doesn't fit in the cell, press the mouse button again and continue to adjust the width of column A by dragging the mouse pointer until the entire **FOLKTALE WORKSHOP** label fits in cell A:A1.

Figure 7-5: The label FOLKTALE WORKSHOP now fits properly in A:A1.

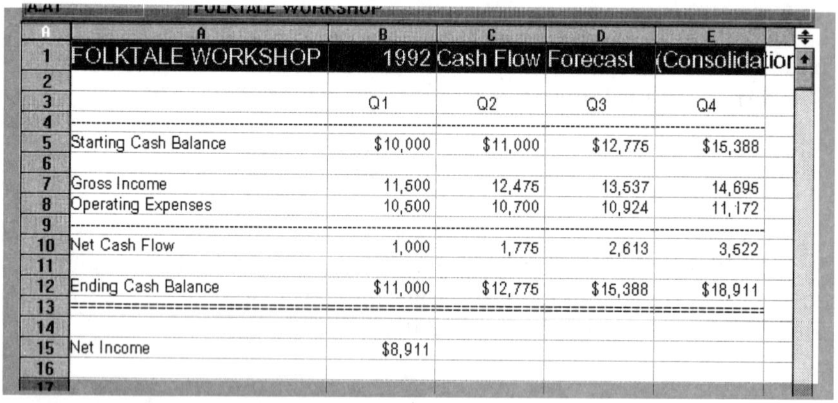

	A	B	C	D	E	
1	FOLKTALE WORKSHOP	1992 Cash Flow Forecast		(Consolidation		
2						
3		Q1	Q2	Q3	Q4	
4						
5	Starting Cash Balance	$10,000	$11,000	$12,775	$15,388	
6						
7	Gross Income	11,500	12,475	13,537	14,695	
8	Operating Expenses	10,500	10,700	10,924	11,172	
9						
10	Net Cash Flow	1,000	1,775	2,613	3,522	
11						
12	Ending Cash Balance	$11,000	$12,775	$15,388	$18,911	
13						
14						
15	Net Income	$8,911				
16						
17						

■ *NOTE:*   The **FOLKTALE WORKSHOP** label set in 14-point Arial MT requires a cell that is at least 26 characters wide. 1-2-3 displays the width of the current cell on the format line of the 1-2-3 control panel. For example, [W26] indicates a cell 26 characters wide.

At this point, 1-2-3 displays the full **FOLKTALE WORKSHOP** label in cell A1. Now, however, we have created another problem: the **(Consolidation)** label in cell A:E1 extends past the right side of the screen; this is definitely not the desired result. It is clear that we cannot use Arial MT 14 for the title and still have it fit on the display. Let's find a way to add emphasis to the title and still keep it on a single screen.

5. Change the worksheet title to bold.

Changing the title to bold should make it stand out from the other data in the worksheet. Since you pre-selected A:A1..A:E1 in the previous step, that range is still highlighted; you can therefore simply choose the next command and operate on the highlighted range. (As part of the operation, you'll also change the font of the title from Arial MT 14 back to the default Arial MT 10.)

Choose:	`Style   Font`
Select:	`Arial MT 10`
	`Bold` *and check the check-box*
	`OK`

Figure 7-6:   Changing the Title to Bold Arial MT 10

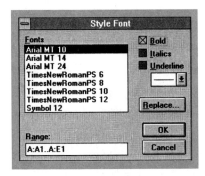

Now 1-2-3 displays the title in Arial MT 10-point bold. The bold works well to highlight the title.

6. Adjust the width of column A.

The extra width that you previously added to column A is now creating unnecessary white space on the worksheet. Reduce the width of column A before continuing. Last time, you used the mouse to change column width; this time, use the Worksheet Column Width command:

Highlight:	cell A:A1
Choose:	`Worksheet   Column Width`
Select:	`Set width to`
Type:	`22` *in the text box*

Select: OK

Figure 7-7:   **Adjusting Cell Width Again**

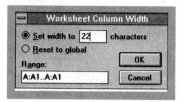

Column A looks good at 22 characters wide. Adjust the width of column A in each of the remaining sheets by first moving to the column A of the worksheet, then executing the following keystrokes:

Choose: `Worksheet    Column Width`

Select: `Set width to`

Type: `22`   *in the text box*

Select: `OK`

■ *NOTE:*   If you did not have the Adobe Type Manager turned on, text in bold would (often) displayed wider than text that was not bold. See "1-2-3 and the Adobe Type Manager" later in this chapter if you have not installed the Adobe Type Manager yet.

Using Borders and Colors

The worksheet title set in bold does look good; but maybe you could set the title off even more by surrounding it with a border. 1-2-3 lets you add single-, double-, or thick-lined borders to any or all sides of a range. You can even add borders to the edges of each cell in a range. Add a single-lined border (an outline) around the entire title range.

■ *NOTE:*   Previously, when you specified the range to format, you did not need to specify the additional cell F1 that contains the rest of the long label `(Consolidation)`. Most Style commands work this in that you only need to specify the cells that actually contain the labels. This is not true way, however, when you add borders or shading to a range. Then, you must specify the entire range as it is displayed.

Highlight: A:A1..A:F1

Choose: `Style    Border`

Select: `Outline`   *and check the check-box*

                 `OK`

1-2-3 creates a single-lined border around the cells in A:A1 through A:F1. But a close look shows that it really doesn't work that well here. First, you can't distinguish the top edge of the outline against the 1-2-3 frame. Second, the right edge of the border (around cell A:F1) is not visible on the screen.

Figure 7-8: Surrounding the Title with a Border

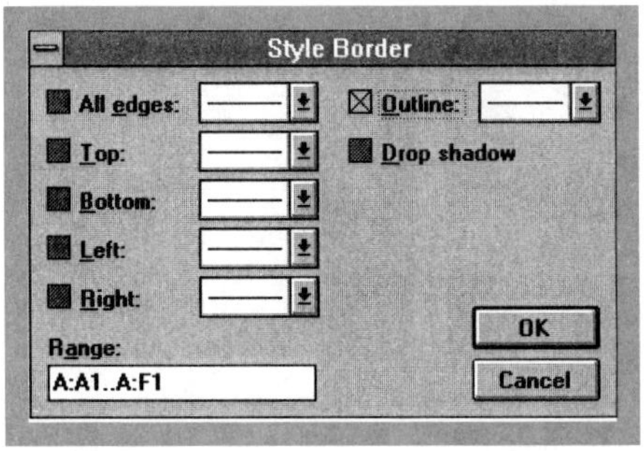

Figure 7-9: The Title with a Border

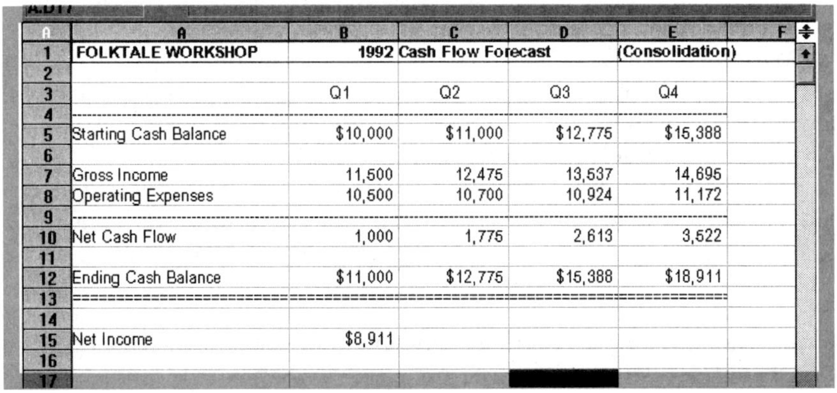

A	A	B	C	D	E	F
1	FOLKTALE WORKSHOP	1992	Cash Flow Forecast		(Consolidation)	
2						
3		Q1	Q2	Q3	Q4	
4	------------------------------	------------	------------	------------	------------	
5	Starting Cash Balance	$10,000	$11,000	$12,775	$15,388	
6						
7	Gross Income	11,500	12,475	13,537	14,695	
8	Operating Expenses	10,500	10,700	10,924	11,172	
9	------------------------------	------------	------------	------------	------------	
10	Net Cash Flow	1,000	1,775	2,613	3,522	
11						
12	Ending Cash Balance	$11,000	$12,775	$15,388	$18,911	
13	==============================	============	============	============	============	
14						
15	Net Income	$8,911				
16						
17						

Maybe, instead of a border, changing the color of the title will be more effective. Try changing the color of the title to Dark-blue. But first, remove the border from the title. (Once again, you are operating on the same range as you did in the previous step and therefore do not have to specify the range.)

Choose: `Style` `Border`

Select: `Outline` *and clear the check-box*

`OK`

1-2-3 removes the border. Now, you are ready to use the Style Color command to change the color of the worksheet title to Dark-blue. This time, you'll change the color for A:A1..A:E1 only, the range that actually contains the title.

Highlight:	A:A1..A:E1
Choose:	Style Color
Click on:	Cell contents
Select:	Dark-blue OK

Figure 7-10:   Changing the Color of the Title

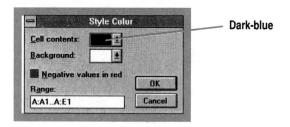

Dark-blue

1-2-3 changes the color of the text in the title to Dark-blue. 1-2-3's format line (the third line of the 1-2-3 control panel) indicates that the current cell is "Bold Dark-blue". And, if you are using a color printer, 1-2-3 will also print the titles in a different color.

Finally, you have a style for titles that really does look good on the worksheet, and one that does not cause other formatting problems. It may seem to you that we took a pretty circuitous route to establish a good-looking style for titles, but it was not an unrealistic route: The styles you use in your worksheets are largely a matter of personal preference, and it probably *will* take you some time to figure out just what styles you like. On the other hand, as you become more accustomed to working with 1-2-3 styles, you'll get to know from experience which styles work well with others, and which work well in particular situations; this will shorten the process.

■ *NOTE:*   If you are using a monochrome monitor (and you have set up Windows for a color display, either when you installed Windows or by using the Windows Setup application), 1-2-3 uses different shades for each color choice. Depending on the monitor you are using, some of the color selections may correspond to shades that do not enhance your display. You may need to try several "color" choices to find the one that you like best. For example, if Dark-blue creates a shading that you do not like, try Red or Yellow. You can replace the current colors using the Window Display Options Palette command.

Now let's turn to another important range in the Cash Flow Forecast and see if we can enhance it using Style commands. To Bob, the net income value on the summary sheet is probably the most significant figure in the application. To make it really stand out, add a double-lined border to the cell that contains net income.

Highlight:	cell A:B15
Choose:	Style Border
Select:	Outline *and check the check-box*

> *the Outline list box*
> *the double outline*
> OK

Figure 7-11: Surrounding the Net Income Figure with a Border

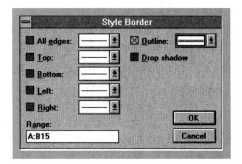

1-2-3 adds a double-lined border to cell A:B15. Add a Cyan (light blue) background color to the net income box you created. The background color should make it even easier to scan the worksheet for this important information.

Choose: Style   Color

Select: Background

              Cyan   *(light blue)*

              OK

Figure 7-12: Adding Background Color to the Net Income Value

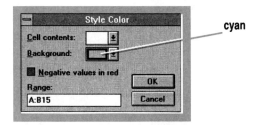

1-2-3 adds a Cyan background to A:B15. Save—but don't close—the Cash Flow Forecast file before you continue with the next section.

Copying and Moving Formats

As you're designing the "look" of your application, you'll want to experiment with different styles in different ranges. The easiest way to do this is to: (1) Copy or move a style to a new range; (2) determine if *that's* the way you want that range to look; then (3) maybe copy or move the style again. 1-2-3 provides many ways to copy and move styles.

- Edit Copy and Edit Move, both of which use the clipboard, copy the style of the copied or moved range as well as the contents of that range.
- Both the Edit Quick Copy and the Edit Move Cells commands have "Styles only" options that allow you to copy and move styles without copying or moving the contents of the cell.
- The "Apply Formatting" icon copies the formatting of the current cell to a specified cell. This is a very convenient way to experiment with the look of an application.

In this section, you'll experiment with all of these techniques and more. You'll use a blank worksheet as a scratch pad for "doodling" with styles.

- **NOTE:**   Just like copying cell contents with the Edit Copy command, copying styles leaves the style in the "from" cell and adds it to the "to" cell. Just like moving cell contents, moving styles removes the style from the "from" cell and adds it to the "to" cell. Another method for copying formats—using named styles—is discussed in "Automating Data Formats with Named Styles," later in this chapter.

1. Open a new blank file.

   Open a new file to use as a "scratch" worksheet.

   Choose: File   New

Figure 7-13: 1-2-3 opens a new file.

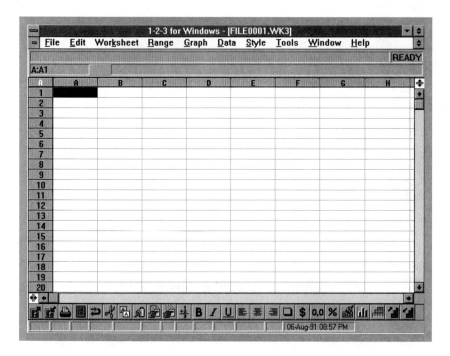

1-2-3 opens a new file entitled FILE0001.WK3 and displays it in a blank Worksheet window.

■ *NOTE:*   The name that 1-2-3 creates for a Worksheet window opened by File New depends upon the number of "new" worksheet files you have previously saved without naming them yourself. The first worksheet file you open with File New is named FILE0001.WK3; if you save that file (without renaming it by using File Save As), 1-2-3 names the next worksheet you open with File New FILE0002.WK3, and so on.

2. Enter and format some test data.

In this exercise, you'll enter the label **TEST** into cell A1; then you'll add a drop shadow, bold, and the color Red as formatting to cell A1. You will use this cell for experimenting with several different methods for copying and moving formatted ranges. You'll use the icon bar for these operations whenever possible.

In this exercise, you'll use the "Drop Shadow" icon, which looks like this:

And, you'll use the "Bold" icon, which looks like this:

Press:	HOME	*to move to cell A1 (if necessary)*
Type:	TEST	↵
Click on:	*the Drop Shadow icon*	
	the Bold icon	
Choose:	Style *Color*	
Select:	Cell contents Red OK	

Figure 7-14:   The label TEST is bold, Red, and has a shadow.

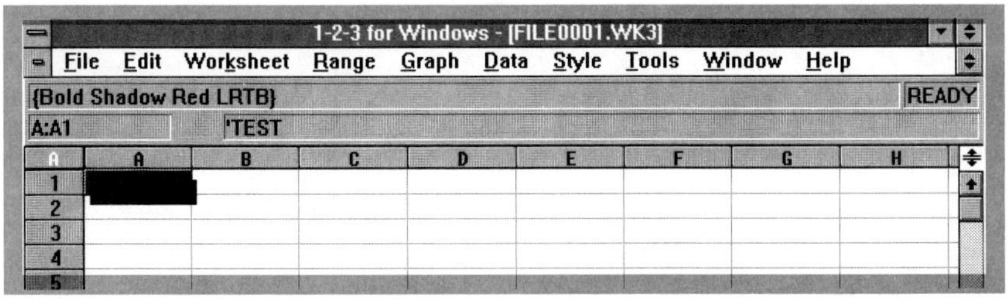

Lotus 1-2-3 At Work

(Paul Campbell is Business Manager for Genetic Screening and Counceling Service in Denton, Texas, a state agency providing genetic laboratory and clinical services. Applications operating on a Novell network and stand-alone comprise a major part of the data processing.)

Lotus is used for financial reporting, budget development, and cost accounting.

The WYSIWYG publishing capability is extremely easy to use for those already familiar with Lotus' style of menus. Using features like multiple fonts, outlines, wide lines, definable row heights, and shadows, reports have a sharp appearance with minimal effort. I have been freed from using dashes and equal signs on their own row to simulate single and double underlines. The automatic compression ability removes much of the burden to get a schedule to fit on a page .

Respectable color is available at low-cost using a dot matrix printer with a multi-color ribbon (not all are color capable). The use of different colors is more than a frill—it can be used to focus attention. My favorite is the ability to use red for negative numbers. Cells can be defined to display or print red only if the number is negative.

1-2-3 inserts the label **TEST** in cell A1, adds a thin-lined border and a drop shadow, and displays the cell's data in bold font and in Red.

- ■ *NOTE:*   If you would prefer to use colors that are not currently available with the Style Color command, you can replace the current colors using the Window Display Options Palette command.

3. Copy cell A1 to cell A3, using the Clipboard.

   Now you'll copy, this timeusing the Clipboard to verify that both the contents *and* the style of the highlighted range are copied. You'll use the "Copy To" icon, which looks like this:

and the "Paste" icon, which looks like this:

Click on: *the Copy To icon*

Press: ⬇ *twice, to move to cell A3*

Click on: *the Paste icon*

Figure 7-15: **1-2-3 copies the style and contents of A1 to A3.**

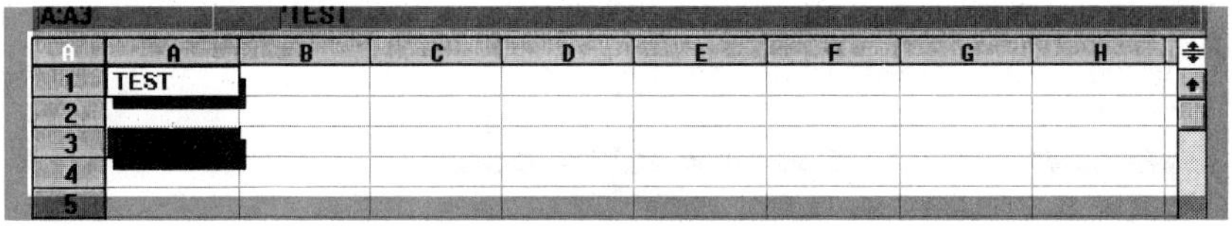

	A	B	C	D	E	F	G	H	
1	TEST								
2									
3									
4									
5									

1-2-3 uses the Clipboard to copy both the data and style format of cell A1 to cell A3. Cell A3 now contains the label **TEST** and is formatted as bold Red with an outline and a drop shadow.

■ *NOTE:*   When you copy and paste using the Clipboard (either by choosing Edit Copy and Edit Paste or using the "Copy To" and "Paste" icon), 1-2-3 copies: (1) The contents of the range; (2) the range's format (such as Currency or Comma); and (3) the style format of the range.

4. Copy the style formatting of cell A3 to cell A5 using Edit Quick Copy.

This time, you'll do a copy using the "Styles only" option of the Edit Quick Copy command. Because you'll be using the "Styles Only" option, only the style format of cell A3 will be copied to cell A5, not its contents.

Choose: Edit   Quick Copy

Select: Styles only   *and check the check-box*

              To:

Specify: cell A5

Select: OK

Figure 7-16:   **Quick Copying Style of A3 to A5**

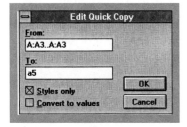

When you click on OK, 1-2-3 copies the style format from the range you specified to the new range. Cell A5 is now formatted as bold Red with a thin-lined border and a drop shadow. Notice that Edit Quick Copy with the "Styles only" option checked follows the same copying rules that the Edit Copy command follows. If you copy information from a range to a cell,

1-2-3 uses the cell as the first cell of the "to" range. You won't be able to see the effect of the contents formatting (bold and Red) until you add some data to the cell.

Move to: cell A5
Type: TEST1

Figure 7-17:   Now you can see the bold and Red formatting.

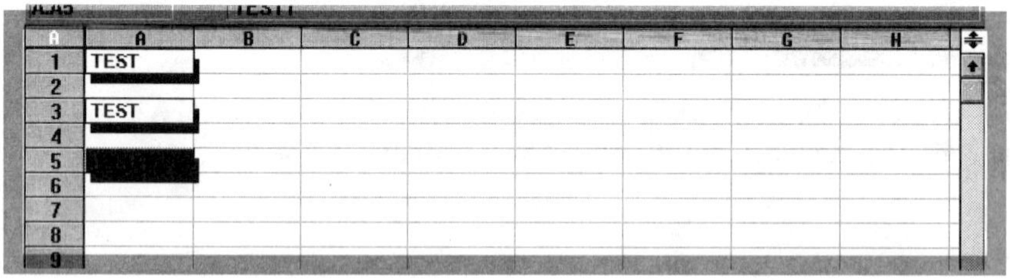

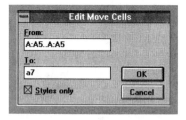

1-2-3 now displays the label **TEST1** in cell A5 in bold and Red.

6. Move a style using Move Cells.

The Move Cells "Styles only" option allows you to move the style formatting from one range to another range without moving the contents. To try this command, move the formatting from cell A5 to cell A7:

Choose: Edit   Move Cells
Select: Styles only   *and check the check-box*
       To:
Specify: cell A7
Select: OK

Figure 7-18:   Moving the Style of cell A5 to cell A7

```
  ─           Edit Move Cells
 From:
 ┌─────────────────────────┐
 │ A:A5..A:A5              │
 └─────────────────────────┘
 To:
 ┌─────────────────────┐   ┌──────────┐
 │ a7                  │   │   OK     │
 └─────────────────────┘   └──────────┘
 ☒ Styles only             ┌──────────┐
                           │  Cancel  │
                           └──────────┘
```

1-2-3 moves only the style format of cell A5 to cell A7. Cell A5 is reset to the default style (no border, drop shadow, bold, or color). Cell A7 takes on cell A5's previous style.
    Enter some data into cell A7 so you see that its contents are formatted in Red.

Move to: cell A7

Type: TEST2   ↵

7. Copy styles using the "Apply Formatting" icon.

The "Apply Formatting" icon applies the formatting of the current cell to a target cell. This offers a very convenient way to copy styles around the worksheet. Use the "Apply Formatting" icon to copy the style format from A7 to A9. The "Apply Formatting" icon looks like this:

Move to: cell A7

Click on: *the Apply Formatting icon*

Move the mouse pointer into the worksheet. The mouse pointer changes to a paintbrush. You'll move to the cell to which you want the current style to be applied, cell A9.

Move to: cell A9

1-2-3 now displays cell A9 as bold Red with a thin-lined border and a drop shadow.

Figure 7-19:   Cell A9 After Applying the Style of cell A7

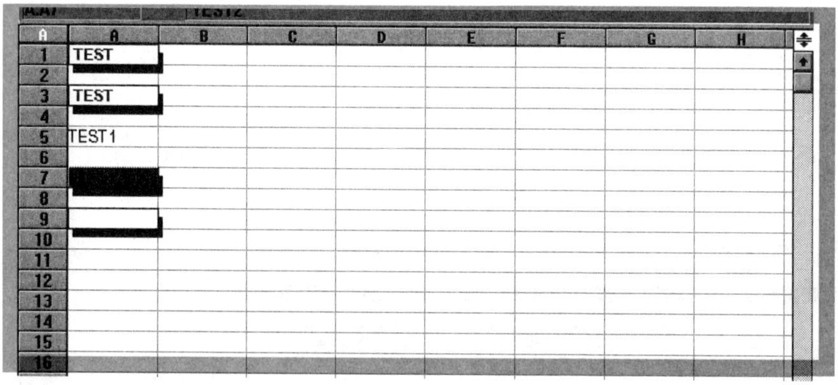

A	A	B	C	D	E	F	G	H	
1	TEST								
2									
3	TEST								
4									
5	TEST1								
6									
7									
8									
9									
10									
11									
12									
13									
14									
15									
16									

8. Remove the style formatting from a range using Edit Clear Special.

As you are experimenting with the design of an application, there will be times when you want to just remove the style format from a range. 1-2-3's Edit Clear Special command has a Styles option to do this. Remove the style formatting from the range A1..A9 using the Edit Clear Special command:

Highlight: A1..A9

Choose: Edit   Clear Special

Select: `Style`   *and check the check-box*

                         `Cell contents`   *and clear the check-box*

                         `Number format`   *and clear the check-box*

                         `OK`

Figure 7-20: Removing a Style with Edit Clear Special

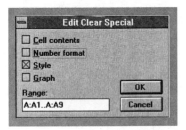

    1-2-3 removes the style formatting from the range A1..A9, leaving the data displayed in the default style format.

    In the previous sections, you learned how to change fonts and use bold and color to change the style of a range of cells. In this section, you learned how to copy and move those styles around the worksheet. In the next section, you'll work with one of 1-2-3's most powerful style-related features: named styles. Before you go on to the next section, close the scratch worksheet file, but don't save it:

Choose: `File`   `Close`

Select: `No`

    1-2-3 closes the Worksheet window for FILE0001.WK3 and displays the Worksheet window for CASHFLOW.WK3.

Figure 7-21: 1-2-3 makes the Worksheet window for CASHFLOW.WK3 active.

	A	B	C	D	E	F
1	FOLKTALE WORKSHOP		1992 Cash Flow Forecast		(Consolidation)	
2						
3		Q1	Q2	Q3	Q4	
4						
5	Starting Cash Balance	$10,000	$11,000	$12,775	$15,388	
6						
7	Gross Income	11,500	12,475	13,537	14,695	
8	Operating Expenses	10,500	10,700	10,924	11,172	
9						
10	Net Cash Flow	1,000	1,775	2,613	3,522	
11						
12	Ending Cash Balance	$11,000	$12,775	$15,388	$18,911	
13						
14						
15	Net Income	$8,911				
16						
17						
18						
19						
20						

Automating Data Formats with Named Styles

Now that you have spent some time working with style formats, you can probably visualize certain styles that you'll want to use often. For example, in an earlier exercise you created a useful format for the worksheet titles: bold and Dark-blue. It would be nice if you could create a special format that automatically set a range in the bold Dark-blue style.

Well, you can. 1-2-3's Style Name command lets you define up to eight separate custom formats. After you've defined one or more styles with Style Name, you can use the Style 1-8 commands to apply those styles to ranges you specify. In this exercise, you will first create a named-style format that displays the contents of a range in bold and Dark-blue, the style that you created for worksheet titles. Then you'll apply the style using the Style 1 command. (If you do not have a Worksheet window opened for CASHFLOW.WK3, open the file before you begin the exercise.)

1. Define the prototype with the format you want.

You define a named-style format by formatting a cell or range as prototype for the name style. That cell or range should have all of the style features you want for the named-style format—font, colors, borders, and so forth. Then you tell 1-2-3 to use the format of that cell (or range of cells) for a named style. Since you have already created a format for titles (bold font displayed in Dark-blue), you can use cell A:A1 as the prototype.

Highlight:	A:A1
Choose:	`Style   Name`

1-2-3 displays the Style Name dialog box which you use to create up to eight named styles. In the Range text box, 1-2-3 proposes A:A1 as the prototype, the range you pre-selected for the Style Name command. You have not created any named styles yet, so choose the first one in the list.

Select:	`1`	*to select the first named style*

Next, enter a name for the namedstyle. Call this style "Titles" and add a description that is more specific. Later, you'll see that the description is displayed in the title bar when the Styles 1-8 command is highlighted.

Type:	`Titles`	*in the Name: text box for style 1. Capitalization counts!*
Select:	*Style 1's Description: text box*	
Type:	`Bold Dark-blue for titles`	
Select:	`OK`	

Now, whenever you want to use the bold Dark-blue format for a range in the Cash Flow Forecast, you can do so simply by selecting Style 1.

2. Use the "Titles" named style.

Use the Style 1 command to apply the named style "Titles" to the titles in the product-specific worksheets of the application.

Highlight: B:A1..E:C1

Choose: Style   1

Figure 7-22:   Creating the Style 1 Format

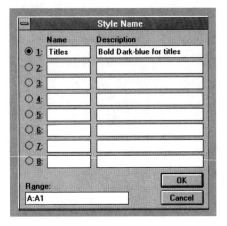

Figure 7-23:   Applying Style 1 Formatting to B:A1..E:C1

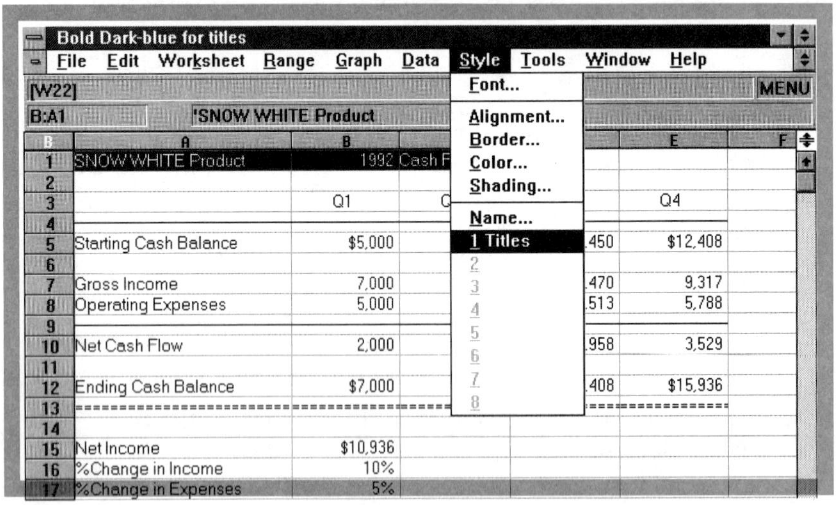

1-2-3 has added Style 1 formatting to the titles of the product-specific worksheets. Page through the worksheets of the application to verify that all titles are formatted in bold and Dark-blue, then return to the summary sheet.

■ *NOTE:*   Although 1-2-3 creates a named style by copying the format of a range you specify, the named-style format is not attached to that range. This means that a named style does not change automatically if you change the formatting of the range that served as the prototype for the named style. For example, if you change the style of A:A1 at this point, the format of B:A1..E:C1 does not change automatically.

Using Graphics for Ruled Lines

Up to now, you have used rows of text characters to create lines in Bob Gordon's Cash Flow Forecast application. In Chapter 5, you divided sections of the application by adding repeating hyphens (\-) to create single-ruled lines and repeating equal signs (\=) to create double-ruled lines. Now you will use the Style Border and the Style Color commands to separate spreadsheet sections and serve as "sub-totals" lines. When you have completed the exercise in this section, the Cash Flow Forecast will look like the one in Figure 7-24. (So you can better see the effect of the graphics, we've turned off the worksheet grid by clearing the "Grid lines" option of the Window Display Options command. You'll learn about this command later in this chapter.)

Figure 7-24:   The Cash Flow Forecast with Graphics Used to Separate Sections

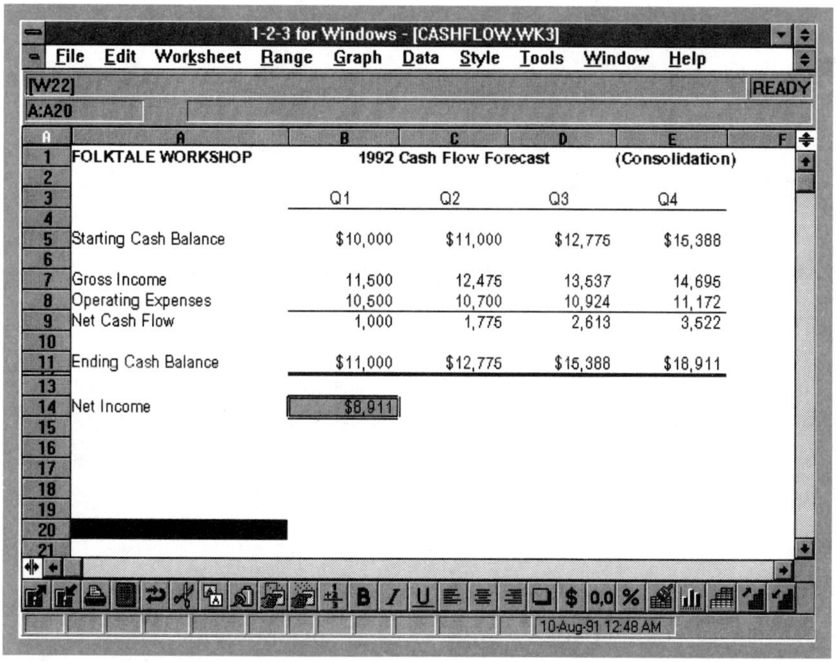

1. Delete row four, containing single-ruled lines.

   You won't be needing the rows of single-ruled lines anymore. Delete them with Worksheet Delete. (You'll deal with the double-ruled lines that you created using repeating equal signs (\=) differently and in a later step.) To delete the fourth row from all of the worksheets in the Cash Flow Forecast, you'll highlight the multi-sheet range A:A4..E:A4. (To delete rows from more than one worksheet, you need to highlight only one cell in the row on each sheet.)

   Highlight: A:A4..E:A4
   Choose: `Worksheet` `Delete`
   Select: `Row` `OK`

   Now, delete the eighth row.

   Highlight: A:A8..E:A8
   Choose: `Worksheet` `Delete`
   Select: `Row` `OK`

Figure 7-25: The Cash Flow Application with Rows of Single-Ruled Lines Removed

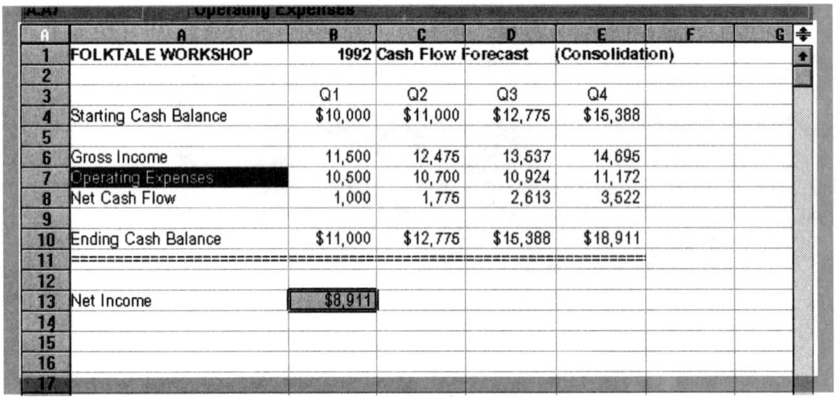

A	A	B	C	D	E	F	G
1	FOLKTALE WORKSHOP	1992 Cash Flow Forecast		(Consolidation)			
2							
3		Q1	Q2	Q3	Q4		
4	Starting Cash Balance	$10,000	$11,000	$12,775	$15,388		
5							
6	Gross Income	11,500	12,475	13,537	14,695		
7	Operating Expenses	10,500	10,700	10,924	11,172		
8	Net Cash Flow	1,000	1,775	2,613	3,522		
9							
10	Ending Cash Balance	$11,000	$12,775	$15,388	$18,911		
11	=========================	===========	===========	===========	===========		
12							
13	Net Income	$8,911					
14							
15							
16							
17							

2. Underline the ranges.

   In place of the single-ruled lines you just deleted, you'll use underlines to indicate subtotals. Again, you must highlight a multi-sheet range. First, add underlines to the labels `Q1` through `Q4` in row three.

   Highlight: A:B3..E:E3
   Choose: `Style` `Border`
   Select: `Bottom` `OK`

   Then, add underlines to the operating expenses figures for the four quarters.

Highlight:	A:A7..E:E7
Choose:	Style Border
Select:	Bottom OK

Figure 7-26: **1-2-3 adds underlines to the worksheets.**

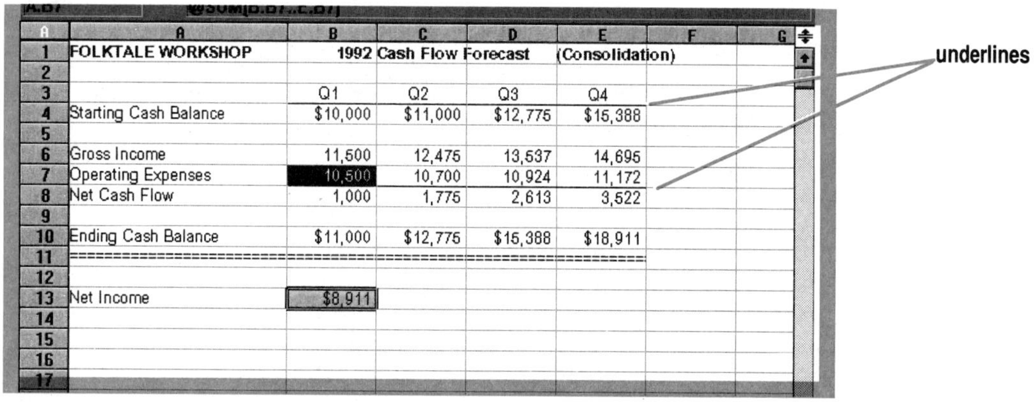

1-2-3 adds underlines to the ranges A:B3..E:E3 and A:B7..E:E7. Take a moment to page through the sheets of the application to look at the underlined ranges, then return to the summary sheet.

3. Erase the double-ruled lines.

In place of the double-ruled lines, you'll add a range of background color. First, erase the double-ruled lines from each of the worksheets:

Highlight:	A:A11..E:E11
Press:	DELETE *to erase the double-ruled lines*

4. Change the background color of the range.

Now, you'll change the background color of the range to Red:

Highlight:	A:B11..E:E11
Choose:	Style Color
Select:	Background Red OK

1-2-3 changes the background color of A:B11..E:E11 to Red. This thick Red bar separates the sections a little *too* well. (See Figure 7-27 on the following page.)

5. Make the separator bar thinner.

Figure 7-27: Now a thick Red bar separates worksheet sections.

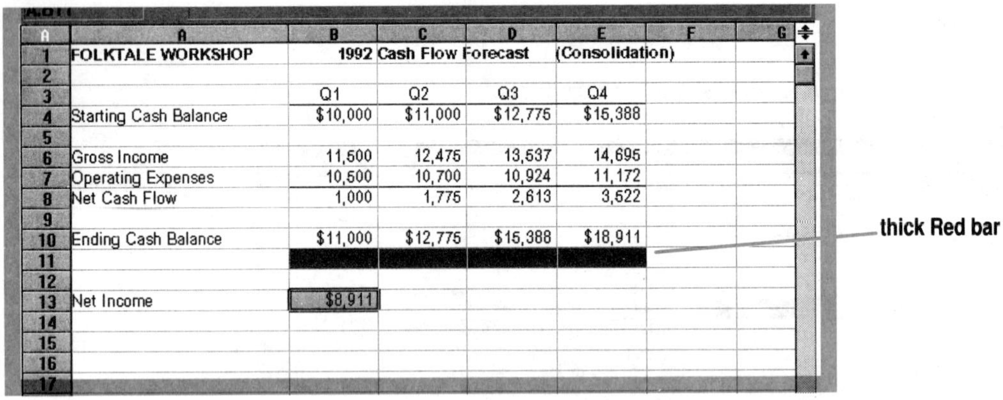

thick Red bar

You'll make the separator in row 11 thinner in all the worksheets by using Worksheet Row Height. First, you'll highlight a range that includes cells from row 11 on each of the worksheets (for example, A:B11..E:B11). Then you'll use the command to set the row heights to two points.

Highlight:	*any range that includes cells from row 11 on sheets A through E*
Choose:	`Worksheet  Row Height`
Type:	`2` *in the Set height text box*
Select:	`OK`

Figure 7-28: The thin Red bar is a good way to separate sections of the worksheet.

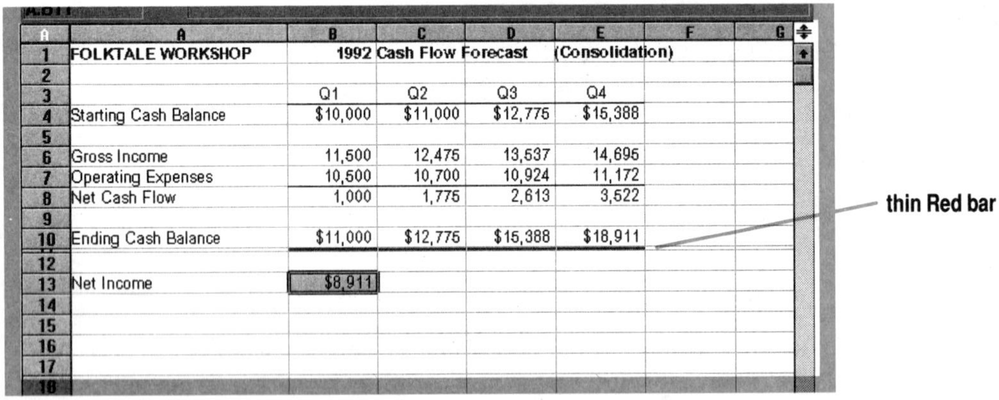

thin Red bar

1-2-3 reduces the height of row 11 to two points; the section separator in row 11 is displayed as a thin Red line.

6. Add a row to spread the data out.

The worksheet looks better with the underlines and the Red row as separators. Adding a row to each of the worksheets under the labels **Q1** through **Q4** might give the data a little more open feel. First, you'll highlight a range that includes cells from row 4 on each of the worksheets (for example, A:A4..E:A4). Then, you'll use the command to add the rows.

Highlight:	*any range that includes cells from row 4 on sheets A through E*
Choose:	Worksheet Insert
Select:	Row OK

Figure 7-29:   1-2-3 inserts a row.

A	B	C	D	E	F	G
1 FOLKTALE WORKSHOP	1992 Cash Flow Forecast		(Consolidation)			
2						
3	Q1	Q2	Q3	Q4		
4						
5 Starting Cash Balance	$10,000	$11,000	$12,775	$15,388		
6						
7 Gross Income	11,500	12,475	13,537	14,695		
8 Operating Expenses	10,500	10,700	10,924	11,172		
9 Net Cash Flow	1,000	1,775	2,613	3,522		
10						
11 Ending Cash Balance	$11,000	$12,775	$15,388	$18,911		
13						
14 Net Income	$8,911					
15						
16						
17						

7. Save the Cash Flow Forecast.

Congratulations! You've done some good work changing the Cash Flow Forecast to use graphics rather than characters as section separators; now save the file.

Selecting and Replacing Fonts

As you've seen in earlier exercises in this chapter, you can use the Style Font command to change the font of a specified range. While doing those exercises, you may have noticed that Style Font lets you select from eight different fonts. These are the eight fonts that make up the *current font set*. When you install 1-2-3, the following eight fonts make up the current font set: Arial MT 10, 14, and 24; Times 6, 8, 10, and 12; and Symbol 12. Choose Style Font now to look at the current font set, then cancel the command and return 1-2-3 to READY mode.

You are not limited to the fonts listed in the Style Font dialog box. You can use the Style Font command's "Replace" option to replace one or more of the fonts in the current font set with any of the fonts that are available under Windows. And since there are lots of ways to install fonts under Windows, there may be *many* fonts available. For example, when you installed the Adobe Type Manager supplied with 1-2-3, you also installed the ATM fonts. You may also have installed additional fonts using the "Fonts" option of the Windows Control

Panel. (Different applications provide the .FON files that you install this way.) Or you might have received additional fonts with your printer or printer driver. For example, the driver for the Hewlett-Packard LaserJet III comes with a number of fonts for that printer.

Any of these fonts are available to you under 1-2-3. Before you can use them, however, you must replace one or more fonts in the current font set with the fonts that you want to use. To do this, you will use the procedures described in this section. After you have done that, if you think your modified current font set will be useful for other worksheets, you can save it as a named font set. You can even make it the default current font set, so that any time you use File New to open a Worksheet window, it will use the new font set.

In this section, you'll use the "Replace" option in the Style Font dialog box to replace default fonts with those that you installed with the Adobe Type Manager. You'll use Bob's Cash Flow Forecast, which should be displayed now in a Worksheet window entitled CASHFLOW.WK3. (If you do not have a Worksheet window open for the Cash Flow Forecast, open one now, using File Open. If you do have a Worksheet window open for the Cash Flow Forecast, but it is not current, make it the current window by choosing Window and selecting the CASHFLOW.WK3, Worksheet window.)

Figure 7-30: The Current Font Set

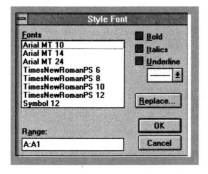

1. Replace Arial MT 10 with TimesNewRomanPS 10.

Choose Style Font again.

Move to:	cell A:A1
Choose:	Style Font

1-2-3 opens the Style Font dialog box. The first font shown in the "Fonts" list is Arial MT 10. This first font is special; it's the default font that 1-2-3 uses to format data you enter into a cell. (As you'll see in a later step, the entire Cash Flow Forecast is, at this time, formatted in Arial MT 10.)

■ **NOTE:** In general, 1-2-3 describes the font of the current cell in the format line of the 1-2-3 control panel. When the current cell is formatted in the font listed first in the Style Font dialog box, however, 1-2-3 does not indicate that in the format line.

Let's see what happens if we use the "Replace" option of the Style Format dialog box to change the first font in the "Fonts" list to something else, such as Courier 10.

Select: Replace

Arial MT 10   *from the Current Fonts list box*

Courier   *from the Available Fonts list box*

10   *from the Size list box*

Replace

Figure 7-31:   Replacing Arial MT 10 with Courier 10

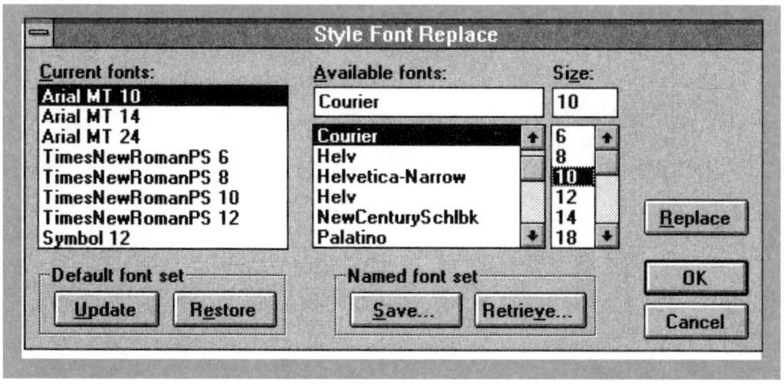

Look at the underlying Worksheet window. (You might want to move the Style Font Replace dialog box to one side for a better view by dragging the dialog box's title bar.) 1-2-3 re-displays the worksheet, and every cell that was Arial MT 10 (and that's every cell in Bob's worksheet!) is now displayed in Courier 10. Close the Styles dialog boxes for a better look.

Select: OK   *two times, to return to 1-2-3 READY mode*

Figure 7-32:   The Cash Flow Forecast in Courier 10

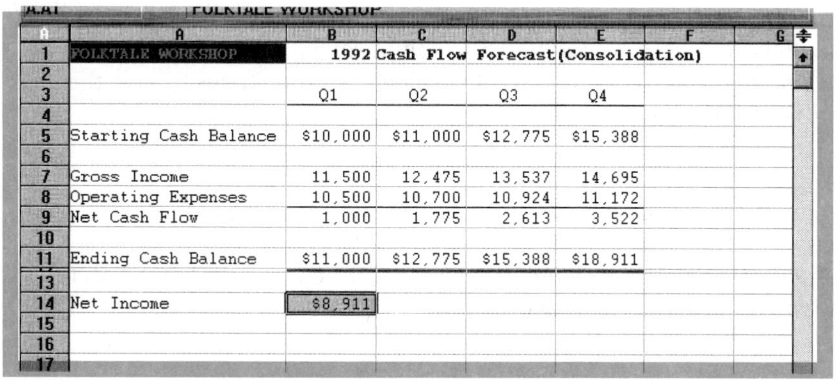

The worksheet looks pretty good in the new Courier font, but let's change it back to the more elegant Arial MT 10.

2. Replace Courier 10 with Arial MT 10.

You'll once again use the "Replace" option of the Style Font command to change the first-listed current font from Courier 10 to Arial MT 10.

Choose:	`Style` `Font`
Select:	`Replace`
	`Courier` *from the Current Fonts list box*
	`Arial MT` *from the Available Fonts list box*
	`10` *from the Size list box*
	`OK` *twice, to return to 1-2-3 READY mode*

Figure 7-33:   Replacing Courier 10 with Arial MT 10

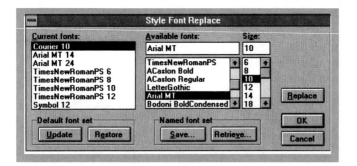

1-2-3 re-displays the worksheet, this time changing all cells back to Arial MT 10. Since you didn't actually make any changes to the Cash Flow Forecast in this exercise, you don't need to save it.

A Note on Saving and Retrieving Named Font Sets   If you found that you liked the set of fonts that includes Courier 10, you could have saved it as a named font set. To do so you choose Style Fonts, and select the "Replace" option. Then, select "Save" to bring up the Style Fonts Replace Save dialog box. Enter the name of the file in which to save the named font set. (The default extension for files of this type is `.AF3.`) Finally, select OK three times to save the named font set and return to READY mode.

Aligning Labels over Columns

1-2-3 Style Alignment commands can align a label within a cell or within a range. Aligning a label within a cell is pretty straightforward; you've done it already by inserting label prefixes. Precede the label with `'` to left-align it, `^` to center-align it, and `"` to align the label with the right side of the cell. When you use the "Align over columns" option of the command, however, Style Alignment becomes quite an interesting tool. In this section, you'll use Style Alignment to align some labels in Bob's Business Contacts database table.

1. Open CONTACTS.WK3.

Use the "File Open" icon to open CONTACTS.WK3. The "File Open" icon looks like this:

Click on: *the File Open icon*

Select: `CONTACTS.WK3  OK`

1-2-3 opens a Worksheet window for CONTACTS.WK3 and makes it active. Move to the Business Contacts database table.

Move to: B:A3

Figure 7-34: The Business Contacts Database Table

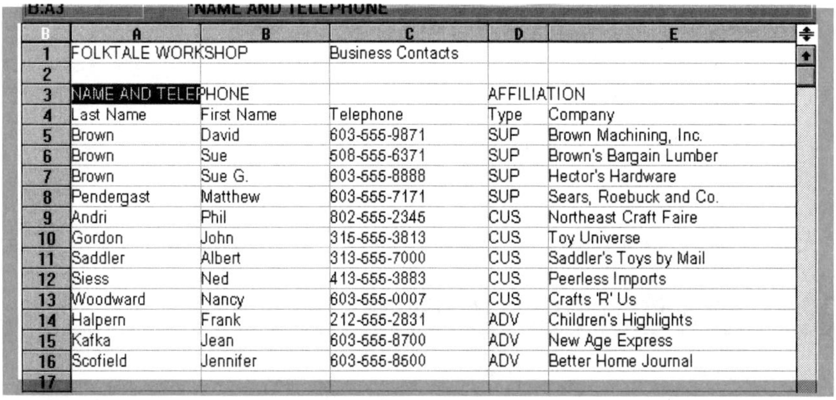

B:A3	'NAME AND TELEPHONE				
B	A	B	C	D	E
1	FOLKTALE WORKSHOP		Business Contacts		
2					
3	NAME AND TELEPHONE			AFFILIATION	
4	Last Name	First Name	Telephone	Type	Company
5	Brown	David	603-555-9871	SUP	Brown Machining, Inc.
6	Brown	Sue	508-555-6371	SUP	Brown's Bargain Lumber
7	Brown	Sue G.	603-555-8888	SUP	Hector's Hardware
8	Pendergast	Matthew	603-555-7171	SUP	Sears, Roebuck and Co.
9	Andri	Phil	802-555-2345	CUS	Northeast Craft Faire
10	Gordon	John	315-555-3813	CUS	Toy Universe
11	Saddler	Albert	313-555-7000	CUS	Saddler's Toys by Mail
12	Siess	Ned	413-555-3883	CUS	Peerless Imports
13	Woodward	Nancy	603-555-0007	CUS	Crafts 'R' Us
14	Halpern	Frank	212-555-2831	ADV	Children's Highlights
15	Kafka	Jean	603-555-8700	ADV	New Age Express
16	Scofield	Jennifer	603-555-8500	ADV	Better Home Journal
17					

2. Center the label `NAME AND TELEPHONE.`

The label `NAME AND TELEPHONE` is a long label (it extends beyond the boundaries of the cell that contains it), and it is aligned flush left (notice the `'` label prefix in the edit line). For the first exercise using Style Alignment, let's center the label over columns A, B, and C:

Highlight: B:A3..B:C3

Choose: `Style   Alignment`

Select: `Center`

                  `Align over columns`   *and check the check-box*

                  `OK`

Figure 7-35: Aligning the Label NAME AND TELEPHONE

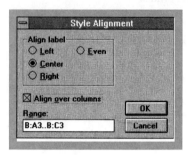

1-2-3 aligns the label **NAME AND TELEPHONE** within the range of B:A3..B:C3. This effectively aligns the label over columns A, B, and C—the columns you labeled **Last Name**, **First Name**, and **Telephone**.

3. Stretch the label **NAME AND TELEPHONE**.

The "even" option of the Style Alignment command stretches a label to fit within a specified range. Stretching the label this way allows it to cover a number of columns without the need for leader or trailer characters, such as hyphens. This time, stretch **NAME AND TELEPHONE** using Style Alignment's "even" option. ("Even" is not displayed until you check "Align over columns".)

Choose: **Style   Alignment**

Select: **Align over columns**   *and check the check-box*

                    Even OK

Figure 7-36: The Label NAME AND TELEPHONE Stretched Over Columns A, B, and C

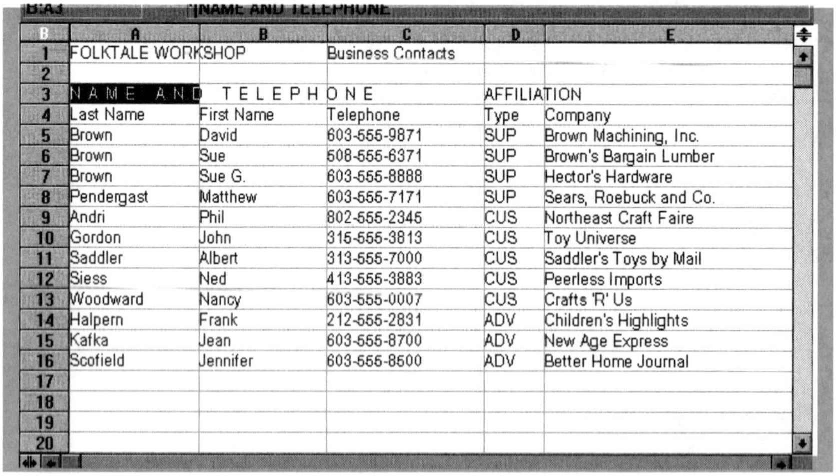

B:A3		NAME AND TELEPHONE		
B	A	B	C	D	E
1	FOLKTALE WORKSHOP		Business Contacts		
2					
3	N A M E A N D T E L E P H O N E			AFFILIATION	
4	Last Name	First Name	Telephone	Type	Company
5	Brown	David	603-555-9871	SUP	Brown Machining, Inc.
6	Brown	Sue	508-555-6371	SUP	Brown's Bargain Lumber
7	Brown	Sue G.	603-555-8888	SUP	Hector's Hardware
8	Pendergast	Matthew	603-555-7171	SUP	Sears, Roebuck and Co.
9	Andri	Phil	802-555-2345	CUS	Northeast Craft Faire
10	Gordon	John	315-555-3813	CUS	Toy Universe
11	Saddler	Albert	313-555-7000	CUS	Saddler's Toys by Mail
12	Siess	Ned	413-555-3883	CUS	Peerless Imports
13	Woodward	Nancy	603-555-0007	CUS	Crafts 'R' Us
14	Halpern	Frank	212-555-2831	ADV	Children's Highlights
15	Kafka	Jean	603-555-8700	ADV	New Age Express
16	Scofield	Jennifer	603-555-8500	ADV	Better Home Journal
17					
18					
19					
20					

Now, 1-2-3 stretches the label **NAME AND TELEPHONE** to fit the range of B:A3..B:C3. You can see exactly which columns contain name and telephone number data.

When used with other Style commands (such as Style Color, Style Font, and Style Border), the Style Alignment command can be very effective in setting off labels that identify columns of data. Take some time now to experiment with the styles of labels in row 3 of the Business Contacts database table. Try different fonts and colors using the Style Font and Style Color commands. Add an underline using Style Border and see if that will give you an effect you like. Be creative and find styles you like. One thing to keep in mind: You don't want your column labels to overpower the database table label FOLKTALE WORKSHOP Business Contacts. When you're done, close and save the **CONTACTS.WK3** file:

Choose: `File Close`

Select: `CONTACTS.WK3`
                `Yes` *to save the file*

More on Worksheet Formatting

The formatting commands you have used so far change selected parts of the worksheet. The Window Display Options commands, which you'll use in this section, change more global settings in the worksheet. For example, you use the Window Display Options commands to view more or less of the worksheet on the screen; remove the grid from the display; and change the display mode from graphics to draft, and from color to monochrome. In this exercise, you'll use Window Display Options to remove the grid from the display, and to view more of the Cash Flow Forecast worksheet in one screen. You'll also change the background color of the display.

■ *NOTE:*   For the exercises below, you'll work with the Cash Flow Forecast in a maximized Worksheet window.

1. Customize the display grid.

First, remove the grid from the display:

Choose: `Window    Display Options`

Select: `Grid Lines` *and clear the check-box*

                `OK`

1-2-3 removes the grid from the display. The worksheet looks cleaner without the grid, but you may find the worksheet more difficult to read. If that's the case, restore the grid lines now:

Choose: `Window    Display Options`

Select: `Grid Lines` *and check the check-box*

                `OK`

1-2-3 adds the grid to the display.

Figure 7-37:   Removing the Grid from the Cash Flow Forecast

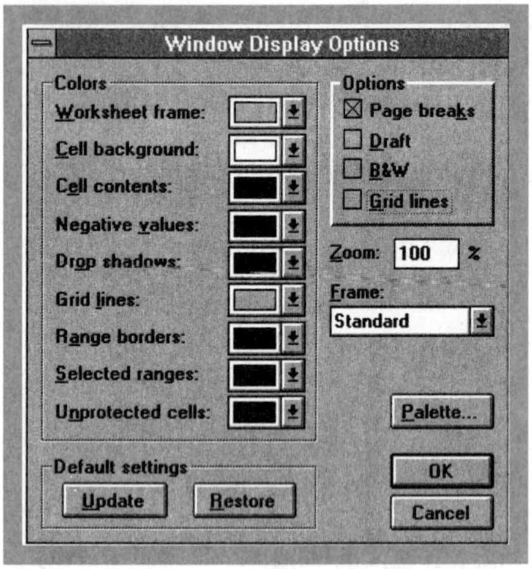

- **NOTE:**   You can also change the color of the grid. To do this, choose Window Display Options again; check the "Grid Lines" option in the "Options" section of the dialog box; and specify the grid color in the "Grid Lines:" option in the "Colors" section of the dialog box. Then, select OK.

2. Increase the displayed worksheet range.

   The Window Display Options "Zoom" option lets you increase the number of cells you can view on the screen. Try reducing the size of the cells to 75% of their normal size. (This will allow you to see approximately one-third more cells on the screen).

Choose:	Window Display Options
Select:	Zoom
Type:	75 *in the text box*
Select:	OK

   1-2-3 reduces the display size of cells so that each is 75% of its normal size. Although you can see that zooming is a good way to see more worksheet data, it's not really necessary for the Cash Flow Forecast at this point. Restore the display to its normal size.

- **NOTE:**   Using Zoom to reduce or enlarge the cell display size does not affect the actual font size used in the cells. You must use Style Font to change the font size.

3. Restore the normal cell size.

   Return the cell display to normal by setting Zoom to 100%:

Choose:	Window Display Options

Figure 7-38: The Display Zoomed to 75% of Full Size

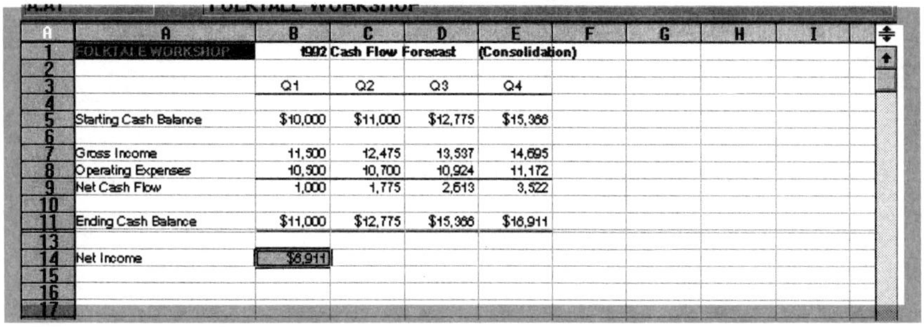

Select:	Zoom	
Type:	100	*to restore the display to normal*
Select:	OK	

4. Change the background display color.

Now, try changing the background color of the display to a color you like. You'll use the options in the "Colors" section of the Window Display Options dialog box to change the colors. You use these "Colors" options to change the colors of many of the components of the display, including the color of the contents of all cells, the color of the worksheet frame, the color of the grid, and the color of the cell pointer. For now, though, change the "Cell background" to a color you like.

Choose:	Window Display Options
Select:	Cell background
	a color you like
	OK

1-2-3 changes the screen display so that the background color becomes the color you selected.

5. Update the default display settings.

Your worksheet now has a different color background and uses the grid or not, depending on your preference. (You may also have changed the grid color.) Update the default display settings to include the new background color and grid settings:

Choose:	Window Display Options
Select:	Update *to update the default setting*
	OK

1-2-3 updates the default window display settings. Now, each time you load 1-2-3, it displays worksheets with the background color you selected, and the grid the way you like it.

■ *NOTE:* When you update the default Window Display Options settings, you change the way 1-2-3 displays all files. That means, for example, that had you updated the default display settings with the display zoomed to 75%, every worksheet you opened would be displayed with the zoomed cell display.

6. Save CASHFLOW.WK3.

Congratulations! You have finished formatting the Cash Flow Forecast worksheet. Now, close and save the file:

| **Choose:** | File   Close |
| **Select:** | Yes   *to save the file* |

Formatting Text

Up to now, you have looked into ways to change the styles of ranges of cells and the look of the Worksheet window. 1-2-3 gives you another, somewhat hidden, way to affect the formatting of the worksheet: the formatting of text. The Styles and Window Display Options menus give you control over some text formatting features. For most of your text formatting, however, you will use the Lotus Classic Wysiwyg menu.

Introducing the Lotus Classic Wysiwyg Menu

In 1-2-3 Releases 2.3 and 3.1 for DOS, you can access many of the commands discussed in this chapter through an add-in called Wysiwyg. Wysiwyg is an acronym for "What You See Is What You Get"; it describes the idea that, with Wysiwyg, the worksheet displayed on the screen has the same look (fonts, size, shading, italics, bold, and so forth) as the printed worksheet (or as nearly as your printer can create that look).

■ *NOTE:* An "add-in" is a program that works closely with 1-2-3, but is not a part of the product. See Chapter 12 for further discussion of add-ins.

/If you've used the Wysiwyg add-in in releases 2.3 or 3.1, you might like the Lotus Classic Wysiwyg menu included in 1-2-3/W. Even if you've never used the Wysiwyg add-in, however, you'll find that a few of the commands available on this menu (and *not* on the regular 1-2-3/W menus) are worth knowing about.

You display the Lotus Classic Wysiwyg menu by pressing the colon key (:). You navigate the menu by using the keyboard. The Lotus Classic Wysiwyg menu does not respond to the mouse for selecting commands; you can, however, use the mouse to select cells and ranges of cells in the worksheet. Open the Lotus Classic Wysiwyg menu now by pressing the colon key (:).

Figure 7-39:   The Lotus Classic Wysiwyg Menu

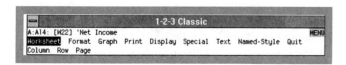

Select Wysiwyg commands either by using the keyboard Left and Right arrows, or by typing the first letter of the command. Look through the menus; you'll see many of the commands that you worked with in this chapter. In the next section, you'll work with the Lotus Classic Wysiwyg :Text commands.

Using Lotus Classic Wysiwyg's :Text Commands

The Lotus Classic Wysiwyg menu allows you to get into a 1-2-3 mode known as Text mode that is not accessible from the main menu. *Text mode* and the text mode commands allow you to specify a range in which you can automatically enter justified text. In a way, the Lotus Classic Wysiwyg :Text commands give you the equivalent of a mini-word processor in 1-2-3. Although they aren't really applicable to the work you've done with Bob Gordon, you will find them useful in other applications.

■ *NOTE:*   For this section, you'll work with the blank Untitled worksheet currently displayed. At the end of the section, you'll discard it. If the Untitled worksheet is not displayed because you have other worksheet files open, save and close those files now.

1. Create a text range.

You can use the Lotus Classic Wysiwyg menu's Text Edit command whenever you want to enter a series of labels, or when you want to create a paragraph-like range of text. You'll select the range you want to use, press colon to bring up the Lotus Classic Wysiwyg menu, then choose Text Edit.

Highlight:	A:A1..A:D10
Press:	`:` **(colon)** *to bring up the Lotus Classic Wysiwyg menu*
Select:	`Text` `Edit`
Press:	`↵`

Figure 7-40: 1-2-3 in Lotus Classic Wysiwyg's Text Mode

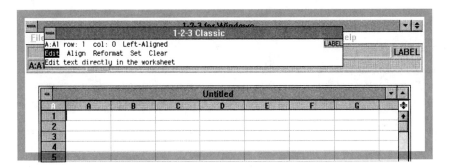

1-2-3 enters Text mode. Although you may not immediately see the difference in the display, a closer look shows you several changes. First, notice that the mode indicator has changed to LABEL, and the cell pointer has changed shape, so that it now resembles a solid bar (|). Finally, you'll see that the first line in the Lotus Classic Wysiwyg control panel indicates the row and column numbers as they relate to the total size of the text range.

When you begin to enter text, you'll find that the row and column numbers in the Lotus Classic Wysiwyg control panel change by character, and not by cell as they do in READY mode. You'll also find that you cannot move the cell pointer beyond the boundaries you established as the text range.

2. Enter text.

Now, enter text in the text range. Type the text exactly as it is shown. Don't worry about reaching the end of a line. 1-2-3 will adjust the text in the range automatically.

Type: `When you enter text in Lotus Classic Wysiwyg's Text mode,` `1-2-3 automatically adjusts the line lengths (and the word` `wrapping) so that all text in the text range is aligned.`

Figure 7-41:   **Entering text in Lotus Classic Wysiwyg Text Mode**

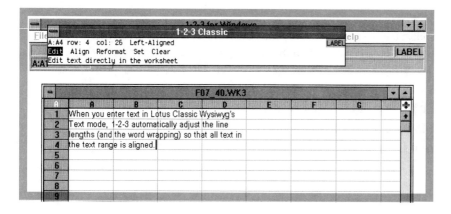

If you make a mistake while you are entering text (or even when you are finished), you can use the regular 1-2-3 cursor-movement keys to move around the text range.

3. Format the text in the range.

When 1-2-3 is in Text mode, you can use F3 (Text Format) to format text in the range so that it is displayed in a different typeface, font, or color. When you format existing text in the range, 1-2-3 considers each line of text as a separate entity. For example, to format the first line of the range so that it is in italics:

Press: `HOME`   *twice,*   *to move to the first character in the first line*

               `F3`

        1-2-3 displays the Text Format menu.

Choose: `Italics`

Figure 7-42:   The first line of text changes to italics.

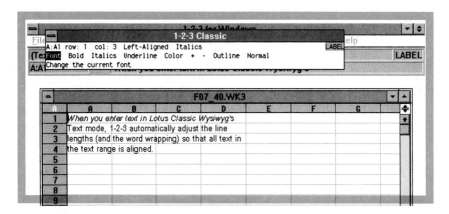

Notice that the first line of text changes to italics, but the balance of the text does not.

4. Experiment with formatting text in the range.

Continue to experiment with formatting the text in the range. For example, try moving the cursor to the middle of a line of text. Then, select a new font for the text. What happens to the line of text? Or, move to the end of the text, press F3, and select the Underline format. Then, type some new text. Only the new text is displayed in underline format.

When you are finished experimenting with the text range, leave Lotus Classic Wysiwyg Text mode.

5. Leave Lotus Classic Wysiwyg Text mode.

Press Escape when you are finished to leave Text mode and return 1-2-3 to READY mode.

Press: ESC

The text remains formatted and aligned correctly in the cells. 1-2-3 retains the Wysiwyg {Text} attribute for each cell that you included in the text range. If you think you will be editing the text again, you should leave the {Text} attributes. Or, if you need to, you can clear the {Text} attribute without destroying the format.

6. Clear the {Text} format.

To clear the {Text} format from a range of cells, select the range to be cleared and select :Text Clear.

Highlight: A:A1..A:D10

Press: : (colon)   *to enter the Lotus Classic Wysiwyg menu*

Choose: Text   Clear

The text remains formatted and aligned correctly in the cells but the {Text} attribute is no longer there. If you want to edit the text as a whole again, highlight the text range and again choose :Edit Text.

7. Remove the scratch worksheet.

Before you leave this chapter, you should take a minute to clean up the display. The worksheet you used to enter text has no particular value, so you can remove it from memory.

Choose: `File`   `Close`

Select   `No`

1-2-3 and the Adobe Type Manager

The Adobe Type Manager is a Windows program that manages the way text is displayed in Windows applications. The main goal of the Adobe Type Manager is to make text displayed on the screen match text that is printed as closely as possible. In addition, the Adobe Type Manager allows you to add fonts to those included by default in Windows.

1-2-3/W includes one diskette associated with the Adobe Type Manager: the ATM Installation Disk. This disk includes INSTALL.EXE, which you use to install the ATM; the Adobe Type Manager itself; the ATM Control program; and a wide variety of fonts.

Once you have installed and turned on the ATM, it controls the way text is displayed and printed from any Windows application including, of course, 1-2-3/W. Once you have installed the fonts included on the ATM Fonts Disk, those fonts are available to any Windows application. Table 7-1 lists and shows samples of the fonts available by default with Windows, and those that are provided on the ATM Fonts Disk.

■ *NOTE:*   Table 7-2 shows fonts as they are printed on a Hewlett-Packard LaserJet IIIP. The same fonts may look different on your printer.

The remainder of this section describes the procedure for installing the Adobe Type Manager, installing the fonts included with 1-2-3/W, and turning on the Adobe Type Manager. If you have not already done so, use the procedure described in this section to install and turn on the Adobe Type Manager (ATM) and the ATM fonts provided with 1-2-3/W. If you have already installed ATM and the fonts, but have not turned it on, use the procedure described in "Turning on the Adobe Type Manager" later in this chapter to do so.

Installing the Adobe Type Manager

In the steps that follow, you're going to close 1-2-3, install the Adobe Type Manager, install the ATM fonts, and then restart 1-2-3. Before you do, however, take a quick look at the fonts that are available now—before installing ATM. When you get back to 1-2-3 after installing ATM, you'll look again at the font selection. You'll be surprised to see how many new fonts the Adobe Type Manager provides.

Table 7-1: Default Windows Fonts and ATM Fonts

Font Name	Example
Windows Fonts:	
Courier	abcdefABCDEF
Helv	abcdefABCDEF
Line Printer	abcdefABCDEF
Modern	abcdefABCDEF
Roman	abcdefABCDEF
Script	abcdefABCDEF
Symbol	αβχδεφΑΒΧΔΕΦ
Adobe Type Manager Fonts:	
Arial MT	abcdefABCDEF
Bodoni BoldCondensed	abcdefABCDEF
BrushScript	abcdefABCDEF
Courier	. abcdefABCDEF
DomCasual	abcdefABCDEF
Letter Gothic	abcdefABCDEF
LinePrinter	abcdefABCDEF
NewsGothic	abcdefABCDEF
Perpetua	abcdefABCDEF
TimesNewRomanPS	abcdefABCDEF

Look at the fonts that are available in 1-2-3 without the Adobe Type Manager installed:

Choose: Style   Font
Select: Replace

1-2-3 displays the Style Fonts Replace dialog box; the Available Fonts list box includes all fonts currently available. Scroll through the list to get a feel for the fonts that are available without the Adobe Type Manager installed. Now you'll install the Adobe Type Manager and the fonts supplied with 1-2-3.

1. Close 1-2-3 and switch to the Windows Program Manager.

Now, close 1-2-3.

Select:	Cancel	*two times, to close the Style Font Replace dialog box and the Style Font dialog box*
Press:	ALT+F4	*to close 1-2-3.*
Select:	Yes	*to save any files currently open*

Windows switches to the Windows Program Manager or—if the Program Manager has been minimized—to the Windows desktop. If Windows *does* switch you to the desktop, restore the Program Manager by clicking the Program Manager icon and selecting Restore, or by simply double-clicking on the Program Manager icon.

2. Install the Adobe Type Manager.

Insert the Adobe Type Manager Program Disk (either 5.25" or 3.5") into drive A. Use the Program Manager's File Run command to run the INSTALL.EXE program on the diskette:

Choose:	File Run
Type:	a:install
Select:	OK

Figure 7-43: ATM Installer

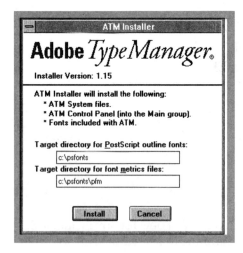

The ATM installation program executes. You can change the directories for the outline fonts and the metric files if you want, then select Install

Figure 7-44: Installing the ATM

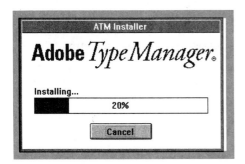

The installation program begins installing the ATM. When the installation is complete, you'll restart Windows.

3. Exit Windows, then restart it.

The ATM control program displays a message box indicating that you must restart Windows before the changes that you made to the Adobe Type Manager will take effect.

Press:	`ALT+F4`	*or choose File Exit to exit Windows*
Select:	`Yes`	*to save changes*
Type:	`win`	*from the DOS prompt, to restart Windows*

Windows starts, this time displaying the Adobe Type Manager icon in the lower left of the screen. (If the Adobe Type Manager is installed, but not turned on, the Adobe Type Manager icon has a slash through it.)

4. Restart 1-2-3 by double-clicking on the 1-2-3 for Windows icon.

5. Look at the fonts that are available now that you have installed and turned on Adobe Type Manager, and installed the ATM fonts provided with 1-2-3.

| **Choose:** | `Style`   `Font` |
| **Select:** | `Replace` |

1-2-3 displays the Style Fonts Replace dialog box. Scroll through the list box. Notice that now, after installing the Adobe Type Manager, there are many more fonts to choose from.

Turning on the Adobe Type Manager

If you have installed the Adobe Type Manager (ATM), but it is not turned on, Windows displays the ATM icon with a slash through it when you start Windows. In that case, use the following procedure to turn on ATM:

1. Close 1-2-3.

Press: `ALT+F4`   *or choose File Exit to close 1-2-3.*

Select: `Yes`   *to save any files currently open*

Windows switches to the Windows Program Manager, or, if you had previously minimized the Program Manager, to the Windows desktop. If the Program Manager *is* minimized, restore it by double-clicking on the Program Manager icon, or clicking on the icon and selecting Restore.

2. From the Windows Program Manager, run the ATM Control program.

Double click: *the ATM Control Panel icon*

Select: `On`   *from the main Adobe Type Manager dialog box*

                     `Exit`

3. Exit and restart Windows.

The ATM control program displays a message box indicating that you must restart Windows for the changes that you made to the Adobe Type Manager to take effect.

Press: `ALT+F4`   *to exit Windows*

Select: `Yes`   *to save the changes*

Type: `win`   *from the DOS prompt, to restart Windows*

Windows starts, this time displaying the Adobe Type Manager icon without the slash in the lower left of the screen.

4. Restart 1-2-3 by double-clicking on the 1-2-3 for Windows icon.

Formatting Tips, Techniques, and Gotchas

This section describes tips and techniques that apply to the Style and Window Display Options commands. It suggests some additional commands available to you beyond those covered in the exercises in this chapter, and encourages you to continue to explore the features available through the Style and Window Display Options menus.

Font Substitution

In most cases, the fonts and formatting you see on the screen very closely resemble the way things will look when you print them. In a few cases, however, your printer may not be able to replicate the fonts you are displaying (or vice versa). If this is the case, 1-2-3 uses the font closest to the one you selected. For example, if your printer cannot print the Arial MT 10 point font, it will print the next closest font available (say, for example, some other sans serif font, such as Modern in 10-point). More information on fonts used in printing can be found in Chapter 9.

Using Draft Display Mode

You can use 1-2-3 in either of two screen display modes, graphic or draft. You select the screen display mode using the Window Display Options menu Drafts option. In *graphic mode*, the screen display closely resembles how the worksheet will be printed. In graphic mode, you also have a choice between displaying your data in color or in a monochrome display. Graphic mode in color is the default screen display mode.

When you are in *draft mode*, 1-2-3 does not display style formats such as bold and italic. So that you can still determine the formatting of the current cell, the style formats are displayed on 1-2-3's format line . You can add style formats in draft mode, but 1-2-3 will not display them. When you print in draft mode, the worksheet is printed exactly like it is in graphic mode.

In draft mode, 1-2-3 can redisplay a screen much faster than in graphic mode. This makes draft mode particularly useful if a worksheet has lots of different style formats or graphs, and it seems slow to redisplay. If your worksheet is slow to redisplay, try switching to draft mode.

Using Other Window Display Options Commands

Although you did not use them in this chapter, you probably noticed several other features available through Window Display Options. Some of the more useful ones include the following:

- *Page Breaks.* You use this command to set page breaks for printing. It is discussed in more detail in Chapter 9.
- *Frame.* This setting determines what information is displayed in the worksheet frame. The default frame shows rows and columns. When you're laying out a worksheet for printing, you might find it useful to have the frame display characters or picas. Before showing a worksheet to others, removing the frame altogether can make for a more elegant presentation.
- *Palette.* The 1-2-3 palette gives you 256 colors from which you can choose any eight for your worksheet. Refer to 1-2-3 for Windows Help for additional information on the palette.

Using Other Styles Options

There are a number of Style options that you did not use in this chapter. It is important to remember, however, that to use each option, you must follow the same procedures you followed when you added an outline or color to a range.

Also, you will find it easiest to format cell entries if you follow some sort of logical order. You might find that it is easiest to work from the inside out. In other words, if you want to format a range with a bold italic font and add a border and shading to the range, specify the bold italic font first, then the shading, and finally the border. This will make it easier for you to see the effect the additional formatting has on what is already there.

Importing Formats

When you save a file that contains formatting, 1-2-3 also creates a separate file, called a *format file*, that contains the format settings. 1-2-3 links the format file to the worksheet file, so that each time you open the worksheet, 1-2-3 can also open the format file. For example, when you saved the Cash Flow Forecast worksheet in the exercises in this chapter, 1-2-3 also created the format file CASHFLOW.FM3.

You can use the File Import From Styles command to copy all the formats from one format file into the format file for the current worksheet. This is useful when you have two or more worksheet files that are identical in setup. For example, if you have five worksheet files that each contain the sales figures for one retail store, you can format one file and then import the settings from that format file into the other four files.

Remember, though, that most formats are specific to ranges in a worksheet. So, if you plan to import a format from another worksheet that is not identical in setup to the one you are working on, be sure you know where those formats will end up.

Also, remember to move or copy format files when you move or copy worksheet files.

At a Glance

In this chapter, you've learned basic skills and concepts for working with style formats, and you've learned to change the display characteristics of the window, including the following:

Task	How To Do It:
Setting row height	Choose Worksheet Row Height and type in the new height for the row. Or move the mouse to the row indicator in the worksheet frame, and drag the row separator up or down.
Changing the font in a range	Choose Style Font and select a font.
Changing cell contents to italic, bold, or underlined	Choose Style Font and select bold, italics, or underline. Or click on the "Bold"," Italics", or "Underline" icons.
Changing cell contents (or cell background) color	Choose Style Color and select the color.
Adding lines or boxes around a range	Choose Style Border and select the type of border, or use the "Drop Shadow" icon.
Adding shading to a range	Choose Style Shading and select the density of shading.
Viewing a larger/smaller portion of the worksheet	Choose Window Display Options and type in the percent value by which to reduce or enlarge the display.
Changing worksheet frame or grid	Choose Window Display Options and select the frame style, or select "Grid lines" to add or remove grid lines.
Copying style formats among cells and ranges	Choose Edit Quick Copy and select "Styles only".
Creating a named-style setting	Choose Style Name, select a number for the named style, and type in a name and a description for the style.
Using a named-style setting	Choose Style 1-8.

■ *NOTE:*   Unless otherwise noted, the descriptions of "How To Do It:" assume that you have highlighted the range you wish to operate on.

Chapter 8

Graphing Worksheets

A worksheet is a good way to manipulate information, and a database is a good way to organize and store it, but neither is necessarily the best way to present that information to other people. For "the big picture," visual aids are often necessary.

When you are looking at screens or pages of numbers, it's easy to get lost in the details and to overlook patterns that would be obvious if seen from a distance. By revealing the patterns in rows and columns of values, a graph can illustrate overall trends and projections more clearly and effectively than the numbers themselves.

1-2-3 lets you draw graphs directly from worksheet data. Each graph is dynamically connected to the data: Change a number and the graph can immediately reflect the change. As you create the graph, you view it in a special 1-2-3 window called a Graph window: You can add new data to the graph, change the scale, or change the graph type (line graph, bar graph, pie graph, and so forth) so it better expresses the points you want to make.

You can enhance a graph by adding text (such as descriptive notes), or graphic information (such as lines, arrows, or even freehand drawings).

You can add a graph to a range in a worksheet. Like graphs in the Graph window, graphs that you add to worksheets can be automatically updated to reflect changes in the underlying data. You print a graph simply by printing the worksheet range that contains the graph. (The printer must be capable of printing graphics.) To print the graph alone, you print only the range that contains the graph. To create a report, you can print one or more ranges that include the graph and other data in the worksheet. (You'll learn about printing graphs in Chapter 9.)

1-2-3 graphs are very flexible. There are seven different basic types of graphs, and there are many variations of shading, color, fonts, and other display elements. Graphs can be displayed horizontally or vertically, and they can be displayed with 3-D effects.

What You'll Learn

In this chapter, you are going to learn about the different kinds of graphs you can draw using 1-2-3. By the time you complete this chapter, you'll know how to perform the following tasks:

- **Create a worksheet table for a graph**

- **Change the graph type**

- **Graph in color**

- **Graph in black and white**

- Create a bar graph, pie chart, and line graph

- Label the x-axis

- Label the slices of a pie chart

- Specify a range of data to be graphed

- View a graph

- Add data range legends

- Add graph titles

- Add data labels

- Change the size of text in the graph

- Add grid lines

- Format the y-axis figures

- Clear current graph settings

- Delete unnecessary graphs

- Add a graph to the worksheet

- Add arrows, text, and other graphic elements

Before You Start

Before you begin the exercises in this chapter, start 1-2-3. Make sure that the cell pointer is in cell A:A1 of a new, maximized, blank worksheet file, and that 1-2-3 has been set up to save files in your 123BOOK directory.

As you work through this chapter, you are going to create graphs and charts using values in the CASHFLOW.WK3 and BUDGET1.WK3 worksheet files that you created earlier in this book. The graphs and charts will remain part of the worksheet files once you have saved them. (A disk containing the worksheets created in this book is also available from the authors.) As in previous chapters, stop at the end of a numbered step or just before the next section heading when you are tired or have something else to do. Be sure to save any modified worksheet files before you stop. If you have more than one active file, write down the names of the files in memory and the order in which they are stored. When you want to continue with the exercises, start up 1-2-3, read in the worksheet files you last used, in the same order they were in before you stopped, then pick up where you left off.

■ **NOTE:** The exercises assume that you have installed the Adobe Type Manager (ATM) and the ATM fonts that are included with 1-2-3, and that you turned on the Adobe Type Manager using the ATM Control Panel. If you have not installed or turned on the Adobe Type Manager, do so by using the procedures in "1-2-3 and the Adobe Type Manager" at the end of Chapter 7.

A Note on Example Layout   As in previous chapters, the examples in this chapter assume that your screen displays 20 rows and eight columns when the Worksheet window is maximized. If your display does not show 20 rows and eight columns, your screens will look somewhat different from the illustrations, but you can still do all the examples. Just be sure to use the cell addresses and ranges specified in the instructions.

A Note on Keystroke Instructions   The keystroke instructions in this chapter often assume you are using a mouse to perform such operations as highlighting a range or selecting an option in a dialog box. You can also use the keyboard to perform the same operations. Many of the keyboard equivalents to mouse operations were described in previous chapters. A few of the most common ones are summarized here. For a complete list of keystroke equivalents to mouse operations, see the 1-2-3 documentation or the 1-2-3 on-line Help.

Keyboard Equivalents to Mouse Operations

Operation	Instruction		Keyboard Equivalent
Complete action and close dialog box	**Select:**	OK	**Press:** `↵`
Cancel action and close dialog box	**Select:**	Cancel	**Press:** `ESC`
Highlight a text box	**Select:**	text box	**Press:** `ALT+`*underlined_letter*
Edit a range in a text box	**Select:** **Specify:**	Range A:A1..C:D4	**Press:** `ALT+`*underlined_letter* `F2` (EDIT)
Edit a number or word in a text box	**Select:** **Specify:** *(or click on text and edit it)*	text box new text	**Press:** `ALT+`*underlined_letter* **Type:** new text *(or press Left arrow and edit text)*
Highlight a range	**Highlight:** A:A1..C:D4		**Move to:** cell A:A1 **Press:** `F4` **Move to:** cell D4 **Press:** `↵`

A Note on the Illustrations in This Chapter

The printed graphs in this chapter were printed on a PostScript printer. The screen illustrations were taken from either a standard or a super VGA display. If you have a different kind of printer or a different kind of display, your graphs may look somewhat different (text may be a different size and placement of legends may vary). However, the numbers and the resulting graphic elements should be basically the same, regardless of the type of display or printer you are using.

Graphing in Color or Black and White

When 1-2-3 displays graphs in color, the program uses different colors to distinguish ranges of graphed data. When 1-2-3 displays graphs in black and white, it uses different *hatch patterns* (cross-hatchings) to distinguish ranges of data. Hardware capable of a color-graphics display can display graphs on the screen either in color or in black and white.

To change the display from color to black and white, choose Window Display Options and check the "B&W" check box. To change the display from black and white to color, select Window Display Options and clear the "B&W" check box.

Graph Types

1-2-3 offers seven types of graphs: line graphs, area graphs, bar graphs (stacked and unstacked), pie charts, XY (scatter) graphs, high-low-close-open (stock market) graphs, and mixed graphs (bar and line). Line, area, bar, and pie graph types are available in both 2-D and 3-D.

All graphs and charts are drawn from data in the worksheet, but each type has different uses. This section describes the graph types in the order in which they appear on the Graph menu. As you work through this chapter, you will create bar graphs, pie charts, and line graphs.

Line Graph

Line graphs display values from the worksheet as a continuous line. They are generally used to show one or more values changing over time. For instance, they can be used to demonstrate trends and projections. Each line usually represents values from a single row or column.

A line graph has two axes: x (horizontal) and y (vertical). The *x-axis* usually defines a specific period of time. The *y-axis* is a numbered scale.

Area Graph

An *area graph* is similar to a line graph; the difference is that the area under the line is filled in either with a color or a hatch pattern. Each area usually represents values from a single row or column. In general, the area graph's differently colored (or hatched) areas are easier to see than are the series of lines displayed in a line graph.

Figure 8-1: Line Graph

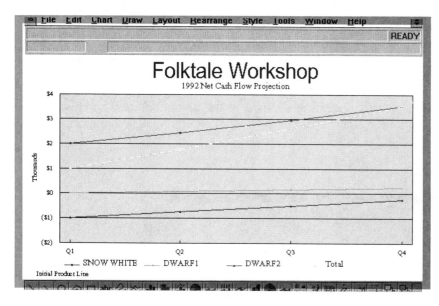

Figure 8-2: 3-D Area Graph

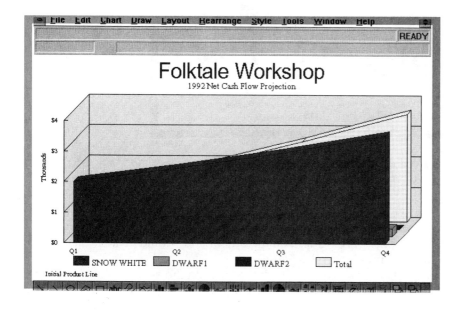

Bar Graph

Bar graphs display information as a series of vertical bars of different heights. Each bar reflects the value of a single worksheet cell.

Bar graphs usually compare values for one item, or for related items. For example, a bar graph prepared for a sales manager might compare annual sales of one or more products for each of the company's regional divisions.

The x-axis of a bar graph has labels that identify the item that each bar, or cluster of bars, represents. Each label can apply to as many as six bars. (A bar graph that displays clusters of bars for each x-axis label is called a *clustered bar graph*.) The y-axis is scaled numerically, according to the worksheet values being represented.

Figure 8-3:   3-D Bar Graph

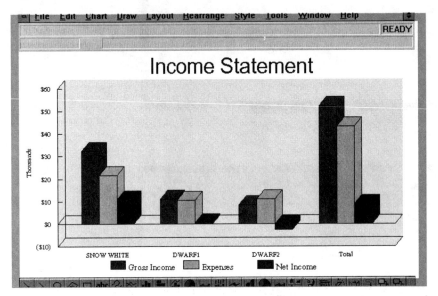

Stacked bar graphs are similar to bar graphs; the difference is that related bars are placed on top of each other (stacked) instead of side by side. Each part of a stacked bar represents a cell value in the worksheet. (See Figure 8-4.)

Stacked bar graphs are often used to compare totals for groups of bars. For example, a stacked bar graph would make it easy to see the total annual sales of three products for each of a company's regional divisions. (A bar graph, on the other hand, would make it easier to compare each of the individual products' sales figures.)

Up to six bars can be stacked. Each stacked bar has a label on the x-axis.

Pie Chart

A *pie chart*, as its name implies, is a circle divided into slices. Each slice represents a cell value in the worksheet. Pie charts show what percentage of the whole each part takes up. If one value is twice as large as another, it gets a slice that is twice as large. For example, a pie chart of classroom grades could display what percentage of the class received As, what percentage Bs, and so on.

You can *explode* (separate and lift out) one or more slices of the pie for emphasis.

Figure 8-4:   Stacked Bar Graph

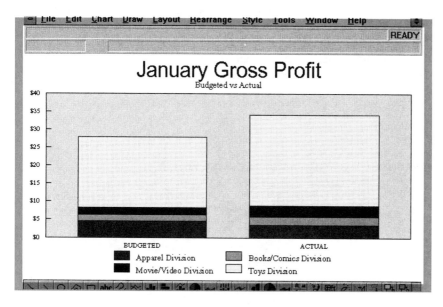

Figure 8-5:   3-D Pie Chart

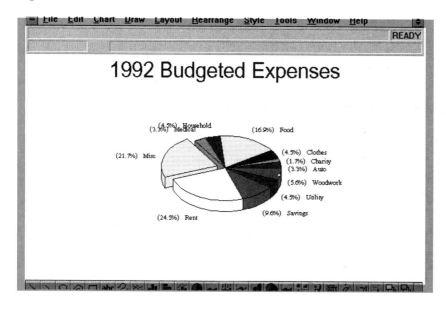

XY Graph

XY graphs display cell values as points. Unlike other 1-2-3 graphs, the XY graph uses both a scaled x-axis and a scaled y-axis. Each point on the graph has an X value and a Y value. The X value determines how far left or right a point is placed on the graph. The Y value controls the vertical placement of a point.

XY graphs are used to show how two different types of data are correlated. For instance, the owner of a small business could make an XY graph that correlated monthly sales with the amount of money spent on advertising. Each point on the graph would represent the sales and advertising figures for a particular month. An engineer could use an XY graph to show experimental results correlating the strength of a test material with temperature; in this case, each point on the graph would represent the strength of the test material at a particular temperature.

XY graphs are also known as *scatter charts* or *scatter diagrams*.

Figure 8-6: XY Graph

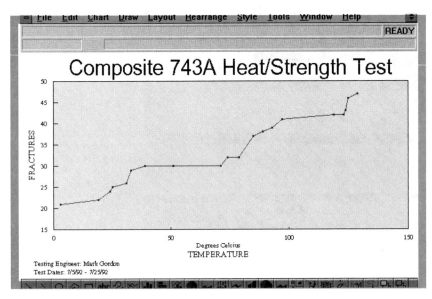

High-Low-Close-Open (HLCO) Graph

High-low-close-open (HLCO) graphs plot up to four related data points as a series of vertical lines. They are also called *stock market graphs*, because they are typically used to track the performance of a stock over time by plotting the high, low, closing, and opening prices of the stock. HLCO graphs can be used to track any kind of data that contains up to four related data points associated with independent variables. For example, an engineer could use a HLCO graph to track the quality of parts coming off a production line. The graph would plot the actual dimensions of a part against the high tolerance, nominal specification, and low tolerance.

Figure 8-7: High-Low-Close-Open (HLCO) Graph

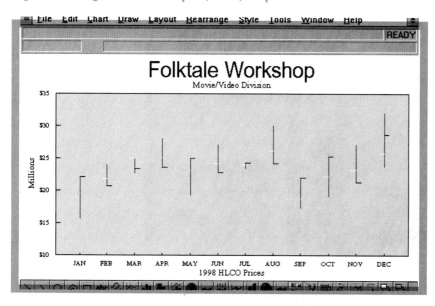

Mixed Graph

Mixed graphs combine bar and line graphs. The lines are used either to accent the information in the bars, or to graph related information. (See Figure 8-8 on the next page.)

For example, you could use a mixed graph to compare actual sales (the bars) with sales quotas (the line). When actual sales exceed sales quotas, the bars extend beyond the line. You could also use a mixed graph to compare sales with profit margin. You could represent the sales figures themselves as a bar chart and graph the corresponding profit margin as a line chart.

Other Graph Features

1-2-3 for Windows also includes special graph features that you can use in combination with the seven graph types. For example, you can:

- rotate the graph so that it is displayed horizontally on the screen
- edit the frame around one or more sides of the graph
- add a table of values to the graph

These graph features and others will be discussed in more detail throughout the chapter.

Creating a Graph

Creating a graph involves several steps:

1. Enter the data to be graphed.

Figure 8-8: Mixed Graph

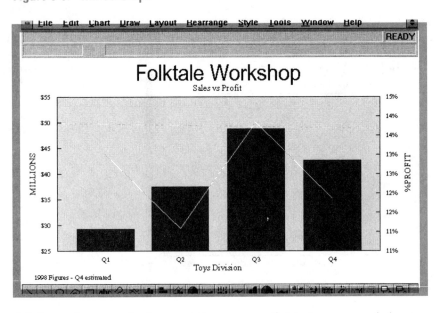

1-2-3 can draw graphs from existing ranges of data in your worksheets, or you can create separate tables, worksheets, or files that contain only the data you want to graph.

2. Create a new graph.

   To create a new graph, you specify a range in the worksheet and tell 1-2-3 to draw a graph based on the values in the range. The range you specify can be a single cell, a one-column range of values, or a multi-column table that you have formatted specifically for graphing. If you create a specially-formatted table, the graph that 1-2-3 creates can be quite full-featured, and can include x-axis labels (or the slices of a pie chart) as well as up to six ranges of graphed data.

3. Choose a graph type.

   1-2-3 creates new graphs as line graphs. If you would prefer a different graph type, choose the one that best illustrates the information you want to graph, or best conveys the points you want to make.

4. Add additional ranges to the graph.

   Once 1-2-3 has created an initial graph, you can specify any additional ranges in the worksheet that contain data to be included in the graph.

5. Identify the graphed data.

   Add titles, legends, and data labels to the graph. Legends identify what bar or line illustrates which value. Data labels usually identify the values at the graph's data points.

6. Refine the graph's appearance.

After you create the basic graph, use additional Graph commands to further refine its appearance. For example, you can change the numeric formatting of the x and y-axis; change the colors or hatch patterns of bars, lines, and pie slices; and edit the frame around the graph. You can also add text and other graphic elements (such as lines, arrows, geometric shapes, and freehand sketches) to the graph.

7. Save the graph.

Graphs are automatically saved when you save the worksheet file from which they are drawn.

The examples in this section build graphs from the worksheet files you have already created. To help Bob Gordon make a more convincing proposal when he approaches banks and potential investors, you are going to create bar and line graphs based on data in the Cash Flow Forecast worksheet file. You will also create a pie chart that reflects data in the Home Budget. This graph will enable Bob and Kathy to literally get a picture of how they plan to spend their money. As you create the bar graph, you will learn many of the basic skills for creating graphs. You'll apply these skills, and pick up additional graphing skills, as you build the line graph and the pie chart.

Bar Graphs

In this section, you are going to create bar graphs that compare the projected financial performance of three of Folktale Workshop's wooden toys. The graphs draw their data from the worksheet file CASHFLOW.WK3 that you created in Chapter 5 and modified in Chapter 7. You will use the main menu's Graph commands and the graph menu's Chart commands described in Table 8-1 to create the bar graphs. The final graph will look like Figure 8-9. (You will print the graphs in Chapter 9.)

Table 8-1:   Commands Used to Build the Bar Graphs

Command	What It Does:
Main Menu Commands	
New	Creates a new graph.
View	Opens a Graph window for a graph in the current file.
Graph Menu Commands	
Type	Changes the graph type (bar, line, mixed, and so on) of the graph.
Range	Changes the ranges of the worksheet on which the x-axis and graph values are drawn.
Data labels	Adds data labels to identify the data points of the graph.
Legend	Adds legends to identify the bars or lines of the graph.
Headings	Adds titles, subtitles, and notes to the graph.

Figure 8-9: The Final Version of One Income Statement Bar Graph

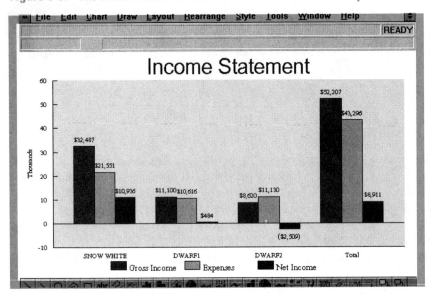

Building a Table to Graph

The bar graphs you are going to draw compare gross income, operating expenses, and net income for each of the three products Bob Gordon plans to manufacture in 1992. This information is already contained in the worksheet file, but it is spread out over several ranges. Although you can construct graphs using existing ranges of data in a worksheet file, it is frequently easier to put all the data you will be graphing in one place. You do this by creating a table in another part of the worksheet file that references the data to be graphed.

In this case, you are going to extend the summary sheet in Bob's Cash Flow Forecast so that it includes a simplified *pro forma* Income Statement. You'll use this Income Statement for several of the exercises in this chapter. (When a business applies for a loan, it often creates a *pro forma* statement. The statement usually consists of an income statement, a balance sheet, and a cash budget. It gives the loan applicant's best estimate of the company's future performance.) This Income Statement shows, in table form, the projected gross income, operating expenses, and net income for each of the SNOW WHITE, DWARF1, and DWARF2 product lines. In addition, it shows these same figures for the company as a whole.

Figure 8-10: Bob's Completed Pro Formal Income Statement

A:D41

	A	B	C	D	E	F
22	FOLKTALE WORKSHOP		1992 Income Statement		(Pro forma)	
23						
24		Gross Income	Expenses	Net Income		
25	SNOW WHITE	$32,487	$21,551	$10,936		
26	DWARF1	$11,100	$10,616	$484		
27	DWARF2	$8,620	$11,130	($2,509)		
28	Total	$52,207	$43,296	$8,911		
29						
30						

Before you create any graphs, follow these steps to add the Income Statement to the Cash Flow Forecast worksheet file:

1. Open the Cash Flow Forecast worksheet file.

Choose:	File Open
Select:	CASHFLOW.WK3 OK

    1-2-3 opens a Worksheet window entitled CASHFLOW.WK3 and makes it the active window.

2. Maximize the Worksheet window.

Click on:	*the Maximize button on the Worksheet window title bar*

3. Enter a title for the Income Statement in row 22.

Use the Edit Quick Copy command to copy the company name, current year, and their formats to row 22.

Highlight:	A:A1..A:B1
Choose:	Edit Quick Copy
Specify:	A:A22 *in the To text box*
Select:	OK

    1-2-3 copies the company name and current year into A:A22..A:B22. Edit Quick Copy also copied the bold Dark-blue style. Now, enter the labels for the remainder of the title.

Move to:	cell A:C22
Type:	Income Statement
Press:	→ *two times*
Type:	'(Pro forma) *make sure you type the label prefix*
Press:	↵

    Next, use the Style 1 command to set the Income Statement and (Pro forma) labels to the bold Dark-blue "Titles" style that you created in Chapter 7.

Highlight:	A:C22..A:E22
Choose:	Style 1

Figure 8-11: The Income Statement Title

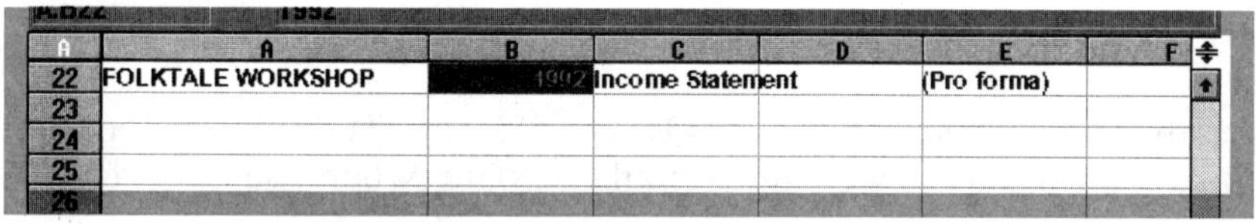

	A	B	C	D	E	F
22	FOLKTALE WORKSHOP		1992 Income Statement		(Pro forma)	
23						
24						
25						
26						

■ **NOTE:**   If you did not create the "Titles" named style in Chapter 7, use Style Font to set the range A:C22..A:E22 to bold, then use Style Color to set that range to Dark-blue.

4. Enter the column and row headings.

Enter labels for the Income Statement data. When you are finished with this step, the screen should look like Figure 8-12.

First, enter the row labels in column A.

Move to: cell A:A25

Type: SNOW WHITE   ↓

DWARF1   ↓

DWARF2   ↓

Total   ↵

Now enter centered column labels in row 24. Make sure you type the label prefix (^) to center the label.

Move to: cell A:B24

Type: ^Gross Income   →

^Expenses   →

^Net Income   ↵

Figure 8-12:   The Income Statement with Column and Row Labels

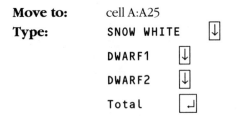

A	A	B	C	D	E	F
22	FOLKTALE WORKSHOP		1992 Income Statement		(Pro forma)	
23						
24		Gross Income	Expenses	Net Income		
25	SNOW WHITE					
26	DWARF 1					
27	DWARF2					
28	Total					
29						
30						

5. Enter a formula for gross income for SNOW WHITE.

The gross income figures in this table are annual figures. They are determined by using formulas that sum the gross income figures for all four quarters. For example, the formula for annual gross income for SNOW WHITE is:

```
@SUM(B:B6..B:E6)
```

This formula adds up the gross income figures for Q1, Q2, Q3, and Q4. Enter this formula using the pointing method, so you can see what the formula is doing. When you have completed entering the gross income formulas for all products and the total gross income formula, the worksheet should look like Figure 8-13.

Move to: cell A:B25

Type: @sum(

Highlight: B:B7..B:E7

Type:) ⏎

■ *NOTE:*   In any of the keystroke instructions that require you to provide ranges, you can either use the pointing method to highlight the ranges or type in the range addresses, as you prefer.

6. Enter the formulas for DWARF1 and DWARF2.

Use similar formulas to calculate the annual gross income for the other two products.

Move to: cell A:B26

Press: @sum (c:b7..c:e7)   ↓

                 @sum (c:b7..c:e7)   ⏎

1-2-3 displays the annual gross income for DWARF1 and DWARF2.

7. Enter the formula for total gross income.

The total gross income is the sum of the annual gross income figures for all three products. This formula is also an @SUM formula.

Move to: cell A:B28

Type: @sum(b25..b27)

Press: ⏎

1-2-3 adds up the annual gross income figures for each product and displays the results in cell A:B28.

Figure 8-13:   The Income Statement with Gross Income Formulas

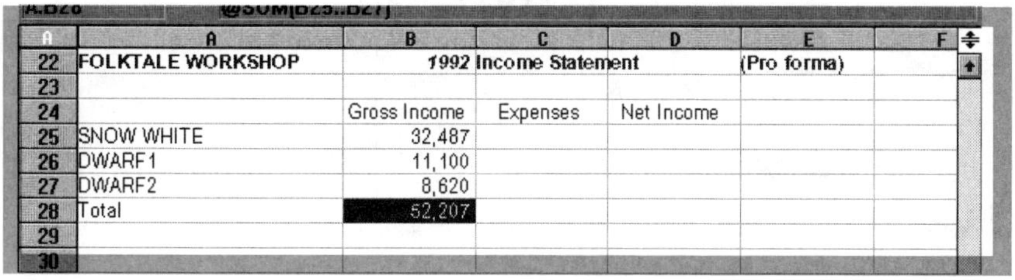

	A	B	C	D	E	F
22	FOLKTALE WORKSHOP	1992 Income Statement			(Pro forma)	
23						
24		Gross Income	Expenses	Net Income		
25	SNOW WHITE	32,487				
26	DWARF1	11,100				
27	DWARF2	8,620				
28	Total	52,207				
29						
30						

8. Enter the formulas for operating expenses for Snow White into column C.

The operating expenses figures in this table are annual figures. They are determined by using formulas that sum the operating expenses figures for all four quarters. For example, the formula for annual operating expenses for SNOW WHITE is:

`@SUM(B:B8..B:E8)`

This formula adds up the operating expenses figures for Q1, Q2, Q3, and Q4. When you have completed adding operating expenses formulas for all products and the formula for total operating expenses, the worksheet will look like Figure 8-14.

Move to: cell A:C25

Type: `@sum(B:B8..B:E8)`

1-2-3 displays the operating expenses for Snow White in cell A:C25.

9. Enter the formulas for DWARF1 and DWARF2.

Use similar formulas to calculate the annual operating expenses for the other two products.

Move to: cell A:C26

Type: `@sum(c:b8..c:e8)`

`@sum(d:b8..d:e8)`

1-2-3 displays the annual operating expenses for DWARF1 and DWARF2.

10. Enter the formula for total operating expenses.

The total operating expense is the sum of the annual operating expenses figures for all three products. This formula is also an @SUM formula.

Move to: cell A:C28

Type: `@sum(c25..c27)`

Figure 8-14:   The Income Statement with Operating Expenses Formulas

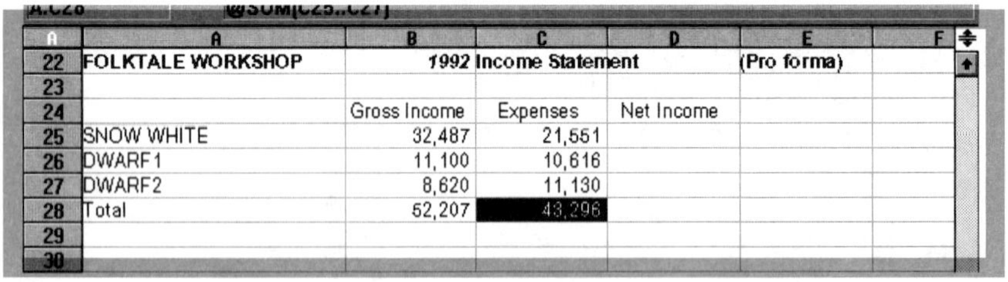

	A	B	C	D	E	F
22	FOLKTALE WORKSHOP		1992 Income Statement		(Pro forma)	
23						
24		Gross Income	Expenses	Net Income		
25	SNOW WHITE	32,487	21,551			
26	DWARF1	11,100	10,616			
27	DWARF2	8,620	11,130			
28	Total	52,207	43,296			
29						
30						

11. Fill in the formulas in column D.

The formulas for the column labeled **Net Income** are merely cell references to the formulas for net income (profit or loss) that already exist in the cash flow worksheets for each individual product. Enter these in column D.

Move to:	cell A:D25	
Type:	+b:b14	*SNOW WHITE's net income*
Press:	⬇	
Type:	+c:b14	*DWARF1's net income*
Press:	⬇	
Type:	+d:b14	*DWARF2's net income*
Press:	⬇	
Type:	+b14	*total net income*
Press:	↵	

1-2-3 displays the figures for net income in column D.

12. Change the numeric display format to Currency, zero decimals.

The figures you entered are currency, so display them with dollar signs.

Highlight:	A:B25..A:D28
Choose:	Range Format
Select:	Currency
	Decimal Places:
Type:	0 *in the text box*
Select:	OK

Figure 8-15: The Income Statement Formatted as Currency

	A	B	C	D	E	F
22	FOLKTALE WORKSHOP		1992 Income Statement		(Pro forma)	
23						
24		Gross Income	Expenses	Net Income		
25	SNOW WHITE	$32,487	$21,551	$10,936		
26	DWARF1	$11,100	$10,616	$484		
27	DWARF2	$8,620	$11,130	($2,509)		
28	Total	$52,207	$43,296	$8,911		
29						
30						

1-2-3 formats the values in rows 25 through 28 as Currency. (Later, you will use some of these numbers as labels on a graph, so the format is important.)

13. Save CASHFLOW.WK3.

Congratulations! You have completed the Income Statement. Save CASHFLOW.WK3.

Choose: File   Save

The next several sections show you how to create and modify a bar graph, using the data in this table. Later on, you'll also see what happens to the graph when you change some of the data in the product-specific worksheets. Finally, you'll add the bar graph to the worksheet.

Create the Initial Graph

Now that you have entered Bob's Income Statement into the summary sheet, the next step is to create an initial graph. So that you can get some practice with the graph-building features 1-2-3 provides, you'll start out small, graphing only the gross income for the three products, and then you'll expand the graph to include all of the information in the Income Statement. You'll use the Graph New command to create the initial graph based on the range of gross income values.

Highlight: A:A25..A:B27   *gross income values*

Choose: Graph   New

1-2-3 displays a dialog box in which it proposes GRAPH1 as the name for the new graph. You'll use the name INCOME instead. (A graph name can be up to 15 characters long and composed of letters, numbers, and the underbar character.)

Select: Graph name:

Type: INCOME

Select: OK

Figure 8-16:   Creating a New Graph

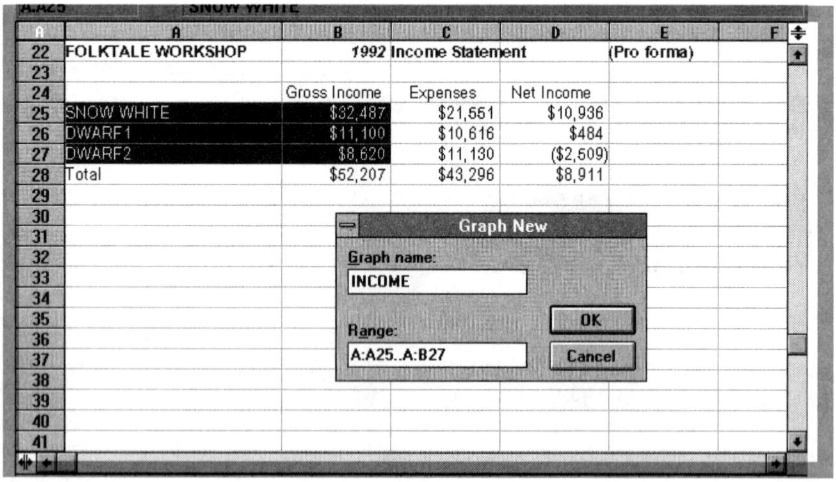

Figure 8-17: The Initial INCOME Graph

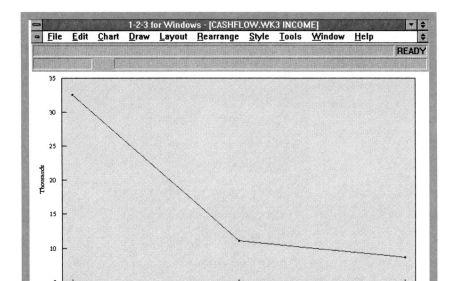

1-2-3 displays graphs in a *Graph window*, not in a standard Worksheet window. The title bar of the Graph window displays CASHFLOW.WK3 INCOME: The name of this graph is INCOME and it will be saved in the file CASHFLOW.WK3 (when you File Save CASHFLOW.WK3).

Notice also that the menu bar has changed. When 1-2-3's active window is a Graph window, the program replaces the main menu (the one you're used to working with) with the *graph menu*. The graph menu gives you the commands you need to expand and customize graphs. You will be working with the commands of the graph menu throughout this chapter.

Check how 1-2-3 changes the menu depending upon whether the active window is a Worksheet window or a Graph window. First, make the Worksheet window for CASHFLOW.WK3 by choosing the Window command and selecting the window to be active. (You can also make a window active by clicking anywhere on that window.) When the Worksheet window for CASHFLOW.WK3 is active, 1-2-3 changes back to the main menu. Then make the Graph window for the INCOME graph active by clicking anywhere on that window. 1-2-3 again puts up the graph menu.

When the active window is a Graph window, the icon palette also changes: 1-2-3 replaces the main menu icon palette with the graph menu icon palette. The icons on this palette let you perform operations with graphs very quickly. You'll be using a number of these icons in the exercises in this chapter. Table 8-2 shows and describes the icons in the graph menu icon palette.

Table 8-2:   The Graph Menu Icon Palette

Icon	Icon Name	Description
	Add arrow	Adds an arrow to the chart.
	Add line	Adds a line to the chart.
	Add ellipse	Adds an ellipse to the chart.
	Add polygon	Adds a polygon to the chart.
	Add rectangle	Adds a rectangle to the chart.
	Add text	Adds text to chart.
	Draw freehand	Allows you to draw freehand on the chart.
	Line graph	Changes the graph to a line graph.
	Bar graph	Changes the graph to a bar graph.
	Horizontal bar graph	Changes the graph to a horizontal bar graph.
	Mixed graph	Changes a graph to a mixed graph.
	Pie graph	Changes the graph to a pie graph.
	Area graph	Changes the graph to an area graph.
	HLCO graph	Changes the graph to a HLCO graph.
	3-D line graph	Changes the graph to a 3-D line graph.
	3-D bar graph	Changes the graph to a 3-D bar graph.
	3-D pie chart	Changes the graph to a 3-D pie chart.
	Select graph type	Allows you to select the type of graph.
	Delete object	Deletes the currently selected object(s).
	Duplicate object	Duplicates the currently selected object(s).
	Rotate object	Rotates the currently selected object(s).
	Flip object backwards	Flips the currently selected object(s) backwards.
	Flip object upside down	Flips the currently selected object(s) upside down.
	Move object to front	Moves the currently selected object(s) to the front of all objects in their space.
	Move object to back	Moves the currently selected object(s) to the back of all objects in their space.

■ *NOTE:* As you work through this chapter, you will be switching often between Worksheet windows and Graph windows. You will also be using commands from both the main menu and the graph menu, as well as icons from the main menu icon palette and the graph menu icon palette. To help you keep your place, we use "graph menu command..." and "main menu command..." quite liberally in text that introduces a keystroke sequence.

Now look at the graph that 1-2-3 has created, using the data in the range A:A25..A:B27. First, notice that it is a line graph. Although you can change the type of INCOME graph at any time (and you will change it to a bar graph in the next step), 1-2-3's Graph New command always builds a line graph.

1-2-3 has added x-axis labels to the graph: `SNOW WHITE`, `DWARF1`, and `DWARF2`. The x-axis labels identify the items that the set of points in the line graph (or cluster of bars in a bar graph) represents. 1-2-3's Graph New command creates x-axis labels automatically; it assumes that the first column of the table that you highlight contains x-axis labels. That's why you high-lighted A:A25..A:A27 along with A:B25..A:B27 when you created the new graph. (If the range that you select for Graph New contains just one column, 1-2-3 assumes that it contains values to be graphed, not labels for the x-axis.)

The program automatically draws a scale on the y-axis. The tick marks (the marks that indicate the scale) are in increments of 5. The top of the scale is 35, which stands for $35,000, just over the gross income value for SNOW WHITE. Notice that 1-2-3 automatically indicates that the scale on the y-axis is in thousands.

The line graph that 1-2-3 has created for INCOME is a good place to start, but it does not yet show the information as clearly as it could. Change INCOME to a bar graph. (Although we're choosing not to use a line graph here, you will be learning all about line graphs in "Line Graphs" later in this chapter.)

Changing the Graph Type

You can change the graph type either by using the graph menu's Chart Type command, or by clicking on the appropriate icon in the graph menu's icon palette. This time, change INCOME from a line graph to a bar graph by using the Chart Type command. The default orientation for a graph is vertical, and the default bar type is side-by-side (not stacked).

Choose: `Chart`   `Type`

Select: `Bar`   *to select the bar type*

               `OK`

1-2-3 converts the INCOME graph to a bar graph and displays it in the Graph window. Each of the x-axis labels (`SNOW WHITE`, `DWARF1`, and `DWARF2`) now refers to a cluster of bars. (At this time, each "cluster" has only one bar in it, representing a single value. In the next sections, you will add bars to each cluster.)

Graphing a Second Data Range

You are going to graph a second data range so Bob Gordon can compare gross income to operating expenses for each product. Each time you add a new data range to a bar graph, you add another bar to each cluster of bars. (One data range produces a graph with single bars along the x-axis, two data ranges produce a graph with two-bar clusters along the x-axis, and so on.)

Figure 8-18: Changing INCOME to a Bar Graph

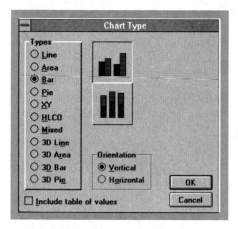

Figure 8-19: INCOME is now a bar graph.

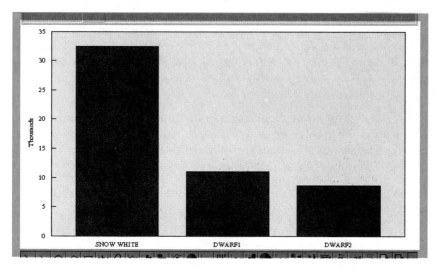

1. Specify an additional range of data to be graphed.

   Each 1-2-3 graph can be based on up to six ranges of worksheet data; in the Chart Ranges command, you use the letters A through F to identify the six ranges. For a bar graph, each cell in a data range adds another bar to the graph. (A one-cell range produces a one-bar graph, a five-cell range produces a five-cell graph, and so on.)

   Choose: Chart   Ranges

1-2-3 displays the Chart Ranges dialog box. The program has filled in values for the X range and for the A range; these are based on the range that you selected when you created the initial graph with Graph New. The X data range text box contains A:A25..A:A27, the range of the x-axis labels **SNOW WHITE**, **DWARF1**, and **DWARF2**. The A data range text box contains the range A:B25..A:B27, the range containing gross income values for the three products. For all 1-2-3 graph types except XY and pie, the X range contains labels for the graph's x-axis, and the A through F ranges contain numbers or values to be graphed. (You'll look at pie charts later in this chapter.)

You'll add the range containing operating expense values as data range B.

Select: B

Specify: A:C25..A:C27   *in the text box*

Select: OK

Figure 8-20:   Adding the B Data Range

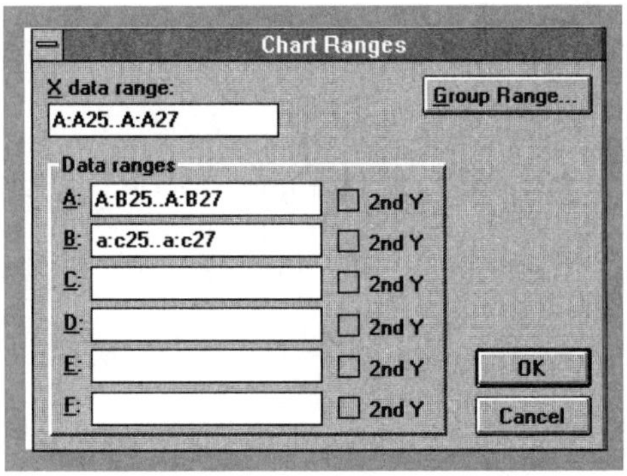

1-2-3 now displays one new bar for each x-axis label. Notice that the program automatically gives each set of bars its own hatch pattern or color. The right bar in each cluster represents operating expenses. (In a later step, you'll add legends to the graph so that color or hatch pattern will be meaningful to anyone viewing the graph.)

Adding Legends

The Graph window's Chart menu includes a number of commands that enhance the appearance of a graph and make it easier to understand. Adding *legends* to the graph is one of the most important of these enhancements. Legends appear below the x-axis. They explain the patterns, symbols, or colors used to identify the A through F data ranges on the graph.

Figure 8-21: The INCOME Graph with Two Data Ranges

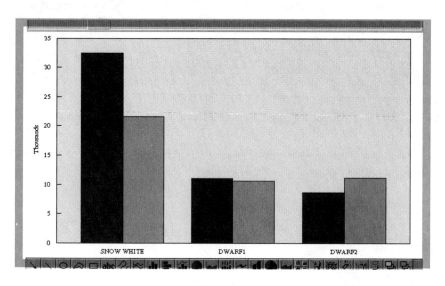

Without legends, most graphs are of limited use. For example, although the bars have different hatch patterns or colors, so far it is not yet clear which bar stands for gross income, and which for operating expenses. Legends for the A and B ranges will clear up this mystery.

Adding legends is a two-step process: (1) Specify the data range to be identified by a legend; and (2) specify the legend.

Name the A range **Gross Income** and the B range **Expenses**.

Choose:	Chart Legend
Select:	A
Type:	Gross Income
Select:	B
Type:	Expenses
Select:	OK

1-2-3 redraws the graph. The legends appear at the bottom of the graph. Each legend represents a bar that has a particular hatch pattern or color. Samples of the hatch patterns or colors appear next to each legend. It is now clear that the leftmost bar of each cluster reflects income values and the rightmost bar reflects expense values. You can see at a glance that the SNOW WHITE product should bring in significantly more money than Bob plans to spend on it, while the other two products should not do nearly as well.

Adding Legends by Using Cell Addresses   Instead of typing a legend, you can type a backslash (\) followed by the address or range name of a cell that contains the text that 1-2-3 should use for the legend.

Figure 8-22: Adding a Legend

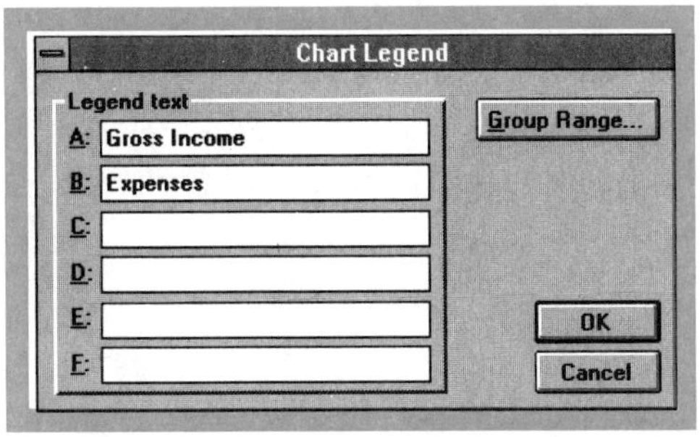

Figure 8-23: The INCOME Graph with Legends Added

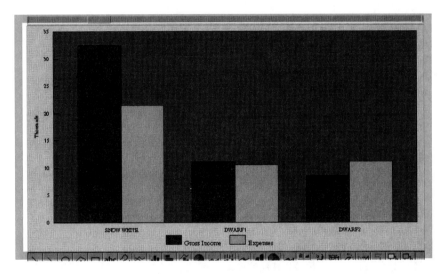

For example, **Gross Income** and **Expenses** are both row labels in the Income Statement. Since **Gross Income** is in cell A:B24 of the Income Statement, you could have typed \A:B24 in the text box instead of typing in the words **Gross Income**. Similarly, you could have typed \A:AC24 instead of **Expenses.**

Using cell addresses instead of typing the text of a legend is a more flexible way to add legends and other text to a graph, because it allows you to synchronize the labels in the worksheet and the legends on the graph. If you change a cell that contains a label used as a legend, the legend changes automatically when the graph is refreshed; you do not have to type in a new legend.

You can use cell addresses for other text elements, too, such as graph headings (which are discussed in the next section). Some of the other examples in this chapter will use cell addresses to add text elements to a graph.

Adding Headings

1-2-3 can print a one-line *title* and a one-line *subtitle* at the top of a graph, and two one-line notes at the bottom left. You use the graph menu's Chart Headings command to create these headings. Like legends, headings can either be typed in directly, or created from cell references. Add the title "Income Statement" above the graph. This time you'll reference cell A:C22, the worksheet cell that contains the label **Income Statement**, instead of typing in the text.

Choose:	Chart	Headings
Select:	Title	
Type:	\A:C22	*don't forget the backslash (\)*
Select:	OK	

Figure 8-24: Adding a Title to a Graph

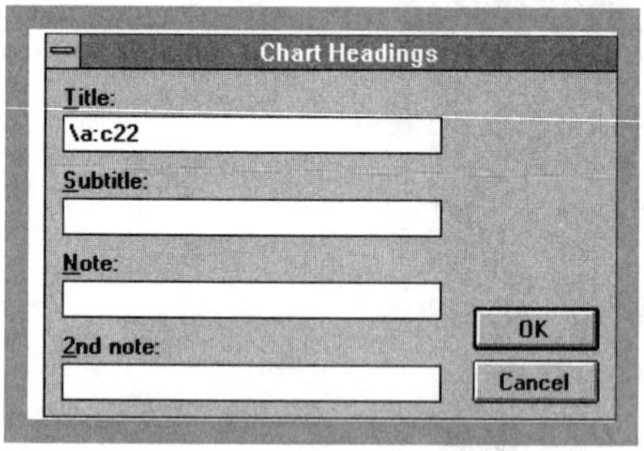

Figure 8-25: The INCOME Graph with a Title

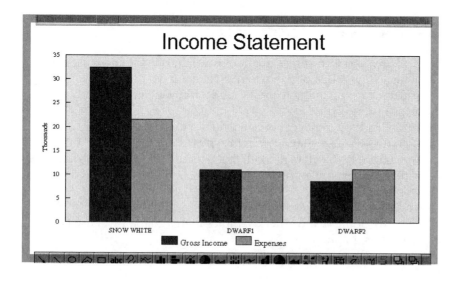

The title "Income Statement" now appears above the bar graph.

The INCOME graph is now complete; the ranges and basic options are in place. You are going to continue to enhance the graph as you work through this chapter, but you should also save the graph at this point. To save a graph, you save the worksheet file from which the graph is drawn. You'll use File Save to save the file. There is, however, one complication.

At this point, the Graph window entitled CASHFLOW.WK3 INCOME is active and 1-2-3 is displaying the graph menu. You must make the CASHFLOW.WK3 Worksheet window active to File Save the file. You can do so: (1) By clicking anywhere on the window; (2) by using the Window command; or (3) by pressing Control+F6 repeatedly until the window you want is active. This time, click on the window. If you can't see the Worksheet window for CASHFLOW.WK3, use Window Cascade to display all windows in cascade mode first. Once you have made CASHFLOW.WK3's window active, save the file.

Choose: `Window   Cascade`   *if necessary*
Click on: *anywhere in the Worksheet window for CASHFLOW.WK3*
Choose: `File   Save`

1-2-3 saves the Cash Flow Forecast worksheet and the INCOME graph in the file CASHFLOW.WK3.

A Note on Saving Worksheet Files with Graphs   As you know, graphs are saved with the worksheet file that contains the data from which the graph is drawn. To save a particular version of a graph, or a version of the graph that reflects a particular state of the underlying data, you can use the File Save As command to save the worksheet file under a different name. You can do this as often as you like, changing the filename each time to save subsequent states of the graph.

Graphing Additional Data

Once you've have created the basic graph, you can easily add more information to it. For instance, you can add an additional bar to each cluster of bars, or you can add a new cluster of bars.

In this section, you are going to add a bar to represent net income to each product's cluster of bars. Then you'll add a cluster of bars for the contents of the Total column.

1. Make the CASHFLOW.WK3 INCOME Graph window active.

This time, you'll use the Window command to make the Graph window for CASHFLOW.WK3 INCOME active. Choose the Window number for "CASHFLOW.WK3 INCOME":

Choose: `Window`
              `CASHFLOW.WK3 INCOME`

1-2-3 makes the INCOME Graph window active and switches to the graph menu.

2. Add net income values to the graph.

The process of adding more data ranges to a graph is the same as the one for adding one range: (1) Assign each new data range; then (2) create a legend for the new range. First, assign the C range to the net income column:

Choose:	Chart	Ranges
Select:	C	
Specify:	A:D25..A:D27	*in the text box*
Select:	OK	

Then, assign a legend to the new range:

Choose:	Chart	Legend
Select:	C	
Type:	Net Income	
Select:	OK	

Figure 8-26:   The INCOME Graph with Bars for Net Income Added

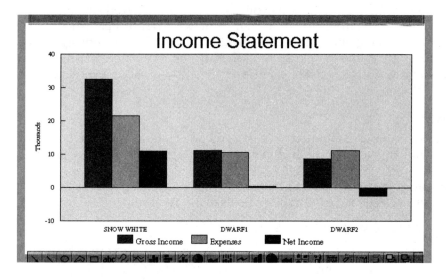

1-2-3 displays the three clusters of bars, each of which now contains three bars. Notice that 1-2-3 has automatically changed the y-axis scale to accommodate the net loss of the DWARF2 product.

3. Graph totals for gross income and operating expenses.

Bob looks over the graph of his Income Statement data and decides he'd like to show the contents of the Total column.

To include the Total column in the graph, you must expand each of the three data ranges (A, B, and C). So that the word `Total` will be printed under the new cluster of bars, you must also expand the X range. First, expand the X range:

Choose: `Chart`   `Ranges`

Select: `X`

1-2-3 proposes the current X range. Expand that range down one row to include the label Total.

Specify: A:A25..A:A28

Select: OK

Then, expand each of the three data ranges, so they include the data from the Total column for each product.

Select: `A`   `Gross Income`

Specify: A:B25..A:B28

Select: `B`   `Operating Expenses`

Specify: A:C25..A:C28

Select: `C`   `Net Income`

Specify: A:D25.A:D28

Choose: OK

Figure 8-27: The INCOME Graph with a Cluster of Bars for Total

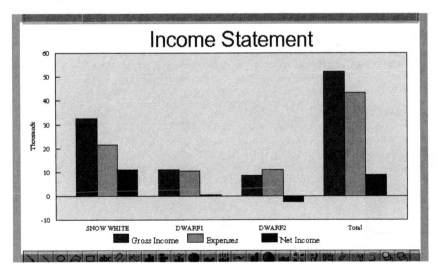

1-2-3 displays the new graph. The graph now includes a cluster of bars for the data in the Total column, as well as an accompanying label along the x-axis. Notice that 1-2-3 has adjusted the y-axis to accommodate the values in the Total column.

■ *NOTE:*   A more common way to represent data in which the total amount is important is as a stacked bar graph. You'll learn to do this in Chapter 10.

4. Save the graph with the worksheet.

Save the modified graph in the worksheet file by saving CASHFLOW.WK3. To switch to the main menu, activate the Worksheet window for CASHFLOW.WK3, and then save the file.

Changing the Frame

Unless you specify otherwise, 1-2-3 displays a frame around the sides of the graph. Although changing this frame does not affect the understanding of the graph or its data, it can create a different effect for a presentation. You change the graph frame using the graph menu's Chart Borders/Grids command. First, make the INCOME Graph window active and maximize it.

1. Make the CASHFLOW.WK3 INCOME Graph window the active window.

Use any of the techniques discussed previously to activate the Graph window for CASHFLOW.WK3 INCOME.

2. Change the graph frame.

Change the graph frame so that there are lines around only the left and bottom sides. Because the default frame includes all four sides, you work backwards to change the frame, deleting the lines you do not want.

Choose: `Chart    Borders/Grids`

Select: `→`   *and clear the check box*

`Top`   *and clear the check box*
`OK`

Figure 8-28:   Changing the Frame on a Graph

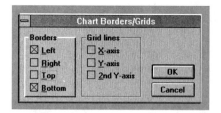

Figure 8-29: The INCOME Graph with the Top and Right Borders Removed

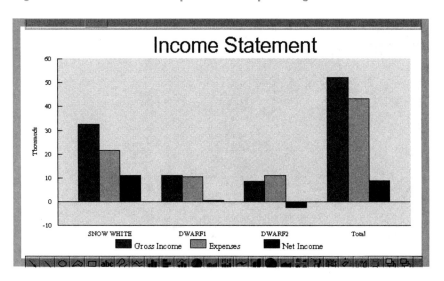

1-2-3 redraws the INCOME graph. Now it has borders only along the left side and on the bottom.

Adding Data Labels

In addition to legends and titles, 1-2-3 allows you to add *data labels* to a graph. Data labels are values or words that appear in the graph itself, next to the data points.

Data labels are drawn from worksheet data. You create them by matching a range that contains data labels to a range of data to be graphed; each cell in the data-label range corresponds to a value in the data range. You can specify a different range of data labels for each range of data you graph.

To add data labels to a graph, you (1) choose Chart Data Labels, (2) associate a range of labels or values in the worksheet with the data ranges you want to label, and (3) choose where you want the labels to be placed in relation to the data points on the graph.

To see how this works, you are going to assign data labels to the INCOME graph. After you have completed the following steps, the graph will look like Figure 8-30.

1. Assign the first range of data labels.

   You are going to use the currency figures in the Income Statement table as data labels for the bars. Using the Chart Data Labels command, you'll specify the values in A:B25..A:B28 to label the gross income bars.

Choose:	`Chart    Data Labels`
Select:	`A` *for Gross Income labels*
Specify:	A:B25..A:B28

Figure 8-30:   Data Labels Allow for Precise Interpretation of the INCOME Graph

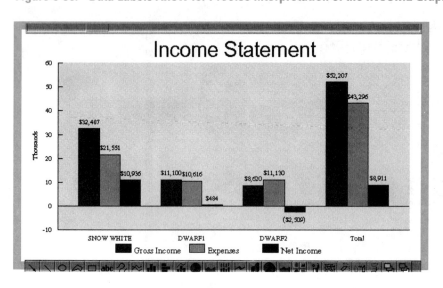

After you have specified the range of cells to be used as labels, you select the position of the label. Selecting Below places the labels inside the bars. Selecting Above places the labels outside the bars (above vertical bars for positive values and below vertical bars for negative values). Place the labels above the bars, then display the graph.

Click on: *the label position box for A*
Select: Above   OK

Figure 8-31:   Specifying Data Labels for Gross Income

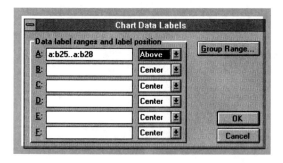

1-2-3 redraws the INCOME graph. It now includes data labels for data range A.

■ *NOTE:*   1-2-3 uses the Chart Data Label command's label position choices "Center", "Left", and "Right" in different ways, depending on the type of graph. For bar graphs, "Center", "Left", and "Right" all do the same thing as selecting "Above": They place the labels outside the bars.

For line, XY, and mixed graphs, "Center" centers data labels over data points, and "Left" and "Right" place labels to the left and right of data points, respectively. You cannot use data labels with pie charts, and you can use data labels only for the E and F ranges of HLCO graphs, not for the high, low, close, and open ranges.

Figure 8-32: The INCOME Graph with Data Labels for Gross Income Added

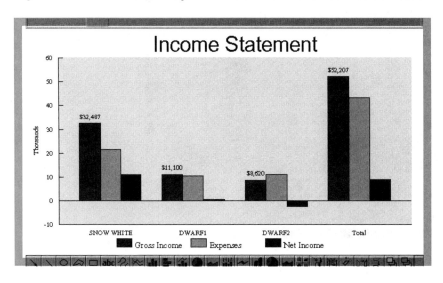

2. Assign data labels to data ranges B and C.

Choose:	Chart Data Labels
Select:	B *for Expenses labels*
Specify:	A:C25..A:C28
Select:	*the label position box for B*
	Above
	C *for Net Income labels*
Specify:	A:D25..A:D28
Select:	*the label position box for C*
	Above OK

The program draws the INCOME graph again, this time including data labels over values in each of the three ranges, Gross Income, Expenses, and Net Income.

3. Save CASHFLOW.WK3.

Congratulations! You have finished creating Bob's bar charts. Leave the Graph menu and save CASHFLOW.WK3 again.

Remember that you must make the Worksheet window entitled CASHFLOW.WK3 active before you can use the main menu's File Save command.

Figure 8-33:   The INCOME Graph with Data Labels for Expenses and Net Income Added

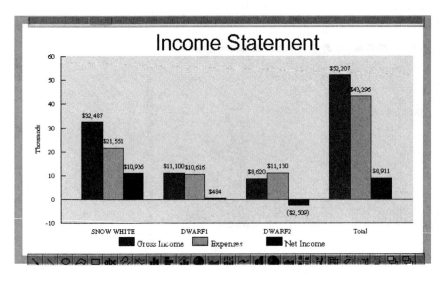

Pie Charts

When you are interested in showing the relationship of values to each other or to a total, a pie chart usually gets the message across more clearly than any other graph type. In this section, you will create a pie chart that shows what portion of their total expense budget Bob and Kathy plan to use for each budgeted item. You'll draw this graph in the Home Budget worksheet you created in Chapters 3 and 4.

To get some practice working with more than one file at a time, you will open the BUDGET1 worksheet while the CASHFLOW worksheet is still open.

Choose: File   Open

Select: BUDGET1.WK3   OK

A Note on Moving Between Worksheets and Worksheet Windows   As you have seen, the Prev Sheet key (Control+Page Down) moves the cell pointer to the worksheet before the current worksheet. When the cell pointer is already in worksheet A and there is only one Worksheet window open (or you are in the first Worksheet window), pressing Prev Sheet causes 1-2-3 to beep because there is no "previous" worksheet to move to. In this case, however, there is a Worksheet window in front of the current one; therefore, the "previous" worksheet is the last worksheet in the previous Worksheet window, CASHFLOW.WK3.

Press: CTRL+PGDN

Pressing Prev Sheet again would move the cell pointer to the second-to-last worksheet of the CASHFLOW.WK3 Worksheet window, and so on.

To return to the Home Budget Worksheet window, press Next Sheet.

Press: CTRL+PGUP

When you press Next Sheet, you tell 1-2-3 to move to the worksheet after the current worksheet. Since worksheet E is the last worksheet of the Cash Flow worksheet file, 1-2-3 moves the cell pointer to the first worksheet of the next Worksheet window, BUDGET1.WK3, and that window once again becomes the active window.

The action of moving between Worksheet windows by moving one worksheet at a time is similar to what you might do if you were to leaf through a group of file folders in a file drawer one page at a time. When you reached the last page in one folder, you would begin leafing through the next folder, starting with the first page. When you reached the last page of that folder, you would advance to the first page of the next folder, and so on. You can also move between worksheet active files a file at a time using the Next File and Prev File keys described briefly later in this chapter, and in detail in Chapter 10.

Creating the Budgeted Expenses Pie Chart

The following steps describe how to create a pie chart of Bob and Kathy's budgeted expenses. When you are done, the completed pie chart will look like Figure 8-34. Although the type of graph you are going to create and the technique for selecting data ranges are different, you are already familiar with all the Graph commands you will need to create this graph.

Figure 8-34:   The Completed EXPENSES Pie Chart

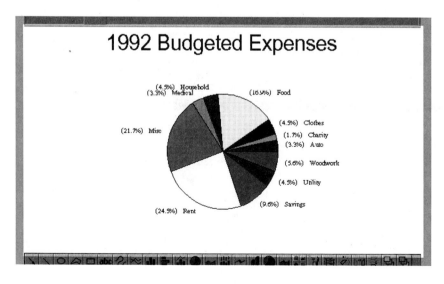

1. Clear worksheet titles.

When you created this worksheet file, one of the last things you did was set worksheet titles. Worksheet titles will make it harder to define one of the ranges you need for the pie chart, so before you start the graph, clear those titles.

Choose: Worksheet Titles

Select: Clear OK

2. Move the cell pointer to the EXPENSES section of the worksheet

To create the INCOME graph in the previous section, you built a table that contained all the labels and values you were going to graph. This time, you'll create the graph from existing label and data ranges. Move the cell pointer to the part of the worksheet that contains the x-axis labels and budget data you are going to graph.

Move to: cell A23

Figure 8-35: The EXPENSES Section of BUDGET1.WK3

	A	B	C	D	E	F	G
20							
21	EXPENSES						
22							
23	Auto	150	150	150	150	150	
24	Charity	75	75	75	75	75	
25	Clothes	200	200	200	200	200	
26	Food	875	700	700	700	875	
27	Household	200	200	200	200	200	
28	Medical	150	150	150	150	150	
29	Misc	1,125	900	900	900	1,125	
30	Rent	1,100	1,100	1,100	1,100	1,100	1,
31	Savings	500	400	400	400	500	
32	Utility	200	200	200	200	200	
33	Woodwork	250	250	250	250	250	
34							
35	Total Expenses	$4,825	$4,325	$4,325	$4,325	$4,825	$4,
36							
37	CASH FLOW						
38							
39	Savings Account						

3. Specify the data range.

A pie chart uses only one numeric data range, range A. Each slice of the graph represents the value in one worksheet cell in the range.

Use the figures in the Annual column of the EXPENSES section as the A range for Bob and Kathy's pie chart.

Highlight: N23..N33

4. Create the initial graph.

Create a graph named EXPENSES using the Graph New command:

Choose:	`Graph    New`
Select:	`Graph Name`
Type:	`EXPENSES` *in the text box*
Select:	`OK`

Figure 8-36: The Initial EXPENSES Graph

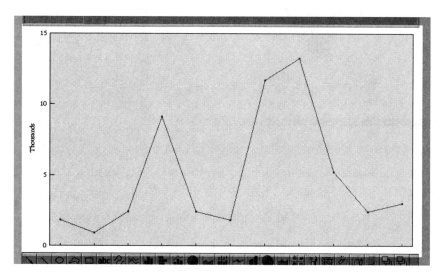

1-2-3 opens a Graph window entitled BUDGET1.WK3 EXPENSES and places it in front of the Worksheet window for BUDGET.WK3. In this window, the program draws a line graph based on the data in the range A:N23..A:N33. Since the range contains only a single column, 1-2 3 interprets it as the A data range (rather than the X data range): the EXPENSES graph, at this point, does not include x-axis labels. Notice that 1-2-3 now displays the graph menu, not the main menu, and the graph menu icon palette rather than the main menu icon palette.

5. Change the graph type to pie.

Bob is interested in seeing his budget as a pie chart. Therefore, change the type of the graph to a 2-dimensional pie graph. This time, use the "2-D Pie Chart" icon, which looks like this:

Click on:	*the 2-D Pie Chart icon*

1-2-3 changes the EXPENSES graph to a pie chart.

Figure 8-37: The EXPENSES graph is changed to a pie chart.

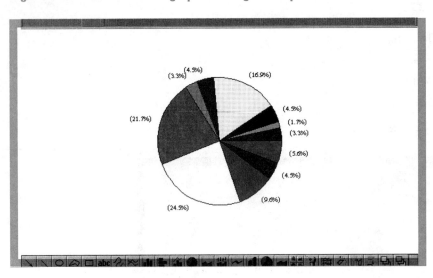

6. Specify the labels for the pie slices.

A pie chart does not have an x-axis, so you can't define one. Instead, 1-2-3 uses the X range for pie slice labels. Use the column of expenses categories in A:A23..A:N33 as the pie slice labels.

Choose:	Chart Ranges
Select:	X *to indicate the X data range*
Specify:	A:A23..A:A33 *in the text box*
Select:	OK

Figure 8-38: The EXPENSES Pie Chart with Labels

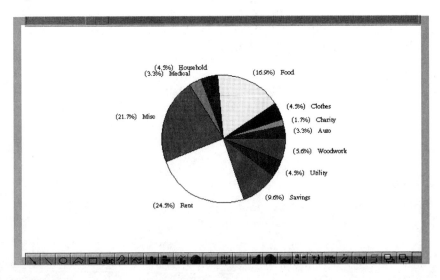

7. Title the pie chart.

Title the pie chart "1992 Budgeted Expenses" using the Chart Titles command.

Choose:	Chart Headings
Select:	Title
Type:	1992 Budgeted Expenses *in the text box*
Select:	OK

Figure 8-39:   The EXPENSES Pie Chart with a Title

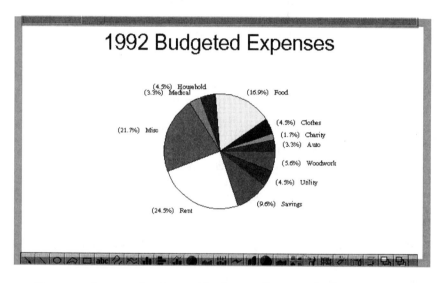

You now have a pie chart with eleven slices. Each slice represents the amount of money Bob and Kathy have budgeted for a particular expense. 1-2-3 automatically calculates each slice's percentage of the Gordons' total budgeted expenses, and displays that percentage on the screen.

8. Restore worksheet titles.

You have finished the pie chart, so you should restore worksheet titles to make the budget easier to use. First, switch to the Worksheet window for BUDGET1.WK3. Then restore titles:

Move to:	cell B5
Choose:	Worksheet Titles
Select:	Both *to freeze both horizontal and vertical titles*
	OK

9. Save BUDGET1.WK3 and close the file.

1-2-3 saves the pie chart with the file.

Congratulations! You have finished working with the Home Budget file for now.

A Note on Pie Charts and Data Ranges   1-2-3 uses the B range of a pie chart to control the colors or hatch patterns of the pie (depending on whether the graph is displayed in color or black and white). The B range also indicates whether a slice should be "exploded" (pulled away from the other slices). If you create a pie chart and the colors or hatch patterns seem strange, or one or more slices of the pie appear to be pulled away from the rest, the B range is probably set to the range of a previous graph. To reset the B range, use the graph menu's Chart Clear command and select to clear the B data range. See "Graphing Tips" later in this chapter for more on controlling the display characteristics of a pie chart.

Line Graphs

Bar graphs are a good way to compare related values, and pie charts are useful for illustrating the relationship of one value to the total of all values. Line graphs, on the other hand, generally show how one or more values change over time.

In this section, you are going to draw a graph that shows how Bob Gordon expects the Net Cash Flow for Folktale Workshop's products to change over the four quarters of 1992. You'll call the graph 1YR_PROJECTION (for "one-year projection"). Bob can see, from this graph, how the products will compare with each other in anticipated performance. He can also use the graph to show potential investors that his company is a good risk (assuming he can justify the assumptions on which his figures are based).

Once again, you'll use the CASHFLOW.WK3 worksheet file. Instead of creating a separate table of ranges to graph, as you did with the INCOME bar graph, you are going to draw the line graph from ranges that are already part of the worksheet file.

In addition to the commands described in Table 8-1, you are going to use the graph menu Chart commands in Table 8-3 to create the line graph. The completed graph will look like Figure 8-40. (You will print the graph in Chapter 9.)

Table 8-3: Graph Menu Chart Commands Used to Build the Line Graphs

Command	Option	What It Does:
Range	X, A-F	Establishes the ranges from which 1-2-3 draws the graph.
	Group Range	Specifies a table on which the graph is based; selects whether 1-2-3 interprets the rows or the columns of the table as containing the ranges to be graphed.
	Clear	Clears one or more graph settings.
Borders/Grids		Adds horizontal, vertical, or horizontal and vertical, grid lines to a graph.
Chart Headings		Adds a title, a subtitle, and notes to the graph.
Axis Y		Changes the display format of numbers along the y-axis scale.

Figure 8-40: The Finished Line Graph

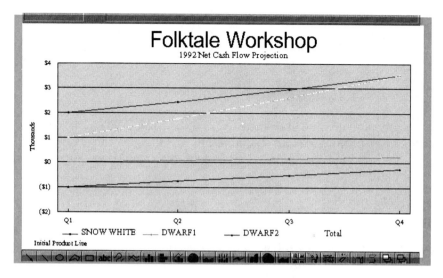

The Worksheet window for CASHFLOW.WK3 should now be active. If it is not, make it the active window, using one of the techniques you've used previously in this chapter.

1. Create an initial graph.

   In this step, you will create an initial graph called 1YR_PROJECTION that is based on data in a randomly selected cell. The initial range doesn't matter; you will actually specify all of the graph's ranges in the next step, using the graph menu's Chart Ranges command.

Move:	*a blank cell in the worksheet*
Choose:	Graph New
Select:	Graph Name
Type:	1yr_projection
Select:	OK

   1-2-3 opens a Graph window entitled CASHFLOW.WK3 1YR_PROJECTION, and makes it the active window. 1-2-3 switches to display the graph menu and the graph menu icon palette.

   You'll be doing a lot of work on 1YR_PROJECTION before you're done, so maximize the Graph window. You can double-click on the Graph window's title bar or select Maximize from the Control menu.

2. Define the X-axis labels.

   Since you are building a line graph, which is the default type, you do not have to specify the chart type; you can start right off specifying the x-axis labels. You use the graph menu's Chart Ranges command to define the X and A-F ranges for the graph. For this graph, the x-axis labels are units of time—the four quarters of 1992. Use the labels **Q1** through **Q4** on the summary worksheet for the X range.

Choose: Chart   Ranges

Select: X

Specify: A:B3..A:E3   *in the text box*

3. Define the A range.

The first three data ranges for the line graph will be the Net Cash Flow values for each of the four quarters, for each of the three products. You will graph the data directly from each product's worksheet, rather than creating and using a supplementary table. Use SNOW WHITE's net cash flow values as data range A.

Select: A   *for the A data range*

Specify: B:B9..B:E9   *in the text box*

Figure 8-41:   Specifying 1YR_PROJECTION's X and A Ranges

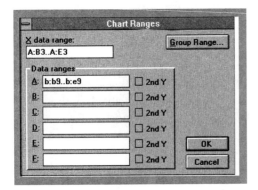

Look at the graph so far.

Select: OK

1-2-3 draws a one-line graph. (See Figure 8-42 on the following page.) It automatically scales the y-axis to the data. The x-axis is labeled with the four quarterly labels. Data points are marked on the graph.

4. Define the remaining data ranges.

You can define the remaining data ranges in the same manner as you defined the A range. In each case, use the Net Cash Flow row of the product's worksheet as the data range.

Figure 8-42: 1YR_PROJECTION with SNOW WHITE Graphed

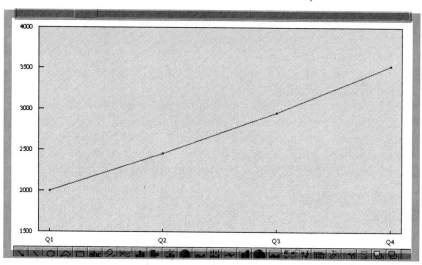

Choose:	Chart	Ranges
Select:	B	
Specify:	C:B9..C:E9	*DWARF1*
Select:	C	
Specify:	D:B9..D:E9	*DWARF2*
Select:	D	
Specify:	A:B9..A:E9	*Total*
Select:	OK	

Figure 8-43: The 1YR_PROJECTION with all Ranges Graphed

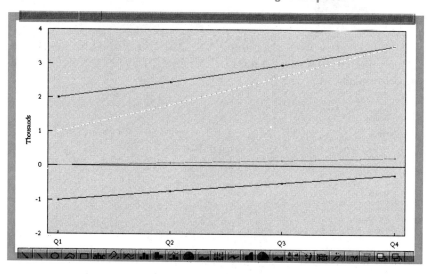

1-2-3 graphs all three products and the Total figures for each quarter. Notice that the y-axis scale has been adjusted to take into account the negative Net Cash Flow values for DWARF2. The data points of each line are marked with a different symbol.

5. Add legends to the graph.

The lines are all drawn, but you still can't really tell which line belongs to what product. Fix this by adding legends to identify the data ranges.

The legends for this graph are the product names and the word **Total**. To save time, you will assign all the legends at once, instead of individually. To do this, use the "Group Range" option of the Chart Legend command. This option assigns a range of labels to a series of data ranges. Each cell in the range of labels provides a legend for one data range. Since you have a range of cells with the proper labels in A:A25..A:A28, you use this as the Group Range for legends.

Choose:	Chart Legend
Select:	Group Range...
	Range
Specify:	A:A25..A:A28
Select:	OK *to return to the Chart Legend dialog box*

Figure 8-44:   Specifying Legends for 1YR_PROJECTION

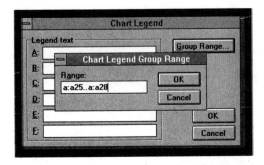

1-2-3 fills in \A:A25 as the legend for the A data range; \A:A26 as the legend for the B data range; \A:A27 for the C data range; and \A:A28 for the D data range. The back-slashes (\) indicate that the text box contains a data range, not text.

Select:	OK *to return 1-2-3 to READY mode*

1-2-3 identifies each of the lines with the appropriate legend, using the data point symbols. (See Figure 8-45 on the following page.) If the graph display is in color, the legend symbols are drawn in the color of the corresponding line.

6. Add a horizontal grid to the graph.

Figure 8-45: The 1YR_PROJECTION Graph with Legends

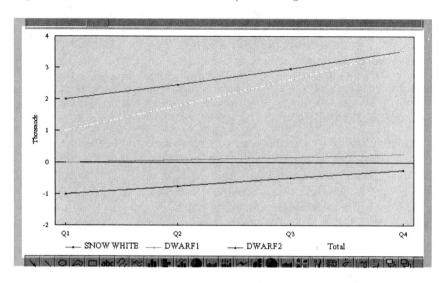

To make it easier to visualize the cash flow changes from quarter to quarter, add a horizontal grid to Bob's graph:

Select: `Chart`   `Borders/Grids`

                        `y-axis`   *and check the check-box*

                        `OK`

Figure 8-46: Now, 1YR_PROJECTION has a grid.

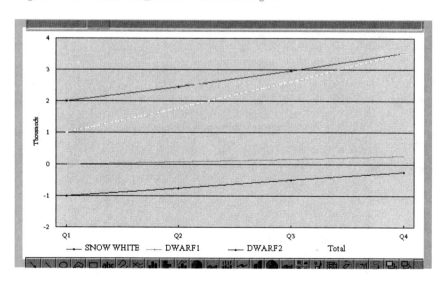

1-2-3 extends the tick marks on the y-axis across the graph.

The horizontal grid makes it easy to see something that the bar graphs you created earlier in this chapter didn't reveal: Although DWARF2 loses money the first year, the product's performance rises faster than the initially more profitable DWARF1 product. Bob finds this encouraging, though he is still not convinced the product is a good risk. (In Chapter 12, you'll have an opportunity to extend the Cash Flow Forecast over three years. Bob will be pleasantly surprised to see how DWARF2 performs.)

7. Add titles, subtitles, and a note to the graph.

You are nearly done with this graph. All that remains is to add some titles and refine the formatting a bit.

First, give the graph a title. Bob will most likely be using this graph in presentations, so give it a title, a subtitle, and a note to make its purpose clear to other users. When you have finished, the graph will look like Figure 8-48 (on the following page).

Choose:	Chart Headings
Select:	Title
Type:	Folktale Workshop
Select:	Subtitle
Type:	1992 Net Cash Flow Projection
Select:	Note
Type:	Initial Product Line
Select:	OK

Figure 8-47:   Adding headings to 1YR_PROJECTION

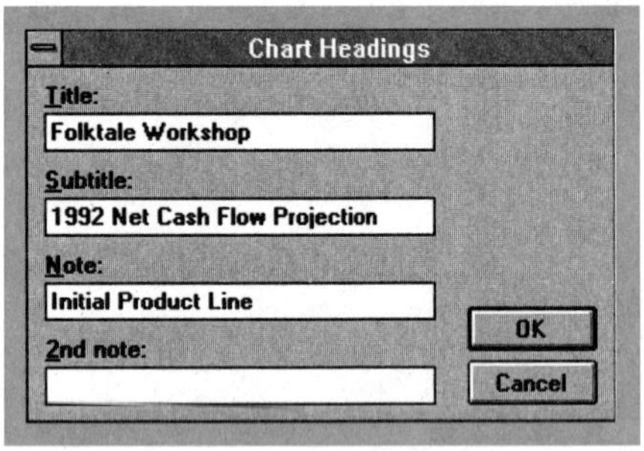

8. Format the y-axis figures.

The graph looks pretty much the way Bob wants it to look. The only remaining task is to change the format of the numbers along the y-axis: They should indicate currency, not numbers.

Figure 8-48:   The 1YR_PROJECTION with headings

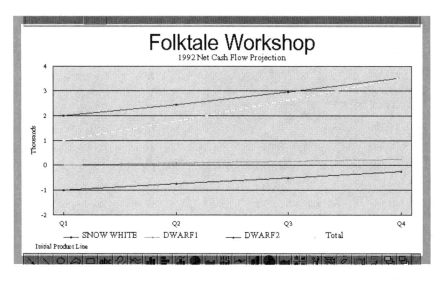

The "Format" option of the graph menu's Chart Axis Y command lets you format the numbers along the y-axis much as you would format the cells in a range. In this case, you are going to format the y-axis numbers as Currency, with zero decimal places.

Choose:	Chart Axis Y
Select:	Format
	Currency *from the Format list*
	Decimal places:
Type:	0 *in the text box*
Select:	OK *twice, to return 1-2-3 to READY mode*

Figure 8-49:   Formatting 1YR_PROJECTION's Y-axis

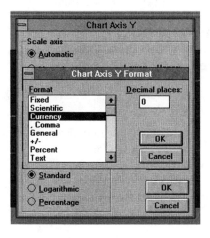

Figure 8-50: 1YR_PROJECTION with the Newly-formatted Y-axis

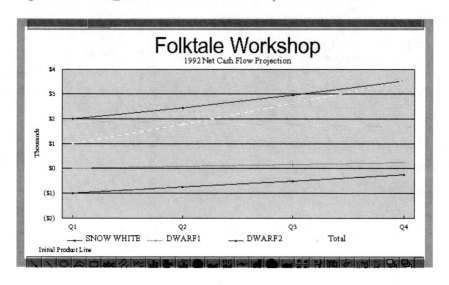

The numbers along the y-axis are now in Currency format with zero decimal places. Notice that negative numbers are in parentheses, just as they are in the worksheet.

9. Close the 1YR_PROJECTION Graph window and save CASHFLOW.WK3.

Close the Graph window for 1YR_PROJECTION using the graph menu's File Close command. Then save the graph in the worksheet file by saving CASHFLOW.WK3 again.

Choose: **File**   **Close**   *to close the Graph window*

                        File   **Save**

1-2-3 closes the Graph window for 1YR_PROJECTION, then saves the Cash Flow Forecast worksheet, the 1YR_PROJECTION graph, and the INCOME graph in the file CASHFLOW.WK3.

If you wish, take some time now to experiment on your own with other graph menu Chart command settings, to further refine the appearance of the line graph. When you are satisfied with your efforts, name the new graph and save the CASHFLOW.WK3 file again. In the following sections, you'll learn how to edit your graphs, and how to incorporate graphs directly into the worksheet. You'll use the Cash Flow worksheet and graphs for these exercises.

What-If Graphing

As you have seen in earlier chapters, what-if analysis uses the worksheet to predict the outcome of a situation, based on the effects of changing one or more assumptions.

1-2-3 is an integrated program, and its automatic recalculation feature extends to graphs. Change a value in the worksheet, and a graph based on that value reflects the change the next time it is drawn. This feature means you can create and test what-if scenarios with graphs. You can even save what-if graphics by saving different versions of the worksheet file, including the graph and its associated data. Later in this chapter, you'll learn how to add graphs to a worksheet with Graph Add to Sheet.. In Chapter 9, you'll print portions of the worksheet, including the added graphs, for a report that Bob is preparing for his investors.

Graphs are particularly useful with what-if analysis. In the following steps, you are going to experiment with using graphs for what-if analysis. First, you will modify the INCOME graph so that it shows only net income values. Then you'll change some of the figures in the Cash Flow Forecast worksheet. As you change graph settings and data, the graph will automatically reflect the changes.

■ *NOTE:*   This section changes data in the worksheet several times to display changes in the graphs. If you have set recalculation to manual, use the "Recalculation" option of the Tools User Setup command to reset recalculation to automatic now.

1. Save the CASHFLOW.WK3 worksheet file under a new name.

You will be modifying values and graph settings in the CASHFLOW.WK3 worksheet file. To make it easy to return to the previous values if you want to, save the file under a new name and make your changes to the new file. You'll name the new file WHATIF1.WK3.

Choose:	File Save As
Select:	File name
Type:	whatif1 *in the text box*
Select:	OK

1-2-3 saves the file as WHATIF1.WK3, and displays WHATIF1.WK3 in the title bar of the active Worksheet window. The latest version of CASHFLOW.WK3 remains on disk.

2. Tell 1-2-3 you want to update graphs automatically.

You can choose one of two ways to update graphs. If you want 1-2-3 to automatically display any changes you make to the graphed data, you can tell 1-2-3 to update graphs automatically. Or, if you would rather make all your changes before 1-2-3 updates the graphs, you can tell 1-2-3 not to update graphs until you are ready. You use the "Updated Automatically" option of the graph menu's Style Display Options command to select how 1-2-3 updates graphs. Since you want to use the graph to try some What-if scenarios, tell 1-2-3 to update graphs automatically.

First, you must open a Graph window for the graph INCOME. Doing so will give you access to the graph menu Style command. To open the Graph window, you will use the main menu's Graph View command.

Choose:	Graph View
Select:	INCOME OK

1-2-3 opens a Graph window entitled WHATIF.WK3 INCOME and makes it the active window. 1-2-3 displays the graph menu and the graph menu icon palette, so now you can use the graph menu's Style command.

Choose: `Style`   `Display Options`

Select: `Updated automatically`   *and check the check-box*

                 `OK`

From now on, any changes you make to the worksheet data on which the INCOME graph is based will automatically be reflected in the graph displayed in the Graph window.

■ *NOTE:*   If you have 1-2-3 is set to manually update graphs, you use the main menu's Graph Refresh command to update the graphs.

3. In the next step, you'll be modifying the INCOME graph. So that you can view the effect of these changes on the graph in the worksheet, switch to tile display mode. Use the graph menu's Window Tile command for this:

Choose: `Window`   `Tile`

Figure 8-51:   1-2-3 tiles the **INCOME** graph and the **WHATIF.WK3** Worksheet window.

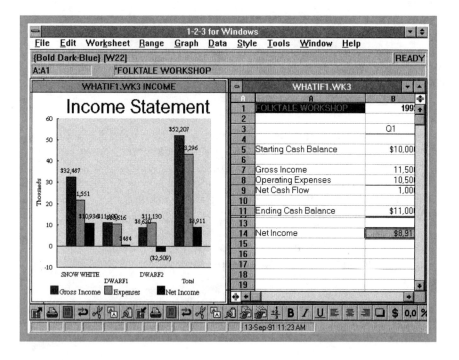

1-2-3 displays a pair of tiled windows—a Worksheet window for WHATIF.WK3, and a Graph window for WHATIF.WK3 INCOME.

4. Clear the A and B data ranges.

Suppose Bob Gordon wants to see how changing some of his estimates affects net income from his wooden toy business. Since Bob is concerned only with profit or loss figures, he wants to eliminate some of the clutter from the Income Statement graph, and pare it down to only the net income bars.

You can do this by using the graph menu's Chart Clear command to clear data ranges A and B, which graph gross income and operating expenses, respectively. Once these ranges have been cleared, only the net income data range will remain.

Choose: Chart   Clear

Select: A   *and check the check-box*

B   *and check the check-box*

OK

Figure 8-52:   The INCOME Graph After Clearing the A and B Ranges

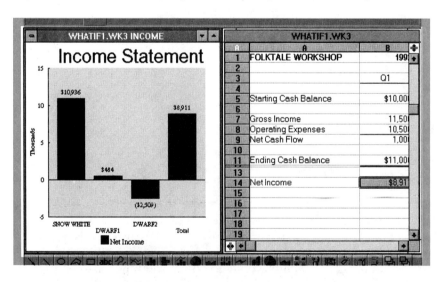

1-2-3 resets data ranges A and B and redraws the WHATIF1.WK3 INCOME Graph window. Notice that the bars for gross income and operating expenses are no longer graphed. Also notice that 1-2-3 has automatically eliminated the legends for these bars from the graph. Data range C, net income, is the only remaining data range.

5. Modify values in the worksheet.

In this step, you will modify data in the WHATIF.WK3 worksheet and view the effect in the tiled WHATIF.WK3 INCOME Graph window. The graph displays only annual net income for each product. See what happens to this graph when you try different scenarios.

For instance, looking at the graph, Bob realizes that he is going to lose money on the DWARF2 product this year. He wonders what would happen to his net income if he didn't use any metal parts in DWARF2.

To find out, change Bob's initial estimate of operating expenses for DWARF2 from $3,000 to $2,000.

Move to: cell D:B8

Type: 2000   ⏎

Figure 8-53:   The INCOME Graph Now Shows DWARF2 with Reduced Expenses

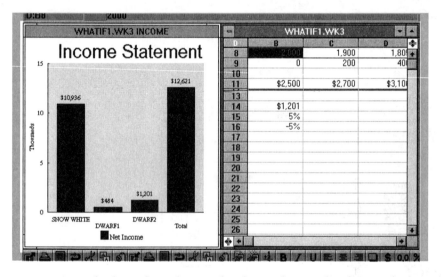

1-2-3 recalculates the values and redraws the graph. The graph shows that instead of losing money, DWARF2 is now earning Bob about $1,200 by the end of the year.

Having looked at the graph, Bob smiles, momentarily satisfied, then realizes he is being overly optimistic. His earlier estimate that expenses for DWARF2 would decrease was based on the assumption that the cost of using metal parts would go down over time, offsetting increases in other costs. With the metal parts no longer in the product, Bob now figures his total costs for DWARF2 will increase over time. He revises his estimate of **% Change in Expenses** from -5 percent to +4 percent.

Move to: cell D:B16

Type: 4%   ⏎

1-2-3 again redraws the graph. This time, the estimate for DWARF2's annual profits is down to $127.

Gritting his teeth, Bob also realizes that eliminating the metal parts will probably affect sales of the product adversely. He cuts both the initial gross income figure and the **% Change in Income** figure down by two percentage points.

Move to:	cell D:B7
Press:	F2 **(EDIT)**
Type:	-2%*2000 ↵
Move to:	cell D:B15
Type:	3% ↵

Figure 8-54: DWARF2 After Reducing Income

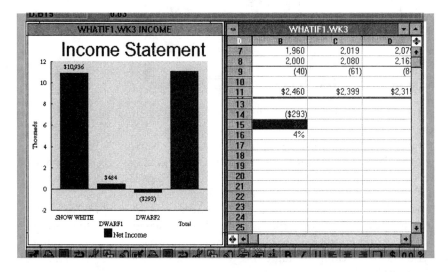

DWARF2's net income drops first to about negative $45, and then to negative $293. Now Bob is a little worried. He decides to call up the line graph of net income projections to see how net income looks over time.

6. Open a Graph window for the 1YR_PROJECTION graph.

Use the Graph View command to view the 1YR_PROJECTION graph, then tile all three windows.

Choose:	Graph View
Select:	1YR_PROJECTION OK
Choose:	Window Tile

Figure 8-55: 1-2-3 Tiles the Two Graph Windows with the Worksheet Window

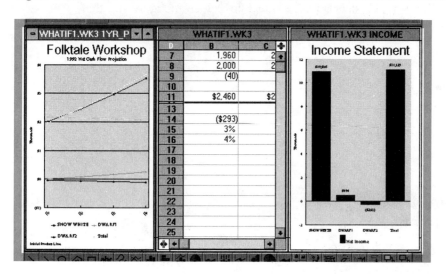

Now both Graph windows and the Worksheet window are simultaneously displayed in the 1-2-3 windows, and Bob can check his data against them.

From the line graph, it is obvious that if Bob follows his present course, DWARF2 will steadily lose money, even though it loses less the first year than it had in his original scenario. Bob realizes that, in the long run, he is probably better off leaving things the way they were. He decides to sleep on it, and see if he can find a better solution another time.

Now, close and save the WHATIF1.WK3 file again. Up to now, you've used File Save to save a file, then File Close to close it. The main menu's File Close, however, is quite useful in that it prompts you to save a modified file before closing it. From now on, you can use whichever closing sequence you choose. You must make the Worksheet window for WHATIF.WK3 active to access the main menu's File Close.

Choose: `File  Close`

Select: `Yes` *to save the file*

1-2-3 saves WHATIF1.WK3, including the modified INCOME graph and the 1YR_PROJECTION graph, and closes all windows it had opened for WHATIF1.WK3.

Adding Graphs to Worksheets

In this section, you are going to use the main menu's Graph Add to Sheet command to add graphs directly to ranges in your worksheet. The ability to add graphs to the worksheet is an important new capability of 1-2-3 for Windows. Once a graph is added to worksheet, you can print the graph on a printer with graphic capabilities simply by printing the range that contains the graph. This allows you to quickly create on-line and printed presentations of your data. (You will be printing graphs in Chapter 9.)

In addition, graphs added to the worksheet are updated just like graphs you view in Graph windows: If you check the "Updated automatically" option of the graph menu's Style Display Options command, the graph is updated whenever the underlying data changes. Otherwise, you must update the graph manually, using the main menu's Graph Refresh command.

You will use the commands described in Table 8-4 to add graphs to the worksheet and then view those graphs.

Table 8-4: Main Menu Graph Commands Used to Add Graphs to the Worksheet

Command	What It Does:
Add to Sheet	Inserts a graph into a range in the worksheet.
Size	Changes the size of a graph that you have added to a worksheet.
View	Opens a graph window for an existing graph.

1. Open the worksheet file CASHFLOW.WK3.

   In this exercise, you will add the INCOME graph to the Cash Flow Forecast. First, open the worksheet file CASHFLOW.WK3:

   Choose: File   Open
   Select: CASHFLOW.WK3   OK

   1-2-3 opens the worksheet file CASHFLOW.WK3, displays the file in a Worksheet window entitled CASHFLOW.WK3, and makes that window active.

2. Add the INCOME graph to the worksheet.

   The main menu command Graph Add to Sheet inserts a graph into the worksheet in the range you specify. You can add any previously created graph. (You can also add a .PIC file or metafile [.CGM file] this way.) As with most 1-2-3 commands that operate on a range, Graph Add to Sheet lets you highlight the worksheet range in which you want the graph displayed, before you choose the command. Remember that 1-2-3 needs to display the graph in the range you specify, so do not pick a range that is too small, or that is shaped in a way that would distort the appearance of the graph..

   Highlight: A:A30..A:E37
   Choose: Graph   Add to Sheet
   Select: INCOME   OK

   1-2-3 adds the INCOME graph to the worksheet in the range you specified. Now you see that the range you specified is too small: The graph is difficult to see.

Figure 8-56: The INCOME Graph Added to the Cash Flow Forecast

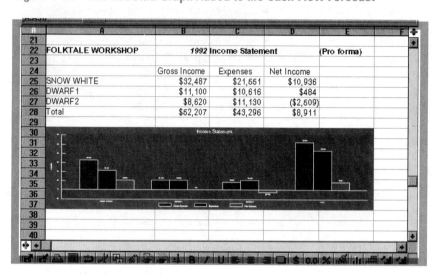

3. Resize the graph on the worksheet.

The main menu's Graph Size command lets you respecify the range in which 1-2-3 draws the graph. Use Graph Size to specify a larger range for the INCOME graph.

Highlight: A:A30..A:E48 *the resized graph range*

Choose: Graph Size

Select: INCOME *as the graph name*

 OK

1-2-3 draws an enlarged INCOME graph to fit the specified range. Although you've now lost the ability to view the graph full-size on a single screen, it *will* fit nicely on a letter-size page, as you'll see when you print this graph in Chapter 9. Bob decides that this is the right approach... he's more interested in how the graph will appear in the printed Income Statement report than in how it looks on his screen.

■ *NOTE:* You can fit the graph on a single screen if you zoom to 70%, using the "Zoom" option of the Window Display Options command.

As Bob peers at the graph, he becomes a little disturbed by that negative net income figure for DWARF2. Maybe he can change the graph to de-emphasize it a bit. He decides to change the y-scale. To do this, you must first open a Graph window for the INCOME graph to gain access to the Graph window menu.

4. Open a Graph window for the INCOME graph.

To open a Graph window, you can use Graph View. Or you can simply double-click anywhere in the range in which the graph is displayed.

Double click: *anywhere in the range A:A30..A:E48*

1-2-3 opens a Graph window for the graph.

5. Manually scale the y-axis.

   Normally, 1-2-3 automatically determines the beginning and ending values for the y-axis. 1-2-3 tries to use ranges that take into account the values you are graphing. Sometimes, however, the values 1-2-3 chooses appear to exaggerate differences, or in some other way convey a different impression from the one you want to convey. And, sometimes, the scale that 1-2-3 selects just doesn't give the data the slant you want it to have. In these cases, you can manually adjust the axes. You use the graph menu's Chart Axis command to change the scale of the y-axis, and, if you are drawing an XY graph, the x-axis.

   Changing the scale involves two steps: (1) Tell 1-2-3 that the scale will be set manually, and (2) select an upper and lower limit for the scale.

Choose:	Chart	Axis	Y
Select:	Manual	*in the Scale axis text box*	
	Lower		
Type:	20000	*in the text box*	
Select:	Upper		
Type:	60000	*in the text box*	
Select:	OK		

Figure 8-57:   The INCOME Chart with Y-axis Set to -20000

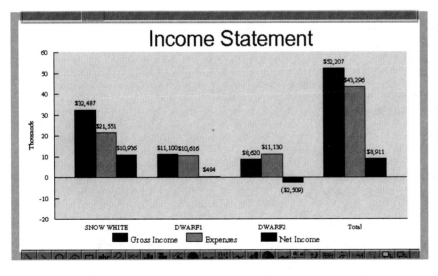

1-2-3 now displays a y-axis on which the scale extends from minus -$20,000 to $60,000.

- ■ **NOTE:** Changing the y-axis to manual scaling is a good technique for sprucing up a presentation version of a graph. It does, however, negatively impact the use of the graph for what-if graphing: The manually-scaled y-axis will not automatically change scales to reflect changes in data.

    Bob decides he wants to add the 1YR_PROJECTION graph to the worksheet as well. That way, he can print a copy of that graph. He's not exactly certain if he'll use this graph in his presentation, so he decides to insert a new sheet into the Cash Flow Forecast and add the 1YR_PROJECTION to that sheet.

- ■ **NOTE:** You can print a graph in 1-2-3 only by adding it to a worksheet. However, you *can* cut the graph from the Graph window to the Clipboard, import it to a graphics program such as, Paintbrush, and print it through that program.

6. Insert a new sheet as the last sheet of the Cash Flow Forecast.

    First, make the Worksheet window for CASHFLOW.WK3 active. Then, move to the last sheet of the file. Finally, insert the new sheet after the current sheet, using the "Sheet" option of the Worksheet Insert command. You'll start by using Control+F6 to make the Worksheet window for the Cash Flow Forecast active.

Press:	`CTRL+F6` *to make the next window active*
Move to:	*anywhere on sheet E*
Choose:	`Worksheet    Insert`
Select:	`Sheet    After    OK`

    1-2-3 inserts a new sheet after sheet E. Now add the 1YR_PROJECTION graph to sheet F.

7. Add the graph 1YR_PROJECTION to sheet F.

    Once again, you'll use the Graph Add to Sheet command to add the 1YR_PROJECTION graph to a range. You'll select the largest range that 1-2-3 can display on a single screen.

Highlight:	F:A1..H20
Choose:	`Graph    Add to Sheet`
Point to:	1YR_PROJECTION
Select:	`OK`

    1-2-3 inserts the 1YR_PROJECTION graph. It'll be there when Bob wants to print it in Chapter 9. (See Figure 8-58.)

8. Save and close the Cash Flow Forecast.

    Save and close CASHFLOW.WK3 with the INCOME graph added to sheet A and the 1YR_PROJECTION added to sheet F.

Figure 8-58:   The 1YR_PROJECTION Graph Added to the Worksheet

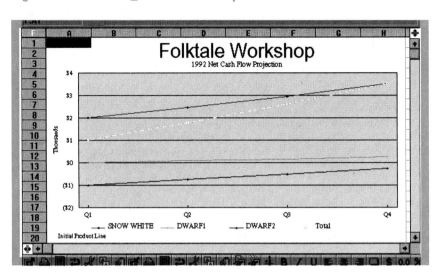

Congratulations! You did some good work adding graphs to worksheets. You might want to take a little break before you continue with the next section on adding text and graphics elements to your graphs.

Adding Text and Graphics Elements

In this section you will use the graph menu's Draw and Style commands to add descriptive text and graphics elements, such as lines and arrows, to the INCOME graph.

Once you've enhanced the graph this way, you can think of it as a chart: A *chart* is 1-2-3's term for a graph to which you've added text and graphics. You'll work with the chart in a Graph window. You will also use the graph menu's Window command to magnify portions of the chart.

You will use the graph menu Window, Draw, and Style commands described in table 8-5 to edit graphs and charts. You will also use the graph menu icon palette extensively in this section; it includes icons to automate many of the procedures for adding text and graphics to graphs.

Table 8-5:   Graph Menu Commands Used to Edit Graphs

Command	What It Does:
Window commands	
Enlarge	Enlarges the display of the contents of a Graph window.
Reduce	Reduces a graph.
Zoom	Enlarges a specified area of a Graph window.

Command	What It Does:
Full	Returns a graph to full size.

Draw commands

Text	Inserts text into a Graph window.
Line	Inserts a line into a Graph window.
Arrow	Inserts an arrow into a Graph window.

Style commands

Add	Adds text and graphics to a graph.
Select	Selects one or more items in the graphic editor.
Edit	Edits selected items in the graphic.
Transform	Sizes and rotates a graphic.
Rearrange	Deletes, moves, and copies items in the graphic editor.
View	Changes the part of the graph you are viewing in the graphic editor.
Options	Changes the size of text in the graphic and displays or hides a grid.
Quit	Returns 1-2-3 to READY mode.

Magnifying the Contents of the Graph window

As you add text and graphics to your graphs, you will be working in the Graph window. To get a closer look at your work—for example, to see how close an arrow head comes to a particular slice on a pie graph—you may want to magnify portions of the graph. The graph menu's Window commands give you several ways to get a closer look at a graph.

In this section, you will work with the graph menu Window commands. You'll enlarge and reduce the graph, zoom in on selected areas of the graph, and then return the graph to normal display size.

1. Open the Cash Flow Forecast worksheet file now:

Choose: File   Open
Select: cashflow.wk3   OK

1-2-3 opens the worksheet file CASHFLOW.WK3, displays it in a Worksheet window entitled CASHFLOW.WK3, and makes that window active.

Move to A:A1. Then page down to look at the INCOME graph that you added in the previous section. Then move to sheet F for a look at the 1YR_PROJECTION graph that you added.

2. Open a Graph window for the INCOME graph.

Use the main menu's Graph View command to open a Graph window for the INCOME graph.

Choose: Graph   View

Select: INCOME   OK

Figure 8-59:   1-2-3 opens a Graph window for the INCOME graph.

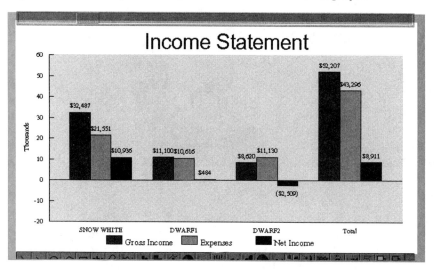

1-2-3 opens a Graph window entitled CASHFLOW.WK3 INCOME, and makes it the active window. 1-2-3 now displays the graph menu and the graph menu icon palette.

Maximize the Graph window by clicking on the Maximize button in the Graph window control panel.

3. Enlarge the graph.

You can use the graph menu's Window Enlarge command to magnify the graph being displayed in the Graph window. A simpler way to activate this command is to use the keypad plus (+) key.

Press: *the keypad plus (+) key two times*

1-2-3 magnifies the graph. (See Figure 8-60; on the following page.) The Graph window now includes scroll bars that you can use to look at other areas of the Graph window. Scroll the graph to the left and right to get a feel for this magnified view of the graph.

4. Return to the full view of the graph.

At this point, this isn't a very helpful view of the graph, so return the display to the original full view. You can either choose Window Full, or press the keypad asterisk (*) key.

Press: *the keypad asterisk (*) key*

1-2-3 returns the display to full size.

Figure 8-60:   An Enlarged View of the INCOME Graph

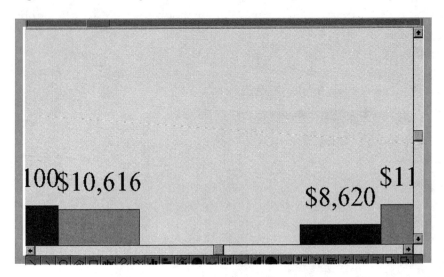

5. Zoom in on the graph.

Another way to magnify a portion of the graph window is to use the Window Zoom command, which you can also access by pressing the at-sign (@) key. This command fills the screen with a specified portion of the graph. Try viewing just a portion of the graph with the at-sign (@) key. You can "zoom" any section of the graph, for an up-close view.

Press: *the at-sign (@) key*

1-2-3 prompts you to "Move to the first corner." You'll move the mouse pointer to one corner of the area you want to view, then click on the mouse button. 1-2-3 then prompts to "Stretch the box". You'll drag the box to encompass the area you want to view. When you release the mouse button, 1-2-3 will redraw the display so that the boxed area fills the screen.

■ *NOTE:*   As you stretch the box, you'll notice that 1-2-3 keeps track of your location with X and Y coordinates in the format bar of the screen. The directions you will follow in these exercises specify approximate X and Y coordinates. Don't worry if you can't locate the exact same coordinates. The results will be the same as long as your coordinates are close to the suggested ones.

You will find that many of the graph menu's commands begin by prompting you for a corner of an area. Think of it as if 1-2-3 were prompting you for the first cell in a range.

Press: *the at-sign (@) key*
Point to: *0,0   the upper left corner of the graph*
Click on: *the mouse button*

1-2-3 prompts you to "Stretch the box."

Drag to: 2000,2000   *around the middle of the graph*

   Notice that as you move the mouse, 1-2-3 drags the rectangle around the area currently selected. When you release the mouse button, 1-2-3 redraws the display so that the boxed area fills the screen.

   Now 1-2-3 displays only the top left quarter of the graph. Don't worry—the graph has not been changed. 1-2-3 has altered only the display. Also notice that 1-2-3 is again displaying scroll bars on the Graph window. You can use the scroll bars to view other portions of the Graph window at the current magnification.

6. Return the graph to normal display size:

Use the keypad asterisk (*) key to return the graph to normal display size.

Press: *the keypad asterisk (*) key*

   1-2-3 returns the graph to normal display size.

Adding and Modifying Text and Lines in a Graph

Now comes the fun part. First, you will add some more text to the Graph window. Then you'll really get serious, and add some descriptive arrows that point out the real meat of the graph.

1. Add a note to the graph.

First, add a note that explains when the graph was created. You could add the note anywhere in the graph, even in the middle of one of the bars, but adding it to the bottom won't interfere with the graph's data. You can add text using either the Draw Text command, or the graph menu icon palette's "Add text" icon, which looks like this:

   This time, use the icon.

Click on: *the Draw Text icon*
Select: `New text`
Type: `Drawn: August 8, 1992.`   *in the text box*
Select: `OK`

   1-2-3 changes the mouse pointer to a black cross. Move to where you want 1-2-3 to enter the text.

Move to: 435,3980   *the lower left corner of the graph*

   1-2-3 adds the text to the Graph window at the specified location. You'll notice that the text is surrounded by "handles," indicating that the text item you created is currently selected.

■ *NOTE:*   In the Graph window, whenever you want to move or edit an item you must first select that item. When you create an item, 1-2-3 automatically selects it.

Figure 8-61: The INCOME Graph with Text Added

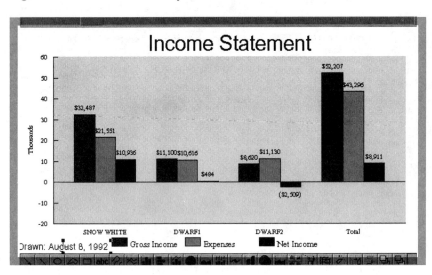

2. Change the font of the text.

The text looks good at the bottom of the graph, but the Arial MT 10 font makes it stand out too much. Try TimesNewRomanPS 10.

Choose: Style   Font

1-2-3 opens the dialog box that contains your font options. The options are identical to those 1-2-3 displays when you choose the main menu's Style Font command.

Select: TimesNewRomanPS 10   OK

Figure 8-62: The note is now in displayed in TimesNewRomanPS 10.

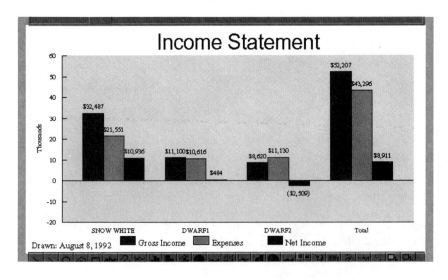

1-2-3 redraws the note in the larger font.

3. Edit the note.

You can edit text that you add to the Graph window using F2 (EDIT). Because the text was the last item you added to the Graph window, it is already selected.

Press: F2   **(EDIT)**

             DELETE

Type: Drawn by: your name

Select: OK

1-2-3 redraws the edited note, adding your personalized touch.

4. Add an arrow to the graph.

Now add an arrow to the graph that points to that troublesome DWARF2 range. Use the "Add arrow" icon, which looks like this:

Click on: *the Draw Arrow icon*

Point to: 2515,1648   *to select the first point*

Click on: *the mouse button*

Drag to: 2778, 2669   *to select the next point*

Double click: *the mouse button*

When you double click, 1-2-3 draws an arrow that points to the DWARF2 data range. When you draw an arrow, the direction will always be toward the last point you specify.

Figure 8-63: The Arrow Points to DWARF2

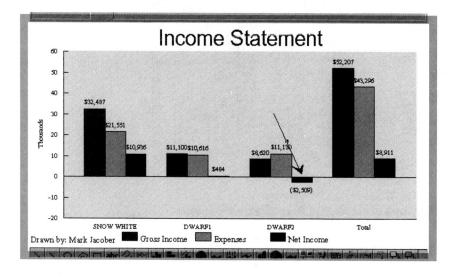

5. Add text to the arrow.

The arrow is nice, but it doesn't tell you why you are highlighting that data bar. Add some descriptive text next to the arrow that explains its significance. Use the "Draw Text" icon, and add the text into the "New" text box.

Click on: *the Draw Text icon*

Type: `This item is losing too much money!`

Select: OK

1-2-3 changes the mouse pointer to a black cross and prompts you to "Place text:". Move the mouse pointer to where you want the text and press Enter:

Press: ↵

Once again, the text is located in the wrong place. You'll need to change the font and move the text closer to the arrow.

Click on: *the text "This item is losing too much money!"*

The mouse pointer changes to a hand, indicating that you can move the selected item by dragging the mouse.

Drag to: 2253,1450   *just above the arrow*

When you release the mouse button, 1-2-3 redraws the text in the correct position just above the arrow.

Figure 8-64:   The Arrow and a Description

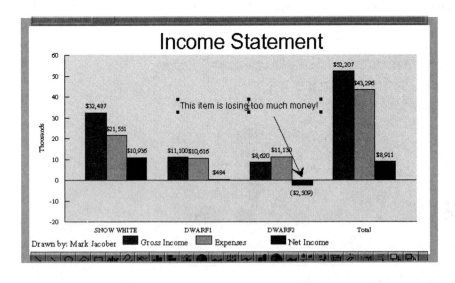

6. Unselect the text.

You are almost finished with the graph, but before you save it, take a final look without any selected items. Remove the handles around the arrow text.

Choose: Edit   Select   None

Well, the graph looks pretty good, but just in case anyone else looks at the worksheet, you should probably get rid of the arrow and text. You can use the graph menu's Edit Delete command to delete text and graphic items from the Graph window, or you can simply click on the item(s) and press Delete.

Click on: *the text "This item is losing too much money!"*
Press: DELETE   *to delete the text*
Click on: *the arrow*
Press: DELETE   *to delete the arrow*

     1-2-3 redraws the graph without the arrow or arrow text.

Figure 8-65: The INCOME Graph with the Arrow and Text Deleted

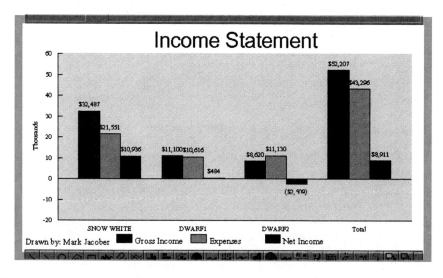

7. Close the Graph window.

You are finished with the graph and ready to return to the worksheet.

Choose: File   Close

     1-2-3 closes the Graph window and makes the Worksheet window entitled CASHFLOW.WK3 active. 1-2-3 displays the main menu and main menu icon palette. The graph is still in the worksheet, and it includes the note you created. A job well done.

8. Save CASHFLOW.WK3.

Congratulations! You have completed your work on the Cash Flow Forecast for now. Save CASHFLOW.WK3.

Graphing Tips

This section describes tips, techniques, and gotchas that apply to 1-2-3 graphs. It suggests some refinements you can make to graphs beyond those covered in the exercises in this chapter, and encourages you to continue to explore the features available through the main menu's Graph command and the commands of the graph menu.

Set up Your Graphs as Tables

In 1-2-3/W, you create graphs using the main menu's Graph New command. Although Graph New will create a graph based on *any* selected data range, it is designed to operate on a table which has the form illustrated in Figure 8-66.

Figure 8-66:   The Form for Graph New Tables

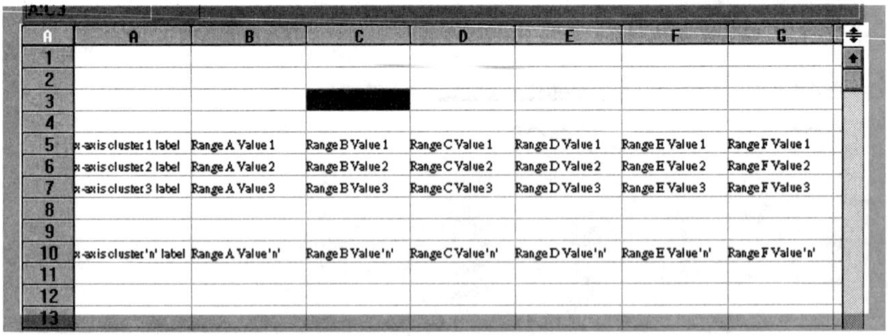

	A	B	C	D	E	F	G
1							
2							
3							
4							
5	x-axis cluster 1 label	Range A Value 1	Range B Value 1	Range C Value 1	Range D Value 1	Range E Value 1	Range F Value 1
6	x-axis cluster 2 label	Range A Value 2	Range B Value 2	Range C Value 2	Range D Value 2	Range E Value 2	Range F Value 2
7	x-axis cluster 3 label	Range A Value 3	Range B Value 3	Range C Value 3	Range D Value 3	Range E Value 3	Range F Value 3
8							
9							
10	x-axis cluster 'n' label	Range A Value 'n'	Range B Value 'n'	Range C Value 'n'	Range D Value 'n'	Range E Value 'n'	Range F Value 'n'
11							
12							
13							

It is almost always easier to graph a table than to graph ranges scattered throughout the worksheet. Just as you might keep one range in a worksheet specifically for macros, you can set up a range to be used only for tables you intend to graph. Use formulas to reference the ranges that contain the actual worksheet data. If you want to preserve a particular graph, first use the "Convert to values" option of The Edit Quick Copy command to convert the table to a table of numbers, then create the graph, giving it a name that identifies what is being graphed.

Flipping a Graph on its Side

By default, 1-2-3 displays graphs so that the x-axis is along the bottom of the graph, and the first y-axis is along the left side. However, some graphs, particularly bar graphs with long labels in the x-axis or long data labels, look better and are easier to read if they are rotated 90 degrees. To rotate a graph 90 degrees, you use Graph Type command or select the "Horizontal bar graph" icon, which looks like this:

Setting Hatch Patterns and Colors on a Pie Chart

When you create a pie chart, 1-2-3 automatically tries to give each slice of the pie a different color or hatch pattern. However, there may be times when you want to assign specific hatch patterns or colors to different slices. For example, assigning the same color or hatch pattern to several related pie slices can help to visually group related quantities together. There may also be times when you want the color of a pie slice to depend on a calculated worksheet value.

To add hatch patterns or colors to the slices, create a new B range. Each cell in the B range contains the hatch pattern or color for the corresponding slice of the graph.

You can display a pie chart in up to eight different colors, or seven different hatch patterns. See Figure 8-67 for the assignment of the hatch patterns. To see the available colors, create a graph with eight slices and use a B data range to assign a different number from 1 to 8 to each slice.

Figure 8-67: Assigning Hatch Patterns

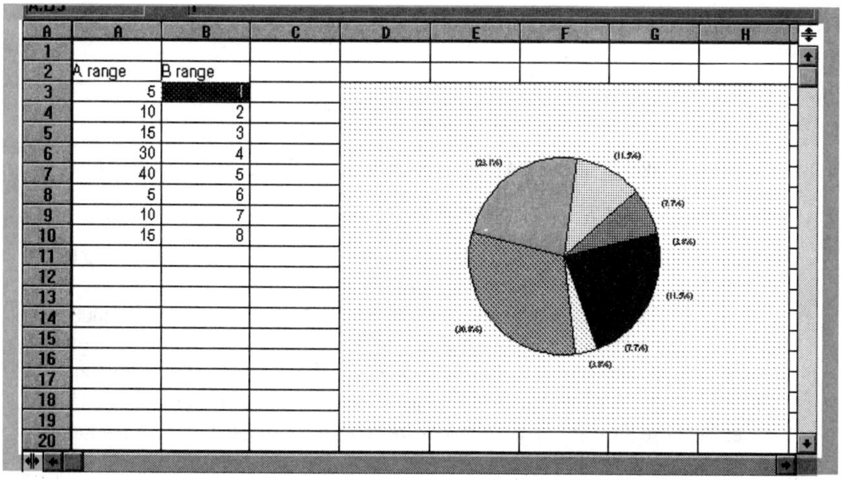

To make a particular slice turn a particular color, depending on a worksheet value, use an @IF formula in the cell that controls that pie slice. For example, the following formula, if placed in the cell corresponding to the color value for woodworking expenses, would turn the pie slice for woodworking red if the value in a cell named WOODWORK were greater than 10% of the value in a cell named TOTAL. Otherwise, the pie slice is displayed in green.

```
@IF(woodwork/total>.1,2,3)
```

Exploding a Slice of the Pie   The advantage to using a B range to set pie slice colors is that the B range also lets you make one or more slices of a pie chart "explode," or break away from, the pie in order to emphasize a particular value or values. To explode a slice of a pie chart, add 100 to the color value for the cell in the B range that corresponds to the slice you want to explode. Like the values that determine colors or hatch patterns, you can use a number, a computed value, a cell reference, or an @IF statement to control whether a slice is exploded. (You can also hide a pie slice by using a negative value in the B range.)

Saving a Graph as a Picture File You may want to insert a 1-2-3 graph into an application other than 1-2-3. For example, a 1-2-3 graph might really spiff up a business report that you create with a word processor. If you use a word processor that can insert .PCX files (picture files) into text you can do that as follows.

First copy the graph to the Clipboard, using 1-2-3's Edit Copy command or the "Copy to Clipboard" Smart Icon. Next, start up the Windows Paintbrush application by clicking on the Paintbrush icon from the Windows Program Manager. Now, paste the contents of the Clipboard—the 1-2-3 graph—into a blank Paintbrush file. Next, save the Paintbrush file as a .PCX file. At that point, you can insert the graph's .PCX file into any application that accepts the .PCX format.

At a Glance

The following table summarizes the tasks presented in this chapter.

Task	How To Do It:
Graphing in color	Clear the "B&W" option to the main menu's Window Display Options command.
Graphing in black and white	Set the "B&W" option to the main menu's Window Display Options command.
Creating a graph	Creating a graph in 1-2-3 requires the following basic steps: (1) Enter the data to be graphed; (2) choose the main menu's Graph New; (3) choose the graph menu's Chart Ranges command to add additional ranges of data you want to graph; (4) choose other graph menu Chart commands to identify the graphed data with titles, legends, and data labels; (5) refine the graph's appearance (for example, change the format of the x-axis and y-axis; change the colors or hatch patterns of bars, lines, and pie slices; and use different fonts and type sizes for titles and legends); (6) save the graph by saving the worksheet file.
Selecting a graph type	Choose the graph menu's Chart Type command or click on the Graph window's "Graph Type" icon.
Labeling the x-axis (or, for a pie chart, the slices)	Choose the graph menu's Chart Ranges command, and type in or highlight the X range.
Specifying a range of data to be graphed	Choose the graph menu's Chart Ranges command, and type in or highlight the A (through F) range(s).
Viewing a graph	Choose the main menu's Graph View command. If the graph has been added to the worksheet, double-click the range that contains the graph.
Adding data range legends	Choose the graph menu's Chart Legend command and either type in the legend or type in a backslash followed by the address of the cell that contains the legend.
Adding graph titles	Choose the graph menu's Chart Headings command and either type in the title or type in a backslash followed by the address of the cell that contains the title.

Task	How To Do It:
Adding data labels	Choose the graph menu's Chart Data Labels command and select the range for the data-range labels.
Adding grid lines	Check the "Show grid lines" option of the graph menu's Style Display Options command.
Formatting the y-axis figures	Select the "Format" option of the graph menu's Chart Axis Y command, and choose a format.
Adding a graph to a worksheet	Choose the main menu's Graph Add to Sheet command.
Deleting unnecessary graphs	Choose the main menu's Graph Name Delete command.
Saving a graph	File Save the worksheet file from which the graph is drawn.
Adding an arrow to a graph	Choose the graph menu's Draw Arrows command, or click on the Graph window's "Draw Arrow" icon.
Adding text to a graph	Choose the graph menu's Draw Text command, or click on the Graph window's "Draw Text" icon.

Chapter 9

Spreadsheet Publishing

This chapter teaches the basic skills of spreadsheet publishing—printing the data from your 1-2-3 worksheets and graphs.

As you work through the exercises in this chapter, you are going to print data from a single worksheet, from multiple worksheets, and from named ranges. You will also print ranges that contain the graphs you added to worksheets in Chapter 8. You'll learn how to set up your printer as well as how to set up the page. Along the way, you'll learn many other aspects of printing with 1-2-3.

What You'll Learn

By the time you finish this chapter, you'll know how to:

- Choose and set up the printer

- Print a worksheet

- Preview a print job

- Use, change, and save the page setup (including margins, page orientation, and using compressed print)

- Print graphs

- Insert and remove page breaks

- Print column and row borders

- Use headers and footers

Before You Start

Before you begin the exercises in this chapter, start 1-2-3. Make sure that the cell pointer is in cell A:A1 of a new, maximized, blank worksheet file, and that 1-2-3 has been set up to save files in your 123BOOK directory.

As you work through the exercises in this chapter, you will modify files named CASHFLOW.WK3 and CONTACT3.WK3 that you created in previous chapters. (A disk containing the worksheets created in this book is also available from the authors.) As in previous chapters, stop at the end of a numbered step or just before the next section heading when you are tired or have something else to do. Be sure to save any modified worksheet files before you stop. If you have more than one active file, write down the names of the files in memory and the order in which they are stored. When you want to continue with the exercises, start up 1-2-3, read in the worksheet files you last used in the same order they were in before you stopped, then pick up where you left off.

■ **NOTE:**   The exercises assume that you have installed the Adobe Type Manager (ATM) and the ATM fonts that are included with 1-2-3/W, and that you turned on the Adobe Type Manager using the ATM Control Panel. If you have not installed or turned on the Adobe Type Manager, do so using the procedures in "1-2-3 and the Adobe Type Manager" at the end of Chapter 7.

A Note on Example Layout   As in previous chapters, the examples in this chapter assume that your screen displays 20 rows and eight columns when the Worksheet window is maximized. If your display does not show 20 rows and eight columns, your screens will look somewhat different from the illustrations, but you can still do all the examples. Just be sure to use the cell addresses and ranges specified in the instructions.

A Note on Keystroke Instructions   The keystroke instructions in this chapter often assume you are using a mouse to perform such operations as highlighting a range or selecting an option in a dialog box. You can also use the keyboard to perform the same operations. Many of the keyboard equivalents to mouse operations were described in previous chapters. A few of the most common ones are summarized here. For a complete list of keystroke equivalents to mouse operations, see the 1-2-3 documentation or the 1-2-3 online Help.

   Throughout this chapter, the Edit Copy and Edit Paste commands are used in the exercises whenever you copy data from one range to another. In all these places, using the Edit Quick Copy command or the "Copy To" icon are perfectly viable alternatives to Edit Copy and Edit Paste. This chapter also instructs you to highlight a range and use the Delete key whenever you have to clear cells. The Edit Clear command or the "Cut" icon would work equally well. In all tasks, feel free to use the approach you find most comfortable.

A Note on the Illustrations in this Chapter   The illustrations for this chapter have been printed on a PostScript printer. If you use a different printer, your printouts may look somewhat different from the illustrations. However, in most cases, the printed values and the basic elements of the page should be the same. Your results should differ significantly only if the printer you use does not support one of the features described here.

   If you follow the keystroke instructions in this chapter and your printouts do not look like the illustrations in the book, you may have established page settings at some earlier time. Use the File Page Setup command to restore the default print settings, reestablish the settings established by the keystroke instructions, and try again.

A Note on Choosing a Printer   Printing in 1-2-3 is easy; the biggest problem most people have is setting up the printer with Windows. When you installed Windows, you were given an opportunity to install your printers. If at that time (or subsequently, using the Windows Control Panel) you installed the printer you plan to use for printing spreadsheets *and* you selected

Keyboard Equivalents to Mouse Operations

Operation	Instruction		Keyboard Equivalent	
Complete action and close dialog box	**Select:**	OK	**Press:**	↵
Cancel action and close dialog box	**Select:**	Cancel	**Press:**	ESC
Highlight a text box	**Select:**	text box	**Press:**	ALT+*underlined_letter*
Edit a range in a text box	**Select:**	Range	**Press:**	ALT+*underlined_letter*
	Specify:	A:A1..C:D4		F2 (EDIT)
Edit a number or word in a text box	**Select:**	text box	**Press:**	ALT+*underlined_letter*
	Specify:	new text	**Type:**	new text
	(or click on text and edit it)		*(or press Left arrow and edit text)*	
Highlight a range	**Highlight:** A:A1..C:D4		**Move to:**	cell A:A1
			Press:	F4
			Move to:	cell D4
			Press:	↵

to use the Window Print Manager, you can proceed directly to the next section, "Worksheet Printing Basics". If not, you should install your printer(s), select to use the Windows Print Manager, and follow the procedures in "Installation of a Printer" in the (*Microsoft Windows User's Guide.*) Then, return to "Worksheet Printing Basics" and do the exercises in this chapter.

Worksheet Printing Basics

This section gives you a basic overview of the process of printing a worksheet. The remainder of this chapter leads you through the process of printing specific worksheets. Briefly, the steps you must take to print out the contents of a worksheet file are:

1. Make sure the printer is ready.

   Make sure the printer is connected to your computer, turned on, and on-line (ready to receive information from the computer). If in doubt, check it out: Make sure you can print a text file using the operating system's PRINT or COPY command before you try to print from within 1-2-3. (If you do not know how to use the COPY or PRINT command see "Printing from the Operating System" at the end of this chapter.)

2. Make sure the paper is at the top of the page.

   If your printer lets you adjust the paper position relative to the *print head* (the part of the printer that actually prints the letters), make sure the top of the paper is lined up with the print head. With most dot matrix printers, this usually means lining up the perforation or top edge of the paper with the top of the ribbon.

3. Tell 1-2-3 which printer to use and, optionally, set up that printer.

Use the File Printer Setup command to select the printer to use. You can also use the File Printer Setup command's "Setup" option to set up that printer. This option lets you configure the printer driver. (You can also configure the printer driver using the "Printer" option on the Window Control Panel.) Each printer model has unique setup. For example, the setup for an HP LaserJet allows you to select graphics resolution (the number of dots per inch printed); the setup for a PostScript printer allows you to select a scaling factor that enlarges or reduces the size of the printed output; and the setup for an Epson FX-80 printer allows you to select whether the paper is sheet-fed or tractor-fed.

If the printer you plan to use with 1-2-3 is not listed when you use File Printer Setup, you have not installed that printer under Windows, and you must use the Windows Control Panel to install the printer. See "Installation of a Printer" in the MWUG for information on how to do that.

4. Designate the range or ranges you want to print.

As with most 1-2-3 commands, you can highlight a single range to print before issuing the File Print command. (You specify multiple ranges *after* you choose the File Print command.)

5. Tell 1-2-3 how you want to format the printed page.

You can use the File Page Setup command to change the page setup for the print job. For example, you can add borders, headers, and footers; specify the page margins; and even specify whether the data is printed length-wise (portrait) or width-wise (landscape) on the page. File Page Setup also allows you to name and save the current page setup, or save the current setup as the default; then, you can use it for future print jobs.

6. Tell 1-2-3 to print.

Choose File Print to start the print job. 1-2-3 sends the print job to the Print Manager. If 1-2-3 or another Windows application is already printing something, the Print Manager puts the current print job in line to be printed. See "Installation of a Printer" in the MWUG for more information on the Windows Print Manager.

■ *NOTE:* Instead of printing to a printer, you can print to a text file or to an encapsulated PostScript file (EPT). Printing to a text file is discussed in Chapter 10. See "Installation of a Printer" in the MWUG for information on printing to an EPT file.

Printing a Worksheet

As a basic introduction to printing in 1-2-3, you will print Bob Gordon's Business Contacts database, which you created in Chapter 6.

Open the Business Contacts database file and move the cell pointer to cell A1:

Choose: `File Open`

Point to: `contacts.wk3`

Move to: cell A1

Figure 9-1: The Business Contacts Database Table

	A	B	C	D	E
1	FOLKTALE WORKSHOP		Business Contacts		
2					
3	NAME AND TELEPHONE			AFFILIATION	
4	Last Name	First Name	Telephone	Type	Company
5	Brown	David	603-555-9871	SUP	Brown Machining, Inc.
6	Brown	Sue	508-555-6371	SUP	Brown's Bargain Lumber
7	Brown	Sue G.	603-555-8888	SUP	Hector's Hardware
8	Pendergast	Matthew	603-555-7171	SUP	Sears, Roebuck and Co.
9	Andri	Phil	802-555-2345	CUS	Northeast Craft Faire
10	Gordon	John	315-555-3813	CUS	Toy Universe
11	Saddler	Albert	313-555-7000	CUS	Saddler's Toys by Mail
12	Siess	Ned	413-555-3883	CUS	Peerless Imports
13	Woodward	Nancy	603-555-0007	CUS	Crafts 'R' Us
14	Halpern	Frank	212-555-2831	ADV	Children's Highlights
15	Kafka	Jean	603-555-8700	ADV	New Age Express
16	Scofield	Jennifer	603-555-8500	ADV	Better Home Journal

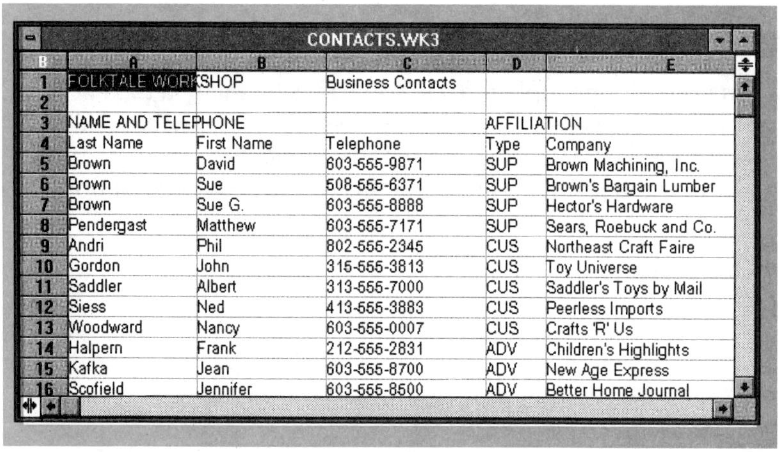

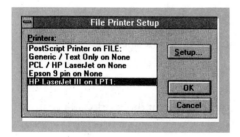

1-2-3 opens the worksheet file CONTACTS.WK3, displays it in a Worksheet window entitled CONTACTS.WK3, and makes that the active window.

Selecting the Printer to Use

You select the printer to use with the File Printer Setup command.

Choose: `File Printer Setup`

Figure 9-2: Selecting the Printer

1-2-3 opens the File Printer Setup dialog box, in which it lists all of the printers you have installed under Windows. Select the printer to use.

■ *NOTE:*   If the list does not include the printer you are planning to use for the print job, or if that printer is not printing on the port you expect, see "Installation of a Printer" in the *Microsoft Windows User's Guide*.

Select: *the printer to use*
                   OK

Specifying the Print Range

You can pre-select a single range to print by highlighting it before you use the File Preview or File Print command. (Later, when you print multiple ranges, you'll specify them in the File Print dialog box.) For your first print job, specify the entire Business Contacts database table. So you can see the entire database table on the screen, first maximize the Worksheet window, and then zoom the display to 50% using the "Zoom" option of the Window Display Options command.

Click on: *the Maximize icon for the Worksheet window*

Choose: Window   Display Options

Select: Zoom

Type: 50   *in the text box*

Select: OK   *or press Enter*

Highlight: B:A1..B:J16

Figure 9-3:   Specifying a Range to Print (Zoomed View)

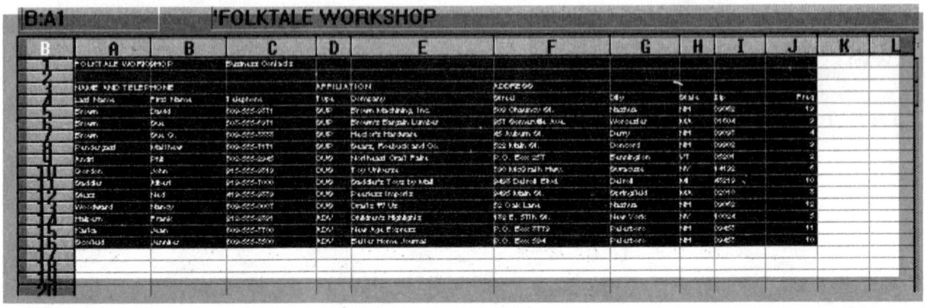

Because you zoomed the display, 1-2-3 now shows the entire Business Contacts database table.

Printing the Worksheet

Once you have selected the printer and the range to print, you can print the worksheet data.

1. Print the selected range.

You use the File Print command to print the selected range.

Choose: File   Print

Select: OK   *or press Enter*

Figure 9-4: Printing the Business Contacts Database Table

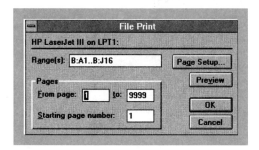

Figure 9-5: 1-2-3 sends the print job to the Windows Print Manager.

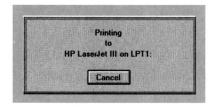

1-2-3 sends the data to the Windows Print Manager. As it does, the program displays a dialog box that identifies the print job and the printer to which it has been sent, and allows you to cancel the print job. When 1-2-3 has completed sending the data for the Business Contacts database table to the Print Manager, it removes the dialog box. If the Print Manager's *queue* (waiting line for jobs to be printed) is empty, the job begins to print nearly immediately on the printer you selected.

■ *NOTE:*   The delay between when 1-2-3 finishes sending the data to the Print Manager and when the printer starts is dependent upon the type of printer. Laser printers, for example, must load an entire page of data before beginning to print. Dot matrix printers and character printers typically start to print almost as soon as they receive any data.

■ *NOTE:*   On the screen, 1-2-3 surrounds the range that you just printed with a dotted gray border. This border indicates the current "print range"—the range that was most recently printed or previewed using File Preview. (You'll learn about File Preview in the next section.) 1-2-3 remembers the print range, and indicates it with the gray border until you highlight another multi-cell range, and either File Print or File Preview that range. If only a single cell is highlighted when you choose File Print or File Preview, 1-2-3 assumes that you want to print or preview the print range—the gray-bordered range—rather than the single cell.

2. Correct any problems in printing.

■ **NOTE:** Execute the keystroke instructions in this step only if the Print Manager has a problem printing. If your file is printing all right, you don't have to do this step.

If the Print Manager has a problem printing the job, 1-2-3 displays a dialog box indicating: (1) That the problem exists, (2) that you should clear the problem, and (3) that you should resume the job from the Print Manager after you have done so.

Figure 9-6:   1-2-3 indicates a problem in printing.

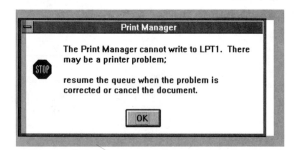

Before you can address the printing problem, you'll have to switch to the Windows Print Manager. To do so, first call up the Windows Task List.

Select: OK   *to close the dialog box*

Press: CTRL+ESC

Figure 9-7:   The Windows Task List

Then, switch to the Windows Print Manager.

Select: Print Manager
                     Switch to   *to switch to the Print Manager*

Windows opens the Print Manager window and makes it active.

The Print Manager window displays the queue for the printer you selected in 1-2-3. The print job is entitled CONTACTS.WK3. After the entry for CONTACTS.WK3, the Print Manager displays a message in brackets indicating the nature of the problem. For example, if the program is unable to send data to the printer, it displays the message "STALLED". "STALLED" might indicate that the printer is jammed, out of paper, or has some other problem.

Figure 9-8: The Windows Print Manager

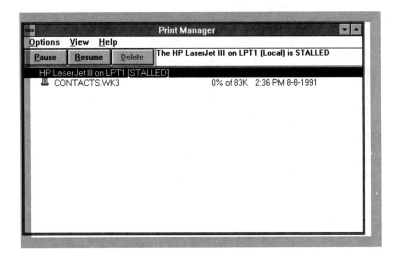

Try to resolve the problem. Look for indicators on the printer, such as a flashing "Paper Out" lamp. Make sure the printer is on-line and that the paper is loaded properly. If you cannot locate and solve the problem, see your printer manual for further information on what to do.

After fixing the printer problem, resume printing, using the Print Manager's Resume command.

Click on: Resume

Now, the Print Manager resumes printing the print job entitled CONTACTS.WK3. You can return to 1-2-3.

Press: CTRL+ESC   *to open the Windows Task List*

Select: 1-2-3 for Windows
              Switch To   *to switch to 1-2-3*

Windows switches to the 1-2-3 window.

3. Look at the printout for the Business Contacts database table.

Notice that 1-2-3 prints Bob Gordon's database table on two sheets of paper. The first sheet (shown in Figure 9-9a) contains all the information in columns B:A through B:F. The second sheet (shown in Figure 9-9b) contains the remainder of the range (columns B:G through B:J).

Figure 9-9a: Page 1 of the Business Contacts Database Table

FOLKTALE WORKSHOP   Business Contacts

NAME AND TELEPHONE			AFFILIATION	
Last Name	First Name	Telephone	Type	Company
Brown	David	603-555-9871	SUP	Brown Machining, Inc.
Brown	Sue	508-555-6371	SUP	Brown's Bargain Lumber
Brown	Sue G.	603-555-8888	SUP	Hector's Hardware
Pendergast	Matthew	603-555-7171	SUP	Sears, Roebuck and Co.
Andri	Phil	802-555-2345	CUS	Northeast Craft Faire
Gordon	John	315-555-3813	CUS	Toy Universe
Saddler	Albert	313-555-7000	CUS	Saddler's Toys by Mail
Siess	Ned	413-555-3883	CUS	Peerless Imports
Woodward	Nancy	603-555-0007	CUS	Crafts 'R' Us
Halpern	Frank	212-555-2831	ADV	Children's Highlights
Kafka	Jean	603-555-8700	ADV	New Age Express
Scofield	Jennifer	603-555-8500	ADV	Better Home Journal

Figure 9-9b: Page 2 of the Business Contacts Database Table

ADDRESS				
Street	City	State	Zip	Freq
509 Chauncy St.	Nashua	NH	03062	13
357 Somerville Ave.	Worcester	MA	01604	3
45 Auburn St.	Derry	NH	03038	4
522 Main St.	Concord	NH	03302	9
P.O. Box 257	Bennington	VT	05201	2
890 McGrath Hwy.	Syracuse	NY	14132	6
3498 Detroit Blvd.	Detroit	MI	48219	10
3435 Main St.	Springfield	MA	02010	8
52 Oak Lane	Nashua	NH	03062	12
182 E. 57th St.	New York	NY	10024	5
P.O. Box 8779	Peterboro	NH	03458	11
P.O. Box 534	Peterboro	NH	03458	10

Congratulations! You have printed your first worksheet.

A Note on How 1-2-3 Splits the Print Range   With the default page setup, 1-2-3 prints eight default-width columns on a line, and 59 default-height rows on a page. If you select to print the worksheet frame using the "Show worksheet frame" option of File Page Setup command, 1-2-3 prints seven default-width columns on a line, and 58 default-height rows on a page.

■ *NOTE:*   If your printer supports landscape orientation or compressed pitch, you can use the File Page Setup command to print all the columns of a wide worksheet on one page. You will do this later in this chapter.

If the range to be printed is too wide to fit on the page, 1-2-3 divides the worksheet into vertical strips. It prints as many columns of data as will fit in one strip, then it prints the next strip, moving down and across the specified range one page-width at a time. This method of printing produces output that you can later tape together into one wide spreadsheet.

Figure 9-10: How 1-2-3 Divides Ranges for Printing

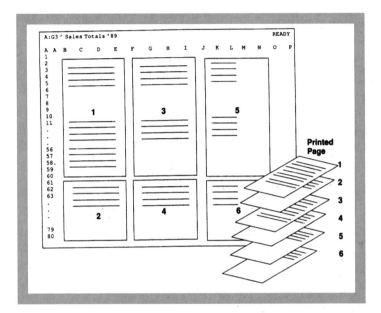

For example, say you want to print a range that is just over twice the width of the default margins (for example, 18 columns wide) and 80 rows long. On the first page, 1-2-3 prints the number of columns that fit on the page, until it has printed the last row that fits on the page. Then, on the next page, 1-2-3 prints the same columns for the remaining rows of the range. When 1-2-3 has printed one vertical strip of the range from top to bottom, the program starts on the second strip. It prints that from top to bottom, then continues on to the third, which in this case is the final strip.

Previewing Print Jobs

In the previous exercise, after selecting the range to print, you immediately chose File Print to print the range. You could have taken a slightly different route: You could have *previewed* the print job before printing it. When you preview a print job, 1-2-3 displays the job on the screen much as it will look on the printed page. The File Preview command opens up a special Preview window in which 1-2-3 displays the print job, one page at a time. The Preview window displays the data, as well as headers, footers, borders, grids, and any other features that you specified for the print job using Page Setup.

Previewing a print job is very useful: If the preview shows that the job will not print as you expected, you can change the ranges that you specified, or the page setup, *before* printing the job. This can save you gobs of time and paper.

■ *NOTE:*   File Preview does not adjust for the printer you have selected, and assumes a printer with full graphic capability. If your printer cannot print graphics, your printout will be different from that in the Preview screen.

To get a feel for the File Preview command, you'll File Preview the current print range in CONTACTS.WK3. Since 1-2-3 remembers that the current print range is B:A1..B:J16, you don't have to pre-select that range before using the File Preview command.

Choose: File   Preview

Select: OK

Figure 9-11:   1-2-3 previews the first page of the Business Contacts database table.

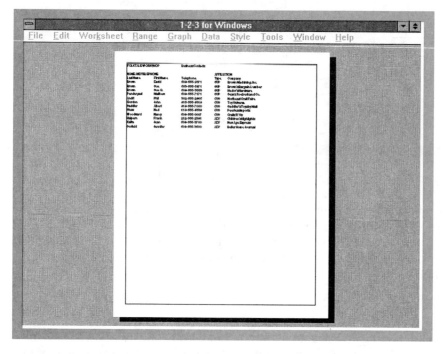

1-2-3 opens the Preview screen and displays the first page of the Business Contacts database table. The screen shows the same information in the same format as the first page of the printed database table. Press Enter to preview the next page.

Press:

Figure 9-12: 1-2-3 previews the second page of the Business Contacts database table.

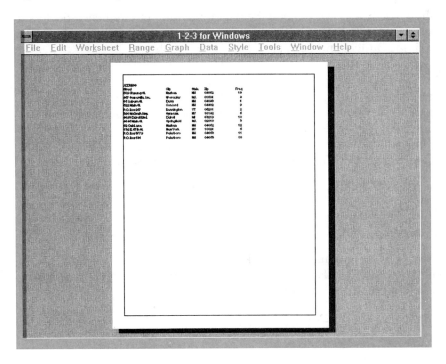

1-2-3 displays the second page of the Business Contacts database table. Again, it looks very much like the printed second page. Had you previewed the Business Contacts database table before printing it, you would have known that it was going to spill onto two sheets. You might have even taken some action to print the entire table on a single sheet, as you will do later in this section. For now, press Enter to return to 1-2-3 READY mode.

Press:

1-2-3 redisplays the Worksheet window for the CONTACTS.WK3.

■ *NOTE:* If there had been additional pages to preview, pressing Enter would have caused 1-2-3 to display the next one. While viewing the Preview screen , you can press Escape any-time to return to the Worksheet window.

Before you go on, save and close CONTACTS.WK3. 1-2-3 remembers the current print range and saves it with the worksheet file. When you next open this file, the print range will be intact.

■ *NOTE:* 1-2-3 also saves the current page settings with the file. In the previous exercise, you used the default page setup. Later you'll change the page setup.

More on Printing Worksheets

The following pages show you how to go beyond the bare minimum requirement (specifying a print range) when you print worksheet data. As you learn more printing skills, you are going to print sections of the Home Budget and Cash Flow Forecast worksheets.

Printing Multiple-Worksheet Ranges

The procedure for printing ranges that span multiple worksheets is the same as the one for printing a single-sheet range: Define the range, establish any other page settings, preview (from now on, we'll preview our print jobs *before* printing them), and print.

To see how 1-2-3 prints multiple-worksheet ranges, follow these steps to print four of the product-specific worksheets from Bob Gordon's Cash Flow Forecast worksheet file:

1. File Open CASHFLOW.WK3 and move the cell pointer to worksheet B.

Choose:	File Open
Select:	cashflow.wk3

   1-2-3 opens CASHFLOW.WK3 and makes its Worksheet window the active window. So you can view the data in the Cash Flow Forecast more clearly, change back to normal display using the "Zoom" option of the Window Display Options command.

Choose:	Window Display Options	
Select:	Zoom	
Type:	100	*in the text box*
Select:	OK	

2. Highlight the multi-sheet range to print.

   To print all of the product-specific information, you'll print the range B:A1..E:E19. This range includes all data for SNOW WHITE, DWARF1, DWARF2, and EVIL QUEEN. (You'll print both the summary sheet and the 1YR_PROJECTION graph added to sheet F later in the chapter.) Notice that this range also includes blank rows 17 and 18. These blank rows will serve to separate the information for each product.

Highlight:	B:A1..E:E19

3. Preview the print range.

   You'll use the "Preview" icon to preview the print job. Previewing will let you determine whether the job will print as you intended. The "Preview" icon looks like this:

Click on:	*the Preview icon*

Figure 9-13:   The Preview of the First Page of the Cash Flow Forecast Printout

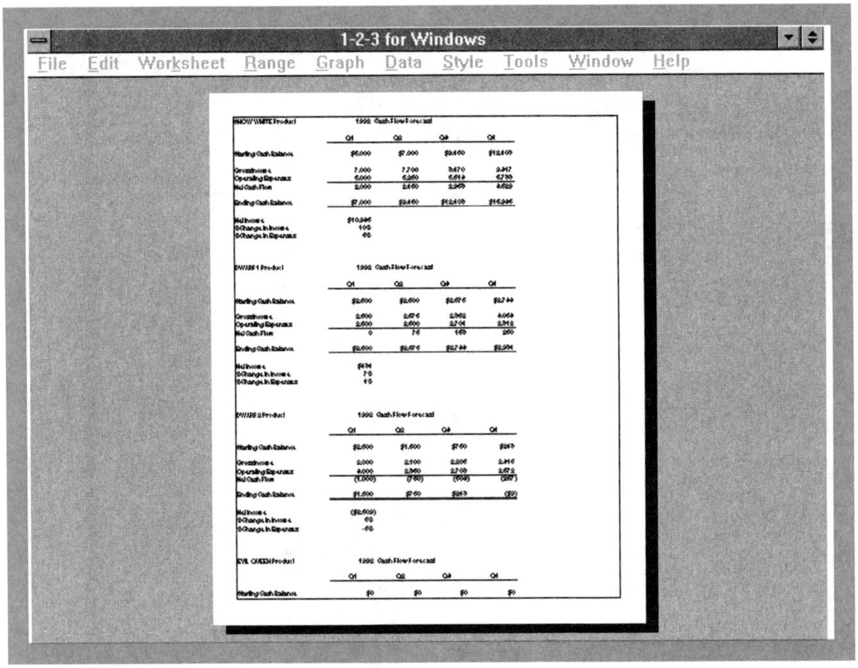

1-2-3 previews the first page of the printout on the Preview screen. This page will contain all information for SNOW WHITE, DWARF1, and DWARF2, and some of the information for EVIL QUEEN. Let's preview the next page (see Figure 9-14):

Press: ⏎

1-2-3 displays the next page of the printout. It contains the remainder of the data for EVIL QUEEN. See if there are any more pages:

Press: ⏎

There are no more pages: 1-2-3 redisplays the Worksheet window.

Well, File Preview has shown that the information for the four products will *not* print as you had hoped: Having EVIL QUEEN's information split across two pages simply will not do! Rather than print the range at this time, go on to the next section. There, you'll learn how to fix this range-splitting problem by inserting a page break into the print range.

■ *NOTE:*   1-2-3 prints (and previews) worksheets in a multiple-worksheet range one after the other, except when the range is too wide for the margins. In that case, 1-2-3 behaves much as it does when it prints a single-worksheet range that is too wide for the margins. It prints as much as fits within the margins until it has printed one strip of the entire range. It then returns to the first worksheet, advances to a new page, and continues printing where it left off, one page-width at a time.

Figure 9-14:   The Preview of the Next Page of the Cash Flow Forecast Printout

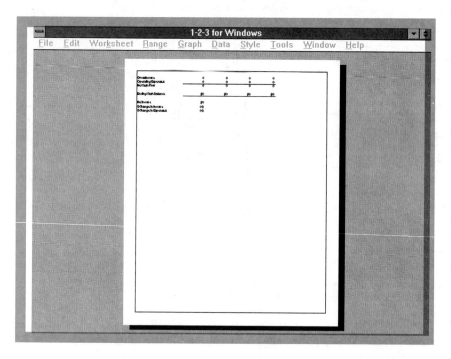

Figure 9-14:   The Preview of the Next Page of the Cash Flow Forecast Printout

Inserting and Removing Page Breaks

Instead of printing a report in a continuous flow, allowing 1-2-3 to break the pages as it sees fit, you can break the printout (either horizontally, vertically, or both) at specific points in the worksheet. You can select the row that you want to be the top row of the new page; the column that you want to be the left-most column of the new page; or the cell that you want to be the top left cell of the new page.

Inserting a page break is simple. Move to: (1) Any cell in the row you want to be the top row of the new page; (2) any cell in the column you want to be the left-most column of the new page; or (3) the cell that you want to be the top left cell of the new page. Then choose Worksheet Page Break. This command's options let you specify whether you want to break the sheet horizontally at the selected cell, vertically at the selected cell, or both horizontally *and* vertically at the selected cell.

In this exercise, you are going to insert a page break into the Cash Flow Forecast print range that you specified in the previous section. This page break will solve the range-splitting problem you saw in that section; the page break will force *all* of EVIL QUEEN's data to print on a separate sheet.

1. Move to cell E:A1 in CASHFLOW.WK3.
   You will insert a horizontal page break in cell E:A1. This should force a page break *before* row 1 of worksheet E.

   Move to: cell E:A1

2. Insert a page break.

   Now, insert the page break, using Worksheet Page Break:

   Choose: Worksheet   Page Break
   Select: Horizontal   OK

Figure 9-15: Inserting a Page Break

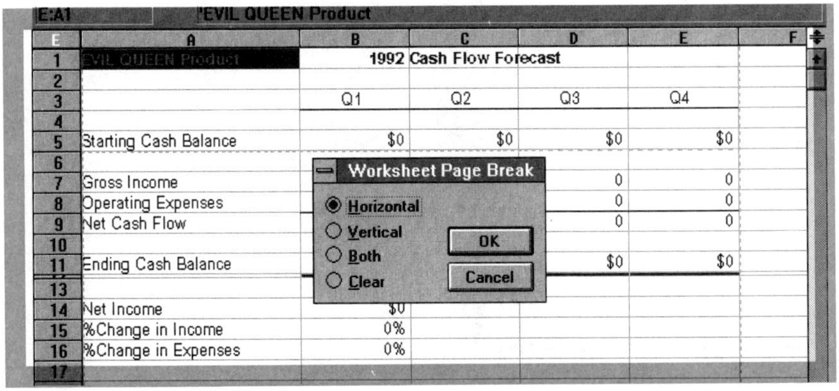

1-2-3 inserts a horizontal page break in row 1 of worksheet E. Notice that the format line says {MPage}, indicating that the current cell contains a page break. 1-2-3 also displays a dotted line in row 1 to show where the page break will occur when the range is printed or previewed.

■ *NOTE:*   If you select to break the worksheet horizontally, 1-2-3 displays a dotted line in the selected row. If you select to break the worksheet vertically, 1-2-3 displays a dotted line in the selected column. If you select both, 1-2-3 inserts both horizontal and vertical dotted lines. You can tell 1-2-3 to hide the dotted lines by clearing the "Page breaks" option of the Windows Display Options command.

■ *CAUTION:*   If this file were in GROUP mode, inserting a page break with the Worksheet Pagebreak command would cause page breaks to be inserted in all of the worksheets.

   To check that the page break will do what's expected, preview the print job.

3. Preview the print job.

Use the "Preview" icon to preview the print job now.

Click on: *the Preview icon*

Figure 9-16:   The First Page of the Product-specific Printout After Inserting the Page Break

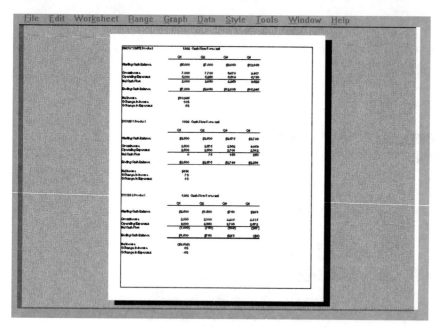

1-2-3 displays the first page of the product-specific information. This time, only the data for SNOW WHITE, DWARF1, and DWARF2 appear on this page. Let's check page two (see Figure 9-17 on the next page).

Press:

1-2-3 displays the second page of the product-specific information. This page now contains *all* of the data for EVIL QUEEN. Inserting the page break has solved the problem. Now, you can print the job. First, press Escape to return to the Worksheet window.

Press:

1-2-3 returns to READY mode.

4. Print the Cash Flow Forecast's product-specific information.

This time, to print the product-specific information from the Cash Flow Forecast, you'll use the "Print" icon. The "Print" icon looks like this:

Figure 9-17: The Second Page of the Product-specific Printout After Inserting the Page Break

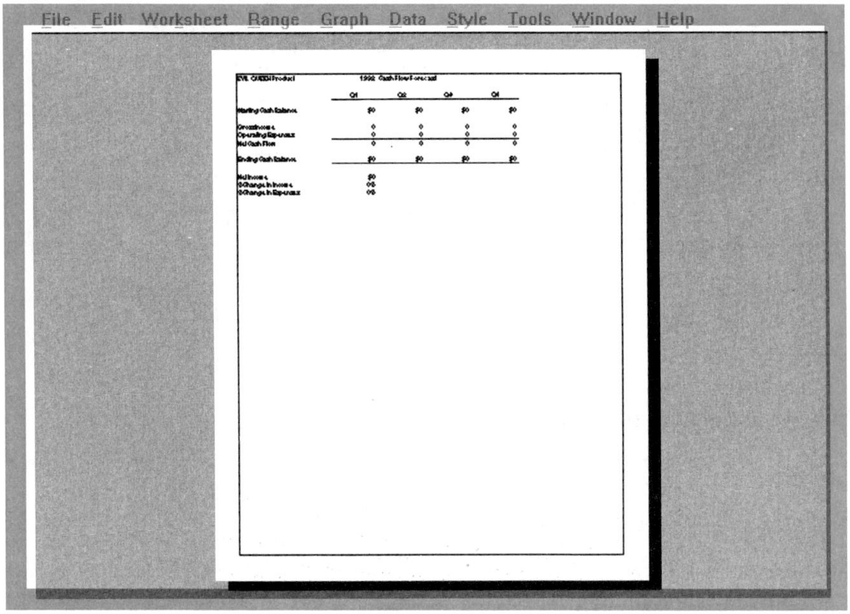

Click on: *the Print icon*

1-2-3 prints the product-specific information from the Cash Flow Forecast. The program has divided the print range onto two pages, just like File Preview indicated it would. Now that you have printed this range, you can clear the page break. It could cause confusion if you later tried to print a different range—say, just EVIL QUEEN.

5. Clear the page break.

To clear a page break that you have established with Worksheet Page Break, move the cell pointer to the row that contains the page break, as identified by the {Page ....} indicator in the format line. Then use the "Clear" option of the Worksheet Page Break command.

Move to: E:A1

Choose: Worksheet   Page Break

Select: Clear

1-2-3 clears the page break in the current cell. If the current cell contains both horizontal and vertical page breaks, the program clears both.

■ *NOTE:*   File Save saves page breaks that you insert with Worksheet Page Break when it saves the file. For a print range that you print often, saving page breaks in that range might be exactly what you want. If you are printing a range to get a one-time printed copy of the data, you'll probably want to clear the page break after printing.

6. Save and close CASHFLOW.WK3.

Later in this chapter, you'll use the Cash Flow Forecast to learn about printing graphs. For now, however, save and close the file to remove it from the 1-2-3 desktop.

Using Page Settings

So far, the printing you have done has been quite straightforward: Define a range, choose File Preview to verify that the range will print as you would like, and then File Print the job. Much of your day-to-day printing, in fact, will be just that simple. However, through the File Page Setup commands and its numerous settings, 1-2-3 provides a number of ways to improve your printed output. For example, you can:

- Print headers and footers on each page
- Change the margins
- Print border rows and columns
- Size the printout by compressing or enlarging it to fit the page
- Select whether the printed page is oriented vertically (portrait mode) or horizontally (landscape mode)
- Determine whether the printout has a grid and a worksheet frame

This section introduces you to 1-2-3's basic Page Setup options. You will use the Page Setup options described here as you work through this chapter. In a later section, you'll also learn how to save a set of customized page settings so that you can use them at any time.

The File Page Setup Options   The File Page Setup command gives you a great deal of control over the way your worksheet data is printed. The File Page Setup options you'll use in this section and in other sections of the chapter are described in Table 9-1.

Table 9-1: The File Page Setup Command Options

Setting	What It Does:
Header	Specifies a header to be printed on each page.
Footer	Specifies a footer to be printed on each page.
Margins	Sets left, right, top, and bottom margins.
Borders	Specifies border columns, rows, or both.
Compression	Specifies whether 1-2-3 reduces or enlarges the printed data to fit the page.
Options	Selects whether the range is printed with or without grid lines and a worksheet frame.
Orientation	Selects portrait (vertical) or landscape (horizontal) printing .

Default Page Settings   When you printed the Business Contacts database and the ranges in the Cash Flow Forecast, 1-2-3 automatically selected a number of page settings for you. These settings are known as the *default page settings.* Before you change any of these page settings, take a moment to examine the defaults. You can view the default page settings by choosing File Page Setup. Look at the default page settings now.

Choose: File   Page Setup

Figure 9-18:   The File Page Setup Dialog Box

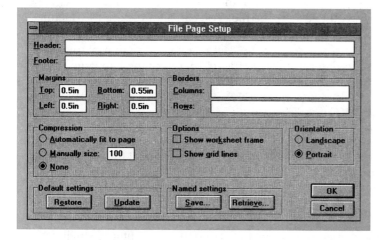

1-2-3 displays the File Page Setup dialog box. The default page settings are described in Table 9-2. (Your settings may differ from the ones in Figure 9-18 and Table 9-2.)

Table 9-2:   Default Page Settings

Setting	Default	Description
Margins	Left 0.5in Right 0.5in Top 0.5in Bottom 0.55in	Printing starts .5 inches from the left edge and stops .5 inches from the right edge. 1-2-3 leaves a margin of .5 inches at the top of the page and .55 inches at the bottom.
Header	*none*	1-2-3 does not print a header.
Footer	*none*	1-2-3 does not print a footer.
Borders	*none*	The printout does not have any borders.
Options	*none*	The printout does not include a grid or a worksheet frame.
Orientation	Portrait	The data is oriented vertically on the page.
Compression	None	The data is neither compressed nor enlarged when printed.

When you are finished looking at the File Page Setup dialog box, return to READY mode.

Select: `Cancel`

A Note on Changing the Page Setup   If you do not change any page settings, 1-2-3 uses the default settings. Just as you can change other default settings, such as the default directory (using Tools User Setup), you can change the default page settings. 1-2-3 allows you to change the page settings in three ways:

- For an individual file, you can override some of the default page settings, and the new settings will be saved when you File Save the file. You can later restore the default settings for that file by using the "Restore" option of the File Page Setup command.
- You can save the settings in a separate .AL3 file using the "Save" option of the File Page Setup command you can later use the "Retrieve" option of the File Page Setup command to establish these as the page settings for *any* worksheet file.
- You can change the default settings permanently, using the "Update" option of the File Page Setup command. The new page settings will become the default for new files (files that you create with File New).

Later in this chapter, after you modify some of the page settings so that the Business Contacts database table prints on a single sheet, you'll save the page settings using the "Save" option of the File Page Setup command.

Printing Column and Row Borders

When 1-2-3 prints a large worksheet, it automatically breaks up the printout into smaller chunks to fit on separate pages. One result of this is that you may lose important row and column labels from the top or left borders of the printout on the second and all following pages. For example, when you printed CONTACTS.WK3 earlier in this chapter, 1-2-3 printed the left half on one page and the right half on another; the labels in column A were not printed on the second page, making it hard to match a contact's name with his or her address.

Figure 9-19:   **"Overflow" from CONTACTS.WK3 printout**

FOLKTALE WORKSHOP			Business Contacts	
NAME AND TELEPHONE				
Last Name	First Name	Telephone	**AFFILIATION**	
			Type	Company
Brown	David	603-555-9871	SUP	Brown Machining, Inc.
Brown	Sue	508-555-6371	SUP	Brown's Bargain Lumber
Brown	Sue G.	603-555-8888	SUP	Hector's Hardware
Pendergast	Matthew	603-555-7171	SUP	Sears, Roebuck and Co.
Andri	Phil	802-555-2345	CUS	Northeast Craft Faire
Gordon	John	315-555-3813	CUS	Toy Universe
Saddler	Albert	313-555-7000	CUS	Saddler's Toys by Mail
Siess	Ned	413-555-3883	CUS	Peerless Imports
Woodward	Nancy	603-555-0007	CUS	Crafts 'R' Us
Halpern	Frank	212-555-2831	ADV	Children's Highlights
Kafka	Jean	603-555-8700	ADV	New Age Express
Scofield	Jennifer	603-555-8500	ADV	Better Home Journal

You can use the "Columns" and "Rows" borderoptions of the File Page Setup command to create a print border. Specified columns and rows at the left and top edges will then print on every page of the printout. These options do for printing what Worksheet Titles does for the Worksheet window: They effectively let you "freeze" certain rows and columns so they are always printed. For example, if the labels for the months of the year are located at the top of the worksheet, as they are in the Home Budget worksheet, you can print that row at the top of every page of the printout.

Take the following steps to print a section of the Home Budget worksheet with column and row borders:

1. Open BUDGET1.WK3.

2. Specify the print range.

You will find it easier to specify print ranges in BUDGET1.WK3 if you turn off worksheet titles.

Choose:	Worksheet Titles
Select:	Clear OK

Now, specify the last quarter and annual totals values of the EXPENSES section of the budget worksheet as the print range:

Highlight:	K21..N36

3. See what happens if you preview the range without using borders:

Click on:	*the Preview icon*

Previewing this range without borders shows that the printout will be only columns of numbers. The data is meaningless without the labels in column A (see Figure 9-20 on the next page).

4. Add borders.

The easiest way to provide meaningful labels for this section of the worksheet is to use column A as the border column and rows 1 through 4 as the border rows, just as you did when you set worksheet titles. You add borders using the "Columns" and "Rows" options of the File Page Setup command (see Figure 9-21).

Choose:	File Page Setup
Select:	Columns
Specify:	A1
Select:	Rows
Specify:	A1..A4
Select:	OK

Figure 9-20: Preview of Fourth Quarter Expenses Without Borders

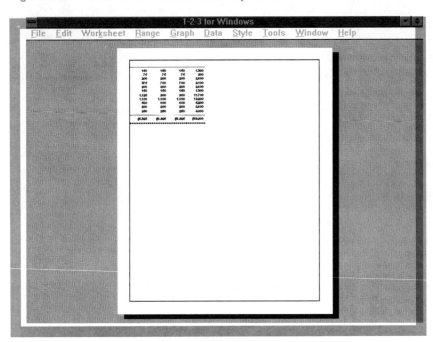

Figure 9-21: Setting Up Borders for the Home Budget Worksheet

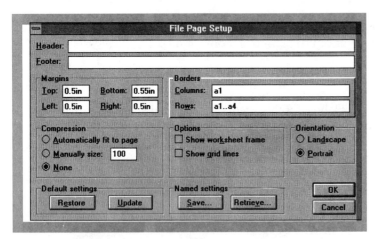

■ **NOTE:** The range of "Columns" you specify must include only one cell from each column you want included as the vertical border in the printout. Likewise, the range of "Rows" you specify must include only one cell from each row you want to include as the horizontal border in the printout.

5. Preview the worksheet data again, then print.

   Click on: *the Preview icon*

   Previewing this range with borders shows that the data will be easy to decipher when you print. Return to the Worksheet window and print.

   Press: ⏎   *to return to 1-2-3 READY mode*

   When you print, each page will start with the cells in the border rows that correspond to the columns being printed. For example, when you print columns K through N, each page will start with cells K1..N4. Also, each row will start with the cell in column A from the same row as the row being printed. For example, row 21 will begin with cell A21.

   Click on: *the Print icon*

Figure 9-22:   Fourth Quarter Expenses with Borders

Bob and Kathy Gordon

	Oct	Nov	Dec	Annual
EXPENSES				
Auto	150	150	150	1,800
Charity	75	75	75	900
Clothes	200	200	200	2,400
Food	875	700	700	9,100
Household	200	200	200	2,400
Medical	150	150	150	1,800
Misc	1,125	900	900	11,700
Rent	1,100	1,100	1,100	13,200
Savings	500	400	400	5,200
Utility	200	200	200	2,400
Woodwork	250	250	250	3,000
Total Expenses	$4,825	$4,325	$4,325	$53,900

   1-2-3 prints the last quarter and annual totals of the EXPENSES section of the Home Budget worksheet. Notice that both the row and column borders print with the range, even though they are not included in the print range itself.

■ *NOTE:*   Do *not* include border ranges in the print range, or 1-2-3 will print the borders twice: Once as borders, and again as part of the print range.

6. Save the BUDGET1.WK3 file.

   You'll be using BUDGET1.WK3 with borders in the next section. At that time, you'll print another part of the worksheet using the same borders, and all you will need to do is specify the new print range. The borders will continue to print on each page. So that you can take a little break at this time, save the file now.

Choose: File   Save

Congratulations!   You have learned to use borders and have saved the current page settings in the file.

Three Ways to Print More Data on a Page

Often, a worksheet is too wide to fit on a single page. Sometimes it's all right to print the wider spreadsheet on more than one page and tape the pages together—for example, when you want to display a large spreadsheet at a meeting. At other times, however, taping together several sheets of paper is inconvenient or inappropriate. 1-2-3 offers three easy ways to print wider spreadsheets on a standard page:

- *Changing the margins.* With any printer, you can make more room on a page for the worksheet simply by widening the left and right margins.
- *Using compressed pitch.* Laser printers and most dot-matrix printers can compress the print by using a smaller font. With compressed pitch, you can print more characters on a sheet.
- *Printing sideways.* Most laser printers support a landscape (sideways) orientation. Landscape orientation with standard pitch allows you to print slightly more than 12 default-width columns and approximately 44 default-height rows on a page. If you combine landscape orientation with compressed pitch, you can print even more data on a page.

The following examples show you how to change margins, use compressed pitch, and use landscape orientation to print wider worksheets so that all the columns fit on one page.

Changing the Margins   To get a feel for how changing the margins can solve some printing problems, you'll again print a portion of the Home Budget Worksheet. (If you don't have the BUDGET1.WK3 file open at this time, open it now.)

1. Select the print range.

You'll print Bob and Kathy's budget for January through August. (They're about to go on summer vacation and want to see how things are going on the financial front.) Remember, the page settings still specify a border consisting of column A1 and rows A1..A4.

Highlight: A:B4..A:I15

2. Preview the print range.

Use the "Preview" icon to preview the print range.

Click on: *the Preview icon*

Figure 9-23: The First Page of the Home Budget Worksheet

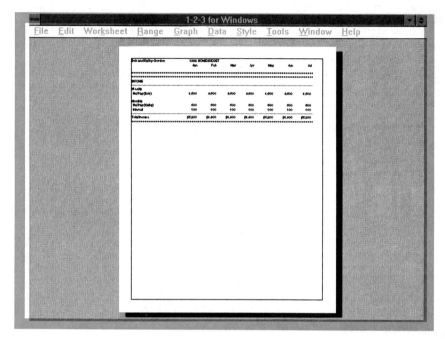

1-2-3 previews the print job in the Preview window. With default margins, not all of the budget is shown on this first sheet. Look at the second page.

Press: ⏎

There's the rest of the budget. (See Figure 9-24 on the next page.) Let's see whether changing the margins will solve the problem.

3. Change the margins to 0".

Change the left and right margins to 0" to see whether you can get the entire January through August budget on a single page.

Choose:	`File   Page Setup`
Select:	`Left`
Type:	`0` *in the text box*
Select:	`Right`
Type:	`0` *in the text box*
Select:	`OK`

4. Preview the print job again.

Click on: *the Preview icon*

Figure 9-24:   The Second Page of the Home Budget Worksheet

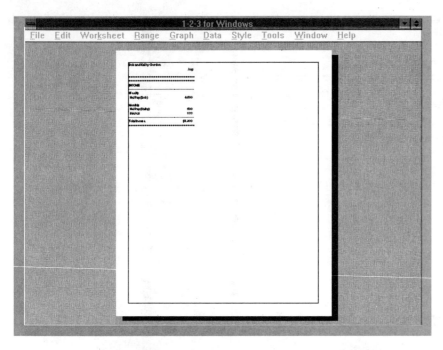

Figure 9-25:   Now the Home Budget worksheet will fit on one sheet.

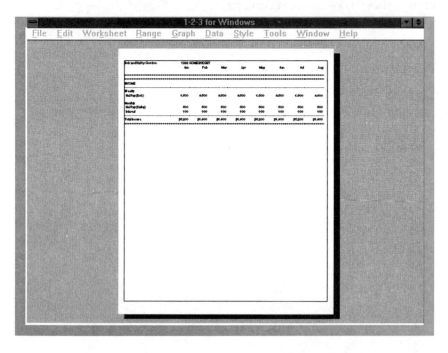

Now 1-2-3 shows that the entire range will print on a single page. The solid black border is near the edges of the pages, reflecting the left and right margins now set to zero inches. Changing the margins was a good way to solve this problem... and it will work with nearly any printer.

5. Print the worksheet using either File Print or the "Print" icon.

6. Save and close the file.

Now you can save and close BUDGET1.WK3. The next time you open this file, the margins will be set to zero inches and the borders will be intact.

Printing with Compressed Pitch   Imagine that Bob Gordon is about to leave on a trip, and he wants to take a printed copy of his Business Contacts database with him. He knows the database table is too wide to fit on a single sheet if he prints with the default page settings, and printing the database on two separate sheets of paper and taping them together is awkward. So Bob decides to print it on one: He is confident that he can find the page settings in 1-2-3 that will work. In his first attempt to fit the Business Contacts database on a single sheet, Bob uses a compressed pitch Page Setup option.

■ *NOTE:*   The example in this section assumes that your default printer is capable of printing compressed pitch. If it is not, and you have a second printer that can handle compressed pitch (most dot-matrix and laser printers can handle compressed pitch), use File Printer Setup to switch to that printer before you start this exercise .

1. Open the file CONTACTS.WK3.

2. Check the print range.

Move to the Business Contacts database table to verify that 1-2-3 saved this table as the most recent print range.

Move to: B:B1

1-2-3 shows the dotted line around the Business Contacts database table; it *was* saved as the print range with the file .

3. Change the "Compression" page setting for CONTACTS.WK3.

You will use the "Manually size:" option of the File Page Setup command to change the page settings for the file so that the printout fits the page. Setting "Manually size:" to 60% should do the trick.

Choose:	`File   Page Setup`
Select:	`Manually size`
Type:	`60` *in the text box*
Select:	`OK`

Figure 9-26: Setting 60% Compression

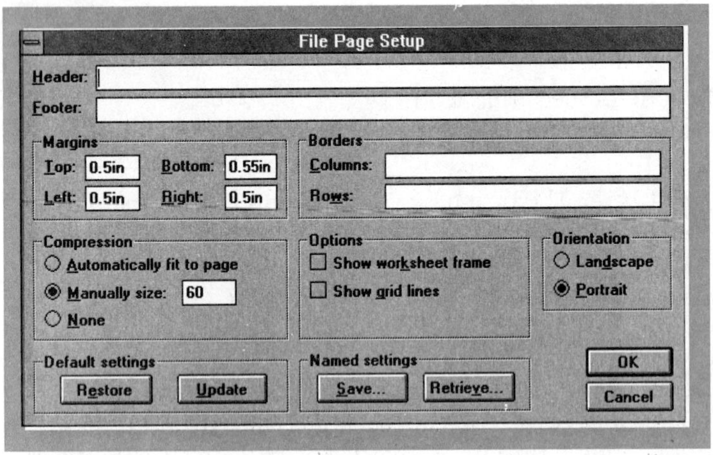

File Page Setup

Header:

Footer:

Margins
Top: 0.5in   Bottom: 0.55in
Left: 0.5in   Right: 0.5in

Borders
Columns:
Rows:

Compression
○ Automatically fit to page
◉ Manually size: 60
○ None

Options
☐ Show worksheet frame
☐ Show grid lines

Orientation
○ Landscape
◉ Portrait

Default settings
Restore   Update

Named settings
Save...   Retrieve...

OK
Cancel

1-2-3 stores the new page settings.

4. Preview the print job.

Use the "Preview" icon to preview the print job.

Click on: *the Preview icon*

Figure 9-27: Compressing the print allows the database table to fit vertically on the page.

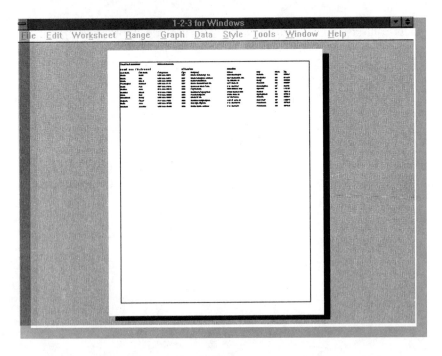

1-2-3 displays the print job on the Preview screen. Notice that the entire Business Contacts database table now fits on a vertically-oriented ("portrait") single page.

Press: ⏎

Since this print job has only one page, pressing Enter brings you back to the worksheet window.

5. Print the worksheet.

Click on: *the File Print icon*

1-2-3 sends the data to the Windows Print Manager.

6. Save the current page settings.

Bob may need to use the current group of page settings again, so save them in a file. Use a filename that will remind you of the purpose of the page settings. The file extension will be .AL3. You can save the .AL3 file in any directory; for this exercise you will save the file in the 123BOOK directory that you set up for worksheets (with Tools User Setup).

Choose: `File   Page Setup`
Select: `Save`   *to save the current page settings*

1-2-3 displays a file selection dialog box in which you will specify the name of the file to save. You'll name the file COMPVERT.AL3 (for "compress vertical").

Select: `Filename`
Type: `compvert`   *in the text box*
Select: `OK`   *to return to the File Page Setup dialog box*

1-2-3 saves the current page settings in the file COMPVERT.AL3 in the 123BOOK directory.

Select: `OK`   *to return 1-2-3 to READY mode*

Using Landscape Orientation   If you have a laser printer that supports landscape orientation, you can print a wide spreadsheet across the wide dimension of the page. Landscape orientation and standard pitch allows you to use a larger type size than compressed pitch and still print wider worksheets on one page. If you combine landscape orientation with compressed pitch, you can print even wider worksheets.

■ *NOTE:*   This exercise assumes you have installed a Hewlett-Packard LaserJet printer as the default printer. If you have another laser printer, try the exercise with your printer. If you do not have a printer that supports landscape orientation, you can still step through the exercise, but 1-2-3 will print the file in portrait mode.

1. Restore the default page settings.

First, restore the default page settings, using the File Page Setup command. This will allow you to create a fresh new page setup for printing in landscape mode.

Choose: `File   Page Setup`

Select: `Restore`   *to restore 1-2-3's default page setup as the current setup for CONTACTS.WK3*

2. Change the orientation page setting to Landscape.

Set the page orientation to Landscape so that rows of data print across the length of the page.

Select: `Landscape`   *as the Orientation setting*

Click on: `OK`

3. Preview the print job.

Use the File Preview icon to preview the print job:

Click on: *the File Preview icon*

1-2-3 displays the print job on the Preview screen. Since you selected landscape mode for the orientation, the preview is showing the page turned horizontally. More of the Contacts database is fitting on the page now, but—still—a second page is required.

Press: `⏎`

1-2-3 displays the second page of the print job. To fit the entire Contacts database on a single page, you'll have to compress the print.

Press: `ESC`   *(or Enter) to return to the Worksheet window*

4. Specify compressed pitch.

Just turning the page horizontally is not enough to get the entire Business Contacts database table on a single sheet (although the table *does* look better printed sideways). You'll still have to compress the print somewhat. This time, let 1-2-3 figure out how much it needs to compress the table.

Choose: `File   Page Setup`

Select: `Automatically to fit to page`   *and check the check-box*

                 `OK`

5. Preview the print job again.

Use the File Preview icon to preview the print job:

Click on: *the File Preview icon*

Figure 9-28: Automatic compression insures a good fit.

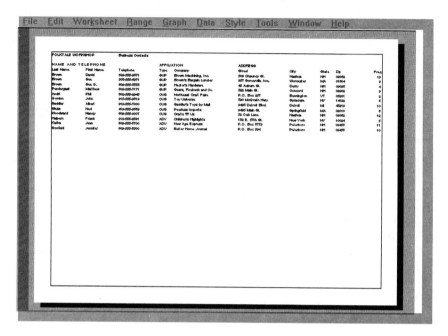

1-2-3 displays the print job on the Preview screen. Compressing the print has done the trick: The database table fits very nicely.

6. Print the worksheet.

You do not need to redefine the print range, since 1-2-3 remembers the last range you specified; simply File Print the job.

Click on: *the Print icon*

1-2-3 sends the worksheet data to the printer. It prints the worksheet using compressed pitch and landscape orientation.

7. Save the page settings.

Save the current page settings to a file using the "Save" option of the File Page Settings command. Use the filename `landscap` (`landscape` won't work: Too many characters for a filename) so that you can easily remember what the settings do.

Choose: File   Page Setup
Select: Save   *to save the current page settings*

1-2-3 displays a file selection dialog in which you specify the name of the file to save.

Select:	Filename
Type:	landscap *in the text box*
Select:	OK *to return to the File Page Setup dialog box*

1-2-3 saves the current page settings in the file LANDSCAP.AL3 in the directory 123BOOK.

| **Click on:** | OK |

If you use the settings from LANDSCAP.AL3 in the future, 1-2-3 will change the orientation to landscape, and compress the printed data automatically to fit the page.

8. Save the CONTACTS.WK3 file.

Using a Range Name to Specify a Print Range

If you are likely to print the same range more than once, it makes sense to name the print range. That way, you can specify a range by typing its name instead of having to highlight the range or type its address each time you want to print it.

Specifying a range name for a print range is the same as specifying any other range name. After choosing Range Name Create, you type in the range name and highlight the range.

1. Open the BUDGET1.WK3 worksheet file.

Use the "File Open" icon to open BUDGET1.WK3.

| **Click on:** | *the File Open icon* |
| **Select:** | budget1.wk3 OK |

1-2-3 opens a Worksheet window for BUDGET1.WK3 and makes it the active window.

2. Clear titles.

| **Choose:** | Worksheet   Titles |
| **Select:** | Clear OK |

3. Name the first quarter of the INCOME section.

To demonstrate printing named ranges, you are going to name some ranges in the Home Budget worksheet file and then print them. First, specify a name for the first three months of the INCOME section of the Home Budget worksheet file. When you specify this range, do *not* include the border rows you specified earlier in this chapter.

Highlight:	B5..D15
Choose:	Range Name Create
Select:	Range name

| **Type:** | `p_q1income` | *in the text box* |
| **Select:** | `OK` | |

1-2-3 names the highlighted range, which you can use in future File Print commands.

4. Name the remaining ranges in the first quarter.

While you are at it, name the first-quarter ranges for the EXPENSES and CASH FLOW sections of the Home Budget worksheet in a similar fashion. (You will use these range names later.)

Highlight:	B21..D36	
Choose:	`Range   Name   Create`	
Select:	`Range name`	
Type:	`p_q1expenses`	*in the text box*
Select:	`OK`	
Highlight:	B37..D52	
Choose:	`Range   Name   Create`	
Select:	`Range name`	
Type:	`p_q1cashflow`	
Select:	`OK`	

Notice that all of these range names start with the characters P_. When you have several named ranges with similar uses, it is a good idea to use the same characters to begin each name. That way, when you press the Name key to display the names, all the ranges with similar purposes are listed together. (There is nothing magical about using P_ for print ranges; the point is to decide on a particular convention and stick to it, so it is easy for you to distinguish the print ranges from other ranges in the worksheet.)

Also notice that none of these range names includes column A. You will use column A as a border column when you print this worksheet, so you should not include the column in the print range. If you do, the cells in column A will print twice, once as the border, and again as part of the print range.

5. Print the income values for January, February, and March.

Printing a named range is the same as printing a range that you highlight or type in, except that you supply 1-2-3 with the range name instead of supplying specific cell addresses.

To select the range name for the first-quarter budgeted income values, use the Name key to display a list of named ranges, and then select P_Q1INCOME.

Choose:	`File   Print`
Select:	`Ranges`
Press:	[F3] (NAME)

1-2-3 displays a list of named ranges in the BUDGET1.WK3 worksheet file. Notice that all the print range names are grouped together in the display.

Figure 9-29: The Named Ranges in BUDGET1.WK3

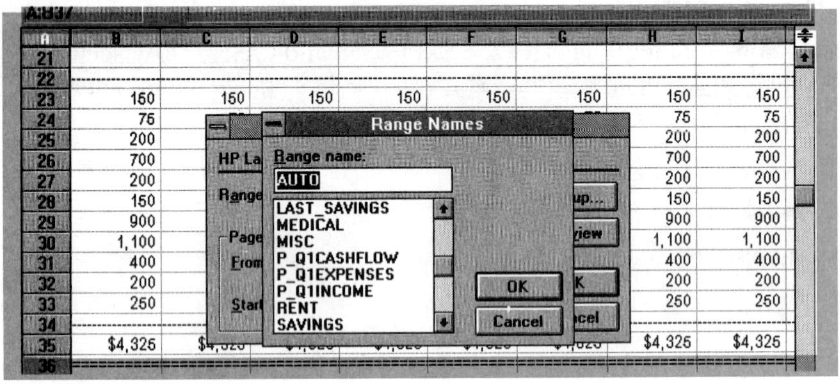

Now, select the name P_Q1INCOME.

Select: p_q1income   OK

1-2-3 displays the range you specified in the "Range" text box. Now, send the range to the printer.

Select: OK

1-2-3 prints the range.

Printing Multiple Ranges

Sometimes, all the data to be printed is contiguous and you can specify a single print range. At other times, however, the data you want to print is in different parts of a worksheet file, or in several active files.

To print multiple ranges, you provide 1-2-3 with a list containing all of the ranges to print, and then do all the printing in a single step. These ranges can come from the same worksheet, from different worksheets in the same file, or from different active files. The entire list of ranges becomes the current print range.

1. Call up the File Print command:

Choose: File   Print

2. Enter the series of print ranges.

Now, enter the ranges. To separate the print ranges, you are going to print a range that contains two blank rows between each data range. You will type cell addresses for the blank-row range, and you will use range names for the other ranges.

Select: Range

■ *NOTE:*   Do *not* click OK until you have given 1-2-3 the whole list of ranges. If you do accidentally click OK before you are finished, re-choose the File Print command and then continue with the keystroke instructions. If you make a mistake when you are creating a list of ranges, you can edit the list by pressing Edit and then using the arrow keys to move to the part you want to change. (The editing and cursor-movement keys work as expected.) You can also press Escape to erase the list.

First, clear the "Ranges" text box:

Press: ESC

Now, specify the range for the current year, the worksheet title, and the months of the year. (1-2-3 will print the labels in A1..A4 as a border, since border columns are still set.)

Type: B1..D4   *in the Ranges text box*

Type a comma to separate this range specification from the next, then type the range name for the INCOME section's first-quarter values. Do not put any spaces between the comma and either of the ranges.

Type: ,p_q1income

Now type a comma to separate this range from the next, then type the address of the range of blank rows—the first cells of the two blank rows at the bottom of the INCOME section screen.

Type: ,a19.a20

Type another comma, then type the range name for the EXPENSES section's first-quarter values.

Type: ,p_q1expenses

Now, type in the following to complete the range list. Notice that the range list scrolls in the control panel to make room for the new characters you type.

Type: ,a19.a20,p_q1cashflow

Finally, select OK to print the job.

Select: OK

1-2-3 sends the multiple-range print job to the Windows Print Manager.

Figure 9-30: Specifying the Multiple-Range Print Job

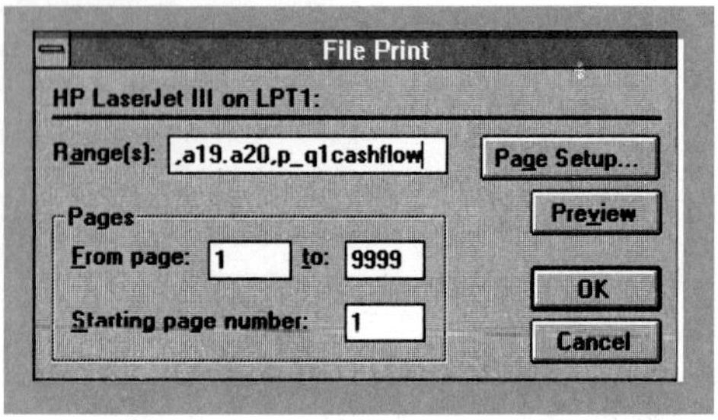

3. Save and close BUDGET1.WK3.

Congratulations! You have completed a multiple-range print job.

A Note on Printing a List of Ranges   1-2-3 prints multiple ranges in a range list one after the other, with one exception: If a range is too wide for the paper, 1-2-3 prints as much of the first range as fits within the margins. It then prints as much of the next range as fits within the margins, and so on. Then it returns to the first range and continues printing, one page-width at a time. This lets you print consecutive ranges on the same page, even when one or more of the ranges is wider than the margins. You can tape the separate pages together to create one large printed spreadsheet.

Printing Headers and Footers

A *header* is a line of text that is printed just below the top margin of each page. 1-2-3 prints the margin, then the header, then skips two lines before it prints the first line of data. A *footer* is a line of text that is printed just above the bottom margin of each page. 1-2-3 prints the last line of data, then skips two lines, then prints the footer, followed by the bottom margin, see Figure 9-31 on the following page.

Headers and footers help to unify a printed report. They can contain text, page numbers, and the current date, in any combination. Headers and footers can be separated into left-aligned, centered, and right-aligned segments, and they can contain as many characters as will print on a single line. Table 9-3 summarizes the special symbols that can be used in headers and footers in addition to text.

Table 9-3: Special Symbols for Headers and Footers

Symbol	Description
# (pound sign)	Prints the current page number in a header or footer.
@ (at sign)	Prints the current date in a header or footer.
\<cell reference>	Uses the contents of the specified cell as a header or footer.
I (vertical bar)	Separates the header or footer into left-aligned, centered, and right-aligned segments: <right_segment>I<centered>I<left_segment>

Figure 9-31: Headers and Footers

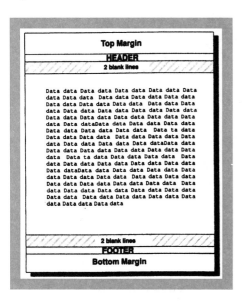

The next three sections give general procedures for including page numbers, dates, and text in headers and footers. Later, you will create a header and a footer for Bob Gordon's Cash Flow Forecast, and then print the Cash Flow Forecast with the header and footer.

Including Page Numbers in Headers and Footers

1-2-3 automatically keeps track of page numbers when printing. To include page numbers in a header or footer, you use the pound sign (#) character. For example, you would use the following keystrokes to print the page number in a footer (don't type these keystrokes now):

Choose:	File Page Setup
Select:	Footer
Type:	# *in the text box*
Select:	OK

By default, 1-2-3 justifies a footer with the left edge of the page. If you prefer to center the page number (or any other footer material), type a vertical bar and then type a pound sign (| #); to align the page number with the right edge, type two vertical bars and then a pound sign (| | #).

Follow the same steps to print the page number as a header, but select "Header" instead of "Footer".

Figure 9-32: Specifying a Footer

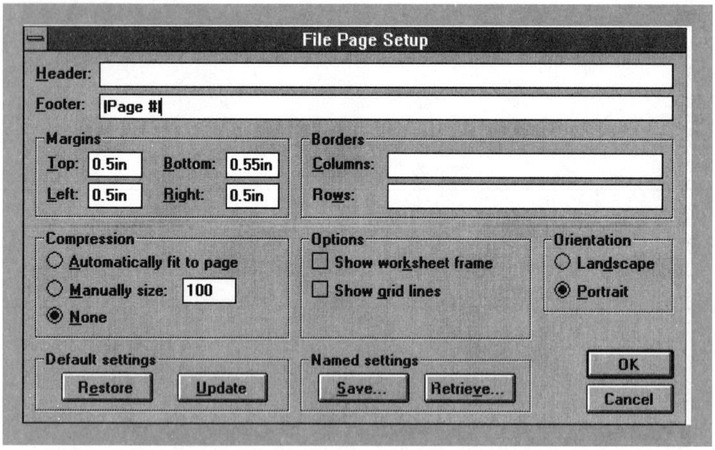

Including the Current Date in Headers and Footers

You can instruct 1-2-3 to print the current date in the header or footer of a printout. Assuming that either your computer has an internal clock or that you entered the date correctly at the operating system prompt, the at sign (@) character specifies the current date.

You would use the following keystrokes to print the current date in a header (don't type these keystrokes now):

Choose:	File Page Setup
Select:	Header
Type:	@ *in the text box*
Select:	OK

The current date would be printed as a left-aligned header. Type | @ to center the date, or | | @ to right-align it. Use the same steps to print the date as a footer, but select "Footer" instead of "Header".

Using Text or Cell Contents in a Header or Footer

You can include text in a header or footer in two ways: By typing in the text, or by using a cell reference.

To print text in a header or footer, select the "Header" or "Footer" option of the File Page Setup command, type in the text, and select OK. Like page numbers and the current date, text in a header or footer can be left-aligned, centered, or right-aligned. Type | before the text to center it, or type | | before the text to right-align it.

To print the contents of a cell in a header or footer; (1) select the "Header" or "Footer" option of the File Page Setup command; (2) type a backslash (\); (3) either point to the cell whose contents you want to appear in the header or footer, or type in its address or range name; and (4) select OK.

■ **NOTE:**   Cell contents must be the only entry in a header or footer.

Figure 9-33: Specifying a Header

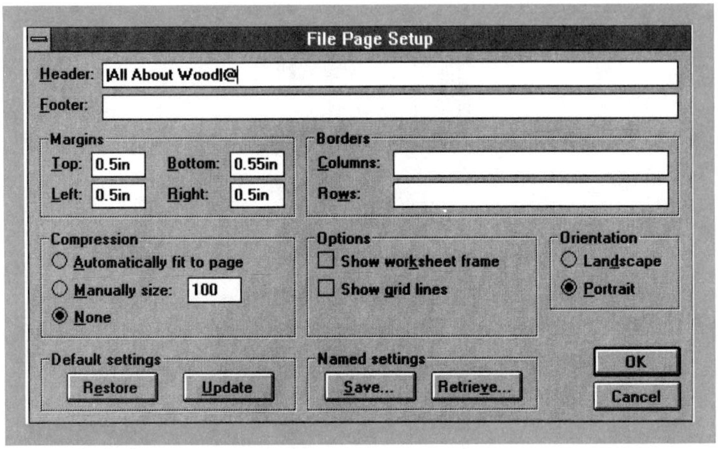

More on File Page Setup

The following pages show you how to control two page settings options: Whether you want to include a grid for the print range, and whether to include the 1-2-3 worksheet frame with the printed data. You will use the Home Budget worksheet for this section.

■ **NOTE:**   If you stopped after the previous section, open BUDGET1.WK3 now.

Adding a Grid to the Print Range

First, you will add a grid to the print range. Grids can help improve the legibility of your print range, particularly if the range contains long rows or columns of numbers.

Choose:	File Page Setup
Select:	Show grid lines *and check the check-box*
	OK

Now, clear titles, select the range to print, and preview the document to see how the grid looks in the print range.

Choose:	Worksheet Titles
Select:	Clear OK
Highlight:	A1.G15
Choose:	File Preview

Figure 9-34: Home Budget Worksheet Preview, with Grid

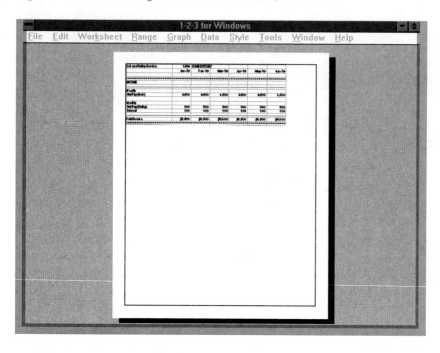

The Preview screen displays the Home Budget worksheet with a grid. Press Escape to return 1-2-3 to READY mode.

Press: `ESC`

Adding a Frame to the Print Range

Next, add the 1-2-3 worksheet frame to the print range. Adding the worksheet frame makes the document look more like the version of the worksheet you see on screen. A worksheet frame, like the grid can make long lists of values easier to read, and it makes it possible to refer to each of the values by cell number directly from the document.

Choose: `File    Page Setup`

Select: `Show worksheet frame`   *and check the check-box*
                `OK`

Now, preview the document to see how it looks with both the grid and worksheet frame.

Click on: *the Preview icon*

Press: `ESC`

When you save the Home Budget file, 1-2-3 will save the grid and frame settings automatically, along with the other page settings for the file.

Figure 9-35: **Previewing the Home Budget with Both a Grid and a Frame**

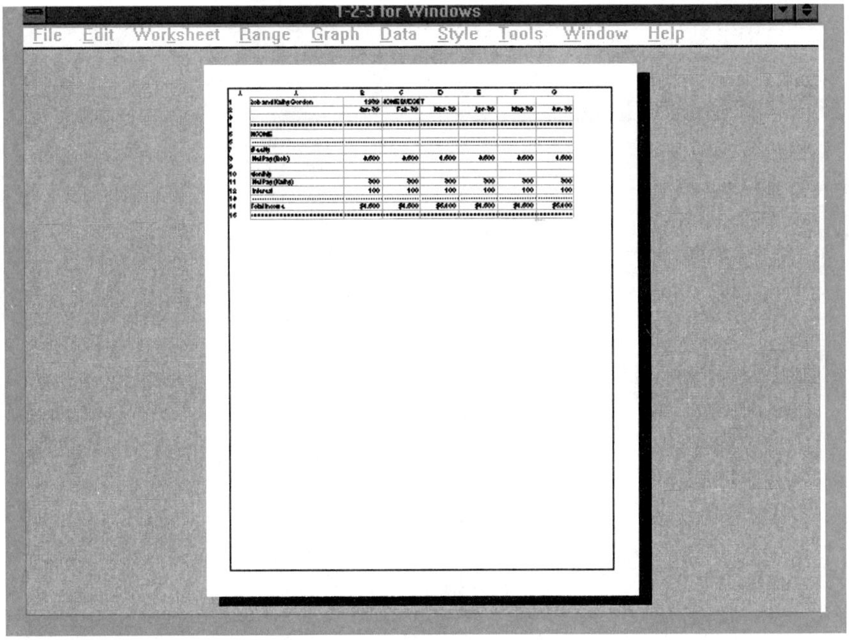

Close and Save the Home Budget File

Use File Save to save the Home Budget file and keep the grid and worksheet frame settings.

Printing Graphs

Printing graphs and reports that contain graphs is one area in which 1-2-3 for Windows really shines. With only a minimum of effort you can create great-looking printed reports.

In this section, you're going to print the Income Statement in Bob's Cash Flow Forecast, including the INCOME graph that you created and added to the worksheet in Chapter 8. Bob will be using this printout as a report for his potential investors. You'll also print the 1YR_PROJECTION line graph that you added to a separate sheet at the end of the file.

1. Open the Cash Flow Forecast.

2. Select the range to print.

   You'll be printing the Income Statement and the INCOME graph that you added to the sheet.

   Highlight: A:A22..A:E48

3. Preview the print job.

   When you preview a print range that contains a graph, 1-2-3 displays the graph as well as the data on the Preview screen.

Click on: *the Preview icon*

Figure 9-36:   Previewing the Income Statement with the Added INCOME Graph

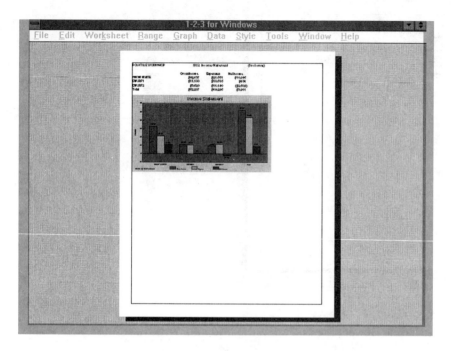

The Preview screen shows the graph as well as the data in the current print range. It looks pretty good, but before we print it, let's add a header and footer to give the report a really finished look.

4. Add a header and a footer.

You'll add a header that gives the name of the report and the date on which it is printed. The footer will identify the page number.

Choose:	Page Setup
Select:	Header
Type:	Folktale Workshop|1992 Projected Cash Flow|@ *in the text box*
Select:	Footer
Type:	Page-# *in the text box*
Select:	OK

5. Print the Income Statement job.

Use the "Print" icon to send the Income Statement print job to the printer.

Click on: *the Print icon*

Figure 9-37:   A Page from Bob Gordon's 1992 Net Cash Flow Forecast

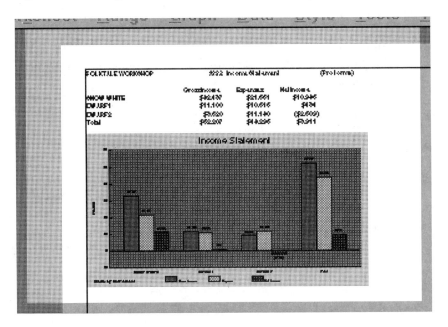

1-2-3 sends the print job to the printer. Now, Bob decides that he wants to get a printed copy of the 1YR_PROJECTION graph that you added to sheet F.

6. Restore the default page settings.

Use the "Restore" option of the File Page Setup command to restore the default page settings.

Choose: `File    Page Setup`

Select: `Restore   OK`

7. Print the 1YR_PROJECTION graph on sheet F.

You added the 1YR_PROJECTION graph to the Cash Flow Forecast just so that you could print it. Remember: The only way you can print a graph with 1-2-3 is to add it to a worksheet.

■ *NOTE:*   You *can* print a graph outside of 1-2-3 as follows: (1) Copy the graph from a Graph window to the Clipboard; (2) paste it into a graphics application such as Paintbrush; and (3) print it out from that application.

Highlight: F:A1..F:H20
Click on: *the Print icon*

1-2-3 prints the 1YR_PROJECTION.

More on the File Print Command

In addition to the File Print command features discussed earlier in this chapter, the command provides the settings described in Table 9-4.

Table 9-4:   The File Print Command Options

Setting	What It Does:
From page	Specifies the last page of the document that you want to print. For example, if you are printing a ten-page document and you only want to begin printing with the third page, you would specify 3 as the "from" page.
To page	Specifies the last page of the document that you want to print. For example, if you are printing a ten-page document and you only want to print the first five pages, you would specify 5 as the "to" page.
Starting number	Specifies the page number for the first page in the print range.

Printing Tips, Techniques, and Gotchas

This section describes tips and techniques that apply to printing in 1-2-3.

Determining the Width of a Print Range

This section describes several easy ways to automate the process of figuring out how wide a print range is.

The fastest (and surest) way to determine the width of the print range is to preview the page, using the File Preview command. File Preview shows you how the page will look when you send it to the printer, and you can make a fairly accurate determination of where to change margins, compression, and so on before you spend any time actually printing.

Another quick way to determine the width of the print range (and of each column in your worksheet), is to let 1-2-3 do the work for you. The "Frame" option of the Windows Display Options command sets a special frame that displays the size of the worksheet in standard measurements. You can tell 1-2-3 to display width and height in inches, in characters, in centimeters, or in points/picas. Figure 9-38 shows a worksheet frame displayed to measure the worksheet in inches.

Figure 9-38:   **The worksheet frame can display inches.**

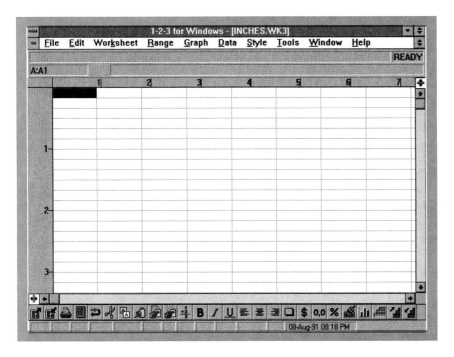

Printing Non-Adjacent Columns

Using sequential print ranges makes it easy to print rows that are separate from each other, one after the other. However, printing two or more groups of columns next to each other, when the groups of columns are separated by columns that you do not want to print, requires a different approach.

There are two easy ways to print two ranges next to each other when they are separated by other columns. One is to specify one range as a border and the other as the print range. For example, to print columns I, J, and K followed by columns P, Q, and R, you would specify columns I, J, and K as the border columns, and columns P, Q, and R as the print range.

The other technique you can use is to hide intervening columns that you do not wish to print. You can also use this technique when you have more than two non-adjacent groups of columns you want to print.

To hide columns in a worksheet, highlight the columns you want to hide, and select Worksheet Hide. (You can also type in the cell addresses or range name of the range of columns you wish to hide in the Worksheet Hide's "Range" text box.) You can include as many columns as you like. When you have specified the range, press Enter. The selected columns disappear, and the cell pointer rests on the column to the right of the hidden range. The hidden columns will not be printed.

You can use the Worksheet Hide command as many times as is necessary to achieve the desired effect. Any columns you have already hidden are displayed with an asterisk next to the column letter while you are highlighting columns: After you have completed the Hide command, the columns are invisible.

Once you have printed the range that contains hidden columns, you can restore the hidden columns with Worksheet Unhide. Again, you can type the cell addresses or highlight the range containing the columns you wish to redisplay. Once you have specified the range, press Enter.

■ *NOTE:*   Hidden columns are displayed whenever you are in POINT mode. Therefore, you can see those columns when you select commands that call for a range, or when you're entering a formula and pointing to the cells. Columns that are temporarily unhidden are marked with an asterisk placed after the column letter on the top border of the worksheet.

Printing from the Operating System

If you cannot cajole your printer into working properly from within Windows, you can test the electrical connection between the computer and the printer by printing directly from the operating system, using either the COPY command or the PRINT command. If the printer prints properly from the operating system, you can be quite certain that the problem is with the way you set up your printer to work with Windows. In that case, see the section "Installation of a Printer" in the *Microsoft Windows User's Guide.*

From the operating system prompt, you can print text files and other print files to a printer using the COPY command. When you use COPY to print a file, you provide the name of the file you want to print as the source file, just as if you were copying the file to another file. As the destination, supply the name of the printer port to which your printer is connected, instead of supplying a file name or directory name. For example, the following command would print the file EXECSUM.PRN on the printer connected to parallel port 1 on your computer.

Type: `copy execsum.prn lpt1:`
Press: ⏎

Using the PRINT command, you can print text files while you are doing other work in DOS. This is know as *background printing.* To use PRINT to print the file EXECSUM.PRN on the printer connected to parallel port 1 on your computer:

Type: `print execsum.prn`
Press: ⏎

If this is the first time you have issued the PRINT command since you last started or rebooted your computer, PRINT will prompt you for the place to which it is to send files. Press Enter to select the default printer port, PRN. If you know that your printer is connected to a different printer port, type the name of that port and press Enter. (PRN is usually LPT1.Other possible printer ports include parallel ports LPT2 and LPT3, and serial ports COM1 and COM2.)

Unlike COPY, which requires you to wait until it has sent your file to the printer, PRINT requires you to wait only until it has lined up your file for printing; it very quickly returns you to the operating system prompt.

Typing PRINT without any file names displays the names of the files PRINT is waiting to print.

Setting the TEMP Variable

When 1-2-3 sends a print job to the Windows Print Manager, the Print Manager creates a set of files on disk in which it temporarily stores portions of the job. These files come and go as the Print Manager sends the job to the printer. If the Print Manager does not have sufficient space on disk to freely create these files, the print job will bog down.

To prevent this problem, you should specify the directory for the Print Manager's temporary files by setting the TEMP variable in your AUTOEXEC.BAT file. You should set TEMP to a directory on the hard disk drive which has the most free space. You can use the operating system "dir" command to determine the amount of free space on each of your hard drives. If you determined, for example, that drive D: had the most free space, you would add the following line to your AUTOEXEC.BAT file to set the TEMP variable to a directory named TEMP on the D: drive:

```
set temp=d:\temp
```

You can use the Windows Notepad to edit AUTOEXEC.BAT to add the line. If the directory you specify does not exist, the system will create it.

At a Glance

This chapter described the basics of printing worksheets and graphs. As you printed the worksheet files you created earlier in this book, you learned many new skills, including those listed in the following table.

Task	How To Do It:
Choosing where to send a print job	Choose File Printer Setup.
Displaying a preview page	Choose File Preview.
Changing default page settings	Choose File Page Setup.
Printing a worksheet (summary)	Printing worksheet data to a printer connected to your computer involves the following basic steps: (1) Make sure the printer is ready (plugged in, connected to your computer, and on-line) and that the correct printer driver is installed; (2) make sure the paper is at the top of the page; (3) highlight the range you want to print; (4) preview the print job by choosing File Preview; (5) print the print job using File Print.
Printing multiple ranges	Specify the multiple ranges in the File Print command's "Range(s)" text box.

Task	How To Do It:
Printing long labels	To print a long label, you must include in the print range the entire range that the label spans. For example, if a label in column C extends into column E on the screen, you must include columns D and E in the print range, or only the part of the label that fits in column C will be printed.
Inserting and removing page breaks	Choose Worksheet Page Break and specify whether the page break is to insert a page break, more to where you want the page to break and thenhorizontal, vertical, or both.Remove a 1-2-3 page break using the "Clear" option of the Worksheet Page Break command.
Using column and row borders	Select the "Columns" and "Rows" Borders option of the File Page Setup command.
Using compressed pitch	Select the "Automatically to fit page" or the "Manual" compression option of the File Page Setup command.
Adjusting page margins	Select the "Margins" options of the File Page Setup command.
Saving current page settings	Select the "Save" named settings option of the File Page Setup command.

Printing headers and footers:

Task	How To Do It:
Printing the page number in headers and footers	Select the "Header" and/or "Footer" option of the File Page Setup command. Use the pound sign (#) in a header or footer to print the current page number.
Printing the date in headers and footers	Use the at sign (@) in a header or footer to print the current date.
Printing text or cell contents in headers and footers	Type in text and press Enter to use text in a header or footer. Type a backslash (\) followed by a cell address to use the cell's contents as a header or footer.
Printing a graph	To print a graph, you must Graph Add the graph to the worksheet, and then print the range that contains the graph.
Printing text and graphs together	Simply print a range or a set of ranges that includes both the graph and text.

Chapter 10

Working with Files and Directories

In this chapter, you are going to learn more about managing files in 1-2-3. You'll learn several general file-management skills, and you'll also build a multiple-file application that consolidates financial information from several branches of Bob Gordon's much-expanded business. At the end of the chapter, you'll learn some tips for handling diskettes and for dealing with "disk full" errors.

What You'll Learn

By the time you finish this chapter, you'll know how to:

■ Retrieve files from directories other than the default directory

■ Temporarily change the current directory

■ Navigate among multiple active files

■ Create a backup file

■ Link worksheet files

■ Graph data from multiple files

■ Change formulas to their current values

■ Erase files on disk from within 1-2-3

■ Create links and transfer data between 1-2-3 and other applications

■ Create text files from 1-2-3 files

■ Import the contents of text files into 1-2-3 worksheets

■ Extract all or part of a worksheet file to another worksheet file

■ Combine all or part of a worksheet file with another worksheet file

Before You Start

Before you begin the exercises in this chapter, start 1-2-3. Make sure that the cell pointer is in cell A:A1 of a new, blank worksheet file, and that 1-2-3 has been set up to save files in your 123BOOK directory.

As you work through the exercises in this chapter, you are going to use several of the small worksheet files you created in Chapter 2. As in previous chapters, stop at the end of a numbered step, or just before the next section heading, when you are tired or have something else to do. Be sure to save any modified worksheet files before you stop. If you have more than one active file, write down the names of the files in memory. When you want to continue with the exercises, start up 1-2-3, read in the worksheet files you last used, and then pick up where you left off.

A Note on Directories and the Exercises in This Chapter   This chapter assumes that the default directory was C:\123 when you began the exercises in this book, and that the files you created in Chapter 2 reside in C:\123. If, when you installed 1-2-3, you specified a different default directory, the files from Chapter 2 will be in the directory Install created, rather than the 1-2-3 program directory. In addition, if you told Install to use a directory other than C:\123 as the 1-2-3 program directory, your 1-2-3 program directory will be the directory you specified.

In the exercises in this chapter, if your initial default directory was not C:\123, substitute the actual directory in which the files you created in Chapter 2 were saved. For example, if you told Install to use D:\123W as the 1-2-3 program directory and to use D:\123W\WORK as the default directory, use D:\123W\WORK when the exercises call for C:\123. Similarly, if the exercises tell you to use the 1-2-3 program directory, and your 1-2-3 program directory is not C:\123, specify your actual program directory instead.

If you are working on files in the directory in which you created the Chapter 2 files and you stop to take a break, be sure to return to that directory before you resume the exercises.

A Note on Example Layout   As in previous chapters, the examples in this chapter assume that your screen displays 20 rows and eight columns when the Worksheet window is maximized. If your display does not show 20 rows and eight columns, your screens will look somewhat different from the illustrations, but you can still do all the examples. Just be sure to use the cell addresses and ranges specified in the instructions.

A Note on Keystroke Instructions   The keystroke instructions in this chapter often assume you are using a mouse to perform such operations as highlighting a range or selecting an option in a dialog box. You can also use the keyboard to perform the same operations. Many of the keyboard equivalents to mouse operations were described in previous chapters. A few of the most common ones are summarized on the next page. For a complete list of keystroke equivalents to mouse operations, see the 1-2-3 documentation or the 1-2-3 online Help.

Accessing Files In Other Directories

So far, most of your work in this book has been in the 123BOOK directory. In general, most people spend most of their time working with 1-2-3 in a particular directory. However, it is frequently necessary to access files in other directories. You can access files in other directories in several ways. You can:

- Provide a full path for the file you want to retrieve
- Back up a level in the directory tree or move down a level to a directory in the default directory

Keyboard Equivalents to Mouse Operations

Operation	Instruction		Keyboard Equivalent	
Complete action and close dialog box	**Select:**	OK	**Press:**	⏎
Cancel action and close dialog box	**Select:**	Cancel	**Press:**	ESC
Highlight a text box	**Select:**	text box	**Press:**	ALT+*underlined_letter*
Edit a range in a text box	**Select:** **Specify:**	Range A:A1..C:D4	**Press:**	ALT+*underlined_letter* F2 (EDIT)
Edit a number or word in a text box	**Select:** **Specify:** *(or click on text and edit it)*	text box new text	**Press:** **Type:** *(or press Left arrow and edit text)*	ALT+*underlined_letter* new text
Highlight a range	**Highlight:** A:A1..C:D4		**Move to:** **Press:** **Move to:** **Press:**	cell A:A1 F4 cell D4 ⏎

- Change to a different directory for the current session
- Change to a different directory for the current session and then make that directory the default directory for subsequent 1-2-3 sessions

You have already learned how to change and save the default directory in Chapter 2. In this section, you are going to learn and use the other methods.

Using a Path in File Operations

If you are saving or retrieving only a file or two in another directory or on another disk, the simplest way to do so is to specify the file's full path as well as the file name. The path includes all the information the operating system needs to find a file: The disk drive, the directory specification, and the file name. For example, suppose you want to retrieve the file FOLKTALE.WK3, which you created back in Chapter 2. You created this file in the default directory in effect when you started the chapter, rather than in the 123BOOK directory. If this directory is \123 on disk drive C, the file's path is C:\123\FOLKTALE.WK3. Retrieve this file using the full path:

Choose: File Open

Type: c:\123\folktale   *in the Filename: text box*

Press:	↵	*or select OK*

■ *NOTE:*   Type the actual directory in which you created FOLKTALE.WK3, rather than `c:\123`, if you told Install to use a different directory as the default directory. You don't have to type the .WK3 file extension.

Although the default directory is still your 123BOOK directory, 1-2-3 retrieves the file FOLKTALE.WK3 from the specified directory.

You can also specify the full path when you want to save a file to another disk drive or directory. For example, suppose you want to make a backup copy of FOLKTALE.WK3 on a diskette in disk drive A. To do so, put a formatted diskette in drive A, close the disk drive door, then use drive A as the destination drive in a File Save As operation:

Choose:	`File Save As`	
Type:	`a:\folktale`	*in the File name: text box*
Press:	↵	*or select OK*

1-2-3 makes a copy of FOLKTALE.WK3 in the root directory of the diskette in drive A and makes A:\FOLKTALE.WK3 the current active file. Before you go on to the next section, close A:\FOLKTALE.WK3

Press:	`CTRL+F4`

Navigating the Directory Tree

If you are not sure of the name of a file in another directory, or you are not sure which directory the file is in, you can quickly navigate the directory tree. Once you have started a File Open operation, clicking on "`..`" (two dots) in the "Directories:" list box moves you one level up the directory tree; pressing Enter or selecting OK when you are highlighting the name of a directory (or double-clicking on the directory name) moves you down the tree, into the highlighted directory. This technique is particularly handy if you need to move around the directory tree quite a bit.

Choose:	`File Open`

1-2-3 displays the worksheet files in the default directory, your 123BOOK directory.

Moving Up the Directory Tree   Move up a level, to the 1-2-3 program directory:

Select:	`Directories:`	
Point to:	`..` *(two dots) in the list box*	
Press:	↵	*or select OK or double-click "..""*

Figure 10-1: Selecting ".." (two dots) moves you up one level in the directory tree.

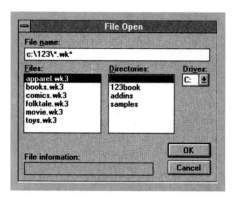

The prompt in the "File name:" text box changes to `c:\123\*.wk*` and 1-2-3 displays the worksheet files in the 1-2-3 program directory, if any. The "Directories:" list box displays two dots at the top of the list box, as well as any directories in the 1-2-3 program directory. Were you to select the two dots once again, 1-2-3 would display files in the root directory of the current drive, as well as all directories in the root directory.

■ *NOTE:* If you created the files from Chapter 2 in the 1-2-3 program directory, 1-2-3 displays the names of those files in the "Files:" list box, as well as any other worksheet files in the 1-2-3 program directory. If you used a different default directory, 1-2-3 will not display the files you created in Chapter 2; they are still in the directory in which you created them.

Temporarily Changing the Default Directory

If you plan to spend most of a session working in a particular directory (as you will for most of this chapter), it is easiest to temporarily make that directory the default directory. As you learned in Chapter 2, you use the Tools User Setup command to change the default directory. In Chapter 2, you changed to the 123BOOK directory and saved those changes in the 1-2-3 configuration file. In this chapter, you will change back to the directory in which you created files in Chapter 2, but you will do so only temporarily. When you exit 1-2-3 and then restart the program, the default directory will still be your 123BOOK directory.

1. Change to the directory where your Chapter 2 files are stored.

Press: ESC *to close the File Open dialog box*

Choose: Tools User Setup

Select: Worksheet directory:

1-2-3 displays the default directory setting (see Figure 10-2). For the duration of this session, change this to the directory in which you created files in Chapter 2:

Type: c:\123 ↵

Figure 10-2:   Changing to a Different Directory

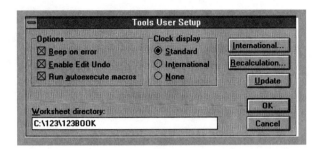

■ **NOTE:**   If your Chapter 2 files are not in C:\123, type the name of the actual drive and directory the files are in instead of typing `c:\123`.

2. Verify that you are in the changed directory.

Now, to verify that you are actually in the correct directory, begin a File Open operation:

Choose: `File   Open`

1-2-3 displays the names of the files you created in Chapter 2. Return to READY mode:

Press: `ESC`   *or select Cancel*

3. Look at the files in the 123BOOK directory.

When you use a File Open or File Save As command, 1-2-3 displays the files in the default directory in the "Files:" list box, and any directories in the default directory in the "Directories:" list box. If you highlight a directory name and press Enter or double-click on the directory name, 1-2-3 displays the files in *that* directory in the "Files:" list box.

Now that C:\123 is the current directory, watch what happens if, after you have begun a File Open operation, you select the directory 123BOOK:

Choose: `File   Open`
Select: `123book`
Press: `↵`   *or double-click 123BOOK*

1-2-3 temporarily moves down a level in the directory tree and displays the worksheet files in the 123BOOK directory. At the moment, you don't want to use any of these files, so return to READY mode again before you go on to the next section:

Select: `Cancel`

■ **NOTE:**   You will use the directory in which you created the Chapter 2 files as the default directory for most of this chapter. If you exit 1-2-3 before you finish the chapter, and then start up the program again later, reissue the Tools User Setup command and change the default directory to the directory in which you created the Chapter 2 files.

Figure 10-3:   Viewing the File Names in a Different Directory

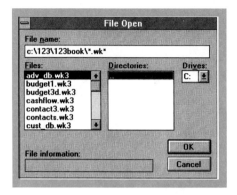

Working With Multiple Files

Most of your work in 1-2-3 in this book has been with a single active file. However, it is easy to work with several files in memory at the same time, and to connect active files both to each other and to other files on disk. This section covers the basics of working with multiple active files, and of using formulas to link cells in one file to cells in another.

What is File Linking?

If your computer has sufficient memory, you can have several files in memory at once, and each file can contain several worksheets. (The maximum number of worksheets, distributed among all the files in memory, is 256.) You can freely move among these active files.

Formulas in one worksheet file can refer to cells in any other worksheet file in memory or on disk. This is called *file linking*. The file that contains the linking formula (and that therefore *receives* the data) is known as the *destination file*. Similarly, the file that contains the range that the linking formula refers to (and that therefore *provides* the data) is known as the *source file*. When you change a value in a source file, any formulas in the destination file that refer to that value also change. For example, suppose a formula in cell A:A5 in a file called DEST.WK3 refers to cell C:D11 in a file called SOURCE.WK3. If you change the value in cell C:D11 of SOURCE.WK3, the value of the linking formula in cell A:A5 in DEST.WK3 is updated, as are any cells that refer to cell A:A5.

A worksheet file can be linked to more than one file, and can contain links to more than one file. A worksheet file can also simultaneously serve both as a source file and a destination file.

■ **NOTE:**   If the destination file is in memory when you modify a source file, 1-2-3 immediately updates formulas in the destination file that refer to the source file. Otherwise, the formulas are updated when you open the destination file. If the source file is no longer in memory when you open the distination file you must choose File Administration Update Links to update the formulas.

Figure 10-4:   When you link files, formulas in the destination file or files reflect changes to data in the source file or files.

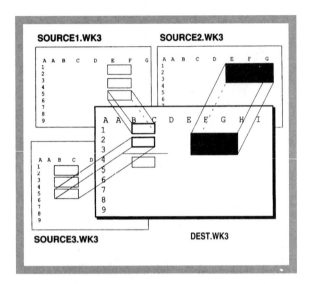

Advantages of File Linking

File linking makes it much easier for a group of people to share information. For example, the managers of several departments may need information from a worksheet database created by the accounting department. Instead of physically incorporating the accounting department's figures into their worksheets, each manager's worksheet can reference the appropriate cells in the accounting department's database. When a new database file comes out of accounting, the department managers' worksheets will automatically contain the latest information the next time they retrieve their worksheet files and update the file links.

By letting you link files in memory to files on disk, 1-2-3 also significantly reduces memory constraints on an application. If you structure an application so that it takes advantage of file linking, the application can conceivably be as large as the available disk storage, instead of being limited to the amount of available memory. In a networked environment, the size of an application is not limited even by local disk storage, since parts of an application can reside on more than one physical disk drive as long as all the pieces are accessible over the network.

Navigating Among Multiple Active Files

Navigating among multiple files in memory is, conceptually, a lot like flipping through folders in a file cabinet. Just as you might pull out several folders, lay them on a desk, and leaf through them while you are looking for the item you want, you can read in several worksheet files, each containing several worksheets, and flip through them with the mouse or keyboard.

Table 10-1 summarizes the keys you can use to move the cell pointer from one active file to another. In addition to the keys described in Table 10-1, you can also use the mouse to move from one file to another by clicking anywhere in the Worksheet window or the title bar of the file you want to move to. Further, you can move to a specific active file by choosing Window, and then choosing the active file's name.

You will have a chance to practice your file navigation skills in this chapter, as you create a multiple-file application.

Figure 10-5: Choosing from a List of Active Files

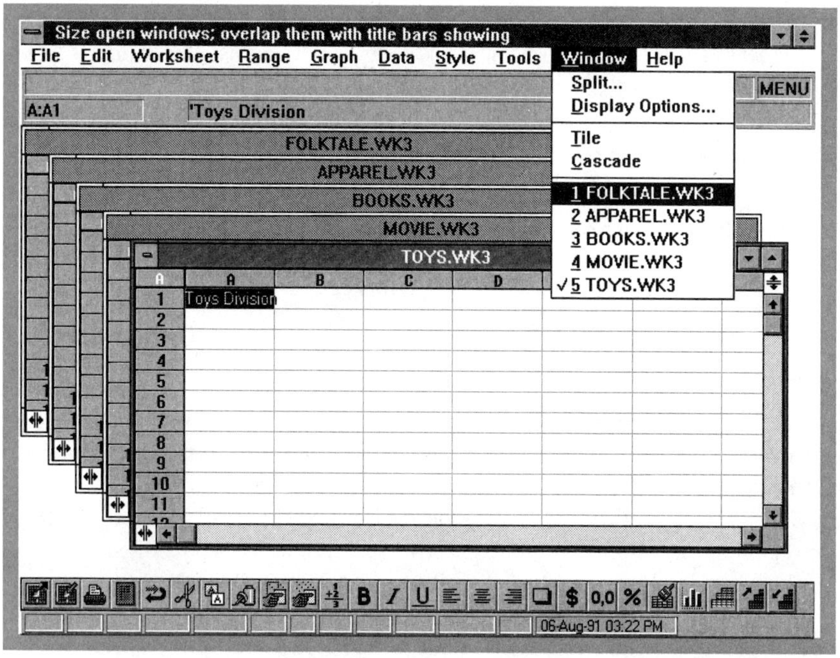

■ *NOTE:* The order of active files in a 1-2-3 session depends on the order in which you open files, and on which file the cell pointer is in when you open another file. The first file you open in a 1-2-3 session is always the first active file.

Table 10-1: File Navigation Keys

Key Name	What It Does:
CTRL+F6	Moves to next worksheet, Graph, or Transcript window in the 1-2-3 window (the same as choosing Next from the Control menu of a window in the 1-2-3 window).
CTRL+END CTRL+PGUP (NEXTFILE)	Moves to the most recent location of the cell pointer in the next active file. If the next file has no active cells, the cell pointer moves to cell A:A1 in that file.
CTRL+END CTRL+PGUP (PREVFILE)	Moves to the most recent location of the cell pointer in the previous active file. If the previous file has no active cells, the cell pointer moves to cell A:A1 in that file.
CTRL+END HOME (FIRSTFILE)	Moves to the most recent location of the cell pointer in the first active file.
CTRL+END END (LAST FILE)	Moves to the most recent location of the cell pointer in the last active file.
CTRL+PGUP (NEXTSHEET)	If the cell pointer is in the last worksheet of the current active file, moves to the most recent location of the cell pointer in the next active file. Otherwise, moves to the next worksheet in the current file.
CTRL+PGDN (PREVSHEET)	If the cell pointer is in the first worksheet of the current active file, moves to the most recent location of the cell pointer in the previous active file. Otherwise, moves to the previous worksheet in the current file.
F5 (GOTO)	Moves to any cell in any active file you specify. If you specify only the file name, moves to the most recent location of the cell pointer in the specified file. If the file has no active cells, the cell pointer moves to cell A:A1 in that file.

The Executive Summary Model

To help you get your feet wet working with file linking, this chapter shows you how to build part of what, in real life, would be a fairly detailed multiple-file application. In the process, it continues the Bob Gordon story.

In Chapter 8, we left Bob as he was about to start looking for additional funding for Folktale Workshop. This chapter picks up eight years later, in the year 2000. In the years since Chapter 8, Bob's business has boomed. Inspired by a Chinese fortune cookie ("Your humble idea will blossom into big enterprise"), and some what-if analysis with Backsolver and Solver (see Chapter 12), Bob convinced two potential investors to put $10,000 each into Folktale Workshop. With their $20,000, and with $10,000 of his own, Bob began larger-scale production and promotion. Business far exceeded his expectations. Within a year, Folktale Workshop was Bob's full-time job. Within two years, his staff had grown to 35. Within four years, Folktale Workshop had branches across the northeastern United States.

This chapter sees Bob at the head of a major corporation, with branches throughout the United States and Canada. While the transformable dolls are still Folktale Workshop's major product line, the company also has a book and comic book division, an apparel division, and a movie/video division (currently at work on their second full-length motion picture). There is even talk about opening a theme park, though that is still a couple of years in the future.

In this chapter, you will construct part of a summary worksheet and supporting worksheet files for Bob's much-expanded business. Its purpose will be to give Bob a bird's eye view of his whole transcontinental operation.

■ *NOTE:*   In real life, an application of this sort would consist of a balance sheet, income statement, and cash flow budget for each of Folktale Workshop's divisions, and an executive summary that rolled up all the significant information in the division-specific worksheet files and summarized it. Each division-specific worksheet file would reference supporting worksheet files or databases. However, the principles you will learn in constructing this simpler example apply equally well to more complex applications.

To build this sample application, you will be working with several files, both in memory and on disk. The basic steps you are going to follow to complete the example are:

1. Create a series of worksheet files for each division of Folktale Workshop.

2. Create an Executive Summary worksheet file that contains links to the division-specific worksheets.

3. Enter data in the division-specific worksheets.

4. Modify values in the division-specific worksheets and see the changes reflected in the Executive Summary.

Building the First Division Worksheet File

You are going to build worksheet files for each of Folktale Workshop's divisions. First, you will build a sample worksheet file for the Apparel Division. From this file, you will create a template. You will use the template to create the files for the Books/Comics, Movie/Video, and Toys divisions. Figure 10-6 shows how the Apparel Division worksheet will look when you have completed it.

Figure 10-6: The Completed Apparel Division Worksheet

	A	B	C	D
1	Apparel Division		2000 Budget (Consolidation)	
2				
3	TOTALS	Jan-2000		
4	(in Millions)	BUDGETED	ACTUAL	%VARIANCE
5				
6	Gross Income	15.70	14.80	-5.73%
7	Gross Expenses	11.20	11.30	0.89%
8				
9	Gross Profit	$4.50	$3.50	-22.22%
10				
11				
12				
13				

The Division files track both budgeted and actual income and expenses. In addition, they show how much above or below expected values the actual income, expenses, and profit are for each month. Column B shows the budgeted amounts, column C the actual amounts, and column D shows the computed variance as a percentage of the budgeted amounts. The worksheet is set up so that, were you to freeze column A, Bob could use Tab or Control-Right to view one month's data at a time. For this exercise, however, you will fill in figures only for the month of January.

■ *NOTE:*   In a real-life application, each of the Division worksheets would most likely summarize values in other worksheets in the same file. However, in this exercise, you will not create any additional worksheets in the Division worksheet files.

Building the Template   Begin by building the worksheet for the Apparel Division of Folktale Workshop.

1. Read APPAREL.WK3 into memory and maximize the Worksheet window.

    You created APPAREL.WK3 in Chapter 2 as a way of learning more about saving and retrieving files. Now, you'll turn the simple file you created in Chapter 2 into an actual application file.

Choose:	`File  Open`
Select:	`apparel.wk3`
	`OK` *or double-click apparel.wk3*

    After you have read APPAREL.WK3 into memory, maximize the Worksheet window.

2. Change the global format and adjust column widths.

    First, you will set up the worksheet so that numbers are displayed in Comma (,) format with two decimal places. Then you'll widen the columns to make room for the labels in column A and to display the values across the screen. First, change the global format:

Choose:	`Worksheet  Global Settings`
Select:	`Format...`
	`Comma  OK`

    Now, change the global column width:

Select:	`Column width:`
Type:	`16` *in the text box*
Select:	`OK`

    Finally, change the width of column A. With the cell pointer anywhere in column A,

Choose:	`Worksheet  Column Width`
Type:	`20` *in the Set width to: text box*

Select: OK

3. Enter labels in rows 1 through 9.

Fill in the labels for the worksheet, using Figure 10-7 as your guide. Make sure you type an apostrophe (') before you type the labels (`in Millions`) and `2000 Budget (Consolidation)`.

Figure 10-7

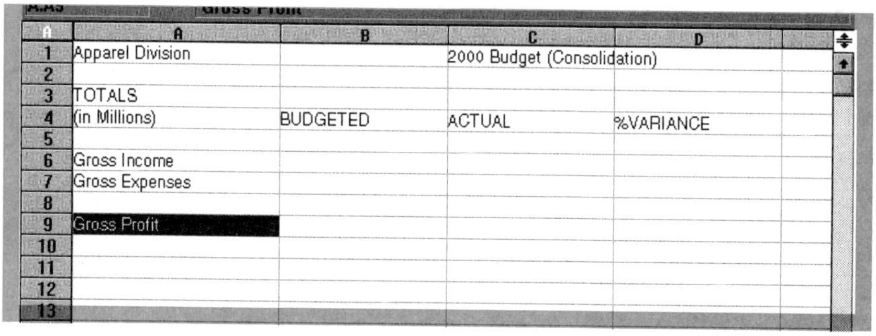

Now, center the labels in cells A3 and A4 (with Style Alignment Center or the "Align Center" icon) and right-justify the labels in B4..D4 (with Style Alignment Right or the "Align Right" icon). When you are finished, your screen should look like Figure 10-8.

Figure 10-8: Right-Aligning the Column Label

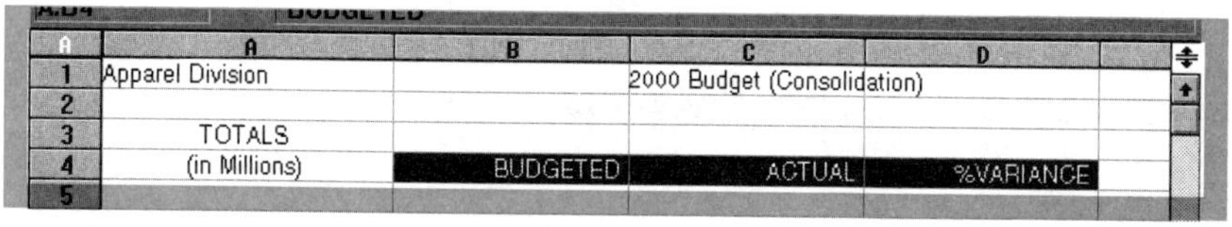

4. Format cell B3 as a date and enter the date 1-Jan-2000.

You will use a date number for the column heading in cell B3. Format the cell as date type 3 and enter the date for the first day of the year 2000. 1-2-3 will accept the date you type as a valid date number and display cell B3 in date type 3 format (MMMYY). Do *not* type a label prefix before `1-jan-2000`.

Move to: cell B3

Choose: `Range Format`

Select: `3: Dec 90 OK`

Type: `1-jan-2000` ↵

Figure 10-9: Typing a Date to Enter a Date Number

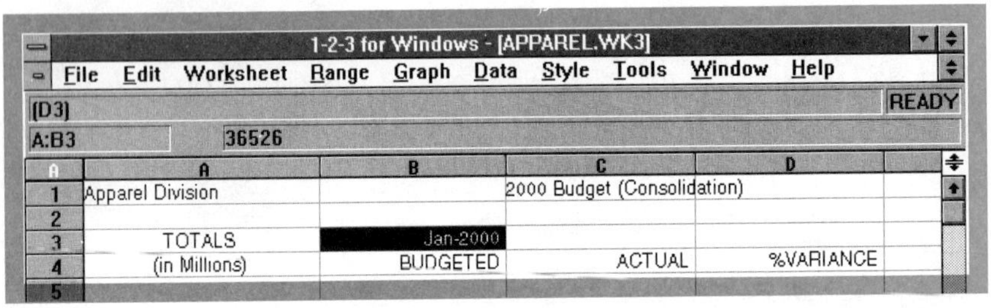

1-2-3 displays the date as **Jan-2000** but shows the date number 36526 in the control panel.

5. Enter values in cells B6..C7.

Fill in values for the Apparel Division's budgeted and actual gross income and gross expenses. Use Figure 10-10 as your guide. You do not have to type in the second decimal place zeros when you enter the value—1-2-3 will add them automatically because the cells are formatted as Comma (,) with two decimal places.

Figure 10-10

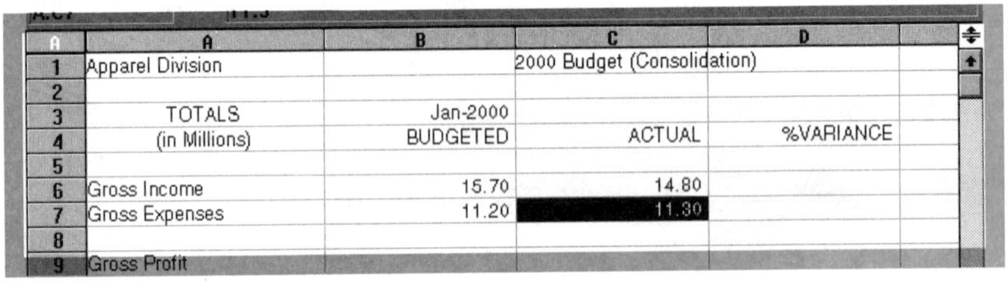

6. Create formulas in cells B9 and C9.

Cell B9 displays the expected gross profit and cell C9 displays the actual gross profit for the month of January 2000. Cells B9 and C9 calculate gross profit using the following equation:

```
Gross Profit = Gross Income-Gross Expenses
```

Unlike similar formulas you have entered in other exercises in this book, the formulas in cells B9 and C9 contain error checking. The error checking tells 1-2-3 to display the characters NA if any of the values on which a formula depends have not been entered. For instance, the formula in cell B9 reads:

```
@IF(B6=""#OR#B7="",@NA,B6-B7)
```

This formula uses two @functions. One, @NA, takes no arguments. It returns the value NA, which means "not available." The other, @IF, takes three arguments: A test, the value of the function if the test is True, and the value of the function if the test is False. In this case, the test is to determine whether either cell B6 or cell B7 is blank (B6=""#OR#B7=""), indicating that data has not yet been entered. The formula evaluates to NA if either cell B6 or cell B7 is blank; otherwise, the formula evaluates to the difference between the values in cells B6 and B7. Cell C9 contains similar error checking.

Enter the formula in cell B9 and then copy it to cell C9. Do not type any spaces between the pairs of quotation marks in the formula. When you are finished, your screen should look like Figure 10-11.

Move to:	cell B9
Type:	`aif(b6=""#or#b7="",ana,b6-b7)` ↵
Choose:	Edit Quick Copy
Specify:	cell C9 *in the To: text box*
Select:	OK

Figure 10-11: Calculating Gross Profit for the Apparel Division

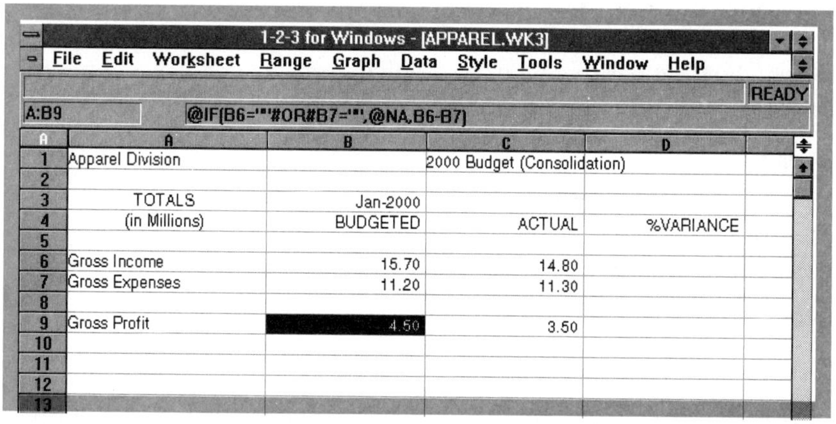

7. Create formulas in column D.

The %VARIANCE column (column D) shows how much above or below the expected values the actual income, expenses, and profit are for the month.

Figure 10-12: Computing the Variance Between Actual and Budgeted Income, Expenses, and Profit

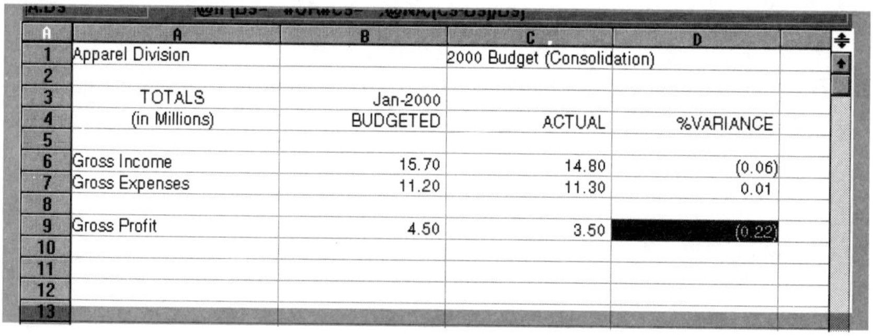

The basic formula in each cell in column D is:

```
%VARIANCE = (ACTUAL-BUDGETED)/BUDGETED
```

Like the formulas in cells B9 and C9, the formulas in column D also contain error checking, so that cells dependent on data that has not yet been entered display NA instead of displaying erroneous values. For example, the formula in cell D6 is:

```
@IF(B6=""#OR#C6="",@NA,(C6-B6)/B6)
```

This formula means: "If cell B6 is blank or cell C6 is blank, the value of this cell is NA. Otherwise, the value of this cell is equal to the difference between cells C6 and B6 expressed as a percentage of the value in cell B6." The other cells in column D contain similar error checking.

Move to: cell D6

Type: `@if(b6=""#or#c6="",@na,(c6-b6)/b6)`   ⏎

Now that you have created the formula in cell D6, use it to create the formulas in cells D7 and D9. If you have a mouse, use the "Copy to Clipboard" and "Paste" icons to copy the formula in cell D6 to cells D7 and D9. Otherwise, use Control+Insert to copy to the Clipboard, and Shift+Insert to paste from the Clipboard, or type the following commands. 1-2-3 automatically adjusts the cell addresses.

Choose: `Edit  Copy`

Move to: cell D7

Choose: `Edit  Paste`

Move to: cell D9

Choose: `Edit  Paste`

8. Format column D as Percent.

Display the values in column D as percent values, with two decimal places. If you have a mouse, do so by highlighting the range D6..D9 and clicking on the "Percent" icon. If not, use the following keystrokes to change the format:

Highlight: D6..D9

Choose: `Range  Format`

Select: `Percent  OK`

9. Format cells B9 and C9 as Currency.

Display the values in cells B9 and C9 as Currency with two decimal places. Again, if you have a mouse, highlight the cells and click on the "Currency" icon. If not, use the following keystrokes:

Highlight: B9..C9

Choose: `Range  Format`

Select: Currency OK

Figure 10-13: **The Apparel Division Spreadsheet with Values Formatted as Percent and Currency**

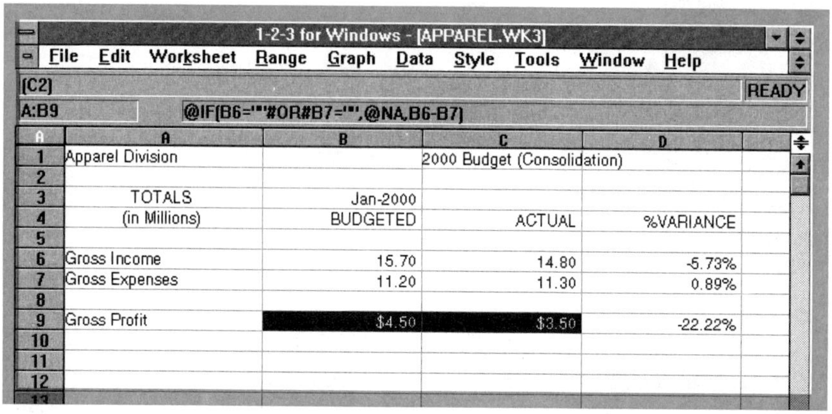

10. Underline rows 4, 7, and 9.

Draw a single underline beneath the data in rows 4 and 7 and draw a double underline beneath the data in row 9. Use the Style Border commands to draw the lines, instead of inserting hyphens or equal signs in the rows beneath the data.

Highlight: A4..D4

Choose: Style Border

Select: Bottom: *and check the check-box*
                 OK

Repeat the same procedure to underline the data in the range A7..D7. Then, draw a double underline at the bottom of cells A9..D9.

Highlight: A9..D9

Choose: Style Border

Select: Bottom: *and check the check-box*

As before, 1-2-3 displays a single underline beside the "Bottom:" check-box. However, you can also select a double underline. To select the double underline from the "Bottom:" drop-down menu, either press Tab to highlight the menu box and then press Down to display the double underline, or click on the "Bottom:" drop-down menu and then click on the double underline.

Select: *the double underline, in the Bottom: drop-down menu*
                 OK   *to complete the operation*

Figure 10-14a: Selecting the Double Underline from the "Bottom:" Option of the Style Border Dialog Box

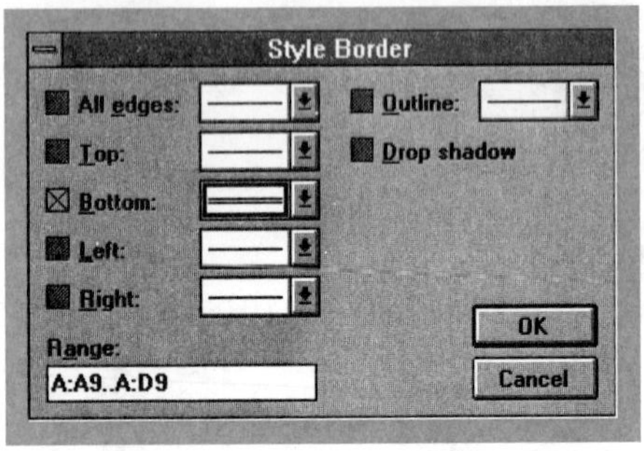

Figure 10-14b: The Apparel Division Worksheet (Completed)

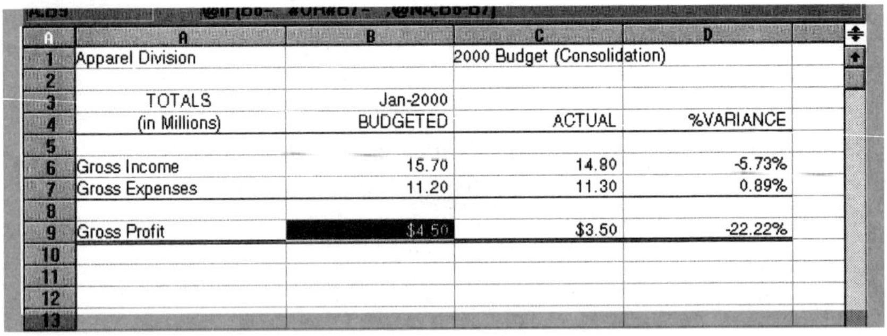

11. Name the values in row 9.

Finally, name the cells in row 9 that contain values. You will refer to these range names in the Executive Summary worksheet file.

First, name cell B9, the budgeted value for January's gross profit:

Move to:	cell B9
Choose:	`Range   Name   Create`
Type:	`jan_profit_bud` *in the Range name: text box*
Select:	`Create`

1-2-3 enters the name in the "Range name:" list. Now, name cells C9 and D9 and then close the dialog box:

Type:	`jan_profit_act` *in the Range name: text box*
Select:	`Range:`
Specify:	cell C9 *in the text box*
Select:	`Create`

Type:	`jan_profit_var`	*in the Range name: text box*
Select:	`Range:`	
Specify:	cell D9	*in the text box*
Select:	`OK`	

12. Save APPAREL.WK3.

A Note on Using Range Names with File Links   Although you can refer to cells and ranges in other files even if the cells and ranges are not named, referring to them by name makes the references easier to understand. Using range names also makes an application less susceptible to error.

Consider what happens when you create a link to a cell in another file, and then move the cell in the other file. When you refer to a source range by address, 1-2-3 always uses this address; if the cell data is moved and the destination file is not active, 1-2-3 has no way to know about the move, and so the file link no longer refers to the correct data.

However, when you use a range name to refer to the source range, 1-2-3 uses the range name to locate the cell. If the cell data is moved, 1-2-3 adjusts the range name to point to the moved data, and so the formula in the destination file still refers to the correct data.

Creating the Remaining Division Worksheets

In this section, you will make a template out of APPAREL.WK3 and then save three more copies of the file, each under a different name. Each of these new copies will become a new division worksheet.

1. Change the worksheet title.

The worksheet file APPAREL.WK3 is now safely tucked away on disk. You are going to modify a copy of this file so that it becomes the first template file. Then, you will save that file as BOOKS.WK3 to create a new Books/Comics Division file.

First, change the title to Books/Comics Division:

Move to:	cell A1	
Type:	`Books/Comics Division`	↵

2. Erase cells B6..C7.

In order to use this file as a template, you are going to erase the values in B6..C7. Because the cells have formatting information that you want to keep, you'll use Edit Clear Special instead of Edit Clear to erase these cells. Edit Clear erases cell contents and any formatting information you have applied, while Edit Clear Special lets you selectively erase cell contents, numeric formatting, any style formatting you have applied, or all three. In this case, you will erase only cell contents.

■ *NOTE:*   If you check the "Graph" check-box, you can also use Edit Clear Special to remove a graph you have embedded in the worksheet.

Highlight:	B6..C7
Choose:	Edit Clear Special
Select:	Number format *and clear the check box*
	OK

Figure 10-15:   Using Edit Clear Special to Erase Only Cell Contents

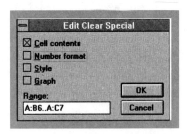

When you erase the contents of cells B6..C7, notice what happens to the values in row 9 and in column D. Erasing the values in cells B6..C7 causes 1-2-3 to display the value NA in the cells of row 9 and column D; as you recall, these cells contain formulas that test whether the cells on which they are dependent are blank. These formulas display NA to indicate that the required data is not yet available.

Figure 10-16:   Because you have erased the data in cells B6..C7, formulas that depend on values in that range now display NA

A	B	C	D	
1 Books/Comics Division		2000 Budget (Consolidation)		
2				
3 TOTALS	Jan-2000			
4 (in Millions)	BUDGETED	ACTUAL	%VARIANCE	
5				
6 Gross Income	██████		NA	
7 Gross Expenses			NA	
8				
9 Gross Profit	NA	NA	NA	
10				
11				
12				
13				

3. Save BOOKS.WK3.

You will save this file as BOOKS.WK3, replacing the existing disk file.

Choose:	File Save As
Select:	File name:
Type:	books *in the text box*

Press: ⏎

Figure 10-17:   The File Save As Message Box

Because a file called BOOKS.WK3 already exists, 1-2-3 asks if you really do want to over-write the existing file. (When you use File Save to save a new version of a file that already exists, 1-2-3 does not take this precaution, since File Save does not allow you to inadvertently specify the name of any other existing file.)

Instead of immediately saving the current file as the new BOOKS.WK3, 1-2-3 asks you if you want to replace the existing file, keep the existing file as a *backup*, or cancel the operation. If you select "Replace," 1-2-3 saves the modified worksheet file by writing over the existing version of the disk file. Selecting "Backup" changes the file extension of the existing worksheet file to .BAK (for backup) and the existing format file to .FMB (for format backup) and then saves the new file under the original file name. Selecting "Cancel" stops the File Save As operation and returns you to READY mode, leaving the disk version of the file BOOKS.WK3 intact.

In this case, you have no further use for the original BOOKS.WK3, so replace it:

Select: Replace

1-2-3 replaces the original BOOKS file with a copy of the file in memory. Notice that the file name in the title bar changes to BOOKS.WK3.

4. Create MOVIE.WK3 and TOYS.WK3

To create the remaining template files, modify the title of the current file and save the file under a new name. First, create a new version of MOVIE.WK3:

Move to:	cell A1
Type:	Movie/Video Division ⏎
Choose:	File Save As
Select:	File name:
Type:	movie *in the File name: Text box*
Press:	⏎
Select:	Replace

Then, create a new TOYS.WK3 file:

Type:	Toys Division ⏎

Choose:	File Save As
Type:	toys *in the File name: text box*
Press:	↵
Select:	Replace

A Note on Saving a File and Retaining a Backup   Normally, when you save a file with File Save or create a new file with File Save As, 1-2-3 saves the file immediately, without question. When you saved the files BOOKS.WK3, MOVIE.WK3, and TOYS.WK3 with the File Save As command, 1-2-3 presented you with the choice of replacing the current file, saving the current file but keeping the original file as a backup, or cancelling the save operation. This was a precaution. 1-2-3 wanted to make sure you weren't accidentally overwriting a file you might want to keep. In the exercise, you told 1-2-3 to replace the existing file with the new one, but at other times you might prefer that 1-2-3 create a backup.

To intentionally save backup files as you work, choose File Save As instead of File Save, and then select "Backup." 1-2-3 renames the original .WK3 file so that it has a .BAK extension, and renames the original .FM3 file so it has the extension .FMB.

It's a good idea to keep a backup when you are making many changes to a worksheet. This technique enables you to have, at any time, three versions of a particular file: The version in memory, the version you have most recently saved, and the version before that. If you make a serious mistake while you are building or modifying a worksheet file, you can go back to either of the previous versions and start again.

To retrieve the backup file, choose File Open and specify the name of the original file with the extension .BAK. For instance, to retrieve the backup of the Apparel Division file, type APPAREL.BAK in the File Open text box and then press Enter or select OK. To save the file, choose File Save As and give the file a different name, without the .BAK extension.

Filling in Values in the Division Files   The file APPAREL.WK3 already has data in it, but the remaining files are still just empty templates. If this were a real application, each of these division files would be completed by someone in that division's office, and then the files would be passed on to the head office for Bob to examine. To simulate this process, read into memory the files you just created and then fill in sample values for the remaining divisions. (If you have a mouse, use the "File Open" icon. Otherwise, follow the keystroke instructions given here.)

1. Read the remaining division files into memory.

First, read APPAREL.WK3 back in:

Choose:	File Open
Select:	apparel.wk3 OK

1-2-3 places APPAREL.WK3 in front of TOYS.WK3. Use the same procedure to read in BOOKS.WK3 and MOVIE.WK3:

Choose:	File Open

Select:	books.wk3 OK
Choose:	File Open
Select:	movie.wk3 OK

Figure 10-18: All the division worksheet files are in memory (Window Cascade view).

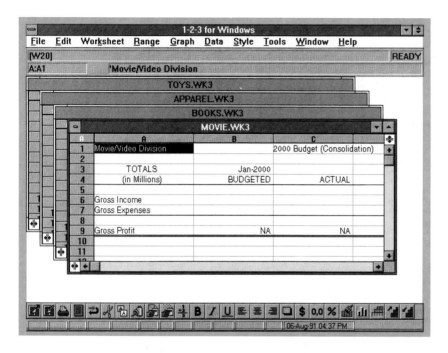

2. Fill in division worksheet values.

Fill in values for the MOVIE.WK3, BOOKS.WK3, and TOYS.WK3 Division files. Enter the values in Setup Table 10-1 in the indicated files. To make it easier to move among the worksheet files as you fill in values, use a tiled display.

Choose: Window Tile

To move from one file to the next, either click anywhere in the file's Worksheet window, press Control+F6, or press Next File or Prev File (Control+End Control+Page Up or Control+End Control+Page Down). Maximize the Worksheet window while you are working in the file, then Restore the Worksheet window before you move on to the next file. Complete this process until you have filled in the values for all the files in memory.

Setup Table 10-1: Division Worksheet Values

Worksheet	Cell B6	Cell C6	Cell B7	Cell C7
MOVIE.WK3	40.1	52.3	38.3	50.2
BOOKS.WK3	10.9	11.5	8.5	9.2
TOYS.WK3	78.27	80.2	58.7	55.1

Figures 10-19a-d show how the four completed worksheets should look when you are finished entering all the values.

Figure 10-19a:　The Apparel Division Worksheet

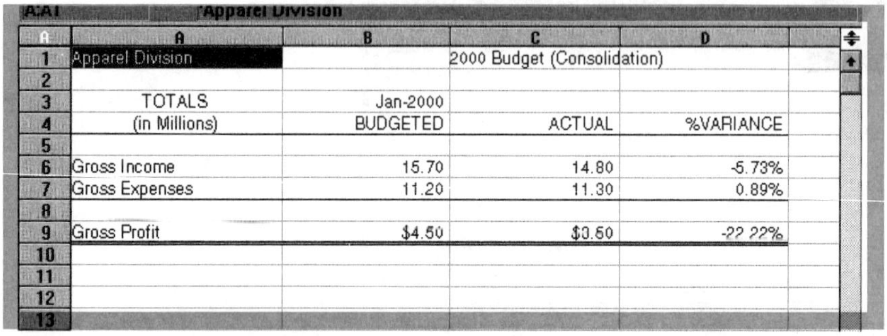

Figure 10-19b:　The Movie/Video Division Worksheet

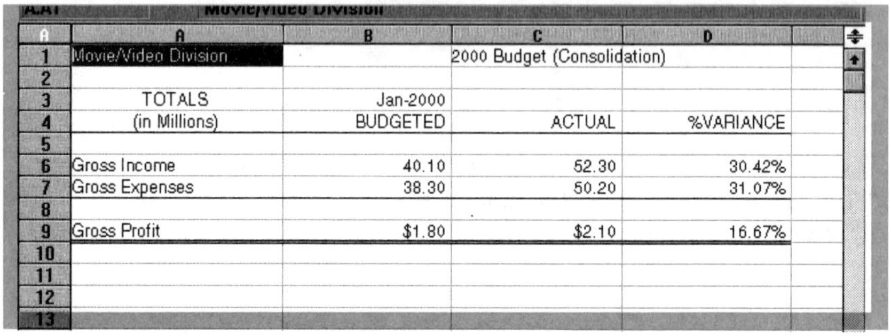

Figure 10-19c:　The Books Division Worksheet

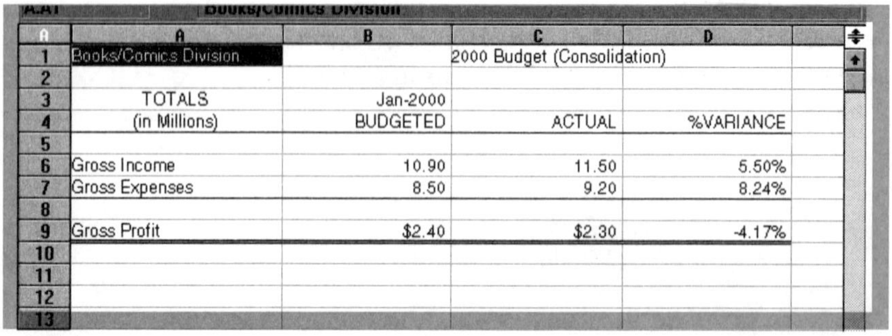

Figure 10-19d: The Toys Division Worksheet

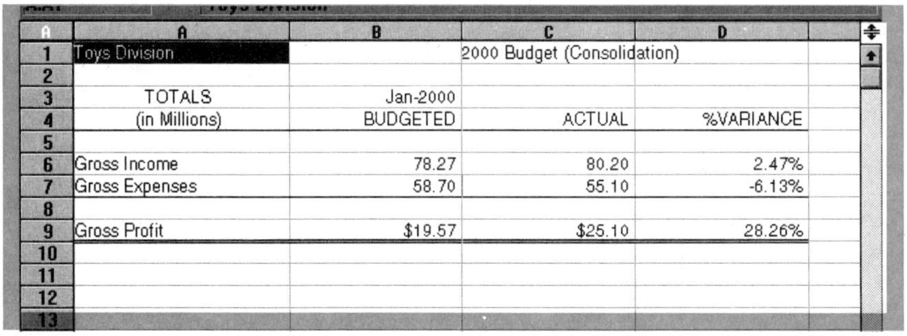

	A	B	C	D
1	Toys Division		2000 Budget (Consolidation)	
2				
3	TOTALS	Jan-2000		
4	(in Millions)	BUDGETED	ACTUAL	%VARIANCE
5				
6	Gross Income	78.27	80.20	2.47%
7	Gross Expenses	58.70	55.10	-6.13%
8				
9	Gross Profit	$19.57	$25.10	28.26%
10				
11				
12				
13				

3. Save all modified files.

The easiest way to save your work is to save all modified files at once:

Choose: File   Save As

Select: Save All

1-2-3 saves all the files that have changed since the last time you saved them—in this case, MOVIE.WK3, BOOKS.WK3, and TOYS.WK3—and then returns to READY mode.

Figure 10-20:   A Tiled View of the Completed Division Worksheet Files

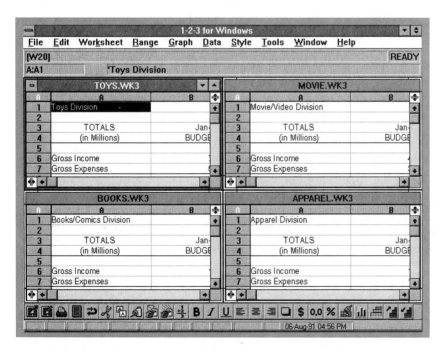

Creating the Executive Summary

In this section, you will create a worksheet file that references named ranges in each of the division worksheets. This file is a fragment of a real application that would roll up all the significant values from each of the division worksheets and compare, contrast, and summarize them. In this exercise, you will be rolling up and totalling only the figures for gross profit.

Figure 10-21: The Completed Executive Summary Worksheet

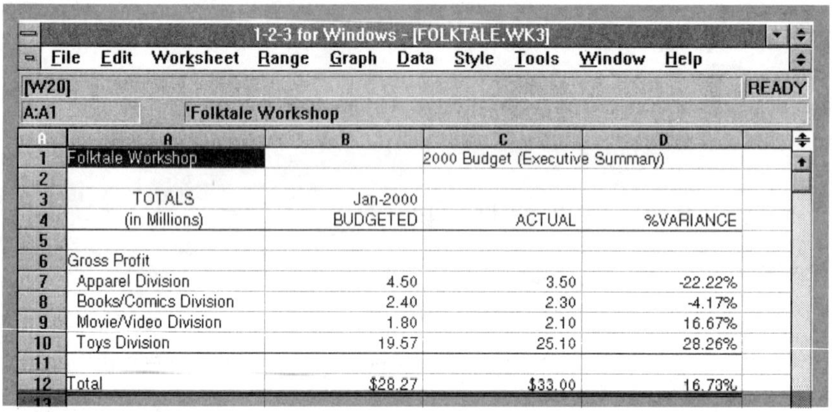

	A	B	C	D
1	Folktale Workshop		2000 Budget (Executive Summary)	
2				
3	TOTALS	Jan-2000		
4	(in Millions)	BUDGETED	ACTUAL	%VARIANCE
5				
6	Gross Profit			
7	Apparel Division	4.50	3.50	-22.22%
8	Books/Comics Division	2.40	2.30	-4.17%
9	Movie/Video Division	1.80	2.10	16.67%
10	Toys Division	19.57	25.10	28.26%
11				
12	Total	$28.27	$33.00	16.73%

1. Save MOVIE.WK3 as FOLKTALE.WK3.

Because some of the global settings and labels you will use in the Executive Summary are the same as those in the division files, using a copy of one of the division worksheet files as a starting point for the Executive Summary is quicker than starting from scratch. Begin constructing the Executive Summary by modifying MOVIE.WK3.

Make MOVIE.WK3 the active window and maximize the Worksheet window. Then, save the file as FOLKTALE.WK3. The new file will overwrite the original file called FOLKTALE.WK3.

Choose: `File Save As`
Type: `folktale` *in the File name: text box*
Press: ↵
Select: `Replace`

2. Enter a new title for the worksheet and the application.

Start to transform the file into the Executive Summary by changing the title row. First, change the name of the worksheet:

Move to: cell A1
Type: `Folktale Workshop`
Press: → *two times*

Then, edit cell C1 so it reads: `2000 Budget (Executive Summary)`.

3. Erase the data in rows 6 through 9.

The Executive Summary does not use the data, cell formats, or style formatting of the original file. Use Edit Clear to remove the cell contents and the formatting information in cells A6..D9 in one operation.

Highlight: A6..D9

Press: DELETE

Figure 10-22: Erasing Unneeded Data and Formatting from the Executive Summary Worksheet

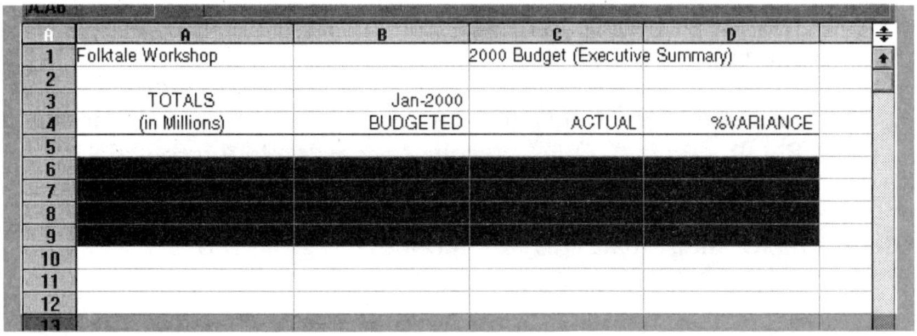

4. Enter labels in cells A6..A12.

Using Figure 10-23 as a guide, enter the labels in column A. Indented labels are indented two spaces.

Figure 10-23: The Executive Summary Labels

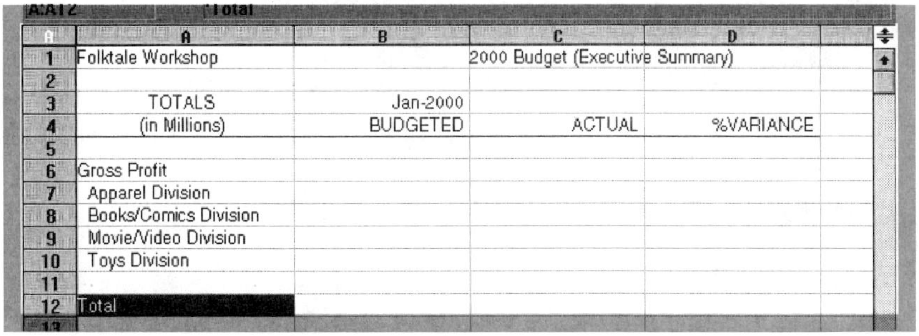

5. Enter file-linking formulas in row 7.

The formulas in cells B7..D10 are all of the same type: They are a simple reference to a cell in one of the division worksheets. The syntax for identifying a location in another file is:

+<<file name>>range. That is, you specify the name of the file, surrounded by double angle brackets, and then the cell or range address. For example, the formula in cell B7 is:

```
+<<APPAREL.WK3>>$JAN_PROFIT_BUD
```

In this case, the file name is APPAREL.WK3 and the cell is named JAN_PROFIT_BUD.

Because you will be copying these formulas to other cells and you do not want the cell addresses to change when you make the copies, the formulas in this worksheet use absolute range names instead of relative range names. Other applications may require relative range names or actual cell addresses.

The file references in this worksheet file also use only the file name, rather than the full path specification. This allows you to move the application to another directory or another disk without having to edit the file names in the cell references. For example, you can move FOLKTALE.WK3 and all the supporting files into your 123BOOK directory without having to change any of the file references in FOLKTALE.WK3.

■ *NOTE:*   When you create a file reference without specifying the full path, 1-2-3 looks in the current directory for the source file. If it finds the file, it displays the value in the specified range. If it does not find the file, it displays ERR.

Begin by creating the formula for the Apparel division's budgeted gross profit:

Move to: cell B7

Type: `+<<apparel.wk3>>$jan_profit_bud`   ↵

Figure 10-24:   The value for the Apparel Division's budgeted gross profit comes from a link to
                APPAREL.WK3

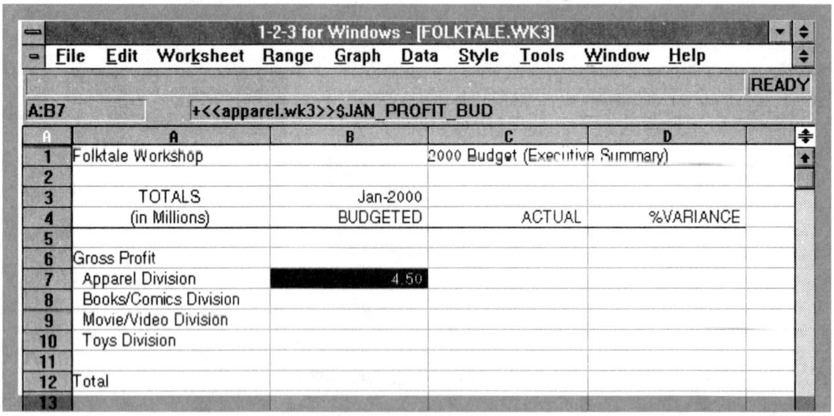

1-2-3 displays the current value for the Apparel division's budgeted gross profit in cell B7. Copy this formula across row 7:

Choose: Edit   Quick Copy

Select:	To:
Specify:	C7..D7 *in the text box*
Select:	OK

Now, 1-2-3 displays the value for the range <<APPAREL.WK3>>$JAN_PROFIT_BUD in all three formula cells. Edit the formulas in cells C7 and D7 so they refer to the named ranges JAN_PROFIT_ACT and JAN_PROFIT_VAR, respectively. First, edit cell C7:

Move to:	cell C7
Press:	F2 **(EDIT)** *or double-click the cell*
	BACKSPACE *three times, to erase BUD*
Type:	act ↵

Then, edit cell D7:

Move to:	cell D7
Press:	F2 **(EDIT)** *or double-click the cell*
	BACKSPACE *three times, to erase BUD*
Type:	var ↵

Figure 10-25: Editing File Links in the Executive Summary Worksheet File

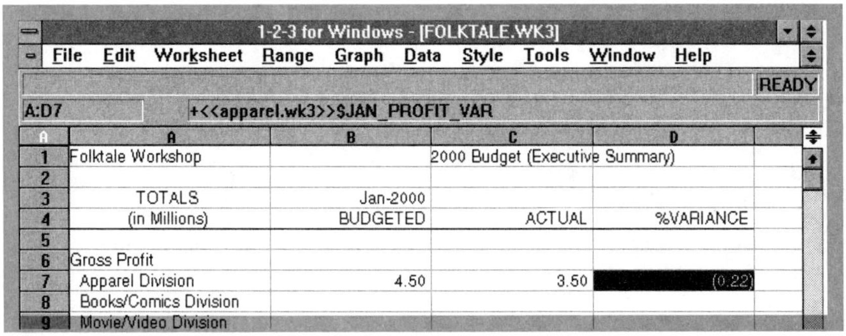

6. Format column D as Percent.

Column D, like column D of the Division worksheets, shows the difference between budgeted and actual values as a percentage of the budgeted value. Format column D as Percent with two decimal places. If you have a mouse, use the "Percent" icon; otherwise, use the following keystrokes:

Highlight:	D7..D12
Choose:	Range Format

Select: `Percent   OK`

7. Copy the formulas in row 7 to rows 8 through 10.

The only difference between the formulas in rows 7, 8, 9, and 10 is the name of the file to which each row's formulas refer (the formulas in row 7 refer to APPAREL.WK3, the formulas in row 8 to BOOKS.WK3, and so on). Copying row 7 to the next three rows will make it easy to create the formulas in those rows.

Highlight: B7..D7
Choose: `Edit   Quick Copy`
Specify: B8..B10   *in the To: text box*
Select: `OK`

Figure 10-26: Temporary formulas all reflect values in apparel.wk3, but you'll fix that in a moment.

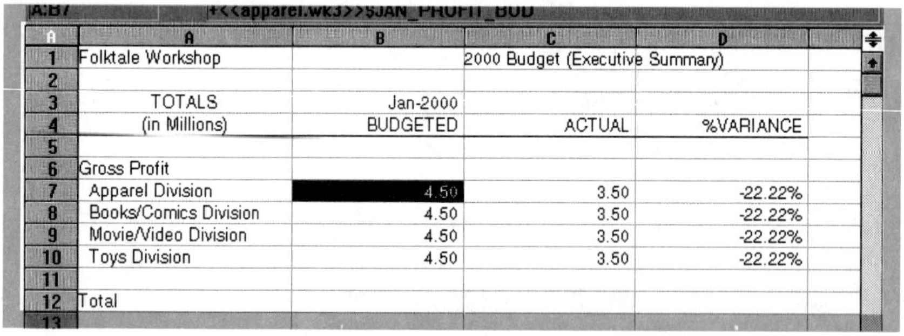

A:B7	+<<apparel.wk3>>$JAN_PROFIT_BUD			
	A	B	C	D
1	Folktale Workshop		2000 Budget (Executive Summary)	
2				
3	TOTALS	Jan-2000		
4	(in Millions)	BUDGETED	ACTUAL	%VARIANCE
5				
6	Gross Profit			
7	Apparel Division	4.50	3.50	-22.22%
8	Books/Comics Division	4.50	3.50	-22.22%
9	Movie/Video Division	4.50	3.50	-22.22%
10	Toys Division	4.50	3.50	-22.22%
11				
12	Total			
13				

1-2-3 displays values from APPAREL.WK3 in all four rows. You will make the formulas point to the correct files in the next step.

8. Use Edit Find to edit the formulas in rows 8 through 10.

The easiest way to edit the formulas in rows 8, 9, and 10 so they refer to the correct files is to use Edit Find. First, correct the formulas in row 8:

Highlight: B8..D8
Choose: `Edit   Find`
Type: `apparel`   *in the Search for: text box*
Select: `Replace with:`
Type: `books`   *in the text box*
Select: `Replace All`

1-2-3 replaces the word APPAREL in cells B8..D8 with the word BOOKS. The formulas for the Books/Comics Division display the correct results. (See Figure 10-27.)

Figure 10-27:   The Corrected Formulas for the Books/Comics Division

	A	B	C	D	
			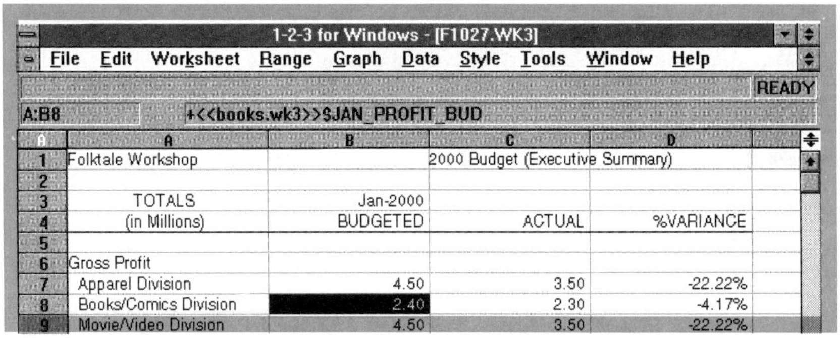 1-2-3 for Windows - [F1027.WK3]		
	File Edit Worksheet Range Graph Data Style Tools Window Help				
					READY
A:B8		+<<books.wk3>>$JAN_PROFIT_BUD			
	A	B	C	D	
1	Folktale Workshop		2000 Budget (Executive Summary)		
2					
3	TOTALS	Jan-2000			
4	(in Millions)	BUDGETED	ACTUAL	%VARIANCE	
5					
6	Gross Profit				
7	Apparel Division	4.50	3.50	-22.22%	
8	Books/Comics Division	2.40	2.30	-4.17%	
9	Movie/Video Division	4.50	3.50	-22.22%	

Use the same technique to correct the formulas in row 9.

Highlight: B9..D9

Choose: Edit   Find

Type: apparel   *in the Search for: text box*

Select: Replace with:

Type: movie   *in the text box*

Select: Replace All

Try correcting the formulas in row 10 on your own, following the example of the keystrokes you used to change row 9. (Instead of changing apparel to movie, change apparel to toys.) When you are finished, the screen should look like Figure 10-28.

Figure 10-28

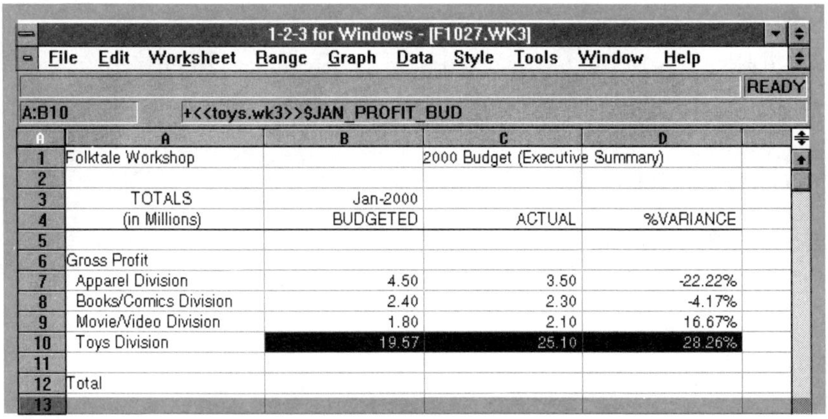

	A	B	C	D	
			1-2-3 for Windows - [F1027.WK3]		
	File Edit Worksheet Range Graph Data Style Tools Window Help				
					READY
A:B10		+<<toys.wk3>>$JAN_PROFIT_BUD			
	A	B	C	D	
1	Folktale Workshop		2000 Budget (Executive Summary)		
2					
3	TOTALS	Jan-2000			
4	(in Millions)	BUDGETED	ACTUAL	%VARIANCE	
5					
6	Gross Profit				
7	Apparel Division	4.50	3.50	-22.22%	
8	Books/Comics Division	2.40	2.30	-4.17%	
9	Movie/Video Division	1.80	2.10	16.67%	
10	Toys Division	19.57	25.10	28.26%	
11					
12	Total				
13					

9. Enter formulas in row 12.

The formulas in row 12 complete the worksheet figures.

Figure 10-29: The Total Formulas for the Executive Summary Worksheet

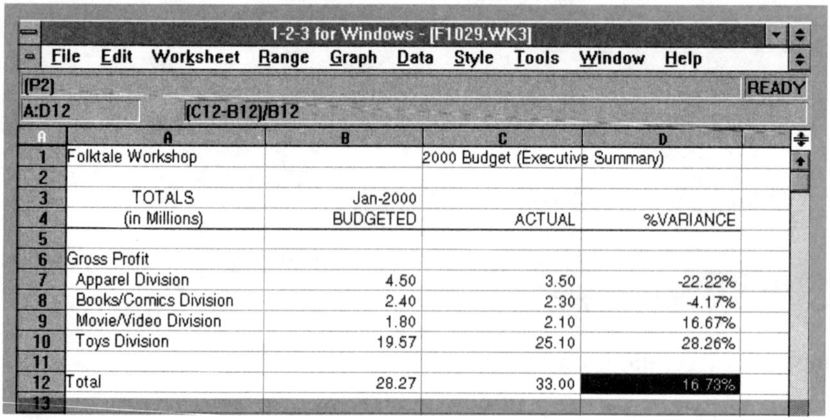

Cells B12 and C12 contain formulas that sum the values in columns B and C, respectively. These formulas add up the gross profit figures for each division, to arrive at a total for the whole company. Cell D12 calculates the variance between Folktale Workshop's expected gross profit and the company's actual profit as a percentage of the expected value. Enter the formula in cell B12 and copy it to cell C12:

Move to:	cell B12
Type:	⏎
Choose:	Edit Quick Copy
Select:	To:
Specify:	C12 *in the text box*
Select:	OK

1-2-3 displays Folktale Workshop's budgeted and actual gross profit for January 2000. Now, enter the formula for %VARIANCE:

Move to:	cell D12
Type:	(c12-b12)/b12 ⏎

1-2-3 shows that Folktale Workshop's gross profit was 16.73% higher than expected.

10. Format cells B12 and C12 as Currency.

Formatting the cells containing the budgeted and actual totals for gross profit completes the Executive Summary worksheet. Use the "Currency" icon to format the range, if you have a mouse. Otherwise, do the following.

Highlight:	B12..C12
Choose:	Range Format
Select:	Currency OK

11. Underline rows 10 and 12.

Highlight:	A10..D10
Choose:	Style Border
Select:	Bottom: *and check the check-box*
	OK
Highlight:	A12..D12
Choose:	Style Border
Select:	Bottom: *and check the check-box*
Click on:	*the Bottom: drop-down menu*
Select:	*the double underline*
	OK *to complete the operation*

Figure 10-30: The Completed Executive Summary Worksheet

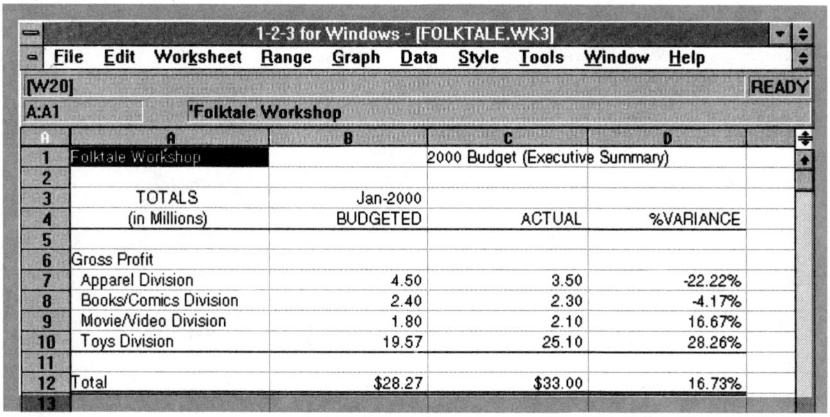

12. Save FOLKTALE.WK3.

Congratulations! You have completed the Executive Summary application. Now, let's see how it works.

Testing the Executive Summary

In this section, you will see how a changed value in one of the division worksheet files is reflected in the Executive Summary. In addition to getting more practice working with multiple files, you will learn how to copy formula values without copying the formulas themselves, and how to annotate formula cells.

Changing the Referenced Cell Values in File Links   When you change a value in a worksheet file, 1-2-3 updates any links to the changed cell. If the file that contains the link to the changed cell is also an active file, 1-2-3 updates the link immediately. Otherwise, 1-2-3 updates the link when you read the file that refers to the changed cell into memory and select File Administration Update Links. Perform the following exercise to see how this works:

1. Save values in B7..D12 of FOLKTALE.WK3 for future reference.

To make it easier to compare old values with new values in FOLKTALE.WK3, make a temporary copy of the current values. Use the "Convert to values" option of Edit Quick Copy to make this copy. The "Convert to values" option works similarly to the normal Edit Quick Copy command, except that it copies only the values in a range, not the formulas that created them. This option is often used to take a snapshot of a set of values, for example, to preserve a set of what-if values or the data for a what-if graph.

Highlight:	A7..D12
Choose:	Edit Quick Copy
Select:	Convert to values *and check the check-box*
Specify:	cell A14 *in the To: text box*
Select:	OK

Figure 10-31:   Using the "Convert to values" Option of Edit Quick Copy to Preserve a Set of Values

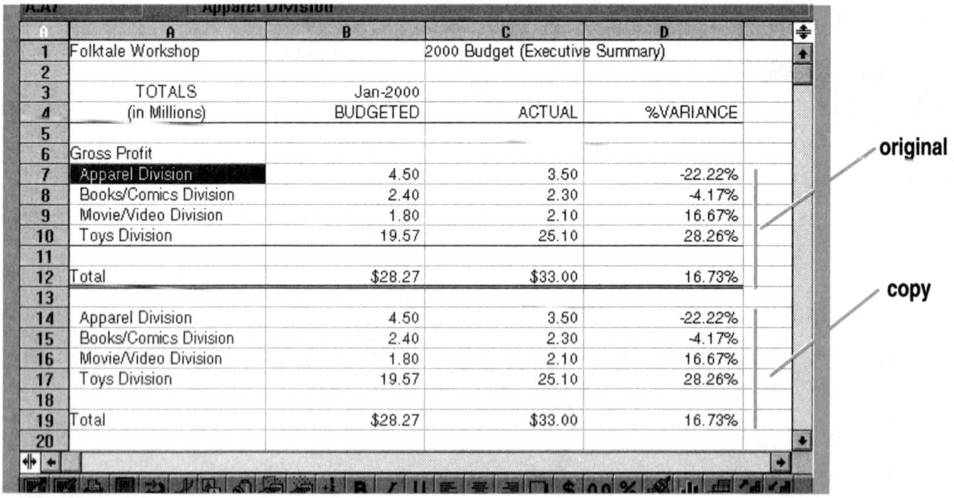

1-2-3 copies the values in A7..D12 to A14..D19. These values will not change when values change in APPAREL.WK3, BOOKS.WK3, MOVIE.WK3, or TOYS.WK3, but the values in rows 7 through 12 will change, as you'll soon see.

2. Save all active files and then close them.

To make the effects on a destination file of changing a value in a source file more obvious, save all modified files and then erase them from memory. (Then, you'll modify one source file and retrieve the destination file.)

First, save all modified active files:

Choose:	File Save As
Select:	Save All

Next, remove all active files from memory. Instead of individually closing each file, use a shortcut from the 1-2-3 Classic menu. Remember, you call up the menu by pressing the slash key (/). To choose commands, either use the arrow keys to highlight the command you want and then press Enter, or press the first letter of the command name.

Press:	⎡/⎤ (slash)
Choose:	Worksheet Erase Yes

1-2-3 simultaneously closes all active files and then leaves a blank, untitled Worksheet window on the screen.

Figure 10-32: **Choosing the Worksheet Erase Yes Command from the 1-2-3 Classic Menu (to Close all Active Files)**

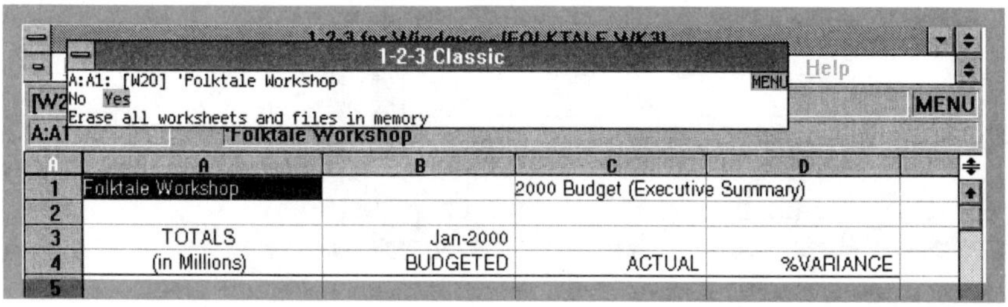

3. Open one division file and modify a value.

As it turns out, the Movie/Video Division manager neglected to include movie receipts from Buffalo, New York, in the January figures. Retrieve MOVIE.WK3 and add one million dollars to the figure to correct the actual value for gross income.

You can add a *comment* to any value cell by placing a semicolon after the value or formula and typing in the comment. This is known as *annotating* the formula. When you update cell C6 with the corrected value, add a comment to the formula, so that the worksheet contains a record of why the value has been modified.

Choose:	File Open
Select:	movie.wk3 *from the Files: list box*
	OK
Move to:	cell C6
Press:	F2 (EDIT)
Type:	+1; Buffalo receipts added
Press:	↵

Figure 10-33: Modifying and Annotating a Cell in MOVIE.WK3

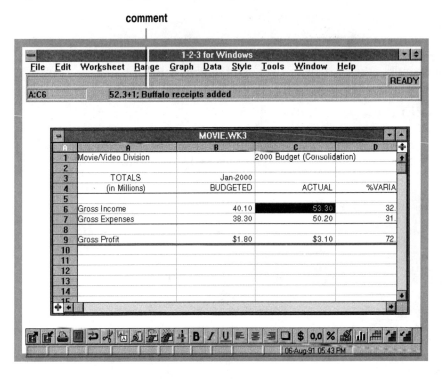

4. Save the modified MOVIE.WK3.

5. Retrieve FOLKTALE.WK3, and then compare new values with saved values.

Choose:	File Open
Select:	folktale.wk3 *from the Files: list box*
	OK

Maximize the Worksheet window entitled FOLKTALE.WK3.

Figure 10-34:   **The upper part of the Executive Summary worksheet reflects the modified values in MOVIE.WK3, while the lower part preserves the old values.**

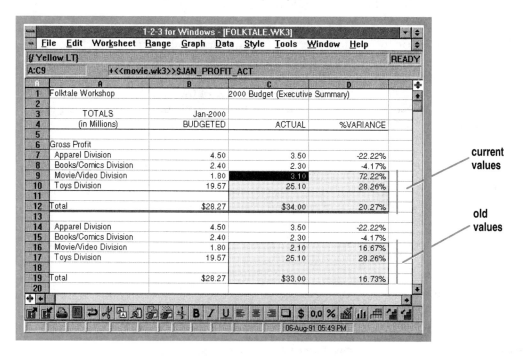

Compare the values in cells C9 and D9 with the previously-saved values for these cells in C16 and D16. Notice that 1-2-3 has recalculated the formulas in cells C9 and D9 to account for the changes you made to MOVIE.WK3. When you read FOLKTALE.WK3 back into memory, 1-2-3 automatically refreshed the file links; it accessed the values from the copy of MOVIE.WK3 in memory and then it displayed them in cells C9 and D9. Notice that any values that depend on the modified values also change automatically.

■ *NOTE:*   If any values in a destination file (such as FOLKTALE.WK3, in this example) are linked to source files that are not in memory, you must choose File Administration Update Links to update those values.

6. (Optional) Experiment with changing values in other division files.

   If you wish, experiment with changing some of the values in cells B6..C7 in the other division files, to see how the changes affect the values in FOLKTALE.WK3. To do this, repeat steps 1 through 5 above. When you are finished, go on to step 7.

7. Erase the duplicate values in FOLKTALE.WK3.

   Clean up the duplicate values in rows 14 through 19:

   Highlight: A14..D19

Choose: Edit   Clear   *or press Delete*

8. Save FOLKTALE.WK3, and then File Close MOVIE.WK3.

Congratulations! You have mastered the basics of file linking and working with multiple files. For additional information on file linking, see "File Linking Tips" at the end of this chapter.

Graphing in the Executive Summary Worksheet File

As a final multiple-file exercise, you are going to graph some of the ranges in FOLKTALE.WK3 that refer to data in the division worksheets. Once you have created the graph, any changes you make to the referenced data in any of the division worksheets will automatically be reflected in the graph.

1. Create a Graph window in the 1-2-3 window.

Before you begin, move the cell pointer to a blank cell, then create a blank Graph window and tile the windows. 1-2-3 will automatically name this graph GRAPH1; accept the name.

Move to: cell A21

Choose: Graph   New

Select: OK

Choose: Window   Tile

Figure 10-35:   Tiled Worksheet and Graph Windows

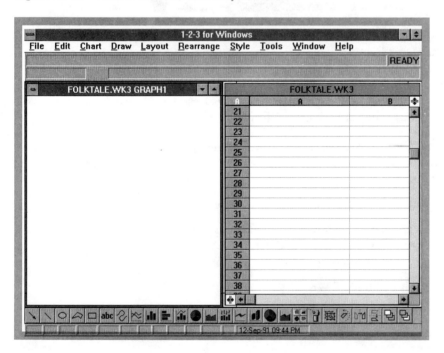

2. Select the graph type.

Bob Gordon wants to be able to compare the budgeted and actual gross profit values side by side. He is interested in the individual totals for each division and also in the grand total for Folktale Workshop.

   A natural choice for this kind of display is a stacked-bar graph. Figure 10-36 shows what the graph will look like when you are finished. Notice that each part of a bar represents the gross profit from one division; the height of the entire bar reveals the gross profit figures for the whole company.

Figure 10-36:   The Completed Budgeted and Actual Gross Profit Graph

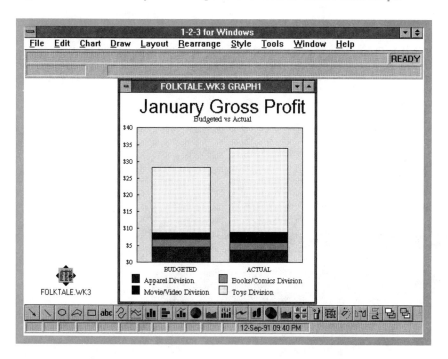

Choose:	Chart Type
Select:	Bar
Click on:	*the stacked-bar icon in the Chart Type dialog box*
Select:	OK

3. Designate the graph ranges.

This bar graph will display only two bars: one for all of the budgeted values and the other for all of the actual values.

The data ranges are the columns of budgeted and actual data. Each row in this range contains one budgeted value and one actual value. For example, the A range is the range B7..C7; it graphs the budgeted and actual values for the Apparel Division.

Because the data is arranged in nearly the form 1-2-3 uses for graphing a table with x-axis and data ranges arranged as rows, the easiest way to designate the data ranges is to designate them as a group. This will temporarily designate an incorrect X range, but you'll fix that right away.

Choose:	`Chart  Ranges`
Select:	`Group range  Row-wise`
Specify:	B6..C10 *in the Range: text box*
Select:	`OK`

1-2-3 fills in the ranges for the X and A through D text boxes. The A through D ranges are okay, but the labels along the x-axis should be **BUDGETED** and **ACTUAL**, taken from the last row of the worksheet title area. Correct the X range and then close the dialog box.

Select:	`Xdata range:`
Specify:	B4..C4 *in the text box*
Select:	`OK`

Notice that 1-2-3 automatically defines the scale along the y-axis.

Figure 10-37: 1-2-3 draws the graph using the X and A through D ranges.

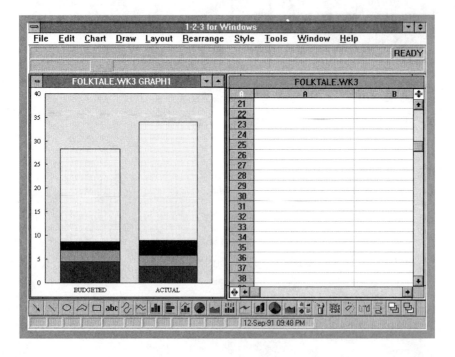

4. Designate the legend range.

You can designate all the legends at once by using a range of labels. Establish legends for the data ranges, to identify which part of each bar represents which division's gross profit figures.

Click on:	*the FOLKTALE.WK3 window*
Highlight:	`A7..A10`
Click on:	*the GRAPH1 window*
Choose:	`Chart  Legend`
Select:	`Group range   OK`

1-2-3 draws the legends in the Graph window.

5. Specify First and Second titles.

Now the graph is legible. To make it more informative, give it a two-line title.

Choose:	`Chart  Headings`
Type:	`January Gross Profit` *in the Title: text box*
Select:	`Subtitle:`
Type:	`Budgeted vs Actual` *in the Subtitle: text box*
Select:	`OK`

6. Modify the y-axis numeric format.

Change the y-axis so that the numbers look like currency.

Choose:	`Chart  Axis`
Select:	`Y  Format... Currency  Decimal places:`
Type:	`0`
Select:	`OK` *two times*

This completes the graph. (See Figure 10-38 on the next page.)

7. Save FOLKTALE.WK3.

You are through with Bob's Executive Summary. If you wish, experiment with changing the budgeted and actual gross profit figures in the division worksheets, and then retrieve FOLKTALE.WK3 to see how these changes affect the graph.

A Note on Graphing Data in Other Files   There are two ways to graph data in other files: (1) You can graph ranges in the current file that refer to ranges in other files, or (2) you can graph ranges in the other files directly.

You used the first of these two methods in the previous exercise, when you graphed the A, B, C, and D ranges of the stacked-bar graph. Each of these ranges is in the same file as the graph (the destination file), but each cell in the range refers to data in another active file (the source files). Figure 10-39 (shown on the next page), illustrates this type of graph.

Figure 10-38: Formatting the Y-axis as Currency Completes the Graph

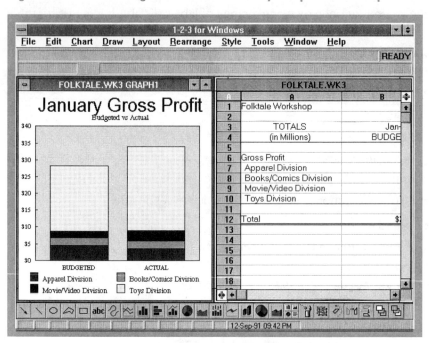

Figure 10-39: Graphing Ranges in the Destination File

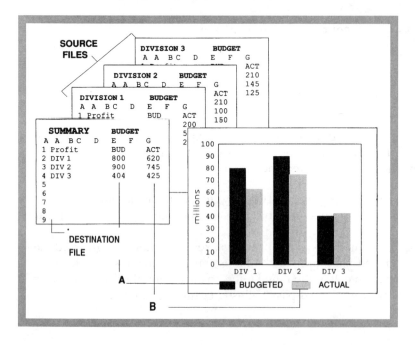

Creating a table in the destination file is usually the easiest way to construct a graph that uses multiple files. However, it is not the only method you can use.

You can also refer to ranges in source files in the graph settings themselves, rather than graphing references to those values in the destination file. For example, you could have created Bob's stacked-bar graph by graphing the row containing the gross profit values in APPAREL.WK3 as the A data range, the row containing the gross profit values in BOOKS.WK3 as the B data range, and so on.

This latter method is not usually as convenient as making a table in the file that contains the graph settings, but it is a technique worth remembering, in case you need it. It is particularly useful when you are comparing similar data in different files. For instance, suppose you have performance data for a number of similar products, and the data for each product is in a separate worksheet file. Each worksheet is structured exactly the same way. A graph to compare all the products might specify an X range from one file and one data range from each file to be included in the comparison graph. Figure 10-40 illustrates this method of creating a multiple-file graph.

Figure 10-40:   Graphing Ranges in the Source Files

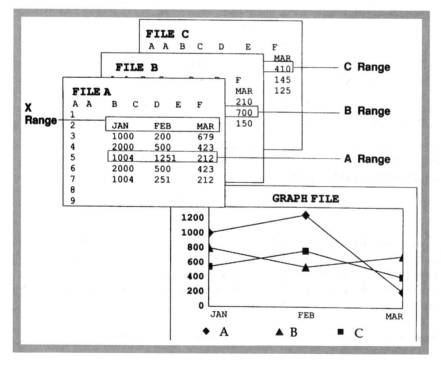

More About Files

In this chapter, you've already learned the basics of navigating directories and multiple files, and of creating applications that link worksheets to other worksheets. There is, however, considerably more to 1-2-3's file management. The next few sections briefly explain how to use 1-2-3 to:

- Use the Clipboard to copy information between 1-2-3 worksheet files and files created by other Windows applications
- Link data in 1-2-3 worksheet files to files created by other Windows applications
- Import ASCII data into a 1-2-3 worksheet file
- Export data to an ASCII file
- Extract part of a worksheet to a separate file
- Combine one worksheet file with another
- Save a worksheet file with a password
- Erase worksheet files from disk from within 1-2-3

Using the Clipboard to Exchange Data with Other Programs

Throughout this book, you've used the Windows Clipboard as a temporary place to store information when you are copying a range of data or an embedded graph to another range. The Clipboard, however, is actually a much more versatile tool. Among its many uses, it provides an easy way to exchange data between 1-2-3 and other Windows programs.

For example, suppose you had a range of values in a 1-2-3 worksheet and you wanted to transfer those values to a memo you were writing in Windows Write. Typing the information in by hand would be tedious. Transferring the data from the worksheet file to the Write file with the Clipboard, on the other hand, is a matter of a few simple steps. To copy data from 1-2-3 to another Windows program (such as Write):

1. In 1-2-3, highlight the range you want to copy from the worksheet to the other program. Choose Edit Copy (or press Control+Insert, or click on the "Copy to Clipboard" icon).

2. If the other program is running, press Control+Escape, highlight the program name in the Windows Task List, and select "Switch to." If the other program is not running, switch to the Program Manager and then start the other program.

3. If the file in the other program into which you want to paste the worksheet data is not yet open, open it.

4. In the other program's file, move the cursor to the location where you want the 1-2-3 worksheet information to start. Press Shift+Insert (or the key combination that pastes information from the Clipboard to the program) or, from the program's menu bar, choose Edit Paste (or the command that the program uses to paste information from the Clipboard). The Clipboard copies the data into the program.

Reversing the process is just as easy. To copy data from another Windows program (such as Write) to 1-2-3:

1. In the other program, highlight the data you want to copy to the worksheet. Choose Edit Copy (or the equivalent command for copying data to the Clipboard), or press Control+Insert (or the equivalent shortcut key for copying data to the Clipboard).

2. If 1-2-3/W is running, press Control+Escape, highlight the 1-2-3 for Windows program name in the Windows Task List, and select "Switch to." If 1-2-3/W is not running, switch to the Program Manager and then start 1-2-3/W.

3. If the worksheet file into which you want to paste the Clipboard data is not yet open, open it.

4. In the worksheet file, move the cell pointer to the upper left corner of the range where you want the Clipboard data to be inserted. (Make sure there is no important data in the range, because 1-2-3 will overwrite whatever is there with the information in the Clipboard.)

5. Press Shift+Insert or, from the 1-2-3 menu bar, choose Edit Paste. The Clipboard copies the data into 1-2-3. 1-2-3 interprets labels as labels and values as values, where possible. (Values in the Clipboard that are delimited by Tab characters are interpreted as numbers by 1-2-3 and are placed in separate columns.)

■ *NOTE:*   You can also use the Clipboard to transfer graphs and graphic objects between 1-2-3 and other programs, if the other program is capable of displaying graphs. For example, you can copy a graph from 1-2-3 to the Clipboard and then paste it into Paintbrush, or create a drawing in Paintbrush, copy it to the Clipboard, and paste it into 1-2-3.

Linking Worksheet Files to Other Programs

When you use the Clipboard to copy information between 1-2-3 and other programs, the information is no longer directly associated with the program that created it. For example, if you copy a range of worksheet data to Windows Write, and then you change the worksheet data, the copy of the data in Windows Write does not change. With many Windows programs, however, you can dynamically link worksheet data to other program files. For example, you could link a range of worksheet data to one or more Microsoft Word for Windows or Lotus Ami Pro documents. When you change the spreadsheet data, the word processing documents would automatically reflect the changes.

The mechanism through which Windows programs can be dynamically linked to one another is called Dynamic Data Exchange (DDE), and the actual link is called a *DDE link*.

A full discussion of creating and maintaining DDE links is beyond the scope of this book. (See the 1-2-3 online Help and the 1-2-3 for Windows *User's Guide* for details.) However, creating a simple DDE link between 1-2-3 and another program that supports DDE is similar to pasting information between 1-2-3 and other programs. The main difference is that both the source and destination files must be active in order to create the link, and both must also be active in order for Windows to update the link.

To link 1-2-3 data to another Windows program that supports DDE (such as Microsoft Word for Windows or Lotus Ami Pro):

1. Start 1-2-3 and open the worksheet file that contains the data you want to display in the other program. Highlight the worksheet range you want to display. Then, copy the range to the Clipboard (either choose Edit Copy, press Control+Insert, or click on the "Copy to Clipboard" icon).

2. While 1-2-3 is still running, switch to the Program Manager and then start the other program (if it is not already running). Open the file into which you want to place the DDE link. Move the

cursor to the upper left corner of the location where you want to display the 1-2-3 worksheet data.

3. In the other program, choose the command that creates a DDE link (for example, in Word for Windows you would choose Edit Paste Link). The program uses information stored in the Clipboard to create the link and then displays the worksheet information at the current cursor location. As long as both the 1-2-3 file and the destination file are active, changes to the 1-2-3 range are reflected in the destination file.

Figure 10-41: **A Word for Windows document and a 1-2-3 for Windows worksheet are linked with DDE. Numeric information in the 1-2-3 Worksheet is reflected in the Word for Windows document.**

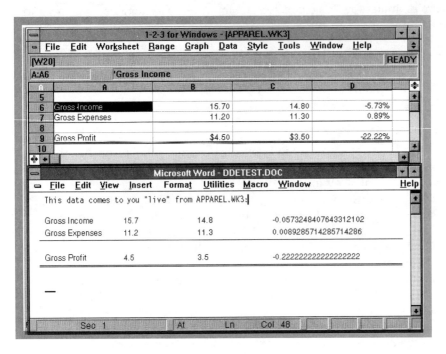

■ *NOTE:* If the DDE link is not created successfully, repeat the procedure.

Reversing the process is just as easy. To create a DDE link from another Windows program that supports DDE to a 1-2-3 worksheet file:

1. Start the other program and then open the file that contains data you want to link to a 1-2-3 worksheet file. Highlight the information in the other program that you want to display in 1-2-3 and then choose the command that copies information to the Clipboard (for example, choose Edit Copy or press Control+Insert).

2. Switch to the Program Manager, start 1-2-3 (if it is not already running), and then open the worksheet file in which you want to display information from the other program. Move the

cell pointer to the upper left corner of the range where you want the information from the other program to appear.

3. In 1-2-3, highlight a range that is large enough to receive the data you want to display, then choose Edit Paste Link. 1-2-3 uses information stored in the Clipboard to create the link, and then it displays the data from the other program. As you change data in the other program, 1-2-3 reflects the change. (You can see this happen if you display the 1-2-3 window and the other application's window simultaneously, as in Figure 10-41 and Figure 10-42.)

Figure 10-42: A Word for Windows document and a 1-2-3 for Windows worksheet are linked with DDE. Numeric information from 1-2-3 is reflected in the Word for Windows document, and text information from the Word for Windows document is reflected in the 1-2-3 worksheet.

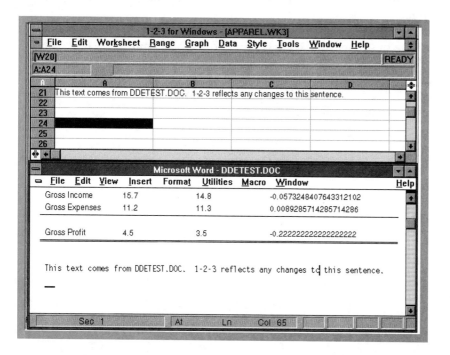

■ *NOTE:* This section described how to create basic links between 1-2-3 worksheet files and the files of other applications. To modify those links, or to create links with characteristics other than the default characteristics, choose Edit Link Options. For more information on DDE links, see the entries in the 1-2-3 online Help entitled "Edit Link Options" and "Linking Files."

Creating and Importing Text Files

This section describes how to use ASCII files as a way to transfer information between 1-2-3 and other software programs.

From time to time, you may need to incorporate worksheet data into a non-Windows program such as a DOS-based word processor, or an application running on another type of computer. From time to time, you may also need to include in a 1-2-3/W worksheet file data that comes from some other source; for instance, you might want to incorporate a table of numbers generated by a FORTRAN program, or a memo created by a word processor, into a worksheet file.

Some programs can read or write 1-2-3 worksheet files directly, and others provide translation utilities between their format and the 1-2-3 worksheet format. Bringing data from 1-2-3 into these programs is no problem. Similarly, 1-2-3 provides a translation utility that allows you to convert some non-1-2-3 files into 1-2-3 files and vice versa. (Converting a dBASE file to a 1-2-3 file was described in Chapter 6.) Also, 1-2-3 can read data in many database formats directly. Here, too, exchanging data between 1-2-3 and another program is no problem.

Many software programs, however, cannot directly use 1-2-3 data, nor is their output directly usable by 1-2-3. Fortunately, there exists one type of file that most programs can both read and write: an *ASCII file.*

ASCII stands for American Standard Code for Information Interchange. In an ASCII file, each character uses one byte of storage, and each is assigned a specific numeric value. For example, the uppercase letter "A" in an ASCII file is represented as the number 65, the lowercase letter "d" is 100, and so on. Table 10-2 shows how printable characters are represented in an ASCII file. (Incidentally, Table 10-2 was itself created with formulas, in 1-2-3, and was then imported into a word processor as an ASCII file.)

Table 10-2: Printable ASCII Characters

32	space	40	(	64	@	80	P	96	'	112	p
33	!	41	)	65	A	81	Q	97	a	113	q
34	"	42	*	66	B	82	R	98	b	114	r
35	#	43	+	67	C	83	S	99	c	115	s
36	$	44	,	68	D	84	T	100	d	116	t
37	%	45	-	69	E	85	U	101	e	117	u
38	&	46	.	70	F	86	V	102	f	118	v
39	'	47	/	71	G	87	W	103	g	119	w
40	(	48	0	72	H	88	X	104	h	120	x
41	)	49	1	73	I	89	Y	105	i	121	y
42	*	50	2	74	J	90	Z	106	j	122	z
43	+	51	3	75	K	91	[	107	k	123	{
44	,	52	<	76	L	92	\	108	l	124		
45	-	53	=	77	M	93	]	109	m	125	}
46	.	54	>	78	N	94	^	110	n	126	~
47	/	55	?	79	O	95	_	111	o		

The following sections show you how to use 1-2-3 to create an ASCII text file (from now on called, simply, a *text file*) from a worksheet, and how to read a text file into a worksheet.

Creating a Text File from a Worksheet   When you need to create an ASCII representation of worksheet data so you can incorporate the data into another program, use the File Extract To Text command.

To try out this command, retrieve FOLKTALE.WK3, if it is not already active. You'll export part of the Executive Summary worksheet to a text file.

Choose: File Open
Select: folktale OK

1. Make sure columns are wide enough for all the data to be extracted to the text file.

1-2-3 extracts only as many characters as would fit in the column, were you to use a mono spaced font. For instance, the width of column A of FOLKTALE.WK3 is 20, so 1-2-3 would extract up to 20 characters from this column. FOLKTALE.WK3 uses a proportional font, and there are more than 20 characters in column A's widest entry. To be sure you will extract all the characters in the widest entries, you must widen column A before you create the text file.

Using either the mouse or the Worksheet Column Width command, widen column A to 26 characters.

2. Highlight the range to extract.

You will extract the entire spreadsheet area of this small worksheet.

Highlight: A1..D12

3. Extract the data to EXECSUM.PRN.

Choose: File Extract To

1-2-3 prompts you for a name for the file. You can create a new file by entering a new file name, or you can overwrite an existing file with a new file by specifying the name of an existing file. If you select an existing file, 1-2-3 prompts to either Replace or Canel. If you choose Replace, 1-2-3 will replace the existing file with the new text file; if you choose Cancel, 1-2-3 will not create a new text file.) In this case, you will create a new file, EXECSUM.PRN. Type only the file name; 1-2-3 automatically gives the file a .PRN extension.

Type: execsum   *in the File name: text box*
Select: Text   *in the Save As option area*

             OK

The disk drive light flashes briefly as 1-2-3 creates the file. EXECSUM.PRN contains all the labels and values in the highlighted range of the file FOLKTALE.WK3. However, the values are now ASCII characters, rather than formulas that evaluate to values. You can import this file into most word processors, print it on most printers, or import it back into 1-2-3, as you'll do in the next section.

Figure 10-43:   The Executive Summary Text File EXECSUM.PRN (Displayed in Windows Write)

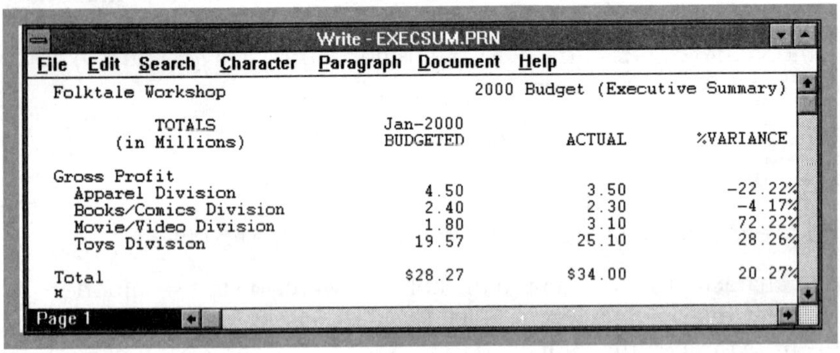

```
┌─────────────────────────────────────────────────────────────────────┐
│ ▭                        Write - EXECSUM.PRN                   ▼ ▲  │
│ File  Edit  Search   Character  Paragraph  Document  Help            │
│   Folktale Workshop                    2000 Budget (Executive Summary) ▲│
│                                                                      │
│              TOTALS              Jan-2000                            │
│            (in Millions)         BUDGETED        ACTUAL      %VARIANCE │
│                                                                      │
│   Gross Profit                                                       │
│      Apparel Division               4.50          3.50      -22.22%  │
│      Books/Comics Division          2.40          2.30       -4.17%  │
│      Movie/Video Division           1.80          3.10       72.22%  │
│      Toys Division                 19.57         25.10       28.26%  │
│                                                                      │
│   Total                           $28.27        $34.00       20.27%  │
│   ▯                                                              ▼  │
│ Page 1          ◄                                              ►    │
└─────────────────────────────────────────────────────────────────────┘
```

Importing a Text File into a Worksheet   The File Import From command let you incorporate other files into 1-2-3 worksheet files. File Import From Text copies a text file such as the one you just created—or created by any program that allows you to print to a text–only printer— into the current worksheet at the location of the cell pointer. Each line of the imported file is converted to a long label. The result is a column of long labels.

To see how this works, try importing the text file you created in the previous section back into 1-2-3. You will import the file into a new worksheet file that you'll call EXECSUM.WK3.

1. Create a new, blank worksheet and save it as EXECSUM.WK3:

Choose: File Save As

Type: execsum   ↵

1-2-3 creates a new file called EXECSUM.WK3.

2. Import EXECSUM.PRN into 1-2-3.

You can import two different types of ASCII files into 1-2-3. One is a simple text file. The other is a file containing numbers and character strings enclosed in quotes. (This type of file, which you import by choosing File Import From Numbers, is described in "A Note on Importing Numbers and Quoted Text into a Worksheet" at the end of this chapter.) EXECSUM.PRN is a text file, so import it as such. With the cell pointer in cell A1 of the new file EXECSUM.WK3:

Choose: File   Import From   Text

1-2-3 prompts you for the name of a file to import and lists any files in the current directory with the .PRN extension. Import EXECSUM.PRN.

Select: execsum.prn   *in the Files: list box*

OK

Figure 10-44: The Imported Text File EXECSUM.PRN

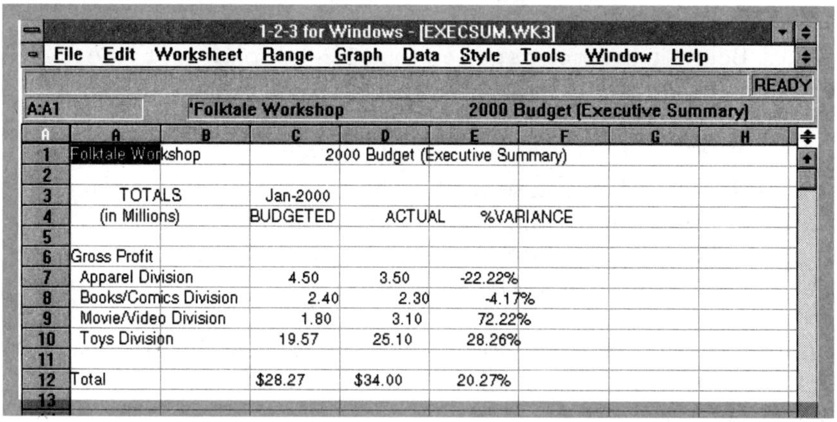

1-2-3 imports the file into the current worksheet as a series of long labels. Notice, for example, that the control panel displays all of row 1, rather than just the words Folktale Workshop. 1-2-3 displays the file in the current font. Since this font is a proportional font (unless you've changed it to one of the monospaced fonts), the columns do not line up properly.

■ *NOTE:*   To import text files with extensions other than .PRN, provide both the file name and the extension when you choose File Import From Text.

Converting Long Labels into Separate Fields   Sometimes, it is useful to import text into a worksheet and leave it as a column of long labels. For example, had the text file you imported been a memo created by a word processor, the format of long labels would be fine. However, if you want to manipulate imported data or incorporate it into a database table, you must convert the data from rows of long labels into rows and columns of text and values. To do so, you use the Data Parse commands.

To *parse* something means to break it down into its component parts. Normally, you use Data Parse to convert strings of text and numbers from a text file into separate fields of a database table. For example, you might have a database program running on a mainframe or minicomputer that creates an ASCII file as a report, and you want to convert that ASCII file into a 1-2-3 database file.

Converting long labels into separate fields involves the following steps:

1. Highlight the column of data to be parsed.

Usually, this is the block of long labels you imported into the worksheet.

2. Choose Data Parse.

1-2-3 displays the Data Parse dialog box. The "Format line" text box is blank, initially.

3. Choose the "Create" option of the Data Parse command.

When you choose "Create," 1-2-3 creates a *format line* that tells how it interprets the labels in the first row of the highlighted range. The format line contains symbols that 1-2-3 will use when it parses the data to distinguish values from labels, and to determine how wide to make columns for labels and values. Below it, in a `monospaced` font, 1-2-3 displays up to the first five labels you are going to parse (see Figure 10-45a).

4. Correct the format line, if necessary.

1-2-3 makes an educated guess for you when you select the "Create" option, based on the contents of the first row of data in the input column. Edit the format line to tell 1-2-3 how *you* want the data to be interpreted. The format line contains asterisks (*) where 1-2-3 finds spaces. 1-2-3 places an L where it finds a character it thinks begins a label, and a V where it finds the beginning of a value. It uses right angle brackets (>) to indicate additional characters in a field (see Figure 10-45b). The other characters that can show up in a format line are D, for a date value; T, for a time value; and S, for a data block that Data Parse should ignore.

5. Specify an area for the parsed data to be copied to.

In the "Output range:" text box, specify the first cell of the range to copy the parsed data to. (You can also specify the entire range, if you prefer.)

6. Parse the data.

Select OK to complete the operation. 1-2-3 parses the data in the input column and copies it to the output range. The input data is unaffected, unless you use the same range for the input column and the output range.

On your own, as a demonstration of Data Parse, try parsing the data in A7..A10 of EXECSUM.WK3. Place the results just below the data itself, so it is easy to compare the input with the output. Leave at least one blank row for a new row of database table field names.

A couple of hints: To correctly parse the data, you'll have to modify the format line so that the space it allocates to the first column of the output range is wide enough to accommodate the longest label in the input column. The initial format line will look like the one in Figure 10-45a (shown on the next page) and the corrected format line like Figure 10-45b. When you are finished parsing the data, your screen will look like Figure 10-46a. Were this a real database table, you would probably format the numeric cells into which the parsed data is copied. Figure 10-46b shows the parsed, formatted output, complete with field names for the database table.

When you have finished, save the file as EXECSUM.WK3, replacing the existing version of EXECSUM.WK3.

■ *NOTE:*   When you parse a database that has been imported as a text file, you usually have to create two format lines: One for the field names and another for the data. 1-2-3 will parse the field names and the data rows at the same time.

A Note on Importing Data Into a Worksheet   The "Numbers" option of the File Import From command lets you import a delimited ASCII file into a worksheet. A *delimited ASCII file* is one in which each item is separated by a delimiter (commas, spaces, colons and semicolons are the usual delimiters), and each text item is enclosed in quotation marks. Several database programs can create output in this format.

Figure 10-45a: The Initial Format Line for Parsing the EXECSUM.WK3 Data

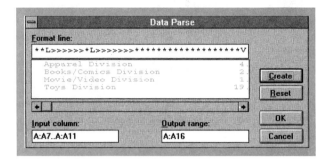

Figure 10-45b: The Corrected Format Line

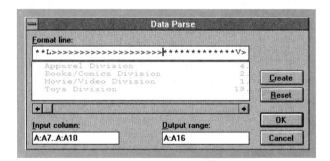

Figure 10-46a: The Parsed Data, Unformatted

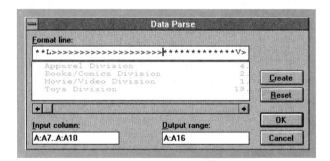

Figure 10-46b: The Parsed Data, Formatted

1-2-3 for Windows - [EXECSUM.WK3]

File Edit Worksheet Range Graph Data Style Tools Window Help

[W18]   READY

A:A15   'DIVISION

	A	B	C	D	E	F
15	DIVISION	BUDGETED	ACTUAL	%VARIANCE		
16	Apparel Division	4.50	3.50	-22.22%		
17	Books/Comics Division	2.40	2.30	-4.17%		
18	Movie/Video Division	1.80	3.10	72.22%		
19	Toys Division	19.57	25.10	28.26%		
20						
21						
22						
23						

When you import a delimited ASCII file, 1-2-3 immediately places the labels and values into the proper type of cell, instead of your having to use Data Parse to convert long labels into columns of text and numbers. 1-2-3 creates a value cell for each number, and a left-aligned label for each quoted label. Non-numeric characters that are not quoted are ignored. Imported data adopts the format and column width of the current worksheet.

Figure 10-47 shows a sample worksheet. This worksheet is part of a log of expenses. Column A contains a check number if the expense was paid by check, and an abbreviation of the type of transaction if the expense was not paid by check (for example, if it was a bank transfer or a VISA charge). The other columns contain the date of the expense, a description, the type of expense, and the amount.

Figure 10-47:   The Expense Log as a Worksheet File

1-2-3 for Windows - [CHECKLOG.WK3]

File Edit Worksheet Range Graph Data Style Tools Window Help

(G) [W4]   READY

A:A1   'No.

	A	B	C	D	E	F	G
1	No.	Date	Description	Type	Amount		
2	571	02-Jan-92	Baby Bonanza	clothes	15.00		
3	572	02-Jan-92	Eastern Mountaineer	clothes	83.80		
4	573	02-Jan-92	Stop and Shop	food	82.24		
5	575	02-Jan-92	Sergio Realty	rent	975.00		
6	TRN	02-Jan-92	Transfer to savings	savings	300.00		
7	576	04-Jan-92	Dr. George Fine	medical	45.00		
8	577	04-Jan-92	Boston Gas	utility	72.62		
9	578	04-Jan-92	Mass. Electric	utility	24.61		
10	579	04-Jan-92	Good Guys Hardware	hobby	12.00		
11	580	09-Jan-92	K-mart	clothes	12.00		
12	581	09-Jan-92	Bloomingdales	clothes	79.34		
13	582	09-Jan-92	Johnny's Foodmaster	food	80.54		
14	TRN	09-Jan-92	Transfer to savings	savings	50.00		
15	583	09-Jan-92	Black & Decker	hobby	790.00		
16	584	10-Jan-92	Walden Books	hobby	60.00		
17	585	14-Jan-92	Cash	misc.	200.00		
18	586	16-Jan-92	Filene's	clothes	200.00		
19							
20							

B I U $ 0.0 %

06-Aug-91 08:21 PM

Figure 10-48 shows how the same worksheet would look as a delimited ASCII file. Notice that text strings are surrounded by double quotes and that numbers are not quoted. Importing this file into an appropriately formatted blank worksheet would recreate the worksheet in Figure 10-47.

Figure 10-48:   The Expense Log as a Delimited ASCII File

```
"No.","Date","Description","Type","Amount"
571,"02-Jan-92","Baby Bonanza","clothes",15
572,"02-Jan-92","Eastern Mountaineer","clothes",83.80
573,"02-Jan-92","Stop and Shop","food",82.24
575,"02-Jan-92","Sergio Realty","rent",975
"TRN","02-Jan-92","Transfer to savings","savings",300
576,"04-Jan-92","Dr. George Fine","medical",45
577,"04-Jan-92","Boston Gas","utility",72.62
578,"04-Jan-92","Mass. Electric","utility",24.61
579,"04-Jan-92","Good Guys Hardware","hobby",12
580,"09-Jan-92","Kmart","clothes",12
581,"09-Jan-92","Bloomingdales","clothes",79.34
582,"09-Jan-92","Johnny's Foodmaster","food",80.54
"TRN","09-Jan-92","Transfer to savings","savings",50
583,"09-Jan-92","Black & Decker","hobby",790
584,"10-Jan-92","Walden Books","hobby",60
585,"14-Jan-92","Cash","misc.",200
586,"16-Jan-92","Filene's","clothes",200
```

Extracting and Combining Worksheet Files

Besides using the File Extract To command to save worksheet data as a text file, you can also use the command to save all or part of a worksheet file to a new worksheet file. If, under "Save as" in the File Extract To dialog box, you select the "Values" option, 1-2-3 saves only worksheet settings, data, and the current values of formulas in the new file. If you select the "Formulas" option, 1-2-3 saves the formulas themselves, instead of their current values (cell addresses in formulas adjust to their new locations in the new file). In either case, the new file contains the current format of the saved cells, but it does not contain range names.

To reverse the process and combine all or part of a worksheet file into the current file, use the File Combine From command. The "Copy" option of the File Combine dialog box tells 1-2-3 to replace the contents of cells in the current file with the contents of the corresponding cells in the file whose name you provide to File Combine From. If you select the "Add" option instead, 1-2-3 adds values in the incoming file to values in the corresponding cells in the existing file (this is one way to consolidate several identically formatted worksheets into a single worksheet). Conversely, if you select the "Subtract" option, 1-2-3 subtracts values in the incoming file from the values in the corresponding cells of the current file; "Subtract" won't attempt to subtract numbers from formulas or labels, but subtracting a positive incoming value from a blank existing cell yields a negative value, since a blank cell is equal to zero.

■ *CAUTION:*   File Combine From changes the current file. To make it easier to recover your work in case you make a mistake in the File Combine From command, save the current file before you use this command.

Saving Files with Passwords

If you have files that are accessible to other people and the files contain sensitive data, you can use password protection to prevent unauthorized users from reading that data. When you attempt to retrieve a password-protected file, you are prompted for the password. Password-protected files can be retrieved only if you provide the correct password. Giving an incorrect password results in an error message and cancels the retrieval.

You add a password to the file when you save it. To save a file with a password:

1. Choose File Save As.

2. Enter the name you want to use for the file.

3. Select "Password protect" and check the check-box.

4. 1-2-3 prompts for a password to use for the file. Type in a password of up to 15 characters (write the password down in a safe place), and then press Enter or select OK. 1-2-3 prompts you to type the password again, to be sure you typed it correctly, then saves the file.

To retrieve a file you have protected with a password:

1. Choose File Open and select the file you want to retrieve.

2. 1-2-3 prompts you to enter the password. Type in the password, and press Enter or select OK to retrieve the file.

To remove a password from a file:

1. Open the file

2. Choose File Save As.

3. Select the "Password protect" check-box and clear the check-box.

4. Select OK to save the file. The file will no longer be password-protected.

■ *NOTE:*   Passwords are case-sensitive: "Open_Sesame" is not the same as "open_sesame."

Erasing Disk Files

Although it is easy enough to use the Windows File Manager to erase files you no longer need, if you need to erase only an occasional file, using the /File Erase command on the 1-2-3 Classic menu is quicker.

/File Erase allows you to erase files on disk from within 1-2-3. Selecting /File Erase produces the following menu:

Worksheet   Print   Graph   Other

The Worksheet, Print, Graph, and Other commands each display a list of the files of the specified type stored in the current directory.

Figure 10-49:   **The /File Erase worksheet command displays worksheets in the current directory and lets you select and then delete one.**

To erase a file, choose the appropriate /File Erase command, point to the name of the file you want to erase, and press Enter. 1-2-3 prompts you to confirm the selection. If you select No, 1-2-3 will return to READY mode without erasing the file. If you are sure you really do want to get rid of the file, select Yes.

If you press F3 (Name), 1-2-3 displays a screen of the names of the files in the current directory. If there are more files in the directory than will fit on the screen, you can press Page Down to see another screen. The lists are displayed in the 1-2-3 Classic window.

■ *CAUTION:*   Be very careful when you erase files! Erasing a file is permanent, and it cannot be undone with Edit Undo. Make sure that you really do not need a file before you erase it.

You can use the question mark (?) and asterisk (*) wildcard characters with /File Erase to pre-select the files you want to erase. These wildcard characters work in file specifications much as they do in database criteria. The question mark matches any single character in the corresponding position in the file name or extension. For example, MOVIE.WK? matches any file in the current directory whose name is MOVIE, and whose extension starts with .WK. The asterisk matches any set of characters from the asterisk to the end of either the file name or the file extension. For example, *.WK3 matches all files with the .WK3 extension, *.BAK matches all backup files, *.* matches all files, and M*.* matches all files whose names start with the letter M, regardless of their file extensions.

You can also use path specifications with /File Erase. To erase a file in a directory other than the current directory, precede the file name with the path.

Figure 10-50:   **Using the Asterisk (*) Wildcard to Display .BAK Files**

■ **NOTE:**   As a safety feature, /File Erase lets you erase only one file at a time. If you wish simply to clean up a diskette or directory, you will find it easier to use the Windows File Manager or DOS's ERASE or DEL command to remove files.

File Tips

This section describes file-related tips, techniques, and gotchas that apply to any work you do in 1-2-3.

File Linking Tips

The following tips add to the information on file linking presented earlier in this chapter.

Linking to Files From Other Releases of 1-2-3 and Symphony   From 1-2-3 for Windows, you can create links to 1-2-3 Release 1A, 2.x, and 3.x for DOS, and to all releases of Symphony. Just use the appropriate file reference, including the extension, in the linking formula. For example, to link to the range named TAXES in the file 92EXPENS.WK1, you would use the following cell reference: <<92EXPENS.WK1>>TAXES.

Many programs besides 1-2-3 save files in the 1-2-3 worksheet format, but not all of them do so perfectly. If you have trouble creating a link to a file created with another program, it may be because the file does not have the correct format. To remedy the problem, retrieve and save that file as a 1-2-3/W file, and then try creating the link again.

Updating File Links on a Network   You can update the linking formulas in the current file any time by selecting File Administration Update Links. This is handy when you are using files on a network and other people have access to the same files; it lets you update your current file's links while you are working in the file, in case someone else changed the value of any of the source cells since you retrieved the current file. If you are sharing files on a network, select File Administration Update Links before saving your linked files.

When 1-2-3 Displays ERR as a Linking Formula's Result.   1-2-3 displays ERR as the result of a linking formula in the following situations:

- When you delete or invalidate a range name referenced in the linking formula
- When you erase or rename the file referenced in the linking formula
- When you omit the path from a file reference (because the file is in the current directory), and then change the current directory (making it impossible for 1-2-3 to locate the file)

To correct the formula, first make sure 1-2-3 can find the file. If the file is where the file reference says it is, verify the range, then update the file links.

Multi-Level File Links   File linking is a great convenience, since it allows you to use data in other files without having to read those files into memory. There is, however, one potential problem with file linking that can lead to incorrect results if you don't watch out.

1-2-3 updates file links to active files when you read in the destination files, and to any file whenever you select File Administration Update Links. 1-2-3 does not, however, attempt to resolve file links that depend on other linked cells. This means that if file A links to file B on disk, and file B links to file C, the links in file A may not be correct if file C has been changed since the last time the links in file B were updated.

To avoid problems with multi-level file linking, either keep your file links to one level, or update files beginning with the lowest level and proceeding to the highest. For example, in the situation just described, to ensure that file A contains accurate information whenever file C is updated, you could: (1) Update file C and save it, (2) retrieve file B, update its links to file C, and then save it, and (3) retrieve file A while file B is still in memory (or retrieve file A and then update its links).

Files Gotchas

Most work with files in 1-2-3 is routine, and there is little to go wrong. When something does go wrong with files, however, the consequences can be serious. Unless you are rigorous about backing up your work onto diskettes, tape cartridges, or some other medium, accidentally erasing a file or running out of disk space can at minimum be an unsettling experience, and can in the worst case mean losing hours or days of valuable work.

This section outlines some of the problems you can encounter when working with disks and files, and describes how to avoid those problems.

File Reservation and Read-only Files   If you are using 1-2-3 on a network, you may occasionally, while reading in a file, be met with an OK/Cancel message box asking you if you want to retrieve the file without a reservation. If you select Cancel, 1-2-3 cancels the operation. If you select OK, 1-2-3 reads in the file and puts a RO (read-only) indicator in the status line. This indicator means that you cannot make changes to the file and save it under the same name; 1-2-3 beeps and displays an error message if you try. This message box is the most obvious manifestation of a feature known as *file reservation.*

File reservation is designed to prevent more than one person or process at a time from modifying the same file. Normally, when you read in a file, you automatically receive what is called a file reservation. This means that you have reserved the right to modify this file. When you stop editing the file, you give up that reservation.

If you encounter the file reservation message box when you are reading a file over a network, it means someone else is editing the file. You can read the file, but you can't make permanent changes to it. If you encounter the file reservation message box and the file is not on a network, it is probably because the file has been made read-only with a DOS command, or you have tried to read in a file that is already active in another 1-2-3 session (for instance, you may be running another version of 1-2-3 as a non-Windows application under Windows). If you are running multiple versions of 1-2-3, exit the new 1-2-3 session and return to the original session in which you edited the file, then continue to work on the file in that session. Change a read-only file to read/write with the DOS ATTRIB command.

File Names to Avoid   In general, DOS file names can contain up to eight characters, and file extensions can be up to three characters long. Although you are safest if you avoid characters in file names that could cause problems in formulas and macros, you can use any characters that are acceptable to DOS. Under DOS (and, therefore, under Windows), file names can contain letters, numbers, and any punctuation characters except the following characters:

| \ , . < > ? : ; " [ ] * + =

The following are characters which, though legal characters in file names, could lead to errors in macros, since they are also used in special ways by 1-2-3:

@ / ~ ! $ % ^ & ( ) #

There are a few file names you cannot use because they are reserved by the operating system and have special meaning to it. Table 10-3 lists names you cannot use:

Table 10-3: File Names You Cannot Use

Name	Meaning
AUX	Serial communications port
CON	System console (the screen)
NUL	Null file
PRN	Default printer port
COM1, COM2, COM3, COM4	Serial communications ports
LPT1, LPT2, LPT3, LPT4	Parallel printer ports

Taking Care of Diskettes   If much of your work is stored on diskettes, be careful how you handle them and where you leave them. Though they are physically quite tough, moisture, oil, magnetism, and heat are their enemies, and each can cause data to be lost.

The coating on a diskette is similar to the coating on an audio or video cassette tapes. It is a magnetic medium, and your files are recorded on this coating using magnetic recording heads inside the computer's disk drives. Because the disk surface is magnetic, it is susceptible to being erased or altered by magnetic forces. Common sources of magnetism that diskettes are likely to encounter include: the telephone (some telephones use an electromagnet when they ring), the computer monitor (an electromagnet controls the movement of the electronic beam that paints the image), paper clips, scissors, stereo speakers, screw drivers, refrigerator magnets, and some equipment used to detect theft in bookstores and libraries.

It is better to be safe than sorry: Keep paper clips, magnets, and telephones away from diskettes; don't leave diskettes on top of computer monitors and television sets, and try not to walk through theft-detection equipment while carrying diskettes that contain significant data. Keep diskettes in closed, nonmetallic containers when you are not using them. Keep 5.25-inch diskettes in their protective sleeves and do not touch the diskette surface; do not open the protective slide of the more rigid 3.5-inch diskettes. Store diskettes at room temperature and keep them dry.

If a diskette is damaged, copy as much of the data as is readable to a hard disk or to another diskette. If the damage is magnetic, rather than physical, the diskette itself can probably be reused if you reformat it. You may also be able to "revive" the diskette with a disk-repair utility such as the Norton Utilities Disk Doctor or PC Tools DiskFix.

The best protection against data loss is to keep a backup copy of important data at a remote location, and to keep that backup up-to-date.

What to Do When You Run Out of Disk Space   If you run out of disk space when you are trying to save a file, DON'T PANIC! Your information is perfectly safe in your computer's memory, as long as the power is on and you remain in 1-2-3. This section describes some of the ways you can preserve your work.

- If you have files you don't mind erasing (such as backup files or old print files), use /File Erase or the Windows File Manager to remove them from the disk, then save your work.
- If, after erasing some files, you still don't have enough room to save your new work, save the work to a diskette. It is always a good idea to keep a few formatted diskettes around for just such an emergency, but if you haven't done so and you have some blank, unformatted diskettes, you are still all right. Switch to the File Manager and then format a new diskette. Once the diskette is formatted, switch back to the 1-2-3 session and save your files to a diskette. Then, clean up your hard disk so you don't have this problem again!

At a Glance

In this chapter, you've learned some new skills for working with files on disk and with multiple files in memory. As a result of reading this chapter and completing the exercises, you now know how to do the following new tasks:

Task	How To Do It:
Retrieving files from directories other than the default directory	Files on disk are organized in directories. To access files in different directories, you can : (1) change the current directory with Tools User Setup and then retrieve the file; (2) choose File Open and specify the full path of the file you want to retrieve; or (3) choose File Open and then navigate through the directory tree when 1-2-3 prompts you for a file. Click on ".." to move up a directory level; highlight a directory name and select OK to move down a level.
Temporarily changing the current directory	Choose Tools User Setup, and either edit the existing directory specification or type a new one.
Navigating among multiple active files	Press Control+F6 to move from one active window to another, Control+End Control+Page Up to move to the next active file, Control+End Control+Page Down to move to the previous active file, Control+End Home to move to the first active file, and Control+End End to move to the last active file. You can also move from active file to active file by clicking anywhere in that file's worksheet window.

Task	How To Do It:
Creating a backup file	To save a new version of a file while maintaining the previous version on disk as a backup, choose File Save As, select OK, and then select "Backup". 1-2-3 renames the original file so that it has a .BAK extension, and saves a copy of the file in memory under the original file name.
Linking worksheet files	Reference cells in files on disk from the current file by typing the file name, enclosed in double angle brackets, in front of the range name or cell address of the cell you want to link to. Precede the file link specification with a plus sign (+). For example, `+<<f1040.wk3>>se_tax` links a cell in the current file to a cell named SE_TAX in the file F1040.WK3. File linking can be especially helpful when consolidating data from several subsidiary worksheets into a summary worksheet. File links can be included in formulas.
Graphing data from multiple files	Create a table in one file that contains file links to the data in other files, and then graph the table. Or, provide a file reference to the data in another file in the data ranges of the Graph Chart Ranges dialog box.
Changing formulas to their current values	Highlight the range you wish to convert to values, choose Edit Quick Copy, and select the "Convert to values" option. Then, specify the range to copy "to" and select OK. To convert a range from formulas to values (when you no longer need the formulas in the worksheet), use the same range as the "from" and "to" range.
Erasing files on disk	Select /File Erase from the 1-2-3 Classic menu to erase any file on disk from within 1-2-3. Use /File Erase Worksheet to erase worksheet files, /File Erase Print to erase .PRN files, /File Erase Graph to erase .PIC files, and /File Erase Other to erase other disk files. /File Erase permanently removes the file from the disk, so use it with care.
Creating links and transferring data between 1-2-3 and other applications	To copy information between 1-2-3 and other Windows applications, use the Windows Clipboard. To transfer 1-2-3 data from a worksheet file to another application, use Edit Copy to place the data on the Clipboard, then switch to or start the other application and move to the place where you want the 1-2-3 data to appear. Choose Edit Paste (or the application's command for copying from the Clipboard) to insert the 1-2-3 information into the other application. To copy information from another application to 1-2-3, reverse the process.

To create "live" links between Windows applications, use Edit Copy and Edit Paste Link in 1-2-3 and the corresponding commands in the other application. (See "Linking Worksheet Files to Other Programs" in this chapter for details.) NOTE: the other application must support DDE (Dynamic Data Exchange). |
| Creating text files from 1-2-3 files | Highlight the range you want to convert to a text file and then choose File Extract To Enter a name for the text file you want to create (1-2-3 supplies the extension .PRN if you don't specify a file extension), and then select the "Text" option and select OK. 1-2-3 creates an ASCII file on disk from data in a worksheet range. |

Task	How To Do It:
Importing the contents of text files into 1-2-3 worksheets	Choose File Import From to bring the contents of an ASCII file into the worksheet as a series of long labels. To divide the long labels into separate cells, highlight the column of long labels and then use Data Parse Create to automatically generate the format line to be used for parsing. Edit the generated format line (if necessary), specify the parsed output's destination range, and then select OK to perform the parse.
Extracting all or part of a worksheet file to another worksheet file	Highlight the range you want to extract, choose File Extract To, and select "Values" to save only labels, numbers, and the results of formulas, or select "Formulas" to save the formulas themselves.
Combining all or part of a worksheet file into another worksheet file	Move the cell pointer to the cell in which you want the combined data to appear and choose File Combine From. Select "Copy" to copy the information from the other worksheet file, select "Add" to add the new values to the existing values, or select "Subtract" to subtract the new values from the existing values. You can combine either the entire file or a specified range of data.

Chapter 11

Working with Macros

A *macro* is a series of instructions to 1-2-3 that can be executed repeatedly. Any 1-2-3 task you can perform, from the simplest to the most complex, can be automated with a macro. With macros, you can:

- *Simplify repetitive tasks and ensure consistency.* For example, a macro can automatically enter the current date, a company name, or any other standard text into a worksheet. Another macro can generate reports by compiling information from different sources and printing that information.
- *Streamline interaction with 1-2-3 using customized menus and prompts.* Interactive macros can begin a procedure, pause for user input, and then continue the procedure. Using macros, you can also display menus containing commands that, when chosen, execute other macros.
- *Create complete macro-driven applications within 1-2-3.* A macro application can manage an entire 1-2-3 session: offer customized menus and icon palettes, prompt for data, create and edit worksheet files, access databases, print reports, and draw graphs. The users of the application do not even have to know they are working with 1-2-3.

In this chapter you are going to learn the principles of creating, testing, and running macros. In the process, you will write some simple keystroke macros, use several of 1-2-3's macro commands, create your own macro menus, build a small library of macros you can use in any worksheet file, and construct a macro that automatically executes each time you start 1-2-3. After covering the fundamentals of creating and using macros, the chapter presents a sample macro application that illustrates more advanced macro features. Finally, it describes how to customize 1-2-3's icon palette so that clicking an icon runs a macro you've assigned to the icon.

What You'll Learn

By the time you complete this chapter, you'll know how to perform these macro tasks:

- Enter, name, and document macros

- Run macros with Control keys and the Run command

- Use all types of macro instructions—single keystrokes, keynames, menu commands, and macro commands—in a macro

- Record macros in the Transcript window

- Create looping macros

- Use macro subroutines

- Create and use macro menus

- Run a macro that is not in the current file

- Create auto-executing macros

- Use an auto-loading file to load a macro library into memory

- Debug (find and correct mistakes in) macros

- Customize the icon palette to run a macro

Before You Start

Before you begin the exercises in this chapter, start 1-2-3. Make sure that the cell pointer is in cell A:A1 of a new, blank worksheet file, and that 1-2-3 has been set up to save files in your C:\123\123BOOK directory.

As you work through this chapter, you are going to use macros to automate some of the tasks you performed in earlier chapters. You will create three new files: Two in which to experiment with macros (MACROS.WK3 and MACTEST.WK3), and one to use as a macro library (UTILITY.WK3). (If you want to experiment with macros but do not want to type in the examples in this chapter, a disk containing all the worksheet files created in this book is available from the authors.)

As in previous chapters, stop at the end of a numbered step or just before the next section heading when you are tired or have something else to do. Be sure to save any modified worksheet files before you stop. If you have more than one active file, write down the names of the files in memory and the order in which they are stored. When you want to continue with the exercises, start up 1-2-3, read in the worksheet files you last used, making sure they are in the same order they were in before you stopped, then pick up where you left off.

A Note on Example Layout   As in previous chapters, the examples in this chapter assume that your screen displays 20 rows and eight columns when the Worksheet window is maximized. If your display does not show 20 rows and eight columns, your screens will look somewhat different from the illustrations, but you can still do all the examples. Just be sure to use the cell addresses and ranges specified in the instructions.

A Note on Keystroke Instructions   The keystroke instructions in this chapter often assume you are using a mouse to perform such operations as highlighting a range or selecting an option in a dialog box. You can also use the keyboard to perform the same operations. Many of the keyboard equivalents to mouse operations were described in Chapters 3 and 4. A few of the most common ones are summarized here. For a complete list of keystroke equivalents to mouse operations, see the 1-2-3 documentation or the 1-2-3 online Help.

Keyboard Equivalents to Mouse Operations

Operation	Command		Keyboard Equivalent	
Complete action and close dialog box	**Select:**	OK	**Press:**	↵
Cancel action and close dialog box	**Select:**	Cancel	**Press:**	ESC
Highlight a text box	**Select:**	text box	**Press:**	ALT+*underlined_letter*
Edit a range in a text box	**Select:** **Specify:**	Range A:A1..C:D4	**Press:**	ALT+*underlined_letter* F2 (EDIT)
Edit a number or word in a text box	**Select:** **Specify:** *(or click on text and edit it)*	text box new text	**Press:** **Type:** *(or press Left arrow and edit text)*	ALT+*underlined_letter* new text
Highlight a range	**Highlight:** A:A1..C:D4		**Move to:** cell A:A1 **Press:** F4 **Move to:** cell D4 **Press:** ↵	

Throughout this chapter, the Edit Copy and Edit Paste commands are used in the exercises whenever you copy data from one range to another. In all these places, using the Edit Quick Copy command or the "Copy To" icon are perfectly viable alternatives to Edit Copy and Edit Paste. This chapter also instructs you to highlight a range and use the Delete key whenever you have to clear cells. The Edit Clear command or the "Edit Cut" icon would work equally well. In all tasks, feel free to use the approach you find most comfortable.

Macro Basics

"Macro" is short for "macro instruction," which literally means "large instruction." Macros are appropriately named: You can execute a macro with as few as two keystrokes, but a single macro can contain dozens or even hundreds of separate instructions to 1-2-3. There are three basic types of macros:

- *Keystroke macros.* Keystroke macros are made up of the characters you would type if you were entering commands and typing data into 1-2-3 yourself. For example, a macro that saves the current file is a typical keystroke macro. Such a macro would choose the File Save command, select the current file as the file to save, and then automatically save the file.
- *Macros that use macro commands.* Macro commands are special 1-2-3 commands that have meaning only within a macro. Macro commands let you create macros that are more flexible and do more than keystroke macros. For example, a macro that asks

you which of several tax forms you want to print and then prints the form would use macro commands to prompt you for information.

- *Macro applications.* Macro applications effectively "take over" 1-2-3. Macro applications are actually computer programs written in 1-2-3's macro command language. Typically, they start up as soon as you retrieve the worksheet containing the application, display their own menus and submenus, and read and write their own files. Many macro applications can be run by people who have little or no familiarity with 1-2-3; the person running the macro application interacts with the macro, which in turn interacts with 1-2-3. A typical macro application might be a 1-2-3 accounting package for a small business.

What's in a Macro?

You enter macro instructions directly into worksheet cells as one or more labels. Any number of macros can be included in a worksheet file. Every macro instruction is either (1) a keystroke you would press in the normal process of entering data, selecting an item from a menu, or responding to a prompt or (2) a macro command. Macros can include any of the components listed in Table 11-1, individually or in combination.

Table 11-1: Macro Components

Macro component	Description
Keystrokes that represent labels or values	To create labels or enter values in a macro, you include the keystrokes you would type to create those labels or values. Indicate pressing the Enter key with the tilde (~) key.
Macro key names	Macros use special key names to represent the Alt key, with which you choose commands in the 1-2-3 menu by their underlined letters, the pointer-movement keys, the function keys, and some other special keys. Key names within a macro are enclosed in braces ({ }). For example, a macro that contains the key name {RIGHT} will move the cell pointer one cell to the right, as if you had pressed the Right arrow key.
Keystrokes that select menu items	In a macro, a series of 1-2-3 commands begins with the Alt key. Menu commands are abbreviated to the first letter of the command. For example, the keystrokes to choose the File Save command would appear in a macro as {ALT}FS.
Keystrokes that select options in dialog boxes	Options in a dialog box are selected by combining the Alt key with the underlined letter in the option. For example, the Alt+S keystroke that would select the Save All option in the File Save dialog box would appear in a macro as {ALT "s"}.
Formulas and @functions	Formulas and @functions work the same way in a macro as they do in the worksheet. For instance, the formula +b5+b6 in a macro adds the contents of cells B5 and B6 as part of the execution of the macro.

Macro component	Description
Macro commands	Macro commands perform operations specific to macros. Like macro key names, macro commands are enclosed in braces ({ }). Some macro commands perform operations similar to commands you can perform with keystrokes, while others do not. For example, the {BLANK} command is similar in function to the Edit Clear command; on the other hand, there is no set of keystrokes that directly corresponds to the {GET} command, which stores a single keystroke in a cell.

Basic Steps in Developing and Running a Macro

This section briefly summarizes the basic steps you should follow to create and run a macro. Read this section to get an overview of the process; each of these steps is described in more detail later in this chapter, when you will actually build some macros.

Figure 11-1: Some Macros You'll Create in This Chapter

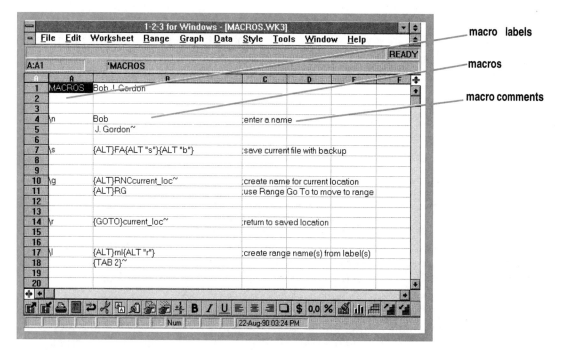

1. Plan the macro.

   It will ultimately save you time and trouble if you plan out what you want the macro to do before you start writing it. First, figure out what you want to accomplish. Next, make a list of the main steps in the task. Then, perform the task manually and write down the keystrokes and macro instructions that could accomplish each step. (In other words, translate your list of steps into macro instructions.)

2. Position the macro in a safe place.

A separate worksheet containing only macros is usually the best place for macros. However, if you create macros in worksheets that contain other data, always place macros in an area that is diagonally opposite the data (for example, below and to the right, or above and to the left, of the data). This prevents the macro from being affected if you delete or insert rows, and makes it less likely to be accidentally overwritten by Copy and Move operations.

3. Document the macro name.

Enter the macro's name in the cell immediately to the left of the first cell the macro will occupy. This reminds you and others who may use the macro of the keystrokes needed to run it. In the cell to the right of the macro, enter comments that describe what the macro is doing.

4. Name the macro.

Although *you* know that the macros you create are macros, 1-2-3 doesn't know it until you assign them range names. Assigning a range name to a macro makes it possible to run the macro by name or to associate it with a Control key combination. Usually the range name you assign is identical to the name you entered in step 3. (For instance, if you create a file-save macro and label it \s, you assign it the range name \S.)

5. Enter the macro.

You create a macro as a column of labels that consist of instructions. Begin the macro in the cell to the right of the macro's descriptive label, and continue it in as many cells below that cell as you need to complete the macro.

6. Test and run the macro.

Test a macro by first "playing computer" (keystroking each part of the macro) and then running it when you are confident the instructions are correct.

When you run a macro, 1-2-3 starts executing the keystrokes and commands that it finds in the first cell of the macro range. After it executes those keystrokes, 1-2-3 automatically continues to the cell below and executes any commands it finds there. 1-2-3 continues to move down the column, executing macro instructions until it encounters a blank cell, at which time the macro ends.

When 1-2-3 is executing a macro, the status indicator in the bottom line of the screen reads Cmd. (Short macros are executed so quickly that this indicator will appear as no more than a flash.)

■ *NOTE:* You can run a macro at almost any time during a 1-2-3 session. However, you cannot start a macro when an error condition exists (1-2-3 has displayed ERROR in the mode indicator), another macro is running, or 1-2-3's on-line Help is active.

7. Debug the macro, if necessary.

If the macro does not do what you want it to, or if an incorrect instruction results in an error message, you will have to *debug* the macro.

When you debug a macro, you examine it for errors in syntax and errors in logic, then you correct the errors. If an error is a syntax error (an incorrect instruction), 1-2-3 usually identifies the incorrect macro instruction when it executes the macro. If the error is a logic error (the macro doesn't do what you want), you will have to identify the problem yourself using techniques and tools described in "Debugging a Macro" later in this chapter.

Rules for Creating Macros

There are two basic rules for creating macros:

1. Macro instructions should be entered as labels.

Almost everything in a macro—keystroke sequences, key names, and macro commands—is a label. 1-2-3 automatically interprets cells that begin with letters, macro commands, and key names entered in braces (for example, {RIGHT}) as labels. If a macro cell begins with any character that 1-2-3 interprets as a value or part of a formula, you must type a label prefix before entering the first character. 1-2-3 ignores each macro cell's label prefix when it executes the macro, so it doesn't matter if you use an apostrophe ('), double quotes ("), or a caret (^) as the label prefix.

2. Macros should be given range names.

In order to run a macro, you have to tell 1-2-3 where the macro is. The easiest way to do this is to name the first cell of the range that contains the macro instructions. You can also execute a macro by pointing to it. (This is described in "Debugging a Macro" later in this chapter.)

You can give macros two types of range names: Descriptive range names (such as SAVE_BACK for a macro that saves the current file and retains the previous version of the file as a backup), or range names composed of a backslash (\) followed by a letter of the alphabet (such as \S). If you give a macro a descriptive name, it is easy to remember what the macro does just by looking at the range name. Normally, you name frequently-used macros with a backslash/letter combination to make them easy to run: Simply hold down the Control key and press the letter you used in the range name to run the macro.

You only need to name the first cell of a macro, even if the macro itself takes up several cells in a column.

Other Conventions for Creating Macros

Besides these two main rules, there are other conventions you should follow when you write macros. Although your macros will usually work if you don't follow these conventions, they will help you create macros that are easy to understand and to modify, and that are safe from accidental modification.

1. Place macros in their own worksheet.

Even though 1-2-3 allows you to place macros anywhere in a worksheet file, it is best to safeguard against accidentally deleting or overwriting your macros by putting them in their own worksheet. When you have finished creating the macros, you can also protect the worksheet, to provide another level of safety. Start all macros in the same column, so that it is easy to find and to name them.

2. Use uppercase for 1-2-3 keywords, keynames, and commands. Use lowercase for everything else.

Type macro keywords, key names, @functions, and menu commands in uppercase. Type range names, cell addresses, labels, and arguments you have defined for macro commands and @functions in lowercase. That way, you can easily distinguish the components of your macros that are part of 1-2-3 from the components that you have made up.

3. Document your macros.

Just as you label values in a worksheet to identify their purpose, you should document your macros. Documentation is the name for information you include in the worksheet that explains what the macro does or how it works. Macros without documentation quickly become indecipherable.

You should always identify the start of a macro by placing a label containing the range name of the macro in the cell immediately to the left of the macro's first cell. Most people also document each macro cell by placing a comment in the cell to its right. You can also enter labels in the cells above the macro to describe the overall purpose of the macro.

4. Adopt a convention for naming macros.

Although 1-2-3 allows you to use any range name to name a macro, you will find it convenient to pick a convention and stick with it. Name your most frequently-used macros with a backslash followed by a single letter; choose a letter that reminds you of the macro's purpose (for example, name a file-saving macro \S). Give longer, more descriptive range names to your other macros. Begin the range names used for macros with the same character, so that you can distinguish range names of macros from other range names. For example, in this book, all macro names will begin with the backslash character. Some suggested conventions for naming parts of macros will be demonstrated throughout this chapter.

Figure 11-2 shows an example of a fully-documented macro. (You'll actually create this macro later in this chapter.)

Figure 11-2: A Fully Documented Macro

	A	B	C	D	E
3		\E - Enter records and, optionally, sort them.			
4		This macro consists of a main routine named \E; a menu			
5		named MENU_E; subroutines named NEWREC_E, GETREC_E, and			
6		SORTREC_E; and a flag named QUITFLG_E. Uses range names			
7		PRIMARY_E and SECONDARY_E as sort keys.			
8					
9	\e	{IF @CELLPOINTER("TYPE")<>"B"}{BEEP}{QUIT}	;Error!		
10		{LET quitflg_e,0}	;Not ready to quit yet		
11		{MENUCALL menu_e}	;Ask what to do next		
12		{IF quitflg_e,1}{CALC}{QUIT}	;User wants to quit?		
13		{BRANCH \E}	;No, so start again		
14					
15					

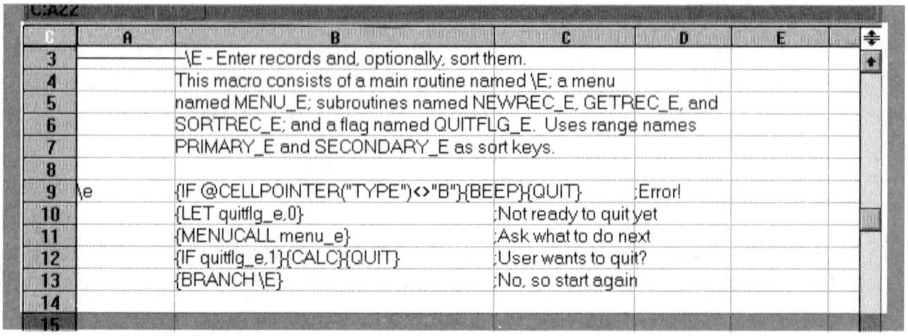

Creating a Keystroke Macro

In this section, you will build a very simple keystroke macro. Keystroke macros are the most basic type of macro, and the easiest to create. They are mostly made up of the actual keystrokes you would type if you were entering commands and typing data into 1-2-3 interactively. Typical uses for keystroke macros include typing a label, number, or formula in a worksheet; saving files; copying a range; adding a column of numbers; changing worksheet, print, or graph settings; and printing reports.

Even the very simplest keystroke macros can save you time. For instance, suppose you often find yourself typing in the same label. You can put the keystrokes in a macro and the macro will type them for you. The following macro types and enters "Bob J. Gordon" wherever Bob needs the name entered.

```
'\n Bob J. Gordon~   ;type a name
```

The label **Bob J. Gordon~** is the actual macro and is the only part of this example that 1-2-3 requires. The label **\n** serves as a title for the macro; it records the macro's name in the worksheet. The label **;type a name** documents the macro instructions.

In this section, you'll create a macro that types your own name in a new worksheet file you will call MACROS.WK3. You will use MACROS.WK3 to experiment with macros. Later, you will use this file to create a macro library that you can use with any worksheet file.

1. Create a title for the MACROS worksheet.

    In a blank, untitled Worksheet window, enter a title for the MACROS worksheet.

    Move to: cell A1
    Type: MACROS   ⏎

2. Label the first macro.

    Now you will build your first macro. Before you start, label the macro. In the cell to the left of the cell into which you are going to enter the macro, enter the name you will use to run the macro. 1-2-3 does not require this label, nor does the label help 1-2-3 execute the macro. However, the label does help you remember the macro's range name so you can invoke it. The label also helps you find the macro later, in case you need to change it.

    Move to: cell A4
    Type: '\n   *don't forget the apostrophe*
    Press: ⏎

Figure 11-3:   A Macro Label

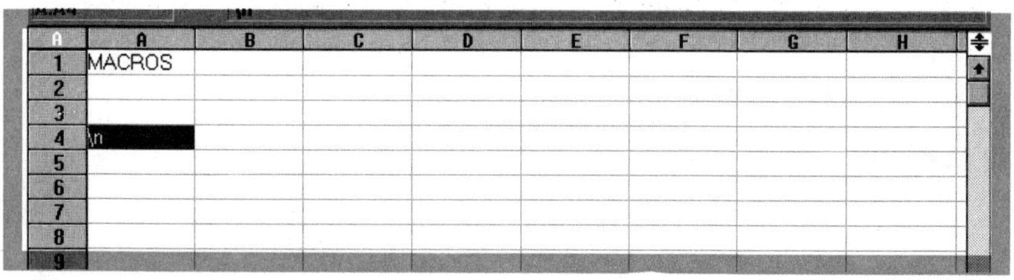

3. Give the macro a range name.

Macro instructions are cell entries; 1-2-3 does not automatically distinguish them from other entries in the worksheet. To identify a cell or column of cells as a set of macro instructions, you assign a range name to the first cell of the macro. Naming the range lets 1-2-3 know where the macro is.

1-2-3 recognizes the letters A through Z, preceded by a backslash (\), as range names for macros that can be executed with an Control key combination; for example, pressing Control+A runs a macro called \A, pressing Control+B runs a macro named \B, and so on. If you give the macro any other type of range name, you can still run it with the Run command, described later in this chapter.

Name this macro \N, for "Name." You can use either Range Name Create or Range Name Label Create to name the macro. Generally, it is easier to use Range Name Label Create to name the macro. With the cell pointer still in cell A4, name cell B4:

Choose: `Range`   `Name`   `Label Create`

Select: `Right`   *as Direction, if necessary*

              `OK`   *or press Enter*

1-2-3 uses the text of cell A4 as the range name for the cell to its right, cell B4.

4. Enter the macro into cell B4.

Finally, enter the macro into cell B4. You'll enter the name "Bob J. Gordon" followed by a tilde, the symbol for the Enter key. (If you wish, type in your own name instead of typing Bob J. Gordon.) Verify that 1-2-3 created the range name by using the Range Goto command.

Choose: `Range`   `Go to`

Specify: `\N`   *in the Range text box*

Select: `OK`   *to move to B4*

Type: `Bob J. Gordon˜`   *in B4 (don't forget the tilde)*

Press: →

5. Document the macro instructions.

When you document a macro's instructions, you provide information so that you or somebody else looking at the macro can quickly figure out what it does and how it does it. Providing good documentation is indispensable if you share your macros with anyone else. It is also useful when you want to modify your own macros at some later time. Macros are not inherently easy to read. After a week or two, macro instructions that seem clear when you create the macro begin to grow hazy. After a few months, the only way you will be able to understand your own undocumented macros is to step through them one keystroke at a time.

In general, it is a good idea to include an overall description of the macro in the cells above the macro instructions, and a comment on each line of macro instructions. In this case, since the macro is only one cell long, a single comment will suffice.

Type: `;enter a name`   ↵

■ *NOTE:*   In this book, comments on individual macro cells will begin with a semicolon (;), to make it easier to distinguish a comment from macro instructions. However, you do not have to use a semicolon (or any other character) to identify macro comments.

6. Widen column B.

Notice that the comment in column C truncates the display of the macro in column B. This has no effect on how 1-2-3 executes the macro, but it does make the macro harder to read. Widen column B so that you have enough space on the screen to display the macro and its comments.

Press:	$\boxed{\leftarrow}$ *to move the cell pointer to column B*
Choose:	`Worksheet    Column Width`
Type:	`30` *in the Set width text box*
Press:	$\boxed{\downarrow}$

Figure 11-4:   Column Width Adjusted to Accommodate Macros

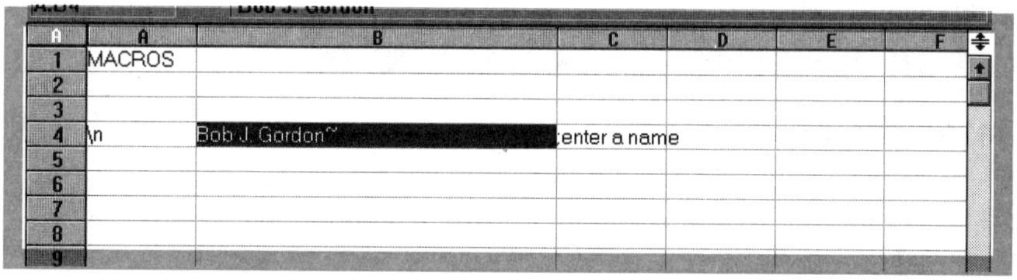

7. Test and run the macro.

Test this simple macro by moving the cell pointer to a blank cell and pressing Control+N:

Move to:	cell A10
Press:	$\boxed{\text{CTRL+N}}$

When you run the macro, 1-2-3 enters Bob's name (or your name) in the current cell. Use the macro to enter the name in several locations in rows 10 through 20 and columns A through E.

Once you have tested the macro, erase the test cells (but not the cells containing the macro).

Highlight:	A10..E20
Press:	$\boxed{\text{DELETE}}$

8. Save the worksheet file as MACROS.WK3.

Congratulations!   You have created and used your first macro. Save the macro by saving the file as MACROS.WK3:

Choose: File   Save As

Type: macros   ⏎

Figure 11-5: Testing the \N Macro

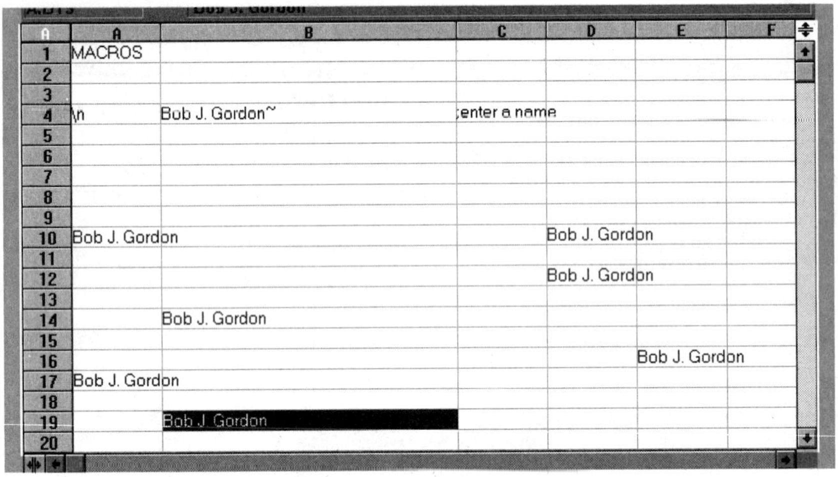

More on Creating Keystroke Macros

The simple macro you just created to type in text contains only alphabetic keys and the symbol for the Enter key. Keystroke macros that type in text are useful, but keystroke macros can do much more; they can take the drudgery out of many other tasks you do all the time. By including in the macro the keystrokes to select options in dialog boxes, function keys, and other special keys, you can automate almost any task you can do from the keyboard.

This section describes the syntax for entering function keys and other special keys, as well as some additional rules for entering macros. Then it shows you how to create three macros that use some of these special keys.

1-2-3 Function Keys and Special Keys in Macros

You enter text, values, and 1-2-3 menu commands in a macro the same way you would type them into 1-2-3. However, the 1-2-3 function keys, pointer-movement keys, and other special keys are represented in macros by name. You type the name of the special key between braces ({ }). For instance:

```
First{RIGHT}Second{RIGHT}Third{HOME}
```

This keystroke macro includes two presses of the Right arrow key and a single press of the Home key. Most keys are represented by the actual names assigned to them in 1-2-3 and used in the keystroke instructions in this book. The main exception to this is the Enter key, which is represented by a tilde (~). Using a single character to represent the Enter key is a convenience, since macros often include many presses of Enter. Be sure to include a tilde wherever you want the macro to press the Enter key. (If you want to indicate the actual tilde character in a macro, use the three-character sequence {~}.)

■ *NOTE:*   If your keyboard does not include the tilde as one of the typing keys, you can create it by pressing Alt+F1 (Compose) and then typing two hyphens.

Table 11-2 summarizes the way special keys are represented in macros. The table also lists abbreviations for keys, if there are any. (You can use an abbreviation in exactly the same way as you would use the full name for the key.) Skim through this table now; refer back to it when you are creating macros. You can also find definitions of all the macro keys in 1-2-3's online Help.

■ *NOTE:*   When you type special keys, you can use either lowercase or uppercase letters. However, as noted earlier, it is helpful to type special keys (as well as menu commands, macro command keywords, and @functions) in uppercase, to distinguish these "built-in" components from the components you define. In this book, all special keys will be typed in uppercase letters when they appear in macro examples.

Table 11-2:   Special Keys in Macros

Key Name	Keystroke	Macro Key	Macro Abbreviation
Editing Keys and Miscellaneous Special Keys			
Backspace	BACKSPACE	{BACKSPACE}	{BS}
Delete	DELETE	{DELETE}	{DEL}
Enter	ENTER	~	
Escape	ESCAPE	{ESCAPE}	{ESC}
Insert	INSERT	{INSERT}	{INS}
Menubar	ALT or F10	{ALT} {MENUBAR}	{MB}
Pointer-movement Keys			
Up	UP	{UP}	{U}
Down	DOWN	{DOWN}	{D}
Left	LEFT	{LEFT}	{L}
Right	RIGHT	{RIGHT}	{R}
Big Left	CTRL+LEFT or SHIFT+TAB	{BIGLEFT}	
Big Right	CTRL+RIGHT or TAB	{BIGRIGHT}	

Key Name	Keystroke	Macro Key	Macro Abbreviation
Home	HOME	{HOME}	
End	END	{END}	
Page Up	PGUP	{PGUP}	
Page Down	PGDN	{PGDN}	
Function Keys			
Help	F1	{HELP}	
Edit	F2	{EDIT}	
Name	F3	{NAME}	
Anchor *(in READY mode)*	F4	{ANCHOR}	
Absolute *(in VALUE or EDIT mode)*	F4	{ABS}	
Goto	F5	{GOTO}	
Pane	F6	{WINDOW}	
Zoom	ALT+F6	{ZOOM}	
Table	F8	{TABLE}	
Calc	F9	{CALC}	
Addin Application Function Keys			
App1	ALT+F7	{APP1}	
App3	ALT+F8	{APP2}	
App4	ALT+F9	{APP3}	
Literal Characters			
Slash	/	/, >, or {MENU}	
Tilde	~	{~}	
Open brace	{	{{}	
Close brace	}	{}}	

Note on Special Keys   The following keys can be typed from the keyboard but cannot be included in a macro: Alt+Backspace (Undo), Alt+F1 (Compose), Alt+F3 (Run), Backtab (Shift+Tab), Num Lock, Print Screen, Scroll Lock, and Shift. You cannot use these keystrokes in macros. Table 11-3 summarizes the functions of these keys and, when an alternative exists, describes other ways a macro can accomplish the tasks these keys perform.

There is also one special keystroke that you can include in a macro for which there is no keyboard equivalent. This is the {CLEARENTRY} macro, abbreviated {CE}. {CLEARENTRY} clears the edit line when you are editing a cell or the text box when you are entering data in a dialog box. Its effect is similar to pressing Escape the number of times necessary to clear the text box or the edit line.

Table 11-3: Keys that cannot be typed in a macro.

Key	Description
BACKTAB (SHIFT+TAB)	Backtab moves the cell pointer one screen-width to the left (in READY mode) or moves the cursor five characters to the left (in EDIT mode). It is functionally equivalent to Big Left (Control-Left). Use {BIGLEFT} in macros.
CAPS LOCK	Caps Lock toggles the letter keys between lowercase and uppercase. A macro cannot turn Caps Lock on and off or determine the current state of the Caps Lock key. Either instruct the macro user to press Caps Lock; type in characters in uppercase, if they are to appear that way in macros; or use the @UPPER function to convert lowercase characters to uppercase within the macro.
COMPOSE (ALT+F1)	Compose allows you to enter characters in 1-2-3 that you cannot type directly from the keyboard. Although you cannot use this key as a macro instruction, you can include characters typed with the aid of the Compose key in a macro, and you can use the @CODE function to convert a number that corresponds to any character into the character.
NUM LOCK	Num Lock changes the functioning of the numeric keypad. As with Caps Lock, a macro cannot determine or change the state of the Number Lock key. You can, however, prompt the user of the macro to press the Number Lock key, and you can sometimes process non-numeric keypad keys as if they were numeric keys (such as interpreting {HOME} as 7 and {PGUP} as 9).
PRINT SCREEN	The Print Screen key normally prints the current screen contents to the Clipboard. You cannot press this key from a macro.
RUN (ALT+F3)	The Run key invokes macros. You can run one macro from within another by branching to the second macro or calling it as a subroutine.
SCROLL LOCK	Scroll Lock changes the function of the pointer-movement keys. As with Caps Lock, a macro cannot determine or change the state of the Scroll Lock key.
SHIFT	The Shift key toggles keyboard typewriter keys between their two functions (lowercase becomes uppercase or uppercase becomes lowercase, depending on Caps Lock). Holding down Shift while typing one of the keys on the numeric keypad also reverses the effect of the Number Lock key.
	A macro cannot determine or change the state of the Shift key. You can, however, display a message in the control panel that asks the macro user to press the Shift key. You can also use @UPPER to convert characters to uppercase and @LOWER to convert characters to lowercase.

Key	Description
STEP (ALT+F2)	The Step key controls 1-2-3's single-step macro execution facility. (It is equivalent to checking or unchecking the "Step" option in the Tools Macro Debug dialog box.) You cannot use the Step key from within a macro, although you can instruct the macro user to turn Step mode on or off.
TAB	Tab moves the cell pointer one screen-width to the right (in READY mode) or moves the cursor five characters to the right (in EDIT mode). Tab is functionally equivalent to Big Right (Control-Right). Use {BIGRIGHT} in macros.
UNDO (ALT+ BACKSPACE)	Undo undoes the effects of commands that change the worksheet file, including the effects of running a macro. A macro cannot press Undo, nor can the user press Undo from within a macro. Pressing Undo after a macro completes or is interrupted by Control+Break will undo all changes made by the macro except those changes to which Undo does not apply, such as saving files and printing.

A Note on {MENU} and {MENUBAR}   1-2-3 for Windows can run macros created with earlier releases of 1-2-3 by executing commands in the 1-2-3 Classic menu. To achieve this compatibility, 1-2-3 uses the {MENU} macro to activate the 1-2-3 Classic menu, rather than the 1-2-3 for Windows menu. Be careful not to use the {MENU} macro unintentionally. To choose commands from the 1-2-3/W menu, you use {ALT}, {MENUBAR}, or {MB}.

A Note on Using a Repetition Factor with Macro Keys   A keystroke sequence frequently includes several consecutive presses of the same key. For example, you may want to move the cell pointer seven cells to the left in a worksheet. Instead of typing {LEFT} seven times, specify a repetition factor: {LEFT 7}. Similarly, instead of typing {END}{HOME}{HOME} to move the cell pointer to the end of the worksheet and then back to the first cell, you can enter {END}{HOME 2} in a macro. Using a repetition factor makes the macro easier to read and takes up less room in the worksheet. It also makes the macro more flexible, since you can use an expression or a cell reference as the repetition factor, as well as a literal number. The following rules apply to repetition factors:

- *The key name must be followed by exactly one space.* Any other number of spaces terminates macro execution with an error message.
- *The repetition factor can be a number, range name, or numeric expression.* If you use a range name or numeric expression, 1-2-3 uses its value at the time the macro is executed. For example {RIGHT A3} would move the cell pointer right 5 times if the number 5 were in cell A3 and 8 times if the number 8 were in cell A3. Similarly, {RIGHT counter*3} would move the cell pointer to the right 15 columns if the value 5 were in a cell named COUNTER.

A Keystroke Macro to Save the Current File with a Backup

Although 1-2-3 provides a File Save command and icon, you may have noticed that there is no quick way to save a file while retaining a backup. Creating a macro to retain a backup when saving the current file lets you do it with one Control key combination.

Create a macro called \S (for "Save a file with backup") in cell B7:

1. Label and name the save-with-backup macro.

Move to:	cell A7
Type:	'\s $\boxed{\downarrow}$
Choose:	Range Name Label Create
Select:	Right *as Direction, if necessary*
	OK *or press Enter*

2. Enter and document the save-with-backup macro.

   To save the current file under its existing name while retaining a backup, you would: (1) Choose File Save As; (2) select the "Save All" option in the File Save As dialog box; and (3) select the "Backup" option when 1-2-3 prompts you to choose between backing up and replacing the file on disk. Create a macro to perform this task, and document your work:

Press:	$\boxed{\rightarrow}$
Type:	{ALT}FA{ALT "s"}{ALT "b"} $\boxed{\rightarrow}$
	;save current file with backup $\boxed{\downarrow}$

Figure 11-6: A macro for Saving the Current File with a Backup

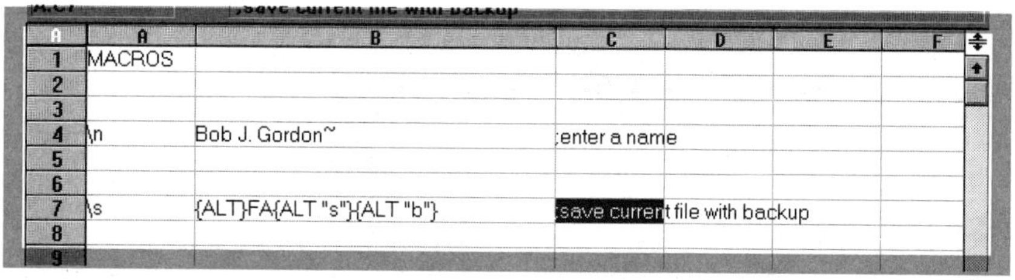

	A	B	C	D	E	F
1	MACROS					
2						
3						
4	\n	Bob J. Gordon~	;enter a name			
5						
6						
7	\s	{ALT}FA{ALT "s"}{ALT "b"}	;save current file with backup			
8						
9						

Pressing Control+S will save the current worksheet file (the file containing the worksheet with the active cell pointer) under its current name, and save the on-disk files (the existing worksheet and format files with extensions .WK3 and .FM3) as backups with the backup file extensions .BAK and .FMB.

■ *NOTE:*   This macro will only work as intended when the current file has already been saved at least once. If the file is currently Untitled, the macro will assign the file the first name available in the sequence FILE0001.WK3, FILE0002.WK3, and so on. Therefore, use this macro only after you have saved the current file at least once. (If you use it inadvertently in an Untitled worksheet file, use File Save As to give the file the name you want.)

3. Save MACROS.WK3 and retain a backup using the save-with-backup macro.

   Test Control+S by using it to save MACROS.WK3.

Press:	$\boxed{\text{CTRL+S}}$

1-2-3 renames the file on disk MACROS.BAK and saves the current worksheet file as MACROS.WK3. From now on, you can use Control+S to save MACROS.WK3.

A Note on Splitting a Macro Between Cells   One cell can hold a macro up to 512 characters in length, and the macro can have as many commands as will fit in the cell. However, it is often better to split a macro into two or more cells. This can make a macro easier to enter, to read, and, if necessary, to debug. The number of cells a macro occupies has no effect on the execution of the macro itself. In other words, it doesn't matter whether you enter as many instructions as possible in one cell, or break up the sequence of instructions into a series of shorter cell entries.

To prove this to yourself, split your first macro into two cells. One cell will contain Bob's first name (or yours). The cell directly below it will contain a space, Bob's (or your) middle initial and last name, and a tilde.

Move to:	cell B4	
Type:	Bob	*or your first name*
Press:	↓	
	SPACEBAR	
Type:	J. Gordon˜	*or your initial, last name, and a tilde*
Press:	↵	

Figure 11-7: A Macro Split Across Two Cells

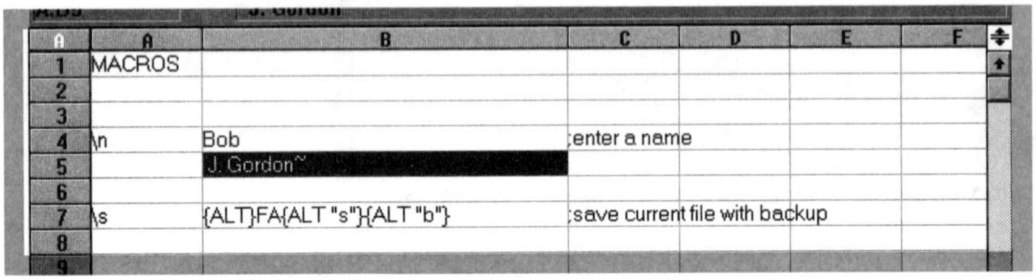

Now move to an empty cell and try out the modified macro.

Move to:	cell B1	
Press:	CTRL+N	

Figure 11-8: Macro split across two cells runs successfully.

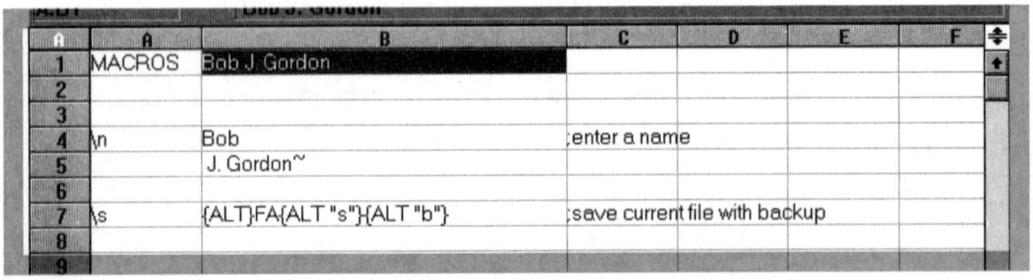

The macro types the name in cells B4 and B5 into cell B1. Notice that the macro still types in the name exactly the same way it did before, even though the name in the macro is now in two cells instead of one.

In general, you can format a macro in whatever way is easiest for you to read and understand. In this book, macros are formatted so that the commands that accomplish a particular task, and the comments on those commands, can be viewed on the same screen. This makes it easier to view simultaneously the macro and its comments. As you work with macros, you will develop your own style.

Note that you cannot break up individual key names (such as {CALC} or {HOME}), or macro commands (such as {GET}), into two or more cells. Any commands enclosed in a set of braces—including repetition factors or macro command arguments—must be entered in one cell. For instance, either of the following two sets of macro instructions will type the words First, Second, and Third in three adjacent cells:

```
First{RIGHT}Second{RIGHT}Third~
```

or

```
First{RIGHT}
Second{RIGHT}
Third~
```

The following division of macro instructions, however, will not work correctly:

```
First{RIGHT}Second{RI
GHT}Third~
```

- **NOTE:** If a you use more than one cell for a macro, enter the macro into consecutive cells in the column, rather than leaving blank cells between cells containing macro instructions. 1-2-3 stops executing a macro when it encounters a blank cell.

A Pair of Keystroke Macros

Many people use simple keystroke macros to speed up building and using worksheets. The file-save macro you constructed earlier in this chapter automates one frequently-performed task. With very little effort, you can construct macros that automate many others. This section shows you how to write two keystroke macros that are designed to work together to simplify another frequently-performed task: Moving to one part of the worksheet file (that you have assigned a range name) to look something up or make an entry, then returning to where you had been working.

Suppose that in a particular worksheet you frequently move to a location you have named TAX_TABLE, and then move back to where you were. To move to TAX_TABLE, you would choose Range Go To or press F5 (Goto), select or type the range name TAX_TABLE, and press Enter or click OK. To get back to where you were, you would have to press Goto, type in the address of the location you had been working in, and then press Enter. If you forgot the original cell pointer location, you would have to page through the worksheet until you got back to where you started. With a couple of keystroke macros, you can accomplish the same task much more quickly and easily.

The following pair of macros illustrates one of several different ways to do this. The macros allow you to press Control+G (for "Go To range") to go to any named range, then press Control+R ("Return to previous location") to return to your previous location. Since you haven't defined a TAX_TABLE range, the Control+G macro (using the Range Go To command) will offer the choice of sending you to a named range called MACROS, and the Control+R macro will allow you to return from MACROS to the previous cell pointer location. (At the moment, the beginning of your macros area and all your named ranges are in sight, and the idea of having a macro to go there and back might not seem especially useful. But imagine these macros as part of an application that includes a large area of the worksheet. In this case, the ability to jump back and forth between one part of the worksheet and another with a couple of keystrokes could save you a significant amount of time and aggravation.)

Figure 11-9: Macros to Move the Cell Pointer to a Named Range and Return It to Its Original Location

```
'-- \G  -Save current location and move cell pointer to MACROS
'\g      {ALT}RNCcurrent_loc~      ;create name for current location
         {ALT}RG                   ;go to a range

'-- \R  -Return to cell pointer location saved by \G
'\r      {GOTO}current_loc~        ;return to saved location
```

The first macro, named \G, has two basic steps: (1) Create the range name CURRENT_LOC to store the current cell pointer location, and (2) use the Range Go To to offer the list of named ranges, then move the cell pointer to the selected range.

The macro is equivalent to the following keystrokes:

Choose:	Range Name Create
Type:	current_loc
Press:	↵ *to accept the name and current location*
Choose:	Range Go To
Select:	*the range to which you want to move in the list box* *OK or press Enter*

The second macro, \R, issues the keystrokes needed to return to the location saved by the \G macro. This macro is equivalent to the following keystrokes:

Press:	F5 **(GOTO)**
Type:	current_loc ↵

1. Give cell A4 the range name MACROS.

It is better to move to a range name in a macro than to a specific cell address because 1-2-3 keeps range names up-to-date when you change the worksheet (by inserting or deleting rows, for example). If you included the cell address A4 in a macro, changes such as inserting or deleting a row in the worksheet would cause the macro to function improperly.

Move to:	cell A4
Choose:	`Range   Name   Create`
Type:	`macros`
Press:	⏎

2. Label and name the \G macro.

   Label the macro you are about to create \G, for "Go to range," then use Range Name Label Create to create a range name from the label.

Move to:	cell A10
Type:	`'\g` *don't forget the apostrophe*
Press:	⏎
Choose:	`Range   Name   Label Create`
Select:	`Right` *if necessary*
	OK

   Now, pressing Control+G will run any macro that begins in cell B10.

3. Enter the \G macro.

   Enter the \G macro into cells B10 and B11. Be sure to include any apostrophes (') and tildes (~) needed in the keystroke instructions. Document the contents of each macro cell as you create the macro. First, create the first line and its comment:

Move to:	cell B10
Type:	`{ALT}RNCcurrent_loc˜`
Press:	→
Type:	`;create name for current location`
Press:	↓ ←

   Then, type in the second line and its comment to complete the macro:

Type:	`{ALT}RG`
Press:	→
Type:	`;use Range Go To to move to range` ⏎

4. Label and name the \R macro.

Label the second macro \R, for "Return to previous location," and create a range name from the label.

Move to:	cell A14
Type:	'\r *don't forget the apostrophe*
Press:	⏎
Choose:	Range Name Label Create
Select:	Right *if necessary*
	OK

You will now be able to run any macro that begins in cell B14 by pressing the Control+R keystroke combination.

5. Enter the \R macro.

Enter the \R macro into cell B14. Be sure to include the tilde (~) at the end of the macro.

Move to:	cell B14
Type:	{GOTO}current_loc~
Press:	→
Type:	;return to saved location
Press:	⏎

Figure 11-10: The \G and \R Macros

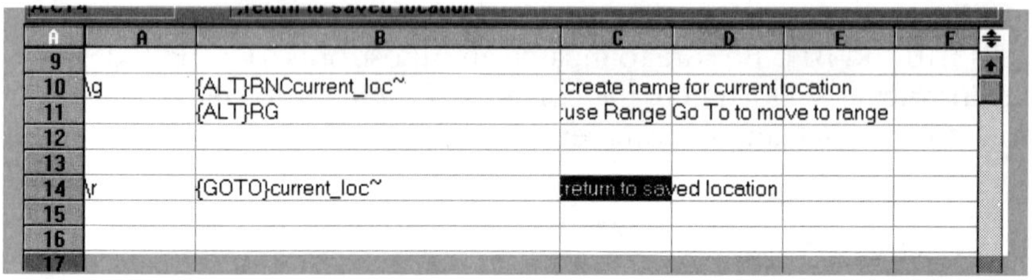

6. Test the \G and \R macros.

To test these macros, you are going to move to a distant part of the worksheet from your current location. You will use \G to mark your place and move to MACROS, and then use \R to move back to the location you marked. First, move to a distant cell and leave your mark:

Move to:	cell DB888
Type:	I was here. ⏎

Figure 11-11: Remote Location in the Worksheet File

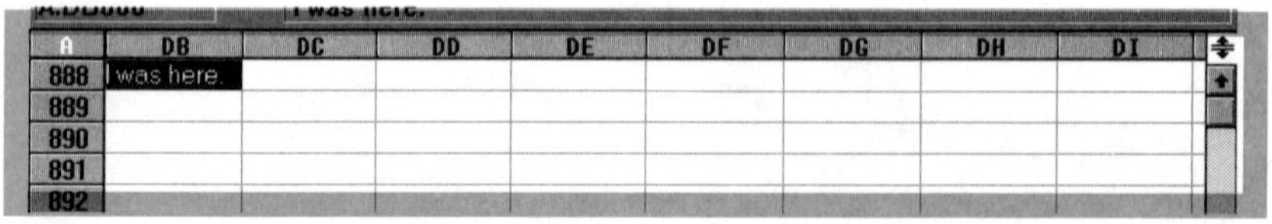

Now use the \G macro to go to the area you have named MACROS:

Press: CTRL+G

Select: MACROS   *in the Range Go To list box*

OK

Figure 11-12: \G moves the cell pointer to cell A4.

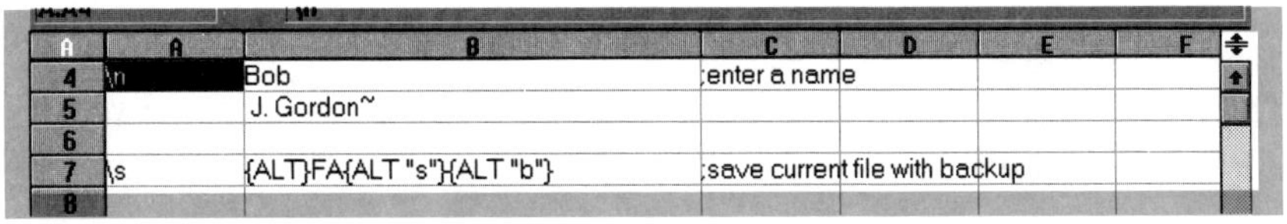

	A	B	C	D	E	F
4	\n	Bob	;enter a name			
5		J. Gordon~				
6						
7	\s	{ALT}FA{ALT "s"}{ALT "b"}	;save current file with backup			
8						

Now use the \R macro to return to cell DB888:

Press: CTRL+R

Figure 11-13: \R returns the cell pointer to DB888.

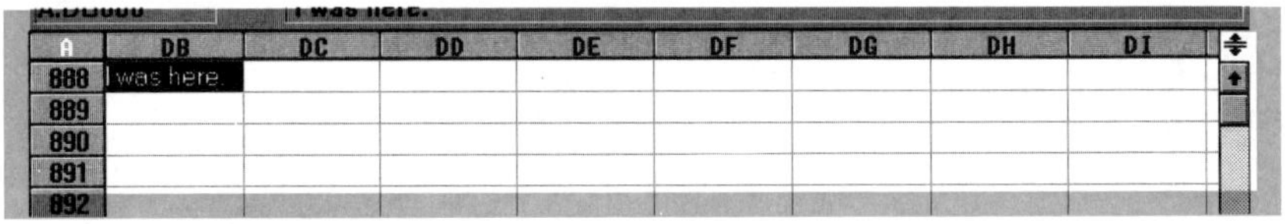

	DB	DC	DD	DE	DF	DG	DH	DI
888	I was here							
889								
890								
891								
892								

1-2-3 immediately moves the cell pointer back to cell DB888. Finally, use \G again to return to the macros area:

Press: CTRL+G

Select: MACROS

OK

7. Save MACROS.WK3.

Use Control+S to save the file (with a backup).

Using the Run Command to Run Macros

So far, you have named your macros so that they can be run by pressing Control and a single letter. This method of naming and running macros is handy, but it has two potential disadvantages: You can only name 26 macros per worksheet file this way (one for each letter of the alphabet), and it is easy to confuse two macros, since a single letter cannot convey much information about the macro's purpose. (Does \E stand for "Enter data" or "Erase worksheet"? Finding out when you press Control+E may be too late!)

Fortunately, you can get around both of these potential problems by giving a macro an ordinary range name. By using the Tools Macro Run command or its keyboard equivalent, Alt+F3 (Run), you can run any macro regardless of how it is named. The ability to run macros by selecting their names means you can have an almost unlimited number of macros in any worksheet file. To run a macro with the Run command or key, you: (1) Choose Run (in either form), (2) select the name of the macro from the list of range names 1-2-3 presents, and (3) select OK or press Enter. Try using the Run command with the first macro you created, just to get the feel of this process:

1. Move to a blank cell in the worksheet.

   Move to: cell A20

2. Choose the Run command.

   Choose: Tools   Macros   Run

   Figure 11-14: Run Command Displays a List of Range Names

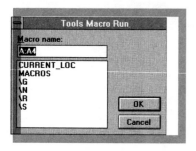

   The list of range names 1-2-3 displays is similar to the display you get when you use the Range Go To command.

3. Select \N from the list of range names.

   Select: \N
                 OK   *or press Enter*

   1-2-3 once again runs the \N macro and types a name in the current cell. Before you go on, delete the name. With the cell pointer still on cell A20,

   Press: DELETE

4. Create another name for the \G macro.

   The Run command is most useful with macros that are not associated with a particular key. You have not created any such macros yet, but you can see how the Run command works with these macros by giving one of your existing macros a new name. Create a more descriptive range name for the \G macro and run that macro again, this time using the Alt+F3 (Run) key.

   Move to: cell B10

Choose:	Range	Name	Create
Type:	\goto_range		
Press:	⏎		

1-2-3 creates a new name for cell B10, \GOTO_RANGE.

5. Run \GOTO_RANGE.

Now use Alt+F3 (Run) to run the macro under its new name:

Press:	ALT+F3	*(RUN)*
Select:	\GOTO_RANGE	*in the list box*
	OK	

1-2-3 executes the macro, just as if you had pressed Control+G. It saves the current cell pointer location and prompts you for a range to move to. Move to MACROS:

Select:	MACROS	*in the Range Go To list box*
	OK	

1-2-3 moves the cell pointer to cell A4. To verify that each step of the macro has indeed been executed, press Control+R to return to the place you were working:

Press:	CTRL+R	*the "Return" macro*

1-2-3 restores the cell pointer position. Now you have three ways to run this particular macro: (1) Press Control+G, (2) choose Run (by pressing Alt+F3 or choosing Tools Macro Run) and select the range name \G, or (3) choose Run and select the range name \GOTO_RANGE.

6. Save MACROS.WK3.

Press:	CTRL+S

Using the Transcript Window to Create a Macro

Most of the time, it is fairly simple to create a keystroke macro by typing commands in the worksheet and writing down the commands as you type them. However, this can be a tedious process if the keystroke macro is a long one, and inconvenient if paper and pencil are not handy. 1-2-3 provides a feature that simplifies creating keystroke macros: the *Transcript window*.

All the time 1-2-3 is running, the program records all your actions as keystrokes in the Transcript window. This window can hold up to 512 characters representing your most recent keystrokes. When the Transcript window is full, the oldest characters in the buffer are effectively "pushed out" to make room for new ones. You can view the contents of the Transcript window at any time with the Tools Macro Show Transcript command.

To create a macro using the Transcript window, you: (1) Erase the Transcript window, so it will contain only the keystrokes for the task you'll be performing; (2) move the cell pointer to the cell where you will start the task, if that location is important; (3) perform the task you want to automate so it's recorded in the Transcript window; (4) copy the working macro from the Transcript window into a worksheet; and (5) label, name, and document the macro in the normal manner. Between the time you record a task and copy it into a worksheet, you also can run a macro in the Transcript window and edit the keystrokes, if necessary.

How 1-2-3 Records Keystrokes and Mouse Clicks

The Transcript window stores letters, numbers, and punctuation characters the same way you type them. It stores mouse actions as their keystroke equivalents, and menu choices as the underlined letters in the command names (Tools Macro Show Transcript becomes {ALT}tms). Selections inside dialog boxes are recorded as the combination of ALT and the selection's underlined letter. (The "Right" option in the Range Name Label Create dialog box is recorded as {ALT "r"}.)

To save space in the buffer, 1-2-3 abbreviates macro key names and uses repetition factors for multiple presses of the same key. For example, {RIGHT} is stored as {R}; three consecutive presses of the Right key would be recorded as {R 3}. 1-2-3 also consolidates consecutive presses of the Escape key into {CE} ({CLEARENTRY}) when the purpose of pressing Escape is to clear the edit line or a text box. When Control+Break is used to exit a menu, {ESC} keystrokes are recorded instead of {BREAK}.

Alt+F1 (Compose), Alt+F2 (Record), Alt+F3 (Run), Alt+F5 (Undo), Break, Caps Lock, Shift, Num Lock, and Scroll Lock are not recorded in the Transcript window. Function keys are recorded as the equivalent macro commands, so 1-2-3 records {GOTO}, not {F5}. If you run a backslash macro such as \G, 1-2-3 records it as {\G}, but does not record the keystrokes that make up \G.

Recording a Macro

To see how this works, use the Transcript window to record a macro that you will use instead of the Range Name Label Create command. Although using the Transcript window for a simple macro such as this one is probably more effort than it's worth, this exercise familiarizes you with the process. For more complicated keystroke macros, recording in the Transcript window and making corrections there can be a real timesaver.

1. Prepare the label and the range name you will use for this macro.

   You'll use "\l" (for Label) as the label and range name.

Move to:	cell A17
Type:	'\l ⏎ *remember the apostrophe*
Choose:	Range Name Label Create
Select:	Right *if necessary*
	OK

2. Display the Transcript window:

Choose: Tools   Macros   Show Transcript

Figure 11-15: The Transcript Window, When First Displayed

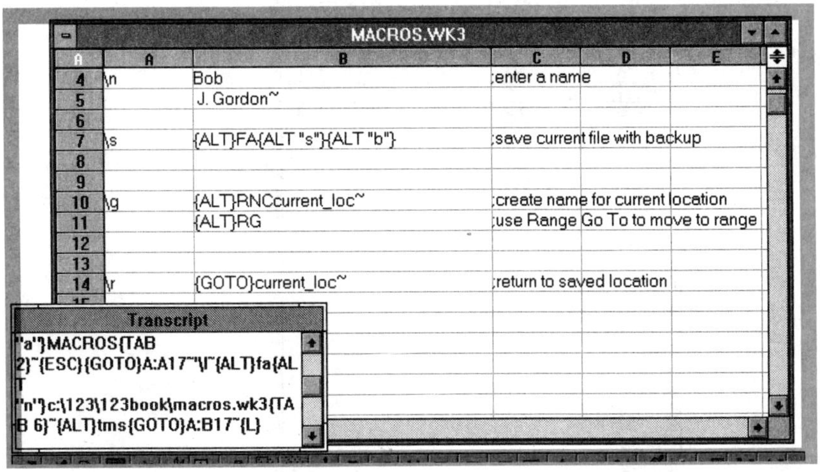

1-2-3 displays the Transcript window, which contains your recent keystrokes. Unlike other windows, the Transcript window does not automatically become the active window when you open it. In order to see the Transcript window and your Worksheet window simultaneously, arrange the windows side by side:

Choose: Window   Tile

3. Make the Transcript window active:

Click on: *anywhere in the Transcript window*

When the Transcript window is active, 1-2-3 displays the Transcript menu in the menu bar. (As with any other window, you could have made the Transcript window active by clicking anywhere in the window, or by choosing the Window command and selecting Transcript.)

4. Erase the current contents.

To start fresh as you record a new macro, erase the current contents of the Transcript window.

Choose: Edit   Clear All

1-2-3 erases the contents of the Transcript window:

5. Make the Worksheet window for MACROS.WK3 active by using the Window command, and perform the task you want to record.

Choose: Window

Select: MACROS.WK3

The cell pointer moves to cell A17 of the MACROS.WK3 Worksheet window.

Choose: Range   Name   Label Create

Select: Right   *even if it is already selected*

               OK

Figure 11-16:   When the Transcript window is active, 1-2-3 displays its menu.

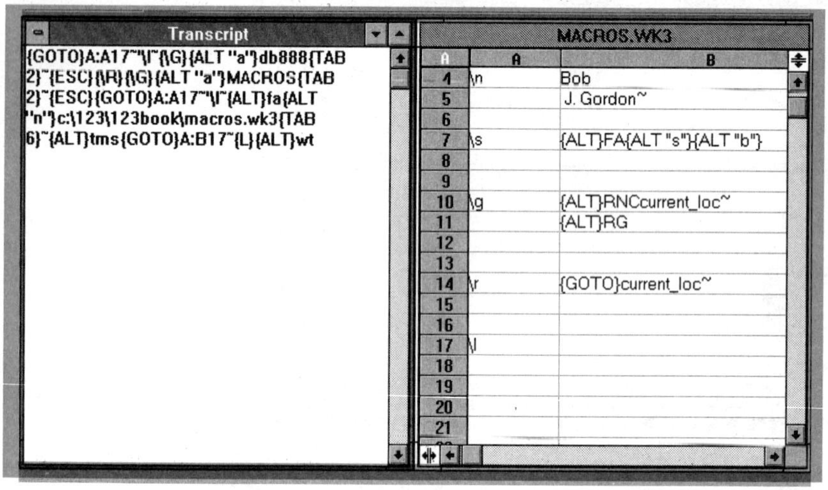

Figure 11-17:   Transcript window is cleared to record a macro.

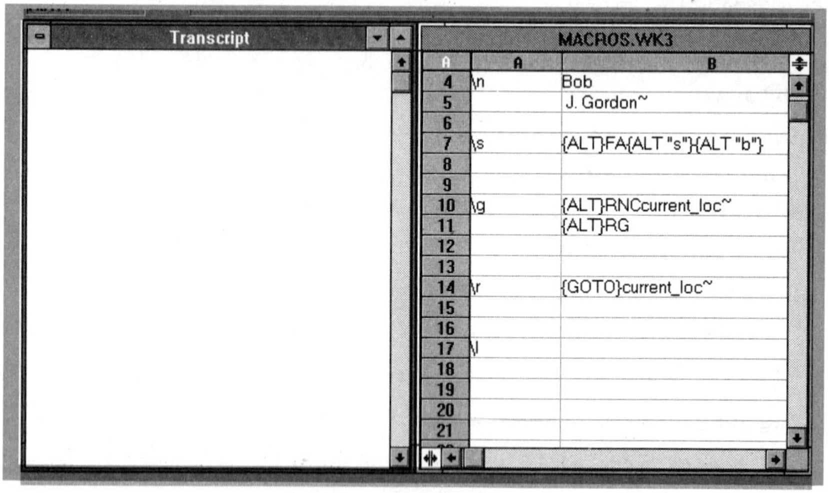

■ *NOTE:*   Selecting the "Right" option button even if it's already selected insures that the option is recorded in the Transcript window. If you didn't select "Right", the effect of the recorded keystrokes would be to accept whatever "Direction" option was selected the last time the Range Name Label Create command was used. The macro would only work when it followed uses of Range Name Label Create where "Right" was selected. In general, when recording keystrokes to create a macro, make sure that all instructions are explicit. Accepting existing settings in the dialog box will cause you problems.

6. Examine the recorded keystrokes in the Transcript window.

The Range Name Label Create is recorded as **{ALT}rnl**. Selecting Right as the direction becomes **{ALT "r"}**. Selecting OK is recorded as pressing Tab the number of times it would take to move from the "Right" option to the OK button, followed by the tilde: **{TAB 2}~**.

Figure 11-18: Transcript Window with Keystrokes for Creating Macro Labels

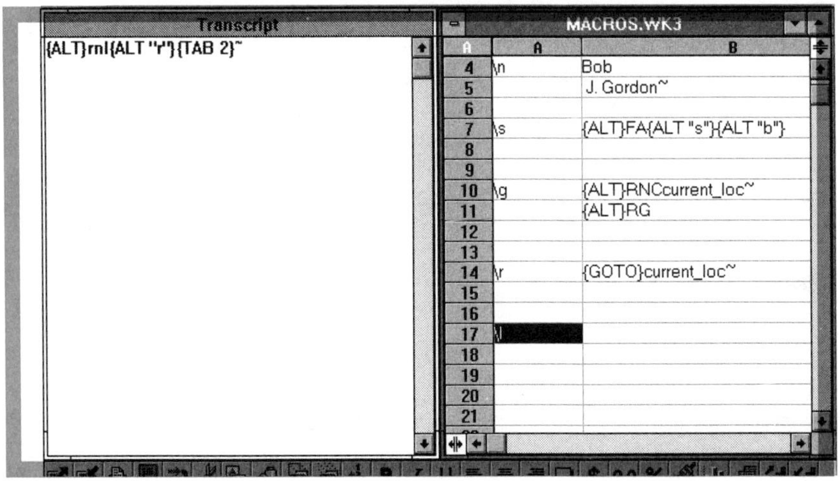

7. Copy the macro from the Transcript window to the worksheet.

Select the recorded keystrokes.

Highlight: *keystrokes shown in Figure 11-19*

Figure 11-19: Keystrokes to Copy from Transcript Window

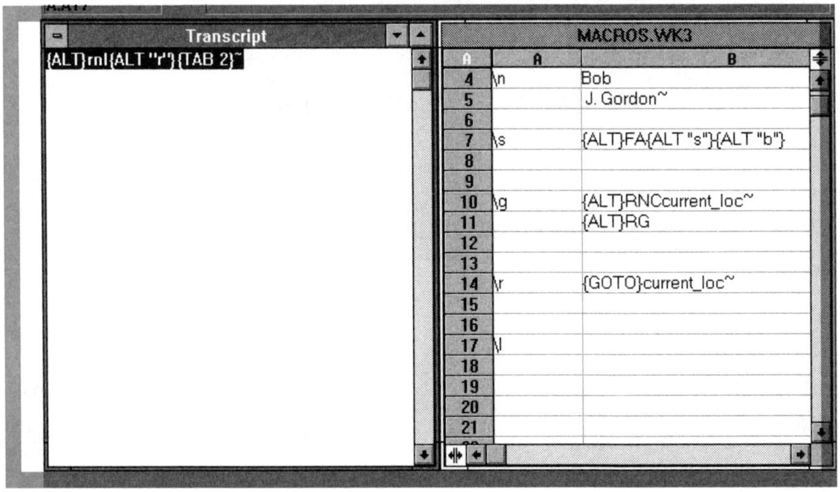

Choose: Edit   Copy

Move to: cell B17   *in MACROS.WK3*

Choose: Edit   Paste

Select: *the Maximize button in MACROS.WK3 window*

     1-2-3 pastes the copied keystrokes into cells B17 and B18.

Figure 11-20: Keystroke Macro Pasted into the Worksheet (Figure Adjusted to Show Column A)

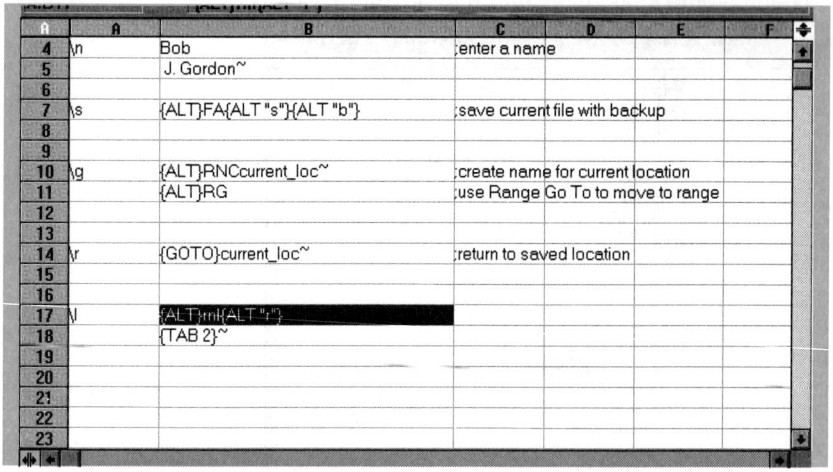

8. Complete the macro by documenting it.

Move to: cell C17

Type: ;create range name(s) from label(s)   ⏎

Figure 11-21: Recorded Macro with Name and Documentation

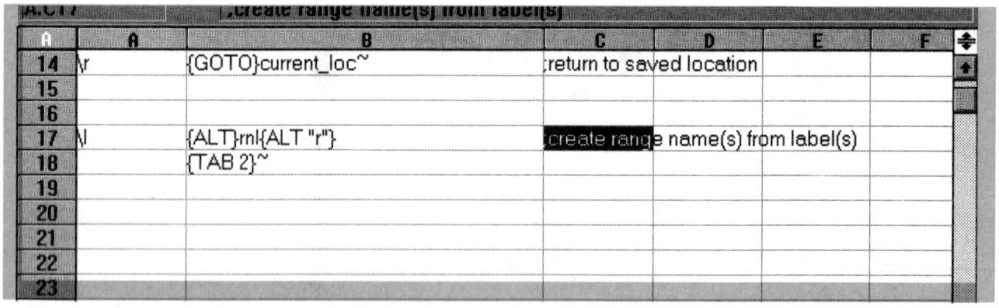

9. Test the macro in the worksheet.

Move to: cell A20

Type: test   ⏎

Press: CTRL+L

Simultaneously verify that the macro worked, and clean up the unneeded label and range name.

Press: DELETE *to delete "test" from cell A20*

Choose: `Range Name Delete`

Select: `TEST`
`OK`

The presence of TEST in the list box confirms that the macro worked. You will use the \L macro throughout the remainder of this chapter.

10. Save MACROS.WK3, retaining a backup.

Press: CTRL+S

Macro Commands

Keystroke macros can save you a lot of time, but it is possible to do much more with macros than just reproduce keystrokes. Alone or in combination with keystrokes, *macro commands* can completely automate almost any 1-2-3 task.

Most operations that a macro can perform using keystroke sequences—such as transferring data from cell to cell, erasing data from cells, or creating and editing new cell entries—can also be accomplished using 1-2-3 macro commands. In fact, in many cases, using macro commands for these purposes is faster and more convenient than using the corresponding keystroke sequence. But macro commands don't just provide an alternative way to accomplish keystroke procedures. They also extend 1-2-3's macro capabilities beyond what can be accomplished with keystroke sequences alone. You can use macro commands to perform an individual task or a complex series of tasks. You can even create macro-driven applications with your own customized menus, commands, and procedures.

Macro Command Syntax

Each macro command uses one of 1-2-3's macro keywords, and derives its name from that particular keyword. In some cases the command consists simply of the keyword enclosed in braces. In most cases, however, one or more arguments are required to complete the command. (Only a few macro commands do not take any arguments.) The arguments appear in the braces along with the macro command.

Figure 11-22: Syntax of a Macro Command

```
{KEYWORD}
or
{KEYWORD argument1,argument2,...argumentn}
```

Open brace   Space   Argument   Close brace

An argument specifies the information the macro command will act upon. You can think of a macro command as a verb in a sentence and the argument as the object. The macro command, like a verb, gives the action; the argument is what is acted upon or used by the macro command. For example, the {BRANCH} command tells 1-2-3 to continue executing macro instructions in another location in the worksheet file. The BRANCH keyword is followed by a single space, then by one argument:

```
{BRANCH totals}
```

Here, the {BRANCH} command tells 1-2-3 to continue executing the macro at the first cell in the range named TOTALS. Macro commands often take more than one argument. The first argument is separated from the macro keyword by one space, and the arguments are separated from each other with commas or semicolons. (This book always uses commas, for consistency. If you work in a setting where the comma is used in decimal numbers, you should use periods or semi-colons to separate arguments.) For instance, the {LET} command enters a label or a value in a cell. The command takes two arguments: A location, and a label or value. The LET keyword is followed by a space, the first argument, an argument separator, and the second argument.

```
{LFT result,37}
```

This particular {LET} instruction assigns the value 37 to a cell named RESULT. The command consists of the keyword LET and two arguments: The cell to receive the value (in this case, the cell named RESULT), and the value itself (in this case, 37).

In general, there should be at most one space character in a macro command; the space used to separate the keyword from the first argument. You cannot put spaces between arguments. Where appropriate, however, you can put space characters within the arguments. For example, the macro command {GETLABEL} displays a prompt and waits for the person running the macro to type in a label. Then it stores the label in a specified worksheet cell. {GETLABEL} needs two arguments. The first argument serves as a prompt. The second argument names a worksheet location in which 1-2-3 is to store the data entered after the prompt. The full syntax of {GETLABEL} is:

```
{GETLABEL prompt,location}
```

The prompt can contain spaces. For example:

```
{GETLABEL "Enter Last Name: ",last_name}
```

This {GETLABEL} command says: "Get a label using the prompt 'Enter Last Name: ' and put the label in the location named LAST_NAME." There is one space between the keyword GETLABEL and the first quotation mark, and there are spaces on either side of the word Last and between the colon and the second quotation mark.

■ **NOTE:** You must enclose the prompt for the {GETLABEL} command in double quotation marks ("") if the prompt includes a comma, semicolon, or colon.

Categories of Macro Commands

Macro commands can be grouped into nine broad categories:

- *Interactive.* Interactive commands control the interaction between the person running the macro and 1-2-3. They "pause" the macro to get input from the keyboard, and they determine whether or not you can break out of a running macro. In addition, they can create customized menus similar to the menus 1-2-3 displays.
- *Data manipulation.* Data manipulation commands enter, edit, and erase cell entries.
- *Flow-of-control.* Flow-of-control commands determine the order in which 1-2-3 executes macro statements. Macro commands for flow-of-control are similar to those in many other programming languages. They include branching, looping, conditional processing, and subroutine calls.
- *Text file manipulation.* Text file manipulation commands create and move data between text (ASCII) files. Using file-manipulation commands, a macro can transfer information between worksheets and text files on a character-by-character or line-by-line basis. (This capability is completely independent of 1-2-3's File and Print commands.)
- *Screen control.* Screen control commands control what you see (and hear) when you run a macro. They can freeze the screen or control panel, change the mode indicator, and also sound a variety of tones to get the macro user's attention.
- *Window Control.* Window control commands move 1-2-3 windows, size them, and make them active. These commands allow you to control the size and layout of your 1-2-3 windows as a macro runs. They also are used to make active a window in which subsequent macro commands are to execute.
- *External Table Control.* External table control commands let you control transactions in external databases to which you connect from 1-2-3.
- *Clipboard.* Clipboard commands cut and copy data to the Windows Clipboard, and paste data from the Clipboard.
- *Dynamic Data Exchange.* Dynamic Data Exchange (DDE) commands allow you to create and manipulate links between 1-2-3 and other active Windows applications.

To give you an idea of the scope of 1-2-3's macro command language, each macro command is briefly described in Table 11-4. For a complete description of specific macro commands, see the 1-2-3 online Help.

Table 11-4: Macro Command Summary

Command	Description
Interactive Commands	
{?}	Pauses macro execution to let you move the cell pointer or enter data. Macro execution resumes as soon as you press Enter.
{BREAK}	Has the effect of pressing Control+Break to return 1-2-3 to READY mode from a menu or submenu. (For example, at the start of a macro, to be sure you are in READY mode.)
{BREAKOFF}	Prevents the current macro from being interrupted by pressing Control+Break.
{BREAKON}	Reverses the effects of {BREAKOFF}, enabling the current macro to be interrupted by pressing Control+Break.
{FORM}	Pauses macro execution so a user can enter data in a specified range, and gives you more control over user input.
{FORMBREAK}	Cancels the current {FORM} command, or, in the case of nested forms, moves up one form level.
{GET}	Pauses macro execution until you press a key, and then stores that keystroke in a cell.
{GETLABEL}	Displays a prompt in the 1-2-3 Classic menu, waits for a response, then enters the response as a label in the specified cell. The response is completed when the user presses Enter.
{GETNUMBER}	Displays a prompt in the 1-2-3 Classic menu, waits for a response, then enters the response as a number in the specified cell. The response is completed when the user presses Enter.
{LOOK}	Checks the type-ahead buffer, in which 1-2-3 stores keystrokes while non-interactive parts of macros are executing. Stores the first keystroke in the buffer, if any, in the specified cell.
{MENUBRANCH}	Displays a customized menu in the 1-2-3 Classic menu, waits for you to select an item, then branches to the macro instructions associated with the selected menu item.
{MENUCALL}	Displays a customized menu in the 1-2-3 Classic menu, waits for you to select an item, then executes the macro instructions in the specified subroutine. After the subroutine has been executed, macro execution continues with the instruction following the {MENUCALL} instruction.
{WAIT}	Pauses macro instruction until the specified time. Time is specified as a time serial number (as explained in the Tips section of Chapter 4). NOTE: You can use @functions to calculate the date and time instead of calculating the numbers yourself. For example, {WAIT @NOW+@TIME(0,1,0)} pauses macro execution for one minute.
Data Manipulation Commands	
{APPENDBELOW}	Copies the contents of a specified source range to the cells immediately below the specified target range.
{APPENDRIGHT}	Copies the contents of a specified source range to the cells immediately to the right of the specified target range.

Command	Description
{BLANK}	Erases the contents of a cell or range. Similar to highlighting a range and pressing Delete.
{CONTENTS}	Copies the contents of one cell to another cell as a label. Combines some of the capabilities of Edit Quick Copy and Range Format.
{LET}	Enters a specified number or label in a specified cell.
{PUT}	Enters a specified number or label in a cell identified by a column/row offset within a specified range.
{RECALC}	Recalculates a specified range, proceeding row by row.
{RECALCCOL}	Recalculates a specified range, proceeding column by column.

Flow-of-Control Commands

Command	Description
{subroutine}	Transfers macro execution to the indicated subroutine. When that subroutine ends, macro execution resumes with the keystroke immediately following the subroutine call.
{BRANCH}	Transfers macro execution to a specified location.
{DEFINE}	Used in subroutines. Allows you to assign arguments passed to a subroutine to worksheet cells, so you can use them.
{DISPATCH}	Transfers macro execution to the cell whose name or address is in the specified location.
{FOR}	Repeats a call to a subroutine a specified number of times.
{FORBREAK}	Used in subroutines called by {FOR} commands to end the subroutine and the {FOR} command. Execution continues at the first character after the {FOR} command.
{IF}	Tests a specified condition. If the condition is TRUE, 1-2-3 executes the remaining keystrokes in the cell containing the {IF} command. If the condition is FALSE, 1-2-3 skips the remaining keystrokes in the cell containing the {IF} command, and immediately executes the keystrokes in the next cell in the column.
{ONERROR}	Transfers macro execution to a specified location if an error occurs.
{QUIT}	Ends a macro and returns 1-2-3 to READY mode.
{RESTART}	Clears the subroutine stack during macro execution. This prevents the subroutine from returning to the calling macro, and causes macro execution to end when either a {RETURN} or the last statement in the subroutine is encountered.
{RETURN}	Used in subroutines to return control to the macro instruction just after the subroutine call or {MENUCALL} command in the calling routine.
{SYSTEM}	Temporarily suspends the 1-2-3 session and executes the specified operating system command. Similar in function to switching to the Windows Program Manager, selecting the Windows DOS prompt icon, issuing a DOS command, exiting DOS, and switching back to 1-2-3.

Command	Description
Text File Manipulation Commands	
{CLOSE}	Closes a text file opened by {OPEN}.
{FILESIZE}	Determines the number of bytes in a text file opened by {OPEN} and enters the number in a specified cell. Ignored if no file is currently open.
{GETPOS}	Determines the position of the byte pointer in a text file opened by {OPEN} and enters it as a number in a specified cell. (The *byte pointer* keeps track of where, in the open file, 1-2-3 is currently reading or writing.)
{OPEN}	Opens a specified text file for processing by the current macro.
{READ}	Copies a specified number of bytes (characters) from a text file opened by {OPEN} into a specified cell.
{READLN}	Copies the remainder of the current line in a file opened by {OPEN} to a specified cell.
{SETPOS}	Sets the byte pointer to a new position in a file opened by {OPEN}.
{TABLE-DISK-FILES}	Pastes into a worksheet range a table showing the files on disk.
{WRITE}	Copies the specified string to a text file opened by the {OPEN} command, starting at the current byte-pointer position.
{WRITELN}	Copies the specified string and an end-of-line sequence to a text file opened by {OPEN}, starting at the current byte-pointer position.
Screen Control Commands	
{BEEP}	Causes the computer to beep in one of four specified tones.
{FRAMEOFF}	Turns off the display of the worksheet frame (column letters, row numbers, worksheet letters, and grid lines) during the execution of the current macro.
{FRAMEON}	Restores the display of the worksheet frame, if it has been turned off by {FRAMEOFF}.
{GRAPHOFF}	Restores the current Worksheet window, reversing the effects of {GRAPHON}.
{GRAPHON}	Without pausing macro execution, displays the current graph in the Graph window, or makes a graph the current graph with or without displaying it. (This command is useful in presenting macro-driven slide shows.)
{INDICATE}	Changes the mode indicator in the control panel to the specified character string.
{PANELOFF}	Freezes the control panel and the status line. Changes 1-2-3 would normally show during execution of the current macro are not displayed.
{PANELON}	Unfreezes the control panel and status line if they had been frozen by {PANELOFF}; otherwise, has no effect.
{WINDOWSOFF}	Freezes the Worksheet window. Changes that 1-2-3 would normally show during execution of the current macro are not displayed.

Command	Description
{WINDOWSON}	Unfreezes the Worksheet window if it has been frozen by {WINDOWSOFF}; otherwise, has no effect.

Window Control Commands

Command	Description
{SELECT-VIEW}	Makes active a Worksheet window, Graph window, or the Transcript window.
{SET "APP"}	Moves the 1-2-3 window and changes its size.
{SET "APP_STATE"}	Minimizes, maximizes, or restores the 1-2-3 window.
{SET "VIEW"}	Minimizes, maximizes, or restores a Worksheet window, Graph window, or the Transcript window.
{SET "VIEW_STATE"}	Move the active window or a specified window and changes the window's size.

External Database Control Commands

Command	Description
{COMMIT}	Commits all pending transactions in a given database, or in all databases if you don't specify any arguments.
{ROLLBACK}	Commits all pending transactions in a given database, or in all databases if you don't specify any arguments.

Clipboard Commands

Command	Description
{EDIT_CLEAR}	Deletes the current selection without copying it to the Clipboard.
{EDIT_COPY}	Copies the current selection to the Clipboard.
{EDIT_COPY_GRAPH}	Copies a graph to the Clipboard.
{EDIT_CUT}	Copies the current selection to the Clipboard, then deletes the selection.
{EDIT_PASTE}	Copies the contents of the Clipboard to the current selection.
{EDIT_PASTE_LINK}	Creates a Dynamic Data Exchange link between the active worksheet file and a file (created with a Windows application that supports DDE) from which the current contents of the Clipboard were cut or copied.

Dynamic Data Exchange Commands

Command	Description
{DDE-ADVISE}	Defines the name of a macro (or subroutine in a macro) that will execute whenever there is a change in data to which a DDE link has been created.
{DDE-CLOSE}	Closes the current DDE conversation.
{DDE-EXECUTE}	Sends a command to the Windows application with which 1-2-3 is having the current conversation.

Command	Description
{DDE-OPEN}	Initiates a conversation with a Windows application and makes it the current conversation.
{DDE-POKE}	Sends an unsolicited range of data from 1-2-3 to a server Windows application.
{DDE-REQUEST}	Requests that data be sent from a Windows application to a range in a 1-2-3 worksheet.
{DDE-UNADVISE}	Cancels the effect of a {DDE-ADVISE} command.
{DDE-USE}	Makes an existing conversation the current conversation.
{LAUNCH}	Starts a Windows application. (You can only have DDE conversations with applications that are currently running; you must launch an application if it is not running.)
{LINK-ASSIGN}	Defines a 1-2-3 range as the destination for an existing link between the active worksheet file and another file created with 1-2-3 or another Windows application.
{LINK-CREATE}	Creates a DDE link between the current worksheet file and another file created with 1-2-3 or another Windows application.
{LINK-DEACTIVATE}	Deactivates, but does not destroy, an existing DDE link.
{LINK-DELETE}	Deletes an existing DDE link.
{LINK-REMOVE}	Cancels the effect of a {LINK-ASSIGN} command, so that a 1-2-3 range is no longer defined as the destination for a link.
{LINK-TABLE}	Pastes into a worksheet range a table showing all existing DDE links for the current worksheet file.
{LINK-UPDATE}	Reactivates a currently deactivated link.

The /X Macro Commands

Early releases of 1-2-3 used a series of commands that began with the characters /X to create macros. All /X commands have corresponding macro commands in 1-2-3/W. The newer macro commands offer greater flexibility in designing 1-2-3 macros; however, to maintain compatibility with previous releases, 1-2-3/W also contains all of the /X commands. These commands and their corresponding macro commands are described in Table 11-5.

■ *CAUTION:* Execute /X commands from within a macro only in READY mode. Executing a /X command in the middle of another 1-2-3 command may produce unexpected results.

Table 11-5: /X Commands and Corresponding Macro Commands

/X Command	Macro Command	Function
/XC*location*	{subroutine}	Calls a subroutine.
/XG*location*	{BRANCH}	Continues macro execution at the specified location.

/X Command	Macro Command	Function
/XIcondition	{IF}	Allows if-then conditional execution.
/XLmessage,location	{GETLABEL}	Displays a message in the 1-2-3 Classic menu, accepts a label entry from the keyboard, and stores the entry in a cell.
/XMlocation	{MENUBRANCH}	Displays a user-defined menu.
/XNmessage,location	{GETNUMBER}	Displays a message in the 1-2-3 Classic menu, accepts a number entry from the keyboard, and stores the entry in a cell.
/XQ	{QUIT}	Quits macro execution.
/XR	{RETURN}	Returns flow of control from a subroutine to the calling routine.

Using Macro Commands

This section introduces you to macros that use macro commands. It begins with a description of how you interrupt a macro that is executing. It then shows you how to create two macros that automatically rerun themselves, and demonstrates how to make a macro behave differently, depending on user input.

Interrupting Macro Execution

From the time a macro starts until it ends, control of the 1-2-3 session belongs to the macro. A typical utility macro runs for a few seconds and then ends, leaving 1-2-3 in READY mode. Macro applications, on the other hand, may run for several minutes or more. At times, you may need to regain control of the session before a macro ends, and some macros, such as the simple looping macros you are going to create in the next section, *must* be interrupted, or they will run indefinitely.

To interrupt a macro while it is running, press Control+Break. 1-2-3 will stop the macro and display an error message. Pressing Escape clears the error and returns you to READY mode.

■ *NOTE:* Sometimes, you may not want to interrupt a macro, but merely pause it. You can pause a macro that sends output to the screen by pressing Control+Num Lock. This is useful when you have to leave the computer for awhile, and you are running a long macro that requires you to interact with it or monitor its results. Pressing any key restarts the macro.

Using the {BRANCH} and {?} Commands in a Looping Macro

In this section, you are going to create a macro that repeats itself until you press Control+Break to end it. This type of macro, called a *looping macro*, is useful when you want to do a series of repetitive tasks; you can use a looping macro instead of running the macro over and over again.

Entering records in a database can be a time-consuming process. 1-2-3 can't type names, addresses, and phone numbers for you, but it can automate the other aspects of creating a database table. The \E (for "Enter records") macro makes it easier to enter data in a database table.

The macro uses the {?} command to wait for input, and the pointer-movement keys to move the cell pointer to the appropriate field. The {?} command is a general-purpose interactive macro command. It pauses macro execution and waits for input from the keyboard (in this case, a field in the record). When you press Enter, macro execution resumes with the instruction following the {?} command.

{BRANCH} is a Flow-of-control command. It tells 1-2-3 to continue executing the macro at a specified location. The {BRANCH} command causes the macro to loop so that, after you've entered one record, the macro automatically repeats so you can enter another.

You will enter the macro in worksheet A of MACROS.WK3. Unlike the other macros you have created so far, this one is tailored to a specific application. In this case, you will build the macro so it can create a simple name and address list in a new worksheet in the MACROS.WK3 file. (Later in the chapter you will modify this macro in different ways to make it more flexible.)

1. Create a new worksheet and title it PHONE LIST.

   First, insert a new worksheet in MACROS.WK3 to hold your new database table. Give it a title and range name:

Select:	`Worksheet    Insert`
Select:	`Sheet`
	`After`
	`OK`
Type:	`PHONE LIST` *in cell A1 of the new worksheet*
Choose:	`Range    Name    Create`
Type:	`phonelist` ⏎ *the range name*
Press:	⬇ *two times*

2. Enter field names for the telephone list.

   Type in the field names for the telephone list so your worksheet looks like Figure 11-23 (shown on the next page). To make the entries easy to read, use Worksheet Global Settings to change the global column width of the worksheet to 14, then use Worksheet Column Width to change the width of column D to 16.

3. Label, then name the data-entry macro using the \L macro you created earlier.

   Place the data-entry macro in worksheet A, along with the other macros you have created in this chapter:

Move to:	*cell A:A21*
Type:	`'\e`
	⏎
Press:	CTRL+L

Figure 11-23: Field Names for a Phone List Database Table

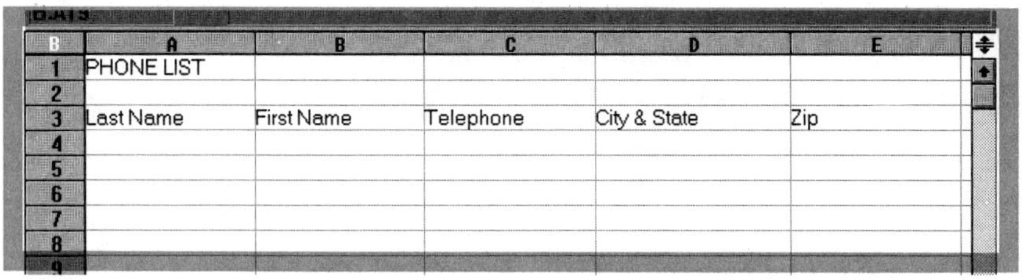

4. Create and document the data-entry macro.

Now enter the macro by typing in the keystrokes in Setup Table 11-1. Except for cells A21, B23, and B26, you do not have to type label prefixes, so they are not indicated in the Setup Table. Notice that you can copy some of the entries, rather than typing them all in from scratch. When you are finished, your screen should look like Figure 11-24.

■ *NOTE:*   The keystrokes shown for cells B23 and B26 in Setup Table 11-1 consist of two single-gle apostrophe (') characters each. The first apostrophe is the label prefix; the second causes the macro to type an apostrophe before numeric entries so that 1-2-3 will interpret them as labels. 1-2-3 will display only the second of the two apostrophes you type in cells B23 and B26.

Setup Table 11-1: A Data-entry Macro

A	B	C
21 \e	{?} {RIGHT}	;enter Last Name
22	{?} {RIGHT}	;enter First Name
23	"	;type a label prefix
24	{?} {RIGHT}	;enter Telephone
25	{?} {RIGHT}	;enter City & State
26	"	;type a label prefix
27	{?}~	;enter zip code
28	{END} {LEFT} {DOWN}	;--> next record
29	{BRANCH\e}	;do it all again.

Figure 11-24: The Data-entry Macro in the Worksheet

	A	B	C	D	E	F
20						
21	\e	{?}{RIGHT}	;enter Last Name			
22		{?}{RIGHT}	;enter First Name			
23		'	;type a label prefix			
24		{?}{RIGHT}	;enter Telephone			
25		{?}{RIGHT}	;enter City and State			
26		'	;type a label prefix			
27		{?}~	;enter zip code			
28		{END}{LEFT}{DOWN}	;–>next record			
29		{BRANCH \e}	;do it all again			
30						
31						
32						

5. Test the data-entry macro.

The macro assumes you are starting out in the leftmost cell of the first record you want to create. Test the macro by moving the cell pointer to the beginning of the first database record and pressing Control+E:

Move to: cell B:A4

Press: CTRL+E

At first, it looks as though nothing has happened. However, if you look at the status line, you will see that the Cmd indicator is turned on, indicating that the macro is running. 1-2-3 is waiting for you to type in the first field of the first record. (Later in the chapter, you'll use the {GETLABEL} macro so the user is prompted to type the data.) Enter a last name:

Type: Brown

Press: ⏎

Figure 11-25: Macro Advances Cell Pointer to the First Name Field

	A	B	C	D	E
1	PHONE LIST				
2					
3	Last Name	First Name	Telephone	City & State	Zip
4	Brown				
5					
6					
7					
8					
9					

1-2-3 enters the name Brown into cell A4 and automatically advances the cell pointer to cell B4. Complete the remainder of the record:

Type: David

Press: ⏎

Type:	6175559871
Press:	⏎
Type:	Cambridge, MA
Press:	⏎
Type:	02138
Press:	⏎

1-2-3 completes the record and automatically moves the cell pointer to cell B:A5, where it waits for you to enter the first field of the next record. Notice that the macro automatically placed a label prefix in front of the numbers you typed in cells B:C4 and B:E4 so that these numbers would be interpreted as labels, not as numbers. If you wish, continue to enter names, addresses, and phone numbers, to get a better feel for running the macro. When you are finished, end the macro by pressing Control+Break:

Press: CTRL+BREAK

⏎ *or click OK, to clear ERROR message*

6. Save MACROS.WK3.

Press: CTRL+S

Creating Conditional Macros with the {IF} Command

Looping macros let you repeat a sequence of commands as many times as you like. *Conditional macros* let you execute a different sequence of commands, depending on a certain worksheet condition (for example, the contents of a particular cell).

You use the {IF} macro command to implement a conditional macro. The {IF} command works somewhat like the @IF function, in that it tests a certain condition. If the condition is TRUE, one thing happens; if the condition is FALSE, a different thing happens.

The syntax of the {IF} command is:

```
{IF condition}
```

Usually, "condition" is a logical formula. If the condition is TRUE (the result of the test is neither zero, ERR, nor NA), 1-2-3 executes the remaining instructions in the cell containing the {IF} command. If the condition is FALSE (the result of the test is 0, ERR, or NA), execution continues with the instructions below the cell containing the {IF} command.

The following simple macro uses the {BLANK} command to erase a cell named QUITFLAG. It then uses the {GET} command to get a single character from the keyboard and put that character in QUITFLAG. The macro tests QUITFLAG: If the character in QUITFLAG is Q or q, the macro quits; otherwise, the macro branches back to the label REPEAT, where it waits for another character to be typed. The macro continues to run until you type the letter Q (or press Control+Break). Executing {QUIT} is a more graceful way to leave a looping macro than pressing Control+Break. Several of the macros later in this chapter use a similar technique to end gracefully.

Setup Table 11-2:   A Macro That Uses the {IF} Command

A	B	C
61 '\q	{BLANK quitflag}	;make sure flag is not Q
62 REPEAT	{GET quitflag}{CALC}	;store input in QUITFLAG and redisplay
63	{IF quitflag="Q"}{QUIT}	;end macro if user said quit
64	{BRANCH repeat}	;else get another character
65 QUITFLAG		;keyboard input goes here

If you wish to try this macro, enter it the MACROS.WK3 worksheet starting in cell A:A61, using Setup Table 11-2 as your guide. Use the \L macro to simultaneously assign the range names \Q, REPEAT, and QUITFLAG to cells A:B61, A:B62, and A:B65, respectively. To do so, highlight A:B61..A:B65, then press Control+L. (You could use the Range Name Label Create command instead of \L, if you preferred.) Run the macro to test it. Type Q or q to end the macro.

Figure 11-26:   Highlighting Multiple Labels to Create Multiple Range Names Using \L

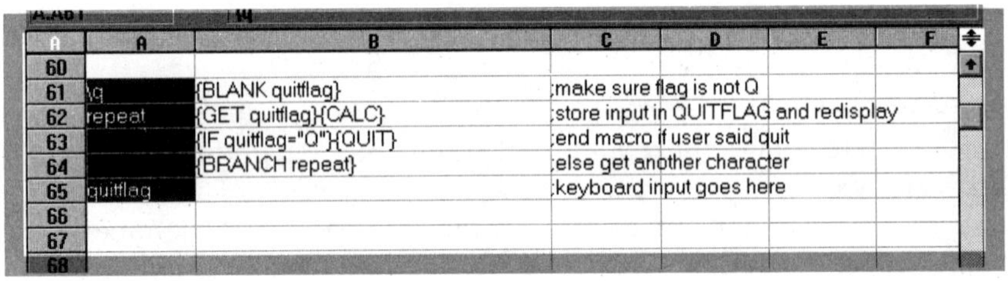

■ **NOTE:**   {IF} commands are often used in conjunction with the {BRANCH} command to control macro execution. If a condition is TRUE, the macro branches to one set of macro instructions. If a condition is FALSE, execution continues with the next cell in the column, and the instructions at the branch location are not executed. By combining several {IF} and {BRANCH} commands, you can test for a series of conditions and have the macro behave differently for each one. The \0 macro in "Automatically Loading a Macro Library" later in this chapter shows a practical use of this technique.

Using Macro Subroutines

You have seen that you can control the order in which 1-2-3 executes macro instructions by using the {BRANCH} and {IF} commands. You can also control macro execution by dividing up the macro into separate parts called *subroutines* and using *subroutine calls* to connect the parts together.

A subroutine is a group of macro instructions like any other group of macro instructions. The difference is in how the instructions are used. While a group of instructions appearing in the middle of many other instructions is executed once, subroutines are often executed several times by the same macro, or even by different macros.

You execute a subroutine by *calling* it from the current macro. To call a subroutine, include the subroutine name in the macro, surrounding it with braces as if the subroutine were a built-in macro command. When 1-2-3 encounters the subroutine call, it starts to execute the instructions in the subroutine. When it has finished executing the subroutine instructions, 1-2-3 returns to the instruction immediately following the subroutine call, and continues to execute the macro there.

A subroutine ends when 1-2-3 encounters a blank cell or a cell with a value. You can also explicitly transfer macro execution from a subroutine back to the routine that called it with the {RETURN} statement.

Calling a subroutine looks like this:

```
\macro          ....            ;start of macro
                ....            ;macro instructions
        ┌─── {subroutine}       ;subroutine call
        │       ... ◄────┐      ;execution continues after subroutine returns
        │       ....     │      ;more macro instructions
        │                │      ;macro ends at blank cell
        │                │
        │                │
subroutine ►    ....     │      ;macro instructions in subroutine
        │       ....     │      ;more macro instructions
        │    {IF condition}     ;conditional return to caller (If TRUE, execute
        │    {RETURN}           ;the following command ({RETURN})
        └───    ....            ;skip to these instructions if condition not TRUE
```

Why Use Subroutines?

There are two main reasons for using subroutines in macros: clarity and economy.

Clarity of Organization   If you are doing a complicated task, it is often easier to understand the task if you divide it into logical steps. Once you understand the larger steps, you can break down each step into the smaller steps required to complete it.

To take an example from life, suppose you have to write a speech. You could sit down and start writing the first word and keep going until you get to the end, but most likely you would not do that. Instead, you would outline the main points you wanted to make, and then flesh out the outline with smaller points and supporting statements. Creating the outline makes it easier to see the whole collection of ideas at a glance, and to skip around as you develop the speech without losing track of the main thread.

Creating a large macro is similar. First, you create a main macro that contains the basic steps the macro is to carry out. Then, you create subroutines, like the parts of a speech you have outlined, to carry out each major step. These subroutines, like the parts of the outlined speech, can be written in any order.

Economy of Construction   The other reason for using subroutines is economy of construction. When your macro must perform the same task more than once, or when the same task must be performed by several macros, you can put the instructions required to do that task into a subroutine and call the subroutine each time the task must be done. This can save a lot of typing, and it also saves memory. Furthermore, using subroutines simplifies macro maintenance: You need only modify a subroutine once, and each part of a macro that calls it is, in effect, automatically updated.

Creating Subroutines

This and the following section briefly introduce you to the technique of creating subroutines in macros. Later in this chapter, you will use subroutines extensively to clarify the construction of the macros you will build. For more information on using subroutines, and on using subroutines with arguments, see the 1-2-3 documentation or a book devoted to writing 1-2-3 macros.

1. Rewrite \E to use subroutines.

   Rewrite the data-entry macro so that it uses a subroutine call to enter each field of a record. Use Setup Table 11-3 as your guide. (To avoid confusion, you may find it easier to erase cells A:B21..A:B29 before you start.)

   Be sure to put a blank row between the GETRIGHT subroutine and the GETLAST subroutine. This will prevent 1-2-3 from executing GETLAST each time GETRIGHT is called. There is no need for a blank row between the main routine and GETRIGHT, since the main routine ends with a {BRANCH} instruction.

■ *NOTE:* The first two keystrokes shown in Setup Table 11-3 for cells A:B28 and A:B30 consist of two single apostrophes ('), not a double quotation mark. The first apostrophe is the label prefix; the second causes the macro to type an apostrophe before numeric entries so that 1-2-3 will interpret them as labels. 1-2-3 will display only the second of the two apostrophes you type in cells A:B28 and A:B30.

Setup Table 11-3: A data-entry Macro With Subroutines

A	B	C
21 '\e	{getright}	;enter Last Name
22	{getright}	;enter First Name
23	{getright}	;enter Telephone
24	{getright}	;enter City and State
25	{getlast}	;enter Zip code
26	{END} {LEFT} {DOWN}	;--> next record
27	{BRANCH \e}	;do it all again.
28 getlast	"{?} {RIGHT}	;get a field,move right
29		
30 getlast	"{?}~	;get last field

Subroutine calls to GETRIGHT replace instructions that get data from the keyboard, and move the cursor one cell to the right. The call to GETLAST in cell B26 gets the last field in the record. Notice that both GETRIGHT and GETLAST type a label prefix before they wait for input from the keyboard. Also notice that the subroutines themselves appear below the macro that calls them. This placement is not required (the subroutines could be anywhere in the worksheet file), but it does make it easier to follow the logic of a macro.

■ *CAUTION:* Do not use a subroutine name that is the same as a macro key name (such as {RIGHT}) or a macro command (such as {QUIT}). If you do, 1-2-3 will execute the subroutine instead of performing the keystroke or macro command.

2. Name the ranges used by \E.

Make sure all the ranges used by the new \E macro are properly named:

Highlight: A:A21..A:A30
Press: CTRL+L

3. Test the new \E macro.

Test the new \E macro the same way you tested the previous version: Move the cell pointer to the first field of the first blank record in the PHONE LIST database (use Control+G phonelist to get to the database), and then press Control+E. Enter several records, and make sure the macro enters each field correctly. When you are satisfied the macro works the same way the earlier version worked, press Control+Break to end the macro.

4. Save MACROS.WK3.

Congratulations! You have used your first macro subroutine. Use Control+S to save the file before you go on to the next exercise.

Using the {FOR} Command with Subroutines

Just as 1-2-3 has a way to specify a repetition factor for macro keys, you can also specify that a subroutine should be called more than once in a row.

The macro you just built calls GETRIGHT four times in a row. The {FOR} command lets you execute the same subroutine several times in a row without having to type in the explicit subroutine call each time. It uses a worksheet cell as a counter to keep track of the number of times the subroutine has been executed. {FOR} requires you to specify the numbers for the counter cell to start at, to stop at, and to increase by, each time the subroutine is executed. These numbers can be actual values, or they can be worksheet cells containing values.

The syntax of the {FOR} command is:

```
{FOR counter,start,stop,step,subroutine}
```

counter	is a cell in which 1-2-3 keeps track of the number of times the subroutine has been executed
start	is the beginning value for the counter
stop	is the end value for the counter
step	is the value by which the counter increases each time 1-2-3 executes the subroutine
subroutine	is the subroutine to be executed by the {FOR} command

For example, the following {FOR} command executes a subroutine called GETRIGHT four times:

```
{FOR counter,1,4,1,getright}
```

In this case, a cell named COUNTER stores how many times the subroutine has been executed. COUNTER automatically starts at 1 (the start value), and—each time GETRIGHT is executed—increases by 1 (the step value). The {FOR} command ends when GETRIGHT has been executed four times (the stop value).

You can use the {FOR} command to streamline the data-entry macro you created earlier. Use Setup Table 11-4 to create a new macro named \F just below the \E macro. This macro uses the {FOR} command to call the GETRIGHT subroutine. After you have typed in the macro instructions, use the \L macro or Range Name Label Create to assign the range names \F, COUNTER, and MAX to cells A:B33, A:B37, and A:B38, respectively.

■ **NOTE:**   The value in cell A:B38 is the number 4, not the label '4. Do *not* type a label prefix before this value.

Setup Table 11-4:   A data-entry Macro With a {FOR} Command

A		B		C
33	'\f	{FOR counter,1,max,1,getright}		;get MAX records
34		{getlast}		;get last record
35		{END} {LEFT} {DOWN}		;get ready for next record
36		{BRANCH \f}		;do it all again
37	counter			;FOR loop counter
38	max		4	;# of times to call GETRIGHT

Besides being considerably shorter than the \E macro, notice that this new macro is more flexible: To adapt the macro to a database with more or fewer fields per record, all you have to do is change the value in the MAX variable in cell A:B38 to one less than the number of fields in a record. Also notice that \F calls the same subroutines you created for the \E macro.

Testing the {FOR} Command Macro   You can test this macro the same way you tested the \E macro. However, if you wish to see how the {FOR} command works, you should split the screen horizontally so you can look at the values change in the counter cell while you enter data in the database table. To do so, take the following steps. Figure 11-27 shows how your screen will look while you are running the macro.

1. Use the Scroll arrow to move cell A:A31 to the upper left corner of the window.

2. Use the Down arrow key to move the cell pointer to row 40.

3. Choose Window Split to split the window into two panes. Select Horizontal as the type of split, and clear the "Synchronize" option.

4. Click anywhere in the lower pane to move the cell pointer to the lower half of the split window. You can use F6 (Pane) if you prefer.

5. Use Control+G or F5 (Goto) to move to cell PHONELIST.

6. Move the cell pointer to the first field of the first blank record in the database table.

7. Press Control+F to start the macro.

As you enter data in the database, watch cell B37 in the upper pane. Notice that the macro first sets this cell to 1, and then increases the value by 1 each time you complete a cell entry.

Figure 11-27: Using a Split Window to View the \F Macro and the COUNTER Cell

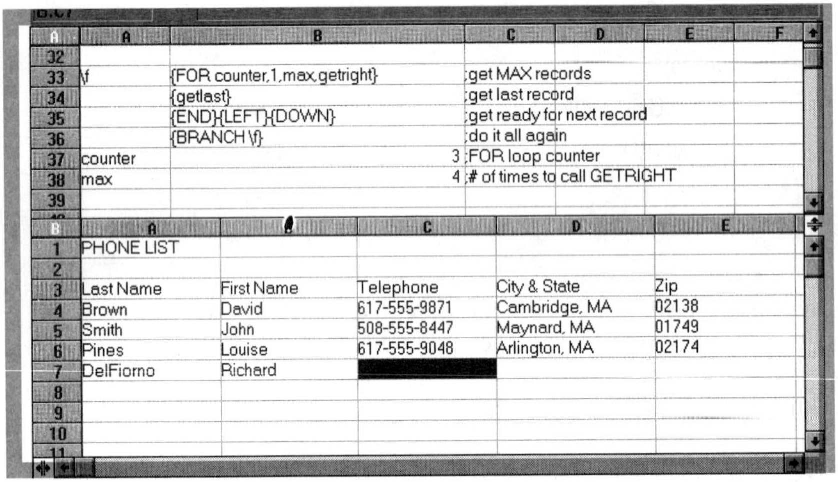

When you are finished experimenting with the \F macro, end it by pressing Control+Break and Escape, then clear the Worksheet windows and save MACROS.WK3:

Choose:	Window	Split
Select:	Clear	*to return to the full-sized window*
	OK	
Press:	CTRL+S	

■ *NOTE:*   This example illustrates the simplest use of the {FOR} command. The {FOR} command actually lets you do much more. See the description of the {FORBREAK} command in the 1-2-3 online Help for some ideas on how to use the {IF}, {FORBREAK}, and {RETURN} commands in conjunction with the {FOR} command.

Creating a Macro Menu

Many tasks involve several specific activities that can easily be presented as items in a menu. Using macro commands, you can create your own menus to do specific tasks. When you select an item from such a menu, the macro automatically executes instructions that perform the task indicated by the menu choice.

For example, a menu for the Business Contacts database you created in Chapter 6 could list a few standard tasks, such as EnterRecord (for entering a new record), Sort (for rearranging records after new ones have been entered), and Quit (for exiting the macro). The macro, when run, would call up this menu. If you selected EnterRecord or Sort, the macro would perform the appropriate operation and then return you to the menu, from which you could make another selection. If you selected Quit, the macro would end, returning you to READY mode.

In this section, you will create a simplified version of such a macro menu, using the small database you created in MACROS.WK3. Later, you will construct a macro menu to enter and sort records in the CONTACTS.WK3 file you created in Chapter 6.

How Macro Menus Work

Macro menus are invoked with the macro commands {MENUBRANCH} and {MENUCALL}. Menus invoked with either of these commands are displayed in the 1-2-3 Classic menu. The menu choices appear at the top of the window. Initially, the first (leftmost) command is highlighted. A one-line description of the highlighted command appears in the next line. You select a menu item by typing the first letter of the menu item, or by highlighting the item (using the Left and Right keys) and pressing Enter. In this case, the macro menu will display the following menu when you press Control+E:

Figure 11-28:   Macro Menu Displayed in the 1-2-3 Classic Menu

■ *NOTE:*   Altogether, a macro menu can have as many as eight menu choices. As long as each choice begins with a different character, you can select a menu item either by highlighting the item and pressing Enter, or by typing the first character of the item.

Building a Macro Menu

In this example, you will create a macro menu that displays a menu with the items EnterRecord (to enter a new record), or Quit (to stop entering records). The EnterRecord item in this macro menu calls a slightly modified version of the \F macro you just created. The Quit item returns you to READY mode without your having to press Control+Break to interrupt the macro.

Build the macro menu in the cells currently occupied by the \E macro. (You no longer need the \E macro, since the new macro does the same thing, only better.)

1. Erase the modified \E macro.

   First, erase the range containing the main loop of the \E macro. You will reuse the subroutines GETRIGHT and GETLAST, so don't erase them!

   Highlight: A:B21..A:C27
   Press: DELETE

2. Move the GETRIGHT and GETLAST subroutines below the \F macro.

You are going to modify the \F macro to make it a subroutine of the macro menu. It will be easier to keep track of what you are doing if you rearrange the worksheet so that the subroutines called by the \F macro are located below the main macro. Move GETRIGHT and

GETLAST below the \F macro. This time, you're going to use the "Move To" icon to move cells. The "Move To" icon looks like this:

Highlight: A:A28..A:C30

Click on: the Move To icon

Move to: cell A40

1-2-3 places the highlighted range in the range beginning at cell A40.

3. Enter and document the macro menu.

Begin to create the new macro in the cell to the right of the \e label. First, type in the {MENUBRANCH} command. The {MENUBRANCH} command takes one argument; the location of the menu items and their related instructions.

Move to: cell A:B21

Type: `{MENUBRANCH datamenu}`

                      `;create menu for record entry`

The menu itself consists of two menu items, EnterRecord and Quit. Each menu item consists of three parts: (1) The menu choice; (2) a one-line description of the menu choice; and (3) the macro instructions necessary to carry out the choice. The menu items are entered in adjacent worksheet columns. The first menu item always goes in the leftmost column of the worksheet area that contains the menu instructions (in this case, column B), with the description and instructions in the cells below it. The next menu item must be entered in the column immediately to the right (column C), with its description and instructions immediately below it. (Each additional menu item goes in the column to the right of the preceding menu item.)

Enter the data-entry menu, using Setup Table 11-5 as your guide. Notice that the EnterRecord menu item contains a call to a subroutine named GETREC. This subroutine is actually the \F macro, which you will rename GETREC after you have modified it for use with the new macro menu.

Setup Table 11-5:   A data-entry Macro With a Menu

A	B	C
21 '\e	{MENUBRANCH datamenu}	;record entry menu
22		
23 datamenu	Enter-Record	Quit
24	Enter a database record	End the macro
25	{getrec}	{QUIT}
26	{BRANCH \e}	

4. Delete blank rows 28 through 32.

For cosmetic purposes, delete some of the blank rows between the macro menu and the \F macro. This will make it easier to view the \E macro and its subroutines on the same screen.

Move to:	*any cell in row 28*
Choose:	`Worksheet   Delete`
Select:	`Row   Range`
Specify:	*cells in rows 28 to 32 as the "Range:"*
Select:	`OK`

5. Modify the \F macro and rename it.

You'll use a slightly modified version of the \F macro to carry out the EnterRecord menu item. Right now, the \F macro is itself a looping macro; however, the looping capability of the \F macro is no longer necessary: Eliminate the {BRANCH} command:

Highlight:	B31..C31
Press:	DELETE

The data-entry macro calls this macro as the subroutine GETREC. Change the label for the macro from \f to getrec, since that is the name you have already used in the DATAMENU macro menu. (You will change the range name for the macro to GETREC in the next step.) When you have finished modifying this macro, your screen should look like Figure 11-28 (shown on the next page).

Move to:	cell A28
Type:	`getrec` ↵

6. Create new range names for the macro menu.

You have finished creating the macro menu. All that remains is to make sure all the range names are correct. The easiest way to do that is with the Range Name Label Create macro:

Highlight: A21..A37
Press: `CTRL+L`

Figure 11-29: \F Macro Converted to GETREC Subroutine

	A	B	C	D	E	F
20						
21	\e	{MENUBRANCH datamenu}	;menu for record entry			
22						
23	datamenu	Enter-Record	Quit			
24		Enter a database record	End the macro			
25		{getrec}	{QUIT}			
26		{BRANCH \e}				
27						
28	getrec	{FOR counter,1,max,1,getright}	;get max records			
29		{getlast}	;get last record			
30		{END}{LEFT}{DOWN}	;get ready for next record			
31						
32	counter		1	;FOR loop counter		
33	max		4	;# of times to call GETRIGHT		
34						
35	getright	'{?}{RIGHT}	;get a field, move right			
36						
37	getlast	'{?}~	;get last field			
38						
39						

7. Test the new version of the data-entry macro.

Carefully examine your worksheet to make sure your macro is the same as the example, then test the macro the same way you have tested the other data-entry macros—by running it.

Begin by moving the cell pointer to the first cell of the first blank row below the PHONE LIST database table. Then, press Control+E to run the macro. 1-2-3 should display the menu in Figure 11-30.

Figure 11-30: Macro menu is displayed for data entry.

	A	B	C	D	E
1	PHONE LIST				
2					
3	Last Name	First Name	Telephone	City & State	Zip
4	Brown	David	617-555-9871	Cambridge, MA	02138
5	Smith	John	508-555-8447	Maynard, MA	01749
6	Pines	Louise	617-555-9048	Arlington, MA	02174
7	DelFiorno	Richard	617-55-3357	Lexington, MA	02179
8					

You can select Enter-Record or Quit. When you select EnterRecord and type in a record, that record is added to the database and the menu is re-displayed.

Choose:	Enter-Record
Type:	Avinger ⏎
	Richard ⏎
	7165554930 ⏎
	Buffalo, NY ⏎
	14221 ⏎

Figure 11-31: Record Added to the Phone List Database Table

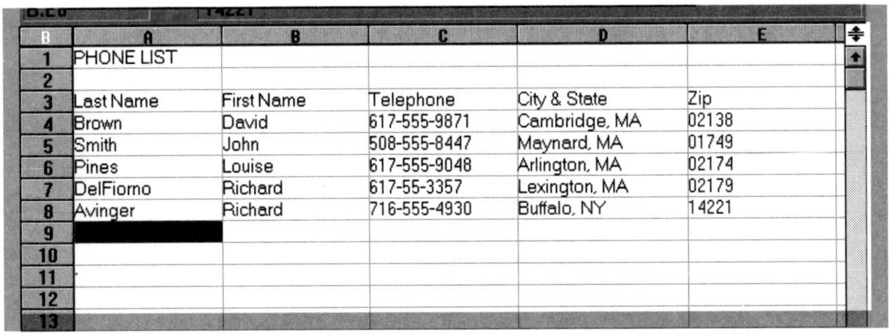

	A	B	C	D	E
1	PHONE LIST				
2					
3	Last Name	First Name	Telephone	City & State	Zip
4	Brown	David	617-555-9871	Cambridge, MA	02138
5	Smith	John	508-555-8447	Maynard, MA	01749
6	Pines	Louise	617-555-9048	Arlington, MA	02174
7	DelFiorno	Richard	617-55-3357	Lexington, MA	02179
8	Avinger	Richard	716-555-4930	Buffalo, NY	14221
9					
10					
11					
12					
13					

Selecting Quit returns you to READY mode:

Choose: Quit

8. Save MACROS.WK3:

Press: CTRL+S

Building and Using a Macro Library

So far, you have built several generally useful macros, and you have somewhat randomly added them to the file MACROS.WK3. In this section, you will start to build a *macro library*. A macro library is a file containing 1-2-3 macros. The library you will begin to build here contains only macros that do not depend on particular worksheet file locations. You will be able to run these macros from any worksheet file and have the macros work correctly, or you will be able to include the macros themselves in any worksheet file.

You are going to build the library from the macros in MACROS.WK3:

1. Create a new file called UTILITY.WK3.

You will build your macro library in a new file, UTILITY.WK3. Building the macro in a new file instead of saving MACROS.WK3 under a new name saves you from having to delete a lot of extraneous range names. It also gives you some practice in the process of transferring macros from one file into another. Create a new file and name it UTILITY.WK3:

Choose:	File	New
Choose:	File	Save As
Type:	utility	
Press:	↵	

2. Widen column B.

Make column B of the new file wide enough to accommodate the macros you will end up storing there, while leaving adequate room for displaying the comments and labels on the same screen. Since you have already debugged these macros, displaying the comments and labels is probably more useful than displaying the actual macro code, so just leave 20 characters for the macros.

Move to:	*any cell in column B*	
Choose:	Worksheet	Column Width
Type:	20	
Press:	↵	

3. Copy the macros in MACROS.WK3 to UTILITY.WK3:

Move to:	cell A:A1 *in MACROS.WK3*	
Highlight:	A:A1..A:C18	
Choose:	Edit	Copy
Press:	CTRL+F6	*to move to UTILITY.WK3*

The cell pointer jumps back to cell A:B1 of UTILITY.WK3. Move left one cell, then paste the copied macros:

Press:	←	
Choose:	Edit	Paste

1-2-3 copies the macros to UTILITY.WK3, but not the range names.

4. Delete the macros you don't want in your library.

You will want to keep and reuse the \S, \G, \R, and \L macros. You can add to these later as you create the macros described later in this chapter. You won't keep \N, so delete it:

Highlight:	*any combination of cells in rows 4 and 5*	
Choose:	Worksheet	Delete
Select:	Row	OK

1-2-3 deletes the \N macro and moves everything up two rows.

5. Give descriptive names to the macros in UTILITY.WK3.

Change the names of the three macros remaining in UTILITY.WK3. Since you may be using them from many files, you will find it much easier to remember what they do if you give them long range names, instead of the two-character names they have in MACROS.WK3.

Label the file-save macro \FILE_SAVE; the "Go to" macro \GOTO_RANGE; the "Return" macro \RETURN; and the "Label" macro \LABEL_RIGHT.

Move to:	cell A5
Type:	'\file_save
Press:	↓ *three times*
Type:	'\goto_range
Press:	↓ *four times*
Type:	'\return
Press:	↓ *three times*
Type:	'\label_right ↵

Figure 11-32: The Macros to Keep: \S, \G, \R and \L

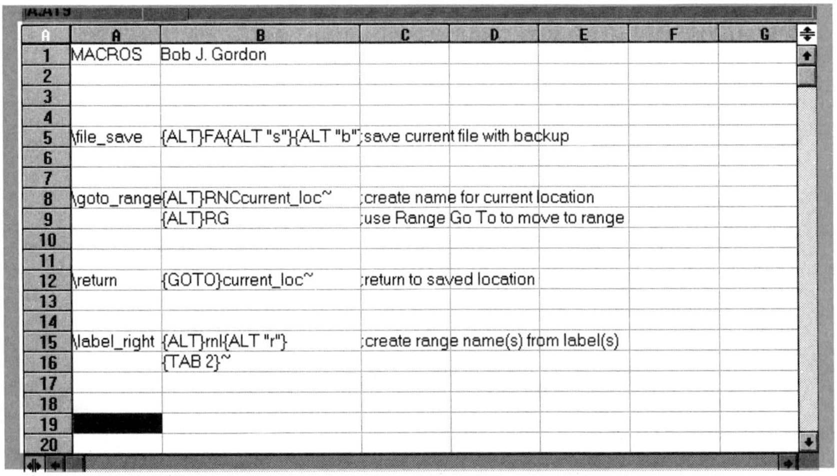

	A	B	C	D	E	F	G
1	MACROS	Bob J. Gordon					
2							
3							
4							
5	\file_save	{ALT}FA{ALT "s"}{ALT "b"}	;save current file with backup				
6							
7							
8	\goto_range	{ALT}RNCcurrent_loc~	;create name for current location				
9		{ALT}RG	;use Range Go To to move to range				
10							
11							
12	\return	{GOTO}current_loc~	;return to saved location				
13							
14							
15	\label_right	{ALT}rnl{ALT "r"}	;create range name(s) from label(s)				
16		{TAB 2}~					
17							
18							
19							
20							

6. Widen column A so you can read these longer macro names more easily:

Choose:	Worksheet Column Width
Type:	13 ↵

7. Name the macros in UTILITY.WK3.

Use Range Name Label Create to create range names for the labelled cells:

Highlight:	A5..A15
Choose:	`Range   Name   Label Create`
Select:	`Right` *if necessary*
	`OK`

This completes the changes to the macros. If you wish, you can further improve the macro library by adding additional comments to the macros, or by creating a Table of Contents on a separate worksheet.

8. Save UTILITY.WK3 using the \FILE_SAVE macro:

Press:	`ALT+F3` **(RUN)**
Select:	`\FILE_SAVE`
	`OK`

9. Create a file to test the macros in UTILITY.WK3.

You are going to create a scratch file in which to test the macros in UTILITY.WK3, to verify that they still work. Open the file CONTACTS.WK3, then save it under a new name to create a test file:

Choose:	`File   Open`
Select:	`CONTACTS.WK3`
	`OK`

1-2-3 opens CONTACTS.WK3 and makes it the current file. Now save the file under a new name:

Choose:	`File   Save As`
Type:	`mactest`
Press:	↵

MACTEST.WK3 is now the current file. UTILITY.WK3 and MACROS.WK3 are still in memory. Close MACROS.WK3 so that only MACTEST.WK3 and UTILITY.WK3 are active. The copy of MACROS.WK3 on disk will remain intact.

Select:	`Window   MACROS.WK3` *to move to MACROS.WK3*
Choose:	`File   Close`

10. Run the macros in UTILITY.WK3 from MACTEST.WK3.

To run a macro from a file that is not the current file, you: (1) Choose Run; (2) double-click the name of the file containing the macro; (3) select the macro from that list; and (4) press

Enter or select OK to execute the macro. With the cell pointer in MACTEST.WK3, use this technique to run the \FILE_SAVE macro:

Move to: <<MACTEST.WK3>>   *if necessary*

Press: | ALT+F3 | **(RUN)**

Double-click: <<UTILITY.WK3>>   *in the list box*

Select: \FILE_SAVE   *as the macro to execute*

OK   *to execute the macro*

The macro saves MACTEST.WK3, retaining a backup.

Figure 11-33:   Running a Macro in UTILITY.WK3 While in MACTEST.WK3

■ *NOTE:*   You must double-click the file name in the list box. Selecting the file and pressing ENTER or selecting OK will not work.

If you find yourself frequently using a macro in a macro library, you can call the macro in the library as a subroutine of a macro in the current file. Perform the following keystrokes to add a call to the \GOTO_RANGE macro in UTILITY.WK3 to a macro in MACTEST.WK3.

■ *NOTE:*   This technique will only work if the file containing the macros is in memory when the macro is run.

First, prepare for this exercise by creating a range name in MACTEST.WK3:

Move to: cell B:A1   *in MACTEST.WK3*

Choose: Range   Name   Create

Type: contacts_db   ENTER

Insert a new worksheet in MACTEST.WK3 and label it MACROS:

Choose: Worksheet   Insert

Select: Sheet
           After

           OK

Type: MACROS
Press: ↓   *three times*

Figure 11-34:   Macros Worksheet in MACTEST.WK3

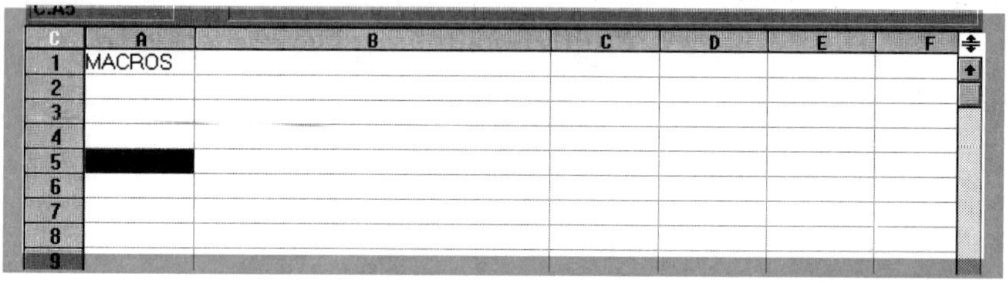

Then label, name, and create the following macro in the new worksheet:

Type: '\G
Press: ↵
Choose: Range   Name   Label Create
Select: Right   *if necessary*

               OK
Press: →
Type: {<<utility.wk3>>\goto_range}
Press: ↵

Figure 11-35 :   A macro is defined as a subroutine call to a macro in another worksheet file.

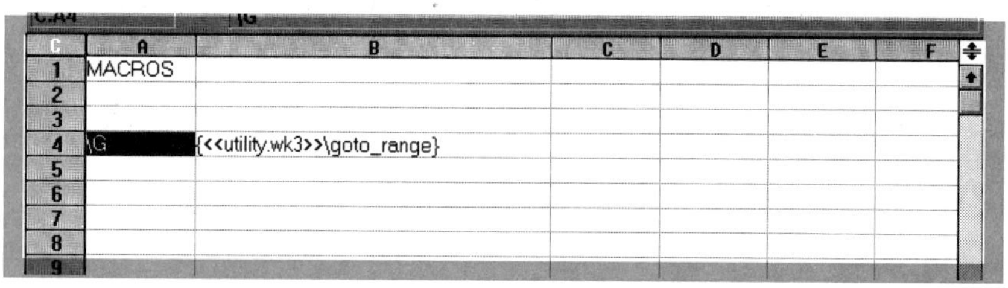

Run the new macro:

Press: CTRL+G

The instructions in cell C:B4 tell 1-2-3 to call the macro \GOTO_RANGE in UTILITY.WK3 as a subroutine of the \G macro. 1-2-3 calls the macro and, once again, prompts you to select a range to move to.

Select: `OⓍNTACTS_DB`

The macro moves the cell pointer to cell B:A1, the contacts database table. If you wish, add other macros to the macro worksheet of MACTEST.WK3, either by copying the macros to the worksheet, typing them into the worksheet, or creating subroutine calls to macros in UTILITY.WK3. Since you've incorporated \GOTO_RANGE as a subroutine call, you might want to copy \RETURN as well.

12. Save MACTEST.WK3, using the \FILE_SAVE macro in UTILITY.WK3:

Press: `ALT+F3` **(RUN)**

Double-click: `<<UTILITY.WK3>>`

Select: `\FILE_SAVE` *in the list box*

               `OK`

Backslash Macro Names in UTILITY.WK3   In creating longer, more descriptive range names for the macros you copied from MACROS.WK3 to UTILITY.WK3, you lost the convenience of the macros' original backslash range names. When a macro in an active (but not current) file is named with a backslash (\) and a single letter, it is possible to run the macro from the current file by pressing Control and the letter used in the macro name, provided no other active files contain the same range name. 1-2-3 searches among the active files for the macro with the specified range name.

Assign a second backslash range name to each of the macros in UTILITY.WK3:

Move to: cell A:B5   *in UTILITY.WK3*

Choose: `Range`   `Name`   `Create`

Type: `\S`   `⏎`   *remember the apostrophe*

Press: `↓` *three times*

                `⏎`

Choose: `Range`   `Name`   `Create`

Type: `\G`   `⏎`

Press: `↓` *four times*

Choose: `Range`   `Name`   `Create`

Type: `\R`   `⏎`

Press: `↓` *three times*

Choose: `Range`   `Name`   `Create`

Type: \L   ⏎

Now that you've assigned \S to the \FILE_SAVE macro, use Control+S to save UTILITY.WK3 with the new range names.

Press: `CTRL+S`

Creating an Auto-Executing Macro

To make a macro execute automatically each time you retrieve a worksheet file, name it \0 (backslash zero). \0 is a special name for an auto-execute macro. This can be a macro that you execute only when you retrieve a file, or it can be a macro that you also run while you are working in a file.

Auto-execute macros are often used to start up a macro-driven application or to customize 1-2-3 before you begin working. You can also use the \0 macro to read in other worksheet files.

For example, if most of the macros you use are in one worksheet file, an easy way to make sure that the macros are in memory is to use the \0 macro to automatically bring the worksheet into memory. To see how this works, create a \0 macro in MACTEST.WK3 that automatically loads UTILITY.WK3 into memory when you read in MACTEST.WK3.

■ *NOTE:*   The "Run auto-execute macros" option must be checked in the Tools User Setup dialog box for a \0 macro to automatically execute. If your \0 macro does not work, choose Tools User Setup, check the "Run auto-execute macros" check box, and select OK. If this fixes the problem, permanently update the 1-2-3 configuration file with this change by choosing Tools User Setup again and selecting the "Update" option.

1. Label, name, and create the \0 macro.

   Create the \0 macro in worksheet C of MACTEST.WK3, which you have previously titled MACROS. First, widen column B to 30:

   Move to: *any cell in worksheet C, column B of MACTEST.WK3*
   Choose: `Worksheet   Column Width`
   Type: `30`
   Press: ⏎

   Then, type the macro into the worksheet, using Setup Table 11-6 on the next page as your guide.

Setup Table 11-6: An Auto-Executing Macro

	A	B	C
7	\0	{ALT}FOc:\123w\123book\utility.wk3~	;read UTILITY.WK3 into memory
8		{FIRSTFILE}	;move back to main file

When you are finished, label and name the macro:

Move to: cell C:A7

Press: CTRL+L   *UTILITY.WK3 must be in memory*

2. Test the Auto-Executing macro.

Using the Run command, save MACTEST.WK3 to save the macro:

Press: ALT+F3   **(RUN)**

Select: <<UTILITY.WK3>>   *in the list box*

OK   *to display macro names in UTILITY.WK3*

\FILE_SAVE   *as the macro to execute*

OK   *to execute the macro*

Then, erase all worksheet files in memory. To do so, you will use the Worksheet Erase command available in the 1-2-3 Classic menu, since there is no equivalent command available in the 1-2-3/W menu bar:

Press: / **(slash)**

Choose: Worksheet   Erase   Yes

Now reopen MACTEST.WK3. 1-2-3 will retrieve MACTEST.WK3 and execute the \0 macro, which will read in UTILITY.WK3 and then move the cell pointer back to MACTEST.WK3.

Choose: File   Open

Select: MACTEST.WK3
OK

Verify that the Auto-Executing macro works as expected by running the \GOTO_RANGE macro in UTILITY.WK3:

Press: ALT+F3   **(RUN)**

Double-click: <<UTILITY.WK3>>   *in the list box*

Select: \GOTO_RANGE   *as the macro to execute*

OK   *to execute the macro*

Figure 11-36:   Macro is Available in MACTEST.WK3 After Auto-executing Macro Runs

1-2-3 begins executing the \GOTO_RANGE macro, which brings up the Range Go To dialog box. Now that you've determined that the macro was called successfully, cancel the rest of the macro:

Press: CTRL+BREAK

Using an Auto-Loading Worksheet File

If you find that you always want a particular set of instructions to be executed, regardless of the file you are retrieving, you can put an Auto-Executing macro into a file named AUTO123.WK3 and place that file in the 1-2-3 global default directory.

AUTO123.WK3 is an *auto-loading* worksheet. When you start up 1-2-3, the program automatically looks for a worksheet named AUTO123.WK3 in the default directory. If 1-2-3 finds such a file, it retrieves it before it does anything else. 1-2-3 will also execute any Auto-Executing macro you include in AUTO123.WK3.

Automatically Reading a Macro Library

Suppose you find that you always want to have your utility macro library in memory when you work in 1-2-3. You can accomplish that task by creating a AUTO123.WK3 file in 1-2-3's default directory and placing a \0 macro in that file that reads the macro library file into memory. When 1-2-3 starts up, it automatically loads AUTO123.WK3 and executes the \0 macro in AUTO123.WK3. The \0 macro, in turn, loads UTILITY.WK3.

If you include the following macro in a file called AUTO123.WK3 in the default directory, 1-2-3 will read a macro library called UTILITY.WK3 into memory and prompt you for the name of a file to open.

Setup Table 11-7:   An Auto-Loading, Auto-Executing Macro

	A	B	C
1	\-	'\0 Read UTILITY.WK3 into memory and prompt for file to open	
2			
3	'\0	{ALT}FOc:\123\123book\utility.wk3~	;Read UTILITY.WK3 into memory
4		{ALT}FO	;prompt for file to open

Debugging a Macro

No matter how carefully you plan a macro, sometimes errors creep in. These can be errors due to carelessness, such as leaving out a macro instruction, an argument, or a tilde, or they can be errors of logic. In either case, these errors are known as *bugs*, and the process of tracking them down and correcting them (in macros, and in computer programs in general) is known as *debugging*.

A complete discussion of macro debugging techniques is beyond the scope of this chapter. However, this section describes the tools 1-2-3 provides for debugging and some basic techniques you can use to debug your work.

1-2-3's Debugging Tools: TRACE and STEP Modes

1-2-3 provides two tools for debugging macros: TRACE mode and STEP mode. Selecting TRACE mode opens a small window in which 1-2-3 displays the macro instructions as they execute. STEP mode causes 1-2-3 to execute macros one instruction at a time, pausing after each instruction until a user's keystroke directs it to execute the next instruction.

TRACE Mode   When a bug is causing a macro to crash, using TRACE mode is often the quickest way to find the bug. When a macro crashes while executing in TRACE mode, the Trace window displays the instruction that made it crash. TRACE mode is especially useful for finding bugs that are caused by a mistyped or forgotten macro command. (It will not provide immediate relief, however, for bugs caused by an error in logic that makes a macro to behave differently from the way you intended.)

To put 1-2-3 in TRACE mode, you select the "Trace" option in the Tools Macro Debug dialog box. 1-2-3 displays the Macro Trace window. Because no macro is executing, the window displays descriptions (<Location> and <Instructions>) of what it will display when a macro executes. Once displayed, the window remains visible when you move to another worksheet or worksheet file.

Because the Trace Macro window is so useful for locating bugs and takes up so little space, you may want to display it whenever you are creating and testing macros.

Figure 11-37: The Trace Macro Window When no Macro is Running

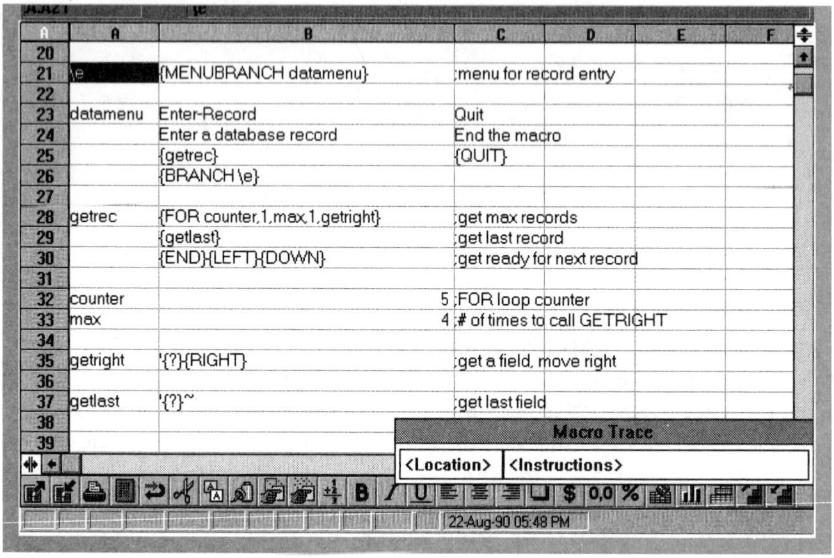

	A	B	C	D	E	F
20						
21	\e	{MENUBRANCH datamenu}	;menu for record entry			
22						
23	datamenu	Enter-Record	Quit			
24		Enter a database record	End the macro			
25		{getrec}	{QUIT}			
26		{BRANCH \e}				
27						
28	getrec	{FOR counter,1,max,1,getright}	;get max records			
29		{getlast}	;get last record			
30		{END}{LEFT}{DOWN}	;get ready for next record			
31						
32	counter		5	;FOR loop counter		
33	max		4	;# of times to call GETRIGHT		
34						
35	getright	'{?}{RIGHT}	;get a field, move right			
36						
37	getlast	'{?}~	;get last field			
38						
39						

Macro Trace — <Location> <Instructions>

22-Aug-90 05:48 PM

STEP Mode   Using STEP mode, you execute a macro one instruction at a time, advancing from one instruction to the next by pressing any keyboard key. Stepping through a macro one instruction at a time allows you to determine the point at which the macro does something unexpected. Using STEP mode in conjunction with TRACE mode lets you see in the Trace Macro window the instruction that is executing at the moment the macro's unexpected behavior occurs.

To put 1-2-3 in STEP mode, you can select the "Single Step" option in the Tools Macro Debug dialog box, or you can press the Alt+F2 (Step) key. 1-2-3 displays the STEP mode indicator in the status line whenever it is in STEP mode.

Debugging Techniques

As you gain experience with 1-2-3, you will create larger and more complex macros. Macros can span hundreds of cells and contain thousands of individual instructions. With such large macros, single-stepping through all the instructions becomes impractical. Logic errors that don't produce crashes become especially difficult and time-consuming to find if you search the entire macro. When debugging a large macro, you want to isolate the part of the macro that contains the error and examine that part in detail. This section describes debugging techniques you can use to isolate problems within a macro. You apply these techniques in conjunction with the TRACE and STEP modes described earlier.

Checking the Macro Before You Run It   The first step in debugging a macro of any size should come before you even run it: Check your work to make sure you have said what you intended to say. Compare the macro you typed in with the steps you laid out when you were planning your work and make sure the instructions you typed do what you want them to do. Play computer: Mentally trace through each of the instructions and write down intermediate values for variables to make sure your logic is correct. You can usually catch the bulk of your errors this way. (This is known as *desk-checking* a macro or computer program.)

Using a Split Window to Display Variables as the Macro Runs   Another useful technique for debugging a macro is to display, while you are running the macro, any variables that the macro changes. For example, say you are running a macro that is supposed to stop when a particular cell being used as a counter is equal to 12. Split the worksheet display so that the part of the worksheet in which the macro does its work is in one window and the counter cell is in the other window. Then move the cell pointer to the window containing the part of the worksheet file in which the macro does its work. Run the macro, watching the counter cell as the macro executes, and see if the counter ever reaches 12. If it does not, then you know that your error is in the part of the macro that is supposed to set the counter. If it does, then you know that your error is in the part of the macro that is supposed to quit when the counter reaches 12.

See "Testing the {FOR} Command Macro" earlier in this chapter for an illustration of this technique.

■ *NOTE:*   Make sure your macro does not issue a {WINDOWSOFF} command, or you will not be able to see the variables change as the macro executes.

Running Subroutines Individually   Macros that have been broken into subroutines are often the easiest to debug because you can execute each subroutine in order, using either Alt+F3 (Run) or Tools Macro Run. Run each subroutine as a separate macro, in the order in which it would be executed by the main routine of your macro. Stop after you have run each subroutine and examine variables and other worksheet cells to make sure that the macro has done what you expected it to do. (See "A Database Record-Entry Macro" later in this chapter for an illustration of this technique.)

Running Segments of Macro Instructions Separately   If your macro is not divided into subroutines, you can still execute it one piece at a time by using *breakpoints*. A break-point is a special instruction that stops execution of a computer program at the indicated place and allows you to see what the program has done so far. You can simulate breakpoints in macros by inserting a blank row or a {QUIT} instruction at the point you think your macro is going astray. When macro execution reaches the blank row or the {QUIT} instruction, the macro will stop, and you can see if it has done what you expected it to do.

The Run command allows you to run any macro that the cell pointer is resting on. To use the Run command in conjunction with break-points to execute parts of a macro, follow the steps listed here.

1. *Insert a blank row beneath the last cell you want to test.* (Alternatively, insert a {QUIT} instruction after the last instruction you want to test.)

2. *Move the cell pointer to the location where you want to test that part of the macro.*

3. *Run the macro fragment.* Do the following to run a particular group of macro instructions: (1) Move to the first cell of the macro fragment; (2) press Alt+F3 (Run); and (3) press Enter to run the instructions at this cell address. Execution stops when 1-2-3 gets to the break-point.

4. *Examine the results.* Check to see if the macro did what you expected it to do. If it did, that part of the macro is probably all right. If it didn't, you've found at least one of your problems.

5. *Delete the breakpoint and set a new breakpoint.* Once you are sure a particular part of the macro is working correctly, delete the breakpoint row or the {QUIT} instruction. Run the macro again. If the macro is still not working perfectly, set a new break-point and repeat the process until you have worked your way through the entire macro.

To use breakpoints successfully, you should be very systematic. You can use either of two methods to determine where to set the breakpoints: (1) Insert a break-point after each logical grouping of instructions, and move progressively further down the macro; or (2) use the "divide and conquer" method.

To use method 1, put your first break-point after the first group of instructions that does a clearly identifiable task. Use Run to run the instructions. If they are okay, delete the break-point row and insert another breakpoint row beneath the next group of instructions the macro would execute. Keep doing this until you have gone through the entire macro.

Alternatively, you can sometimes find a bug very quickly by progressively dividing the macro in half (method 2). Instead of setting your first breakpoint at the first logical grouping of instructions, insert a blank row approximately in the middle of the macro, then run the macro. If the macro does what it is supposed to do up to that point, you know that your problem is in the latter half of the macro. If the macro misbehaves when you test the first half, you know that the problem is in the first half. Once you have identified the half of the macro that probably contains the bug, subdivide that half with a blank row, and run it. If the bug shows up before the new breakpoint, the error is in the instructions before the breakpoint. If the error does not show up before the breakpoint, it is most likely in the other half of this smaller group of instructions. Repeat this procedure as many times as is necessary to isolate the bug.

A Sample Macro Application

To this point, you've learned enough of 1-2-3's macro commands and many of the concepts you need to understand in order to create and debug macros. The sample database application in this section gives you more practice creating macros that do useful work. It demonstrates some additional techniques for developing macros.

Macros can play an extremely useful role in databases. This section contains a more sophisticated version of the data-entry macro you created earlier in the chapter for the CONTACTS.WK3 database file. Once you have this macro working properly with the Business Contacts database, you can easily adapt it to other databases.

A Database Record-Entry Macro

Data records are usually very similar, and they must be entered and formatted in a standard manner. By using a macro to facilitate data entry, you can speed up and simplify the process, and eliminate the need to format the data with a separate set of commands. You can also use macros to help others who will be entering data into the database, but who may not be as familiar with the type of data to be entered or the formatting requirements.

You will create a macro to be used with the database you created in the Database chapter. This macro is similar in function to the database macro you created earlier, except that in addition to letting you enter new records, it also automates the process of sorting the new records into the database. The macro also introduces several new macro commands, shows you how to incorporate error-checking into your macros, and prompts for the fields as you enter new data. You will call this macro \E, for "Enter data."

The \E macro has a main routine, a macro menu, and several subroutines. The main routine performs the following steps:

1. Checks to make sure the cell pointer is on a blank cell.

   The macro assumes that you have positioned the cell pointer in the first field of a new record. It uses @CELLPOINTER("TYPE") to determine whether the current cell is blank. If the cell is not blank, the macro issues a beep and quits. If it is blank, the macro continues.

2. Zeros a variable that signals whether the user wants to quit the macro.

   The Quit menu choice sets a variable to 1. The macro initially sets this variable to 0. (Variables that are used to signal a condition are often called *flags*).

3. Displays a menu that lets you enter a record, sort records, or Quit.

   \E uses {MENUCALL} instead of {MENUBRANCH} to create a menu. {MENUCALL} works similarly to {MENUBRANCH}, except that instead of branching to a macro menu, {MENUCALL} calls the macro menu as a subroutine. When the task is completed, control returns to the instruction following the {MENUCALL} command.

   The menu calls one subroutine to enter a record if the user selects Enter-Record, and another to sort records if the user selects Sort. If the user selects Quit, the menu sets a flag to 1.

4. Checks to see if the user selected Quit.

   The macro checks to see if the value of the flag cleared at startup but has been set by the Quit menu choice. If it has, the macro ends. If not, the macro branches back to the start and re-displays the menu.

   The macro contains three subroutines: NEWREC_E, GETREC_E, and SORTREC_E. Each is described in Table 11-6.

Table 11-6: Subroutines for the Data-Entry Macro

Subroutine	What It Does:
NEWREC_E	Freezes the window and control panel, copies the last record of the database to the next row, and erases the new row. In this way, NEWREC_E preformats the row to contain the new record. Then, NEWREC unfreezes the window and control panel. (The CONTACTS database requires this subroutine because the Telephone and Street fields need to be preformatted as labels. Such a routine would also be useful when a field contains currency values.)
GETREC_E	Uses the {GETLABEL} and {GETNUMBER} commands to get input from the keyboard. {GETLABEL} prompts for input and automatically stores that input as a label. {GETNUMBER} prompts for input and automatically stores that input as a number. When the last field has been filled, GETREC_E advances the cell pointer to the start of the next new record.
SORTREC_E	Sorts the records by primary and secondary keys, using the same sort keys as those established in Chapter 6. The subroutine uses range names that you must define *before* you start the macro to establish the primary and secondary keys; you can change the sort order by redefining these range names. It counts on the data range having already been established, but extends the data range by as many records as you add. It assumes all rows beneath the database are blank.

The following steps describe how to create the data-entry macro in the CONTACTS file.

1. Retrieve CONTACTS.WK3 and add a new worksheet.

   You will enter this macro in a new worksheet in the file CONTACTS.WK3. Retrieve the file, move to the last worksheet in it, and insert a new worksheet:

Choose:	File Open
Select:	CONTACTS.WK3 OK
Move to:	any location in worksheet B (if necessary)
Choose:	Worksheet Insert
Select:	Sheet After
	OK

   Give the worksheet the title MACROS:

Type:	MACROS ⏎ *in cell C:A1*

2. Widen columns B and C.

   To make it easier to read the macro, widen column B to 30 characters and column C to 13 characters:

Move to:	*any cell in column B*
Choose:	Worksheet Column Width

Type:	30	
Press:	↵	
	→	
Choose:	Worksheet	Column Width
Type:	13	
Press:	↵	

3. Enter the macro and documentation beginning in cell C:B3 using Setup Table 11-8 as your guide.

You will name this macro \E, for "Enter data." Instead of creating a range name for the macro now, you are going to wait until you have finished typing in the macro, then you'll use \LABEL_RIGHT macro (or Range Name Label Create) to simultaneously name the macro and any variables.

Setup Table 11-8:   Data-entry Macro for CONTACTS.WK3

	A	B	C	D
3	\'	\E Enter records and, optionally, sort them.		
4		This macro consists of a main routine named \E; a menu		
5		named MENU_E; subroutines named NEWREC_E, GETREC_E, and		
6		SORTREC_E; and a flag named QUITFLG_E. Uses range names		
7		PRIMARY_E and SECONDARY_E as sort keys.		
8				
9	'\e	{IF @CELLPOINTER("TYPE")<>"B"}{BEEP}{QUIT}		;Error!
10		{LET quitflg_e,0}	;Not ready to quit yet	
11		{MENUCALL menu_e}	;Ask what to do next	
12		{IF quitflg_e,1}{CALC}{QUIT}	;User wants to quit?	
13		{BRANCH \e}	;No, so start again	
14				
15				
16				
17		VARIABLES Cells used as variables		
18	quitflg_e		;set to 1 to quit, else 0	
19				

	A	B	C	D
20				
21		MENU_E Enter next record, Sort entries, or Quit.		
22				
23	menu_e	Enter-Record	Sort	Quit
24		Enter next record	Sort records	End this macro
25		{newrec_e}	{PANELOFF}	{LET quitflg_e,1}
26		{getrec_e}	{sortrec_e}	
27			{PANELON}	
28				
29		NEWREC_E Create a new record.		
30				
31	newrec_e	{WINDOWSOFF}{PANELOFF}	;Freeze display	
32		{UP}{ANCHOR}{END}{R}~{ALT}EC	;Copy last record	
33		{D}{ALT}EP~{ANCHOR}{END}{R}~	;Paste into next row and highlight	
34		{ALT}RNCtemp~{BLANK temp}	;Create range name and blank it	
35		{WINDOWSON}{PANELON}	;Unfreeze display	
36				
37				
38		GETREC_E Get a record, one field at a time.		
39				
40	getrec_e	{GETLABEL "Last name: ",@CELLPOINTER("ADDRESS")}{RIGHT}		
41		{GETLABEL "First name: ",@CELLPOINTER("ADDRESS")}{RIGHT}		
42		{GETLABEL "Telephone: ",@CELLPOINTER("ADDRESS")}{RIGHT}		
43		{GETLABEL "Type: ",@CELLPOINTER("ADDRESS")}{RIGHT}		
44		{GETLABEL "Company: ",@CELLPOINTER("ADDRESS")}{RIGHT}		
45		{GETLABEL "Street: ",@CELLPOINTER("ADDRESS")}{RIGHT}		
46		{GETLABEL "City: ",@CELLPOINTER("ADDRESS")}{RIGHT}		
47		{GETLABEL "State: ",@CELLPOINTER("ADDRESS")}{RIGHT}		
48		{GETLABEL "Zip code: ",@CELLPOINTER("ADDRESS")}{RIGHT}		
49		{GETNUMBER "Frequency: ",@CELLPOINTER("ADDRESS")}~		

	A	B	C	D
50		{END}{LEFT}{DOWN}		
51				
52				
53		SORTREC_E Extend the sort range, sort records.		
54		Requires that PRIMARY_E, and SECONDARY_E, range names be created.		
55				
56	sortrec_e	{ALT}DS{END}{DOWN}~	;Extend sort range to include new records	
57		{ALT "p"}primary_e{ALT "d"}	;primary key = Type field, descending	
58		{ALT "s"}secondary_e{ALT "e"}	;secondary key = Last Name, ascending	
59		~	;sort the database table	

4. Name the macro, its subroutines, and its variables.

Use the \L macro you created earlier (or Range Name Label Create, if UTILITY.WK3 is not active) to simultaneously turn all the variables and subroutine labels in column A into range names for the cells immediately to their right. (You'll name the range names used by the sort routine later.)

Highlight: C:A9..C:A56
Press: CTRL+L

5. Test the NEWREC_E subroutine.

Because this is a somewhat complex macro, it is easiest to test it by first testing each of the individual subroutines. Test the NEWREC_E subroutine first, to make sure that it properly copies the last record in the database to the first blank row and then erases the contents of that row.

Before you test the subroutine, delete all the rows below row 17, to be sure that they are truly blank and unformatted. First, move the cell pointer to cell B:C17:

Move to: cell B:C17

Look at the control panel. Notice that it contains the format indicator (L). This is because, in Chapter 6, you formatted that cell as a Label cell. The NEWREC_E subroutine will correctly format all fields in each new record by copying the cell format from the previous record. To make sure the subroutine is working properly, clear the formats for row 17 and the rows beneath it by deleting the rows:

Highlight: B:C17..B:C20
Choose: Worksheet   Delete
Select: Row   OK

Figure 11-38: Cell is formatted as label from your work in Chapter 6.

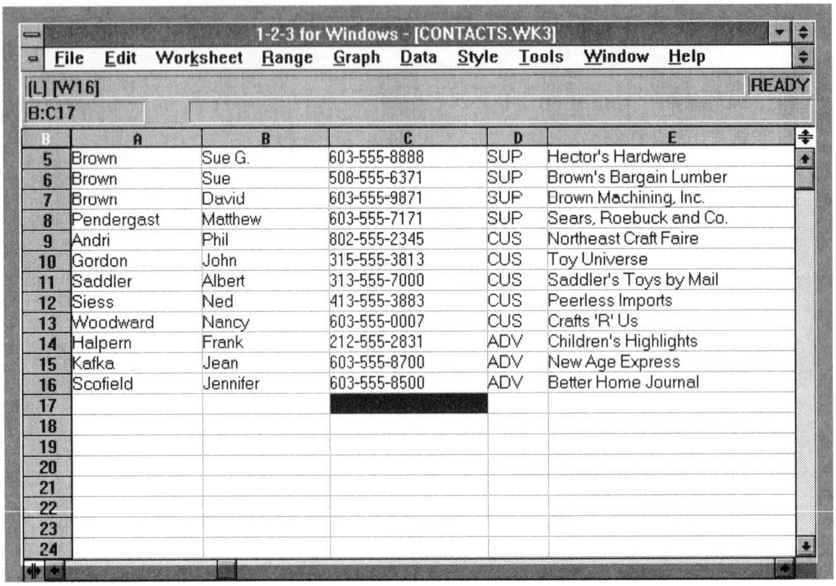
1-2-3 for Windows - [CONTACTS.WK3]
File Edit Worksheet Range Graph Data Style Tools Window Help
(L) [W16]
READY
B:C17
B A B C D E
5 Brown Sue G. 603-555-8888 SUP Hector's Hardware
6 Brown Sue 508-555-6371 SUP Brown's Bargain Lumber
7 Brown David 603-555-9871 SUP Brown Machining, Inc.
8 Pendergast Matthew 603-555-7171 SUP Sears, Roebuck and Co.
9 Andri Phil 802-555-2345 CUS Northeast Craft Faire
10 Gordon John 315-555-3813 CUS Toy Universe
11 Saddler Albert 313-555-7000 CUS Saddler's Toys by Mail
12 Siess Ned 413-555-3883 CUS Peerless Imports
13 Woodward Nancy 603-555-0007 CUS Crafts 'R' Us
14 Halpern Frank 212-555-2831 ADV Children's Highlights
15 Kafka Jean 603-555-8700 ADV New Age Express
16 Scofield Jennifer 603-555-8500 ADV Better Home Journal
17
18
19
20
21
22
23
24

Notice that the control panel no longer displays the (L) format indicator.

Now run the NEWREC_E subroutine:

Move to:	cell B:A17	*first field of new record*
Press:	RUN **(ALT+F3)**	
Highlight:	NEWREC_E	
Press:	↵	

The screen should flicker briefly as 1-2-3 freezes the control panel and window, copies row 16 to row 17, then erases the contents of cells B:A17 to B:J17. Although it will appear that nothing has happened, row 17 should now be formatted exactly the same as the other rows of the database table. To verify this, move the cell pointer to cell B:C17:

Press:	→	*two times*

The control panel once again displays the (L) indicator, verifying that cell B:C17 has been formatted in Label format.

6. Test the GETREC_E subroutine.

Once you are satisfied that the NEWREC_E routine works as expected, test the next routine that the macro would normally execute, GETREC_E. Test this routine the same way you tested NEWREC_E by positioning the cell pointer where the macro expects it to be when the routine begins (in this case, in cell B:A17), pressing Alt+F3 (Run), and selecting GETREC_E.

Figure 11-39:   Formatting Removed

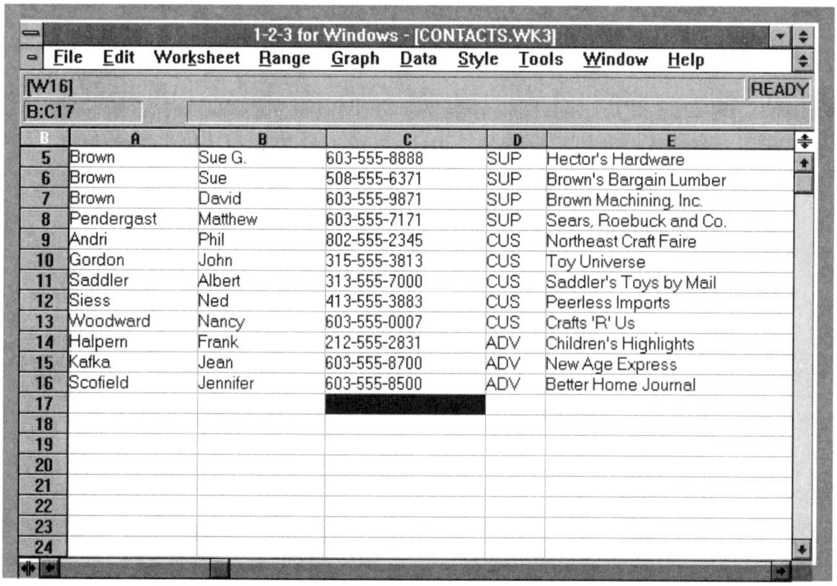

Figure 11-40:   Formatting is restored by the NEWREC_E subroutine.

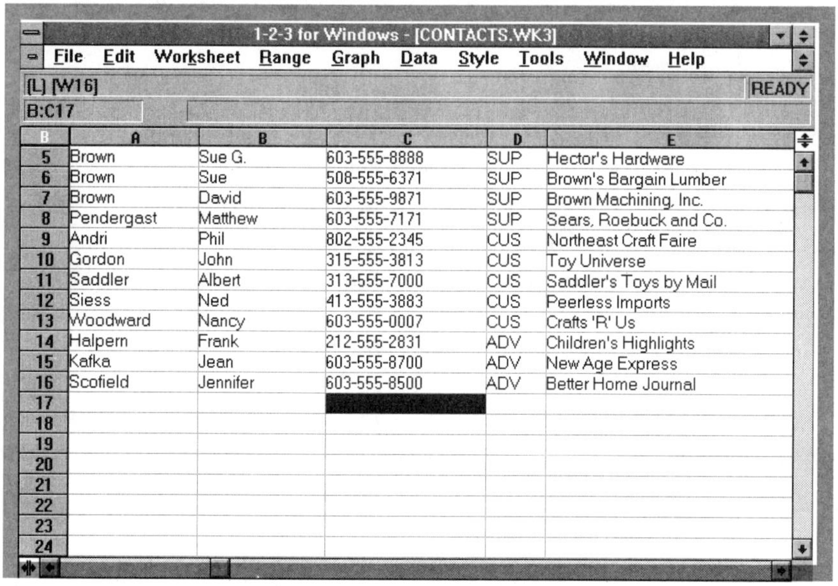

The subroutine should prompt you for a new record, one field at a time. Enter your name, telephone number, and so on. After you have entered the last field, the subroutine should move the cell pointer to the first cell of the next record. If the subroutine does not work correctly, debug it before you move on to the next step.

7. Name the fields used as sort keys and test the SORTREC_E subroutine.

The SORTREC_E subroutine requires you to name two ranges; a range for the primary sort key and a range for the secondary sort key. You are going to use the range names PRIMARY_E and SECONDARY_E for these keys.

■ *NOTE:*　In this case, you will use the same fields for the primary and secondary keys as you used when you sorted the database back in Chapter 6; the Type field for the primary key and the Last Name field for the secondary key. To sort on different fields, you would change the definitions for the range names to the new fields before running the macro.

Create the range names now. First, create the name for the primary key:

Move to:	cell B:D8　*or any Type field in the table*
Choose:	Range　Name　Create
Type:	primary_e　⏎

Then, create the range name for the secondary key:

Lotus 1-2-3 for Windows At Work

(Mary Troupe, an accountant, was formerly Accounting Manager at New England Development in Newton, Massachusetts. New England Development is a real estate development and management company, which develops and manages regional shopping centers principally in the New England area.)

　　In order to manage cash in the most efficient manner, it is extremely important that a cash flow report be prepared for each separate shopping center by the fifth working day of the month detailing the prior month's activity. To accomplish this magnitude of work on time, we download a cash basis trial balance from the IBM AS400 to a Lotus file for each individual center. The trial balance is downloaded to a cash flow report which we have designed with formulas in each income and expense account, referencing the monthly balances from the trial balance.

　　In the past we had to run several reports off the AS400 and manually keypunch the monthly cash receipts and cash disbursements into a Lotus file; this was an extremely time-consuming task. Downloading the trial balance has enabled us to meet our monthly deadline with a minimum amount of work.

Press:	⭠	*three times, to cell B:A8*
Choose:	Range Name Create	
Type:	secondary_e	⏎

Now test the subroutine by positioning the cell pointer where GETREC_E left it (in cell B:A18), choosing Run, and selecting SORTREC_E. SORTREC_E assumes that the database has been sorted at least once before. It uses the End Home key combination to extend the data range to include any records added since the last time the database was sorted.

1-2-3 should sort the new record you have entered into the appropriate position in the database. If it does not, you have problems in SORTREC_E, and you should debug the routine before you go on.

8. Test the main macro.

Finally, test the main macro by running \E. First, test the error-checking code by putting the cell pointer on a non-blank cell and pressing Control+E. The macro should cause 1-2-3 to beep and quit the macro without even displaying the macro menu.

Now, move the cell pointer to cell B:A18 and press Control+E again. This time, the macro should display the macro menu. Enter several records, sort them, and select Quit from the macro menu to end the macro.

9. Save CONTACTS.WK3.

When you have \E working correctly, use the \FILE_SAVE macro in UTILITY.WK3 to save the current file:

Press: CTRL+S

■ *NOTE:*   A useful menu addition to the data-entry macro would be a menu choice that lets you save the current file.

Customizing the Icon Palette

You've already learned how to create macro menus that allow a user to choose among a set of commands. 1-2-3/W also allows you to customize the icon palette to include a SmartIcon that runs a macro you have written when a user clicks on the icon. This section presents an overview of the icon palette, and describes how you would add a custom icon to the icon palette.

SmartIcons and the Icon Palette

When it is first installed, 1-2-3 presents the icon palette shown in Figure 11-41 at the top of the work area. In an earlier chapter, you selected the "Bottom" option in the Tools SmartIcons dialog box to change the position of the icon palette to the bottom of the work area.

Figure 11-41: 1-2-3's Default Icon Palette

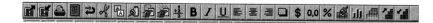

The other position options of the Tools SmartIcons command (shown in Figure 11-42) can place the icon palette at the right or left edge of the work area, or specify a floating palette. The right- and left-edge positions display fewer icons than the top- or bottom-edge positions. The floating option immediately accommodates more icons than any other position, and also can be resized to accommodate still more. If you were to create an icon-based application with many macros, the floating position would offer the greatest flexibility. (The "Hide palette" option suppresses the display of the icon palette completely.)

Figure 11-42:   Position Options Offered by the Tools SmartIcons Command

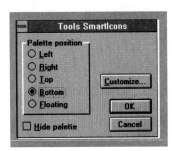

The "Customize" option in the Tools SmartIcons dialog box allows you to tailor the icon palette in other ways. In the Available Icons scroll box, 1-2-3 presents all its predefined SmartIcons. The Current Icons scroll box shows the icons currently being displayed in the icon palette. The Custom Icons scroll box shows SmartIcons beyond the default set that 1-2-3 offers. You can create icons in a draw or print program such as Microsoft Windows Paintbrush and add it to the set of custom icons. Then, after associating a 1-2-3 macro with the icon, you can add the icon to the set of Current Icons.

Adding a Custom Icon to the Icon Palette

The following procedure takes you through the process of removing an icon from the set of current icons, associating a macro with the custom icon, and adding the custom icon to the set of current icons. It does not describe how the custom icon was created in Paintbrush. (See the Windows Paintbrush documentation for those instructions.)

This procedure presupposes the existence of a file called LABEL_RT.BMP (for the \LABEL_RIGHT macro in UTILITY.WK3) in the C:\123\SHEETICO directory. To serve as a SmartIcon, a picture must be 24-by-24 pixels (1/4 inch by 1/4 inch), and be stored in a file in the Windows Bitmap format (indicated by a .BMP file extension) in either the C:\123\SHEETICO or C:\123\GRAPHICO directory. Icon files in the \SHEETICO directory can be used in the worksheet icon palette. Icon files in the \GRAPHICO directory can be used in the graph icon palette that 1-2-3 displays when you use Graph commands.

Figure 11-43: The Customize Dialog Box

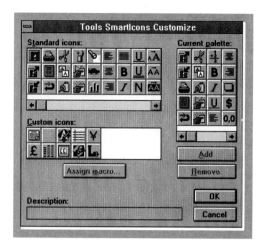

1. Remove an icon from Current Icons so you can put the \LABEL_RIGHT icon in its place.

   Since you have defined a \FILE_SAVE macro as an alternative to the File Save command and icon, you will remove the File Save icon. Before doing so, move to the UTILITY.WK3 file that contains the \LABEL_RIGHT macro. Since the macro you will assign to the custom icon is there, making UTILITY.WK3 the current file makes the macro available later in this procedure.

   Move to: *any location in worksheet A in UTILITY.WK3*

   Remove the Save File icon:

   Choose: `Tools    SmartIcons`
   Select: `Customize`
                 File Save icon in Current Icons scroll box.
                 `Remove`

2. Select the \LABEL_RIGHT Icon in the Custom Icons scroll box.

   The \LABEL_RIGHT macro is represented by an "L" followed by a right-pointing arrow. (Remember that the icon appears in the Custom Icons box because the LABEL-RT.BMP file is in the C:\123\SHEETICO directory.)

   Click on: *the \LABEL_RIGHT icon to select it*

Figure 11-44: File Save icon Selected for Removal

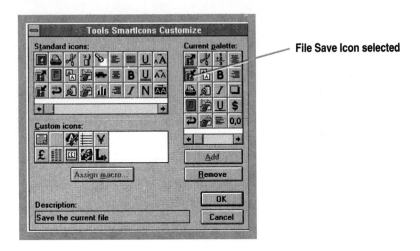

File Save Icon selected

Figure 11-45: \LABEL_RIGHT Icon Selected in the Custom Icons Box

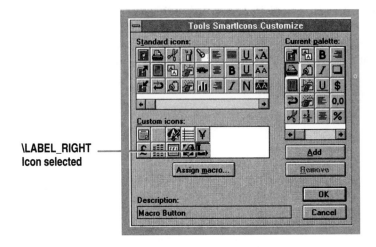

\LABEL_RIGHT
Icon selected

3. Associate the \LABEL_RIGHT macro with the icon:

Select: Assign macro

1-2-3 presents the Assign Macro dialog box.

Select: Range
Specify: A:B15..A:B16

Select: Get macro

Figure 11-46: Assigning the **\LABEL_RIGHT** Macro as the Custom Icon

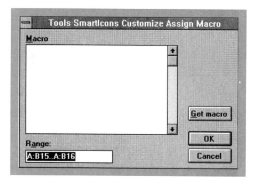

■ *NOTE:*   When you specify a range to assign a macro, you must specify all the cells that contain the macro instructions, not just the first cell (as you would to run the macro).

Figure 11-47: 1-2-3 Retrieves the **\LABEL_RIGHT** macro.

1-2-3 requires only the macro instructions, not the label or documentation, so you include only the two cells in column B that contain the \LABEL_RIGHT macro instructions.

Select: OK   *to exit the Assign macro dialog box*

4. Add the \LABEL_RIGHT icon to the Current Icons.

Back in the Customize dialog box, add the now-complete \LABEL_RIGHT icon to the current icons:

Select: Add

OK   *twice, to return to READY mode*

Figure 11-48:   \LABEL_RIGHT Icon Now Appears in the Icon Palette

\LABEL_RIGHT
icon

At a Glance

This chapter has presented a great deal of information about 1-2-3's macros facility. Having completed the chapter, you now have the following concepts and skills under your belt:

Task	How To Do It:
Entering, naming, and documenting macros	(1) Plan the macro: Decide what you want the macro to do and how it will accomplish the task; (2) decide on a worksheet location for the macro (ideally in a separate worksheet); (3) enter the macro instructions; (4) assign a range name to the macro; (5) label and document the instructions; (6) test the macro; (7) (if necessary) debug the macro.
Running macros with the Control key and the Run command	If a macro name consists of a backslash and a single letter, such as \S, simultaneously press Control and the letter (for example, press Control+S). If the macro has a longer name, choose Tools Macro Run or press Alt+F3 (Run), point to the name of the macro, and select OK or press Enter. If the macro has no name, highlight the first cell in the macro, choose Run, and select OK or press Enter.
Using all types of macro instructions—single keystrokes, keynames, menu commands, and macro commands—in a macro	Macros can include both keystroke instructions and macro commands. Keystroke instructions duplicate keystrokes you can type at the keyboard, such as typewriter keys, function keys, 1-2-3 menu commands, and dialog box selections. Macro commands allow you to incorporate many different programming techniques in your macros. For example, the {?} command lets you suspend macro execution temporarily to get input from the user.
Creating looping macros	The {BRANCH} command lets you create macros that repeat over and over until you press Control+Break, or a specified "IF" condition is met.
Using macro subroutines	Place a group of instructions in their own worksheet area and name the cell containing the first instruction. Call those instructions as a subroutine by surrounding the name in braces. For example, {routine} calls a subroutine named ROUTINE. The {FOR} command lets you execute the same subroutine a specific number of times.
Creating and using macro menus	Use the {MENUBRANCH} and {MENUCALL} commands to create macro menus that give the user a choice of tasks to perform.

Task	How To Do It:
Running a macro that is not in the current file	To run any macro from a file that is not the current file, you: (1) Press Alt+F3 (Run) or choose Tools Macro Run; (2) double-click the name of the file containing the macro; (3) select the macro from that list; and (4) select OK or press Enter to run the macro. If the macro has a backslash/letter name (such as \S), you can execute the macro by pressing Control+*letter* (as in Control+S), provided no other active file contains a range with the same name.
Creating auto-executing macros and an auto-loading file	Create a worksheet file named AUTO123.WK3 in 1-2-3's default directory. In this file, place a macro that reads the macro library into memory and give this macro the range name \0. Save AUTO123.WK3. Whenever you start up 1-2-3, the program will automatically read in AUTO123.WK3 and execute \0 macro, which will read the macro library into memory.
Debugging (finding and correcting mistakes in) a macro	1-2-3 provides STEP and TRACE modes as tools for debugging. In conjunction with these tools, you can apply a number of debugging techniques to locating and correcting problems in macros.
Adding a custom icon that runs a macro to the icon palette	(1) Remove an icon from the current icons (if you need the space). (2) Assign a macro to an icon you created in a paint or draw program. (3) Add the icon to which you've assigned the macro to the set of current icons.

Chapter 12

Backsolver, Solver, and Add-In Applications

This chapter discusses three 1-2-3 Tools commands that provide advanced spreadsheet capabilities: Backsolver, Solver, and Add-ins.

Backsolver provides additional ways to do what-if analysis. Essentially, it works backwards from the way you'd do manual what-if analysis. With manual analysis, you adjust the value in one cell until a related cell has a desired value. With Backsolver, you specify the desired value in one cell, and the tool automatically adjusts the value in the related cell until you get that value. In the Backsolver exercises in this chapter, you'll let Bob Gordon pick an income that he would like to earn, and then have Backsolver tell him how much starting cash he'd need to earn that income.

Solver is also a what-if analysis tool. Although somewhat more complex to use than Backsolver, it can solve more sophisticated spreadsheet problems. Where Backsolver adjusts a single cell to achieve a single desired result, Solver can:

- Adjust the values of more than one cell.
- Solve for a set of values in a specified cell as well as an optimal (either maximum or minimum) value. This way, you can analyze a range of solutions to the problem.
- Apply constraints to the problem. For example, you might set up constraints that "You can't work more than 40 hours per week" or "the maximum number of pieces produced for any given product in the product line is 10,000 per-month".

In your work with Solver in this chapter, you'll first expand Bob Gordon's Cash Flow Forecast to reflect business over a 3-year period, and then you'll use Solver to divide the starting cash among the SNOW WHITE, DWARF1, and DWARF2 products to maximize the return.

Finally, the chapter gives you an overview of add-in applications. Add-in applications (generally called, simply, add-ins) are separate programs that you attach to 1-2-3 to provide new capabilities.

What You'll Learn

By the time you finish this chapter, you'll know how to:

- Use Backsolver to solve for a single value
- Use Solver to find a set of values that meet the goals of a spreadsheet

■   **Load and remove add-ins**

■   **Run add-ins**

Before You Start

Before you begin the exercises in this chapter, start 1-2-3. Make sure that the cell pointer is in cell A:A1 of a new, maximized, blank worksheet file, and that 1-2-3 has been set up to save files in your 123BOOK directory.

As you work through this chapter, you are going to expand the Cash Flow Forecast worksheet file that you built earlier in this book. (A disk containing the worksheets created in this book is also available from the authors.) The exercises are quite comprehensive; you'll use many of the skills that you learned in previous chapters of this book. As in previous chapters, stop at the end of a numbered step or just before the next section heading when you are tired or have something else to do. Be sure to save any modified worksheet files before you stop. If you have more than one active file, write down the names of the files in memory and the order in which they are stored. When you want to continue with the exercises, start up 1-2-3, read in the worksheet files you last used, in the same order they were in before you stopped, then pick up where you left off.

■ *NOTE:*   The exercises assume that you have installed the Adobe Type Manager (ATM) and the ATM fonts that are included with 1-2-3/W, and that you turned on the Adobe Type Manager using the ATM Control Panel. If you have not installed or turned on the Adobe Type Manager, do so using the procedures in "1-2-3 and the Adobe Type Manager" at the end of Chapter 7.

A Note on Example Layout   As in previous chapters, the examples in this chapter assume that your screen displays 20 rows and eight columns when the Worksheet window is maximized. If your display does not show 20 rows and eight columns, your screens will look somewhat different from the illustrations, but you can still do all the examples. Just be sure to use the cell addresses and ranges specified in the instructions.

A Note on Keystroke Instructions   The keystroke instructions in this chapter often assume you are using a mouse to perform operations such as highlighting a range or selecting an option in a dialog box. You can also use the keyboard to perform the same operations. Many of the keyboard equivalents to mouse operations were described in previous chapters. A few of the most common ones are summarized on the next page. For a complete list of keystroke equivalents to mouse operations, see the 1-2-3 documentation or the 1-2-3 online Help.

Backsolver

In this section, Bob is planning for a meeting with potential investors and financial advisors. He realizes that if he can present the Folktale Workshop proposal with higher profits, he's more likely to attract investments. He decides to use 1-2-3's Backsolver to assist him in presenting the Cash Flow Forecast in its best light.

Keyboard Equivalents to Mouse Operations

Operation	Instruction		Keyboard Equivalent	
Complete action and close dialog box	**Select:**	OK	**Press:**	↵
Cancel action and close dialog box	**Select:**	Cancel	**Press:**	ESC
Highlight a text box	**Select:**	text box	**Press:**	ALT+*underlined_letter*
Edit a range in a text box	**Select:**	Range	**Press:**	ALT+*underlined_letter*
	Specify:	A:A1..C:D4		F2 (EDIT)
Edit a number or word in a text box	**Select:**	text box	**Press:**	ALT+*underlined_letter*
	Specify:	new text	**Type:**	new text
	(or click on text and edit it)		*(or press Left arrow and edit text)*	
Highlight a range	**Highlight:** A:A1..C:D4		**Move to:**	cell A:A1
			Press:	F4
			Move to:	cell D4
			Press:	↵

Backsolver makes the value of one cell equal to a value you specify by adjusting the value of a related cell. Essentially, you give Backsolver the "answer" you want, and the program figures out what value you need to get that answer. This is often exactly what you're aiming for with what-if analysis.

Before Backsolver can work, the cells that you specify must be related by a formula. To see how this works, you'll do a few short experiments using the blank, untitled worksheet now displayed in the current Worksheet window.

■ *NOTE:*   If you have any other Worksheet windows or Graph windows open, close them now. You will do your first Backsolver experiments using only the Untitled worksheet.

First, you'll use Backsolver to "back-solve" a simple problem. In cell A3, enter the formula to add the contents of cells A1 and A2:

Move to: cell A3
Type: +a1+a2   ↵

1-2-3 displays the value 0 in cell A3. Now, enter the value 5 in cell A1:

Move to: cell A1
Type: 5   ↵

1-2-3 displays 5 in cell A3. This is, of course, the sum of the contents of cells A1 and A2. Now, move back to A3 and choose Tools Backsolver:

Move to:　　cell A3

Choose:　　`Tools　Backsolver`

Figure 12-1: The Backsolver Dialog Box

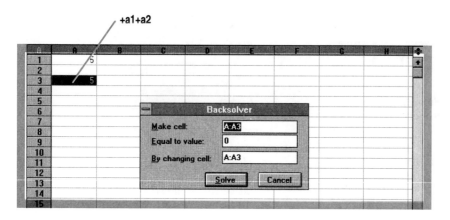

+a1+a2

1-2-3 displays the Backsolver dialog box. It includes text boxes for the "Make cell," the "Equal to value," and the "By changing cell." You should read this dialog box as a sentence: "Make cell *XXX* equal to value *YYY* by changing cell *ZZZ*". Now, tell Backsolver that you want it "Make cell A3 equal to value 8 by changing cell A2". (Because you highlighted A3 before choosing Backsolver, the program correctly recommends A3 as the "Make cell:".)

Select:　　`Equal to value:`

Type:　　8　*in the text box*

Select:　　`By changing cell:`

Type:　　A2　*in the text box*

Select:　　`Solve`

Backsolver determines that if cell A2 (the "By changing cell:") has a value of 3, then cell A3 (the "Make cell") will have the value 8 (the "Equal to value"). Backsolver has done its job.

Pretty simple, you say. *You* knew that you could solve for A2 by subtracting A1 from A3 and *you* knew that 8 minus 3 equals 5! Well, before you decide never to use Backsolver again, let's give it a little freer reign and see what it comes up with. First, let's have Backsolver solve for a different result in A3, say 133.

Choose:　　`Tools　Backsolver`

Figure 12-2: Setting Up a Simple Backsolver Problem

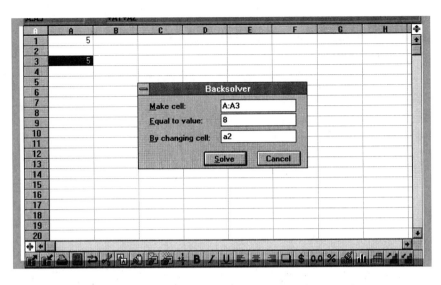

Figure 12-3: Backsolver calculates the value of cell A2.

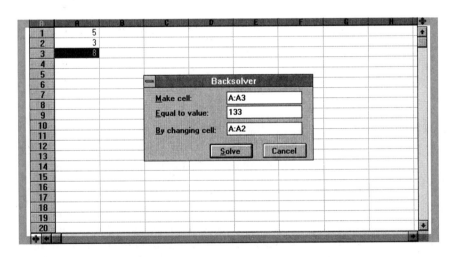

Notice that Backsolver has maintained the values it last used.

Select:	`Equal to value:`
Type:	`133` *in the text box*
Select:	`Solve`

Figure 12-4:   Setting Up a More Complex Problem

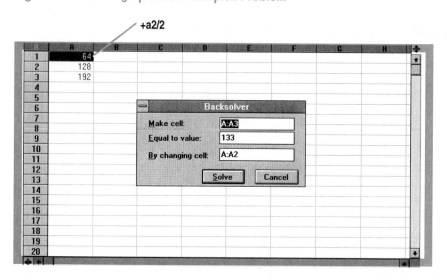

+a2/2

Now Backsolver has entered the value 128 in cell A2; and the formula in A3 yields 133. Still no big deal, right? OK, let's complicate things a bit by making A1 dependent upon A2 (see Figure 12-4).

Move to:	cell A1
Type:	+a2/2 ⏎
Choose:	Tools Backsolver
Select:	Solve

Backsolver finds that if cell A2 is assigned a value of 88.6666.., cell A1 will have a value of 44.3333... and that this will result in the desired value 133 in cell A3. Now *that's* fairly impressive. So Backsolver *can* do more than add a couple of values. Let's see what it can do for Bob Gordon's Cash Flow Forecast.

■ *NOTE:*   When Backsolver executes, it changes the value in the "By changing cell:". Depending upon how cells in the application are related, the result of this change may be felt throughout the application. If you want to preserve the application's state, save the file before running Backsolver. You may also want to use File Save As to save the file under different names between Backsolver runs.

In the following exercise, you're going to use Backsolver to determine how much starting cash Bob would need to earn $100,000 in his first year. (Bob knows that this is ridiculously optimistic, but he's having a good time playing "what-if".) Before you can actually call upon Backsolver to address this problem, you'll have to modify the Cash Flow Forecast somewhat. You'll enter formulas so that the money apportioned as starting cash to each of the products is related to a central starting cash figure. You'll also enter formulas to relate the net income for each of the products to the starting cash for that product.

1. Open a Worksheet window for the CASHFLOW.WK3 worksheet file.

2. Look over the application to refresh your memory of the Cash Flow Forecast. Notice that the starting cash balance in cell A:B5 shows that the worksheet is based on $10,000 starting cash. Now, look at SNOW WHITE.

Move to: cell B:B5

Figure 12-5:   SNOW WHITE gets $5,000 starting cash.

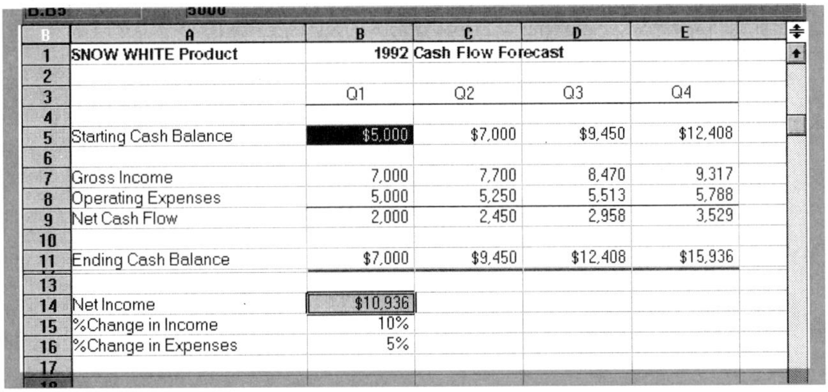

	A	B	C	D	E
1	SNOW WHITE Product		1992 Cash Flow Forecast		
2					
3		Q1	Q2	Q3	Q4
4					
5	Starting Cash Balance	$5,000	$7,000	$9,450	$12,408
6					
7	Gross Income	7,000	7,700	8,470	9,317
8	Operating Expenses	5,000	5,250	5,513	5,788
9	Net Cash Flow	2,000	2,450	2,958	3,529
10					
11	Ending Cash Balance	$7,000	$9,450	$12,408	$15,936
13					
14	Net Income	$10,936			
15	%Change in Income	10%			
16	%Change in Expenses	5%			
17					

Bob has set up the worksheet so that $5,000 goes as starting cash to the SNOW WHITE product. Notice that you entered the $5,000 as a fixed value, not a formula. (You're going to have to change this before you can run Backsolver on the application.) Move to cell C:B5, then to cell D:B5. Notice that Bob has put $2,500 in DWARF1 and $2,500 in DWARF2, and that you also entered each of these as a fixed value, rather than a formula.

Now look over the gross income and operating expenses for each of the products. (B:B7 and B:B8 contain gross income and operating expenses for the SNOW WHITE product; C:B7 and C:B8 contain gross income and operating expenses for DWARF1; and D:B7 and D:B8 contain gross income and operating expenses for DWARF2.) Again, you entered each of these figures as a fixed value, not a formula.

You'll recall from the exercises that you did at the start of this section that Backsolver can really be put to use only if the cells that it works with are related by formulas. At this point, that is not the case with the Cash Flow Forecast: Each of the product-specific starting cash balances, gross income and operating expenses values is fixed.

In the next two steps, you're going to modify the Cash Flow Forecast to use formulas rather than fixed values. First, you'll enter formulas for gross income and operating expenses. Then, you'll enter formulas for starting cash balances. Once you've completed these modifications, you'll be able to run Backsolver on the Cash Flow Forecast to calculate how much starting cash Bob will need to reach any desired net income goals... and Bob is starting to have some pretty lofty goals.

3. Enter formulas for gross income and operating expenses.

In this step, you're going to enter formulas for gross income and operating expenses for each of the products; the formulas will relate each of these values to the starting cash balance for the product. The formulas you enter will yield the same result as the fixed values currently in the worksheet.
Enter the gross income and operating expenses for SNOW WHITE:

Move to:	cell B:B7
Type:	+b5*7000/5000 ↵
Move to:	cell B:B8
Type:	+b5*5000/5000 ↵

Now, enter the gross income and operating expenses for DWARF1:

Move to:	cell C:B7
Type:	+b5*2500/2500 ↵
Move to:	cell C:B8
Type:	+b5*2500/2500 ↵

Finally, enter the corresponding values for DWARF2:

Move to:	cell D:B7
Type:	+b5*2000/2500 ↵
Move to:	cell D:B8
Type:	+b5*3000/2500 ↵

■ *NOTE:* There are a number of ways that you could enter formulas that would yield the same result as those above. For example, you could express the relationship between D:B5 and D:B7 by entering **+b5*80%** or **+b5*20/25** in D:B7.

When you are done, the worksheets in the Cash Flow Forecast for SNOW WHITE, DWARF1, and DWARF2 should look like those in Figures 12-6a, 12-6b, and 12-6c.

Figure 12-6a: SNOW WHITE After Entering Formulas

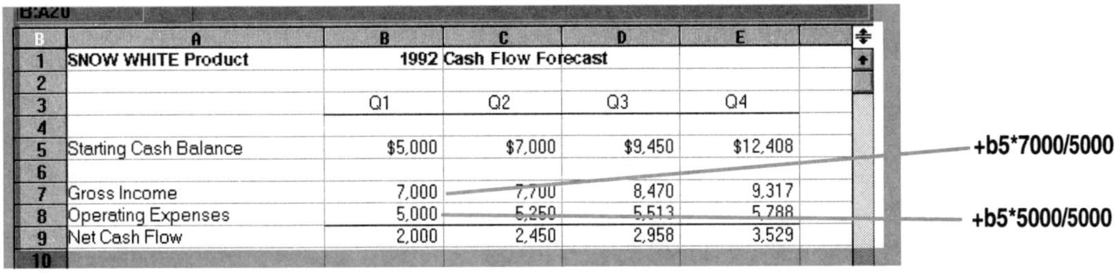

	A	B	C	D	E	
1	SNOW WHITE Product	1992 Cash Flow Forecast				
2						
3		Q1	Q2	Q3	Q4	
4						
5	Starting Cash Balance	$5,000	$7,000	$9,450	$12,408	+b5*7000/5000
6						
7	Gross Income	7,000	7,700	8,470	9,317	
8	Operating Expenses	5,000	5,250	5,513	5,788	+b5*5000/5000
9	Net Cash Flow	2,000	2,450	2,958	3,529	

Figure 12-6b: DWARF1 After Entering Formulas

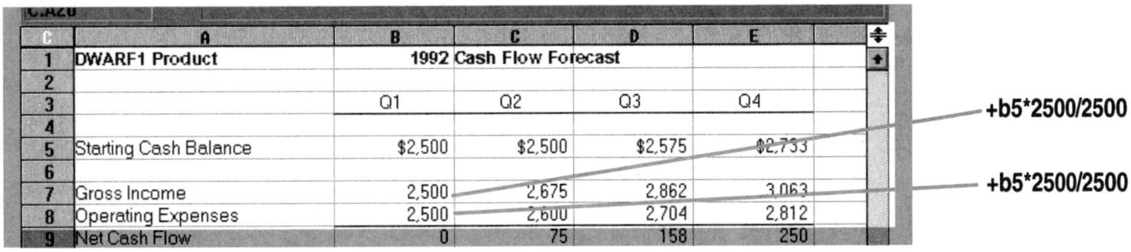

	A	B	C	D	E	
1	DWARF1 Product	1992 Cash Flow Forecast				
2						
3		Q1	Q2	Q3	Q4	
4						
5	Starting Cash Balance	$2,500	$2,500	$2,575	$2,733	+b5*2500/2500
6						
7	Gross Income	2,500	2,675	2,862	3,063	+b5*2500/2500
8	Operating Expenses	2,500	2,600	2,704	2,812	
9	Net Cash Flow	0	75	158	250	

Figure 12-6c: DWARF2 After Entering Formulas

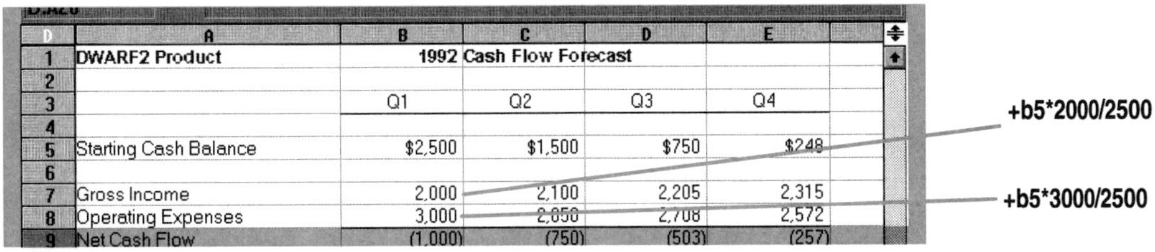

	A	B	C	D	E	
1	DWARF2 Product	1992 Cash Flow Forecast				
2						
3		Q1	Q2	Q3	Q4	
4						
5	Starting Cash Balance	$2,500	$1,500	$750	$248	+b5*2000/2500
6						
7	Gross Income	2,000	2,100	2,205	2,315	+b5*3000/2500
8	Operating Expenses	3,000	2,050	2,708	2,572	
9	Net Cash Flow	(1,000)	(750)	(503)	(257)	

4. Enter a variable for starting cash.

In a later step, you'll create formulas to tie the starting cash for each of the products to the total starting cash. Now, create a variable for total starting cash, format it as currency, and give it the range name START_CASH so that you can easily reference it later in formulas. First, you'll add a label and the variable:

Move to:	cell A:A16
Type:	`Starting Cash` ↵
Move to:	cell A:B16
Type:	`10000` ↵

Now, format the variable as currency:

Choose:	Range Format
Select:	Currency
	Decimal places
Type:	0 *in the text box*
Select:	OK

Figure 12-7:   Adding the Starting Cash Variable

A:B16		10000				
	A	B	C	D	E	
1	FOLKTALE WORKSHOP		1992 Cash Flow Forecast		(Consolidation)	
2						
3		Q1	Q2	Q3	Q4	
4						
5	Starting Cash Balance	$10,000	$11,000	$12,775	$15,388	
6						
7	Gross Income	11,500	12,475	13,537	14,695	
8	Operating Expenses	10,500	10,700	10,924	11,172	
9	Net Cash Flow	1,000	1,775	2,613	3,522	
10						
11	Ending Cash Balance	$11,000	$12,775	$15,388	$18,911	
13						
14	Net Income	$8,911				
15						
16	Starting Cash	$10,000				
17						

Finally, create the range name START_CASH for the variable in cell A:B16.

Choose:	Range Name Create
Select:	Range name:
Type:	start_cash *in the text box*
Select:	OK

Figure 12-8   Creating the Range Name START_CASH

5. Save CASHFLOW.WK3 as CASH1.WK3.

In the section on the Solver tool later in this chapter, you'll be needing a version of the Cash Flow Forecast application that looks very much like this one does now. To save having to later undo the work in the following steps, use File Save As now to save the current state of the application as CASH1.WK3.

Choose:	`File    Save As`
Select:	`File name:`
Type:	`cash1` *in the text box*
Select:	`OK   Replace`

Now, save the file again as CASHFLOW.WK3 so that: (1) The Worksheet window displays the correct file name, and (2) you can simply File Save to CASHFLOW.WK3 next time without mistakenly overwriting CASH1.WK3.

Choose:	`File    Save As`
Select:	`File name`
Type:	`cashflow` *in the text box*
Select:	`OK`

6. Enter formulas for starting cash.

Next, you're going to change the application so that starting cash is divided among the products by formulas: SNOW WHITE gets 50% of the total starting cash ($5,000) and DWARF1 and DWARF2 each get 25% ($2,500).

Figure 12-9: CASHFLOW.WK3 with Formulas for Starting Cash

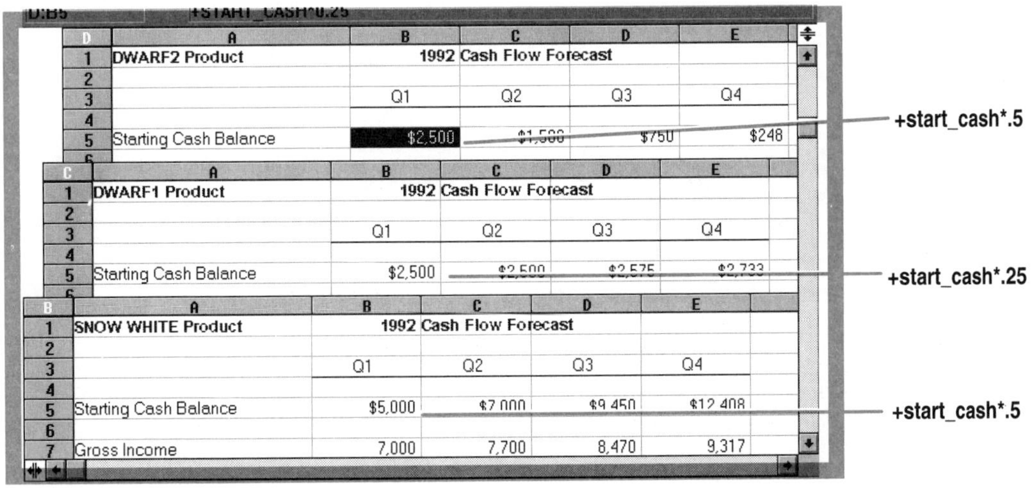

Move to: cell B:B5

Type: +start_cash*.5 ⏎

Move to: cell C:B5

Type: +start_cash*.25 ⏎

Move to: cell D:B5

Type: +start_cash*.25 ⏎

7. Use Backsolver to calculate starting cash for $100,000 net income.

Finally, you're going to get to use Backsolver to help Bob out. Knowing that he can earn $8,911 (as displayed in cell A:B14) with $10,000, Bob wants to see how much starting cash he would need to earn $100,000. To solve this problem, you'll move to the cell containing total net income (cell A:B14), then call up Backsolver to determine how much starting cash (in cell A:B16) is required to earn $100,000.

Move to: cell A:B14

Choose: Tools   Backsolver

Select: Equal to value:

Type: 100000   *in the text box*

Select: By changing cell:

Type: B16   *in the text box*

Select: Solve

Figure 12-10:   Cashflow Forecast for $100,000 Net Income

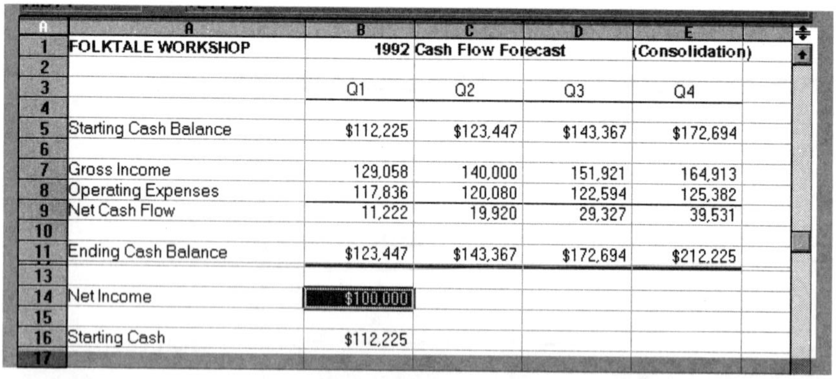

	A	B	C	D	E	
1	FOLKTALE WORKSHOP	1992 Cash Flow Forecast		(Consolidation)		
2						
3		Q1	Q2	Q3	Q4	
4						
5	Starting Cash Balance	$112,225	$123,447	$143,367	$172,694	
6						
7	Gross Income	129,058	140,000	151,921	164,913	
8	Operating Expenses	117,836	120,080	122,594	125,382	
9	Net Cash Flow	11,222	19,920	29,327	39,531	
10						
11	Ending Cash Balance	$123,447	$143,367	$172,694	$212,225	
13						
14	Net Income	$100,000				
15						
16	Starting Cash	$112,225				
17						

After Backsolver executes, the worksheet shows that Bob would need $112,225 starting cash (as displayed in cell A:B16) to earn $100,000 in his first year. Although you certainly *could* have calculated this value manually, using Backsolver has made it a snap.

8. Save CASHFLOW.WK3 and close the Worksheet window.

The Cash Flow Forecast now shows what it would take to make $100,000 in a single year. The plan is too aggressive and Bob knows it. He decides that the goal—although fun to ponder—requires more starting cash than he can go to his investors for. He decides to look for an additional $20,000, figuring roughly that a total of $30,000 in starting cash will give him a first year's income that he and his family can live on. In the next section, Bob will extend the Cash Flow Forecast for three years—hoping that a longer projection will be more convincing to the potential investors—and you'll call upon the Solver tool to see how he can optimize his profits.

Before you begin the next section, save and close CASHFLOW.WK3.

Solver

1-2-3's Solver lets you perform more sophisticated what-if problems than does Backsolver. Like Backsolver, this tool adjusts certain values in the worksheet. There are, however, several key differences between Solver and Backsolver:

- *Solver can work with multiple adjustable cells.* Unlike Backsolver, which adjusts the value of a single cell (the "By changing cell:") when it runs, Solver can adjust the values of more than one cell.

  The differences between these two methods is illustrated by the exercises you do in each of the sections. In the previous section's exercise, Backsolver adjusted only one cell, the cell of the Cash Flow Forecast which contains the total starting cash. In the problem you'll do in this section, Solver will adjust the starting cash for each of the products; Solver will adjust *three* cells. And you'll see that Solver can change the values in each of the adjustable cells independently, bound only by the constraints you may wish to impose.

- *Solver lets you apply constraints.* Constraints define boundaries for the problem, such as a maximum cost that cannot be exceeded, or a minimum number of articles that can be produced. Constraints make the what-if problem fit real-world conditions. You can make constraints as simple or as complex as required to fully describe the conditions of the problem. In this section, you will set up a Solver problem whose constraints specify that: (1) You can't exceed the starting cash, (2) SNOW WHITE must get at least 30% of the starting cash, and (3) DWARF1 and DWARF2 must each get 20% of the starting cash.

- *Solver can find multiple solutions for a problem.* Solver does not stop when it finds a single solution to the problem; it can generate a set of solutions.

- *Solver can (optionally) find an optimum solution.* For some problems, you may be looking for only for a range of answers. For others, you'll want to know which of the answers results in a maximum or minimum value in a related cell. In the problem in this section, you *will* be concerned about an optimum solution: you'll want to know how starting cash can be divided among the products to produce maximum net income.

■ Solver can generate a report that describes the details of the analysis. Much of the information in the report is quite complex, dealing with *how* Solver reached its conclusions. Some of the information, however, is interesting even for more casual analysis of the problem.

In this section on Solver, Bob Gordon is getting very serious about going to investors for additional capital. He's looking for an additional $20,000. (He just *knows* that—with additional funds—Folktale Workshop can make it very big.) After looking at the Backsolver analysis in the previous section, Bob has decided that he'll have his best chance to win over the investors if he can show his products generating increased revenues over an extended period. He decides to extend the Cash Flow Forecast over a three-year period. Bob also figures that he would like to show the starting cash divided among SNOW WHITE, DWARF1, and DWARF2 in a way that yields the highest revenues. He knows that 1-2-3's Solver tool can handle such a problem. And, although it will take a bit of setting up, he decides to use Solver to optimally divide the starting cash over his three premier products. Before Bob can get on to using Solver, you'll have to extend the Cash Flow Forecast to cover the three-year period from 1992 through 1994.

Extending the Cash Flow Forecast for Three Years

Before actually running Solver, you're going to extend the Cash Flow Forecast so that it shows cash flow for a three-year period.

1. Open CASH1.WK3.

In the previous section, you saved the Cash Flow Forecast under the name CASH1.WK3 for use in your work with Solver. Open that file now.

Choose: File   Open

Select: cash1.wk3   OK

1-2-3 opens a Worksheet window entitled CASH1.WK3 and makes it current. In the series of steps that follow, you are going to expand the Cash Flow Forecast to cover a three-year period. When you have completed these steps, the Consolidated Cash Flow Forecast will look like the zoomed screen in Figure 12-11.

Figure 12-11

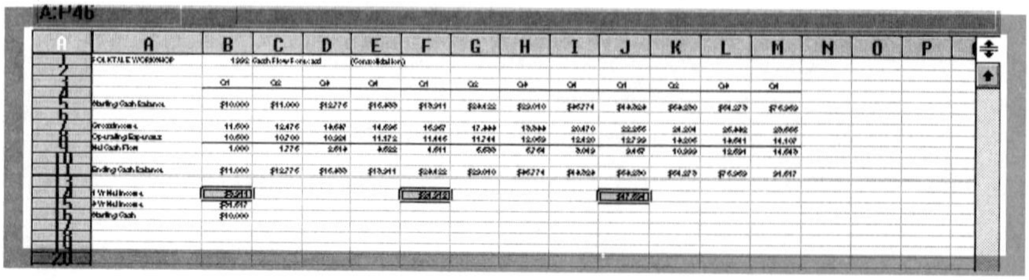

2. Extend the labels Q1, Q2, Q3, and Q4 for three years.

Your first task is to extend the Q1, Q2, Q3, and Q4 labels to cover the three-year period of the revised forecast. You'll use the "Copy to Clipboard" icon, which looks like this:

and the "Paste" icon, which looks like this:

to do this task.

Highlight:	A:B3..A:E3
Click on:	*the Copy to Clipboard icon*
Highlight:	A:F3..D:I3 *(use the keyboard rather than the mouse)*
Click on:	*the "Paste" icon*
Highlight:	A:J3..D:M3 *(use the keyboard)*
Click on:	*the "Paste" icon*

Figure 12-12:   The Summary Sheet with Labels Q1, Q2, Q3, and Q4 Extended for Three Years (Zoomed View)

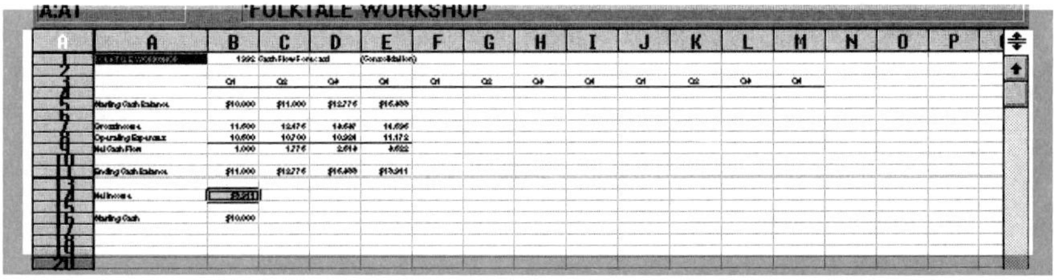

1-2-3 extends the labels Q1, Q2, Q3, and Q4 into the range A:J2..D:M3.

■ *NOTE:*   You have to paste labels twice, once into A:F3..D:I3, and then again into A:J3..D:M3. If you try to paste the contents of the Clipboard into A:F3..D:M3, then the range A:J3..D:M3 will end up blank.

3. Extend the quarterly formulas in the summary sheet for three years.

Next, you'll extend the starting cash balance, gross income, operating expenses, and net cash flow formulas on the summary sheet to cover the three-year period. You'll copy the formulas in A:E5..A:E12 out for three years.

Highlight:	A:E5..A:E12
Click on:	*the Copy to Clipboard icon*
Highlight:	A:F5..A:M12
Click on:	*the Paste icon*

Figure 12-13: **The Summary Sheet After Extending the Quarterly Formulas (Zoomed View)**

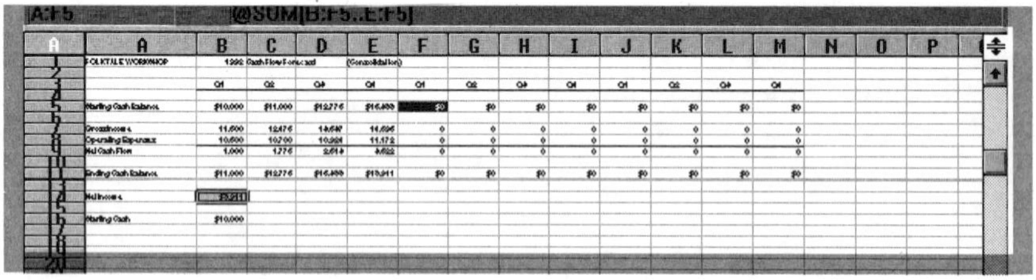

1-2-3 extends the formulas out to cover the three-year period. Since you haven't yet applied any formulas to the extended periods of the product-specific worksheets, the new formulas yield 0's.

4. Extend the quarterly formulas in the product-specific worksheets for three years.

Now, you're going to extend the starting cash balance, gross income, operating expenses, and net cash flow formulas in SNOW WHITE, DWARF1, and DWARF2 to cover the new period. Again, you'll use the "Copy to Clipboard" and "Paste" icons.

Highlight:	B:E5..B:E12
Click on:	*the Copy to Clipboard icon*
Highlight:	B:F5..D:M12
Click on:	*the Paste icon*

Figure 12-14: **The SNOW WHITE Worksheet After Extending Quarterly Formulas (Zoomed View)**

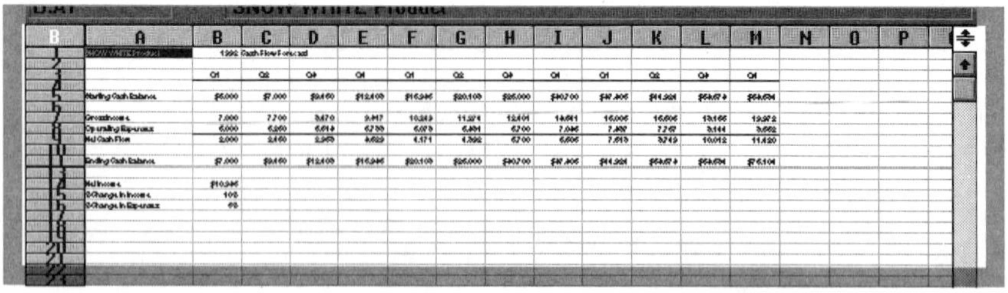

1-2-3 extends the quarterly formulas out to cover the three-year period. Now move back to the summary sheet to see the values that 1-2-3 has entered. Cell A:M11 shows an ending cash balance of $91,517. Things are looking better than Bob expected. But he wants to know the net income for each of the years.

Figure 12-15: A Portion of the Summary Sheet After Extending Quarterly Formulas

A	H	I	J	K	L	M	N
1							
2							
3	Q3	Q4	Q1	Q2	Q3	Q4	
4							
5	$29,010	$35,774	$43,823	$53,280	$64,278	$76,969	
6							
7	18,833	20,470	22,255	24,204	26,332	28,655	
8	12,069	12,420	12,799	13,206	13,641	14,107	
9	6,764	8,049	9,457	10,999	12,691	14,548	
10							
11	$35,774	$43,823	$53,280	$64,278	$76,969	$91,517	
13							
14							
15							
16							
17							

5. Create net income formulas for each of the years.

In this step, you'll create net income formulas for each of the years. Since the spreadsheet already has a formula for net income, you'll just copy it into the appropriate cells.

Move to:	cell A:B14
Click on:	*the Copy to Clipboard icon*
Highlight:	A:F14..D:F14 *the second year's net income*
Click on:	*the Paste icon*
Highlight:	A:J14..D:J14 *the third year's net income*
Click on:	*the Paste icon*

Take a quick look at DWARF2 worksheet to confirm that the copy procedure went as you expected.

Move to:	cell D:J1

■ **NOTE:**   You'll notice that the cells containing the extended net income formulas are formatted with a Cyan background and a border, just like A:A14. If you'd prefer these cells to be plain, you can remove the formatting using Style Color and Style Border, or using the "Apply Formatting" icon.

In the next step, you're going to enter formulas to show the net income over three years. But before you do that, modify the current net income labels to indicate that they represent one-year values only.

Figure 12-16: A Portion of the DWARF2 Worksheet After Extending the Net Income Formulas

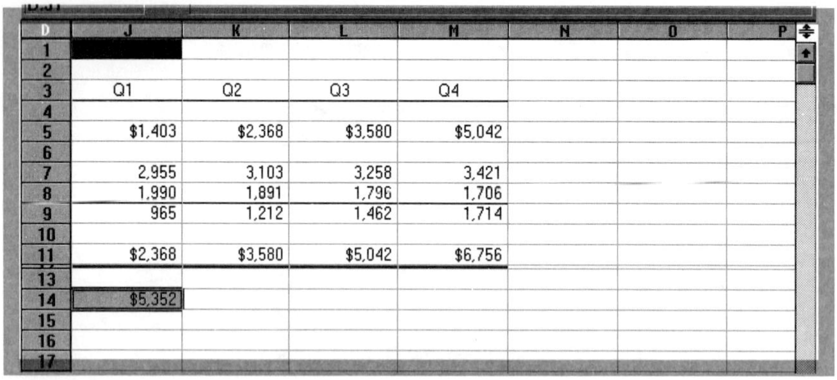

	J	K	L	M	N	O	P
1							
2							
3	Q1	Q2	Q3	Q4			
4							
5	$1,403	$2,368	$3,580	$5,042			
6							
7	2,955	3,103	3,258	3,421			
8	1,990	1,891	1,796	1,706			
9	965	1,212	1,462	1,714			
10							
11	$2,368	$3,580	$5,042	$6,756			
13							
14	$5,352						
15							
16							
17							

Move to:	A:A14
Type:	'1 Yr Net Income ↵
Click on:	*the Copy to Clipboard icon*
Highlight:	B:A14..D:A14
Click on:	*the "Paste" icon*

6. Enter labels and formulas to show three-year net income.

The three-year net income formula for each sheet will simply add the one-year net income values on the sheet. You'll enter the labels in cell A15 on each of the sheets and the formulas in cell B15 on each of the sheets. First, you'll have to insert a new row before row 15 on sheets B, C, and D.

Highlight:	*a range that includes one or more cells from row 15 on each of sheets B, C, and D*
Choose:	Worksheet Insert
Select:	Row OK

Next, enter labels on each of the sheets.

Move to:	A:A15
Type:	'3 Yr Net Income ↵
Click on:	*the Copy to Clipboard icon*
Highlight:	B:A15..D:A15
Click on:	*the Paste icon*

1-2-3 displays the **3 Yr Net Income** labels. Now enter the formula for 3-year net income on the summary sheet and format the cell for Currency.

Move to: A:B15

Type: `@sum(b14,f14,j14)` ↵

Choose: `Range` `Format`

Select: `Currency`

`Decimal places`

Type: `0` *in the text box*

Select: `OK`

Figure 12-17: The summary sheet shows net income over three years.

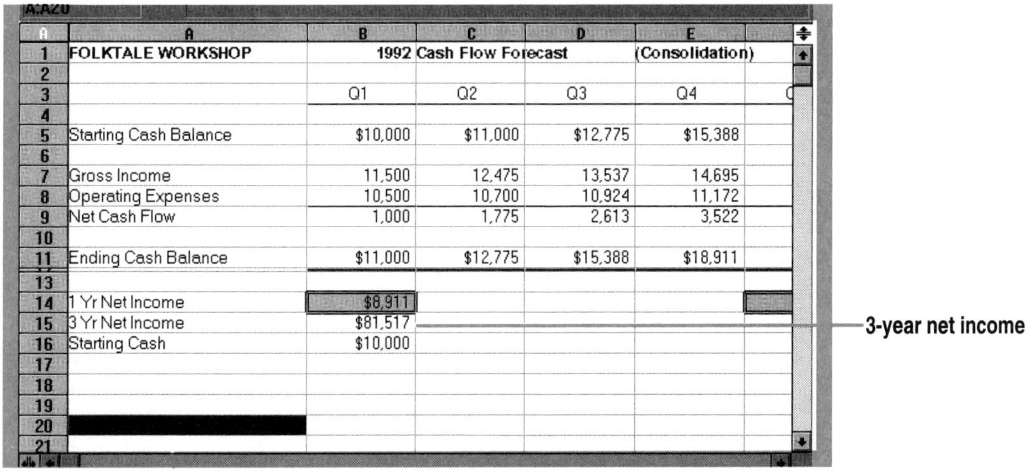

A	A	B	C	D	E
1	FOLKTALE WORKSHOP	1992 Cash Flow Forecast			(Consolidation)
2					
3		Q1	Q2	Q3	Q4
4					
5	Starting Cash Balance	$10,000	$11,000	$12,775	$15,388
6					
7	Gross Income	11,500	12,475	13,537	14,695
8	Operating Expenses	10,500	10,700	10,924	11,172
9	Net Cash Flow	1,000	1,775	2,613	3,522
10					
11	Ending Cash Balance	$11,000	$12,775	$15,388	$18,911
13					
14	1 Yr Net Income	$8,911			
15	3 Yr Net Income	$81,517			
16	Starting Cash	$10,000			
17					
18					
19					
20					
21					

Next, copy the three year net income formula to the sheets B, C, and D.

Click on: *the "Copy to" icon*

Highlight: B:B15..D:B15

Click on: *the "Paste" icon*

1-2-3 displays the results of the three-year net income formulas. Congratulations! You have extended the Cash Flow Forecast to cover three years, and you've used many of the techniques you learned earlier in this book.

Creating a Graph to Project 3 Years In Chapter 8, you created a line graph that showed cash flow projected over one year. You called that graph 1YR_PROJECTION and inserted it into sheet F of the Cash Flow Forecast. Bob would find it very interesting to extend the 1YR_PROJECTION graph for the three-year period. If you were to do so, it would look like Figure 12-18.

Figure 12-18:   The 1YR_PROJECTION Graph Extended For 3 Years

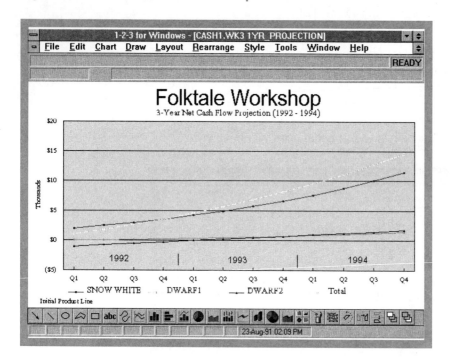

As an exercise, you might try to create this graph. Its easier than you probably think: (1) Open a Graph window for the 1YR_PROJECTION graph; (2) use the Graph menu's Chart Ranges command to extend the current X and A-D ranges so they include columns B through M; (3) use Chart Heading to change the subtitle; and (4) use the Graph menu's Draw commands (or the appropriate Graph menu SmartIcons) to add the text and graphics.

General Solver Setup

At this point, with the Cash Flow Forecast properly extended to cover a three-year period, let's look at some Solver basics. After this discussion, you'll go back to the Cash Flow Forecast problem of optimizing Folktale Workshop profits by dividing starting cash among the SNOW WHITE, DWARF1, and DWARF2 products.

To use Solver, you must define: (1) adjustable cells, (2) constraint cells, and (3) optionally, the optimal cell.

Adjustable cells are those whose values Solver changes as it solves the what-if problem. Like the single adjustable cell used by Backsolver, Solver's adjustable cells must be related directly or indirectly to be meaningful. The number of adjustable cells you specify is limited only by your computer's available memory and how complex the worksheet is.

Constraint cells restrict the problem by defining the boundaries within which Solver can assign values to the adjustable cells. For example, if you were setting up a problem to determine the number of people required to do a particular job, you might set one constraint that each person could work no more than 40 regular hours per week ,and another constraint that each could work no more than 30 overtime hours per month.

Each constraint cell specifies a single constraint. The number of constraint cells you specify is limited only by your computer's available memory and how complex the worksheet is.

A constraint cell contains a *logical formula* that defines the restriction. You use 1-2-3's logical operators to define the formula. (See the online Help for a list and description of 1-2-3's logical operators.) For example, the formula:

```
HOURS_WORKED<=40
```

would define the constraint that each worker could put in no more than 40 hours per week, assuming that the range name HOURS_WORKED refers to a cell whose value reflects the number of hours worked. HOURS_WORKED might itself be an adjustable cell, or it might be related to an adjustable cell.

Because constraints are defined by logical formulas, they yield either *True* or *False*. True implies that the conditions specified by the logical formula are met; False implies that they are not. For instance, in the example above, if the cell whose range name is HOURS_WORKED contains a value less than or equal to 40, the formula yields True. If HOURS_WORKED contains a value greater than 40, the formula yields False. 1-2-3 displays a **1** in a cell whose logical formula yields a True result, and a **0** in a cell whose formula yields False.

The *optimal cell* is optional; it defines a single cell whose value you want Solver to maximize or minimize while solving the problem. The optimal cell must also be related directly or indirectly to the adjustable cells.

After you run Solver, it returns *answers.* Each answer is a set of values for adjustable cells that satisfy *all* constraints you define. If you define an optimal cell, Solver identifies which answer yields the highest (or lowest) value in that cell, depending on whether you specify a maximized or minimized optimal cell.

Entering the Solver Constraints

In this section, you'll enter the constraints to the what-if problem of optimally dividing starting cash among the SNOW WHITE, DWARF1, and DWARF2 products. There are four constraints:

- The sum of the starting cash allotted to each product cannot exceed the total starting cash.
- The starting cash given to the SNOW WHITE product must be at least 30% of the total starting cash.
- DWARF1 must be given at least 20% of the total starting cash.
- DWARF2 must be given at least 20% of the total starting cash.

Now, let's enter logical formulas for these constraints.

1. Enter a label for Solver constraints.

So that you can easily recognize the constraint section on the worksheet, enter a label on the summary sheet and format it using the Titles named style that you created in Chapter 7.

Move to: A:A50

Type: `Solver Constraints` ⏎

Choose: `Style 1` *to select Titles*

Select: OK

2. Enter the first constraint.

The first constraint states that the sum of the starting cash for SNOW WHITE, DWARF1, and DWARF2 can't exceed the total starting cash. First, you'll enter a label to identify this constraint, then you'll enter the formula for the constraint.

Move to: A:A52

Type: `Can't exceed starting cash` ⏎

Move to: A:C52

Type: `@sum(b:b5..d:b5)<=start_ cash` ⏎

Figure 12-19: **1-2-3 displays the first solver constraint.**

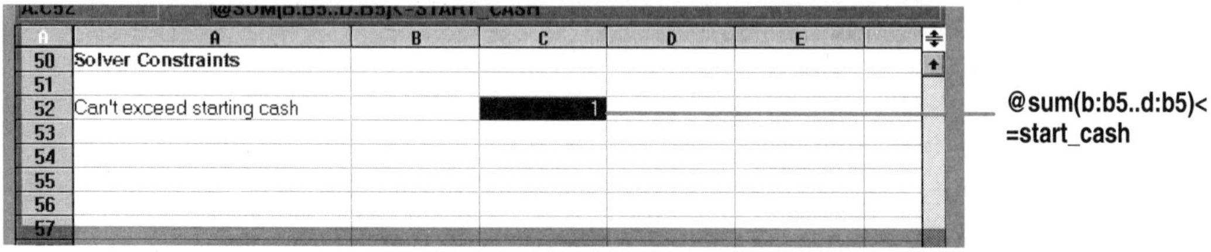

1-2-3 displays a **1** (to indicate True) in cell A:C52. The **1** indicates that the sum of the starting cash allocated to SNOW WHITE, DWARF1 and DWARF3 does not exceed the total starting cash. This makes sense since, in the previous section, you entered $5,000 manually into cell B:B4, and $2,500 into C:B5 and D:B5.

3. Enter the second constraint.

From research that he has done, Bob feels that the SNOW WHITE product is likely to be the best seller. He determines that at least 30% of his starting money should go towards that product. To model this, the second constraint states that at least 30% of the starting cash should be allocated to SNOW WHITE. Again, you'll first enter a label to identify this constraint, then you'll enter the formula for the constraint.

Move to:	A:A53
Type:	SNOW WHITE at least 30% of starting cash
Move to:	A:C53
Type:	+b:b5>=start_cash*.3

Figure 12-20: The second Solver constraint is added.

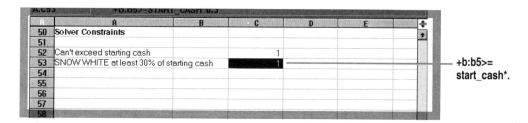

1-2-3 displays a **1** (to indicate True) in cell A:C53 to indicate that at least 30% of the starting cash has been allocated to the SNOW WHITE product. You know that this is true, as well, since currently SNOW WHITE is receiving 50% of the total starting cash. (Later, you're going to ask Solver to optimize this split, and the percentages of starting money allocated to each product will change.)

4. Enter the third and fourth constraints.

Bob's market research also indicates that unless he devotes at least 20% of the starting cash to DWARF1 and 20% to DWARF2, he won't be able to supply all of his retailers with dolls of each of the three types.

Move to:	A:A54
Type:	DWARF1 at least 20% of starting cash
Move to:	A:C54
Type:	+c:b5>=start_cash*.2
Move to:	A:A55
Type:	DWARF2 at least 20% of starting cash
Move to:	A:C55
Type:	+d:b5>=start_cash*.2

1-2-3 displays 1's (to indicate True) in cells A:C54 and A:C55 to indicate that at least 20% of the starting cash has been allocated for DWARF1 and 20% for DWARF2.

Now the Cash Flow Forecast is ready for Solver. In the next step, you'll run the tool.

Figure 12-21: The third and fourth Solver constraints are added.

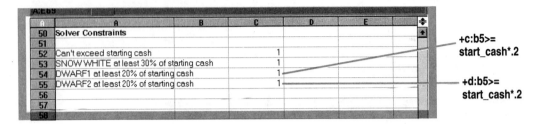

	A	B	C	D	E	
50	Solver Constraints					
51						
52	Can't exceed starting cash		1			
53	SNOW WHITE at least 30% of starting cash		1			
54	DWARF1 at least 20% of starting cash		1			
55	DWARF2 at least 20% of starting cash		1			
56						
57						
58						

+c:b5>=
start_cash*.2

+d:b5>=
start_cash*.2

Entering the New Starting Cash

Since Bob is going to ask his potential investors for an additional $20,000, the problem for Solver is to figure how to best divide $30,000 starting cash ($10,000 of Bob's money plus $20,000 investor's money) among the three products. Change the starting cash figure to $30,000.

Move to:	START_CASH	*the range name for A:B16*
Type:	30000	↵

1-2-3 enters $30,000 for starting cash.

Running Solver

Once you've set up the application to define the adjustable cells, the constraint cells, and (optionally) the optimal cell, you can run Solver to solve the problem. It's very useful to be able to view the underlying worksheet(s) while Solver is running. To view as much meaningful information as possible for *this* problem you will: (1) Move to A:A1; (2) choose Window Split Perspective and clear the "Synchronize" option to put sheets A, B, and C in unsynchronized perspective mode; (3) view the 3-year net income figure on the summary sheet; (4) start Solver; and (5) drag the Solver Definition dialog box to the lower right of the screen so that you can view the underlying worksheets.

Move to:	A:A1	
Choose:	Window Split	
Select:	Perspective	
	Synchronize	*and clear the check-box*
	OK	
Move to:	A:A11	*and scroll the worksheet A window until A:A16 is in view*
Choose:	Tools Solver	
Point to:	*the title bar of the Solver Definition dialog box*	
Drag to:	*the lower right corner of the screen*	

Figure 12-22 shows how your screen should look after you've completed these instructions.

Figure 12-22: Running Solver

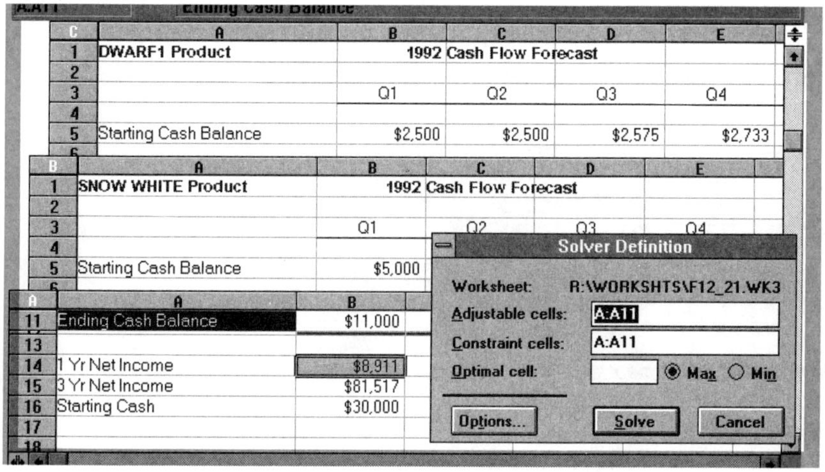

1-2-3 displays the Solver Definition dialog box. It includes text boxes in which you define the adjustable cells, the constraint cells, and (optionally) the optimal Cell. First, you'll specify the adjustable cells—the cells that hold the starting cash for the SNOW WHITE, DWARF1, and DWARF2 products.

Select:	Adjustable cells:
Specify:	B:B5..D:B5

Next, specify the constraint cells. These are the cells that hold the logical formulas for each of the four constraints.

Select:	Constraint cells:
Specify:	A:C52..A:C55

Then specify the Optimal cell. For this problem, you'll use the three-year net income figure on the summary sheet for the Optimal cell, and you'll want Solver to maximize this value.

Select:	Optimal cell:
Specify:	A:B15
Select:	Max *if necessary*

Finally, tell Solver to solve the problem.

Select:	Solve

Figure 12-23: The Solver Progress Dialog Box

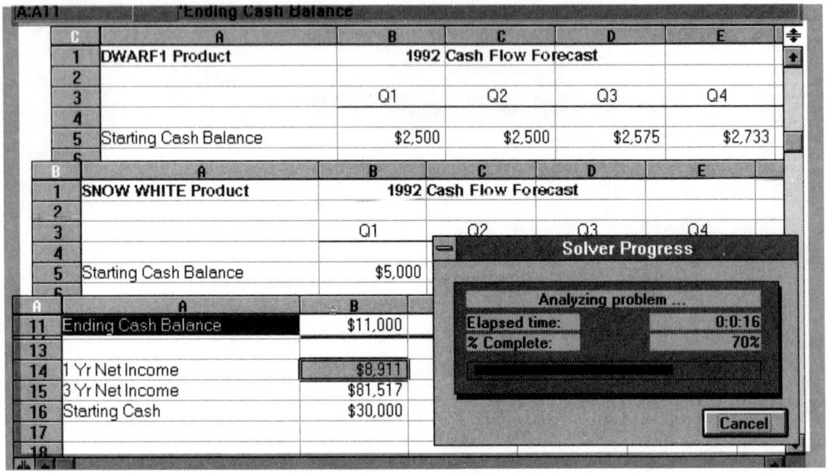

Solver displays the Solver Progress dialog box in which it shows the time elapsed during the analysis of the problem and the search for answers.

■ **NOTE:**   If 1-2-3 displays a message indicating that it has run out of memory: 1) close all open applications (other than 1-2-3); 2) disable Undo using the Tools User Setup command; and 3) run Solver again.

Looking at the Answers

When Solver has found all possible answers, it displays the Solver Answer dialog box.

Figure 12-24: The Solver Answer Dialog Box

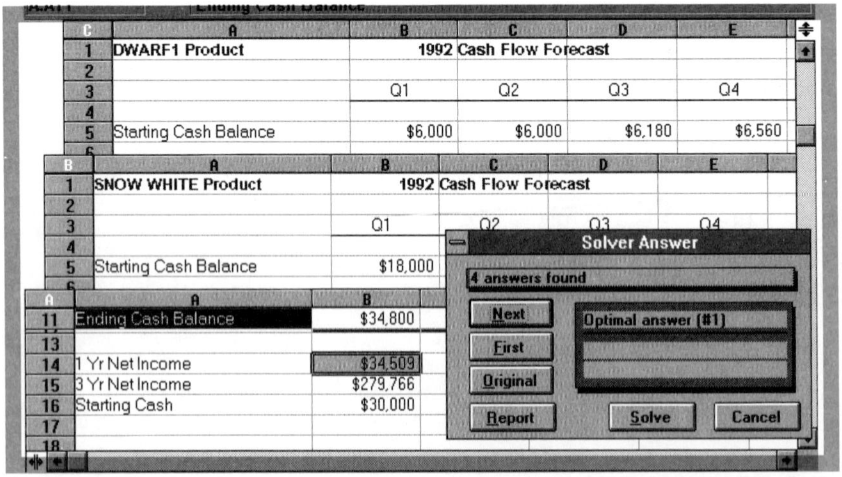

At this point, the adjustable cells now contain the values that Solver found as the optimal answer (#1). Solver has found that the optimal answer produces a three-year net income of $279,766 as shown in cell A:B15. You can also see that Solver has allocated $18,000 for SNOW WHITE and $6,000 for DWARF1. Although you can't see the starting cash figure for DWARF2, you can quickly calculate that it's also $6,000 ($30,000-$18,000-$6,000=$6,000).

To look at the next answer, select the "Next" option.

Select: Next

The adjustable cells now contain the starting cash values that Solver found as sample answer #2. If you continue to select "Next," you can look at each of the four answers Solver found to this problem, or you can use Solver Reports.

Solver Reports

Solver Reports allow you to look at all answers at once. To generate a report of the analysis, choose Tools Solver then select "Report".

Choose: Tools   Solver   *if necessary*
Select: Report

Figure 12-25:   The Solver Report Dialog Box

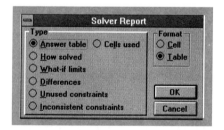

The Solver Report dialog box gives you numerous options for specifying the kind of report you want. The default generates an "Answer table" report in "Table" format.

Select: OK

1-2-3 works for several minutes before it opens a Worksheet window that contains the Solver Report. At the top of the report, you'll see the values for the optimal cell as well as those for each of the adjustable cells for each of the four answers to this problem.

Figure 12-26: A Portion of the Solver Report

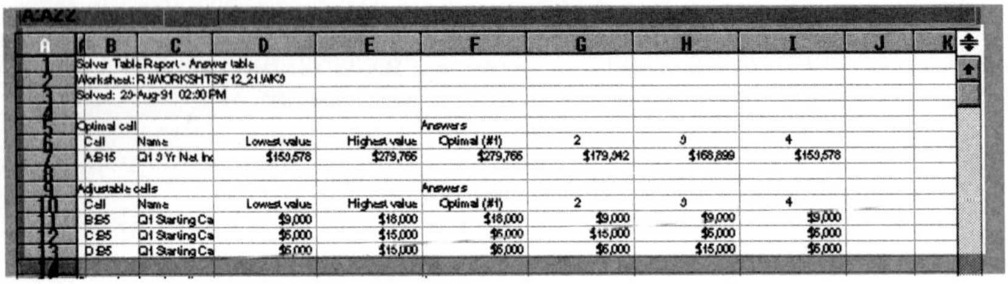

Solver Table Report - Answer table								
Worksheet: R:\WORKSHTS\F12_21.WK3								
Solved: 20-Aug-91 02:30 PM								
Optimal cell				Answers				
Cell	Name	Lowest value	Highest value	Optimal (#1)	2	3	4	
A:B16	Q1 3 Yr Net Inc	$150,578	$279,766	$279,766	$179,042	$168,899	$150,578	
Adjustable cells				Answers				
Cell	Name	Lowest value	Highest value	Optimal (#1)	2	3	4	
B:B5	Q1 Starting Ca	$9,000	$18,000	$18,000	$9,000	$9,000	$9,000	
C:B5	Q1 Starting Ca	$5,000	$15,000	$5,000	$15,000	$5,000	$5,000	
D:B5	Q1 Starting Ca	$5,000	$15,000	$5,000	$5,000	$15,000	$5,000	

If you want, you can examine this report to see more of how Solver handled this problem.

Congratulations! You have used 1-2-3's Solver tool to solve a real-world spreadsheet problem. For further information on Solver, see the Lotus 1-2-3 for Window's *Solver Guide.*

Add-In Applications

Add-ins come in two major categories: add-in applications and add-in macros and @functions. Add in applications are actually separate programs that "attach" themselves to 1-2-3 and use 1-2-3's resources and work space to accomplish their tasks. Add-in macros and @functions work just like the built-in ones except that they perform additional functions.

Some add-in applications augment what you can do with the worksheet, and work closely with 1-2-3: They can perform statistical analysis, fill worksheet cells with data acquired from realtime devices or databases, create fancier graphs, compress worksheet files, save your work at specified intervals, write formulas, or generate reports. Others add completely new features to the product, such as word processing, spellchecking, project management, outlining, form letter generation, risk analysis, and telecommunications. Often, add-in applications also provide additional @functions, as well.

Each 1-2-3 add-in has a .ADW file extension. You load an add-in with Tools Add-In Load. Once it is loaded, an add-in works much like a part of 1-2-3. (In fact, a number of 1-2-3 features that are now built into the product, such as Undo and optimal recalculation in Natural order were originally introduced as add-ins.) You can use any number of add-ins, provided your computer has enough memory; when you are finished using an add-in, you can detach it with Tools Add-In Remove, and free up the memory it used. You can clear all add-ins from memory with Tools Add-In Remove All. To invoke an add-in application, press ALT+F10.

■ ***NOTE:*** A catalog listing hundreds of enhancements to Lotus products, including dozens of add-ins, is available from Lotus Developer Marketing. This catalog is called the *Lotus Enhancement Products Directory.* Many of these products are also available through *LOTUS Selects,* a catalog of computing products available to Lotus users. For more information on the *Lotus Enhancement Products Directory,* contact Lotus Developer Marketing. For more information on *LOTUS Selects,* call 1-800-635-6887.

At a Glance

In this chapter you have learned how to use the 1-2-3's Backsolver and Solver tools, as well as how to use 1-2-3 add-ins. You have also learned how, specifically, to perform the 1-2-3 tasks listed in the following table.

Task	How To Do It:
Solving a what-if problem using Backsolver	(1) Modify the worksheet so that one adjustable cell (the "By changing cell") is related directly or indirectly to one cell whose value you want to set (the "Make cell"); (2) choose Tools Backsolver; (3) specify the "Make cell," the "By changing cell," and the "Equal to value," and (4) select "Solve."
Solving a what-if problem using Solver	(1) Identify one or more adjustable cells; (2) create constraint cells with logical formulas that provide boundaries for the values in the adjustable cells; (3) optionally identify an optimum cell whose value Solver will maximize or minimize; (4) choose Tools Solver and specify the "Adjustable cells," the "Constraint cells," and (optionally) the "Optimal" cell; (5) select "Solve." It's useful to position and size worksheet windows to show as much meaningful data as possible before calling Solver.
Looking at Solver answers	If necessary, cancel out of the Solver dialog boxes and move through the worksheet to look at values of the adjustable cell. Choose Tools Solver and select "Next" for the next set of answer values.
Generating a Solver report	Choose Tools Solver and select "Report." Select the report options from the Solver Report dialog box, then select OK. Wait for a few moments until 1-2-3 generates the report.
Loading an add-in	Select Tools Add-In Load.
Removing an add-in	Select Tools Add-In Remove.
Running an add-in application	Press Alt+F10, then choose Invoke.

Glossary

@function   A built-in formula that performs a specialized calculation.

absolute cell address   A cell address or range name in a formula that always refers to the same cell or range, even when you /Copy the formula to a different part of the worksheet file. To make a cell address absolute, prefix the row and column with a dollar sign ($)—for example, $AX$2. To make a range name absolute, prefix the name with a dollar sign—for example, $TAX_RATE.

absolute reference   A reference to an absolute cell address or to an absolute range name.

active area   The part of the current worksheet into which you have entered data or have formatted cells. The active area starts at cell A1 and ends at the bottommost and rightmost filled or formatted cell.

add-in   A computer program that resides in memory with 1-2-3 and extends 1-2-3's capabilities. You attach, invoke, and remove add-ins through the /Addin menu.

advanced macro command   See *macro command.*

anchored range   A range in which one corner is fixed. You can adjust the other corner with the pointer-movement keys. To anchor a range, press the period key (.).

AND search   You conduct an AND search on a database when you want 1-2-3 to find records that match every criterion you specify in the criteria range.

argument   Information provided in an @function or macro command to tell 1-2-3 what the function or command should work on. Arguments can be strings, values, cell and range locations, or conditions. @Function arguments follow the function name and are enclosed in parentheses. Macro command arguments follow the macro keyword and are separated from it by one space. Multiple arguments to the same @function or macro command are separated from each other by a comma (,) or a semicolon (;).

ascending order   Database records or other worksheet data can be sorted in either ascending or descending order. Ascending sorts labels in alphabetical order and values from lowest to highest.

at function   See @function.

attach   Load an add-in into memory.

auto-loading worksheet   A worksheet file that 1-2-3 automatically reads in on start-up. If you name a worksheet file AUTO123.WK1 and place it in 1-2-3's default directory, 1-2-3 will automatically read it into memory each time you start the program.

background printing   Background printing allows you to do other work while 1-2-3 sends your data to the printer. To use background printing, execute the BPRINT command before you start 1-2-3.

backup   An earlier version of a .WK1 file. A backup file has the original file name, with a .BAK extension. 1-2-3 creates backup files when you save a file and select Backup. To create the backup, 1-2-3 renames the copy of the file on disk with a .BAK extension and saves the active file with the current file name and extension.

   Also, a copy of your working files on another medium (such as diskettes or tape cartridges).

bar graph   A graph that shows numeric data as a series of vertical bars of different height evenly spaced along the x-axis. Each bar reflects the value of a single worksheet cell. The x-axis of a bar graph has labels that identify what each bar represents. The y-axis is scaled numerically, depending on the worksheet values being graphed.

baud rate   The speed at which information is transmitted over a serial port. the higher the baud rate, the higher the rate of transmission.

breakpoint   In computer programming, a special instruction that stops execution of a program at an indicated place and allows you to examine intermediate results of calculations. You can simulate a breakpoint in a macro by inserting a {QUIT} instruction or a blank row at the point you think your macro is going astray. When macro execution stops at the breakpoint, you can examine your worksheet file and see if the macro has done what you expected it to do.

bug   An error in a macro or formula. Bugs can be caused by simple carelessness (such as using an incorrect argument or leaving out a tilde) or by an error in programming logic (such as reversing the sense of a test or failing to account for all possible types of user input).

byte pointer   A place marker that keeps track of the current position in a text file opened by the {OPEN} macro command. 1-2-3 uses the byte pointer in some of the file-manipulation macro commands.

call   You execute a macro subroutine by calling it. To call a subroutine, include the subroutine name in the macro, surrounding it with braces ({ }).

cell   The intersection of a column and a row in a 1-2-3 worksheet. The cell is the basic unit of a worksheet.

cell address   A cell's location in the grid of worksheet column/row intersections. The cell address consists of the column letter plus the row number. For example, the cell in the first column and first row of a worksheet has the cell address A1.

cell format   The way 1-2-3 displays values on the screen. You can set cell formats globally, with the Worksheet Global Format commands, or locally, with the Range Format commands.

cell pointer   The highlighted rectangle in the worksheet display area that marks the current cell. You can move the cell pointer with the mouse, the arrow keys, and a number of other keys.

cell tracking   The border row of letters and the border column of numbers on the worksheet display have highlighted areas that move as you move the cell pointer. The movement of the border highlights is called cell tracking. Cell tracking makes it easier for you to identify the current cell.

character string   Any group of contiguous characters (letters, numbers, punctuation marks, special symbols, and so on) enclosed in quotation marks and used in formulas and macros.

clustered bar graph   A bar graph that plots more than one set of data for each x-axis item. Two or more bars appear over each label on the x-axis.

collating sequence   The collating sequence determines how labels are sorted (numbers before letters, letters before numbers, or by character value). By default, 1-2-3 sorts numbers before letters; you can choose a different collating sequence when you run Install.

comma format   A global or a local format that adds commas to numbers larger than 999 and places negative values in parentheses.

complete   After you type an entry in the second line of the control panel, you press either the Enter key or a pointer-movement key to complete it—that is, to enter the data in the current worksheet cell.

compound logical operator   The logical operators #NOT#, #OR#, and #AND#. #NOT# negates a logical expression; #OR# and #AND# join two logical expressions.

compressed pitch   A printing mode in which characters print smaller than standard characters. Most dot-matrix and laser printers support a compressed pitch that allows you to print up to 132 characters on an 8.5 inch line.

conditional macro   A macro that executes a different sequence of commands depending on the result of a tested worksheet condition (for example, the contents of a particular cell).

configuration file   A permanent storage place for global default settings that control how 1-2-3 communicates with printers and disk drives and how it performs standard procedures. 1-2-3 stores these settings in a file named 123.CNF. You can also create and use alternate configuration files.

context-sensitive help   1-2-3 provides help appropriate to the activity you are currently engaged in by sensing the context in which the Help key (F1) is pressed. For example, if you are in the middle of a command and you press Help, 1-2-3 provides help on that command; if you are typing in an @function and you press Help, 1-2-3 provides help on @functions.

control panel   The top three lines of the 1-2-3 display area. The control panel is where you enter data and give commands to 1-2-3. It also displays information about the current cell and displays indicators that reflect what 1-2-3 is doing at any given moment.

criteria range   The criteria range contains selection criteria that tell 1-2-3 which records in the input range to search for during a database query. The criteria range must contain exact copies of the field names from the input range.

currency format   A global or a local format that prefixes numbers with dollar signs, adds commas to numbers larger than 999, and places negative values in parentheses.

cursor   The underscore character (_) that shows the position of the next character to be typed when you are entering data or editing an entry in the control panel. In READY, POINT, and FIND modes, the cursor appears in the current cell.

data   Information stored in a 1-2-3 worksheet.

data label   Values or words that appear next to, above, or below the data points on a graph.

data range   The range of cells containing the data records to be sorted or graphed.

data range command   Commands on the Graph menu (X, A-F) that let you specify ranges of labels for the x-axis and ranges of worksheet data to be graphed.

database   A collection of items of information about a group of people, places, or things. A 1-2-3 database is a single database table that consists of a row of field names above up to 8,191 rows of data.

database table   A collection of related data arranged in rows and columns in a worksheet. A 1-2-3 database table consists of fields and records; fields are arranged in columns and records in rows.

date number   1-2-3's internal method of keeping track of dates. 1-2-3 starts its calendar at January 1, 1900. It assigns the number 1 to that date, 2 to January 2, 1900, and so on. The last date in the 1-2-3 calendar is December 31, 2099 (date number 73050).

date serial number   See *date number.*

debug   To make corrections in a macro so that it performs correctly.

default print settings   The print settings 1-2-3 uses unless you tell it to use different settings. These settings are stored in the 1-2-3 configuration file.

descending order   Database records or other worksheet data can be sorted in either ascending or descending order. Descending order sorts labels in reverse alphabetical order and values from highest to lowest.

disk file   A permanent copy of your work, written on a hard disk or a diskette. To make a change to a disk file, retrieve it, make the changes, and then resave it under the same file name.

display card   A printed circuit board inside the computer that controls how the screen displays text and graphics.

documentation   Text that you include in the worksheet to explain what a formula or macro does and how it does it. Formulas and macros without documentation quickly become indecipherable.

driver   A special file that allows 1-2-3 to communicate with your hardware.

driver set   A file that contains drivers. The driver set tells 1-2-3 how to communicate with your hardware (screen, printers, and math coprocessor). You create the driver set by running Install, and you can create several alternate driver sets to use with different equipment. The default driver set is 123.SET.

edit   To change a cell entry. You modify a cell entry by pressing the Edit (F2) key, which displays the entry in the second line of the control panel so that you can make changes to it. Press Enter to complete an edited entry.

explode   To separate and lift out one or more slices of a pie chart for emphasis.

field   Categories in a database record. For example, in a phonebook record, the fields would be name, address, and phone number. In a 1-2-3 database table, fields are labeled columns.

field name   The labels in the first row of a database table that identify the contents of each field. For example, an employee database usually contains field names such as First Name, Last Name, and Employee Number.

file extension   A suffix to a file name consisting of a period (.) followed by up to three characters. File extensions usually tell you something about how a file is used, rather than describing the contents of the file. 1-2-3 Release 2.x worksheet files have the extension

.WK1 (meaning "1-2-3 worksheet"); print files have the extension .PRN; Wysiwyg format files have the extension .FMT; and graph files have the extension .PIC. 1-2-3 automatically adds these extensions when you create the worksheet, print, or graph files.

file linking   Creating a formula in one file that references a cell or range in another makes the file containing the formula dependent on the file containing the referenced cell or range. This dependency is known as a link, and the process of linking files is called file linking.

font   A typeface of a particular size used to display or print text.

footer   A line of text that 1-2-3 prints above the bottom margin of each page. You create footers with /Print Printer Options Footer.

format   See cell format.

format file   A file with the same name as the worksheet file but with the extension .FMT. This file is created by the Wysiwyg add-in when you save a file with Wysiwyg loaded in memory. The format file contains the Wysiwyg formats and graphics.

formula   A mathematical expression that performs calculations on values in the worksheet. Formulas can contain numbers and arithmetic operators, as well as cell addresses, range names, and @functions.

free corner   The adjustable corner of an anchored range.

global default directory   The directory 1-2-3 saves files in and retrieves files from, unless you specify a different directory. You establish a default directory with /Worksheet Global Default Directory and temporarily change the default directory with /File Directory.

global setting   A setting that controls the operation of the 1-2-3 program or the basic format of a worksheet. Global settings that control a particular worksheet (such as the global column width) or all the worksheets in a file (such as the global recalculation setting) become part of the worksheet file. Global default settings, which modify the behavior of 1-2-3 itself (such as the global default directory), are saved in the 1-2-3 configuration file with /Worksheet Global Default Update.

graph   A visual way to present data. A graph can often illustrate overall trends and projections more clearly and effectively than worksheet numbers themselves.

graph file   A file in which you store a graph for use outside of 1-2-3. The graph file can then be printed or edited by other software programs, such as Lotus Freelance Plus, or it can be included in the worksheet with Wysiwyg. Unless you are using Wysiwyg, graph files cannot be retrieved or printed from within 1-2-3; instead, use PrintGraph. 1-2-3 automatically gives graph files the extension .PIC when you save them with /Graph Save.

graphics mode   A video mode that displays an image dot-by-dot. This allows both text and graphics to appear on the screen at the same time.

hatch pattern   Cross-hatchings used to distinguish different ranges of graphed data when the graph is displayed on a black and white monitor or printed on a printer that does not print color.

header   A line of text that 1-2-3 prints below the top margin of each page. You establish a header with /Print Printer Options Header.

high-low-close-open (HLCO) graph   A graph that plots up to four data points as a series of vertical lines. HLCO graphs typically are used to track the performance of a stock over time. They plot the high, low, closing, and opening prices of the stock. They are also called stock market graphs.

image density   The degree of darkness or detail of a printed graph. In PrintGraph, you can select either draft or final quality image density.

input cell   A cell into which a user is expected to enter data. Also, a cell into which 1-2-3 temporarily places the results of calculations it makes while creating a data table.

input range   The range 1-2-3 searches when it is performing a Data Query command. The input range must include the field names of the database table being searched as well as the data records themselves.

installation   The process through which you tell 1-2-3 what kind of equipment you have. You must install 1-2-3 before you can use it. When you add or change equipment, you should run the Install program again to let 1-2-3 know about the new equipment. 1-2-3 stores the information it needs to access your hardware in a driver set.

integrated   1-2-3 is an integrated package in the sense that its three major components (spreadsheet, database, and graphics) all work together and all use the same environment, command structure, and worksheet files.

keystroke macro   A macro that consists of instructions that map to keys on the keyboard. When 1-2-3 executes a keystroke macro, the effect is the same as if you had typed in the keystrokes yourself.

label   Any cell that begins with a letter or a label-prefix character is a label. Generally, labels are titles, captions that describe what is in a column or row, or non-numeric database table entries. Macros are also labels. Unless you specify otherwise, 1-2-3 assumes that an entry beginning with a letter is a label and an entry beginning with a number is a value. To force an entry to be interpreted as a label, begin it with a label prefix.

label prefix   Indicates that a cell entry is a label, as opposed to a value. Label prefixes include the apostrophe (') for left-aligned labels, the quotation mark (") for right-aligned labels, the caret (^) for centered labels, the backslash (\) for repeating labels, and the vertical bar (|) for printer set-up strings.

landscape orientation   A printer mode that causes text and graphs to be printed sideways on the page, across the long dimension. Selected with /Print Printer Options Advanced Layout Orientation.

learn range   The area in which 1-2-3 records keystrokes after you have activated Learn by pressing Alt-F5.

legend   Legends explain the patterns, symbols, and colors used to identify the A through F data ranges on a graph. The legends and patterns, symbols, and colors appear beneath the graph.

line graph   A graph that represents worksheet values as a continuous line, a sequence of symbols, or both. Line graphs are generally used to show one or more values changing over time. The x-axis defines a specific period of time; the y-axis is a numbered scale.

local format   The format for a specific cell or a range of cells. Local formats always override global formats.

logical operator   Used in formulas to test for equality, inequality, and other conditions. The logical operators are: <, <=, >, >=, =, <>, #NOT#, #OR#, and #AND#. A logical formula evaluates to either TRUE (1) or FALSE (0).

long label   A label that is longer than the column width of the cell. If the cells to the right of the long label are blank, 1-2-3 displays the entire long label. Otherwise, 1-2-3 truncates the long label display. You can see the entire long label in the control panel when you highlight the cell that contains the label.

looping macro   A set of macro instructions that executes repeatedly. The macro commands {BRANCH} and {FOR} can create a loop in a macro.

macro   A set of instructions for automating a 1-2-3 task. Macros include keystrokes, macro commands, values, and labels. They can duplicate simple keyboard operations but can also be self-contained applications; any 1-2-3 task you can perform can be automated with a macro.

macro application   A macro that manages the entire 1-2-3 session. The macro user interacts with the macro, which in turn interacts with 1-2-3; users need not even know they are working with 1-2-3.

macro command   A special 1-2-3 command that has meaning only within a macro. A macro command tells 1-2-3 to perform a built-in programming function. Each macro command consists of a keyword and its arguments (if any), enclosed in braces. Also known as advanced macro commands.

macro library   A special file, created by the Macro Library Manager, that contains 1-2-3 macros. When a macro library is in memory, any other file in memory can run the macros in the library.

menu   A list of commands that appears in a line across the top of the 1-2-3 display area after you press slash (/) or move the mouse pointer to the menu area while 1-2-3 is in READY mode.

menu pointer   The highlight you use to select a menu item and display its description. To select a menu command, use the pointer-movement keys to move the pointer and then press Enter, use the mouse to move the pointer and click the left mouse button, or type the first letter of the command.

mixed cell address   A cell address in which part of the address is relative and part is absolute. A dollar sign ($) precedes the part of the address that is absolute. When a mixed cell address is used in a formula and the formula is copied, the relative part of the address adjusts to the new location while the absolute part stays the same.

mixed graph   A bar and line graph combined. The lines are used either to accent the information in the bars or to graph related information. A mixed graph can include up to three lines and three sets of bars.

mode indicator   A highlighted indicator that appears at the upper right corner of the control panel. The mode indicator lets you know what 1-2-3 is doing at any given time. For example, it displays ERROR when you've made a mistake, WAIT when 1-2-3 is busy, and READY when 1-2-3 is ready for you to enter data or tell it to do something.

name   You can name files, ranges, and collections of graph settings. Range names and named graphs are saved when you save the worksheet file so that you can use them in future work sessions.

named graph   A collection of graph settings identified by a name. Using a named graph causes the named graph's settings to replace the current graph settings.

OR search   You conduct an OR search on a database when you want 1-2-3 to find records that match any criterion in the criteria range.

order of precedence   The order in which an arithmetic operation will be performed unless you use parentheses to explicitly change that order.

output range   The range into which 1-2-3 copies extracted records when you select /Data Query Extract. The first row of the output range must contain one or more field names from the database table.

parse   To break something down into its component parts. In 1-2-3, you use /Data Parse to convert rows of long labels into labels and values (for example, after importing a text file into a worksheet).

pie chart   A graph in the form of a circle divided into slices, where each slice stands for a value in the A range. Pie charts show what proportion of the total each graphed value represents; if one value is twice as large as another, it gets a slice that is twice as large.

pitch   The amount of space a character and its surrounding white space takes up on a line. Pitch is usually described in terms of characters-per-inch (cpi).

pointer-movement key   A key that moves the cell pointer, menu pointer, or cursor. Pointer-movement keys include the arrow keys, the Goto key, Page Up, Page Down, and other key combinations.

pointing   Moving the cell pointer or highlight to a cell; menu choice; file, graph, or range name; or Help screen choice.

portrait mode   A printer orientation in which the printer prints across the short dimension of the page, from the top to the bottom. Selected with /Print Printer Options Advanced Layout Orientation.

primary key   When you sort a database, you select a primary key to tell 1-2-3 what field to base the main sort on.

print head   The part of a printer that forms the characters on the paper. For example, in a dot-matrix printer, the print head uses small wires to form the image of each character just before the character is printed; the print head moves across the page and pushes against the paper, through the ribbon, each time the printer prints a character. Other printers use plastic wheels containing characters or print the characters dot by dot with a laser or ink jet.

print range   A range you tell 1-2-3 to print. A print range can be a single cell or a range. If you are using Wysiwyg, a print range can include graphs you have added to the worksheet.

print spooler   A computer program or hardware device that intercepts characters intended for a printer, temporarily stores them either in memory or on disk, and then sends the characters to the printer. 1-2-3 includes the BPRINT spooler for use with local printers; networked printers usually have their own spoolers. If you are using a print spooler with 1-2-3, you will be able to Quit 1-2-3 before your print jobs have actually finished printing. (However, in some cases, the jobs may not start to print as soon as you select Go, as they would if no print spooler were operating.)

printer control code   Code used in printer set-up strings. Printer control codes vary from one printer to another. Refer to the reference manual for your printer for correct printer control codes.

protect   You protect a worksheet, file, or range to avoid accidentally erasing or changing cell contents and settings. To protect a worksheet, enable global protection with /Worksheet Prot Enable. Then, allow certain cells to be modified by unprotecting them with /Range Unprot.

query   To query a database is literally to ask questions of it. When you query a database, you search for specific database records by establishing selection criteria and using Data Query commands.

quit   To leave a menu or to leave the 1-2-3 program and return to the operating system prompt. You quit a menu by selecting Quit from the menu choices. To quit 1-2-3, return to READY mode, press the slash key (/) and select Quit from the main menu, and then select Yes to confirm.

range   A cell or a group of contiguous cells in the worksheet file. A range can be one cell, a single row or column of cells, or a block of cells composed of many rows and columns. A range must be a rectangular block.

range name   The name you give to a single cell or to a range of cells. A range name can be up to 15 characters long.

recalculation   The process 1-2-3 uses, after a cell entry has changed, to update worksheet values that depend on other cells. Formulas that contain references to changed cells are automatically recalculated if the default recalculation setting is Automatic (the initial setting). If you set recalculation to Manual (with /Worksheet Global Recalculation Manual), recalculation is performed only when you press the Calc key (F9).

record   A collection of items of information pertaining to a particular person, place, or thing. A database is made up of a number of records, and a record is made up of a number of fields. In a 1-2-3 database, a record is contained in a single row.

relative cell address   A cell address in a formula that changes when you copy the formula to a different part of the worksheet file. To determine the location of the referenced cell, 1-2-3 uses the relative positions of the cell being referred to and the cell containing the reference. (Using a relative cell address is like saying, as a way to identify the location of a particular house, "Go up two streets and take a right; it's the second house from the corner.")

relative reference   A reference to a relative cell address or range name. See *relative cell address*.

repeating label or character   Beginning a label with a backslash (\) followed by a character or character string causes the character or string to be repeated for the width of the column. Repeating characters are often used to draw lines in the worksheet.

scatter chart   See *XY graph*.

secondary key   You select a secondary key when you need to specify the sort order of records whose primary keys are the same. For example, if Last Name is the primary key, you would need to specify First Name as the secondary key to put Jane Smith ahead of Sara Smith in a database sort.

set-up string   A series of characters that controls printer settings such as font size, line spacing, or other printer characteristics. You can provide a default set-up string, and you can embed set-up strings in the worksheet. An embedded set-up string consists of a sequence of printer control codes, prefixed with the vertical bar character. (Do not use set-up strings in combination with Wysiwyg; instead, use Wysiwyg commands and formatting sequences to control the way your worksheet prints.)

simple logical operator   Simple logical operators are used in formulas to compare values. They are: <, <=, >, >=, =, and <>.

sort   Sorting records arranges them in a particular order, according to specific sort keys. For example, you might sort an employee database so that the records appear in alphabetical order by last name. You might also sort such a database by Social Security number. 1-2-3 sorts data in ascending order (A - Z, 0 - 9) or descending order (Z - A, 9 - 0).

sort key   Specifies a field on which to base a sort.

source file   A file that contains a cell or range to which a formula in another file refers.

spreadsheet   A structure used for numeric or financial calculations. Spreadsheets contain columns and rows that intersect to form a pattern of boxes, called *cells*, each of which can hold a value. The 1-2-3 worksheet is often used as an electronic spreadsheet.

stacked bar graph   A bar graph in which related bars are placed on top of each other (stacked) rather than placed side by side. The height of the stack of bars usually represents a total.

status line   The status line appears at the bottom of the 1-2-3 screen. The left side displays the current file name or the current time and date. 1-2-3 also displays error messages there. The middle of the status line displays a variety of indicators that describe the status of the worksheet file (for example, CMD means you are executing a macro). The right side of the status line displays indicators to remind you that certain keys have been pressed (for example, NUM means you have pressed the Num Lock key).

stock market graph   See high-low-close-open graph.

string concatenation operator   The ampersand (&) is the only string operator in 1-2-3. It combines two strings in a formula. (Combining two strings is called concatenation.)

structure   The framework of a worksheet, as opposed to the data the worksheet manipulates. Worksheet structure includes titles, labels, and the formatting specifications that control the worksheet's appearance.

submenu   A list of additional commands available when you select a main menu command. Many menu commands bring up a submenu. Some submenu commands, in turn, bring up additional submenus.

subroutine   A set of macro instructions that perform a specific task. Subroutines are executed from one or more macros. When the subroutine is called, control passes to the subroutine. After 1-2-3 completes the instructions in the subroutine, control returns to the instruction following the subroutine call.

subroutine call   A macro instruction that transfers control to a subroutine.

target file   A file that contains a formula that refers to a cell or range in another file.

template   A piece of plastic that comes with the 1-2-3 package and fits over your computer's function keys. The template indicates the special uses of those keys in 1-2-3. Also, a worksheet that contains the structure of an application but that does not contain the data to be manipulated.

text mode   A video mode that displays text character by character. You cannot display graphics at the same time as text.

tick mark   The markings that indicate the scale used on a y-axis or any numbered x-axis.

title   Rows or columns frozen in place on the top, left, or top and left of the worksheet display. Titles always remain in view as you scroll through the worksheet. Also, a descriptive phrase for a graph. Graph titles can be placed above a graph, below a graph, and along the right and left sides of the graph.

unanchoring   Releasing the cell-pointer from the fixed corner of an anchored range. Press the Backspace key or the Escape key to unanchor a range.

unprotect   Unprotecting a cell or a range of cells in a worksheet lets you make changes to cell contents even when the worksheet itself is protected. 1-2-3 highlights the contents of unprotected cells so that the cells are easy to identify. Use /Range Unprot to unprotect a range. Use /Worksheet Global Protection Disable to remove global protection from a worksheet.

updating   Saving global default settings in the 1-2-3 configuration file is called updating the file. You update the 1-2-3 configuration file when you have made changes to global defaults that you want to use in subsequent sessions. Select /Worksheet Global Default Update to update the configuration file.

value   A number or a formula that evaluates to a number. Values begin with a number or one of the following symbols: + - @ . (# $.

variable   A general term for an item that can have any one of a set of values. In 1-2-3, a worksheet cell that contains one of a set of values you enter into the cell. Changes to the value in the cell are reflected elsewhere in the worksheet file.

variables area   An area of a worksheet in which numbers used by formulas elsewhere in the worksheet file are stored. Worksheet templates often have a variables area. Users of the template assign their own values to the variables, and these values are manipulated by the formulas and macros in the template.

what-if analysis   The process of changing worksheet values and seeing the effect of the changes in the worksheet. Changes you make to the worksheet are automatically recalculated.

what-if graphing   The process of changing worksheet values and seeing the effect of the changes reflected in a graph.

what-if scenario   A calculation that uses variables in formulas to determine potential outcomes of different hypothetical situations.

wildcard character   /Range Search, /File commands, and /Data Query commands use wildcard characters to generalize search operations. The /Range Search and /File wildcard characters are the question mark (?) and the asterisk (*). the /Data Query wildcard charcters include the asterisk, the question mark, and the tilde (~). You use wildcard characters to select characters, files, or records that do not match exactly. For example, to find the records of all customers whose last name begins with S, enter S* as the database search criteria. Similarly, selecting /File Erase and entering *.BAK in response to the prompt for a file name causes all files in the current directory with the .BAK extension to be displayed.

worksheet   A grid of 256 columns by 8,192 rows. You use the worksheet to enter and manipulate spreadsheet data and database table entries.

worksheet display   The area you work in when you use 1-2-3. The worksheet display contains a series of rows and columns that intersect to form cells. It also includes a control panel and status line.

worksheet window   The means through which 1-2-3 displays information. Initially, the worksheet window fills most of the screen. 1-2-3 can display two horizontal or vertical windows that contain different parts of the same worksheet. If you use Wysiwyg, you can also display one or more graphs or graphics in the worksheet.

x-axis   The horizontal axis of a graph. In a line graph, the x-axis usually defines a specific period of time. In an XY graph, the x-axis is a numbered scale. In a bar graph, the x-axis has labels that identify what each bar represents.

XY graph   A graph that displays cell values as points. XY graphs use both a scaled x-axis and a scaled y-axis, so each point on the graph has an X value and a Y value. XY graphs are used to show how two different types of data are correlated. They are also known as scatter charts.

y-axis   The vertical axis of a graph. The y-axis is a numbered scale. 1-2-3 graphs can have one or two y-axes.

About the Authors

David J. Bookbinder has been writing about computers for 11 years and about Lotus 1-2-3 for five. His most recent books include *The Lotus Guide to 1-2-3 Release 3* and *Lotus 1-2-3 for DOS At Work.*

Mark Jacober has been a technical writer and trainer in hardware and software for 20 years. He has been a technical writer at Lotus Corporation for 2 years.

Kevin McDonough is a freelance technical writer based in Arlington, Massachusetts. He has been writing about software for 6 years, specializing in PC software for the last year and a half.

SPECIAL OFFER

Companion diskette to *Lotus 1-2-3 for Windows At Work*

All of the examples and macros in *Lotus 1-2-3 for Windows At Work* are available on either 5 1/4" or 3 1/2" diskettes. In addition, the companion diskette contains intermediate versions of the applications, keyed to figures and setup tables, so you can pick up the exercises at any point.

　　If you would like a companion diskette, please photocopy or clip out the coupon below, fill it in completely, and mail it to:

David J. Bookbinder
P.O. Box 5264
Albany, NY 12205

Make checks payable to *David J. Bookbinder*. Allow three to six weeks for delivery in the United States.

- -

　　　　Please send me the companion diskette for *Lotus 1-2-3 for Windows At Work*.

Name _____

Address _____

City _____ State _____ Zip _____

Desired disk format:　　3 1/2"　　5 1/4" (high density)　　5 1/4" (low density)

Send me _____ copies of the companion diskette at $20 each.　_____

Shipping/Handling:　　Domestic @ $2.50/disk:　　_____

　　　　　　　　　　　Foreign @ $5.00/disk:　　_____

　　　　　　　　　　　New York State residents please
add sales tax:　　_____

　　　　　　　　　　　　　　　TOTAL:　　_____

- -

Do You Have a Favorite Software Package?

Would You Like to Write an *At Work* Sidebar?

If so,

please send us a letter at:

At Work Series Editor
Addison-Wesley Publishing Company, Inc.
Trade Computer Books
5 Jacob Way
Reading, MA 01867

In your letter please provide your name, address, and phone number, and mention the software packages with which you are familiar.